Business Basics
for Law Students

Business Basics for Law Students

Essential Terms and Concepts

Second Edition

Robert W. Hamilton
Minerva House Drysdale Regents
Chair in Law
University of Texas

Richard A. Booth
Professor of Law
University of Maryland

ASPEN LAW & BUSINESS
A Division of Aspen Publishers, Inc.

Permissions
Aspen Law & Business
1185 Avenue of the Americas
New York, NY 10036

Printed in the United States of America

4 5 6 7 8 9 0

Library of Congress Cataloging-in-Publication Data

Hamilton, Robert W., 1931-
    Business basics for law students / Robert W. Hamilton,
Richard A. Booth.
    p. cm.
    Includes index.
    ISBN 1-56706-528-7
    1. Business law — United States. 2. Business. 3. Business
enterprises — Law and legislation — United States. I. Booth,
Richard A., 1950-   . II. Title.
KF889.H238   1998

About Aspen Law & Business, Law School Division

In 1996, Aspen Law & Business welcomed the Law School Division of Little, Brown and Company into its growing business—already established as a leading provider of practical information to legal practitioners.

Acquiring much more than a prestigious collection of educational publications by the country's foremost authors, Aspen Law & Business inherited the long-standing Little, Brown tradition of excellence — born over 150 years ago. As one of America's oldest and most venerable publishing houses, Little, Brown and Company commenced in a world of change and challenge, innovation and growth. Sharing that same spirit, Aspen Law & Business has dedicated itself to continuing and strengthening the integrity begun so many years ago.

ASPEN LAW & BUSINESS
A Division of Aspen Publishers, Inc.
A Wolters Kluwer Company

SUMMARY OF CONTENTS

V

◇

FINANCIAL MARKETS AND INVESTMENTS   381

VI

◇

THE PRACTICE OF CORPORATE LAW   507

CONTENTS

I

BASIC FINANCIAL CONCEPTS — 1

III

◇

ACCOUNTING, VALUATION, AND TAXATION   125

CHAPTER 6

FUNDAMENTAL ACCOUNTING PRINCIPLES   127

CHAPTER 7

HOW TO READ AND USE FINANCIAL STATEMENTS   167

Contents

CHAPTER 8

◆ VALUATION OF AN ONGOING BUSINESS   193

CHAPTER 9

◆ FEDERAL TAXATION   225

IV

◇

BUSINESS FORMS

CHAPTER 10

◆

A SURVEY OF BUSINESS FORMS

Contents

CHAPTER 11

◆

CORPORATE SECURITIES   305

V

CHAPTER 16

OPTIONS, COMMODITIES, FUTURES, AND OTHER ESOTERICA   475

VI

◇

THE PRACTICE OF CORPORATE LAW   507

CHAPTER 17

THE PRACTICE OF LAW AS A BUSINESS   509

ACKNOWLEDGMENTS

We would like to thank the editorial staff at Aspen Publishing for their faith in and assistance with the book. In particular, we would like to thank Paul Christman for his superb work editing the final version.

We gratefully acknowledge the permission granted to reproduce excerpts from the following materials.

The Wall Street Journal. Reprinted by permission of *The Wall Street Journal* © 1997 Dow Jones & Company, Inc. All rights reserved worldwide.

◆ INTRODUCTION

This book is written primarily for the benefit of law students who have no prior business background and who feel insecure in law school classes dealing with corporations, securities, taxation, and similar matters. It discusses the fundamentals of business activity and of business law. It also discusses the practice of corporation law and the concepts and tools with which every successful corporate practitioner must be familiar. These concepts are partly financial in nature and partly legal, and they partly address the relationship between lawyers and sophisticated clients.

Students do not begin law school with a common background in business, economics, or finance. Some law students have a head start on others: They may have gained experience running their own business or through employment. They may have taken courses in accounting, finance, or business in undergraduate or graduate school. A few may have been fortunate enough to have inherited money that they have invested and as a result may have learned something in the process. A few law students have had substantial careers before going to law school, for example, as certified public accountants or as employees of banking or brokerage firms.

When students with varying backgrounds are brought together in a large law school class on corporations or income taxation or other subjects dealing with business and financial concepts, students without a business background tend to feel overwhelmed and fail to participate in class. At the same time, the more experienced students dominate class discussion, causing the instructor to believe that the level of sophistication of the class is higher than it really is. As a result, the insecurity of the less sophisticated student is increased rather than decreased by the classroom experience.

This book is designed to relieve this insecurity. It provides an introduction to business concepts for law students with little or no prior experience or knowledge. It concentrates on practical fundamentals that underlie the modern business world and draws shamelessly from several different courses that regularly appear in the law school curriculm. The book is designed to be a morale builder as well as an educational tool. Throughout there is an emphasis on vocabulary. Words such as *amortize, accounts receivable,* and *balloon notes* may strike fear in the heart of the uninitiated: Such terms are defined and discussed in this book.

Many students may find some of the discussion in this book to be elemen-

tary: On the other hand, it is unlikely that anyone will find all of this book elementary. Although it will not make a corporation lawyer out of the reader, this book does discuss many things that a corporation lawyer must understand, and it should enable the reader to talk with such a lawyer with some confidence.

Regrettably, the law applicable to business and corporate transactions is often complex, uncertain, and confusing. Indeed, for someone faced with difficult business choices in the face of massive uncertainty, the complexity and uncertainty of legal rules surrounding transactions is often frustrating. Fortunately for the lawyer, business as it relates to law is easier to understand than law as it relates to business. A lawyer should always be able to understand what goal a client is pursuing and the means he or she is using to get there.

This book is not a substitute for standard treatises in subjects such as corporations and securities regulation that are part of the traditional law school curriculum. Again, however, it does contain background information and discussion of fundamental principles in those specific areas, which should help students who are concerned that they lack the business background to understand these subjects. Also to some extent, this book may give a brief sketch of some of the issues discussed in those courses. Although this book is intended primarily as a reference work, it can be used as the primary text for a course on basic business concepts. Indeed, in an earlier incarnation it has been used as such a text at several law schools. Such courses, like this book, are designed for law students who think they need extra preparation before diving into business-related law school courses. We hope that the availability of this book will encourage more law schools to offer these courses.

Although this book is written primarily for law students and beginning lawyers, it will also be useful to business students, college students generally, and persons not in school at all, who feel a need for a better grasp of the subjects here discussed. As hinted above, this is in fact the second edition of this book, which was first published in 1989 under the title *Fundamentals of Modern Business* (Student Edition) by Professor Robert Hamilton of the University of Texas School of Law. The book aged well, but the business world changes rapidly. Thus, Professor Richard Booth of the University of Maryland School of Law undertook to revise and update the original work in collaboration with Professor Hamilton. (In the end, both authors reviewed virtually everything in this new edition.) Anyone who is already familiar with the first edition will note that this book is substantially revised. There have been revolutionary changes in the law of business organizations since 1989, explosive growth in the use of limited liability companies (LLCs), limited liability partnerships (LLPs), and other limited liability forms of organization. The hostile takeover virtually disappeared because of state anti-takeover statutes and defensive measures such as poison pills, but there are just as many (if not more) huge deals in the works (albeit friendly) as this book goes to press as there were in 1989. Moreover, hostile takeovers seem to be somewhat more common than they were for many years in the interim. There have also been significant changes in the securities and commodities markets, particularly in connection with the development of derivative products. Finally, although the basic concepts of time value of money, insurance and annuities, financial accounting, valuation, and so forth have not changed, we have extended the discussion of even these to include a wider array of approaches and applications.

Business Basics
for Law Students

I

BASIC FINANCIAL CONCEPTS

CHAPTER 1

DEBT AND INTEREST

§1.1 Introduction

The concept of **interest** is one of the most fundamental ideas in all of business. At its simplest, interest is the amount charged for the use of some amount of money for some period of time. Although the question might sound quite elementary, it helps at the outset to ask why it is routine (at least in most cultures) to charge interest on a loan. Perhaps the simplest answer is that one charges interest because one can. Other lenders receive interest, so it is foolish—at least in commercial transactions—not to insist on the going rate of return. Obviously, that answer is circular, but that does not make it invalid. A more sophisticated but still circular reason for charging interest is that rather than lending some sum to another, one could put the money in the bank and receive interest on it. To lend it without a comparable rate of return is to lose the money that one could have made. In other words, interest is compensation for the opportunity cost of allowing someone else to use your money. Forgone interest is not only lost interest; it is in effect interest paid. Although this answer is better than the first one, it is still circular because it depends on the fact that a bank or other financial institution pays interest on amounts deposited (which they only do because they can lend money to those who want to borrow). Perhaps the best answer to the puzzle of interest is that money is power. It can be used to buy things that can be used for productive and pleasurable purposes.

3

A lender must forgo exercising the power of the money while the borrower enjoys its benefits. Interest is thus compensation for opportunity costs.

If lenders routinely insist on interest, then why does anyone invest in something that pays no interest? Why do people take their savings out of the bank to start a business? Why do investors put their money in so-called growth stocks that pay no dividends? The simple answer is that people make these investments because they expect the eventual returns on such risky investments to be even greater than the interest they could receive from a bank account, savings bond, or other similar investment.

Thus, interest is only a subset of the even more basic concept of **return on investment (ROI)**. Although people do not usually think of returns from investments such as small businesses and stocks in terms of an equivalent interest rate, all investment returns are in fact part of a single continuum with lower rates of return paid in connection with safer investments (and called interest) and higher rates of return paid on riskier investments (and called **profits** or **dividends**). The line between interest and other forms of return is quite fuzzy, although the distinction can be quite important for tax and other purposes, as will be seen in later chapters. Generally speaking, however, the word "interest" refers to the return paid on an enforceable obligation to pay money. With other forms of investment, the return tends to be much more variable, and the investor has no promise of either the payment of a return or the repayment of the amount invested. (Variability in the rate of return and whether it will be paid at all is called "risk.") The greater the risk, the greater the return that the investor demands.

Assume, for example, that an investor agrees to purchase a 50 percent interest in a small business for $500,000. Such a purchase (usually described as an **equity** investment) entitles the investor to 50 percent of all distributions by the business and 50 percent of the proceeds when the business is sold or dissolved. The transaction is not at all like a loan to the business, because there is no promise of periodic payments and no promise of repayment at a definite time. The risk being taken by such an investor is much greater than that taken by a bank lending funds, and the investor naturally expects a greater return. After all, if the business had broken even the first year, the investor would probably have received no distribution at all, while a bank would still need to be paid.

Because most readers probably understand the idea of debt much more firmly, the remaining sections of this chapter focus quite narrowly on interest and how it is calculated. However, it should be kept in mind that many of the same concepts discussed here are directly applicable to other investments as well.

§1.2 The Uses of Debt

For individual consumers, the purchase of houses, cars, washing machines, and other big ticket items would be very difficult without credit. This is also true of both small and large businesses. Virtually every business today relies on debt to finance its operations. The notion that the best business is a debt-free business is now obsolete (if it ever was really true). From a business standpoint,

there are substantial tax incentives and economic forces (including the need for more capital than owners can sometimes provide) that encourage every business to use borrowed money. It is often more profitable for businesses to use debt in their operations and pay interest rather than to raise additional permanent capital.

Entrepreneurs that own their own businesses often find that the use of borrowed capital permits greater growth and greater returns. Debt, in short, is not only a practical necessity for most businesses, it also fuels economic growth and helps to maximize earnings. On the other hand, debt is dangerous. A business that incurs debt also assumes fixed commitments that may run many years into the future. Economic conditions may change and debt incurred in an earlier era may become a crushing burden. In short, debt increases risk.

A preliminary examination of debt and interest is appropriate for another reason. Many business transactions that do not involve loans in the traditional sense involve an immediate exchange of money for rights to receive (it is hoped) larger sums of money in the future (see the example in the previous section). The purchase of an existing business, for example, involves an immediate payment today for the right to receive the profits the business earns in the future. The process of determining whether a contemplated purchase is desirable involves comparing the value of future payments with the payments required to be made today; this calculation turns out to be integrally related to the concept of debt and interest.

§1.3 Simple Interest and Compound Interest

The concept of **interest** on a debt is familiar to most people. Interest is the amount that a borrower pays for the use of the lender's money. Interest is the cost of a loan to a borrower; it is the return to the lender. The amount of interest that a borrower pays is a function of three variables: (1) the amount borrowed, (2) the period for which it is borrowed, and (3) the rate of interest. In addition, to determine how much interest is to be earned on a specific loan, one must know the periods over which interest is to be computed, and, if the loan is to continue for more than one interest period, whether the interest is to be calculated as simple interest or compound interest.

The most common practice is to quote interest rates on an annual basis. The manner in which the actual computation is to be made, however, is not uniform. Interest quoted at the rate of 6 percent per year may actually mean interest calculated at 0.5 percent per month due at the end of each month, or it may mean interest at the rate of 1.5 percent per quarter due at the end of every three-month period, 3 percent semiannually due at the end of six months, or 6 percent due at the end of a year. Usually, these different calculations lead to different results. The times when payments are to be made on a loan may or may not coincide with the times when interest is calculated.

The computation of interest over several periods also involves an assumption as to whether the earned interest is in effect withdrawn every period so that each period's interest is computed on a stable principal, or whether the earned interest from the previous period is left with the borrower and treated

as principal thereafter, itself to earn interest in the future period. The former is called **simple interest** and the latter **compound interest**.

A good example of compound interest involves the deposit of money with a bank. In this transaction, the depositor is the lender and the bank is the borrower who pays the lender interest at a specified rate. Let us assume that you have $10,000 that you deposit with a bank that advertises that it pays 8 percent per year, compounded quarterly. The word "quarterly" means that although the bank quotes its interest rate as 8 percent per year, it actually calculates interest at the rate of 2 percent for each accounting period of three months and adds that amount of interest to your account at the end of that period. Thus, if you left your $10,000 with the bank for three months, you would be credited with $200 (2 percent of $10,000), which you could withdraw without reducing your account below $10,000.

Suppose you let the bank keep (use) your money for another three months. If the bank computed its obligation on a simple interest basis, you would simply earn another $200 during the second three months. If the bank computed its obligation on a compound interest basis (as most banks do and as your bank expressly promised to do when it advertised that its 8 percent rate was "compounded quarterly"), it would consider that you had $10,200 on loan to it throughout the second quarter, and interest would be calculated on this amount at the end of six months, so that you would earn $204 during this period rather than simply $200. This is compound interest. The additional $4 reflects interest on the last period's interest. Over several accounting periods, the difference between compound and simple interest becomes increasingly significant. If you left your compound interest investment with the bank for a full year, you would have an account worth $10,824.32; at the end of two years, it would be worth $11,716.59. If only simple interest were paid, the investment would be worth $10,800 after one year and $11,600 after two years. At the end of ten years, your investment will be $22,080.40 at compound interest; if only simple interest were paid, the account would be worth $18,000. The compounding of interest thus significantly increases the growth rate of capital. If the interest rate is 6 percent (compounded quarterly), the investment doubles in 11.75 years; at 8 percent, in about 9 years; at 10 percent, in about 7 years. (A trick for determining roughly when an amount of money will double from compounding of interest is the Rule of 72. If one divides 72 by the interest rate, the resulting number is the approximate number of years it takes to double the amount deposited or invested.)

If the bank had calculated the interest it owed you on a simple interest basis, in effect it would be ignoring the interest earned in previous periods in calculating the current period's interest. To put it another way, the bank would assume that you had withdrawn the interest earned at the end of each accounting period even though you had not in fact done so. Presented in this way, it seems clear that compound interest more accurately reflects the reality of loan transactions over several accounting periods than does simple interest. The continued existence of simple interest computations here and there in the economy probably reflects a lack of sophistication by some lenders, the somewhat greater complexity of compound interest calculations as compared with simple interest calculations, and possibly an illogical remnant of the historical

antipathy to the payment of interest at all. One can imagine, for example, a creditor making a two-year, 6 percent loan, and concluding that he should receive the original principal of the loan plus an aggregate of 12 percent in interest at the end of two years. The creditor may not realize that he is in fact charging less than 6 percent per year; or in other words that he is worse off setting up the transaction this way than if he made a one-year loan at 6 percent for that year and then "rolled over" that entire loan—principal and interest— at the end of that year into a second one-year loan at 6 percent for the second year.

The apparent complexity of compound interest transactions may have been a serious problem when calculations were made with paper and pencil, and some lenders may have concluded that the additional interest was just not worth the trouble. This calculation problem, however, has been entirely eliminated by the development of compound interest tables and with the development of inexpensive electronic calculating devices and computers.

One of the peculiarities of compound interest calculations is that whenever interest is compounded more frequently than the quoted annual rate, the actual interest rate earned for the year is more favorable to the lender than the quoted rate. If, for example, the quoted rate is 8 percent, the actual rate of return for the first year is 8.243 percent. The quoted rate is sometimes also called the **nominal rate**, while the actual rate earned is usually called the **effective rate** of interest or the **yield** or the **annual percentage rate (APR)**. Some advertisements set forth both rates in seeking to attract potential depositors.

Interest that lending institutions pay is usually compounded for periods of less than one year, though rates are usually quoted on an annual basis. Many financial institutions advertise that their interest is compounded daily, meaning that interest is computed each day and is added to principal to compute the following day's interest. Because compound interest rate calculations rapidly approach a limit as the interest rate and the time period are divided into smaller and smaller segments, the daily compounding of interest increases the productivity of money only slightly compared with quarterly compounding. For example, if you invest $10,000 with a borrower offering to pay 8 percent per year compounded daily, your investment after three years will be worth $12,712.14. If the interest had been compounded quarterly, your investment would be worth $12,682.42. If it were compounded only annually, it would have been worth $12,597.12. If it were compounded hourly, every day and night for the three years, it would be worth $12,712.36, almost exactly the same as it would on the basis of daily compounding.

Bankers also distinguish between **ordinary interest** and **exact interest**. These terms arose in connection with the computation of interest for periods of less than one year. When calculations were made by paper and pencil, and many loans were for days, weeks, months, or fractions of years, it greatly simplified matters to consider a year as 360 days based on 12 months of 30 days each. Interest computed on the basis of these simplifying assumptions is ordinary interest and is still used by many banks, and in the computation of interest on corporate, agency, and municipal bonds. Exact interest treats the year as consisting of 365 or 366 days, as the case may be, and ignores months. The computation of exact interest, like the calculation of compound interest,

has been greatly simplified, though it is obviously more complicated to count the specific number of days in each month than it is to assume that each month has 30 days. Although the difference involved is usually relatively small, one suspects that many banks and financial institutions continue to use ordinary interest because it imparts a small upward bias in the amount of interest charged borrowers. Finally, when calculating interest, it is customary to exclude the day the loan is made and include the day in which it is repaid.

§1.4 Formulas Used to Calculate Compound Interest

The examples so far make one important point about compound interest problems: The calculation of compound interest appears to be complex because it involves more than simple arithmetic or multiplication. Indeed, if one were to compute the interest at the end of each period, add it to the previous balance, and then compute the interest for the next period, the calculation would be quite laborious. There is, however, a formula for computing compound interest that has frightened generations of nonmathematicians:

$$FV = P \times (1 + i)^t$$

where i is the interest rate, t is the number of time periods, P is the principal and FV is the future value after t periods.

For many years, lenders used printed tables that set forth compound interest computations. Table 1-1 is an example of a compound interest table. It shows the future value of $1 (including return of principal) at various interest rates for 50 time periods. Assume you deposit $1,000 in a bank that pays 8 percent per year compounded quarterly. If you leave the money there for ten years, how much will be in the account after ten years? Because the interest is compounded quarterly, the question involves a calculation over 40 periods at 2 percent per period. Looking in the "40" row and "2%" column, we see that $1 will grow to $2.2080 after 40 periods. Hence, $1,000 will have grown to $2,208. Another question: Assume you will need $10,000 in five years for law school tuition. If a bank will guarantee a 6 percent rate compounded semiannually, how much must you deposit today to have $10,000 in five years? This requires a calculation over 10 periods at 3 percent. Using the "10" row and "3%" column, we find that $1 deposited today will have grown to $1.3439 in five years. Hence you must deposit $10,000/1.3439 = $7,441.03. Note that these hypotheticals are not entirely realistic. First, no account is taken of the income tax that would be due on the periodic interest earned. Second, most banks today will not guarantee a fixed interest rate over time, although other financial devices exist that may permit "locking in" a fixed rate.

Calculators are available with compound interest and other calculations built into their memories. One has only to enter any three of the four variables: the interest rate per period, the number of periods, the original principal amount, and the future value. The calculator supplies the missing variable.

One common question is how much of a payment on a loan is interest and how much is principal. The question obviously arises if one desires to pay off a

Table 1-1
Future Value After n Periods of $1 Invested Today

No. of periods	2%	3%	4%	5%	6%	7%	8%
1	1.0200	1.0300	1.0400	1.0500	1.0600	1.0700	1.0800
2	1.0404	1.0609	1.0816	1.1025	1.1236	1.1449	1.1664
3	1.0612	1.0927	1.1249	1.1576	1.1910	1.2250	1.2597
4	1.0824	1.1255	1.1699	1.2155	1.2625	1.3108	1.3605
5	1.1041	1.1593	1.2167	1.2763	1.3382	1.4026	1.4693
6	1.1262	1.1941	1.2653	1.3401	1.4185	1.5007	1.5869
7	1.1487	1.2299	1.3159	1.4071	1.5036	1.6058	1.7138
8	1.1717	1.2668	1.3686	1.4775	1.5938	1.7182	1.8509
9	1.1951	1.3048	1.4233	1.5513	1.6895	1.8365	1.9990
10	1.2190	1.3439	1.4802	1.6289	1.7908	1.9672	2.1589
11	1.2434	1.3842	1.5395	1.7103	1.8983	2.1049	2.3316
12	1.2682	1.4258	1.6010	1.7959	2.0122	2.2522	2.5182
13	1.2936	1.4685	1.6651	1.8856	2.1329	2.4098	2.7196
14	1.3195	1.5126	1.7317	1.9799	2.2609	2.5785	2.9372
15	1.3459	1.5580	1.8009	2.0789	2.3966	2.7590	3.1722
16	1.3728	1.6047	1.8730	2.1829	2.5404	2.9522	3.4259
17	1.4002	1.6528	1.9479	2.2920	2.6928	3.1588	3.7000
18	1.4282	1.7024	2.0258	2.4066	2.8543	3.3799	3.9960
19	1.4568	1.7535	2.1068	2.5270	3.0256	3.6165	4.3157
20	1.4859	1.8061	2.1911	2.6533	3.2071	3.8697	4.6610
21	1.5157	1.8603	2.2788	2.7860	3.3996	4.1406	5.0338
22	1.5460	1.9161	2.3699	2.9253	3.6035	4.4304	5.4365
23	1.5769	1.9736	2.4647	3.0715	3.8197	4.7405	5.8715
24	1.6084	2.0328	2.5633	3.2251	4.0489	5.0724	6.3412
25	1.6406	2.0938	2.6658	3.3864	4.2919	5.4274	6.8485

Table 1-1 (*cont.*)
Future Value After n Periods of $1 Invested Today

No. of periods	2%	3%	4%	5%	6%	7%	8%
26	1.6734	2.1566	2.7725	3.5557	4.4594	5.8074	7.3964
27	1.7069	2.2213	2.8834	3.7335	4.8223	6.2139	7.9881
28	1.7410	2.2879	2.9987	3.9201	5.1117	6.6488	8.6271
29	1.7758	2.3566	3.1187	4.1161	5.4184	7.1143	9.3173
30	1.8114	2.4273	3.2434	4.3219	5.7435	7.6123	10.0627
31	1.8476	2.5001	3.3731	4.5380	6.0881	8.1451	10.8677
32	1.8845	2.5751	3.5081	4.7649	6.4534	8.7153	11.7371
33	1.9222	2.6523	3.6484	5.0032	6.8406	9.3253	12.6760
34	1.9607	2.7319	3.7943	5.2533	7.2510	9.9781	13.6901
35	1.9999	2.8139	3.9461	5.5160	7.6861	10.6766	14.7853
36	2.0399	2.8983	4.1039	5.7918	8.1473	11.4239	15.9682
37	2.0807	2.9852	4.2681	6.0814	8.6361	12.2236	17.2456
38	2.1223	3.0748	4.4388	6.3855	9.1543	13.0793	18.6253
39	2.1647	3.1670	4.6164	6.7048	9.7035	13.9948	20.1153
40	2.2080	3.2620	4.8010	7.0400	10.2857	14.9745	21.7245
41	2.2522	3.3599	4.9931	7.3920	10.9029	16.0227	23.4625
42	2.2972	3.4607	5.1928	7.7616	11.5570	17.1443	25.3395
43	2.3432	3.5645	5.4005	8.1497	12.2505	18.3444	27.3666
44	2.3901	3.6715	5.6165	8.5572	12.9855	19.6285	29.5560
45	2.4379	3.7816	5.8412	8.9850	13.7646	21.0025	31.9204
46	2.4866	3.8950	6.0748	9.4343	14.5905	22.4726	34.4741
47	2.5363	4.0119	6.3178	9.9060	15.4659	24.0457	37.2320
48	2.5871	4.1323	6.5705	10.4013	16.3939	25.7289	40.2106
49	2.6388	4.2562	6.8333	10.9213	17.3775	27.5299	43.4274
50	2.6916	4.3839	7.1067	11.4674	18.4202	29.4570	46.9016

Table 1-1 (*cont.*)
Future Value After n Periods of $1 Invested Today

No. of periods	9%	10%	11%	12%	13%	14%	15%
1	1.0900	1.1000	1.1100	1.1200	1.1300	1.1400	1.1500
2	1.1881	1.2100	1.2321	1.2544	1.2769	1.2996	1.3225
3	1.2950	1.3310	1.3676	1.4049	1.4429	1.4815	1.5209
4	1.4116	1.4641	1.5181	1.5735	1.6305	1.6890	1.7490
5	1.5386	1.6105	1.6851	1.7623	1.8424	1.9254	2.0114
6	1.6771	1.7716	1.8704	1.9738	2.0820	2.1950	2.3131
7	1.8280	1.9487	2.0762	2.2107	2.3526	2.5023	2.6600
8	1.9926	2.1436	2.3045	2.4760	2.6584	2.8526	3.0590
9	2.1719	2.3579	2.5580	2.7731	3.0040	3.2519	3.5179
10	2.3674	2.5937	2.8394	3.1058	3.3946	3.7072	4.0456
11	2.5804	2.8531	3.1518	3.4785	3.8359	4.2262	4.6524
12	2.8127	3.1384	3.4985	3.8960	4.3345	4.8179	5.3503
13	3.0658	3.4523	3.8833	4.3635	4.8980	5.4924	6.1528
14	3.3417	3.7975	4.3104	4.8871	5.5348	6.2613	7.0757
15	3.6425	4.1772	4.7846	5.4736	6.2543	7.1379	8.1371
16	3.9703	4.5950	5.3109	6.1304	7.0673	8.1372	9.3576
17	4.3276	5.0545	5.8951	6.8660	7.9861	9.2765	10.7613
18	4.7171	5.5599	6.5436	7.6900	9.0243	10.5752	12.3755
19	5.1417	6.1159	7.2633	8.6128	10.1974	12.0557	14.2318
20	5.6044	6.7275	8.0623	9.6466	11.5231	13.7435	16.3665
21	6.1088	7.4002	8.9492	10.8038	13.0211	15.6676	18.8215
22	6.6586	8.1403	9.9336	12.1003	14.7138	17.8610	21.6447
23	7.2579	8.9543	11.0263	13.5523	16.6266	20.3616	24.8915
24	7.9111	9.8497	12.2392	15.1786	18.7881	23.2122	28.6252
25	8.6231	10.8347	13.5855	17.0001	21.2305	26.4619	32.9190

Table 1-1 (*cont.*)

Future Value After n Periods of $1 Invested Today

No. of periods	9%	10%	11%	12%	13%	14%	15%
26	9.3992	11.9182	15.0799	19.0401	23.9905	30.1666	37.8568
27	10.2451	13.1100	16.7386	21.3249	27.1093	34.3899	43.5358
28	11.1671	14.4210	18.5799	23.8839	30.6335	39.2045	50.0656
29	12.1722	15.8631	20.6237	26.7499	34.6158	44.6931	57.5755
30	13.2677	17.4494	22.8923	29.9599	39.1159	50.9502	66.2118
31	14.4618	19.1943	25.4104	33.5551	44.2010	58.0832	76.1435
32	15.7633	21.1138	28.2056	37.5817	49.9471	66.2148	87.5651
33	17.1820	23.2252	31.3082	42.0915	56.4402	75.4849	100.6998
34	18.7284	25.5477	34.7521	47.1425	63.7774	86.0528	115.8048
35	20.4140	28.1024	38.5749	52.7996	72.0685	98.1002	133.1755
36	22.2512	30.9127	42.8181	59.1356	81.4374	111.8342	153.1519
37	24.2538	34.0039	47.5281	66.2318	92.0243	127.4910	176.1246
38	26.4367	37.4043	52.7562	74.1797	103.9874	145.3397	202.5433
39	28.8160	41.1448	58.5593	83.0812	117.5058	165.6873	232.9248
40	31.4094	45.2593	65.0009	93.0510	132.7816	188.8835	267.8635
41	34.2363	49.7852	72.1510	104.2171	150.0432	215.3272	308.0431
42	37.3175	54.7637	80.0876	116.7231	169.5488	245.4730	354.2495
43	40.6761	60.2401	88.8972	130.7299	191.5901	279.8392	407.3870
44	44.3370	66.2641	98.6759	146.4175	216.4968	319.0167	468.4950
45	48.3272	72.8905	109.5302	163.9876	244.6414	363.6791	538.7693
46	52.6767	80.1795	121.5786	183.6661	276.4448	414.5941	619.5847
47	57.4176	88.1975	134.9522	205.7061	312.3826	472.6373	712.5224
48	62.5852	97.0172	149.7970	230.3908	352.9923	538.8065	819.4007
49	68.2179	106.7190	166.2746	258.0377	398.8818	614.2395	942.3108
50	74.3575	117.3909	184.5648	289.0022	450.7359	700.2330	1083.6574

loan early. The straightforward method is to calculate the interest due on the unpaid balance at the time each payment is made, and the excess part of the payment is credited to principal. This is usually called the simple interest method and is undoubtedly the fairest way to determine the unpaid balance.

Another method widely used in many states is the **Rule of 78** or **sum of digits** method of calculating interest. This method of calculating is much more favorable to the creditor than the simple interest method. Using a 12-month loan as an example, assign the numbers 1 through 12 to the months the loan is outstanding and add the numbers together. The total is 78. If the borrower pays off or refinances the mortgage after one payment, he or she is assumed to have paid 12/78th of the total interest owed; after two payments, 23/78th of the interest has been paid off, and so forth. On a 2-year loan, the digits 1 through 24 would be added together to form the denominator. This method allocates a significantly higher portion of the total payments to interest in the early months than the simple interest method, and therefore increases the amount of principal that remains unpaid under the simple interest method.

The Rule of 78 maximizes the inflation of interest about a third of the way through a loan. When a large, long-term loan is involved, the inflation can amount to thousands of dollars. For example, on a $30,000 15-year loan to purchase a mobile home at 16 percent interest, a borrower who refinances the loan after the end of five years would discover that he has paid an additional $4,595 in interest (and therefore not reduced principal by that amount) by using the Rule of 78 rather than the simple interest calculation.

One of the quirky aspects of the Rule of 78 is that because the formula applies so much of the interest to the early periods of the loan, the effective interest rate applied on later payments drops steadily. It may make little sense, for example, to refinance the mobile home loan after ten years because the payments thereafter represent primarily principal and the effective interest rate on the balance of the loan is much lower than the interest rate on a loan obtained to refinance that obligation.

Before deciding to refinance and prepay an outstanding loan, one should determine whether the Rule of 78 will be applied to the transaction. If so, one should take into account the cost involved before deciding whether prepayment is desirable. The method of calculation may be determined most simply by asking the lender to estimate in writing the amount that would be due if the loan were prepaid on a specified payment date, and to describe the method of calculation. It is possible that the original loan documents will indicate that the Rule of 78 is to be applied in calculating prepayments, but this does not have to be done, and inquiry is therefore necessary.

The Rule of 78 is widely viewed as unfair to consumers, and its use is barred in many states. When negotiating a loan in a state in which its use is permitted, it is sometimes possible to insist that a simple interest calculation be incorporated in a new loan.

The Rule of 78 apparently developed in the 1930s as a matter of convenient calculation of interest on proposed prepayments. At that time, most loans were relatively short term, and the differences between the Rule of 78 and simple interest were small. That is not true today, however, when five-year automobile loans are practically standard.

§1.5 The Variety of Interest Rates

How are interest rates established in the real world? If one compares banks and other lending institutions and reads the financial press, it quickly becomes apparent that a jungle of inconsistent rates all simultaneously exist side by side. To take some examples:

1. Credit cards often charge 1.5 percent per month on the unpaid balance, or roughly 18 percent per year.
2. A bank may make a small loan — say $5,000 — to a good customer at 12 percent per year.
3. In many states, an unsatisfied judgment earns interest at the rate of 6 percent per year, although the rate is 12 percent in some states.
4. A family desiring to purchase a residence may need to pay interest of 8 percent on a loan for 80 percent of the cost of the residence, while the owner of the house next door may have a loan at 6 percent.
5. A large investor-owned electric utility might borrow $65,000,000, with repayment due in 30 years, at about 8 percent per year, while on the same day a large oil company might borrow $300,000,000 at 7 percent, repayable half in 10 years and half in 20 years. On the same day, a city with a population of about 300,000 may borrow $60,000,000 at interest rates ranging from 4 percent for obligations maturing in 5 years to 5 percent for those maturing in 20 years.

Several factors help to explain the diversity in numbers. First, interest rates have varied widely during different historical periods. Many financial transactions — such as many loans to purchase a house — involve fixed interest rates, even though they may be outstanding for 30 years. Much of the diversity of rates simply reflects the historical level of rates when the transaction giving rise to the loan occurred. In recent years, devices that permit periodic adjustment of interest rates have been used increasingly, though many long-term, fixed-rate obligations continue to be written. Fixed rates add an element of gambling to transactions. This point is well illustrated by the example of the homeowner described above who has a 6 percent loan on his house when current market rates for new house loans are 8 percent or more. The below-market-value loan is itself a valuable asset that enhances the value of the home — if the owner can convey the benefits of that loan to a purchaser. On the other hand, the homeowner's asset is the lending institution's albatross. How do you think the lender at 6 percent feels today, knowing that if it could get the homeowner to pay off the balance of his mortgage, the money could be reinvested at 8 percent by lending to a new buyer?

Second, some interest rates described above are established by government fiat and reflect statutory policies rather than market rates. For example, the government might choose to favor the government-designated groups, such as veterans buying homes.

Third, when one considers market rates of interest, wide variations occur because of differences in risk. Other things being equal, an investor demands a

higher return from more risky investments than from investments that are less risky. The difference in rates that the utility and the oil company in the previous example pay may reflect a difference in risk, although the probability of default by either is slight. More likely, the difference is attributable to the length of time over which the loan will be outstanding and the risk that interest rates will rise in the meantime. The possibility that a borrower will not be able to repay the obligation when it matures is called **default risk**. There are independent rating services that determine the default risk for many publicly traded debt securities. Bond ratings provided by Moody's and Standard & Poor's are the most widely followed. These ratings assign alphabetical designations to risk categories. AAA refers to the strongest and most secure securities, sometimes called gilt-edged securities. More speculative debt securities are assigned successively lower designations, such as AA, A, BBB, BB, B, CCC, and so forth, down to C and D (to use the Standard & Poor's designations). The latter ratings are assigned to highly speculative securities that may already be in default or seem unlikely to be repaid. The classification of a debt security in one risk category or another materially affects the interest rate that the borrower has to pay. Obviously, a guarantee of repayment by the federal government significantly reduces the risk that a borrower will default, and therefore reduces the interest cost to the borrower.

Fourth, debt securities that state or municipal borrowers issue are usually exempt from federal income tax. This favored tax status of state or municipal borrowers largely explains why the city with a population of 300,000 described in the previous example may borrow at a significantly lower rate than large corporations.

Tables 1-2 and 1-3 are taken from the *Wall Street Journal* and illustrate some of the points made in this section. Table 1-2 sets forth interest rates for various types of loans and short-term investments as of October 31, 1996. Table 1-3 shows the relationship between loan duration and interest rate.

§1.6 The Market for Money

There is an active market for lendable funds. Interest is the factor that balances the supply and demand for money in this market, in which the sellers of money are commercial banks and other financial institutions and the buyers are individuals and commercial enterprises. This is a retail market for money to distinguish it from the market in which commercial banks obtain funds — a wholesale market (in which individuals and businesses may themselves be sellers). The basic interest rate in the retail market is called the **prime rate**. That is the rate that is usually (although not accurately) defined as the rate large commercial banks charge the biggest and safest borrowers for whom there is no risk of default. Competition requires large commercial banks throughout the United States to maintain a largely uniform prime rate; however, the rate often changes, and there may be periods of transition in which some banks quote the old rate while others quote the new. If the demand for funds appears to be increasing, one or more banks may announce a quarter-point or even a half-point increase in the prime rate. If other banks believe the higher rate is

Table 1-2

MONEY RATES

Thursday, October 30, 1997

The key U.S. and foreign annual interest rates below are a guide to general levels but don't always represent actual transactions.

PRIME RATE: 8.50% (effective 3/26/97). The base rate on corporate loans posted by at least 75% of the nation's 30 largest banks.

DISCOUNT RATE: 5.00%. The charge on loans to depository institutions by the Federal Reserve Banks.

FEDERAL FUNDS: 5 5/8% high, 5 3/8% low, 5 7/16% near closing bid, 5 1/2% offered. Reserves traded among commercial banks for overnight use in amounts of $1 million or more. Source: Prebon Yamane (U.S.A.) Inc.

CALL MONEY: 7.25% (effective 3/27/97). The charge on loans to brokers on stock exchange collateral. Source: Dow Jones.

COMMERCIAL PAPER placed directly by General Electric Capital Corp.: 5.53% 30 to 45 days; 5.50% 46 to 59 days; 5.52% 60 to 73 days; 5.59% 74 to 119 days; 5.54% 120 to 146 days; 5.53% 147 to 179 days; 5.52% 180 to 239 days; 5.50% 240 to 270 days.

COMMERCIAL PAPER: High-grade unsecured notes sold through dealers by major corporations: 5.53% 30 days; 5.53% 60 days; 5.58% 90 days.

CERTIFICATES OF DEPOSIT: 5.24% one month; 5.28% two months; 5.28% three months; 5.59% six months; 5.77% one year. Average of top rates paid by major New York banks on primary new issues of negotiable C.D.s, usually on amounts of $1 million and more. The minimum unit is $100,000. Typical rates in the secondary market: 5.57% one month; 5.70% three months; 5.76% six months.

BANKERS ACCEPTANCES: 5.47% 30 days; 5.53% 60 days; 5.51% 90 days; 5.54% 120 days; 5.54% 150 days; 5.54% 180 days. Offered rates of negotiable, bank-backed business credit instruments typically financing an import order.

LONDON LATE EURODOLLARS: 5 21/32% - 5 17/32% one month; 5 3/4% - 5 5/8% two months; 5 3/4% - 5 5/8% three months; 5 3/4% - 5 5/8% four months; 5 25/32% - 5 21/32% five months; 5 25/32% - 5 21./32% six months.

LONDON INTERBANK OFFERED RATES (LIBOR): 5 21/32% one month; 5 25/32% three months; 5 13/16% six months; 5 29/32% one year. The average of interbank offered rates for dollar deposits in the London market based on quotations at five major banks. Effective rate for contracts entered into two days from date appearing at top of this column.

FOREIGN PRIME RATES: Canada 5.25%; Germany 3.68% (eff. 10/30/97); Japan 1.625%; Switzerland 3.875% (eff. 10/30/97); Britain 7.00%. These rate indications aren't directly comparable; lending practices vary widely by location.

TREASURY BILLS: Results of the Monday, October 27, 1997, auction of short-term U.S. government bills, sold at a discount from face value in units of $10,000 to $1 million: 4.97% 13 weeks; 5.08% 26 weeks.

OVERNIGHT REPURCHASE RATE: 5.53%. Dealer financing rate for overnight sale and repurchase of Treasury securities. Source: Dow Jones.

FEDERAL HOME LOAN MORTGAGE CORP. (Freddie Mac): Posted yields on 30-year mortgage commitments. Delivery within 30 days 7.28%, 60 days 7.33%, standard conventional fixed-rate mortgages; 5.625%, 2% rate capped one-year adjustable rate mortgages. Source: Dow Jones.

FEDERAL NATIONAL MORTGAGE ASSOCIATION (Fannie Mae): Posted yields on 30 year mortgage commitments (priced at par) for delivery within 30 days 7.23%, 60 days 7.27%, standard conventional fixed rate-mortgages; 6.50%, 6/2 rate capped one-year adjustable rate mortgages. Source: Dow Jones.

MERRILL LYNCH READY ASSETS TRUST: 5.09%. Annualized average rate of return after expenses for the past 30 days; not a forecast of future returns.

supportable by the market for funds, they also announce an increase, and the movement becomes nationwide. If other banks do not go along, the innovative banks will probably rescind the increase in order to ensure that their large borrowers do not go elsewhere for funds. A similar pattern appears when the demand for lendable funds appears to be slack and a decline in the prime rate is being considered.

Many borrowers are not candidates for a prime rate loan. However, all such

Table 1-3

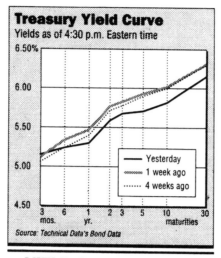

Treasury Yield Curve

Yields as of 4:30 p.m. Eastern time

Legend:
— Yesterday
.... 1 week ago
····· 4 weeks ago

Source: Technical Data's Bond Data

YIELD COMPARISONS

Based on Merrill Lynch Bond Indexes, priced as of midafternoon Eastern time.

	10/30	10/29	52 Week High	52 Week Low
Corp.-Govt. Master	6.06%	6.11%	7.02%	6.03%
Treasury 1-10yr	5.71	5.76	6.65	5.66
10+ yr	6.19	6.25	7.26	6.19
Agencies 1-10yr	6.09	6.16	7.08	6.04
10+ yr	6.35	6.50	7.56	6.35
Corporate				
1-10 yr High Qlty	6.14	6.19	7.18	6.12
Med Qlty	6.39	6.43	7.39	6.36
10+yr High Qlty	6.68	6.71	7.75	6.68
Med Qlty	6.98	7.04	8.05	6.98
Yankee bonds(1)	6.60	6.64	7.51	6.55
Current-coupon mortgages (2)				
GNMA 6.50%	6.73	6.77	7.93	6.73
FNMA 6.50%	6.80	6.84	7.87	6.80
FHLMC6.50%	6.81	6.85	7.88	6.81
High-yield corporates	8.45	8.47	9.65	8.29
Tax-Exempt Bonds				
7-12-yr G.O. (AA)	4.73	4.74	5.32	4.59
12-22-yr G.O. (AA)	5.13	5.16	5.87	5.02
22+yr revenue (A)	5.33	5.36	6.01	5.27

Note: High quality rated AAA-AA; medium quality A-BBB/Baa; high yield, BB/Ba-C.

(1) Dollar-denominated, SEC-registered bonds of foreign issuers sold in the U.S. (2) Reflects the 52-week high and low of mortgage-backed securities indexes rather than the individual securities shown.

borrowers are affected by changes in the prime rate, because interest rates for less secure commercial borrowers are usually tied to the prime rate.

For example, a retail bookstore with sales of $10,000,000 per year may have a line of credit of $1,000,000 to finance inventory from a local bank at three quarters of a point above the prime rate. A line of credit is a very common kind of open arrangement between a bank and a customer by which the customer — in this case the bookstore — may borrow money as needed up to the stated limit of $1,000,000. To take care of the possibility that there are slightly different prime rates being quoted on the last day of the month, such agreements usually specify which bank's quotations of prime rates should be looked to. In this arrangement, of course, the interest rate is flexible and over time varies with the prime rate — and therefore the market price for bank-made

commercial loans also varies. If the business is cyclical, the store may need the line of credit for only part of each year. If not, the store may have loans under the line of credit close to or at the maximum all year round.

Similarly, a small store owner may obtain a signature loan of, say, $5,000. A **signature loan** is also a very common arrangement between a commercial bank and an individual with a good credit rating: It is simply an unsecured loan made solely on the borrower's signature. Two years ago, the store owner borrowed the same amount and was charged 7.5 percent interest. This time, the interest rate is 11 percent. "After all," the friendly banker apologetically explains, "two years ago the prime rate was 6.5 percent; today it is 10 percent." The store owner is in effect being charged one point over the prime rate.

§1.7 The Federal Government and Interest Rates

The federal government uses interest rates and the supply of money in commercial banks as devices to fight inflation and unemployment and to encourage a high level of economic activity. (The fact that these may be partially conflicting goals need not detain us.) This control is exercised principally by the Federal Reserve Board (the Fed) through several devices, the most important of which are (1) open market transactions in federal securities, (2) reserve requirements, (3) federal debt management transactions, and (4) the discount rate.

A detailed discussion of how reserve requirements, open market transactions, and similar devices influence the supply of money and the prime rate is beyond the scope of this book. These devices all operate generally by increasing or decreasing the amount of funds banks have available to lend to customers. The fourth, the discount rate, is more visible because it is an interest rate that the Federal Reserve System charges on loans to commercial banks. The discount rate is set by the Federal Reserve System partly on political and partly on economic considerations: Changes in this rate receive even more publicity than changes in the prime rate and can dramatically affect prices in the stock and bond markets. From a bank's perspective, the discount rate is a wholesale rate and the prime rate is a retail rate for money. The spread between the discount and prime rate is usually about 2 percentage points. Thus, if the Fed raises the discount rate, the prime rate also usually rises.

§1.8 Debts, IOUs, and Promissory Notes

There is more to lending and borrowing money than calculating interest payments. When one person (the creditor) lends money to another (the debtor), one question that arises is what evidence of that debt the creditor should demand. Small noncommercial loans are frequently evidenced simply by a cancelled check, or acknowledged by a handshake, or a simple "thank you." Of course, a debt exists any time there is a loan, even if it is not evidenced by any writing or formality, and the creditor may enforce the repayment obligation upon proving that a loan was in fact made and not repaid.

A slightly more formal arrangement might be for the debtor to execute an IOU—a written acknowledgment by the debtor that a debt exists. The initials "IOU" simply stand for "I owe you." An IOU may simplify the evidentiary requirements otherwise imposed on a creditor seeking to enforce a debt but it is not, by itself, a promise to repay the debt on any particular terms.

Debts may be freely sold, assigned, or traded without the prior consent of the debtor. A person purchasing or otherwise acquiring a debt is known as an assignee and may enforce the creditor's claim against the debtor, subject to whatever defenses arising out of the same transaction the debtor may have against the original creditor. The debtor, however, may also agree in the original transaction to waive defenses he or she may have in a suit brought by an assignee, and such a waiver will be given effect in most circumstances.

A higher level of formality and potentially greater legal consequences occur when the debtor is required to sign a **promissory note**. A promissory note states that the debtor "promises to pay to the order of" the creditor the amount of the debt, usually together with interest. Unlike an IOU, a promissory note itself embodies a promise to make a payment at some future time.

A promissory note may be made payable to the order of a specific person or to the "bearer." A **bearer note** is payable to whoever has physical possession of the piece of paper; the debt is transferred simply by physical transfer of the paper. A promissory note payable to the order of a person is usually transferred by **endorsement**. The payee of the note writes on the back of the note "Pay to the order of Y," signs his or her name, and delivers the note to Y. Y can then enforce the note as though he or she were the payee, or may endorse the note to Z by following the same process.

A promissory note is said to be in **negotiable form** if it meets minimal statutory requirements: It must (1) be signed by the maker (the debtor), (2) contain only an unconditional promise to pay a certain sum in money, (3) be payable on demand or at a definite time, and (4) be payable to order or bearer. Most notes used in commercial transactions are in negotiable form. The advantage of a note in this form is that, if the person acquiring the note is a **holder in due course** (i.e., is a person who acquires the note for value and without knowledge of possible defenses), he or she is able to enforce the promise of payment set forth in the note free of certain defenses that the debtor might have had if suit had been brought directly by the creditor on the underlying transaction. The negotiation of a promissory note to a holder in due course results in a debt becoming an article of commerce largely freed from the underlying transaction that gave rise to it: The debt ceases to be a personal obligation between the creditor and debtor.

To illustrate: Assume that a seller of certain computer equipment originally received cash for a portion of the purchase price and lent the buyer the balance, taking a negotiable promissory note that the buyer executed. The buyer, however, has stopped making payments on the ground that the equipment did not perform as warranted. Obviously, if the seller directly seeks to enforce the buyer's promise to pay the balance of the purchase price, the defense of breach of warranty will be raised. It may not be completely ethical, but if the seller can negotiate the promissory note to a holder in due course, for example, a bank, the buyer will not be able to assert the defense of breach of warranty against

the holder in due course. In other words, in the hands of a holder in due course, the promissory note is enforceable in and of itself without regard to the underlying commercial transaction that gave rise to it. If the buyer is forced to pay the holder in due course in full, he or she may then turn around and sue the seller for breach of warranty, so that at least theoretically, the wrongdoer — the seller whose product did not conform to his or her warranties — ends up ultimately being held responsible. In the process, however, the innocent purchaser of the promissory note is permitted to enforce it in accordance with its terms, and the defense of breach of warranty can only be asserted against the other party to the original transaction in a separate lawsuit.

It is, of course, possible in the preceding hypothetical that the holder in due course will be unable to get satisfaction from the buyer even though he or she obtains a judgment. The seller, who endorsed the note to the holder in due course, is then liable to take back the note from the holder in due course and return any consideration paid, because an endorser warrants that the instrument will be honored when it is presented. Other persons in the chain of transfer may also be liable if they transferred the instrument with knowledge of the maker's insolvency. In other words, if the buyer refuses to pay and the holder in due course is compelled to seek satisfaction from the seller/endorser or earlier transferees on their warranties, the same result is reached — the wrongdoer ends up holding the bag.

The cutting-off of defenses described in the previous paragraphs does not apply to certain **real defenses**, such as forgery or duress. Also, if the person acquiring the note is not a holder in due course or if the transaction is cast as an **assignment** of a note rather than as a **negotiation**, no defenses are shut off (unless the maker agrees to waive them) and the holder of the note stands in precisely the same shoes as the original lender. The difference between assignment ("I hereby assign the attached note to Z") and negotiation ("pay to the order of Z") may seem to be mere semantics; however, different legal consequences often flow from different words. The detailed rules about the negotiation of promissory notes and other types of commercial paper, who qualifies as a holder in due course, and the rights of such a holder all appear in Articles Three and Four of the Uniform Commercial Code and are covered in detail in advanced law school courses in commercial law.

Almost all commercial loan transactions are evidenced by promissory notes. Most of them are in negotiable form. Forms for negotiable promissory notes can readily be found in form books, and printed promissory notes in negotiable form with blanks to be filled in can be obtained from a legal stationer.

Bonds and **debentures** are gussied-up promissory notes that corporations use to borrow long-term funds. Such instruments are often publicly held and widely traded. These are discussed in more detail in the chapter on corporate securities.

§1.9 Secured and Unsecured Loans

Creditors often are not satisfied with the simple right to sue for payment even as a holder in due course of negotiable commercial paper. Such a creditor

is unsecured: His or her right to collect on the claim depends on the debtor being able to pay the amount due when a judgment is obtained. The time when collection is sought is more critical than the time the transaction occurred: A debtor may have numerous assets when the debt is created but business reverses or unwise transactions may make the debt uncollectible when enforcement is sought. A holder in due course is no better off than the original creditor in this regard, because even if the holder gets a judgment on the promissory note, he or she still has to collect on the judgment. Not even a holder in due course can squeeze blood from a turnip.

Creditors increase the likelihood of repayment by requiring, at the time of the transaction, that the debtor grant an interest in some or all of his or her property to secure the repayment of the loan. If the transaction involves the sale of goods on credit, the seller will normally take a **security interest** in the goods sold. In other types of transactions, the security interest may involve various kinds of tangible or intangible property or rights. Typically, the property or assets remain in the control of the debtor until a default on the loan occurs, when the creditor may take judicial steps or self-help to seize the property or rights in order to satisfy the debt. Historically, these creditor-owned interests in debtors' property were called **liens** or **chattel mortgages**. Under the Uniform Commercial Code, they are called **security interests** or **purchase money security interests**, though references to liens still regularly appear in cases involving personal property. Basically, a lien or security interest is an intangible property interest that allows the creditor, if the loan is not repaid, to seize the property subject to the lien to satisfy the unpaid loan; usually the property is sold and the proceeds are applied against the unpaid loan.

Notice of a security interest in the debtor's property is publicly made by filing with a public office to perfect the security interest against claims of subsequent creditors. (There are some important exceptions to the filing requirement for **perfection**. Where an exception is applicable, the security interest is perfected either by other means, such as taking possession of the collateral, or automatically.) A failure to perfect means that subsequent creditors may obtain competing security interests senior to the unfiled interest or that a bankruptcy trustee may be able to avoid the unfiled security interest, reducing the creditor to unsecured status.

The process by which a secured creditor realizes upon the security is usually described as **foreclosure**, though in the case of consumer goods it may involve **repossession**. Typically, the seized property is sold and the proceeds applied to the payment of the debt. If the proceeds of the sale of seized property are not sufficient to discharge the loan (as is usually the case), the creditor continues to have an unsecured claim against the debtor for the balance, usually called a **deficiency** or **deficiency judgment**. If the proceeds exceed the loan balance, unpaid interest, and allowable fees or charges (often including attorney's fees), the debtor is entitled to the balance.

Everyone has heard of hard-hearted creditors repossessing automobiles or washing machines from luckless debtors or the equipment and land of farmers being put up for sale at auction at the direction of one or more creditors. Although such events do obviously happen with some regularity when debtors are individuals, most enforcement efforts involve something less than foreclo-

sure. For one thing, as a device to encourage payment, creditors often take security in property of dubious value but of personal value to the debtor. Second-hand furniture probably will not bring very much upon resale, but the threat of foreclosure could mean the potential loss of a family's cherished items and only furniture, and payment of the secured loan may be made to ensure that the furniture is not lost. Many secured creditors threaten and cajole: They may make numerous threatening telephone calls or even post property for foreclosure. Foreclosure, however, is not free of cost and is usually a last resort. Automobile repossession in many areas is an exception because of the relative mobility and ease of marketability of the collateral.

Even though substantial businesses that raise capital by borrowing are also often required to pledge machinery and other business assets as security for the loans, foreclosure is even less common in the case of businesses than in the case of individuals. A business is typically worth more as a going enterprise than it is broken up and sold in parts. Thus, when a substantial business runs into financial difficulty and secured creditors begin making threatening noises to seize the railroad's freight cars or the manufacturer's machinery and equipment, the debtor usually seeks protection from foreclosure in the federal bankruptcy courts by filing a petition for reorganization so its operating assets can be preserved as a single unit. Although secured creditors holding liens on operating assets are in a better position than unsecured creditors in a reorganization proceeding, there is no assurance that in bankruptcy a secured creditor will be able to realize directly upon his or her security.

Much of the law relating to obtaining and perfecting security interests appears in Article Nine of the Uniform Commercial Code and is covered in detail in advanced commercial law courses in law school. However, legal problems relating to security interests also involve bankruptcy, collection practices, and the like.

§1.10 The Importance of Interest in Commercial Transactions

There are numerous vehicles for investment available to persons with excess capital, either on a short- or long-term basis. Many of these investment vehicles permit the earning of interest on a daily basis. In reflecting on the concept of interest as compensation for the use of funds, it should be apparent that it is uneconomic to leave large amounts of capital in non-interest-bearing form for any period of time. The most common example of a non-interest-bearing form is the simple checking account. Other examples are cash in a sock, a mattress or safe deposit vault, or investments in jewels, works of art, or gold. Of course, one needs to retain cash in a checking account to pay current bills and to avoid bank service charges, but in this day of electronic fund transfers and flexible investment vehicles, excess cash should generally be earning interest rather than lying idle in some form. It is not uncommon for businesses to have an average daily balance in the tens or hundreds of thousands of dollars. In such cases, more effective cash management may permit a steady interest income to be developed where none presently exists.

It is also important to recognize that even one day's interest on a large sum of money involves enough dollars to dictate careful planning. Assume, for example, that your client has successfully negotiated the sale of his solely owned business for $25,000,000 in cash, payable by bank certified check at the closing. The closing should be scheduled early enough in the day to permit investment of the $25,000,000 the same day. Something like $5,000 in interest for one day will be lost if a closing is scheduled at 4:00 p.m. after local banks are closed. That may sound astonishing, but it is true: Large sums generate an appreciable amount of interest each day. Similarly, to set up an escrow account for $10,000,000 without providing for investment of the escrowed amount and a clear statement as to who is entitled to the interim interest is so negligent as to border on malpractice. Of course, clients with large sums of money are usually well aware of the cost of leaving funds idle for even short periods of time and will insist on appropriate investment provisions.

When very large sums are involved, even payment schedules are apt to become a matter of negotiation, because interest may be earned on interest payments. The creditor will usually seek payments quarterly or even monthly to take advantage of this fact. Correspondingly, the debtor may opt for semi-annual or even annual payments, if he or she can. Assume, for example, that your client owns a large hotel and apartment complex on the beach, complete with swimming pool and 18-hole golf course. He has negotiated a sale of the entire property for $100,000,000 on the following terms: $10,000,000 down with the balance payable over 5 years, $15,000,000 per year at 6 percent compound interest per year. Your client proposes that payments of principal and interest be made quarterly each year; the buyer is equally adamant that there be a single $15,000,000 payment plus interest payable on each anniversary date only. If your client can earn more than 6 percent on alternative investments, quarterly payments permit investment at the higher rate sooner than an annual payment. Even a one percent additional yield on investments above the 6 percent rate makes the quarterly payment plan worth $30,000 more than the annual payment plan in the first year alone. Because the purchaser can also earn more than 6 percent per year on alternative investments, it is to his or her decided advantage to place the funds to be used to make payments in these alternative investments, leave them there as long as possible, and make payments as late as possible. In a very real sense, time is money.

CHAPTER 2
PRESENT VALUE

§2.1 Introduction

One of the most fundamental financial concepts is that money to be paid or received in the future is not worth as much as money to be paid or received today. Relatively simple formulas permit a direct comparison of the value of amounts to be paid at different times. This chapter discusses this concept, which underlies much of financial theory and much of current business practice. The process by which amounts payable at different times are made comparable is usually referred to as discounting future payments to **present value**. The word **discounting** in this context simply means reducing. Another phrase that describes this concept is **time value of money**.

§2.2 The Basic Concept

What is the right to receive $1,000 a year from now worth today? Assuming that there is no risk that the payer will default, it is clear that the right is worth something less than $1,000. If one had $1,000 today, one could invest it for a year in a riskless investment and thereby earn one year's interest in addition to the original $1,000. Thus, $1,000 payable a year from now has to be worth somewhat less than $1,000 in hand today. How much less? One way to answer such a question is to approach it from the point of view of a hypothetical

investor: If that investor can make 12 percent per year on his or her money in a riskless investment, how much should the investor pay today for the right to receive that $1,000 in a year? So phrased, the issue becomes an algebraic calculation:

$$x + .12x = \$1,000$$

$$1.12x = \$1,000$$

$$x = \frac{\$1,000}{1.12} = \$892.86$$

To such an investor, the right to receive $1,000 a year from now is worth precisely $892.86. But, it may be rejoined, why choose a 12 percent return? Why not, say, an 8 percent return, in which case the calculation becomes:

$$x + .08x = \$1,000$$

and the value of the right to receive the $1,000 in 12 months becomes $925.93? The difference between these two amounts is significant. Of course, there is no one single rate of return that is correct in an absolute sense. But that element of uncertainty as to what the correct value is should not hide certain basic truths that these simple examples reveal: (1) because interest rates are positive, a dollar in the future is always worth less than a dollar today, and (2) the higher the interest that can be earned on a riskless investment, the lower is the current value of a right to receive a future payment. In other words, there is an inverse relationship between interest rates and current values of future payments. This leads to yet a third basic truth: (3) the riskier the investment, the lower the current value of a right to receive the future payment. Why? Because the riskier the investment, the higher the rate of return on which the investor will insist.

The present value of a future sum is the reverse of the **future value** of a present sum invested at the same interest rate. For example, assume that one plans to buy a $1,000 stereo a year from now; how much do you have to put aside today in an account earning 12 percent per year to have $1,000 in one year? The answer, of course, is the now familiar amount, $892.86; determining that the present value of $1,000 payable one year from now is $892.86 is simply looking at the same transaction from a different perspective.

When speaking of the earning power of a present amount over time, one usually speaks of the interest rate. When going the other way and computing the present value of a future payment, one usually speaks of the discount rate. However, it is the same rate, because the present value of a future sum and the future value of a present sum involve precisely the same calculation, examined from opposite perspectives.

§2.3 Present Value Calculations Over Multiple Periods

Following the same line of reasoning, what is $1,000 payable two years in the future worth today? If we again assume a 12 percent interest rate, it turns

out that a $797.19 investment today grows to $892.86 after one year and to precisely $1,000 after two years. Thus, the present value of $1,000 payable two years from today is $797.19 at 12 percent interest. This involves a compound interest calculation, because the comparison is with a $797.19 investment today that is left untouched until the end of the two-year period. A formula to determine present values of future payments over multiple periods, derived from the formula for compound interest, is:

$$PV = \frac{FV}{(1 + i)^n}$$

where PV = present value; FV = future value; i = the interest rate; and n = the number of periods. The calculations of one-year present values set forth earlier are simply special applications of this formula.

Despite the apparent mathematical certainty of the formula, it is important to recognize that the precise calculation of the present value of a future sum over a specified period depends both on the applicable interest or discount rate and the number of subperiods within the period over which interest is compounded. In other words, in order to get mathematical precision, one must know both the applicable discount rate and whether interest is compounded quarterly, annually, or over some other set of subperiods during the two-year period in question. In the foregoing calculations, it is assumed that interest is compounded only annually so that the number of periods is two. In most calculations like this, involving relatively short time periods, the number of subperiods used does not change the results significantly. For example, if one calculates a 12 percent discount rate compounded quarterly over the two-year period, interest is compounded eight times at 3 percent per quarter, and the present value of $1,000 payable two years from now is $789.41 as compared with the $791.19 obtained above on the assumption that interest is compounded only annually. Do you see why increasing the number of subperiods reduces the present value of a future payment?

§2.4 Examples of Present Value Calculations

Table 2-1 indicates what $1,000 payable at various times in the future is worth today at 12 percent and at 6 percent. Several fundamental relationships described in this table should be emphasized:

First, the longer the period before the payment is to be received, the smaller the value.

Second, the present value of the right to receive even large sums of money in the far distant future is not worth very much, if anything. For example, how much should you pay for the right to receive $100,000 in a lump sum 100 years from now? Not very much: According to the above tables, you should pay no more than one dollar at a 12 percent discount rate and $294 at a 6 percent rate.

Third, in making these present value computations, the discount rate that

Table 2-1

Number of years	Value of $1,000 at 12%	Value of $1,000 at 6%
1	892.90	943.40
2	797.20	890.00
3	711.80	839.60
4	635.50	792.10
5	567.40	747.30
10	322.00	558.40
25	58.80	233.00
50	3.50	54.30
100	0.01	2.94

is chosen has a tremendous effect on the outcome of the calculation. One can manipulate answers obtained by minor changes in that number.

Table 2-2 shows the present values of one dollar payable at various time periods in the future at most plausible interest rates. Note that the numbers in Table 2-2 are all decimals less than one, while in Table 1-1 all the entries are one or larger. That is because each entry in Table 2-2 is the reciprocal of each entry in Table 1-1. In other words:

$$\text{Present Value} = \frac{1}{\text{Future Value}}$$

A simple illustration of the use of Table 2-2 might involve a person planning to set aside a sum of money today to provide $10,000 of law school tuition five years from now. Suppose that an investment earns interest at the rate of 6 percent compounded semiannually. One simply has to look up the discount factor for 3 percent over 10 periods in Table 2-2, which yields 0.7441, and multiply by $10,000 to get $7,441.

One of the most egregious examples of failure to recognize the time value of money can be seen in the advertising for lottery jackpots. A prize may be quoted as $1,000,000 although it is paid out at the rate of $50,000 per year for 20 years. If so, the prize is not in fact $1,000,000 but some lesser number depending on the appropriate rate of interest. The higher the rate of interest the lower the lump sum value of the payment.

The decimal numbers in Table 2-2 are sometimes called **discount factors**, because they can be added together to determine the present values of future payments as the following section illustrates.

§2.5 A Preliminary Look at Annuities

An **annuity** is a stream of constant payments to be made at fixed intervals. This section provides a preliminary examination of the underlying concept. Annuities are treated in detail in Chapter 4.

The present value of the right to receive $1,000 each year, beginning next year and continuing for five years at 12 percent compounded annually can be

Table 2-2
Present Value of $1 Payable After n Periods in the Future

No. of periods	2%	3%	4%	5%	6%	7%	8%
1	.9804	.9709	.9615	.9524	.9434	.9346	.9259
2	.9612	.9426	.9246	.9070	.8900	.8734	.8573
3	.9423	.9151	.8890	.8638	.8396	.8163	.7938
4	.9238	.8885	.8548	.8227	.7921	.7629	.7350
5	.9057	.8626	.8219	.7835	.7473	.7130	.6806
6	.8880	.8375	.7903	.7462	.7050	.6663	.6302
7	.8706	.8131	.7599	.7107	.6651	.6227	.5835
8	.8535	.7894	.7307	.6768	.6274	.5820	.5403
9	.8368	.7664	.7026	.6446	.5919	.5439	.5002
10	.8203	.7441	.6756	.6139	.5584	.5083	.4632
11	.8043	.7224	.6496	.5847	.5268	.4751	.4289
12	.7885	.7014	.6246	.5568	.4970	.4440	.3971
13	.7730	.6810	.6006	.5303	.4688	.4150	.3677
14	.7579	.6611	.5775	.5051	.4423	.3878	.3405
15	.7430	.6419	.5553	.4810	.4173	.3624	.3152
16	.7284	.6232	.5339	.4581	.3936	.3387	.2919
17	.7142	.6050	.5134	.4363	.3714	.3166	.2703
18	.7002	.5874	.4936	.4155	.3503	.2959	.2502
19	.6864	.5703	.4746	.3957	.3305	.2765	.2317
20	.6730	.5537	.4564	.3769	.3118	.2584	.2145
21	.6598	.5375	.4388	.3589	.2942	.2415	.1987
22	.6468	.5219	.4220	.3418	.2775	.2257	.1839
23	.6342	.5067	.4057	.3256	.2618	.2109	.1703
24	.6217	.4919	.3901	.3101	.2470	.1971	.1577
25	.6095	.4776	.3751	.2953	.2330	.1842	.1460

Table 2-2 (cont.)
Present Value of $1 Payable After n Periods in the Future

No. of periods	2%	3%	4%	5%	6%	7%	8%
26	.5976	.4637	.3607	.2812	.2198	.1722	.1352
27	.5859	.4502	.3468	.2678	.2074	.1609	.1252
28	.5744	.4371	.3335	.2551	.1956	.1504	.1159
29	.5631	.4243	.3207	.2429	.1846	.1406	.1073
30	.5521	.4120	.3083	.2314	.1741	.1314	.0994
31	.5412	.4000	.2965	.2204	.1643	.1228	.0920
32	.5306	.3883	.2851	.2099	.1550	.1147	.0852
33	.5202	.3770	.2741	.1999	.1462	.1072	.0789
34	.5100	.3660	.2636	.1904	.1379	.1002	.0730
35	.5000	.3554	.2534	.1813	.1301	.0937	.0676
36	.4902	.3450	.2437	.1727	.1227	.0875	.0626
37	.4806	.3350	.2343	.1644	.1158	.0818	.0580
38	.4712	.3252	.2253	.1566	.1092	.0765	.0537
39	.4619	.3158	.2166	.1491	.1031	.0715	.0497
40	.4529	.3066	.2083	.1420	.0972	.0668	.0460
41	.4440	.2976	.2003	.1353	.0917	.0624	.0426
42	.4353	.2890	.1926	.1288	.0865	.0583	.0395
43	.4268	.2805	.1852	.1227	.0816	.0545	.0365
44	.4184	.2724	.1780	.1169	.0770	.0509	.0338
45	.4102	.2644	.1712	.1113	.0727	.0476	.0313
46	.4022	.2567	.1646	.1060	.0685	.0445	.0290
47	.3943	.2493	.1583	.1009	.0647	.0416	.0269
48	.3865	.2420	.1522	.0961	.0610	.0389	.0249
49	.3790	.2350	.1463	.0916	.0575	.0363	.0230
50	.3715	.2281	.1407	.0872	.0543	.0339	.0213

Table 2-2 (*cont.*)
Present Value of $1 Payable After n Periods in the Future

No. of periods	9%	10%	11%	12%	13%	14%	15%
1	.9174	.9091	.9009	.8929	.8850	.8772	.8696
2	.8417	.8264	.8116	.7972	.7831	.7695	.7561
3	.7722	.7513	.7312	.7118	.6931	.6750	.6575
4	.7084	.6830	.6587	.6355	.6133	.5921	.5718
5	.6499	.6209	.5935	.5674	.5428	.5194	.4972
6	.5963	.5645	.5346	.5066	.4803	.4556	.4323
7	.5470	.5132	.4817	.4523	.4251	.3996	.3759
8	.5019	.4665	.4339	.4039	.3762	.3506	.3269
9	.4604	.4241	.3909	.3606	.3329	.3075	.2843
10	.4224	.3855	.3522	.3220	.2946	.2697	.2472
11	.3875	.3505	.3173	.2875	.2607	.2366	.2149
12	.3555	.3186	.2858	.2567	.2307	.2076	.1869
13	.3262	.2897	.2575	.2292	.2042	.1821	.1625
14	.2992	.2633	.2320	.2046	.1807	.1597	.1413
15	.2745	.2394	.2090	.1827	.1599	.1401	.1229
16	.2519	.2176	.1883	.1631	.1415	.1229	.1069
17	.2311	.1978	.1696	.1456	.1252	.1078	.0929
18	.2120	.1799	.1528	.1300	.1108	.0946	.0808
19	.1945	.1635	.1377	.1161	.0981	.0829	.0703
20	.1784	.1486	.1240	.1037	.0868	.0728	.0611
21	.1637	.1351	.1117	.0926	.0768	.0638	.0531
22	.1502	.1228	.1007	.0826	.0680	.0560	.0462
23	.1378	.1117	.0907	.0738	.0601	.0491	.0402
24	.1264	.1015	.0817	.0659	.0532	.0431	.0349
25	.1160	.0923	.0736	.0588	.0471	.0378	.0304

Table 2-2 (*cont.*)
Present Value of $1 Payable After n Periods in the Future

No. of periods	9%	10%	11%	12%	13%	14%	15%
26	.1064	.0839	.0663	.0525	.0417	.0331	.0264
27	.0976	.0763	.0597	.0469	.0369	.0291	.0230
28	.0895	.0693	.0538	.0419	.0326	.0255	.0200
29	.0822	.0630	.0485	.0374	.0289	.0224	.0714
30	.0754	.0573	.0437	.0334	.0256	.0196	.0151
31	.0691	.0521	.0394	.0298	.0226	.0172	.0131
32	.0634	.0474	.0355	.0266	.0200	.0151	.0114
33	.0582	.0431	.0319	.0238	.0177	.0132	.0099
34	.0534	.0391	.0288	.0212	.0157	.0116	.0086
35	.0490	.0356	.0259	.0189	.0139	.0102	.0075
36	.0449	.0323	.0234	.0169	.0123	.0089	.0065
37	.0412	.0294	.0210	.0151	.0109	.0078	.0057
38	.0378	.0267	.0190	.0135	.0096	.0069	.0049
39	.0347	.0243	.0171	.0120	.0085	.0060	.0043
40	.0318	.0221	.0154	.0107	.0075	.0053	.0037
41	.0292	.0201	.0139	.0096	.0067	.0046	.0032
42	.0268	.0183	.0125	.0086	.0059	.0041	.0028
43	.0246	.0166	.0112	.0076	.0052	.0036	.0025
44	.0226	.0151	.0101	.0068	.0046	.0031	.0021
45	.0207	.0137	.0091	.0061	.0041	.0027	.0019
46	.0190	.0125	.0082	.0054	.0036	.0024	.0016
47	.0174	.0113	.0074	.0049	.0032	.0021	.0014
48	.0160	.0103	.0067	.0043	.0028	.0019	.0012
49	.0147	.0094	.0060	.0039	.0025	.0016	.0011
50	.0134	.0085	.0054	.0035	.0022	.0014	.0009

computed in several ways. First, one may simply add up the present values of each of the first five payments in Table 2-1 ($892.90 + $797.20 + $711.80 + $635.50 + $567.40). The sum $3,604.80 is the present value of the right to receive an aggregate amount of $5,000 in increments of $1,000 per year over the next five years. It seems odd that the right to receive $100,000 in a lump sum 100 years from now, also discounted at 12 percent, is worth only one dollar, while the right to receive only $1,000 per year over the next five years is worth thousands of times as much. Yet that is the magic of the time value of money.

A second way to calculate the present value of the same annuity is to add up the first five discount factors in Table 2-2 under 12 percent (.8929 + .7972 + .7118 + .6355 + .5674 = 3.6048) and multiply the product by $1,000.

An even simpler method exists. Table 2-3 is a table of the present values of annuities (payable at the end of each period). To get the present value of the 12 percent, five-year annuity, one simply looks up the "five year" row and "12 percent" column to find the number 3.6048. Obviously, Table 2-3 may be obtained from Table 2-2 by a process of systematic summing of amounts.

For those mathematically inclined, a nice complex formula to derive the present value of a stream of constant payments in the future is:

$$PV = \frac{P(1 - (1 + i)^{-n})}{i}$$

where P = the recurring payment; PV = the present value; i = the interest rate; and n = the number of periods.

Many calculators have been programmed to compute present and future values of annuities directly, but one should understand the underlying theory. No matter how one calculates it, however, the assumption that the payments are identical in amount and evenly spaced should be kept in mind.

§2.6 The Value of a Perpetual Annuity

Assume that an annuity will continue to pay $1,000 per year forever. One might think that such an annuity must be worth an infinite amount because both the number of payments and the total amount paid are infinite. Not so.

For simplicity, let us assume that an appropriate discount rate is 12 percent, so that we know that the first five years of the annuity is worth $3,604.80. If you turn back to Table 2-2, it appears that the "infinity" answer may be wrong because the present value of future payments drops off dramatically. Similarly, if one looks at Table 2-3 under the 12 percent column, the present value of a 45-year annuity is $8,282.50, while the present value of a 50-year annuity is $8,304.50. In other words, from the 45th to the 50th year, the five years of $1,000 payments increase the present value by only $22. By extension, it is clear that the value of a perpetual annuity is not infinite.

The present value of a perpetual stream of fixed payments is precisely equal

Table 2-3
Present Value of an Annuity of $1 Payable at the End of Each Period for n Periods

No. of periods	2%	3%	4%	5%	6%	7%	8%
1	.9804	.9709	.9615	.9524	.9434	.9346	.9259
2	1.9416	1.9135	1.8861	1.8594	1.8334	1.8080	1.7833
3	2.8839	2.8286	2.7751	2.7232	2.6730	2.6243	2.5771
4	3.8077	3.7171	3.6299	3.5460	3.4651	3.3872	3.3121
5	4.7135	4.5797	4.4518	4.3295	4.2124	4.1002	3.9927
6	5.6014	5.4172	5.2421	5.0757	4.9173	4.7665	4.6229
7	6.4720	6.2303	6.0021	5.7864	5.5824	5.3893	5.2064
8	7.3255	7.0197	6.7327	6.4632	6.2098	5.9713	5.7466
9	8.1622	7.7861	7.4353	7.1078	6.8017	6.5152	6.2469
10	8.9826	8.5302	8.1109	7.7217	7.3601	7.0236	6.7101
11	9.7868	9.2526	8.7605	8.3064	7.8869	7.4987	7.1390
12	10.5753	9.9540	9.3851	8.8633	8.3838	7.9427	7.5361
13	11.3484	10.6350	9.9856	9.3936	8.8527	8.3577	7.9038
14	12.1062	11.2961	10.5631	9.8986	9.2950	8.7455	8.2442
15	12.8493	11.9379	11.1184	10.3797	9.7122	9.1079	8.5595
16	13.5777	12.5611	11.6523	10.8378	10.1059	9.4466	8.8514
17	14.2919	13.1661	12.1657	11.2741	10.4773	9.7632	9.1216
18	14.9920	13.7535	12.6593	11.6896	10.8276	10.0591	9.3719
19	15.6785	14.3238	13.1339	12.0853	11.1581	10.3356	9.6036
20	16.3514	14.8775	13.5903	12.4622	11.4699	10.5940	9.8181
21	17.0112	15.4150	14.0292	12.8212	11.7641	10.8355	10.0168
22	17.6580	15.9369	14.4511	13.1630	12.0416	11.0612	10.2007
23	18.2922	16.4436	14.8568	13.4886	12.3034	11.2722	10.3711
24	18.9139	16.9355	15.2470	13.7986	12.5504	11.4693	10.5288
25	19.5235	17.4131	15.6221	14.0939	12.7834	11.6536	10.6748

26	10.8100	11.8258	13.0032	14.3752	15.9828	17.8768	20.1210
27	10.9352	11.9867	13.2105	14.6430	16.3296	18.3270	20.7069
28	11.0511	12.1371	13.4062	14.8981	16.6631	18.7641	21.2813
29	11.1584	12.2777	13.5907	15.1411	16.9837	19.1885	21.8444
30	11.2578	12.4090	13.7648	15.3725	17.2920	19.6004	22.3965
31	11.3498	12.5318	13.9291	15.5928	17.5885	20.0004	22.9377
32	11.4350	12.6466	14.0840	15.8027	17.8736	20.3888	23.4683
33	11.5139	12.7538	14.2302	16.0025	18.1476	20.7658	23.9886
34	11.5869	12.8540	14.3681	16.1929	18.4112	21.1318	24.4986
35	11.6546	12.9477	14.4982	16.3742	18.6646	21.4872	24.9986
36	11.7172	13.0352	14.6210	16.5469	18.9083	21.8323	25.4888
37	11.7752	13.1170	14.7368	16.7113	19.1426	22.1672	25.9695
38	11.8289	13.1935	14.8460	16.8679	19.3679	22.4925	26.4406
39	11.8786	13.2649	14.9491	17.0170	19.5845	22.8082	26.9026
40	11.9246	13.3317	15.0463	17.1591	19.7928	23.1148	27.3555
41	11.9672	13.3941	15.1380	17.2944	19.9931	23.4124	27.7995
42	12.0067	13.4524	15.2245	17.4232	20.1856	23.7014	28.2348
43	12.0432	13.5070	15.3062	17.5459	20.3708	23.9819	28.6616
44	12.0771	13.5579	15.3832	17.6628	20.5488	24.2543	29.0800
45	12.1084	13.6055	15.4558	17.7741	20.7200	24.5187	29.4902
46	12.1374	13.6500	15.5244	17.8801	20.8847	24.7754	29.8923
47	12.1643	13.6916	15.5890	17.9810	21.0429	25.0247	30.2866
48	12.1891	13.7305	15.6500	18.0772	21.1951	25.2667	30.6731
49	12.2122	13.7668	15.7076	18.1687	21.3415	25.5017	31.0521
50	12.2335	13.8007	15.7619	18.2559	21.4822	25.7298	31.4236

Table 2-3 (*cont.*)
Present Value of an Annuity of $1 Payable at the End of Each Period for n Periods

No. of periods	9%	10%	11%	12%	13%	14%	15%
1	.9174	.9091	.9009	.8929	.8850	.87723	.8696
2	1.7591	1.7355	1.7125	1.6901	1.6681	1.6467	1.6257
3	2.5313	2.4869	2.4437	2.4018	2.3612	2.3216	2.2832
4	3.2397	3.1699	3.1024	3.0373	2.9745	2.9137	2.8550
5	3.8897	3.7908	3.6959	3.6048	3.5172	3.4331	3.3522
6	4.4859	4.3553	4.2305	4.1114	3.9975	3.8887	3.7845
7	5.0330	4.8684	4.7122	4.5638	4.4226	4.2883	4.1604
8	5.5348	5.3349	5.1461	4.9676	4.7988	4.6389	4.4873
9	5.9952	5.7590	5.5370	5.3282	5.1317	4.9464	4.7716
10	6.4177	6.1446	5.8892	5.6502	5.4262	5.2161	5.0188
11	6.8052	6.4951	6.2065	5.9377	5.6869	5.4527	5.2337
12	7.1607	6.8137	6.4924	6.1944	5.9176	5.6603	5.4206
13	7.4869	7.1034	6.7499	6.4235	6.1218	5.8424	5.5831
14	7.7862	7.3667	6.9819	6.6282	6.3025	6.0021	5.7245
15	8.0607	7.6061	7.1909	6.8109	6.4624	6.1422	5.8474
16	8.3126	7.8237	7.3792	6.9740	6.6039	6.2651	5.9542
17	8.5436	8.0216	7.5488	7.1196	6.7291	6.3729	6.0472
18	8.7556	8.2014	7.7016	7.2497	6.8399	6.4674	6.1280
19	8.9501	8.3649	7.8393	7.3658	6.9380	6.5504	6.1982
20	9.1285	8.5136	7.9633	7.4694	7.0248	6.6231	6.2593
21	9.2922	8.6487	8.0751	7.5620	7.1016	6.6870	6.3125
22	9.4424	8.7715	8.1757	7.6446	7.1695	6.7429	6.3587
23	9.5802	8.8832	8.2664	7.7184	7.2297	6.7921	6.3988
24	9.7066	8.9847	8.3481	7.7843	7.2829	6.8351	6.4338
25	9.8226	9.0770	8.4217	7.8431	7.3300	6.8729	6.4641

26	9.9290	9.1609	8.4881	7.8957	7.3717	6.9061	6.4906
27	10.0266	9.2372	8.5478	7.9426	7.4086	6.9352	6.5135
28	10.1161	9.3066	8.6016	7.9844	7.4412	6.9607	6.5335
29	10.1983	9.3696	8.6501	8.0218	7.4701	6.9830	6.5509
30	10.2737	9.4269	8.6938	8.0552	7.4957	7.0027	6.5660
31	10.3428	9.4790	8.7331	8.0850	7.5183	7.0199	6.5791
32	10.4062	9.5264	8.7686	8.1116	7.5383	7.0350	6.5905
33	10.4644	9.5694	8.8005	8.1354	7.5560	7.0482	6.6005
34	10.5178	9.6086	8.8293	8.1566	7.5717	7.0599	6.6091
35	10.5568	9.6442	8.8552	8.1755	7.5856	7.0700	6.6166
36	10.6118	9.6765	8.8786	8.1924	7.5979	7.0790	6.6231
37	10.6530	9.7059	8.8996	8.2075	7.6087	7.0868	6.6288
38	10.6908	9.7327	8.9186	8.2210	7.6183	7.0937	6.6338
39	10.7255	9.7570	8.9357	8.2330	7.6268	7.0997	6.6380
40	10.7574	9.7791	8.9511	8.2438	7.6344	7.1050	6.6418
41	10.7866	9.7991	8.9649	8.2534	7.6410	7.1097	6.6450
42	10.8134	9.8174	8.9774	8.2619	7.6469	7.1138	6.6478
43	10.8380	9.8340	8.9886	8.2696	7.6522	7.1173	6.6503
44	10.8605	9.8491	8.9988	8.2764	7.6568	7.1205	6.6524
45	10.8812	9.8628	9.0079	8.2825	7.6609	7.1232	6.6543
46	10.9002	9.8753	9.0161	8.2880	7.6645	7.1256	6.6559
47	10.9176	9.8866	9.0235	8.2928	7.6677	7.1277	6.6573
48	10.9336	9.8969	9.0302	8.2972	7.6705	7.1296	6.6585
49	10.9482	9.9063	9.0362	8.3010	7.6730	7.1312	6.6596
50	10.9617	9.9148	9.0417	8.3045	7.6752	7.1327	6.6605

to the reciprocal of the discount rate multiplied by the payment. To state the formula in algebraic terms:

$$PV = \frac{1}{i} \times P$$

In the hypothetical, $1/.12 = 8.333$. The reciprocal of the discount rate is often called the **multiplier**. To calculate the present value of a perpetual annuity, one simply multiplies the payment by the appropriate multiplier. Plugging in the numbers from the hypothetical:

$$PV = 8.333 \times \$1{,}000 = \$8{,}333.33$$

Although many find it more convenient to calculate the multiplier first, the formula can be considerably simplified to: $PV = P/i$. Again, plugging in the numbers from the above hypothetical: $PV = \$1{,}000/.12 = \$8{,}333.33$.

   Either way, the present value of the right to receive \$1,000 per year forever (at a 12 percent discount rate) is \$8,333.33. This should become intuitively obvious when you realize that \$8,333.33 invested at 12 percent yields almost \$1,000 per year ($\$8{,}333.33 \times .12 = \$999.99$), year after year, forever. Because the present value of a 50-year annuity on those terms is \$8,304.50, it follows that the present value of the right to receive every payment, from the 51st year on to infinity, is only \$25.50. When one values a long-term annuity, for example, one for 15 years or more, a simple way to approximate its value is to assume that it is infinite, and multiply by the reciprocal of the discount factor.

§2.7 Valuing Variable Future Payments

   Skill in discounting future payments to present value is useful in a variety of contexts. Clients are sometimes faced with selecting the most attractive of several offers that involve payments at different times and in different amounts, or choosing between two or more strategies that involve payments of various amounts at various times under various assumptions. To avoid the common mistake of comparing oranges and apples, that is, of comparing dollars payable at different times without taking into account the time value of money, it is necessary to reduce all future payments to current values. In doing this, one must select one or more discount rates. If all the payments are to be made by the same entity under apparently constant circumstances, it is customary to use a single discount rate for all calculations. Consider the following example: Your client owns a valuable piece of real estate. He is considering three offers that involve the following terms:

   a) \$90,000 cash;
   b) \$10,000 down, \$1,000 per month for 120 months; and
   c) \$25,000 down, \$1,200 per month for 72 months.

   The total payments to be received under the first offer are \$90,000. Under the second, the total payments to be received are \$130,000 (\$10,000 plus 120

times $1,000). The contract presented by the hopeful purchaser to your client ignores the interest component entirely and states, as the purchase price, the full $130,000. Under the third alternative, the total payments are $111,400 ($25,000 plus 72 times $1,200). However, because of the time value of money, this comparison of gross amounts to be received is misleading. Calculation shows that at a 9 percent interest rate, and ignoring income taxes, the present value of $1,000 per month for 120 months is $78,941.69 and the present value of $1,200 per month for 72 months is $66,572.22. Thus, the present values of the three offers are:

a) $90,000;
b) $88,941.69; and
c) $91,572,22.

Even though the second alternative yields the largest gross amount, it has the smallest present value. This occurs because the immediate down payment in alternative b is rather small and periodic payments continue over ten years rather than six years as in the third alternative. On the other hand, because the present values of the three offers are very close, most people would probably recommend that the all-cash offer be accepted on the theory that there is some advantage in being immediately disentangled from a property. However, it certainly is not intuitively obvious that this is the most sensible solution.

In this hypothetical, different conclusions may be reached if a different discount rate is chosen. For example, if one computes the present value of the three payment options using a discount rate of 6 percent rather than 9 percent, the results are as follows:

a) All cash — $90,000;
b) $10,000 down, $1,000 per month over 120 months — $95,366; and
c) $25,000 down, $1,200 per month over 72 months — $94,990.

Suddenly, the payments to be spread out over a period of time have become more attractive, because the present value of future payments is higher at lower discount rates, so that at the lower discount rate the future payments become relatively more valuable compared with the down payments than when a higher discount rate is used. As noted before, there is an inverse relationship between value and discount rates: The higher the rate, the less a future payment is worth.

§2.8 Choosing a Discount Rate

Why was the interest rate of 12 percent used in most of the above calculations? In the last example comparing three different payment schedules, why were the rates compared unexpectedly changed to 9 percent and 6 percent? Where do rates in the real world come from anyway?

Unfortunately, there is no simple answer to the question of which discount rate to use in all circumstances in the real world. The choice depends on the current level of market interest rates, the investment alternatives available to the parties, and the risk in the loan or investment to be made. As described above,

the differences in results reached vary significantly depending on the rate chosen, though the differences between choosing a 6 or a 6.5 percent rate are nowhere near as substantial as the difference between choosing between 6 and 12 percent, as Table 2-1 illustrates. However, that does not give much guidance as to whether a 6 or a 12 percent rate should actually be used.

Most real-life problems in determining present values come down to a choice among one of the four following rates:

1. The market interest rate for essentially risk-free investments (e.g., the yield on short-term debt securities issued by the federal government).
2. The highest interest rate that a person could obtain for a deposit within his or her means at a local financial institution.
3. The lowest interest rate that a person would be charged in order to borrow funds of the same magnitude as the transaction involves.
4. The return that a business has determined it must make on an investment in order to be willing to enter into a transaction.

When a person of doubtful wealth has the obligation to make a future payment, an appropriate upward adjustment may be made to the discount rate. Of course, the greater the risk, the higher the discount rate (and the lower the present value of that payment) will be. In most instances, however, the calculations are made using one of the four basic rates set forth above without express adjustment in the discount rate for the risk of nonpayment. Indeed, most readily ascertainable rates already include some adjustment for the possibility of default. Where the risk of default is higher than normal, however, that risk is usually taken into account in a subjective way in deciding whether to enter the transaction at all, even if the calculation shows the value of the transaction to be attractive.

§2.9 Capital Budgeting by Businesses

Traditional books on finance used in business schools present considerably more sophisticated models for financial decision-making by businesses than those described here. The problem is generally addressed in terms of a business facing alternative investment choices, each of which involves certain outflows (or payments) and inflows (or receipts). The problem addressed is for the business to select, on a rational basis, which projects it should pursue and which it should not. The size of outflows and inflows may be fixed or they may be uncertain (though some way must be found to quantify the uncertainty).

If outflows and inflows occur over various periods of time, the calculation of capital budgeting can become complex even if the element of uncertainty is absent. However, the underlying theory is directly based on the time value of money described in this chapter. There are two widely accepted methods of capital budgeting.

The **internal rate of return (IRR)** is defined as a discount rate that equates the present value of the expected cash outflows with the expected cash inflows. Assume, for example, that a business is faced with an immediate cash outlay of

$20,000 that is expected to yield inflows of $6,000 per year over each of the next five years thereafter. The internal rate of return is that discount rate that makes the present value of the future inflows equal to the present value of the outflow. In this instance, that rate is approximately 15 percent. If similar calculations are made for each of the alternative projects the business is considering, the business should select those with the highest internal rate of return. The calculation of internal rates of return may involve successive estimations, or iterations, of the appropriate rate when done by hand, but here again, calculators and computer programs are readily available that perform such calculations. Comparison of internal rates of returns of alternative ventures provides a useful means of determining which ventures are most attractive for a business.

The net present value technique involves establishing a minimum rate of return on projects that the business has determined is necessary for its financial health. When this discount rate is established, all outflows and inflows are reduced to present values using this discount rate and outflows are subtracted from inflows: The project is attractive if the net present value is positive; if it is zero or negative, the project is unattractive.

These capital budgeting theories, as well as many other present value calculations, often contain a hidden assumption that may affect the accuracy of the calculation. That assumption is that interim payments to be received may be reinvested at the same interest rate that was applicable when the transaction was originally entered into. The following simplified example makes this point: Assume that you are the financial vice president of an insurance company with $100,000 to invest. You know that five years from now you must have on hand $190,000 to pay anticipated life insurance claims. A reliable borrower offers to borrow that $100,000 for five years, with annual interest payments at 14 percent per year. In other words, each year the borrower will pay you the amount of the interest due for that year. If one simply calculates the future value of $100,000 at the end of five years at an interest rate of 14 percent, that value is $192,541. There is, however, a critical assumption hidden in this example: this calculation assumes that your company will be able to invest consistently the $14,000 annual interest payment each year, also at the steady rate of 14 percent per year. That assumption, of course, may not be correct; if interest rates decline, you may be able to invest some interest payments at only 8 percent, say, and your company then will not have the $190,000 available as expected. Although this problem of reinvesting interim payments may seem to be self-evident after it is pointed out, it is an implicit assumption in many capital budget calculations that is not always fully appreciated.

II

◇

APPLICATIONS

CHAPTER 3

THE CREATIVE USE OF DEBT: REAL ESTATE

§3.1 Introduction

The purchase and sale of real estate are among the most common and most important commercial transactions. They typify many other commercial transactions because they are complex business transactions that almost always involve money borrowed from third persons or from the seller to finance the purchase price. This is true of both residential and commercial real estate, but this chapter concentrates on financing arrangements that primarily apply to commercial transactions.

This chapter considers real estate from the standpoint of a developer or owner. It does not discuss the relationship of landlords and tenants or the rights and duties of tenants. Although this chapter deals primarily with the financing of commercial real estate transactions, many of the matters discussed here also apply to commercial transactions involving the purchase and sale of whole businesses, of components or segments of businesses, of individual business assets, of controlling shares of stock in corporations, and of valuable personal property.

§3.2 Commercial Real Estate Investments Yield Cash Flows

Commercial real estate transactions differ in several respects from residential transactions. For one, commercial transactions tend to be much larger than residential transactions, often involving large tracts of land and construction of large and expensive buildings involving millions of dollars. However, the most important difference by far is that commercial real estate generates funds on a recurring basis, usually in the form of rent that commercial or residential tenants pay, or by the subdivision and sale of parts of the tract. Homeowners receive no such income.

Some commercial real estate investments, however, do not fit into this general pattern. For example, a person speculating in commercial real estate may purchase a tract of land and simply hold it, hoping for appreciation in value; such an investment usually has no positive cash flow until the property is sold. Or a person may buy land and build houses, apartments, or other structures, planning to resell the real estate as improved. Houses or apartment complexes built on this basis are usually referred to as built **on spec** (for "speculative" or "speculation"); the cash flow in this situation is likely to be sporadic and unpredictable. Or a business may buy or develop a commercial real estate tract to use for its own purposes — say, as its manufacturing plant or to house its own offices — thereby, it is hoped, reducing costs that the business would otherwise incur if it rented equivalent space. Such an investment does not create an identifiable cash flow, because the benefits that a business generates through the use of its own real estate are usually not segregated on the books of the business as arising specifically from the use of the commercial real estate. Rather, these benefits are viewed as part of the overall profitability of the business.

§3.3 Cash Flows Are Not Identical to Income or Loss

The funds that a commercial real estate project generates are often referred to as its **cash flow**. If the project produces more cash inflow than the cash outflow necessary to operate the project, it is said to have a positive cash flow. If disbursements exceed receipts, the project has a negative cash flow. A negative cash flow means that the cash being generated by the project is not sufficient to cover its cash needs—and that is usually bad. In some new ventures, however, a negative cash flow may be anticipated in the first few years of operation, and provision may be made for the additional capital infusions in the original planning. In other words, it is entirely possible for a good investment, one with net positive **income** over time, to have a negative cash flow for a while. The situation in which a positive cash flow is projected but does not materialize is most serious, because the investor then faces the painful and unexpected choice of making an additional unplanned capital investment or permitting the project to go into default.

A simplified cash flow projection for a duplex might look as follows:

Duplex — Purchase 12/31/96

Purchase price: $120,000
Mortgage: $100,000
Closing costs: $4,000

Table 3-1 is the critical one. Table 3-2 shows how the income tax saving line of Table 3-1 is calculated. (The assumption of a 50 percent tax bracket may be somewhat high for many investors, but is close to the maximum rate that the highest bracket investors pay if one considers federal, state, and local income taxes.) Table 3-3 reconciles the entries for mortgage payments in Table 3-1 and

Table 3-1
Cash Flow

	1996	1997	1998	1999
Gross receipts	-0-	$10,260	$10,773	$11,312
Less expenses		2,500	2,625	2,756
Net operating income (NOI)		7,760	8,148	8,555
Less mortgage payments (PI)		11,850	11,850	11,850
Cash flow before tax		(4,090)	(3,702)	(3,294)
Income tax saving (from Table 3-2 below)		8,351	7,595	6,826
Cash flow after tax	$(24,000)	$ 4,261	$ 3,893	$ 3,532

Table 3-2
Calculation of Tax Saving

	1996	1997	1998	1999
Net operating income (NOI)		$ 7,760	$ 8,148	$ 8,555
Mortgage interest		(11,501)	(11,457)	(11,407)
Depreciation		(12,960)	(11,880)	(10,800)
Net gain (loss) (NOI — interest — depreciation)		(16,701)	(15,189)	(13,652)
Tax saving on other real estate income (50% bracket)		$ 8,351	$ 7,595	$ 6,826

Table 3-3
Mortgage Analysis

	1996	1997	1998	1999
Mortgage payments (PI)		$11,850	$11,850	$11,850
Interest		11,501	11,457	11,407
Principal reduction		$ 349	$ 393	$ 443

mortgage interest in Table 3-2. Net operating income in Table 3-2 is calculated in the third line of Table 3-1. In Tables 3-1 and 3-3, "Mortgage Payments (PI)" is the monthly payment on the mortgage. ("PI" means simply principal and interest.)

Most investors are accustomed to income or profit-and-loss statements that show the earnings (or lack thereof) of a venture on an annual or monthly basis. Such statements are discussed in some detail in later chapters. The net cash flow statement set forth in Table 3-1 is not an income or profit-and-loss statement in the traditional sense (though the calculation of taxable income in Table 3-2 is a form of income statement). Rather, it is a cash-in and cash-out analysis that simply compares the dollars coming in with the dollars going out. The net cash flow statement differs from a profit-and-loss statement in several respects:

1. Principal payments on a mortgage (the amount that each monthly payment reduces the balance due on the mortgage) reduce the cash available from the venture and therefore negatively affect the cash flow statement for that period. However, these payments do not affect the income statement, because the repayment of a loan, in the eyes of an accountant, is a reduction in a liability but not an expense of doing business. Thus, the reduction of principal of $349 in 1997, $393 in 1998, and $443 in 1999 all affect the cash flow statement but not the income statement.

2. Some expense items such as depreciation are considered to be expenses for profit-and-loss purposes, but because they do not involve any cash payments by the project, they do not affect the net cash flow statement. **Depreciation** may be thought of for this purpose as amounts subtracted from income in order to reflect the gradual using up of the building. It may be an expense appropriately taken into account in determining profit and loss, but it does not involve any payment of cash.

The hypothetical duplex above reflects a common pattern of commercial real estate projects. It shows a loss on the income statement but a positive cash flow after taxes. An investor in a project with negative income (loss) can, for tax purposes, use the negative income on his or her federal income tax return as a tax deduction to shelter the taxable income from other real estate projects from tax. Before 1987, such negative income could be used to shelter income of all types from tax. This led to numerous real estate investments (like the duplex in the hypothetical) by high-income individuals to get tax deductions without additional investment, a practice that was sharply limited by the 1986 Tax Act.

In the hypothetical, the duplex is an attractive investment only because the income tax savings significantly exceed the negative cash flow from the duplex itself. It assumes that the owner is consistently in the 50 percent tax bracket each year. Of course, the investor has invested $24,000 in the duplex in 1996 and the total after-tax cash flows from 1997 through 1999 do not equal that amount. However, the investor owns the duplex (subject to the mortgage) and should recoup all or most of this investment when the property is sold. Strictly

speaking, this outflow and inflow of capital should also considered in deciding whether to make the investment.

To repeat, "cash flow" and "income" are not synonymous. Income assumes there is some matching of income and expense in an accounting sense, while cash flow is a pure checkbook concept. Any kind of cash receipt increases cash flow and any kind of cash payment decreases it.

§3.4 The Purchase of Commercial Real Estate

The goal of a person purchasing commercial real estate differs from that of a person purchasing residential real estate. The goal in purchasing residential real estate is largely personal satisfaction — finding a good place to live given the constraints of the person's financial resources. In contrast, the goal of a person purchasing commercial real estate is usually purely economic, based on the hoped-for financial return in light of the required investment, and is usually (though not always) unrelated to personal considerations of taste or aesthetics.

The ability of commercial real estate to generate gross cash flows usually makes a **bootstrap acquisition** possible. By borrowing most of the cost of the land and improvements, the developer of the property may use the later cash flows to repay the loans and thereby pay for the land and improvements with no further personal investment. When commercial real estate is being acquired, a developer customarily persuades a lender to lend money to finance the project primarily by developing estimates of the later cash flow that show that it will be sufficient to repay the loan. These estimates may be in the form of computer-generated spreadsheets or documents with titles such as **projected cash flow** or **pro forma cash projections**. The hypothetical cash flow projection set forth in the previous section might well have served to convince a lender.

Because commercial real estate loans are typically made or refused primarily on the basis of projected cash flows, analysis of these projections is usually vital to the success of a contemplated project. The question that a commercial real estate developer asks is not primarily "Is this a good project?" but rather "Can I persuade a lender that they should make a large loan on it?" To a very substantial extent, decisions regarding whether or not projects will go forward are made by the sources of possible financing, not by the developer itself. For this reason, the developer of commercial real estate often seeks to obtain letters of intent from potential tenants — particularly the major tenants or **anchor tenants** — in order to improve the reliability of the cash flow projections in the eyes of possible lenders. Such letters are usually not binding in a legal sense, but are indications of interest in the project.

No traditional minimum cash down payment is required for a commercial real estate project. If the cash flows are high enough, a developer may be able to persuade one or more lenders to lend 100 percent, or even more, of the acquisition and development cost of the project. Generally, it is in the interest of the developer to obtain the largest loan possible in order to make the project self-sufficient and reduce the amount of personal capital the developer must

invest in the project. After all, the duplex purchaser in the previous section needed to come up with $24,000 in cash; he doubtless would have preferred to invest a smaller amount. The way to do that is to get a larger mortgage. If a loan for 80 percent of the purchase price is desirable, then a 90 percent loan is usually preferable, and a 100 percent loan may be ideal from the investor's standpoint. In the 100 percent mortgage case, of course, the developer owns a project with essentially a zero capital investment. However, even when a capital investment is required of the developer, if the cash flows develop as planned or, even better, if they exceed the original estimates, the developer may be able to recoup his or her original investment in a relatively brief period of time. The developer will then own a project (subject of course to the lender's interest) that may be worth millions of dollars with a zero capital investment. It is like magic—making money for oneself using other people's money. Many real estate fortunes have been made on the basis of the simple principle of borrowing as much as possible and then making the project a success.

Most lenders are concerned that the developer not get a totally free ride, and they therefore do not usually give 100 percent mortgages. On the other hand, projected cash flows from a commercial project are often sufficient to justify more than a single mortgage on the project. Junior mortgages from different sources, often called second or third mortgages depending on their priority, may permit a developer to approach or exceed 100 percent financing in specific situations even if the senior lender refuses to fund more than 70 or 80 percent of the project's anticipated cost. Because junior mortgages are risky, a junior lender may insist on receiving a percentage of the ownership as a condition of making the loan.

The fact that a developer may be able to justify loans exceeding the cost of a project illustrates that the project's real value lies in its cash flow. It is quite possible, of course, that the cash flow of a project will be less than expected and that the cost of development will be greater than the project's value. Obviously, such projects should be avoided, but anticipated cash flows must be estimated long in advance of completion of the project, and it is easy to be overly optimistic or to fail to anticipate some event that greatly reduces the anticipated cash flow. The trick to real estate development is finding projects in which the value of cash flows is greater than the cost of development and avoiding those in which the opposite is true.

Even if a lender is confident that a project's value will exceed the cost of development, however, many lenders prefer that a developer invest some equity in the project, that is, some value over and above the amount of the loans against the project. This equity investment will be lost if the project fails, and it therefore creates an incentive for the developer to make the project a success and to pay back the lender. The lender will be concerned not only about the loan it has made but also about all other loans that the developer may obtain that are secured by the project. Even though the primary lender has retained the right to be paid first in the event the project goes under, the primary lender has additional default risk foisted on it by virtue of subsequent junior loans that reduce the incentives for the developer. For this reason, loan agreements typically contain numerous covenants that are designed to restrict further borrowing

as well as many other potential courses of business and that require that periodic reports about the project be sent to the lender.

The foregoing discussion assumes that the developer is personally responsible to repay the loan. In some cases, however, a lender will agree in connection with real estate loans not to hold the developer personally liable in the event of default and to look only to the property for repayment. Such a loan is called a **nonrecourse loan**. Even when the developer has a nonrecourse loan, however, the developer still has an interest in maintaining his or her reputation with lenders. If the developer "walks" away from an unsuccessful project, he or she will find it difficult to find favorable loans in the future. In a sense, the developer's reputation is an additional asset that has been pledged as security, though a developer may be willing to sacrifice this asset if the cost is too great or if the developer does not anticipate any future projects.

The only safe generalizations are that down payments on commercial real estate purchases usually comprise a lower percentage than that required on residential real estate purchases, that the amount of capital that a developer must invest in a commercial project is inversely dependent on the attractiveness of the cash-flow projections, and that nonrecourse financing may be available in whole or in part to commercial developers if a project is sufficiently attractive.

The possibility that the cash that a project generates may not cover the costs of the loans, leading to default, and the possible personal liability of the developer on these various mortgages, is discussed further below.

§3.5 Permanent and Interim Loans for Real Estate Development

In many situations, a person plans to use the proceeds of a loan to construct improvements on the raw land that he or she already owns. In other instances, a single loan may cover both the acquisition of the raw land and the construction of the improvements. In this case, the lender will usually advance the land acquisition cost separately from the funds needed to construct the improvements.

Where loan proceeds are to finance construction, it is quite common for two different lenders that provide basically different services to participate in the transaction. These two lenders are usually called the **construction lender** and the **permanent lender**, respectively.

The construction lender advances funds as construction proceeds to enable the contractor to complete the construction; in advancing these funds, the construction lender relies on architects' or engineers' certificates as required by the construction loan agreement to ensure that work to date has been performed properly and that a designated stage or percentage of completion has been attained. Payments made by that lender are often called **progress payments**. When the project is completed, the construction loan is usually paid off in full with the proceeds of the permanent loan. The construction lender therefore usually makes no investigation of the economics of the completed project; rather, it relies on the unconditional commitment of the permanent

lender to make the permanent loan upon the project's completion. If there is no commitment from an acceptable permanent lender, there is usually no construction loan available.

The permanent lender in effect agrees to make the long-term loan on the property when the project is completed. In other words, the permanent lender examines the cash flow projections submitted with the loan application and determines the project's viability. It performs the functions of the lender described in the preceding sections in assessing the long-term economics of the project and the financial strength of the borrower. In the balance of this chapter, "lender" refers to the permanent lender and not the interim lender.

In some instances, the same lending institution may serve as both the interim and the permanent lender. Typically, however, such a lending institution has two staffs, one skilled in the responsibilities of an interim lender and the other skilled in the responsibilities of a permanent lender.

§3.6 Real Estate Loans Are Secured by Liens

A loan made to enable the borrower to purchase or develop real estate is represented by a promissory note that is usually on a standard printed form. The promissory note is usually secured by a lien on the real estate that is the subject of the transaction. The lien is usually created in a separate document, either a **mortgage** or **deed of trust**, which is executed simultaneously with the note at the closing. The terms of these documents are so standardized that printed forms are usually used with a few blanks filled in. (Typed-in clauses referring to special terms such as prepayment privileges are also sometimes added.) These standardized forms are typically prepared by the lender, who usually resists making changes in them. A deed of trust differs from a mortgage in only minor respects: The type of instrument used in a particular state or community depends more on tradition or convention than on the differences between the two forms of instruments. Hereafter, the word "mortgage" will be used to refer to both types of instruments.

The lien created by a mortgage covers the entire property that is the subject of the transaction. It covers the improvements as they are constructed as well as the land itself. Liens have both a geographic and a temporal aspect. If the transaction involves a commercial development that includes the installation of streets and utilities followed by a sale of lots, it is necessary to arrange, in the mortgage, a procedure by which the developer can obtain the release of individual lots from this lien when they are sold. Otherwise, the purchasers of the lots purchase subject to the lien of the mortgage covering the whole project and will be unable to arrange first lien financing to construct improvements on the lot. Similarly, temporal rights, such as the rights of a lessee under a ten-year lease, are subject to the lien of the mortgagee, although in the event of a default the mortgagee usually will not want to dispossess tenants. In some cities, rent control laws may limit the power of owners to dispossess tenants even when they wish to do so.

§3.7 Is Anybody Liable on the Real Estate Loan?

The promissory note secured by a real estate mortgage is, of course, a promise by the person signing it to pay the amount set forth. In most commercial (and practically all residential) real estate transactions, the developers or owners are required to sign the note individually so that they will be personally liable if a default occurs. That is, in addition to losing the property, the developer or owner will be liable for any further amount that may be owed to the lender after the property is sold. In commercial real estate, however, it is not unknown for the lender to agree to look solely to the property as the source of payment and not require the developer to assume personal liability. This may be done by having some third person — a **straw party** — or a corporation without substantial assets sign the note. The same result may be reached by a non-recourse loan in the note that limits the power of the holder to recover from the maker in the event of default. In the case of such a loan, if there is a default, the developer is faced with the loss of the property, including whatever equity he or she has in the property, but is not personally liable for the debt.

Even where the developer is personally liable on the note, individual investors may not be. It is quite common for developers to sell participations in a project through the medium of a corporation or a limited partnership in which the individual investors risk their original investments but have no personal liability in excess of that amount.

Finally, individual liability on real estate notes may be discharged through the bankruptcy process if the individual is insolvent.

§3.8 The Economics of the Traditional Real Estate Mortgage

This section begins with the classic level-payment real estate loan, widely used for both commercial and residential real estate financing. It then considers the numerous variations that have arisen since 1970.

A traditional real estate mortgage is for a long term — 25 or 30 years — at a fixed interest rate established at or close to the market rate of interest at the time the loan is made. Monthly payments are required, and interest is computed on the unpaid balance each month. The loan is amortized over the period of the loan by these monthly payments, which are fixed in advance and remain constant throughout the life of the mortgage. The words **amortize** and **amortization** are fancy terms that simply mean the loan is set up so that a portion of each monthly payment is applied to principal as well as interest: In the classic mortgage of this type, the monthly payment is computed so that the final level payment—the 360th in a 30-year mortgage—reduces the loan balance to zero.

The first payment on a traditional mortgage represents virtually all interest with a few dollars being applied to principal; the second payment consists of a tiny bit less interest (because the first payment reduced the principal slightly) and therefore a tiny bit more is available to be applied to reduce principal. This

process continues over the life of the mortgage, with each payment representing a somewhat larger amount of principal and smaller amount of interest than the previous one.

To illustrate: on a $75,000 loan at 9 percent, the level monthly payment is $603.47 over the 30 years. The first payment reduces principal by $40.97 (the remaining $562.50 is interest); the second payment reduces principal by $41.27 (the remaining $562.19 is interest); and so on. The 12th payment reduces principal by $44.48; after this payment, the principal has been reduced to $74,487.60. The payment made on the 5th anniversary of the mortgage (the 60th payment), reduces principal by $63.66 and the mortgage then has been reduced to $71,910.10. Obviously, only a small amount of the unpaid balance is amortized in the early years of the mortgage. After 10 years, the principal has been reduced to $67,072.31; after 15 years, it has been reduced to $59,497.86; after 20 years to $47,638.70; after 25 years to $29,071.04. During the last five years, most of each payment is principal, and upon making the 360th payment, the principal is reduced to zero. As with compound interest, tables, calculators, and computer programs are readily available that give the level payment amount per dollar borrowed at various rates of interest over various periods.

The fixed-interest, level-payment loan described here is so common and so widely used that it is sometimes referred to as a **conventional loan**. (The term conventional is also sometimes used in a different context to describe residential real estate loans made by a savings and loan association or other lender in contrast to loans guaranteed under federal programs such as those administered by the FHA or VA.) Until the late 1970s, the level-payment loan was the only mortgage arrangement available for residential real estate and was used almost universally in commercial real estate as well. With the very high interest rates that prevailed in the late 1970s, a number of alternative mortgages were created that departed from the level-payment structure. Some of these alternative mortgages are widely used today in connection with commercial real estate mortgages.

The basic premises underlying the level-payment mortgage appear to be (1) that the person making payments on the mortgage has a level income over the term of the mortgage, (2) that interest rates are going to remain relatively stable over the term of the mortgage, and (3) that there is no inflation in the system. These premises obviously have not been true in the recent past, and they seem particularly inappropriate for commercial real estate with its open-ended potential for producing cash flow. Indeed, a very common cash flow pattern in commercial real estate is relatively small gross receipts in early years followed by gradual improvement as the project becomes established and successful. It would seem sensible to structure mortgage payments for commercial loans not on a fixed level over the term of the mortgage, but on a basis that increases over time. Once lenders escaped from the traditional thinking underlying the level-payment mortgage, several variations were commonly offered:

1. The simplest pattern involves interest-only payments for a period of several years followed by an increase in the payments to permit amortization of the principal over the balance of the mortgage when the

interest-only period ends. This results in an abrupt increase in the size of the payments when amortization of the principal begins.

2. There is no reason why the initial payments must fully cover the interest costs of the initial years as long as the payments are thereafter increased sufficiently to pay off the whole mortgage when it is due. So-called **negative amortization** loans provide initial payments below the interest-only level with the unpaid interest added to principal so that the outstanding balance of the mortgage increases in the early years of the mortgage. Later payments obviously must increase in amount to cover both the negative amortization in the early years and the regular amortization of the principal in the remaining years. Payments often increase gradually to ease the impact on cash flow in later years.

3. There is also no reason why the interest rate on a mortgage must be fixed for the life of the mortgage. The **adjustable rate mortgage (ARM)** provides for adjustments to the effective interest rate on the mortgage periodically based on changes in a specified market interest rate.

4. Another real estate financing technique involves balloon notes. A **balloon note** is a simple idea: It is a note that requires periodic payments, but the unpaid balance comes due long before the payments amortize the borrowed amount. In the real estate context, a balloon note might come due in 5 or 10 years, but the periodic monthly payments are computed based on a 25-year or 30-year amortization schedule. Such a note might be described as a 5-year balloon with payments based on a 25-year 10 percent amortization schedule. This means that monthly payments are computed on the 25-year 10 percent table, but the loan itself comes due in 5 years. Of course, when it comes due, there is a huge final payment that is due — the balloon — because monthly payments have mostly gone to the payment of interest and the principal has been reduced only slightly. Because most borrowers do not have the funds to pay the balloon in cash when it comes due, the property is often resold or refinanced. **Refinancing** may involve a second balloon note, which in turn may lead to a third. If interest rates have risen or fallen when the balloon comes due, the new mortgage covering the balloon is written at the then-current market rate. A balloon note, in other words, is not unlike the ARM discussed above in ultimate economic effect. The difference is that with a balloon note, the burden is on the borrower to find substitute financing. Most balloon notes are probably carried by sellers of property, though a number of financial institutions also accept short-term balloon notes. Many balloon notes appear as part of second mortgages in creative financing transactions discussed below.

5. A wide variety of short-term mortgages known as **bridge loans, mezzanine financing,** or simply short-term **interim financing** exist. Such loans usually provide for interest-only payments with no reduction of principal for periods as short as one year, but often running three to five years. Like the balloon note, such loans usually result in refinancing of the project when the note comes due. Sometimes these short-term loans may be unsecured.

In the world of commercial real estate financing, these various types of mortgage terms may be combined in a variety of ingenious ways.

§3.9 Junior Mortgages

Many commercial real estate transactions involve second, third, and sometimes even more **junior mortgages**. The rights of junior mortgages in case of default are described below. This section describes why purchasing commercial real estate often involves such financing.

Many lenders are constrained by statute, regulation, or internal policy to make only **first mortgages** that cover a designated fraction or less of the value of the project, sometimes called the **loan-to-value (LTV)** ratio. These first mortgage lenders are commercial banks, savings and loan associations, and other lenders subject to some degree of state or federal regulation. The usual pattern of commercial real estate financing is to obtain a first mortgage from one of these lenders. This mortgage may be a traditional fixed-interest rate, level-payment mortgage, or it may be an ARM or some other type of innovative financing. Nevertheless, it is for a long term and provides only a large fraction of the needed financing. The difference between the amount of the mortgage and the estimated cost of the project must come either from the developer as a large capital investment or from other lending sources.

Junior mortgages usually provide most of the remaining financing needed to develop the project. The junior mortgages carry significantly greater risk of nonpayment if the project does not work out as well as the developer projects. As a result, they usually carry higher interest rates. In addition, the most risky of these mortgages may carry an equity kicker, the right of the holder to purchase a portion of the developer's interest in the project, usually at a bargain price. Two somewhat similar variations are deals (1) in which the lender receives a specified amount to be applied against the loan or as additional compensation for making the loan and (2) in which the lender shares in the increase in value upon the sale or refinancing of the project but does not participate in the cash flow.

An example might be helpful. Assume that Jones, a real estate speculator and developer, owns land that is suitable for apartment development: She bought the land two years ago for $15,000 cash and now has an independent appraisal that the current value of the land is $26,000. She plans to build a 45-unit apartment that she estimates will cost $950,000 after making due allowance for all contingencies. After discussions with lenders, Jones works out the following financing arrangements:

1. A 75 percent (of $950,000) first mortgage from a savings and loan association for 30 years at 10 percent. This first mortgage provides $712,500 of the cost.
2. A $150,000 second mortgage, from a commercial lending company engaged in speculative but not unduly risky investments, for 10 years at 14 percent, adjustable after 3 years on the basis of an index based on the average discount rate on 26-week Treasury bills as announced by

the U.S. Treasury Department following sale of these securities. (Treasury bills and discount rates are discussed in a later chapter; simply assume for present purposes that this average rate is a reliable indication of market interest rates for commercial first mortgage loans.)

These two mortgages leave Jones $87,500 short of the $950,000 she needs ($950,000 − 712,500 − 150,000 = $87,500), well within striking distance. She obtains a bridge loan for this amount from a privately owned investment firm that specializes in high-risk loans. The bridge loan carries an interest rate of 16 percent, with monthly payments of interest only for three years. At the end of three years, the $87,500 of principal is due. In addition, Jones is required to give the investment firm the option to purchase a 25 percent interest in the project for $87,500 at that time. If the project is successful, the holder of the third mortgage will probably exercise its option, which will precisely cancel the principal payment due on the third mortgage. The holder thereafter will not get interest but will have a substantial equity participation in the project. If the project is not sufficiently successful, the holder of the third mortgage will not exercise its option and Jones will (1) have to come up with $87,500 cash, (2) negotiate with the holder of the third mortgage for an extension of that mortgage, or (3) suffer a default and likely foreclosure on that mortgage. If the option is not exercised, the renegotiation alternative is probably the most likely.

On the basis of the foregoing, Jones has invested $26,000 in the form of the value of the land and has borrowed $950,000 to finance the improvements. Her equity investment is therefore about 3 percent, a not unusual figure for commercial projects in real life.

Calculations will reveal that for the first three years after the completion of the project the required monthly cash flow to service the indebtedness is $9,748.35: $6,252.70 on the first mortgage, $2,329.00 on the second, and $1,166.67 on the third. This is only $216.63 per apartment. Of course, there are other items of disbursement in addition to debt service, and it is possible that if the discount rate on Treasury bills rises, the second mortgage payments may increase. If the project appears to be successful and the holder of the third mortgage exercises its option to purchase 25 percent of the project, the payments will drop to $8,581.70 per month after three years, or about $190.70 per apartment. To continue with the mathematics of this example, at the end of three years the first two mortgages will have been paid down to $699,330.48 and $124,279.50 respectively or a total of $823,610. The decision by the holder of the third mortgage whether to exercise its option must be based on his or her estimate of the difference between the value of the project and this indebtedness.

§3.10 Economic Equivalents to Mortgages

A complicating factor in real estate financing is that there are many different interests in land that are not formally designated as mortgages but that have the same economic effect as mortgages. For example, a person planning to develop a tract of land might sell the land to an investor for a lump sum and

take back a long-term ground lease for 99 years. The lump sum that the developer receives is similar to mortgage proceeds, and the obligation to pay rent for 99 years on the ground lease is analogous to monthly payments on a mortgage. In the event of nonpayment, cancellation of the lease is analogous to foreclosure of a mortgage. (Undivided interests in the ownership of the land subject to the ground lease may even be sold to investors who participate in the yield from cash flow as well as possible appreciation in the value of the land.) The developer may thereafter place one or more conventional mortgages on his or her interest in the ground lease; these mortgages in effect are second or third mortgages (because the lease payments on the ground lease are superior to the rights of the nominal first mortgage on the interest in the leasehold).

If the property has existing improvements, the owner may be able to sell the land but not the improvements to one investor and the improvements but not the land to a second investor, in both cases taking back long-term leases. One or more conventional mortgages may then be placed on the leaseholds. Transactions in which interests are carved up among several layers or tiers of sales and leasebacks and then mixed with traditional mortgages on the developer's interests may be exceptionally complex and difficult to analyze. Indeed, it may sometimes be difficult to establish the precise priorities of various lenders.

In the following sections, the possibility that one or more layers of financing may be represented by sale and leaseback interests is ignored; for simplicity, the assumption is that only traditional mortgages are involved.

§3.11 Default

What happens when there is a **default** on a mortgage? The answer can be best developed by considering what might happen if the apartment development described in §3.9 does not work out as projected.

It is important to recognize that not all defaults lead immediately to foreclosure on the property and lawsuits brought to recover missed payments. Loan instruments often provide for **grace periods** in which missed payments may be made up, often upon the payment of an additional fee or charge. In addition, legal action is expensive, and taken only as a matter of last resort. It is not uncommon for lenders to threaten foreclosure, and even post property for sale under the procedures set forth in the mortgage without completing the threatened action. As will be seen in more detail below, foreclosure may well lead to the lender purchasing the property at the foreclosure sale. What does the lender do with the property then? If the developer could not make a go of it, will the lender be able to do any better? Probably not, and it may very well do even worse. Also, a lender must worry about its own bottom line. If a lender forecloses on property that cannot be resold at a high enough price to cover the unpaid portion of the loan, the lender must recognize the difference as a loss. A troubled lender may therefore prefer to retain problem loans or noncurrent loans in its portfolio rather than closing them out by foreclosure. For these various reasons, defaults often lead to negotiation between the lenders and the developer in an effort to work out a revised schedule of payments that is realistic

under the circumstances. Indeed, many lenders maintain work out groups that may try to avoid foreclosure by temporarily assuming control over a project and supervising disbursements to persons other than the lender. The final steps of foreclosure, described below, usually occur only after all these preliminary solutions prove unworkable.

§3.12 Foreclosure

An uncured default usually permits the lender to declare the entire unpaid balance due. A default on a mortgage may lead to foreclosure and ultimately public sale of the property by auction after public announcement. The procedures to be followed for sale of the property are set forth in the mortgage itself; usually no judicial order is required before the sale. The proceeds of the sale, after deduction of expenses, are applied to the mortgages in default. Two critical rules about the effect of a foreclosure of one mortgage on other mortgages are (1) a foreclosure of a junior mortgage does not affect a senior mortgage and the purchaser at the foreclosure sale takes the property subject to the senior mortgage, and (2) the sale of the property following foreclosure of a senior mortgage automatically extinguishes the liens of all junior mortgages. Thus, if Jones defaults only on the third mortgage, the rights of the first two mortgagees are unaffected, and the purchaser at the foreclosure sale takes the property subject to the prior rights of the holders of the first and second mortgages. If that purchaser fails to make the payments necessary to keep those mortgages current, another foreclosure may occur. However, if Jones defaults on the first mortgage, all junior mortgagees are in imminent danger of losing their interest in the apartment building. Thus, a default on a senior mortgage is typically also a violation of covenants in junior mortgages, so that a default on a senior mortgage usually triggers defaults on junior mortgages.

Assume that the apartment project fails to meet the cash-flow projections, and that after one year Jones does not have the necessary cash to make all three payments. Knowing that she is going into default, she does not make any further payments on any of the mortgages. At this time, the unpaid principal balances on the three mortgages are approximately as follows:

First mortgage	$708,500
Second mortgage	142,500
Third mortgage	87,500
Total loans	$938,500

Assume further that the holder of the first mortgage declares a default and that the property is put up for sale. What happens at the sale depends on the value of the property after deduction of foreclosure expenses. At the public foreclosure sale, each of the creditors and Jones herself may bid on the property. In addition, third persons hoping to find a bargain may also enter bids. If we assume that the value of the property is $950,000 (exceeding the sum total of the three mortgages of $938,500), the foreclosure of the first mortgage should

lead to some spirited bidding at the sale. The holder of the first mortgage, knowing that the value of the property exceeds its interest in the property, bids the amount of the unpaid balance of the first mortgage: $708,500. If this holder bids any higher than the amount of its debt, the surplus goes not to it but to holders of the inferior mortgages or to Jones. The holder of the second mortgage bids up to $851,000 in order to protect its interest in the property. If it acquires the property, it will need to pay the first mortgagee $708,500 to pay off the first mortgage, and therefore it should bid another $142,500 to cover its own debt. If the holder of the second mortgage bids any more, the surplus goes not to it but to the holder of the third mortgage or to Jones. The holder of the third mortgage has a similar motivation to bid up to $938,500 but no more: $708,500 to pay off the first mortgage, $142,500 to pay off the second, and up to $87,500 to protect its own interest. If it bids any more, the surplus simply goes to Jones.

Because Jones has a positive equity in the property of $11,500 (the hypo-thetical value of the property, $950,000, minus the unpaid balances on the mortgages, $938,500), in theory she should bid on the property to preserve her equity (i.e., the difference between the mortgages and the market value of the project). Of course, if Jones could not meet the monthly payments, she probably will not be able to raise $938,500 to pay off the loans at the foreclosure sale in cash. As a result, whatever equity she has in the project is, as a practical matter, probably gone. A third person could theoretically bid $938,501 and get Jones's $11,500 equity for $1. It would be unusual, however, for someone to invest $938,501 in a problematic venture in order to secure the equity owner-ship of an interest worth $11,500. Where the owner's equity is larger, however, it is quite possible that a third person or the defaulting owner may be able to raise the necessary funds through a short-term loan that may be paid off when the purchaser refinances or resells the property. One thing is clear: If the owner has a substantial equity in the foreclosed property, she must scramble: If she does not, someone else—either one of the lending institutions or some oppor-tunistic third person—will obtain a bargain at her expense.

If the hypothesized market value is only $650,000, no one other than the holder of the first mortgage will bid, because the value of the property is less than the first lien balance of $708,500. The security for the second and third mortgages as well as Jones's equity is simply gone upon the foreclosure sale. If the hypothesized market value is $750,000, the holder of the second mortgage should end up purchasing the project.

These examples are somewhat unrealistic because it is difficult to estimate the fair market value of a defaulted project. It is therefore not uncommon for bidders to make mistakes. Some things can, however, be said with confidence. Although it is theoretically possible to find bargains, in the real world secured debts usually exceed the market value for projects in foreclosure. Thus, because in the typical case there is no positive equity, the only bidders are the repre-sentatives of the lenders. After all, if there were any significant equity in the project, the owner probably could have paid on time or could find substitute financing.

Although many foreclosure sales involve bidding only by existing creditors, deciding how much to bid is not necessarily a simple matter. Assume that the

property is worth $650,000 and the balance on the first lien is $708,500. How much should the first lien holder bid? The fair market value of the property, the amount of the loan, or something in between? If the lender hopes to collect the deficiency from the developer, the lender probably should bid low in order to preserve its rights against the developer. When the developer is not personally liable on the mortgage, or is insolvent, the lender is likely to bid the full amount of the mortgage. As long as the bid is less than $708,500, in one sense it does not matter if the bid is above market value because the holder of the first lien is in effect paying itself back out of the purchase price. However, estimates of fair market value are always uncertain, and the lender may wish to defer recognition of any loss on its own financial statements until the property is finally disposed of. The most likely scenario therefore is that the lender would bid precisely $708,500 even though it believes the property is worth less.

Once the holder of the first lien acquires the property, what happens to it? The new owner is unlikely to dispose of it at a fire sale price; after all it has $708,500 invested in it and does not want to take a loss. It may manage the apartment complex on its own or it may try to find someone willing to buy it for $708,500 or more. This may be practical because the new owner is itself a financial institution and may grant a new purchaser favorable financing terms (e.g., no money down or interest deferred for some period of time) in order to persuade the potential purchaser to take over the project. Favorable financing in effect lowers the price, although such sales might not always need to be recognized as losses by the lender for accounting purposes. If things do not work out, the original holder of the lien might need to foreclose again, but it is not significantly worse off than if it owns the defaulted project. And in the meantime it does not have the headache of managing an apartment complex.

As far as our developer Jones is concerned, it is possible that she may not be personally liable on the mortgages; if she is not, she can walk away from the project, sacrificing only her initial investment. If, as is more commonly the case, Jones is personally liable on the mortgages, she may be insolvent or judgment-proof. Often, if one project that a developer owns goes bad, other projects have gone bad or will do so in the near future. The developer's liabilities therefore may greatly exceed her assets. In addition, if Jones is pursued vigorously in an effort to collect from her personal assets, she may always take refuge in the federal bankruptcy courts. Further, as a practical matter, Jones is liable only for any deficiency between the realized value of the collateral (the apartment building project) and the amount of the indebtedness. Foreclosure may take several months, and suit must then be brought on the **deficiency** (the amount by which the proceeds of the sale after expenses of collection are less than the unpaid balance on the mortgage). Only then must a developer be concerned about his or her liability on the promissory notes.

§3.13 Debt and Leverage

Developers of commercial real estate usually want to finance their projects with the largest possible loan. The use of debt may be prompted simply by the

developer's lack of funds to invest in a larger equity interest. A more important reason for using debt, however, is **leverage**.

Jones's apartment building described in the preceding sections provides a clear illustration of the concept of leverage. The total cost of the apartment house, including the land contributed by Jones, is $976,000. Assume that under Jones's cash-flow projections, the apartments should rent for $400 each, and that (for simplicity) 100 percent occupancy can be expected. There are 45 units, the monthly gross revenue is $18,000, and the annual revenue is $216,000, from which operating expenses, real estate taxes, insurance, upkeep, and similar items must be deducted. Assume that Jones projects that these expenses (exclusive of mortgage loan payments) will be approximately $27,000 per year. Accepting their accuracy, however, one can investigate the cash-flow return Jones will receive on the basis of various assumptions about financing:

1. If Jones builds the project entirely with her own cash and obtains no loans at all, she will have invested a total of $976,000, from which there will be a positive annual cash flow of $189,000 per year ($216,000 gross cash flow minus $27,000 of expenses, real estate taxes, insurance, etc.). On the $976,000 that she invested, Jones will receive a return of about 19 percent on a cash-flow basis before income taxes.

2. If Jones builds the project with only the first mortgage as financing (face amount of $712,500 and monthly payments of $6,252.70), she will have invested a total of $263,500 and the expected cash flow will be reduced to $113,967.60 for a yield on each dollar that Jones invests of about 43 percent on a cash-flow basis. (The $263,500 figure is obtained by subtracting from $976,000 the amount of the first mortgage ($712,500); the $113,967.60 cash flow is obtained by taking the $189,000 cash flow from an all-cash investment and subtracting the annual payments on the first mortgage; again no account is taken of income taxes.)

3. If Jones builds the project with both the first and second mortgages as financing, her cash investment will be reduced to $113,500 ($263,500 minus $150,000 for the second mortgage) and her annual cash flow will be reduced to $86,019.60 ($113,967.60 minus $27,948, the total annual payment on the second mortgage). Even so, this increases the yield on Jones's cash investment to 76 percent on a cash-flow basis.

4. If Jones builds the project with all three mortgages, as she originally contemplated, her cash investment is reduced to $26,000 (the fair market value of the land), and the cash flow will be reduced to $72,019. This is a 277 percent return; while Jones has a large payment coming due on the third mortgage in a couple of years, the cash flow should be ample to cover it.

Leverage reflects the fact that the more Jones borrows, the higher the percentage return is on each dollar that she has invested. In the foregoing example, every dollar invested in the project yields a cash flow of about $0.19 each year. When Jones borrows on the first mortgage, she is borrowing a dollar at an interest cost of $0.10 per year and receiving $0.19 on that dollar. The

additional $0.09 is additional return on the dollars that Jones herself invests. Hence, her return on each dollar she invests is improved by each additional dollar she borrows. No wonder borrowing is attractive under such circumstances. Indeed, if Jones can obtain loans for 100 percent of her cost at an interest rate of less than 19 percent per year, she should do so; she then has a zero investment in the project and an infinite return on that investment.

The secret of leverage is that if a borrowed dollar yields a greater cash flow than the cost of borrowing it, you should borrow it. The excess is then allocable to the dollars you do invest, increasing the return, often dramatically. Leverage, in short, involves the productive use of other people's money. As we shall see, the concept of leverage applies to virtually all aspects of finance, not just real estate.

§3.14 The Danger of Debt

Leverage is a two-edged sword. By increasing the number of borrowed dollars "working" for the developer, the rate of return on the dollars he or she actually invests may be greatly increased. As long as the per dollar return from the venture exceeds the interest cost, it appears to be sensible to borrow. On the other hand, these assertions take no account of the possibility that the developer might miscalculate and the per dollar return might be less than the interest cost. If this occurs, the leveraged transaction may be a disaster for the investor, because the fixed interest costs must still be met in any event. Indeed, most of the spectacular collapses of real estate ventures have been the result of excessive leverage and a miscalculation by the developer of the return from a venture.

In the hypothetical based on Jones's apartment complex, a number of calculations were based on optimistic cash-flow projections: rents of $400 per apartment, out-of-pocket costs of $27,000 per year, and 100 percent occupancy rates. Assume, however, that because of an unexpected economic downturn in the local economy a large surplus of apartments develops, and Jones finds that she actually has a 60 percent occupancy rate and an average rent of $360 per month per apartment. Costs other than financing, furthermore, turn out to be $3,000 per month, or a total of $36,000 per year rather than the $27,000 projected. These are dramatic shortfalls in the projections, but in real life it is not uncommon for rosy cash-flow projections to turn bleak in such a dramatic fashion. These misfortunes bring the net cash flow from the project before financing costs to $77,400 per year rather than the projected $189,000.

In the unleveraged transaction (Jones investing all $976,000 in cash) the result is extremely disappointing but not disastrous: Rather than the project showing the expected 20 percent return on a cash-flow basis, the return is a little under 8 percent. Similarly if Jones takes out the first mortgage and invests capital of $263,500, the result is again disappointing but not disastrous: The interest payments on the first mortgage consume virtually the entire cash flow, reducing it to only $2,367 per year, and Jones is receiving a cash-flow return of less than one percent on her $263,500 investment. If, however, she has "leveraged up" the project, the results become increasingly disastrous. If she

takes out the first two mortgages and invests $113,500 in cash, the project has a negative cash flow after financing costs of over $25,000 per year. In other words, she has the choice of watching her $113,500 disappear without a trace or coming up with an additional $25,000 per year, with no end in sight unless the apartment rental market improves dramatically. If she takes out three mortgages involving monthly cash payments of over $9,000 per month, both she and the project are in deep trouble: The negative cash flow increases to nearly $40,000 per year. At this point, the critical question becomes whether Jones is personally liable on those three mortgages. If she is, Jones's personal wealth may well be drawn down the drain. If she is not, she can walk away from the project losing only the original land value she contributed to the project.

§3.15 Leverage Generally

In the remaining chapters of this book, we will encounter the concept of leverage in a number of different guises. In many transactions involving securities, for example, a portion of the purchase price may be borrowed. Such transactions are leveraged because the investor buys (or sells) a larger amount of the security in question than he or she could without borrowing. The investor is in effect gambling that the price movement (and cash return if any) will more than offset the interest cost of the borrowing. As a result, any change in the price of the security has a correspondingly greater effect on a borrowing investor than on one who invests the same amount of capital but does not borrow in order to increase the size of the investment. Similarly, a corporation uses leverage whenever it finances expansion of its productive capacity by borrowing funds at fixed interest rates rather than by selling additional shares of common stock. There are many other examples of business transactions involving the borrowing of capital in order to improve the profitability of the transaction to equity holders.

CHAPTER 4
COMMERCIAL ANNUITIES
AND RETIREMENT PLANS

§4.1 Introduction

A stream of payments payable at specified intervals in the future is called an **annuity**. Annuities affect the lives of most people in the United States at some time, even though many may not even know what the word means. Annuities are an essential part of pensions and retirement plans, often supplementing social security and related public benefit programs. This chapter introduces the annuity in a logical but indirect way, dealing first with simple and somewhat artificial examples, and then progressing to retirement annuities.

§4.2 Commercial Annuities in General

Some annuities are purchased by individuals, usually from life insurance companies. If payments are of fixed amounts for a fixed period, the determination of the present values of such payments is a straightforward application of the time value of money, that is, the principle of discounting future payments to present values, applying an appropriate discount rate to each payment to determine the present value of each payment, and then adding up those present values (as explained more fully above in the chapter on present value).

Most commercial annuities are designed not to make payments for a fixed

period but rather to continue for the lifetime of one or more persons. The pricing of such annuities requires an estimate of the probable lifespans involved, which in turn involves reliance on mortality or life expectancy tables. Indeed, if the word "annuity" conjures up any image at all to the average person, it is probably one of an elderly person receiving a payment each month for the balance of his or her life. Mortality and life expectancy tables are discussed briefly in Chapter 5. Retirement programs often rely on commercial annuities, usually by the purchase of a lifetime annuity shortly before the employee's retirement. An annuity for the life of a person is in a sense the converse of life insurance on the life of that person: The annuity pays for the lifetime of the person and ends upon that person's death, while life insurance becomes due and payable on death and provides for the period following the death of the person.

In the discussion of commercial annuities below, the person creating the annuity is often referred to as the **contributor**. The person receiving the annuity is referred to as the **annuitant**; the annuitant and the contributor can, of course, be the same person. The person or entity agreeing to make the payments is referred to as the **writer** of the annuity: As noted, many life insurance companies are also in the business of selling annuities.

§4.3 Single-Premium Fixed Annuities

The simplest kind of annuity does not involve any mortality calculation. For example, suppose that your client, a rather well-to-do elderly widow, is considering the purchase of an annuity. For $100,000 cash paid to a large life insurance company, the company will agree to pay $1,200 per month each year for 10 years to her or her estate. The $100,000 represents the bulk of her current liquid resources: It may have resulted from a lifetime of incremental saving, from life insurance proceeds on the life of her deceased spouse, or from other sources. The theory behind the 10-year provision is that in 10 years she will begin receiving retirement income from other sources: social security payments and a lifetime annuity from an employee pension plan. The 10-year annuity is thus a stopgap. There is no gambling on the death of your client in this example; payments are guaranteed for 10 years, whether or not your client is alive. If she dies within the 10 years, the payments will continue to be made to her estate, or to whomever she directs in her will, for the balance of the 10-year term. At the end of ten years, the obligation of the writer of the annuity ends.

It should be obvious in this example that each monthly payment that your client receives consists partly of return of her principal and partly of interest earned on the balance of the money. Without taking into account the time value of money, it appears that she is investing $100,000 and receiving back a total of $144,000 ($1,200 per month times 120 months). However, the discussion in Chapter 2 should make clear the fallacy of that approach. The reason that this is economical from the standpoint of the life insurance company is that each month it is earning interest on that portion of the $100,000 that it has not yet repaid to your client. In other words, each payment except for the last has an interest component as well as a return of principal component. A computation

(difficult with pencil and paper but easy with a calculator) reveals that your client is actually receiving a 7.75 percent return on her $100,000 investment over 10 years. In other words, the sum of the present values of the 120 payments of $1,200 each computed at 7.75 percent is almost precisely $100,000. Mathematically, at 7.75 percent, the first monthly payment of $1,200 (the first annuity payment) constitutes $645.83 of interest on the $100,000 and $554.17 return of principal. The second payment consists of $642.25 of interest (one month's interest on $99,445.83 ($100,000 − $554.17)) and $557.75 return of principal; the third payment consists of $638.65 of interest (one month's interest on $98,888.08 ($99,445.83 − $557.75)) and $561.35 of principal. And so on, for each of the remaining payments until the last $1,200 payment, which consists almost entirely of principal and finally exhausts the original $100,000 of principal. In each month, the remaining principal is calculated by subtracting the amount of principal repaid the previous month. (If these figures look vaguely familiar, compare the analysis of the conventional level-premium mortgage in Chapter 3. From the mortgagee's perspective, an "annuity" is being received from the mortgagor.)

If the current market rate for riskless investments is 9 percent at the time of the proposed purchase, this annuity at first glance does not appear to be a very attractive deal. Your client would apparently be better off simply investing the money in a federally insured bank account at the higher market interest rate of 9 percent, and withdrawing each month the accumulated interest and a portion of principal necessary to yield her $1,200 per month. In the discussion below, this will be referred to as a "do-it-yourself annuity." The economic difference between the life insurance company's product and the do-it-yourself annuity can be made graphic by considering the composition of the first few payments. If the same amount were invested at 9 percent, the first month's interest would have been $750, and only $450 would have had to be drawn from principal to make the $1,200 payment. The life insurance company only gave your client credit for interest of $645.83 and repaid her $554.17 from her principal. At 9 percent, the interest for the second month would be $746.63 and the amount of principal that would have to be drawn out would be $453.38. Corresponding figures for the life insurance company annuity are $642.25 of principal and $557.75 of interest. In each month thereafter the performance of the do-it-yourself annuity is superior, reflecting the fact that the dollars are invested at a 9 percent annual rate rather than at a 7.75 percent annual rate. At the end of the 10-year pay-out period, the bank account would still have $12,918 in it, while the commercial annuity would have been exhausted.

Why might a person be interested in buying a commercial annuity at apparently disadvantageous terms rather than simply investing the money in a bank? There are several possible advantages. For one thing, it is more convenient simply to receive a check each month, rather than to visit the bank and withdraw $1,200. There is also the matter of self-discipline. Does your client have the mental resolve to follow the routine each month without taking out "a little extra, just this time"? Third, an elderly person with a large bank account may be defrauded by a smooth-talking swindler; investment of funds in an annuity provides protection to the annuitant against such unwise dissipations of assets.

These factors may not appear to be of great importance in this simple example, but in individual cases they may well justify the decision to purchase a commercial annuity rather than to simply turn over a large sum of money to someone who must rely on that sum over a long period of time to provide his or her livelihood. In other words, an annuity can be rather like a spendthrift trust.

A much more substantial advantage of the life insurance company annuity from the standpoint of your client is that the return of 7.75 percent is guaranteed for the next 10 years; someone opening the bank account implicitly assumes that the 9 percent market rate will remain stable for that period, obviously a very dubious assumption. If the market rate of interest were to drop to 6 percent a year after the annuity arrangement was created, your client would have been considerably worse off electing to "do-it-herself." Correspondingly, if interest rates go up, the life insurance company gets fat from investing your client's funds at (say) 15 percent while continuing to make fixed payments at a rate of 7.75 percent. It obviously suffers if interest rates drop and the insurance company earns 5 percent on invested funds while being required to pay your client 7.75 percent. In effect, the insurance company takes the risk of market fluctuations in the interest rate. The company is able to do this profitably because it can diversify against this risk; it enters into many different arrangements and many different investments of varying maturities and varying yields at different times. It probably would be difficult or impossible for your client to find a riskless 10-year investment that would be guaranteed to continue to pay 9 percent and would also permit monthly withdrawals. In a word, the insurance company provides an important service in packaging the investment to meet your client's needs.

A countervailing factor is the possibility of insolvency: The do-it-yourself annuity is invested in insured savings accounts, but the right of your client to receive payments from the insurance company under the commercial annuity is not secured in any way and is dependent on the continued solvency of the insurance company. This may seem to be theoretical because life insurance companies rarely go under, but major companies writing single-premium annuities have been known to become insolvent after promising annuity payments at higher interest rates than could be maintained. On the other hand, banks and thrifts also become insolvent, and although funds on deposit are typically insured, interest payments are not.

A second countervailing factor to consider is the possibility that your client may become ill and need a significant portion of her principal back immediately rather than in bits of $1,200 per month. This, of course, is not a problem with the do-it-yourself annuity. Most commercial single-premium annuities, however, allow cancellation of the annuity and a refund of most of the remaining unpaid principal. Although cancellation may entail a significant penalty, it at least permits most financial emergencies to be met.

On balance, it appears that a fixed-return annuity can provide a considerable amount of convenience and security at the cost of some loss of yield. One way of looking at this transaction is that for a premium of 1.25 percent, the insurance company is assuming the administrative costs of handling the transaction as well as the risk that interest rates may decline during the next 10 years.

Other legal devices exist that may be a substitute for a commercial single-

premium annuity. For example, you might consider creating an inter vivos trust for your client's benefit that would invest and disburse the $100,000. The relatively small amount involved, however, and attendant fees and expenses probably would make this alternative unattractive.

§4.4 Single-Premium Deferred Annuities

The example set forth in the preceding section involved payments to the annuitant commencing immediately upon purchase of the annuity. It is also possible, however, to purchase a single-premium annuity that does not begin to make payments to the annuitant for a period of years.

Assume that a contributor makes a single, lump-sum payment of $100,000 when he is 35 years old for an annuity commencing at age 65. The contributor may be seeking to fund or supplement retirement by making a long-term investment. Traditionally, most annuities of this type provided a fixed-dollar return beginning at the age of 65. In other words, both the interest rate being paid on the $100,000 contribution over the 30 years before the first payment comes due and the interest rate that determines the amount of the annuity to be paid each month thereafter were set forth in the original contract. Nowadays, it is more typical for a series of elections to be provided so that before the annuitant reaches the age at which the first payment is due to be made, he or she may select a payment option. Typical options are payments for the balance of the contributor's life, for the lives of the contributor and his or her spouse, or for the contributor's life with a guaranteed period of payments in the event the contributor dies shortly after retirement.

The growth that naturally occurs over the 30-year period between the time the annuity is purchased and the time the first payment is due is called the buildup. Mathematically, the buildup over 30 years on $100,000 is very substantial: If the insurance company agrees to pay 4 percent per year, the amount available at age 65 would be $331,349.80; at 6 percent, it is $602,257.22; and at 8 percent, $1,093,572.96. Thus, if the contributor can afford to put aside a substantial sum at a relatively young age, there is quite a pot at the end of the rainbow.

Thirty years is, of course, a long time. A similar investment over 10 years shows results that are not as spectacular, but are still substantial. A $100,000 investment made at age 55 with payments to begin in ten years grows to $149,083.27 at 4 percent; to $181,939.67 at 6 percent; and to $221,964.02, at 8 percent.

§4.5 The Risk of Insolvency

An annuity written by an insurance company (or any other writer for that matter) is an unsecured promise by the writer to make certain payments in the future. If the writer becomes insolvent, the annuitant has an unsecured claim that may or may not lead to a partial payment of funds invested in the annuity. The risk of insurance company insolvency is not entirely theoretical. In the late

1980s, three large insurance companies failed because of disastrous junk bond or real estate investments. The parent corporation of another major insurer also failed, although the insurance subsidiary was not directly affected.

Insurance companies are generally regulated and insured (in a limited fashion) under state rather than federal law. It was doubtful that the available state insurance funds were adequate to cover the potential losses of insureds and annuitants arising from these failures, let alone possible additional failures. The insolvency risk when one deposits funds with an insurance company is a real one. The failure of an insurance company is most likely to occur during a period of financial crisis in real estate or securities values (as arguably occurred in the late 1980s) but may also conceivably occur anytime if insurance company assets are lost through massive fraud.

It is therefore important to make an assessment of an insurance company's solvency before investing significant funds. Unfortunately, that is not easy to do. Insurers are allowed to carry most of their investments at cost rather than present market values. Hence, the impact of significant market declines of insurance company assets may not be ascertainable from insurance company financial statements. Further, organizations such as A.M. Best Co., which rate the solvency of insurance companies, may use data that are more than 12 months old, and may rely to some extent on book values in making the assessment. Some companies that rate insurers also charge a fee for supplying anything more than nominal information. Proposals continue to be made to value assets of insurers—particularly troubled loans where terms have been renegotiated or less than full performance accepted—at current market value rather than at cost. These proposals, however, have only been implemented to a limited extent.

Some $150 to $200 billion in retirement funds are currently invested in so-called **guaranteed investment contracts (GICs)** issued by insurance companies. These contracts are essentially naked promises by the insurance company to pay certain amounts in the future and are uninsured in the event of the insolvency of the insurance company. GICs may be found in many employer-provided retirement plans (which are described more fully in a following section). They may also be found in terminated defined benefit plans in which the employer has sought to recapture excess pension funds, substituting GICs for the funds in the plan.

Because of the risk of insurance company insolvency, many employers spread the risk by purchasing contracts from several different insurance companies; others place new funds in more secure alternative investments. Insurance companies may also create separate funds in which retirement funds may be invested directly in securities, presumably free of the credit risk of default by the insurance company. The status of these pools of assets in the event of insurer insolvency, however, is uncertain. These "funded GICs" are called "synthetic GICs" within the insurance industry.

Annuities are also offered for sale by banks. The first commercial annuities that banks offered were in fact written by insurance companies. For example, commercial annuities offered in the lobbies of Security Pacific Bank were actually written by Colonial Penn Life Insurance Company. Many banks also offer annuities written by companies affiliated with the banks. However, none of these annuities are guaranteed by the bank itself or protected by federal deposit

insurance. Commercial annuities today are offered through banks and thrift institutions as alternatives to passbook savings accounts, certificates of deposit, or other traditional investment alternatives offered by banks. The principal advantage of these bank-related annuities is convenience, because most customers regularly visit bank offices.

An annuity contract written by an insurance company may be transferred to another company under the practice generally known as assumption reinsurance. Following such a transaction, the assigning company usually takes the position that it is no longer obligated on the contract. Annuity contracts in which significant amounts have been invested may thus be assigned to weaker companies, materially increasing the risk of default. A person owning such an annuity contract should be particularly vigilant and object to any assignment that appears to increase the default risk on the annuity.

§4.6 The Concept of Tax Deferral

Earlier, a commercial annuity was compared with a do-it-yourself annuity providing essentially the same benefits. The do-it-yourself possibility, while viable for a single-premium annuity with payments to commence immediately, is not attractive when compared with a deferred annuity such as the one described above. The reason is the difference in the income tax treatment of an annuity on the one hand and a savings account on the other.

If our hypothetical 35-year-old contributor were to try to create a do-it-yourself annuity, he might open a savings account and deposit $100,000 in it, planning to allow it to accumulate for 30 years. However, he would be required to pay income taxes each year on the interest earned on that account, whether or not any amount was withdrawn. Assuming that the depositor was in the 28 percent bracket, the interest income each year would need to be reduced by 28 percent when evaluating the do-it-yourself annuity. As a practical matter, if the depositor created a do-it-yourself annuity, it is likely that he would not actually reduce the account by the 28 percent tax but would simply pay the taxes out of other earnings or other assets, allowing the account to grow unconstrained. However, it should be obvious that from a total net worth standpoint, these tax payments must be viewed as part of the cost of the do-it-yourself alternative.

In the case of the commercial annuity, no income tax is due from the contributor on the interest on the $100,000 until the annuitant actually begins to receive payments at age 65. In other words, a **deferred annuity** offers **tax deferral**, whereas the savings account does not. Because of the 28 percent tax rate differential, an 8 percent do-it-yourself deferred annuity accumulates at about the same rate as a 6 percent commercial deferred annuity. This advantage, however, is not permanent. The tax deferral under the annuity continues only during the period of the buildup. Once payments on the annuity commence, a significant portion of each payment becomes subject to income tax. On the other hand, the person creating the do-it-yourself annuity has been paying taxes all along, and a much smaller proportion of each subsequent payment will be subject to tax.

The underlying concept of tax deferral (which applies to many different

kinds of transactions) does not mean that the 30 years of buildup escapes tax forever. Tax is merely put off until the time the contributor receives his or her first payment under the annuity after reaching the age of 65. At that time, taxation of the buildup begins. Each payment under the annuity is viewed as having two different components: Part of the payment is a refund of a portion of the $100,000 contribution that the contributor makes and part of the payment represents a distribution from the buildup. The first portion of each payment is viewed as a tax-free return of capital and the second portion is taxed as ordinary income. The ratio is called the exclusion ratio and the Internal Revenue Code and the regulations issued thereunder contain precise rules for calculating it. That ratio, however, is calculated only once at the time of the first payment and is thereafter applied to each payment. Assuming that the exclusion ratio is properly computed, that all the contemplated payments are made as scheduled, that the annuity is for the lifetime of the contributor, and that the contributor lives precisely to his or her life expectancy, then the annuitant ultimately pays income taxes on every dollar of the buildup.

A single-premium annuity with payments to commence immediately is taxed the same way as a deferred annuity. Thus, even though the creator of the do-it-yourself annuity does not defer taxes during the buildup, an exclusion ratio is created to reflect the interest component earned after the annuity begins paying out.

Investors in commercial annuities gain tax deferral, not tax avoidance. Ultimately, the buildup is subject to tax; the only difference between it and the taxation of a do-it-yourself savings account is that the income is taxed immediately. Why is tax deferral so advantageous if—come the millennium—the contributor's tax position is unchanged? The answer lies in part in the time value of money. When tax deferral is available, the contributor has the use of the funds otherwise needed to pay taxes in order to earn additional interest for an extended period. A dollar today is always worth more than a dollar in the future. A dollar not paid in tax today is worth more than the same dollar paid in tax in 30 years. For this reason alone, tax deferral is almost always advantageous. Furthermore, because the tax deferral in an annuity usually extends over several years, the buildup occurs at an accelerated rate because subsequent earnings on prior years' tax deferrals are also tax deferred. Tax deferral offers other possible advantages as well. For example, tax rates may be lower by the time the tax payments begin than they were during the buildup. Another possible advantage is that after retirement, persons may be in a lower tax bracket than they were when employed, and thus the deferral may again result in the application of lower tax rates.

There is nothing inherent in the concept of an annuity that requires it to be tax-deferred. Indeed there are many investments such as zero-coupon bonds (which are discussed in some detail in Chapter 14) that pay no return until maturity but that nonetheless generate taxable income during their life. Although the favored tax-deferral treatment of annuities is usually justified as a way to encourage private savings and private arrangements to provide retirement income, there are many other investment vehicles that could be made tax deferred for the same reason. Thus, the favored treatment of annuities may be

more a reflection of the influence of the insurance industry in Congress than anything else.

§4.7 Variable Annuities

The fixed-rate annuities described in the previous sections lost much of their attractiveness during the period of high interest rates in the late 1970s and early 1980s. Even with the advantage of tax deferral, an investment yielding perhaps 4 percent per year is unattractive when compared with riskless market investments yielding 12 or 14 percent per year, as was the case in the early 1980s. A person who has invested in such a fixed annuity will naturally seek to suspend or terminate the annuity, even at a sacrifice if necessary, in order to invest the remaining proceeds at the higher market interest rate. Secondly, the relatively high level of inflation during this period made fixed-rate annuities extremely unattractive: The contributor was making a payment with 1965 dollars, say, in order to receive an annuity of a fixed amount in deflated dollars starting in 1995. These two problems are related because higher inflation levels tend to cause higher interest rates; together they make any long-term, fixed-payment investment relatively unattractive.

There is no inherent reason why the company writing an annuity must gamble on interest and inflation rates. The gamble arises from the decision to pay interest at a fixed rate established in advance. Why not let the company put all payments for future annuities into an investment fund and have the amount of the ultimate annuity depend on how much the company actually earns from this fund? This proposal eliminates much of the gamble on interest rates that inevitably occurs whenever a long-term investment is made at a fixed interest rate. On the other hand, this arrangement makes retirement planning less precise, because the amount of the ultimate annuity to be paid becomes expressly dependent on the fund's investment success. Commercial annuities based on this novel but sensible approach are called **variable annuities**.

The earliest versions of variable annuities date back to the 1950s. They eliminated the fixed-return feature, but assumed that the premium would be invested in traditional fixed income investments. The "variable" feature resulted only from changes in yields of such fixed investments over the years. However, once the variable annuity concept was recognized, it was a relatively small additional step to relax the requirement that investments be in long-term interest-yielding investments. Any kind of investment might be appropriate for the fund. Further, it took only a series of relatively small additional steps (1) to create several different funds with different investment goals, (2) to permit contributors to designate which fund or funds in which they would like the $100,000 to be placed, and (3) to allow for changes in the investment mix from time to time. The final step in increasing flexibility was to allow contributors to borrow back a portion of their initial contribution whenever they wanted. Now that the amount of the ultimate annuity was not fixed but was dependent on investment results, such borrowing became essentially a matter of indifference to the writer of the annuity. If the loan was never repaid, the annuity was

simply reduced appropriately. If the loan was repaid, it reduced principal for the period it was outstanding, which reduced the amount of the buildup but did not affect the company's long-term obligation.

At this point, it is useful to step back and look at what the annuity has become. The power to make decisions regarding the investments to be made during the buildup period and the power to withdraw contributions makes the plan not terribly different from an income-producing bank deposit or an investment in a mutual fund. Yet tax deferral is still available. During the 1970s, the Internal Revenue Service (IRS) resisted the argument that such an account should be subject to deferred taxation as an annuity, but eventually the IRS lost that argument. As a result, the earnings are still tax-deferred (because the transaction is cast in the form of an annuity), and human ingenuity has created an investment vehicle that competes with other savings plans but retains tax deferral. Needless to say, this type of investment quickly became very attractive in the early 1980s because of this feature.

Of course, there are administrative costs associated with all annuities. It has been estimated that the yearly administrative costs associated with the management of a variable annuity are about 2 percent of the contributions and buildup. In addition, heavy **surrender charges** of up to 7 percent may be applicable upon early withdrawal. These charges typically decline over time and disappear entirely after the annuity contract has been in existence for a specified period—typically, after seven years. Because of these initial penalties, a variable annuity should remain undisturbed for an extended period so that the tax-deferred compounding can offset the high initial fees. A ten-year holding period for a variable annuity is a good rule of thumb. Some variable annuities soften these surrender charges by permitting a 10 percent withdrawal each year without penalty. Variable annuities also typically permit the transfer of funds into a lifetime annuity without penalty.

Annuity contracts may also carry other insurance-related charges that reduce the earnings. In addition, to the extent funds may be invested in stock or bond mutual funds, the nature and costs of these funds should be considered. The promotional advertising for variable annuities may entirely ignore this second layer of hidden charges. All in all, given the limited nature of the available investment choices and the steep termination costs during the early years of the annuity, one suspects that this type of investment is being oversold.

Variable annuities are often sold as tax-deferred mutual fund investments, which in some ways they resemble. There are, however, important differences: Variable annuity fees are higher, the alternative investments that are available are fewer, and one is locked in, as a practical matter, for a much longer time. Advertisements for variable annuities regularly compare the growth of a tax-deferred annuity with a taxable certificate of deposit or other fixed-income investments. This comparison is potentially misleading, because no account is taken of the deferred tax obligation on the buildup. The comparison, in other words, is stacked against the taxable investment. "What they're really selling you is a compounded interest table," one financial planner has stated.

Earnings taken out of a variable annuity before the investor reaches the age of 59½ are subject to a 10 percent federal tax penalty (which may be avoided if the investor takes a lifetime annuity). There is no similar penalty applicable

to mutual funds. Because a variable annuity is an interest in a fund, there is probably little default risk in the purchase of such an investment. If the investor elects to take a lifetime annuity, the interest in the fund disappears and the continued payment of that annuity depends on the continued solvency of the insurance company. Despite these disadvantages, variable annuities are attractive to many persons.

As noted, variable annuities are similar to mutual funds, but traditionally they have been much more expensive than mutual funds in terms of the various fees that are charged against the fund or upon surrender. In 1995, several no-load variable annuities were introduced with no sales charge, no redemption fee, and lower insurance company fees (for commissions and actuarial services). Some so-called no-loads do, however, charge annual contract fees. In addition, there are significant differences in the way these two similar investments are taxed. These differences were narrowed in the 1980s when Congress provided that any borrowing from an annuity must be treated as a distribution from the buildup rather than a loan out of the original contribution; other changes in the tax treatment of annuity payments themselves were also made to reduce further the attractiveness of deferred annuities from a tax standpoint. As a result, much of the bloom has gone from this rose. In 1992, the Bush tax plan proposed the elimination of the tax-deferred feature of annuities. The proposal was promptly dropped following a hail of criticism.

Several companies continue to offer single-premium, variable-interest-rate annuities, sold largely on the basis of their favorable tax-deferral characteristics and relatively high initial rates of interest. These rates expressly are not guaranteed in later years and in fact appear to be "teaser rates" designed primarily to attract business. Interest rates on these annuities in later years have been significantly lowered even while higher initial rates continue to be advertised for new annuities.

Although fixed annuities waned in popularity during the 1980s because of extremely high interest rates, their popularity increased dramatically when interest rates were at historic lows in the early 1990s. Many investors found that the rates of return available on these investments were higher than on investments of supposedly comparable risk—such as certificates of deposit (CDs).

It is not entirely clear that the default risk in these two products is comparable. Although the risk with an annuity may be small, it is nonetheless real. The principal on a CD, on the other hand, is typically insured—up to $100,000 per depositor per institution—by federal deposit insurance (and in practice the Federal Deposit Insurance Corporation (FDIC) has generally made good on all deposits even in excess of that amount). On the other hand, interest payments are not insured by the FDIC. Annuities are generally not insured at all, although some protections comparable to federal deposit insurance are provided at the state level when an insurer becomes insolvent. In the end, the relative safety of insurance companies, together with state-level protections, may roughly balance out with the somewhat limited scheme of deposit insurance available at banks and savings and loans.

Considerations of risk aside, insurance companies are able to pay higher rates of return on annuities because they contain an insurance component. That is, the agreed return is paid only to those who survive until the time of each

payment. Because some number of people who buy annuities can be expected to die prematurely, the returns that would have been paid to those who die can in effect be transferred to those who survive. This is not to say that fixed annuities (or variable annuities for that matter) are a bad deal. Indeed, they may be a very good deal particularly if you are a survivor. The fact that an annuity diverts the returns of those who die to those who survive explains the favorable rates paid on them.

§4.8 Multiple-Premium Annuities

Consider the situation of a 35-year-old man who lacks the resources to make a $100,000 investment but who desires to make some provision for retirement in 30 years. Commercial insurance companies have long offered annuity plans that are designed to meet the needs of such a person. They involve monthly payment plans under which the contributor gradually builds up a nest egg; the payments accumulate and are converted into an annuity shortly before retirement.

Perhaps this person feels he can contribute $5,000 per year toward retirement. Traditionally, a fixed interest rate was involved, so that the amount accumulated after the 30 years of payments can be calculated mathematically. For simplicity, let us assume that each payment is made at the end of the year, that the person plans to retire at the end of the 30th year, that interest is compounded annually, and that the insurance company guarantees a 7 percent annual return. The value in 30 years of the stream of $5,000 payments is then equal to the future value of $5,000 over 30 years plus the future value of $5,000 over 29 years plus the future value of $5,000 over 28 years, and so forth. This calculation is made much simpler by tables showing the future value of annuities. To determine the amount that will be available in this example for the purchase of an annuity in 30 years, one need merely look in the 30 row and 7 percent column of Table 4-1. The number (94.4608) is simply multiplied by $5,000 to determine that the amount available for the retirement annuity will build up to $472,304 in 30 years.

Three important points should be made about the accumulation aspects of this kind of transaction. First, any kind of regular contribution made over a long period of time builds up to a large amount in absolute terms over 30 years. Whether or not this is considered advantageous, however, depends on what assumptions one makes about inflation over 30 years. If inflation remains low, a comfortable retirement may be expected; under the worst inflation scenarios, $472,304 may be only the cost of a haircut in 30 years. Second, the interest rate that is used in the accumulation phase has an immense impact on the amount of the ultimate annuity. Third, if the buildup phase involves monthly payments and monthly compounding of interest (rather than annual payments and compounding, as in the previous hypothetical), the amount of the buildup is significantly increased.

This kind of annuity seems to be precisely the type envisioned by the Internal Revenue Code when it granted the advantages of tax deferral. The earnings from the investment of the $5,000 payments accumulate without

Table 4-1
Future Value of a Stream of $1 Payments Made at the End of Each Period After n Periods

No. of periods	2%	3%	4%	5%	6%	7%	8%
1	1.0000	1.0000	1.0000	1.0000	1.0000	1.0000	1.0000
2	2.0200	2.0300	2.0400	2.0500	2.0600	2.0700	2.0800
3	3.0604	3.0909	3.1216	3.1525	3.1836	3.2149	3.2464
4	4.1216	4.1836	4.2465	4.3101	4.3746	4.4399	4.5061
5	5.2040	5.3091	5.4163	5.5256	5.6371	5.7507	5.8666
6	6.3081	6.4684	6.6330	6.8019	6.9753	7.1533	7.3359
7	7.4343	7.6625	7.8983	8.1420	8.3938	8.6540	8.9228
8	8.5830	8.8923	9.2142	9.5491	9.8975	10.2598	10.6366
9	9.7546	10.1591	10.5828	11.0266	11.4913	11.9780	12.4876
10	10.9497	11.4639	12.0061	12.5779	13.1808	13.8164	14.4866
11	12.1687	12.8078	13.4864	14.2068	14.9716	15.7836	16.6455
12	13.4121	14.1920	15.0258	15.9171	16.8699	17.8885	18.9771
13	14.6803	15.6178	16.6268	17.7130	18.8821	20.1406	21.4953
14	15.9739	17.0863	18.2919	19.5986	21.0151	22.5505	24.2149
15	17.2934	18.5989	20.0236	21.5786	23.2760	25.1290	27.1521
16	18.6393	20.1569	21.8245	23.6575	25.6725	27.8881	30.3243
17	20.0121	21.7616	23.6975	25.8404	28.2129	30.8402	33.7502
18	21.4123	23.4144	25.6454	28.1324	30.9057	33.9990	37.4502
19	22.8406	25.1169	27.6712	30.5390	33.7600	37.3790	41.4463
20	24.2974	26.8704	29.7781	33.0660	36.7856	40.9955	45.7620
21	25.7833	28.6765	31.9692	35.7193	39.9927	44.8652	50.4229
22	27.2990	30.5368	34.2480	38.5052	43.3923	49.0057	55.4568
23	28.8450	32.4529	36.6179	41.4305	46.9958	53.4361	60.8933
24	30.4219	34.4265	39.0826	44.5020	50.8156	58.1767	66.7648
25	32.0303	36.4593	41.6459	47.7271	54.8645	63.2490	73.1059

Table 4-1 (*cont.*)
Future Value of a Stream of $1 Payments Made at the End of Each Period After n Periods

No. of periods	2%	3%	4%	5%	6%	7%	8%
26	33.6709	38.5530	44.3117	51.1135	59.1564	68.6765	79.9544
27	35.3443	40.7096	47.0842	54.6691	63.7058	74.4838	87.3508
28	37.0512	42.9309	49.9676	58.4026	68.5281	80.6977	95.3388
29	38.7922	45.2189	52.9663	62.3227	73.6398	87.3465	103.9659
30	40.5681	47.5754	56.0849	66.4388	79.0582	94.4608	113.2832
31	42.3794	50.0027	59.3283	70.7608	84.8017	102.0730	123.3459
32	44.2270	52.5028	62.7015	75.2988	90.8898	110.2182	134.2135
33	46.1116	55.0778	66.2095	80.0638	97.3432	118.9334	145.9506
34	48.0338	57.7302	69.8579	85.0670	104.1838	128.2588	158.6267
35	49.9945	60.4621	73.6522	90.3203	111.4348	138.2369	172.3168
36	51.9944	63.2759	77.5983	95.8363	119.1209	148.9135	187.1021
37	54.0343	66.1742	81.7022	101.6281	127.2681	160.3374	203.0703
38	56.1149	69.1594	85.9703	107.7095	135.9042	172.5610	220.3159
39	58.2372	72.2342	90.4091	114.0950	145.0585	185.6403	238.9412
40	60.4020	75.4013	95.0255	120.7998	154.7620	199.6351	259.0565
41	62.6100	78.6633	99.8265	127.8398	165.0477	214.6096	280.7810
42	64.8622	82.0232	104.8196	135.2318	175.9505	230.6322	304.2435
43	67.1595	85.4839	110.0124	142.9933	187.5076	247.7765	329.5830
44	69.5027	89.0484	115.4129	151.1430	199.7580	266.1209	356.9496
45	71.8927	92.7199	121.0294	159.7002	212.7435	285.7493	386.5056
46	74.3306	96.5015	126.8706	168.6852	226.5081	306.7518	418.4261
47	76.8172	100.3965	132.9454	178.1194	241.0986	329.2244	452.9002
48	79.3535	104.4084	139.2632	188.0254	256.5645	353.2701	490.1322
49	81.9406	108.5406	145.8337	198.4267	272.9584	378.9990	530.3427
50	84.5794	112.7969	152.6671	209.3480	290.3359	406.5289	573.7702

Table 4-1 (*cont.*)

Future Value of a Stream of $1 Payments Made at the End of Each Period After n Periods

No. of periods	9%	10%	11%	12%	13%	14%	15%
1	1.0000	1.0000	1.0000	1.0000	1.0000	1.0000	1.0000
2	2.0900	2.1000	2.1100	2.1200	2.1300	2.1400	2.1500
3	3.2781	3.3100	3.3421	3.3744	3.4069	3.4396	3.4725
4	4.5731	4.6410	4.7097	4.7793	4.8498	4.9211	4.9934
5	5.9847	6.1051	6.2278	6.3528	6.4803	6.6101	6.7424
6	7.5233	7.7156	7.9129	8.1152	8.3227	8.5355	8.7537
7	9.2004	9.4872	9.7833	10.0890	10.4047	10.7305	11.0668
8	11.0285	11.4359	11.8594	12.2997	12.7573	13.2328	13.7268
9	13.0210	13.5795	14.1640	14.7757	15.4157	16.0853	16.7858
10	15.1929	15.9374	16.7220	17.5487	18.4197	19.3373	20.3037
11	17.5603	18.5312	19.5614	20.6546	21.8143	23.0445	24.3493
12	20.1407	21.3834	22.7132	24.1331	25.6502	27.2707	29.0017
13	22.9534	24.5227	26.2116	28.0291	29.9847	32.0887	34.3519
14	26.0192	27.9750	30.0949	32.3926	34.8827	37.5811	40.5047
15	29.3609	31.7725	34.4054	37.2797	40.4175	43.8424	47.5804
16	33.0034	35.9497	39.1899	42.7533	46.6717	50.9804	55.7175
17	36.9737	40.5447	44.5008	48.8837	53.7391	59.1176	65.0751
18	41.3013	45.5992	50.3959	55.7497	61.7251	68.3941	75.8364
19	46.0185	51.1591	56.9395	63.4397	70.7494	78.9692	88.2118
20	51.1601	57.2750	64.2028	72.0524	80.9468	91.0249	102.4436
21	56.7645	64.0025	72.2651	81.6987	92.4699	104.7684	118.8101
22	62.8733	71.4027	81.2143	92.5026	105.4910	120.4360	137.6316
23	69.5319	79.5430	91.1479	104.6029	120.2048	138.2970	159.2764
24	76.7898	88.4973	102.1742	118.1552	136.8315	158.6586	184.1678
25	84.7009	98.3471	114.4133	133.3339	155.6196	181.8708	212.7930

Table 4-1 (*cont.*)
Future Value of a Stream of $1 Payments Made at the End of Each Period After n Periods

No. of periods	9%	10%	11%	12%	13%	14%	15%
26	93.3240	109.1818	127.9988	150.3339	176.8501	208.3327	245.7120
27	102.7231	121.0999	143.0786	169.3740	200.8406	238.4993	283.5688
28	112.9682	134.2099	159.8173	190.6989	227.9499	272.8892	327.1041
29	124.1354	148.6309	178.3972	214.5828	258.5834	312.0937	377.1697
30	136.3075	164.4940	199.0209	241.3327	293.1992	356.7868	434.7451
31	149.5752	181.9434	221.9132	271.2926	332.3151	407.7370	500.9569
32	164.0370	201.1378	247.3236	304.8477	376.5161	465.8202	577.1005
33	179.8003	222.2515	275.5292	342.4294	426.4632	532.0350	664.6655
34	196.9823	245.4767	306.8374	384.5210	482.9034	607.5199	765.3654
35	215.7108	271.0244	341.5896	431.6635	546.6808	693.5727	881.1702
36	236.1247	299.1268	380.1644	484.4631	618.7493	791.6729	1014.3457
37	258.3759	330.0395	422.9825	543.5987	700.1867	903.5071	1167.4975
38	282.6298	364.0434	470.5106	609.8305	792.2110	1030.9981	1343.6222
39	309.0665	401.4478	523.2667	684.0102	896.1984	1176.3378	1546.1655
40	337.8824	442.5926	581.8261	767.0914	1013.7042	1342.0251	1779.0903
41	369.2919	487.8518	646.8269	860.1424	1146.4858	1530.9086	2046.9539
42	403.5281	537.6370	718.9779	964.3595	1296.5289	1746.2358	2354.9969
43	440.8457	592.4007	799.0655	1081.0826	1466.0777	1991.7088	2709.2465
44	481.5218	652.6408	887.9627	1211.8125	1657.6678	2271.5481	3116.6334
45	525.8587	718.9048	986.6386	1358.2300	1874.1646	2590.5648	3585.1285
46	574.1860	791.7953	1096.1688	1522.2176	2118.8060	2954.2439	4123.8977
47	626.8628	871.9749	1217.7474	1705.8838	2395.2508	3368.8380	4743.4824
48	684.2804	960.1723	1352.6996	1911.5898	2707.6334	3841.4753	5456.0047
49	746.8656	1057.1896	1502.4965	2141.9806	3060.6258	4380.2819	6275.4055
50	815.0836	1163.9085	1668.7712	2400.0182	3459.5071	4994.5213	7217.7163

taxation until the annuity becomes due; at that point, an exclusion ratio is calculated and a portion of each payment is subject to taxation and a portion is excluded as a return of capital. In calculating this ratio, the capital invested is the total amount contributed without adjustment for the time value of money — 30 payments of $5,000 each.

For the reasons set forth in the preceding section, the fixed interest rate is not an essential aspect of the multiple-premium annuity. The multiple-payment annuity can readily be a variable annuity dependent on the investment results obtained through actual experience in the manner described in the previous section. Indeed, variable annuity plans usually permit contributors to make discretionary payments from time to time.

§4.9 Employee Retirement Plans: Before-Tax and After-Tax Dollars

The preceding section considered an example in which a person agreed to make annual payments of $5,000 per year to fund a retirement annuity. It was implicitly assumed that the payments would be made voluntarily each year, presumably by a check drawn on the contributor's available funds. Such a plan has some of the disadvantages of a do-it-yourself annuity in that payments require discipline on the part of the contributor. It also suffers, however, from a more fundamental problem.

Let us assume—as will usually be the case—that the contributor plans to make the payments out of his or her current earnings from employment. This plan is financed with after-tax dollars. This means simply that the contributor must pay income tax on the dollars he or she earns, and then must make the contribution to fund the annuity out of the dollars that remain. In other words, an employee who is in the 28 percent bracket must earn about $1.39 in order to make a $1 contribution to the retirement plan (and even that does not reflect other income or payroll taxes that may apply).

If the contributor's employer has created a pension or profit-sharing plan that meets the requirements of the federal **Employee Retirement Income Security Act (ERISA)** and the Internal Revenue Code, contributions may be made by the employer directly for the employee's retirement program without the contributions being included in the employee's tax return and without affecting the deductibility of the contributions as business expenses of the employer. A plan that meets the requirements of these federal statutes is referred to as a **qualified plan**. Such a plan provides for a much greater degree of tax deferral than a plan financed with after-tax dollars, because no tax is imposed on either the employer's contribution or on the buildup from such contributions until the employee retires (unless the funds are withdrawn before retirement). At the same time, the employer continues to deduct currently on its federal income tax return the gross amount of salary paid to the employee plus the amounts contributed by the employer for his or her benefit to the qualified plan.

A qualified plan requires that the employer in some way set aside the funds to be used for retirement purposes. Usually the employer makes contributions

directly to a trust or other entity that invests the funds for the benefit of employees. Upon retirement, the fund may either pay annuity benefits directly or may purchase a commercial annuity for the employee.

Federal law imposes a number of very specific requirements on qualified retirement plans. These requirements include vesting (which deals with the question whether the retirement benefits will be paid if the employee quits before retirement) and nondiscrimination (which ensures that lower paid as well as higher paid employees are covered by the plan). It is not necessary to describe these technical requirements: The important point is to recognize the significant degree of additional tax deferral that results from the creation of a qualified retirement plan.

In a qualified plan, everyone appears to gain at the expense of Uncle Sam. The obvious justification for these significant tax benefits is that they provide employers with an incentive to make adequate provision for the retirement of their employees, supplementing the social security system. And, indeed, qualified retirement plans are an important source of retirement income for most working people today.

Qualified retirement plans are divided into defined benefit plans and defined contribution plans. In a **defined benefit plan**, the size of the employer's contribution is determined on an actuarial basis to provide employees with designated benefits: An example might be a defined retirement benefit equal to 2 percent of the employee's average salary over the last 3 years of his or her employment multiplied by the number of years of employment. Thus, an employee with 30 years of service would receive a retirement benefit equal to 60 percent of his or her average 3-year preretirement salary. The military retirement plan is a well-known defined benefit plan.

A **defined contribution plan**, on the other hand, does not establish the amount to be paid by the employer on the basis of the benefits ultimately to be conferred on employees. Rather, the amount is established by reference to extrinsic information during each period, such as the employer's profits, or the actual salary paid to the employee during the period in question. For example, a defined contribution plan might provide an annual contribution by the employer equal to 7 percent of the employee's salary each year. The employee receives 100 percent of his or her salary. The employer contributes an additional 7 percent of this amount to the qualified plan and claims as a deduction for tax purposes 107 percent of the employee's salary. The 7 percent each year builds up in a fund until retirement. The amount in that fund upon retirement cannot be ascertained until retirement: Whatever the amount is, it will then be used to purchase a commercial annuity for the life of the retired employee. The amount of that annuity is determined solely by the amount in that employee's fund.

Some qualified plans are funded by contributions defined by reference to the contributing company's profits or to the value of a specified number of shares of the company's stock. These plans are called **profit-sharing plans** or **stock bonus plans** (respectively), but in the end they are simply special types of defined contribution plans.

In addition to the more traditional retirement plans discussed above, several new types of plans have emerged since 1980 that may eventually replace traditional plans altogether. These new types of plans include the **individual retire-**

ment account (IRA), the **Keogh plan**, **401(k) plans**, and **403(b) plans**. Generally speaking, IRAs are available to employees who are not covered by a retirement plan, while Keogh plans are available to self-employed individuals, and 401(k) and 403(b) plans (which are named for the Internal Revenue Code sections authorizing them) may be set up by employers in lieu of traditional plans and may allow for employees to make additional pretax contributions up to certain limits. (The 401(k) plan is available to private sector employers, while the 403(b) plan is available to public sector employers.) IRAs may also be used on a limited basis by individuals otherwise covered by a retirement plan, but contributions are made in after-tax dollars. Such plans differ from traditional plans in that they vest immediately and therefore are not lost if the employee changes jobs.

Finally, brief mention should be made of a device that has some limited usefulness in certain family-related or tax-oriented transactions. A **private annuity** is created by the transfer of property to a person in exchange for a promise by that person to make fixed periodic payments for the life of the transferor. The rights must be unsecured and the transferor cannot be in the business of writing annuities. In other words, it is an annuity based on the credit of a private individual not in the business of writing annuities. Private annuities may offer tax benefits by deferring the taxation of the transaction.

§4.10 Annuities for One or More Lifetimes

Most annuities are payable for the life or lives of one or more persons. They involve actuarial calculations as well as the time value of money. Actuaries calculate average life expectancies on the basis of mortality records that show numbers of persons of various ages and occupations who die each year. These records form the basis for widely used tables of life expectancies of persons of various ages that in turn form the backbone of both the life insurance industry and the annuity industry. The IRS has also published a table of life expectancies to be used for the calculation of the tax consequences of transactions involving annuities and lifetime interests.

Assume that an employee has reached the age of retirement after participating for many years in a plan that provides tax-deferred benefits arising upon retirement. Specifically, the employer has contributed to a noncontributory qualified pension plan for 25 years. The plan is a defined contribution plan; the most recent statement from the plan shows that the tax-deferred savings credited to the employee's account is $200,000. Now 67, the employee has decided to retire. He must now choose what to do with the $200,000 nest egg. The plan provides the following alternatives upon retirement:

1. Take the total accumulation in cash;
2. Elect a single life annuity payable for his life;
3. Elect a life annuity for the life of the employee with payments for 10 years guaranteed; that is, if he dies within 10 years, payments will continue to be made to his beneficiary;
4. Elect a life annuity for the combined lives of the employee and his

spouse (i.e., the payments are to continue while either the employee or his spouse are alive);

5. Elect a life annuity for the combined lives of the employee and his spouse with a guaranteed 10-year period; or
6. Elect a life annuity for the combined lives of the employee and his spouse with a further election that if the employee dies first, (i) the annuity drops to two-thirds of the level at which it was paid while both are alive; or (ii) the annuity drops to half of the level at which it was paid while both are alive.

The election must be made before the date of retirement, and once it is made and payments have commenced, it is usually irrevocable.

At first glance, these choices may seem confusing and complicated, but they really are not. They are familiar to persons who give financial advice to employees contemplating retirement. Choice 1 is obvious and the simplest, though often not the most advantageous; because the plan was noncontributory, the employee has made no contributions into the plan and the entire amount of $200,000 will be taxable to him upon the date of receipt. Moreover, if the employee elects this option, he then faces the problem of providing for himself and his spouse; there is always some risk with a do-it-yourself retirement plan that the money may run out while one or both of the beneficiaries are still alive.

Choice 2 requires knowledge of two factors: the life expectancy of a 67-year-old man and the interest rate used by the commercial insurance company in calculating the amount of a lifetime annuity for a single person of a specified age. Table 4-2 is a pre-1986 IRS table showing the expected return on an ordinary life annuity. The term **multiple** as used in the table refers to the number of years a person of a given age may be expected to live on average and thus to the number of annual payments that can be expected to be made under an annuity. Table 4-2 expressly takes the sex of an annuitant as well as his or her age into account as do most nongovernmental mortality tables. Because females live longer on the average than males, a contribution of a fixed amount made for the benefit of a female annuitant leads to a smaller monthly payment under this table than if the same payment were made for the benefit of a male. In 1986, the IRS adopted a revised "unisex" table (Table 4-3) that governs present annuity calculations.

In the present example, one may determine the life expectancy of a 67-year-old under the current IRS expected return schedule. From Table 4-3 one sees that the employee's life expectancy is an additional 18.4 years. Basically, the plan is purchasing a single-premium annuity commencing immediately and continuing for the life of the employee, but in determining how much is to be paid, the writer of the annuity assumes that the annuitant will precisely live out his life expectancy. If we assume that an interest rate of 6 percent is used, a $200,000 payment for 18.4 years yields a monthly payment of $1,495.54. It is important to recognize that the payments in this amount continue for the balance of the employee's life, no matter how long or how short that life in fact turns out to be. A particularly long-lived annuitant causes a loss to the insurance company, while one who dies tomorrow gives the company a gain. From the standpoint of the insurance company that writes the annuity, however, the use

Table 4-2
Pre-1986 Internal Revenue Code Table
Ordinary Life Annuities—One Life—Expected Return Multiples

Ages			Ages			Ages		
Male	*Female*	*Multiples*	*Male*	*Female*	*Multiples*	*Male*	*Female*	*Multiples*
6	11	65.0	41	46	33.0	76	81	9.1
7	12	64.1	42	47	32.1	77	82	8.7
8	13	63.2	43	48	31.2	78	83	8.3
9	14	62.3	44	49	30.4	79	84	7.8
10	15	61.4	45	50	29.6	80	85	7.5
11	16	60.4	46	51	28.7	81	86	7.1
12	17	59.5	47	52	27.9	82	87	6.7
13	18	58.6	48	53	27.1	83	88	6.3
14	19	57.7	49	54	26.3	84	89	6.0
15	20	56.7	50	55	25.5	85	90	5.7
16	21	55.8	51	56	24.7	86	91	5.4
17	22	54.9	52	57	24.0	87	92	5.1
18	23	53.9	53	58	23.2	88	93	4.8
19	24	53.0	54	59	22.4	89	94	4.5
20	25	52.1	55	60	21.7	90	95	4.2
21	26	51.1	56	61	21.0	91	96	4.0
22	27	50.2	57	62	20.3	92	97	3.7
23	28	49.3	58	63	19.6	93	98	3.5
24	29	48.3	59	64	18.9	94	99	3.3
25	30	47.4	60	65	18.2	95	100	3.1
26	31	46.5	61	66	17.5	96	101	2.9
27	32	45.6	62	67	16.9	97	102	2.7
28	33	44.6	63	68	16.2	98	103	2.5
29	34	43.7	64	69	15.6	99	104	2.3
30	35	42.8	65	70	15.0	100	105	2.1
31	36	41.9	66	71	14.4	101	106	1.9
32	37	41.0	67	72	13.8	102	107	1.7
33	38	40.0	68	73	13.2	103	108	1.5
34	39	39.1	69	74	12.6	104	109	1.3
35	40	38.2	70	75	12.1	105	110	1.2
						106	111	1.0
36	41	37.3	71	76	11.6	107	112	.8
37	42	36.5	72	77	11.0	108	113	.7
38	43	35.6	73	78	10.5	109	114	.6
39	44	34.7	74	79	10.1	110	115	.5
40	45	33.8	75	80	9.6	111	116	0

of reasonably accurate mortality tables eliminates virtually all of the underlying risk, because if many annuities are written, longer-lived annuitants are balanced and cancelled out by the shorter-lived ones. In other words, the insurance company has diversified away the risk that would attend writing a single annuity. As will be seen, the concept of diversification, like time value of money and

Table 4-3
1986 Internal Revenue Code Table
Ordinary Life Annuities—One Life—Expected Return Multiples

Age	Multiple	Age	Multiple	Age	Multiple
5	76.6	42	40.6	79	10.0
6	75.6	43	39.6	80	9.5
7	74.7	44	38.7	81	8.9
8	73.7	45	37.7	82	8.4
9	72.7	46	36.8	83	7.9
10	71.7	47	35.9	84	7.4
11	70.7	48	34.9	85	6.9
12	69.7	49	34.0	86	6.5
13	68.8	50	33.1	87	6.1
14	67.8	51	32.2	88	5.7
15	66.8	52	31.3	89	5.3
16	65.8	53	30.4	90	5.0
17	64.8	54	29.5	91	4.7
18	63.9	55	28.6	92	4.4
19	62.9	56	27.7	93	4.1
20	61.9	57	26.8	94	3.9
21	60.9	58	25.9	95	3.7
22	59.9	59	25.0	96	3.4
23	59.0	60	24.2	97	3.2
24	58.0	61	23.3	98	3.0
25	57.0	62	22.5	99	2.8
26	56.0	63	21.6	100	2.7
27	55.1	64	20.8	101	2.5
28	54.1	65	20.0	102	2.3
29	53.1	66	19.2	103	2.1
30	52.2	67	18.4	104	1.9
31	51.2	68	17.6	105	1.8
32	50.2	69	16.8	106	1.6
33	49.3	70	16.0	107	1.4
34	48.3	71	15.3	108	1.3
35	47.3	72	14.6	109	1.1
36	46.4	73	13.9	110	1.0
37	45.4	74	13.2	111	.9
38	44.4	75	12.5	112	.8
39	43.5	76	11.9	113	.7
40	42.5	77	11.2	114	.6
41	41.5	78	10.6	115	.5

leverage, has application in many other contexts and especially in investment strategies.

Choice 3 is like Choice 2 except that payments are guaranteed for 10 years. This also involves an actuarial computation. A moment's thought should reveal that the $200,000 payment will purchase a smaller monthly payment under Choice 3 than under Choice 2. The reason is that the premature death of the

annuitant under Choice 3 does not benefit the writer of the annuity as it does under Choice 2; as a result, the total obligation of the writer of the annuity is increased. In the above example, the monthly payment under Choice 3 will be approximately $1,400 per month. The $95 difference from the annuity payable under Choice 3 compensates the writer of the annuity for the possibility that the annuity must continue for a full 10 years even if the annuitant dies before then.

Choice 4 is obviously somewhat more complicated, because payments are to continue while either the annuitant or his spouse are alive. Tables 4-4 and 4-5 are portions of the "ordinary joint life and last survivor annuity" tables published by the IRS. Table 4-4 is the pre-1986 table taking the sex of the joint lives into account, while Table 4-5 is the unisex table in current use. In order to ascertain the amount of the monthly payment if this choice is elected, one must know the age of the spouse as well as of the principal annuitant. If we apply the current table and assume an age of 60 for the wife and 67 for the husband, the expected duration of the annuity is 27.0 years (from Table 4-5). This table is read by selecting one annuitant's age from the horizontal axis and the other annuitant's age from the vertical axis. At 27.0 years of expected return, the monthly payment (at 6 percent) is $1,246.73. Obviously, the difference between this amount and the $1,495.54 that would be payable for the life of the husband alone (Choice 2) is likely to affect significantly the lifestyle of the retirees. The reduction is large because of the younger age of the wife. Under the pre-1986 tables, younger wives had an even greater impact on their husbands' annuities.

Choice 5 is a compromise between preserving current lifestyles in the immediate postretirement period and not leaving the surviving spouse, most likely a younger wife, in dire straits following the death of her husband. The amount of the monthly payments under these plans may be readily determined on an actuarial basis, though the calculations are more complex than those set forth above.

The selection of any of these options must take into account the peculiar needs of the retiree and his or her spouse, their ages, their general health, other available assets, and insurance. These matters are discussed further in the chapter on life insurance.

Retirement plans that offer a variety of lifetime annuity arrangements sometimes describe the effect of the various arrangements as a percentage of a standard benefit. A plan widely used by institutions of higher education to provide retirement benefits for faculty and administrators, for example, estimates the benefit that would be payable on the basis of a life annuity with 10-year guaranteed payments as 100 percent. If the annuitant is 65 at the age of retirement, the election of a lifetime annuity with a 20-year guaranteed payment pays 93 percent of the base annuity. A single life annuity without guaranteed payments pays 104 percent of the base annuity. An annuity for the life of both a 67-year-old husband and his 60-year-old wife, and the survivor of them, with a guaranteed 10-year payment, pays 85 percent of the base amount. These percentages are sometimes more meaningful in the eyes of a person selecting irrevocably among these bewildering choices than dollar figures based on a hypothetical example.

Table 4-4
Pre-1986 Internal Revenue Code:
Ordinary Joint Life and Last Survivor Annuities—Two Lives—Expected Return Multiples

Ages Male	Ages Female	61 / 66	62 / 67	63 / 68	64 / 69	65 / 70	66 / 71	67 / 72	68 / 73	69 / 74	70 / 75	71 / 76	72 / 77	73 / 78
35	40	39.4	39.3	39.2	39.1	39.0	38.9	38.9	38.8	38.8	38.7	38.7	38.6	38.6
36	41	38.5	38.4	38.3	38.2	38.2	38.1	38.0	38.0	37.9	37.9	37.8	37.8	37.7
37	42	37.7	37.6	37.5	37.4	37.3	37.3	37.2	37.1	37.1	37.0	36.9	36.9	36.9
38	43	36.9	36.8	36.7	36.6	36.5	36.4	36.4	36.3	36.2	36.2	36.1	36.0	36.0
39	44	36.2	36.0	35.9	35.8	35.7	35.6	35.5	35.5	35.4	35.3	35.3	35.2	35.2
40	45	35.4	35.3	35.1	35.0	34.9	34.8	34.7	34.6	34.6	34.5	34.4	34.4	34.3
41	46	34.6	34.5	34.4	34.2	34.1	34.0	33.9	33.8	33.8	33.7	33.6	33.5	33.5
42	47	33.9	33.7	33.6	33.5	33.4	33.2	33.1	33.0	33.0	32.9	32.8	32.7	32.7
43	48	33.2	33.0	32.9	32.7	32.6	32.5	32.4	32.3	32.2	32.1	32.0	31.9	31.9
44	49	32.5	32.3	32.1	32.0	31.8	31.7	31.6	31.5	31.4	31.3	31.2	31.1	31.1
45	50	31.8	31.6	31.4	31.3	31.1	31.0	30.8	30.7	30.6	30.5	30.4	30.4	30.3
46	51	31.1	30.9	30.7	30.5	30.4	30.2	30.1	30.0	29.9	29.8	29.7	29.6	29.5
47	52	30.4	30.2	30.0	29.8	29.7	29.5	29.4	29.3	29.1	29.0	28.9	28.8	28.7
48	53	29.8	29.5	29.3	29.2	29.0	28.8	28.7	28.5	28.4	28.3	28.2	28.1	28.0
49	54	29.1	28.9	28.7	28.5	28.3	28.1	28.0	27.8	27.7	27.6	27.5	27.4	27.3
50	55	28.5	28.3	28.1	27.8	27.6	27.5	27.3	27.1	27.0	26.9	26.7	26.6	26.5
51	56	27.9	27.7	27.4	27.2	27.0	26.8	26.6	26.5	26.3	26.2	26.0	25.9	25.8
52	57	27.3	27.1	26.8	26.6	26.4	26.2	26.0	25.8	25.7	25.5	25.4	25.2	25.1
53	58	26.8	26.5	26.2	26.0	25.8	25.6	25.4	25.2	25.0	24.8	24.7	24.6	24.4
54	59	26.2	25.9	25.7	25.4	25.2	25.0	24.7	24.6	24.4	24.2	24.0	23.9	23.8
55	60	25.7	25.4	25.1	24.9	24.6	24.4	24.1	23.9	23.8	23.6	23.4	23.3	23.1

56	61	25.2	24.9	24.6	24.3	24.1	23.8	23.6	23.4	23.2	23.0	22.8	22.6	22.5
57	62	24.7	24.4	24.1	23.8	23.5	23.3	23.0	22.8	22.6	22.4	22.2	22.0	21.9
58	63	24.3	23.9	23.6	23.3	23.0	22.7	22.5	22.2	22.0	21.8	21.6	21.4	21.3
59	64	23.8	23.5	23.1	22.8	22.5	22.2	21.9	21.7	21.5	21.2	21.0	20.9	20.7
60	65	23.4	23.0	22.7	22.3	22.0	21.7	21.4	21.2	20.9	20.7	20.5	20.3	20.1
61	66	23.0	22.6	22.2	21.9	21.6	21.3	21.0	20.7	20.4	20.2	20.0	19.8	19.6
62	67	22.6	22.2	21.8	21.5	21.1	20.8	20.5	20.2	19.9	19.7	19.5	19.2	19.0
63	68	22.2	21.8	21.4	21.1	20.7	20.4	20.1	19.8	19.5	19.2	19.0	18.7	18.5
64	69	21.9	21.5	21.1	20.7	20.3	20.0	19.6	19.3	19.0	18.7	18.5	18.2	18.0
65	70	21.6	21.1	20.7	20.3	19.9	19.6	19.2	18.9	18.6	18.3	18.0	17.8	17.5
66	71	21.3	20.8	20.4	20.0	19.6	19.2	18.8	18.5	18.2	17.9	17.6	17.3	17.1
67	72	21.0	20.5	20.1	19.6	19.2	18.8	18.5	18.1	17.8	17.5	17.2	16.9	16.7
68	73	20.7	20.2	19.8	19.3	18.9	18.5	18.1	17.8	17.4	17.1	16.8	16.5	16.2
69	74	20.4	19.9	19.5	19.0	18.6	18.2	17.8	17.4	17.1	16.7	16.4	16.1	15.8
70	75	20.2	19.7	19.2	18.7	18.3	17.9	17.5	17.1	16.7	16.4	16.1	15.8	15.5
71	76	20.0	19.5	19.0	18.5	18.0	17.6	17.2	16.8	16.4	16.1	15.7	15.4	15.1
72	77	19.8	19.2	18.7	18.2	17.8	17.3	16.9	16.5	16.1	15.8	15.4	15.1	14.8
73	78	19.6	19.0	18.5	18.0	17.5	17.1	16.7	16.2	15.8	15.5	15.1	14.8	14.4

Table 4-5
1986 Internal Revenue Code Table
Ordinary Joint Life and Last Survivor Annuities
Two Lives—Expected Return Multiples

Ages	55	56	57	58	59	60	61	62	63	64
55	34.4	33.9	33.5	33.1	32.7	32.3	32.0	31.7	31.4	31.1
56	33.9	33.4	33.0	32.5	32.1	31.7	31.4	31.0	30.7	30.4
57	33.5	33.0	32.5	32.0	31.6	31.2	30.8	30.4	30.1	29.8
58	33.1	32.5	32.0	31.5	31.1	30.6	30.2	29.9	29.5	29.2
59	32.7	32.1	31.6	31.1	30.6	30.1	29.7	29.3	28.9	28.6
60	32.3	31.7	31.2	30.6	30.1	29.7	29.2	28.8	28.4	28.0
61	32.0	31.4	30.8	30.2	29.7	29.2	28.7	28.3	27.8	27.4
62	31.7	31.0	30.4	29.9	29.3	28.8	28.3	27.8	27.3	26.9
63	31.4	30.7	30.1	29.5	28.9	28.4	27.8	27.3	26.9	26.4
64	31.1	30.4	29.8	29.2	28.6	28.0	27.4	26.9	26.4	25.9
65	30.9	30.2	29.5	28.9	28.2	27.6	27.1	26.5	26.0	25.5
66	30.6	29.9	29.2	28.6	27.9	27.3	26.7	26.1	25.6	25.1
67	30.4	29.7	29.0	28.3	27.6	27.0	26.4	25.8	25.2	24.7
68	30.2	29.5	28.8	28.1	27.4	26.7	26.1	25.5	24.9	24.3
69	30.1	29.3	28.6	27.8	27.1	26.5	25.8	25.2	24.6	24.0
70	29.9	29.1	28.4	27.6	26.9	26.2	25.6	24.9	24.3	23.7
71	29.7	29.0	28.2	27.5	26.7	26.0	25.3	24.7	24.0	23.4
72	29.6	28.8	28.1	27.3	26.5	25.8	25.1	24.4	23.8	23.1
73	29.5	28.7	27.9	27.1	26.4	25.6	24.9	24.2	23.5	22.9
74	29.4	28.6	27.8	27.0	26.2	25.5	24.7	24.0	23.3	22.7
75	29.3	28.5	27.7	26.9	26.1	25.3	24.6	23.8	23.1	22.4
76	29.2	28.4	27.6	26.8	26.0	25.2	24.4	23.7	23.0	22.3
77	29.1	28.3	27.5	26.7	25.9	25.1	24.3	23.6	22.8	22.1
78	29.1	28.2	27.4	26.6	25.8	25.0	24.2	23.4	22.7	21.9
79	29.0	28.2	27.3	26.5	25.7	24.9	24.1	23.3	22.6	21.8
80	29.0	28.1	27.3	26.4	25.6	24.8	24.0	23.2	22.4	21.7
81	28.9	28.1	27.2	26.4	25.5	24.7	23.9	23.1	22.3	21.6
82	28.9	28.0	27.2	26.3	25.5	24.6	23.8	23.0	22.3	21.5
83	28.8	28.0	27.1	26.3	25.4	24.6	23.8	23.0	22.2	21.4
84	28.8	27.9	27.1	26.2	25.4	24.5	23.7	22.9	22.1	21.3
85	28.8	27.9	27.0	26.2	25.3	24.5	23.7	22.8	22.0	21.3

86	28.7	27.9	27.0	26.1	25.3	24.5	23.6	22.8	22.0	21.2
87	28.7	27.8	27.0	26.1	25.3	24.4	23.6	22.8	21.9	21.1
88	28.7	27.8	27.0	26.1	25.2	24.4	23.5	22.7	21.9	21.1
89	28.7	27.8	26.9	26.1	25.2	24.4	23.5	22.7	21.9	21.1
90	28.7	27.8	26.9	26.1	25.2	24.3	23.5	22.7	21.8	21.0
91	28.7	27.8	26.9	26.0	25.2	24.3	23.5	22.6	21.8	21.0
92	28.6	27.8	26.9	26.0	25.2	24.3	23.5	22.6	21.8	21.0
93	28.6	27.8	26.9	26.0	25.1	24.3	23.4	22.6	21.8	20.9
94	28.6	27.7	26.9	26.0	25.1	24.3	23.4	22.6	21.7	20.9
95	28.6	27.7	26.9	26.0	25.1	24.3	23.4	22.6	21.7	20.9
96	26.6	27.7	26.9	26.0	25.1	24.2	23.4	22.6	21.7	20.9
97	28.6	27.7	26.8	26.0	25.1	24.2	23.4	22.5	21.7	20.9
98	28.6	27.7	26.8	26.0	25.1	24.2	23.4	22.5	21.7	20.9
99	28.6	27.7	26.8	26.0	25.1	24.2	23.4	22.5	21.7	20.9
100	28.6	27.7	26.8	26.0	25.1	24.2	23.4	22.5	21.7	20.8
101	28.6	27.7	26.8	25.9	25.1	24.2	23.4	22.5	21.7	20.8
102	28.6	27.7	26.8	25.9	25.1	24.2	23.3	22.5	21.7	20.8
103	28.6	27.7	26.8	25.9	25.1	24.2	23.3	22.5	21.7	20.8
104	28.6	27.7	26.8	25.9	25.1	24.2	23.3	22.5	21.6	20.8
105	28.6	27.7	26.8	25.9	25.1	24.2	23.3	22.5	21.6	20.8
106	28.6	27.7	26.8	25.9	25.1	24.2	23.3	22.5	21.6	20.8
107	28.6	27.7	26.8	25.9	25.1	24.2	23.3	22.5	21.6	20.8
108	28.6	27.7	26.8	25.9	25.1	24.2	23.3	22.5	21.6	20.8
109	28.6	27.7	26.8	25.9	25.1	24.2	23.3	22.5	21.6	20.8
110	28.6	27.7	26.8	25.9	25.1	24.2	23.3	22.5	21.6	20.8
111	28.6	27.7	26.8	25.9	25.0	24.2	23.3	22.5	21.6	20.8
112	28.6	27.7	26.8	25.9	25.0	24.2	23.3	22.5	21.6	20.8
113	28.6	27.7	26.8	25.9	25.0	24.2	23.3	22.5	21.6	20.8
114	28.6	27.7	26.8	25.9	25.0	24.2	23.3	22.5	21.6	20.8
115	28.6	27.7	26.8	25.9	25.0	24.2	23.3	22.5	21.6	20.8

CHAPTER 5

◆ INSURANCE

§5.1 Introduction

This chapter deals with the subject of insurance. The bulk of the chapter is devoted to life insurance, addressing first the basic concept of life insurance, the relationships among the parties to life insurance contracts, the actuarial process, and some of the peculiar tax aspects of insurance. The last few sections of the chapter address other forms of insurance. As will be seen, life insurance companies depend on time value of money in order to offer the products they do. But they also depend on diversification of risk. Other forms of insurance, such as property and casualty insurance, automobile insurance, and health insurance, depend much less on time value of money and much more on diversification. Finally, this chapter briefly addresses the importance of insurance in business and the effect that the availability of insurance has had on legal rules.

In thinking about insurance, one should keep in mind the peculiar treatment that insurance enjoys under federal tax law. Generally speaking, one pays

for insurance with taxable dollars and collects benefits tax free. This pattern is, of course, precisely the opposite of the pattern found in many of the retirement plans discussed in the last chapter. But the logic of tax law as it relates to insurance makes sense considered in isolation. Congress is generally reluctant to grant deductions, and it is thus not surprising that no deduction is allowed for insurance premiums (unless they constitute business expenses). Moreover, insurance benefits are, in many cases, merely compensation for a loss of some sort and should thus not be seen as income. The same thing is generally true with tort damages. Insurance benefits have traditionally been viewed primarily as a way of putting the insured back in his or her original position, although it is clear that many consumers use insurance as a substitute for savings. Thus, innovations such as the variable annuity have been able to offer tax-free growth of sums invested, because they grew at least partially out of the idea of insurance.

§5.2 Life Insurance Generally

One of the most familiar applications of the concept of time value of money is life insurance. For example, a 45-year-old man might agree to pay a premium of $1,000 per year for a life insurance policy that pays his wife $100,000 in the event of his death. How can the insurance company afford to enter into such a deal? One answer is that on the average 45-year-old men live an additional 31 years to the age of 76 (see Table 5-1). Thus, assuming the insurance policy calls for level premiums over the entire life of the insured and assuming the insured continues to make these payments as required, on the average the insurance company will enjoy 31 years of receiving $1,000 per year in exchange for the obligation to pay $100,000 whenever the insured dies. Looking back at Table 4-1, one can determine the value to the insurance company of each dollar received for a given period of years into the future at a given interest rate. As it turns out, at a 7 percent interest rate, the value of one dollar per year to the insurance company will be $102.0703 at the end of 31 years, and the value of $1,000 per year will be $102,070.30. Thus, assuming that the insurance company's costs in administering the policy do not exceed $2070.30 by the end of 31 years, the insurance company at least breaks even in the deal if it can earn 7 percent on the premiums received from the insured.

There is, however, more to insurance than simply the time value of money. It should be apparent in the preceding example that the insurance company assumes a significant risk in writing the policy as described. If the insured dies at any time before the end of 31 years, the insurance company loses money. Of course, if the insured lives beyond 31 years the insurance company makes money. However, insurance companies, like other businesses, are risk averse. The possibility of losses weigh more heavily in deciding whether to enter into a particular deal than does the possibility of gains. After all, if the insurance company writes only the one policy described, there is a 50-50 chance that the company will lose money on the policy.

So how does the insurance company protect itself against this risk? The answer in a word is **diversification**. By selling many policies to many 45-year-old men (or indeed many men and women of differing ages), the insurance company

Table 5-1
Expectation of Life at Various Ages in the United States, 1991-1994

Age	1991			1992			1993*			1994†		
	Male	Female	Total	Male	Female	Total	Male	Female	Total	Male	Female	Total
0	72.0	78.9	75.5	72.3	79.1	75.8	72.1	78.9	74.5	72.1	78.8	75.5
15	58.1	64.8	61.5	58.3	65.0	61.7	58.1	64.7	61.4	58.1	64.6	61.4
25	48.9	55.1	52.1	49.1	55.2	52.2	48.8	55.0	52.0	48.9	54.9	52.0
35	39.8	45.5	42.7	40.0	45.6	42.9	39.8	45.3	42.6	39.8	45.3	42.6
45	30.9	36.0	33.6	31.1	36.2	33.8	30.9	35.9	33.5	31.0	35.9	33.6
55	22.5	27.1	24.9	22.7	27.2	25.1	22.5	27.0	24.9	22.6	26.9	24.9
65	15.3	19.1	17.4	15.4	19.2	17.5	15.3	18.9	17.3	15.3	18.8	17.2
75	9.5	12.1	11.1	9.6	12.2	11.2	9.4	12.0	10.9	9.4	11.9	10.9
85	5.3	6.5	6.2	5.3	6.6	6.2	5.2	6.3	6.0	5.1	6.3	5.9

Note: Some data are revised.
* Provisional.   † Estimated.
Sources: National Center for Health Statistics, U.S. Department of Health and Human Services, and Metropolitan Life Insurance Company.

can reduce and actually eliminate the risk that premium payments will be insufficient to meet the demand for benefits. For example, if the insurance company sells 1,000 policies such as the one described above, it will take in $1 million in premiums in the first year. As long as fewer than ten policy holders die during the first year, the insurance company is ahead. In addition, the insurance company can control risk by varying the terms of the insurance contract. In the example of the 45-year-old man, the risk of death rises as he gets older while the value of premium dollars to be received in the future falls. Thus, the insurance company might try to sell a policy that lasts only for (say) five years, at which time it must be reviewed and may be renewed at a higher premium rate. Indeed, the insurance policy described in the above example would be quite unusual if it is available at all. It would be much more common for the amount of the insurance to decline or for the premiums to increase periodically, as is described more fully in the following section on term insurance.

Until the 1970s, the life insurance industry sold a limited number of products. These traditional products are called **term insurance** and **whole life insurance**, although there are a number of subvariations of these basic types of insurance. Together they are often described as **ordinary life insurance**. These traditional products were designed basically to provide protection against the unexpected death of wage earners and their spouses and, in the case of whole life policies, to encourage savings in low-yielding investments in the guise of providing lifetime life insurance protection. The twin factors of high inflation and high interest rates in the period between the late 1960s and early 1980s shook up the life insurance industry. The traditional policies became less attractive, and new types of life insurance were developed: **flexible premium life insurance** (often called **universal life insurance** or **adjustable life insurance**), and more importantly, **variable life insurance** (often called **single premium insurance**), a type of policy that contains significant tax shelter benefits. Even though tax legislation in the 1980s has generally attempted to eliminate or minimize tax shelter and tax-deferral devices, the tax benefits of variable life insurance were not affected by this legislation, and it remains as one of the few legitimate tax shelter devices to survive the Tax Reform Act of 1986. Much of the recent growth in the purchase of life insurance products has been fueled by these new, tax-oriented policies.

§5.3 Why Buy Life Insurance?

Death may strike a person at any age. The most serious family crises are likely to arise from the unexpected death of a person who is the sole or principal income producer for young and dependent children and a spouse who lacks salable job skills. Life insurance obviously provides essential benefits in this type of situation, and as a result it is not surprising that traditionally most life insurance was sold to "breadwinners" in the classic sense. Today, it is not uncommon for both spouses to work even when the children are relatively young, but life insurance may still provide essential protection because the loss of one income may have devastating consequences. Even when one spouse

remains home to care for young children, it is increasingly recognized that his or her services are also essential to the family unit and costly to replace. Thus, life insurance protection is often purchased for both spouses.

Even when the death of the insured does not create an immediate financial crisis, life insurance is often a desirable component of financial planning, because it provides liquidity upon the death of the insured. Many persons have assets that may have substantial value if they can be disposed of in an orderly way but relatively little value if they must be sold immediately at "fire sale" or "distress" prices. Good examples of such assets include real estate such as the family home, a closely held business, or shares of stock in a family corporation. In addition, a person's heirs may desire to retain certain assets for their own use after the death of the insured, such as the family home, a cabin in the mountains, or an art collection. Whether this is practical may depend on whether the estate has other liquid assets sufficient to cover taxes, expenses, cash bequests, and outstanding indebtedness. If the estate does not, something must be sold and what is most salable is often precisely what the heirs desire to keep for their own use. Life insurance provides liquidity in the form of ready cash that may be of inestimable value in simplifying the immediate post-death affairs of the deceased person's estate and his or her heirs.

§5.4 Death and Taxes

In addition to the life insurance company that writes the policy, every life insurance policy involves three actors: the **insured**, the **beneficiary**, and the **policy owner**. The insured is the person whose death triggers the obligation of the insurance company to pay the face value of the policy, and the beneficiary is the person to whom the face value is paid. The beneficiary of the policy is often the insured's spouse or children, but it may also be the insured's estate or persons unrelated to the insured. The owner of the policy is the person who has the power to exercise a number of options with respect to the policy: to name or change the designation of the beneficiary, to borrow against the policy or pledge it as security for a loan (if it has a cash surrender value), and to surrender the policy or decide to let it lapse for nonpayment. Usually, the owner of the policy is the person who pays the premiums. The owner and the insured may be the same person, but they need not be, and indeed it is often advantageous from a tax standpoint for them to be different persons. Under the federal estate tax law, if the insured has retained the incidents of ownership (e.g., the right to change beneficiaries or to pledge the policy as security for a loan) at the time of death, the policy is includable in his or her estate. This is true even if the beneficiary of the policy is a spouse, other family member, or another individual.

Life insurance that is payable to the decedent's estate is, of course, available for the payment of estate obligations, while life insurance that is payable to an individual usually is not. However, the proceeds of an insurance policy are includable in the estate of the decedent for federal estate tax purposes if the policy is payable to the estate of the decedent, no matter who owns the policy.

The use of life insurance to improve the liquidity of the estate may therefore increase the taxes imposed on the estate.

The rules about when life insurance must be included in the taxable estate of the decedent for federal estate tax purposes are not as important today as they were a few years ago. Changes in federal tax laws during the 1980s greatly reduced the impact of this tax, and it now affects only the most wealthy individuals. Moreover, there is a substantial exemption under federal estate tax law increasing from $600,000 for individuals dying in 1997 to $1 million for individuals dying in 2006 (plus an additional amount for closely held business interests) that effectively shelters most estates from tax.

§5.5 Gambling, Risk, and Life Insurance

Some people undoubtedly view life insurance (and perhaps other types of insurance as well) as a form of ghoulish gambling. In this view, the person buying life insurance is betting that he or she will not live beyond his or her life expectancy, while the insurance company is betting that the insured will live to a ripe old age. There are, however, limitations on such gambling. In order to purchase an insurance policy on someone else's life, the purchaser must have an **insurable interest** in that other person's life. Needless to say, one spouse has an insurable interest in the other. A corporation may also have an insurable interest in its high-level managers. Thus corporations sometimes purchase **key person insurance** policies. But one cannot purchase a life insurance policy on some randomly selected individual, in part precisely because such agreements are viewed as gambling and in part because the availability of insurance in such circumstances could lead to many forms of advantage-taking that insurers could not control.

It is important to recognize that from the life insurance company's standpoint, life insurance is not gambling at all. Consider, for example, the situation where a new insured, Jane Doe, aged 30 with three small children, pays her first premium but is hit and killed by a truck ten minutes later while leaving the insurance agent's office. The face amount of the policy is almost certainly due in this situation, because an insurance company typically gives its agents authority to bind the company on prospective policies while the company assesses the risk and decides whether to issue a permanent policy. (A **binder**, in other words, is a kind of temporary insurance policy.)

The unexpected demise of Jane Doe does not mean that the insurance company writing the policy lost a gamble. The foundation of life insurance is the existence of reliable mortality tables for members of the population as a whole. The earliest such tables date from the late 1600s and early 1700s, and data have been collected on a regular basis ever since. Actuarial science generally governs the translation of this information into tables that permit the determination of theoretical premiums to be charged an average person for a life insurance policy in a specified amount on his or her life. The principal variable is, of course, age, but other more controversial variables also reliably assist actuaries in predicting mortality rates. For example, sex and race may be used, because mortality tables are available for these subgroups of the population. In

addition to relying on actuarial tables, insurance companies diversify and reduce risk by writing many policies on many different people in many different situations. As long as the population of insureds drawn from a specific risk group that a specific company covers resembles the population of that risk group as a whole, and the premiums are established on an actuarial basis to cover not only the risk but also the insurance company's costs and expenses, the element of gambling is eliminated. Indeed, in this perspective, the premature death of our unfortunate Jane Doe is not an unexpected event at all. The mortality tables build in the fact that on average a certain number of 30-year-old women of Jane Doe's race will die in motor vehicle accidents each year. From the perspective of the actuary, this tragedy is a predictable statistic.

Although insurance is often depicted as one of the most boring topics conceivable, it is important to understand how beneficial it can be. From the consumer's point of view, untimely death is a significant risk. Although the chances may be slim, the consequences may be devastating. But the insurance company does not itself assume risk when it writes a policy protecting a consumer from the financial consequences of untimely death. It can eliminate its risk altogether through diversification. Just as with leverage, the process seems almost like magic. By combining numerous discrete risks, the insurance company can avoid risk and provide a valuable service to society.

Even when a person lets an insurance policy lapse and never collects a dime from it, the insured has received a benefit. Insurance must be viewed from what economists call the **ex ante** perspective, that is, from the point of view of someone who does not know how things will turn out, rather than from the **ex post** perspective of hindsight. The value of insurance is that it reduces uncertainty. It has nothing to do with how things turn out other than to the extent that the likelihood of various future events and their consequences must be assessed in deciding whether and how much insurance to buy.

Table 5-1 sets forth data on the expectation of life at various ages in the United States by sex. Table 5-2 describes the historical changes in life expectancies during the 20th century by race and sex. Insurance companies use considerably more elaborate tables to develop premiums for specific applicants, but the general relevance of these tables for purposes of life insurance should be obvious. As long as the individuals being insured by a life insurance company reflect the mortality experience of the population from which they are drawn, premiums may be safely calculated on the basis of available statistics on average mortality tables or life expectancies.

Of course, insurance companies must assess individual risks to make sure that the risk is an average one and not unique in some way. An insurance company must always be careful that risks are randomly obtained and are not self-selected. For example, a life insurance company could easily go broke if it wrote standard insurance policies on a disproportionately large number of persons with serious heart disease and persons engaged in ultrahazardous activities like motorcycle racing, skydiving, and bomb disposal. For exactly the same reason, property casualty companies generally refuse to write flood insurance, because only persons living in flood-prone areas are likely to request such insurance, while persons living on top of the hill realize that they do not need the insurance and do not apply for it. It is impossible when writing flood

Table 5-2
Life Expectancy
Expectation of Life at Birth in the United States (Years)

Year	White			All Other			Total		
	Male	Female	Total	Male	Female	Total	Male	Female	Total
1900	46.6	48.7	47.6	32.5	33.5	33.0	46.3	48.3	47.3
1910	48.6	52.0	50.3	33.8	37.5	35.6	48.4	51.8	50.0
1920	54.4	55.6	54.9	45.5	45.2	45.3	53.6	54.6	54.1
1930	59.7	63.5	61.4	47.3	49.2	48.1	58.1	61.6	59.7
1940	62.1	66.6	64.2	51.5	54.9	53.1	60.8	65.2	62.9
1950	66.5	72.2	69.1	59.1	62.9	60.8	65.6	71.1	68.2
1960	67.4	74.1	70.6	61.1	66.3	63.6	66.6	73.1	69.7
1965	67.6	74.7	71.0	61.1	67.4	64.1	66.8	73.7	70.2
1970	68.0	75.6	71.7	61.3	69.4	65.3	67.1	74.7	70.8
1971	68.3	75.8	72.0	61.6	69.8	65.6	67.4	75.0	71.1
1972	68.3	75.9	72.0	61.5	70.1	65.7	67.4	75.1	71.2
1973	68.5	76.1	72.2	62.0	70.3	66.1	67.6	75.3	71.4
1974	69.0	76.7	72.8	62.9	71.3	67.1	68.2	75.9	72.0
1975	69.5	77.3	73.4	63.7	72.4	68.0	68.8	76.6	72.6
1976	69.9	77.5	73.6	64.2	72.7	68.4	69.1	76.8	72.9
1977	70.2	77.9	74.0	64.7	73.2	68.9	69.5	77.2	73.3
1978	70.4	78.0	74.1	65.0	73.5	69.3	69.6	77.3	73.5
1979	70.8	78.4	74.6	65.4	74.1	69.8	70.0	77.8	73.9

1980	70.7	78.1	74.4	65.3	73.6	69.5	70.0	77.4	73.7
1981	71.1	78.4	74.8	66.2	74.4	70.3	70.4	77.8	74.1
1982	71.5	78.7	75.1	66.8	74.9	70.9	70.8	78.1	74.5
1983	71.6	78.7	75.2	67.0	74.7	70.9	71.0	78.1	74.6
1984	71.8	78.7	78.3	67.2	74.9	71.1	71.1	78.2	74.7
1985	71.8	78.7	75.3	67.0	74.8	71.0	71.1	78.2	74.7
1986	71.9	78.8	75.4	66.8	74.9	70.9	71.2	78.2	74.7
1987	72.1	78.9	75.6	66.9	75.0	71.0	71.4	78.3	74.9
1988	72.2	78.9	75.6	66.7	74.8	70.8	71.4	78.3	74.9
1989	72.5	79.2	75.9	66.7	74.9	70.9	71.7	78.5	75.1
1990	72.7	79.4	76.1	67.0	75.2	71.2	71.8	78.8	75.4
1991	72.9	79.6	76.3	67.3	75.5	71.5	72.0	78.9	75.5
1992	73.2	79.8	76.5	67.7	75.7	71.8	72.3	79.1	75.8
1993*	73.0	79.5	76.3	67.4	75.5	71.5	72.1	78.9	75.5
1994†	N.A.	N.A.	N.A.	N.A.	N.A.	N.A.	72.1	78.8	75.5

Note: Some data are revised.
* Provisional.   † Estimated.   N.A. = Not Available.
Sources: National Center for Health Statistics, U.S. Department of Health and Human Services, and Metropolitan Life Insurance Company.

insurance for the persons at risk to avoid **self-selection** (sometimes also called **adverse selection**).

The major ways used by an insurance company to ensure that risks are randomly selected are physical examinations (which are often but not always required) and questions on the application form relating to medical histories, occupations, and hobbies. A person who can demonstrate that he or she is in reasonably good health and engages in activities of average risk is said to be **insurable**, while a person who cannot is said to be **uninsurable**. These are not black-and-white categories, however. Insurance companies often write **extra-risk insurance** policies for persons with known medical problems, such as apparently controlled cardiovascular disease or cancer that has been successfully treated. Such policies carry higher premiums, of course, and are written only after careful assessment of the applicant's medical condition. A person with controlled high blood pressure is insurable on an extra-risk basis, because insurance companies have had sufficient experience with mortality rates of persons with that medical condition to permit the writing of actuarially sound insurance.

Persons engaged in hazardous occupations may also often obtain life insurance only upon the payment of a higher premium. Many insurance companies now give discounts for nonsmokers; a "discount" in this situation is simply a reduction in premiums for nonsmokers or, phrased differently, the establishment of a somewhat higher premium rate for insurance applicants who smoke.

Questions on the application form for life insurance are carefully devised to provide the insurer accurate information as to the risks involved. Questions usually relate not only to medical histories and known medical conditions but also involve open-ended inquiries that may lead to further investigation, such as whether the applicant has been denied life insurance in the past or whether the applicant has recently been under the care of a physician for any reason. An applicant for life insurance has every incentive to "fudge" on the application form or to omit reference to medical facts or hazardous activities in order to obtain insurance at favorable rates (or in some cases, to obtain insurance at all). Material omissions or misstatements constitute fraud and, if discovered, usually lead to the cancellation of the policy. On the other hand, insurance companies may be tempted to renege on policies that have been in effect for a long period of time for nondisclosure of material facts in the original application form. Such a practice may deprive insureds of benefits even though they have dutifully paid premiums for years and have not sought substitute insurance because they thought the original policy was valid. Life insurance regulation (which is a matter of state law) prevents insurance companies from cancelling policies for nondisclosure after the lapse of a specified period of time. These so-called **incontestability clauses** are a kind of statute of limitations. They permit life insurance companies only a limited time to raise defenses; after that time has expired, the obligation to insure is binding and cannot be avoided for misrepresentation or nondisclosure in the application. These clauses are mandated by state law. The Texas statute, for example, states that each life insurance policy must contain provisions that state that it and the application form "shall constitute the entire contract between the parties and shall be incontestable after

it has been in force during the lifetime of the insured for two years from its date, except for nonpayment of premiums, and which provisions may, at the option of the company, contain an exception for violation of the conditions of the policy relating to naval and military service in time of war."

In addition to the judicious evaluation and acceptance of individual risks, insurance companies may diversify their portfolio of risks by **reinsurance**, through which an insurance company may transfer certain risks to other insurance companies in exchange for a sharing of premiums. Through this process, imbalances of risks may be distributed throughout the life insurance industry. A specific insured is unlikely to be aware that his or her policy has been transferred through reinsurance to another company.

A somewhat similar insurance company practice is the transfer of hundreds of thousands of policies from one insurer to another, with the acquirer taking on the entire insurance obligation of each assigned policy. Insureds are usually notified that their policies have been transferred and are directed to make future premium payments to the acquiring company. This practice is known as **assumption reinsurance**. Policy transfers of this type affect the insureds if the acquiring life insurance company becomes insolvent and disclaims further responsibility on the policies. The original issuing company in these circumstances is likely to argue that its liability under the policy ended with the assumption. The standard legal argument made by policy holders in response is that they did not consent to the assignment or the release of the original insurer who therefore remains liable on its original obligation. In short, the argument is over the scope of the legal doctrine known as novation. An inference that a novation occurred may be drawn if the insured has knowledge of the transfer, does not object to it, and thereafter makes payments to the assignee, particularly if the notice of assignment gives accurate information as to the financial condition of both the assigning and the assuming companies. There has been no definitive resolution of these legal arguments.

Assumption reinsurance may be subject to regulation by state insurance regulatory agencies. Insureds who are adversely affected may also have claims against state insurance guaranty funds. However, until the rights of insureds in this situation are adequately protected, it may be sensible to object to any assignment of policies in writing, stating that the insured will make payments to the assigning company but does not release the assigning company from liability under the policy. This precaution seems particularly justified where the credit rating of the assuming company is lower than the credit rating of the assigning company.

As Mark Twain said, "There are lies, damn lies, and statistics." It is important in dealing with all statistics to understand their limitations and to consider all factors that might affect the data. This is well illustrated by Tables 5-1 and 5-2. Why have life expectancies increased steadily during the 20th century? The obvious factors are improvements in medical care, the development of antibiotics, and the like. However, much of the increase in the life expectancy of a white male (which was less than 50 years if he was born in 1900 and 73 years if he was born in 1993) is due to decreases in infant and child mortality rather than improvements in adult health care.

Another contentious statistical issue: Is it appropriate (or constitutional)

for life insurance companies to use sex-based and race-based tables? The accumulated statistics that support these distinctions provide valid predictors, but they have come under increasing criticism. The reason for this is more political than economic, because sometimes the use of separate tables benefit women and minorities and sometimes they do not. In 1994, a 65-year-old male had a life expectancy of 15.3 years, while a female of the same age had a life expectancy of 18.8 years. If we assume that both the male and the female retire at the same time and have precisely $100,000 to invest in a lifetime retirement annuity that is based on their respective life expectancies, the male would receive monthly payments that are significantly higher than the female. On the other hand, if the transaction contemplates the purchase of life insurance, on the same assumptions the female would be charged a significantly lower premium for the same amount of insurance, because she will, on average, be paying premiums for several more years and the insurance company will have the use of her money for a longer period.

It may seem unfair to charge different rates to persons who cannot control the factors that cause them to be more or less at risk. On the other hand, it is sometimes difficult to draw the line between what can and cannot be controlled. Single male drivers under the age of 25 generally pay the highest rates for auto insurance. Clearly they cannot control their sex or age, though they can in theory decline to drive until they get older or married. On the other hand, a recent study disclosed that single male drivers under 25 tend to drive many more miles per year than female drivers and in fact pay less per mile driven than female drivers.

Similar issues arise in connection with health insurance. Is it appropriate for insurance companies to deny coverage for preexisting conditions or to charge much higher rates to the elderly because they are more likely to get sick? If it is not, what is to keep the younger and healthier from simply not buying insurance until they get older and sicker or indeed from forming their own insurance company? One solution to these problems may be to require insurance companies to accept all applicants, but it may then also be necessary to require everyone to be insured.

§5.6 Term Insurance

Term insurance is a traditional type of life insurance that provides basic life insurance protection. It provides solely death protection for a fixed period of time such as one, five, or ten years. The face amount of the policy is paid only if the insured dies within the time or term stated in the policy. Term insurance is pure insurance, based on actuarial data on the probability of death occurring within the fixed period of the policy. There is no cash value buildup, and hence there is no savings or investment component as there is with some other forms of insurance. As the insured gets older, the probability of his or her death during the current time period obviously increases; thus the cost of term insurance increases with the age of the person involved. At about age 65, the cost of pure term insurance becomes prohibitive. However, for a 35-year-old breadwinner with a nonworking spouse and two or three young children to

support—perhaps the prototypical individual needing life insurance—term insurance provides a very large degree of temporary protection at a relatively
modest cost.

Even though term insurance is based on actuarial principles, there may be
wide variations in price quotations, based on different assessments of risk,
different premium structures, different commission rates payable to agents, and
so forth. In addition, a variety of options may be offered in connection with a
term policy: double payment in the event of accidental death, for example, or
an option to convert term insurance at a later date into other types of insurance
without a new medical examination.

Term insurance policies usually require a medical examination, though
some companies may write term policies for younger persons solely on the basis
of written health-related questions. Persons in certain risky occupations or
having risky avocations may not be able to obtain term insurance at all, or may
be able to obtain it only by paying an additional premium. Term insurance
policies are usually renewable for additional terms (at higher premiums) without
another medical examination or questionnaire. Many policies provide for level
premiums for periods of up to five years, with the level premium during this
period being approximately equal to the average of annual premiums over the
period for a person of the age in question. Term insurance is also often sold at
bargain prices in connection with or as a sweetener for other types of life
insurance.

Group life insurance is a type of term insurance that employers usually
provide for their employees. It is also often offered by membership organizations, such as fraternal organizations, trade associations, social clubs, and investment clubs. The premium for group life insurance is usually lower than the
premium for the equivalent amount of term insurance that could be purchased
individually. There are several reasons for this. The administrative costs of
insuring a group may be significantly lower than the cost of insuring members
individually: selling and advertising costs are usually nominal and the employer
or organization arranging for the group insurance may assume some of the
administrative costs. Second, the risk characteristics for the group in question
may be more favorable than for the population generally. For example, a group
of accountants may be able to obtain term insurance at more favorable group
rates than as individuals because the accountants as a group have a better life
expectancy than the population as a whole: They eat better, they are not
subjected to employment-related risks that most blue collar workers face, and
they are probably less likely to engage in hazardous activities such as motorcycle
racing or skydiving. Third, in some cases the insurer may be willing to quote
lower rates because the volume of term policies generated improves its diversification of risk or because it wishes to retain important business relationships
with the employer. Finally, by selling to groups, insurance companies avoid some
of the risks of self-selection.

Term insurance may be either **face amount insurance** (in which event the
face amount is constant and the premium increases periodically) or **declining
balance** (in which event the premium remains constant but the face amount of
insurance coverage declines as the person gets older). A very common kind of
declining balance insurance is mortgage insurance, sold in connection with a

mortgage on a home, or credit insurance, offered by many lenders when they make small consumer loans. The theory behind such mortgage and credit insurance is that for a small additional monthly payment, life insurance equal to the unpaid balance of the loan is maintained to make sure the loan is repaid in the event the borrower dies before the indebtedness is paid. The charges for this type of insurance are often significantly higher than the cost of a straight term policy. Moreover, the insured or his or her estate has no power to determine how the proceeds of such policies will be used. It should come as no surprise that many consumer loan organizations maintain relationships with insurers and try to have these insurers write all of this lucrative type of insurance.

Declining balance term insurance is also sold through magazine or newspaper advertisements that promise small amounts of insurance and claim that premiums will not increase before a person reaches some specified age. These policies are usually extremely expensive for the coverage provided. A giveaway that declining balance term is being advertised is usually that the amount of the insurance is either not set forth or is described as up to some specified amount.

§5.7 Whole Life Insurance

The most common type of traditional life insurance sold today is **whole life**. These policies, unlike the tax-oriented variable or universal life insurance policies described in later sections, provide a fixed benefit on the death of the insured. Further, unlike term insurance, the premiums remain level from the date of the inception of the policy until the maturation of the policy upon the death of the insured. They differ significantly from term insurance in three important, indeed fundamental, respects.

First, the premiums for whole life policies for relatively young adults (or rarely, young children) are initially much higher than for term insurance for the amount of insurance protection for a person of the same age. For example, a 35-year-old man will typically pay an annual premium of $15 or $20 per $1,000 of coverage for a whole life policy, while a comparable one-year renewable term policy would cost somewhere between $2 and $5 per $1,000. To be sure, the premiums on term insurance increase with the age of the insured. But if our hypothetical 35-year-old man retained the same amount of term insurance year after year, he would be in his early 60s before the annual term insurance premium equaled the annual premium for his whole life policy.

Second, even though the premiums remain constant, the face amount of insurance that a whole life policy provides also remains constant. Whole life insurance is unlike declining balance term insurance in this respect.

Third, whole life policies develop cash values or cash surrender values each year after the policy has been in existence for a specified initial period. Much of the initial excess premium over the cost of term insurance goes to building up this value.

The logic underlying a whole life policy is simple. The premiums during the early years of such a policy are much higher than the amount needed to buy only death protection (i.e., term insurance). A portion of this excess is set aside in a kind of savings account for later use by the owner of the policy. A whole life policy, unlike a term policy, thus combines a savings element as well

as a life insurance element. This savings element gradually increases as the years go by and more premiums are paid. As described below, the owner of the policy may borrow this cash value, and it will be paid to him or her if the policy is surrendered and the insurance lapses. When the insured dies, however, the company pays only the face value of the policy, not the face value plus the cash value. Thus, the payment of the face value of the whole life policy upon the death of the insured in part comes from the savings account inherent in the cash value concept and in part from true life insurance. As the years go by and the cash surrender value increases, the company needs to provide a decreasing amount of pure life insurance protection. At some point when the insured reaches a ripe old age, the savings account reaches the amount of the face value of the policy and the obligation to pay premiums ends. Such a policy is fully paid up, because the savings account equals the face value of the policy and there is no remaining component of life insurance to be paid from premiums.

This description is in some ways an oversimplification. Typically, cash values in a whole life policy build very slowly: There is usually no cash value after one or two years of premiums, and it may be three or four years before the entire cash value equals the amount of the premium due in any single year. Thereafter, the cash value builds more rapidly, fueled in part by the premium payments and in part by earnings on the money already invested. Cancellation of the policy during its first years therefore may involve a substantial financial penalty. Furthermore, if a policy lapses and an attempt is made to replace it at a later date, the insured will find that the premium is increased because he or she is placed in an older age group when applying for the new insurance. These costs are often used by insurance agents as arguments against cancelling a whole life policy, or allowing it to lapse, when they learn that an insured is having difficulty making the payments.

At first glance, it may seem backward that the buildup of cash value in the earliest years is the lowest, given that the pure insurance cost for protection in the earliest years is also the lowest. Several factors help to explain this structure: the administrative costs of writing a policy (including the cost of a medical examination); the commission structure for the life insurance agent (typically one half or more of the first year's premium goes to the agent as a commission for selling the policy); and the desire to establish a premium structure that encourages retention of a policy rather than surrendering it.

As indicated above, the cash value of a whole life policy increases gradually each year after the first year the policy is in effect. A whole life policy is an investment, an asset of the owner of the policy, much like a bank account or a deposit in a mutual fund. A whole life policy may be assigned to a creditor as security for a loan; the creditor may name itself as beneficiary so that it will receive the proceeds from the policy upon the death of the insured and repay the loan from the proceeds. The remaining balance, if any, presumably belongs to the estate of the insured or his or her heirs. During the lifetime of the insured, the creditor may also surrender the policy for its cash surrender value if a default on the obligation occurs. Although loans secured by assignments of life insurance are not uncommon, it is a mark of some desperation by the borrower, because he or she may be depriving the family of needed insurance protection in order to arrange a loan.

While alive, the owner of the policy can also borrow all or part of the cash

value from the insurance company. A loan of the cash surrender value does not increase the insurance risk from the standpoint of the insurer, because if the insured dies while a loan is outstanding, the insurer simply subtracts the out-standing loan from the face amount of the policy and pays the beneficiary the difference. Traditionally, the interest rate on such loans is very low, often 5 percent in the case of older policies. It is important to recognize that this is a very peculiar loan because the insurance company is already holding the cash surrender value in order to make a death payment at some future time. Thus loans of the cash surrender value are more like advances than loans. In one respect, loans of the cash surrender value may adversely affect the insurance company. Its cash flow comes from two sources: premium payments and the return from investments. Loans of cash surrender values reduce the amount available for investment by the insurance company and may reduce its cash flow. This occurs on every such loan whenever the market interest rate on investments is higher than the interest rate charged to the policy owner.

After a whole life policy has been in effect for several years, loans from the cash surrender value may be used to pay future premiums. This practice may permit an insured to keep a policy in effect over long periods without paying premiums, but subject to a gradual reduction of the death benefit that will ultimately be paid.

In addition to the traditional whole life policy, many other life insurance policies are offered that combine savings and life insurance protection in varying degrees. For example, an **endowment policy** involves premiums for a specified period, perhaps 20 or 30 years; at that point the cash value equals the policy face amount and the insurance is fully paid up. A paid-up-at-65 policy is similar to an endowment policy, except that the period during which premiums must be paid ends at age 65. Obviously, substantially higher premium payments are required for all types of endowment or **paid-up policies** than for a whole life policy. As a result, these policies enjoy limited attractiveness.

A study prepared by the Federal Trade Commission in 1979 attempted to estimate the rate of return on a whole life policy viewing its cash value as an investment. This is not a simple computation, because a portion of each pre-mium must be allocated to the insurance feature of the whole life policy. The study concluded that the return was negative—that is, the cash value was less than the amount invested—for over 10 years; after 20 years the rate of return was only 2 percent. Thus as a savings vehicle, the whole life policy is inferior even to an insured savings account. Indeed, a strategy of "buy term and invest the rest" (a phrase used by critics of the traditional insurance industry) usually yields a significantly larger investment after 20 years than buying a whole life policy. This strategy is somewhat similar to the do-it-yourself annuities discussed in the previous chapter, and both suffer from some of the same problems. For example, while the buying term and investing the difference yields superior results, the specific results are based on the assumption that a savings account will yield a definite return, and this cannot be guaranteed. A decline in the rate of interest on the savings component may make the differences much less dramatic. Also, savings through life insurance premium payments is convenient and there is a built-in incentive not to let the insurance lapse. Many persons might lack the discipline to make the same payments into a savings account

without the need to preserve their insurance. Whole life policies also contain some significant options that cannot be replicated in a do-it-yourself plan: A waiver of premiums in the event of disability, for example, is generally available at no additional cost and is tremendously valuable in the rare situation where disability occurs. Other valuable rights may include such options to purchase annuity rights and the ability to use the cash surrender value to buy additional paid-up insurance without a medical examination. Finally, accumulations in a "buy term and invest the rest" plan are subject to federal income taxes each year, while the growth of cash value within a whole life policy is tax deferred.

An argument can be made that it is unrealistic to analyze a whole life policy as being divided into an insurance component and a savings component. One can argue that the whole life insurance contract should be viewed as an undifferentiated whole, and that it consists of buying insurance protection on a level-premium installment plan, in which young people prepay their premiums in the earlier years for protection they will receive many years later when the actual insurance costs greatly exceed the premium then being paid. One basic problem with this analysis is that it gives little weight to the phenomenon of the growth of the cash value within a whole life policy, which is a central feature of whole life insurance. Furthermore, this approach toward whole life raises new questions: It ignores the time value of the money that is prepaid, and also gives no weight to the possibility of inflation and increased earning capacity in later years. If this were the sole explanation of whole life insurance offered to most persons, it is likely that they would opt for term insurance and invest the difference.

§5.8 Variable Life Insurance

The chaotic economic conditions of the 1970s and 1980s were marked by high inflation rates and rapidly increasing interest rates. These developments created unprecedented pressures on traditional forms of life insurance, particularly the whole life policy, the mainstay of the domestic life insurance industry. The prospect of high inflation rates made the savings account feature of cash surrender values relatively unattractive. People realized that they were investing current dollars in exchange for repayments many years later in dollars that were worth much less because of inflation. Further, the relatively low effective rates of return on the cash surrender value made whole life unattractive when compared with competing, riskless investments. The earliest indication of difficult times ahead for the insurance industry was the increase in cash surrender value loans as policy owners borrowed against cash surrender values at 5 percent per year in order to invest the proceeds in much higher yielding investments in the open market. Furthermore, between 1977 and 1981, whole life policies, while still the largest single selling type of insurance, declined significantly as a percentage of the total amount of ordinary life insurance outstanding, with growth in term insurance accounting for most of the increase. It was apparent from these trends that the insurance industry would have to come up with new products if it wished to prosper.

The first new products that the insurance industry developed were relatively

modest. A variable premium life policy was offered, which provided that future premiums would be decreased if the company's investment income increased from rising interest rates and inflation. In effect, the company offered to share with policyholders a portion of the windfall that rising interest rates generated by reducing the premium in later years. An adjustable life insurance policy was also developed that allowed an individual to switch protection from term to whole life, or back. Perhaps the most popular innovation of this sort, however, was the development of universal life insurance policies. Under a **universal life policy**, the insurance and savings components are, in effect, uncoupled. This allows the insured to decide how premium payments are to be allocated within broad limits. Moreover, under a universal life policy, the insurance company pays a market rate of interest on the savings portion. These policies also offered some flexibility in the timing and amount of premium payments, and they provided for periodic readjustments to take into account mortality charges, that is, the cost of the insurance component, based on the actual experience of the insurer in paying death benefits.

More recently, the insurance industry struck a popular chord when it developed a new life insurance policy that is now generally known as **single premium variable life insurance (SPVL)**. SPVL has significant tax deferral benefits and is sold more for the tax and investment benefits than for the insurance benefits. The policy can be analyzed as containing two interrelated components: a term life insurance component and an accumulation component analogous to the traditional cash surrender value of a whole life policy. At the outset, the applicant must deposit a certain amount in an accumulation account to finance the insurance component, and may make a larger initial deposit or may thereafter make additional deposits. The accumulation account is virtually an investment account. The applicant may direct how the accumulation account is to be invested within limited alternatives provided by the insurance company or an associated brokerage firm. The choices typically include most popular investment strategies, such as stock funds and bond funds. As the accumulation account increases, the amount of insurance that must be purchased also increases, but at a much slower rate. The owner of the policy may also borrow the amount of the excess accumulation account.

The driving principle behind this insurance policy is that, like the accumulation of cash surrender values in a traditional whole life policy, the growth of the accumulation account is not subject to federal income tax as long as the policy remains outstanding. Hundreds of thousands of dollars may be deposited in the accumulation account to grow on a tax-exempt basis. Further, the accumulation is exempt from income taxation upon the death of the insured. In other words, this policy is really a tax-deferred or tax-sheltered investment vehicle packaged as insurance.

The amount of term insurance that the package provides is the minimum amount required by Internal Revenue Code provisions to ensure that the package is taxed as an insurance policy rather than as an investment account. However, in practice the amount of insurance is not the dominant or driving factor, but is incidental. It is determined by the tax laws and the amount the applicant has invested in the accumulation account.

It may be recalled that single-premium annuities may also serve as tax-shel-

tered investment vehicles. In 1986, Congress restricted the tax advantages of annuities by providing that loans or extraordinary distributions to the annuitant are deemed to be from the income component of the fund, and therefore fully taxable. In 1988, a similar change was made in the Internal Revenue Code as it relates to SPVL. Still, SPVL has the advantage that upon the death of the insured, the proceeds may be excludable from the insured's estate for federal estate tax purposes (as well as for probate purposes), much as any other type of insurance if the policy is not owned by the deceased and is not payable to his or her estate.

The disadvantages of SPVL are the fees and charges imposed by the insurance company. In addition, premature termination of the policy may result in a significant investment loss (as well as tax gain in some circumstances). Moreover, restrictions are placed on what percentage of the value of an accumulation account may be borrowed by the insured. And SPVL necessarily entails the purchase of increasing amounts of term life insurance as the accumulation account increases even though that purchase might not be justified in the absence of the tax-deferral aspect of the plan. Finally, there is some lingering concern that Congress may decide to limit the tax-deferral advantages of these life insurance policies if they become too popular. Certainly, Congress has consistently tried to limit tax shelters that are believed to be abusive or involve the loss of substantial revenue: The single premium variable life insurance policy may be found to fall within this category in the future.

During the 1980s, when interest rates were high, many middle-aged and older individuals purchased **vanishing premium life insurance**. These cash value life policies involved very substantial premiums for a limited number of years. Thereafter, on the assumption that interest rates would remain at then-current levels, the insurer projected that earnings from the cash value of the insurance would cover the premiums; the premium would "vanish." Unfortunately, the projections used assumptions that turn out to have been unrealistic: the high interest rates of the 1980s on which projections were based have declined steadily in the 1990s. The result is predictable: The premium does not "vanish," but continues or resumes as the earnings fall short of covering the premium. This prospect, of course, does not affect term policies at all and is unlikely to affect ordinary whole life policies in which the insured expects to continue to make payments for many years. For a person expecting to buy permanent life insurance in relatively few years, however, the decline in interest rates has come as a sore disappointment.

Advertising for vanishing premium insurance policies generally disclosed that the performance of the policy was based on projections and that performance was not guaranteed. However, this fact was certainly not emphasized. An individual called upon to resume premium payments in order to preserve the insurance policy may be able to exercise other options, such as reducing the death benefit, that may enable the policy to be continued without additional investment. It is generally undesirable to cancel such a policy and either take the cash-surrender value or create a new policy at a lower death benefit because of policy terms that make cancellation financially less attractive than restructuring the policy by exercising available options.

Another similar product is **level premium term insurance**. Because of

changing regulations, it is likely that level premium insurance will be difficult to find in those states that require larger reserves because of the significant risks in writing such policies. Insurers may respond by offering policies with shorter guarantee periods that are merely projected to remain level throughout the rest of the policy's life. Level premium insurance often includes a so-called re-entry privilege. Those who qualify after a physical examination are allowed to purchase a subsequent policy at a preset and attractive rate, while those whose health has declined may renew only at very much higher rates that are limited only by the maximum stated in the policy. Those who simply continue year to year, rather than signing on for another term, also pay somewhat higher rates. This, of course, inclines many to commit to buying for the longer term.

§5.9 Mutual Life Insurance Companies and Stock Companies

There are two types of life insurance companies writing policies today: mutual companies and stock companies. Today, mutual companies write about 40 percent of all life insurance. A **mutual company** does not have shareholders, its policyholders elect its board of directors, and excess earnings of the company are paid to its policyholders in the form of annual dividends. In a broad sense, the "owners" of a mutual life insurance company are the policyholders. One should not put too much weight on this "ownership," however. Policyholders are widely scattered and unorganized and as a result have virtually no voice in how a mutual company is actually managed. Also, most policyholders are indifferent to management issues as long as their individual policies are not adversely affected. Management of a mutual company can therefore run the company with almost complete freedom from oversight by the owners, the only discipline being provided by the need to offer relatively competitive products compared with those offered by other insurance companies.

The second type of insurance company is a **stock company**. In form, it is a traditional corporation with shareholders who purchase stock in the company and who are entitled to elect the company's board of directors. Dividends in a stock company are paid to the shareholders, not to the policyholders as in a mutual company. In a stock company, policyholders are more analogous to customers of the corporation than to owners.

Policies that are entitled to share in dividends are called **participating policies**, and such policies are usually written by mutual companies. In effect, each year when the premium notice is sent, the amount of the dividend is set forth and the owner of the policy may elect to have the dividend credited against the amount of next year's premium. In mutual companies, dividends may be paid on all types of life insurance outstanding or only on specified classes or types of policies. Policies written by stock companies are usually nonparticipating, that is, they are not entitled to receive dividends. The amount of the annual premium is fixed and is not subject to reduction by a dividend. In making comparisons between various life insurance policies and the costs of similar policies issued by different companies, it is necessary to take into account whether the proposed policy is participating or nonparticipating. Although the

amount of a dividend on a participating policy is apt to be rather small in contrast with the amount of a premium, it tends to be stable and reasonably predictable.

Even though a mutual company pays dividends to policyholders while stock companies pay dividends to shareholders, one should not assume that mutual companies usually offer cheaper products. Both types of companies compete vigorously for the same insurance dollar. It is not uncommon for a stock company to offer a cheaper policy even after the mutual company dividend is taken into account.

A few insurance companies offer **low load** or **low commission insurance** without the services of an insurance agent. Distribution costs of ordinary policies run 20 to 25 percent over the full life of a policy; they run 5 to 10 percent in the case of low load policies. Low load policies include universal and whole life insurance and annuity contracts. Companies offering low load policies tend to be small. It may not be easy to locate them, because life insurance agents, for obvious reasons, do not tout them.

§5.10 Comparing Insurance and Other Investment Vehicles

Traditional life insurance (such as a whole life or universal policy) is a combination of true insurance coverage and an investment vehicle or savings plan of some sort. Although many insurance companies pay adequate returns on the investment portion of such plans, it is extremely difficult to obtain accurate information about such investments that is comparable to information about other similar investments (e.g., mutual funds). And even if one obtains such information, the investment component of a policy is tied to the insurance component. Thus, one component of a plan may be attractive while the other is not, and the task of finding the optimal package can be complicated. Indeed, the optimal package may not even be available in the sense that the best deal on insurance may be from a source wholly different from the best deal on investment (even though many insurance companies offer a variety of different investment funds that are typically managed in-house).

Another basic problem is that insurance is governed by state law, which varies from state to state, while most comparable investment vehicles (e.g., mutual funds) are regulated by federal law and thus are subject to standardized disclosures. Some states have attempted to require disclosure of investment performance by insurance companies, but these steps in the direction of full disclosure fall far short of the information available on free-standing mutual funds and other investment companies.

For these reasons, the market for the various forms of insurance with cash value is much less competitive than the market for insurance alone or investments alone, and the consumer is usually the loser. Perhaps the primary reason that such forms of insurance continue to be purchased is that they may (but do not always) offer tax deferral on investment returns. Now that other methods of tax-deferred investment (such as individual retirement accounts (IRAs)) are available, traditional insurance is far less important as an investment vehicle.

On the other hand, insurance products such as variable annuities and single

premium life insurance offer the advantage of tax-deferred investing without the limits on contributions that go with IRAs and similar plans. The problem is that such investments necessarily come in a package with insurance, because, as a matter of law, if the investments do not contain a significant insurance component, they will be classified as mutual funds and become subject to federal disclosure and tax regulations covering investment companies.

California requires that insurers disclose a yield comparison index for whole life and universal life policies. The index is meant to give consumers some idea of what their return would be if the policy was surrendered a given number of years in the future, taking into account returns in the form of possible death benefits as well as investment returns. Although the index appears to be useful as a way of comparing one policy with another, especially insofar as commissions affect the value of the policy, the payoff's hybrid nature makes it useless for purposes of comparison to other investment vehicles.

Churning is usually thought of as excessive trading of securities to generate commissions for the broker, but churning is also a problem in life insurance. Specifically, insurance agents may urge consumers to trade in policies with high cash value primarily in order to generate commissions. Often, insureds will not be aware that a portion of the cash value is being used to pay a commission on the new policy to an agent and may not learn of it at all unless they attempt to take out a loan against the policy or otherwise gain access to the cash value. (And where a loan is already outstanding and the policy is traded in and the loan forgiven, there may be taxable income to the insured without any distribution of cash with which to pay the tax.) State regulators have attempted to monitor such practices.

§5.11 Life Insurance and the Terminally Ill

Many individuals owning life insurance have later become infected with the HIV virus and subsequently have become terminally ill with full-blown AIDS. In many instances, death has been preceded by prolonged illnesses for months or even years, during which the individual has been unable to work and has rapidly exhausted whatever financial resources he or she had. It would appear reasonable that a person in this position should be able to use life insurance benefits to cover medical and housing expenses before he or she dies. Based on this reasoning, many traditional life insurance companies offer customers who are terminally ill the chance to get their death benefits while they are still alive. Most companies, however, will advance death benefit payments only if the prognosis is that the patient has less than six months or at most a year to live. Prudential Insurance Company, for example, offers to pay 90 percent of the face value of a life insurance policy if the patient's physician certifies that he or she will not live more than six months.

A number of smaller companies have also entered this field. These companies offer to buy the life insurance policies of terminally ill patients at reduced values so the patients can use the cash that will become payable upon their inevitable death during their last illnesses. Unlike the program of the larger insurers, these companies pay the patient anywhere from 50 to 90 percent of the face value of the policy, depending on how long the patient is expected to

live. Although most of the patients taking advantage of this new industry have been AIDS patients, the program is available to any terminally ill individual.

Some of the companies have raised funds from the general public by arranging to sell life insurance policies on individual patients to investors who then become the beneficiaries of the policy. In effect, an investor can reap varying amounts of profits depending on how soon a specific patient dies. The sooner the patient dies, the more profitable the arrangement is from the investor's standpoint. Some companies, moreover, provide a selection of patients to choose from, along with medical information on each. Apart from obvious questions of privacy, the legality of this arrangement must be viewed as doubtful at best under traditional concepts of insurable interest. A number of companies involved in the purchase of life insurance policies from terminally ill patients do not sell policies to outside investors, but raise capital in more traditional ways. Companies in this new industry are called **viatical companies**.

§5.12 Insurance and the Diversification of Risk

There are many forms of insurance other than life insurance. Automobile insurance, homeowners insurance, and health insurance are just a few examples. Other less familiar kinds of insurance include product liability insurance, malpractice insurance for professionals (sometimes called **errors and omissions insurance**), and **directors and officers liability insurance (D&O insurance)**.

These other forms of insurance differ from life insurance in that they do not depend primarily on life expectancy for the insurance company to determine premium rates to be charged to various insureds. To be sure, many of the events that give rise to the payment of benefits under such insurance policies may involve a death. For example, the estate of someone killed in an automobile accident may receive benefits under an accident policy and may also receive payments from insurance policies carried by other motorists involved in the accident. If the accident was caused by some sort of mechanical defect, the estate may ultimately receive payment from an insurer of the manufacturer. The estate may, of course, also receive payment under a life insurance policy on the life of the deceased, which in fact may be doubled as benefits often are in the event of accidental death.

The rates charged for some of these other types of insurance are based on actuarial models about the likelihood of certain kinds of accidents or other events. For example, premiums for health insurance are based on models that attempt to predict the frequency with which certain diseases or medical conditions are likely to strike the insured. These other forms of insurance, however, are based almost purely on risk diversification as opposed to being based in part on the time value of money, as is life insurance. (This is not to say that insurance companies writing these other forms of insurance do not bother to invest their available funds at the highest possible rate between the time premiums are received and benefits are paid out.)

Perhaps the easiest way to see the difference between life insurance (at least whole life) and other forms of insurance is that with other forms of insurance, most policyholders do not collect as much in benefits as they pay in premiums. This does not mean, however, that other forms of insurance are bad deals.

Indeed, quite the contrary is true. People buy insurance to protect themselves against catastrophic events for which individual wealth is likely to be inadequate. For example, a homeowner is unlikely to have $100,000 in cash to rebuild his or her house if it is destroyed by fire. Homeowners insurance allows many homeowners, in effect, to pool their money in order to compensate those few homeowners whose houses actually do burn down. And the insurance company profits by facilitating the transaction.

These types of insurance are a **zero sum game** (except for the expenses of administering them and the profits earned by the insurance company). The monetary value of insurance to a homeowner is the amount of the benefit times the probability of fire or other damage. Assume that one is only worried about fire and that the chances of fire are 1 in 1,000. If the house in question is worth $100,000, the strictly monetary value of the insurance benefit is $100, that is, the value of the benefit times the probability that it will be received. Nevertheless, most homeowners would quite willingly spend more than $100 per year to protect against the possibility of fire. Indeed, one can well imagine that a homeowner might be willing to pay $150 or even $200 per year for such protection.

The fact that people purchase insurance suggests that they perceive a gain from buying insurance. What is the source of the gain? The answer is the elimination of risk. Many insurance company tout the "peace of mind" that comes from being insured. That is just a colloquial way of saying that people tend to be **risk averse**. The possibility of a significant loss, particularly one that is so large that the individual could not soon regain the same lifestyle, tends to weigh more in deciding what to do with $100 per year than does the possibility of using the same money to somehow enhance one's life in the present (say) by buying a new tennis racquet or installing a skylight. There is no real financial gain to the insured who gets precisely what is paid for—or actually a little less—that is, a 1 in 1,000 chance for a payment of $100,000. Still, because the insured has eliminated a worrisome risk, it is a good deal. What is magical about insurance is that the risk is simply gone. By pooling their small annual contributions through the insurance company, the participating homeowners have simply eliminated the risk of financial loss by fire. Of course, one could also argue that the insureds have collectively just figured out a way to pay for the damage in advance and, in effect, have assumed that the worrisome event will occur somewhere sometime. But in fact statistics indicate that it will, and accurately predicting the likelihood and consequences of such events is how insurance companies make money. The value of insurance, from the point of view of any given homeowner, is eliminating the possibility that such random-seeming events will happen to him or her. This view of insurance suggests that premium payments should be made deductible from income for tax purposes in the same way that the benefits of insurance are viewed as not being taxable income, that is, merely a way of making the insured whole. After all, casualty losses are deductible. Nevertheless, insurance premiums are not deductible, and the policy behind the casualty loss deduction is apparently limited to minimizing the devastating effects of larger losses on uninsured or partially insured tax-payers.

The benefits of some types of insurance extend beyond the insured's simply receiving a check for the amount of a loss. Where someone else is or may be

legally responsible for the loss, the insurance company will typically pay the insured victim promptly and then seek to recover that amount from the wrong-doer. Thus, insurance offers convenience and prompt payment, as well as avoiding the risk that a lawsuit may not succeed. Because insurance companies thus depend to some extent on getting back amounts they have paid out from wrongdoers (if any), insurance policies routinely provide for **subrogation**. Subrogation means that the insurance company obtains the right to sue in the name of the insured when it pays a claim. The insured must also undertake to cooperate with the insurance company in pursuing the case. However, from the point of view of a defendant, the insured remains the plaintiff, partly because in most cases the defendant may not introduce evidence of insurance because of the effect it might have on the jury's deliberations.

Where the insured is a defendant (in a case in which there is coverage for the harm done), most liability policies require the insurance company to provide a defense at its expense. It is, of course, in the interest of the insurance company to do so, given that the insured would prefer to settle for the amount of the coverage just to avoid the inconvenience of the lawsuit. Nevertheless, the provision of a defense has some value even to the insured in that the insurance company may often avoid the award of damages exceeding the limits of the policy.

§5.13 No Fault Insurance Systems

Where both (or all) parties to an accident are insured, any legal action that arises out of the accident will involve one insurance company suing another. One may question whether such lawsuits make much sense, given that over large numbers of insureds, automobile accidents (like mortality) become quite predictable. Indeed, in many cases an insurance company may end up on both sides of the same accident, in which case it becomes apparent that the company will pay no matter how the lawsuit turns out. Why bother? It is this logic that has led to the institution of **no fault insurance**. The fact that the involved motorists may be insured by different insurers makes little difference in the end in that as far as each insurance company is concerned, it will be on the winning and losing side of cases a predictable number of times. Thus, it would seem eminently sensible for all insurance companies to get together and simply agree to pay the legitimate claims of their own insureds and agree not to sue each other for reimbursement. Of course, no single company will unilaterally give up the right to sue, for to do so would put it at a competitive disadvantage. In the language of economists, there is a **barrier to contract** or **market failure** that requires an act of the legislature, that is, a statute, if the parties are to enjoy the benefits of a rational bargain.

Ironically, a no fault insurance system in which one's own company pays for most claims gives rise to the need for a residual form of coverage against the possibility that someone involved in the accident may not have bought insurance and may seek to sue the driver who is covered. Such **uninsured motorist coverage** is now required in most states, but it is quite cheap because it only applies in rare circumstances.

Unfortunately, the phrase "no fault" has been appropriated for use in other

contexts (such as no fault divorce laws) in which much of its original sense is lost. The logic of no fault automobile insurance is that litigation is wasteful in a setting in which accidents are highly predictable and recoveries between insurance companies net out over time. There is no such logic that seems to apply in the context of divorce law.

§5.14 Common Coverage Issues

Many individuals purchase **umbrella policies** that protect against awards in excess of lower limits on both auto and homeowners insurance policies. Umbrella policies also provide for some additional coverage (as President Clinton discovered when his insurance company agreed to provide a defense in connection with sexual harassment claims made against him). In some cases, especially in connection with umbrella policies and professional malpractice coverage, the insurance company will deduct the cost of providing a defense from the coverage available under the policy. Thus, if one has a $1 million umbrella policy and it costs $200,000 in attorney fees and court costs to defend a case, the amount available under the insurance policy to pay any damages award will be reduced to $800,000. In most cases, umbrella policies provide a total of the face amount of coverage for the policy year and do not cover for multiple claims once the policy is depleted. Automobile insurance, on the other hand, tends to have only per-occurrence limits.

One of the issues that arises in connection with umbrella policies and more often with professional malpractice and product liability policies is how to determine which claims are covered. For example, a claim made in 1997 may be the result of events that occurred in 1995. Is the claim covered by a 1997 or a 1995 policy? For a variety of reasons, many umbrella policies and almost all malpractice policies and product liability policies are written on a **claims-made basis**, that is, they cover the insured for claims formally made during the policy year irrespective of when the events giving rise to the claims occurred. Claims-made policies avoid controversy about precisely when the claim arose and the problem of claims arising years after a policy has expired. On the other hand, a claims-made policy, rather than some sort of **occurrence coverage**, requires that the insured continue to buy insurance against claims that may have arisen in the past, and it requires the insurance company to cover risks that may not be currently evident or indeed may be unknown to the insured. Although these problems may not be serious in the case of an insured who renews with the same company year after year, they create difficulties in certain settings. For example, a company that has stopped manufacturing a particular product may need to continue to buy insurance for claims that may be made in connection with the old product at least until the statute of limitations has run. In many states, the statute of limitations on claims based on injuries caused by defective products does not begin to run until the injury occurs. Insurance against later claims, called **tail insurance**, may be available in some instances but may be difficult or impossible to obtain.

In the context of malpractice insurance, a claims-made policy means that a lawyer who leaves a law firm will usually cease to be covered for claims made in connection with his or her practice at the former firm and, if the lawyer moves

to another firm, claims may be asserted against the new firm's policy for his or her conduct while at the former firm. The end result has sometimes been that an aggrieved client may recover from both firms for the value of both policies (to the extent they have not been depleted by other claims, of course). A lawyer or other professional who leaves a firm should be aware of the need for continuing protection, and a professional firm that takes on a new partner or employee should be aware that he or she may sometimes carry along liabilities. Tail coverage is sometimes available to cover these types of risks.

§5.15 Overinsurance, Self-Insurance, and Moral Hazard

The primary rationale for buying insurance (including term life insurance) is to spread the risk of various catastrophic events that one cannot afford to cover out of pocket. It should thus be apparent that in some situations, insurance makes little or no sense even though an insurance company may urge you to buy it. Extended warranties on products offer a good example, although they may not be usually thought of as insurance. Anyone who ever attempts to make a claim under an extended warranty quickly discovers that such plans operate very much like insurance policies. Extended warranties for relatively cheap household goods usually make little sense given the cost, the contractual limitations, the difficulties in collecting under them, and, most important, the fact that the item thus "insured" can be repaired or replaced with little financial disruption. If a person purchased an insurance policy against all the minor losses that he or she might suffer in any given year, assuming that these losses could even be catalogued, the cost of the insurance would far exceed the cost of paying out of that person's own pocket for the random events that actually occur.

Separate insurance to pay debt obligations (mortgage insurance is the best example) seldom makes economic sense. To be sure, the mortgage needs to be paid if one dies (assuming that the family home is not to be sold), but if one is adequately insured through other policies, there is nothing peculiar about the need to pay the mortgage that constitutes a unique risk. Indeed, it is arguable that insurance companies create confusion about what constitutes risk as a way of selling more insurance. (It should be emphasized that the mortgage insurance described here is not so-called **private mortgage insurance (PMI)** that lenders sometimes require as a condition for making a loan. PMI is a separate guaranty of payment that lenders require for their own benefit if they consider the risk of default to be high.)

For similar reasons, many large businesses self-insure in connection with risks for which individuals rationally buy insurance. For example, many large employers do not actually purchase health insurance for their employees. Instead, they simply pay for medical care as the need arises, because there are so many employees that the likelihood of certain conditions arising is roughly the same as it is in the population as a whole. Because the company only covers its employees and is not in the business of selling insurance, there is little risk that persons who know that they are more at risk than the average person will seek out jobs with the company in order to take advantage of its health insurance.

From the employee's perspective, employer self-insurance of health care is usually indistinguishable from an insurance plan purchased from an independent

insurance company. In most cases, a self-insuring employer contracts with an insurance company to administer the plan. Thus, the employee may be required to fill out the same forms that are required of others who are in fact insured by an independent company. The only difference is that when a bill is paid, it comes out of the employer's account rather than that of the insurance company.

It should be obvious that the gains from buying insurance are limited to the value of the property at risk. It makes no sense to buy more insurance than one needs. Indeed, insurance companies refuse to insure for amounts that exceed the value of the property insured, and if the insured attempts to buy policies from more than one company in order to double-cover a risk (and in effect bet on the destruction of the property), insurance contracts generally provide that each insurer will pay only a pro rata share of the claim (which is also the reason that medical insurance forms typically ask if there is other coverage).

If one were able to overinsure (and collect), it would create perverse incentives to engage in reckless behavior and even to destroy the insured property, for example, through arson. The insurance industry depends to a great extent on the natural tendency of insureds to avoid the events insured against anyway. Few people are indifferent to being involved in an automobile accident just because they are insured. And indeed, insurance companies are quite active in campaigning for insureds to engage in safer behavior. A basic concern in writing all kinds of insurance is that it should not somehow increase the risk of the event insured against. Thus, life insurance policies routinely exclude claims arising from suicide. On a subtler level, most liability policies exclude coverage for awards of punitive damages against the insured. Why? Punitive damages typically arise because of some form of intentional bad behavior on the part of the defendant from which the defendant hoped to gain (such as various forms of fraud). Such claims thus involve risks created by the insured and are thus excluded, although most insurance policies cover punitive damages assessed purely vicariously against an employer who did not participate in or induce the misdeeds of the employee. (Ironically, insurance companies themselves have been the frequent target of punitive damages claims in connection with failure to pay claims. The courts have recognized that one way an insurance company might make a bit more money is to refuse to pay or delay paying legitimate claims.)

There are generally no limitations on the amount of life insurance one may buy or the number of different insurance companies with whom one may deal. Of course, when it comes to life insurance, it may seem difficult to say how much a life is worth. But insurance cannot compensate for the personal and intangible loss of life. The point of life insurance is to protect not only against financial losses (usually the loss of earning power) but also other sorts of financial losses as well. If one thinks rationally about life insurance, it is possible to determine the amount of life insurance one should have. If, for example, one is living comfortably on $50,000 per year, including paying the mortgage and various bills as they become due, then adequate life insurance would be in an amount that would allow for a return of $50,000 per year if it is invested. Of course, there may be extraordinary expenses that should be considered, such as sending the children to college a few years hence or even paying for excess

medical expenses or funeral expenses. And it may be that one would want to provide for a better standard of living for one's survivors in order to make the loss of a life a bit more bearable. It is entirely possible, however, to estimate these numbers. Having estimated the cash needs of one's survivors and having taken into account other sources of potential income, such as income from existing investments and social security benefits, deciding how much insurance to buy becomes in essence a simple present value calculation: How much of a lump sum is necessary to generate the needed amount per year? The urge to buy any more insurance than that should be resisted, because the cash that is used to buy insurance could also be used to live better in the present, or simply be saved. For similar reasons, it makes little sense to purchase insurance on someone who is not earning a living or providing services on which others depend. Thus, it makes little sense for a retired person to buy life insurance or for a parent to buy life insurance on a child.

§5.16 Insurance and the Law

In many situations, insurance is required either by law or contract. For example, all auto owners are required to carry insurance (although there is usually an exemption for owners who can demonstrate that they have sufficient personal wealth to pay damages up to a specified amount). And, as a usual condition of obtaining a mortgage on a personal residence, the homeowner must insure the property against fire and other sorts of sudden damage. In the case of both auto insurance and homeowners insurance, the concern is that drivers and homeowners will be unable or unwilling to make good on their obligations. An automobile accident can result in hundreds of thousands of dollars of claims. The responsible individual would need to work for many years to pay off a large claim if indeed he or she would ever be able to pay it off. An obvious alternative is simply to declare bankruptcy and walk away from the obligation (if the claim is one that can be discharged in bankruptcy).

An individual is said to be **judgment proof** if he or she has no significant personal wealth with which to pay legal judgments. For example, most mortgages on individual residences specify that the mortgagor is personally liable on the note, but personal liability is not worth much if the person is not worth much. For this reason, many insurance policies require that a property be insured for at least 80 percent of its value. An insurance company may also make large checks payable jointly to the insured and the mortgagee. Both of these restrictions are designed to ensure that the proceeds of insurance are used for their intended purpose and not diverted for other purposes.

Insurance companies face the possibility that as a result of insurance, the insured will be less careful than he or she might otherwise be (a form of so-called moral hazard), or that the insured will make claims for very minor events that cost more in time and effort to administer than they are worth. One way of dealing with claims for minor events is to specify a deductible or require co-payment. With a deductible, the insured must pay the first $100, $250, $500, or other specified amount in connection with the claim. This is a very common arrangement in connection with **collision insurance** for automobiles,

the insurance that protects the auto owner against damage to his or her own car. There are, however, no deductibles in connection with liability coverage, that is, coverage for damage done to others. Why? Because insurance does not make one any less vigilant about avoiding accidents involving other automobiles or property. But one may be tempted to make a claim for minor dents and dings that could be avoided through a bit more care.

A **co-payment** is slightly different in that it requires the insured to pay some percentage of every claim. This is much more common in connection with health insurance, which also often specifies some deductible amount (e.g., $100 per year per individual). A typical health insurance policy (at least one that operates by reimbursement of the insured) might cover medical care only after the insured has paid out the first $100 and only then to the extent of 80 percent of further expenses.

Although liability insurance is not generally mandatory for businesses, there are certain risks for which insurance is required, such as unemployment and workers compensation. And, of course, there are certain lines of business that require special forms of insurance, such as deposit insurance for banks, or simple accident insurance for a trucking company. The availability (or not) of insurance has affected the development of the law dramatically in recent years. For example, one of the arguments that underlies the growth in consumer rights to sue for injuries suffered from defective products is that the manufacturer is in a better position either to spread the cost of such accidents by obtaining insurance (or self-insuring) and increasing the price of the product somewhat to offset the increased cost. If the availability of insurance is a factor to be considered in deciding whether a business is liable for a particular harm, the practical effect is to require the business to buy insurance or self-insure (which is to say pay the claim out of its own pocket).

Similarly, the law has long held that an employer is liable for damages that an employee causes while acting within the scope of employment. This doctrine is sometimes called by its original Latin name **respondeat superior** and is a kind of **vicarious liability**. Although many arguments have been advanced historically for why employers should be held liable for the accidents caused by their employees, one economic argument is that employers and employees would usually agree to have it so because the employer is in a better position to spread the cost by paying for accidents and reducing wages a bit to make up for it or by buying insurance. In effect, there is a hypothetical agreement by which the employer agrees to insure the employee in exchange for a lower wage or salary. As with commercial insurance, it is a matter of indifference to the employer whether it pays a lower wage and pays out a claim now and then or whether it pays a higher wage and lets the employees pay their own claims, assuming, of course, that the employer has an adequate number of employees performing more or less repetitive tasks so that the employer can accurately assess the risk. Indeed, the employer may gain from such an arrangement, because the employer may be able to assess risks more accurately than employees or even an outside insurance company and may be able to take steps to control these risks through various safety incentives and so forth that would not be instituted by the employees on their own. Thus, it may be argued that the law of employer liability mandates the agreement that ordinarily employer and

employee would freely enter into unless they were conspiring to avoid responsibility altogether. One problem with this theory is that the law gives the employer the right to seek indemnification (reimbursement) from the employee in most situations, though few employers ever do. One notable exception is the federal government, which has by statute given up the right to sue its own employees for indemnification in connection with accident claims.

Another example of how insurance affects the law relates to the benefit of limited liability when doing business in the form of a corporation or limited liability company. With these forms of business, the owners of the business are not personally responsible for debts of the business. But in the case of corporations at least, the courts, in situations in which they conclude that the corporate form has somehow been abused, may **pierce the corporate veil** and hold the shareholders of the corporation personally liable. One of the factors that courts cite in piercing cases involving torts is that the corporation was undercapitalized in the sense that there were insufficient funds available to pay claims that should have been foreseen as likely in the line of business in question. Many courts have noted that the purchase of insurance obviates the **undercapitalization** argument in such cases. The net effect is that, practically speaking, a business that fails to insure against likely harms it may cause runs an enhanced risk of personal liability for its owners in cases of tortious conduct, although not in cases of contractual liability.

III

ACCOUNTING, VALUATION,
AND TAXATION

CHAPTER 6

FUNDAMENTAL ACCOUNTING PRINCIPLES

§6.1 Introduction

As business and financial transactions occur, they are usually recorded in financial books and records. The results of the operation of the business are periodically communicated through financial statements that are usually based on these financial books and records. Accounting thus involves the collection, summarization, and reporting of financial data by a business, as well as the computation of profit and other measures of a business's financial health. The creation and maintenance of financial records are usually performed or overseen by persons with backgrounds in accounting, and the language in which the results of business operations are communicated is typically the language of the accountant. Every lawyer should have working familiarity with this language.

In addition, in order to understand what is being communicated in financial statements, one has to understand not only the underlying principles on

which modern accounting systems are based but also the major limitations on, or more accurately, the major policy decisions that underlie, these accounting systems. Because financial statements can be prepared on any number of different accounting systems, one also has to know what principles were followed in the creation of the specific financial statements under consideration, whether they depart from accepted accounting principles, and if they do, the extent to which the differences affect the results being reported. The standard set of accounting principles that forms the norm for financial reporting in the United States is known as **generally accepted accounting principles (GAAP)**. These principles must be followed by most publicly held corporations in the United States in publicly reporting the results of their operations. GAAP is not officially set down anywhere in the form of a code. Instead, GAAP is a loose set of rules and principles that outlines a range of reasonable and permissible treatments of many transactions.

GAAP has a hierarchy of principles, standards, and practices. First, the most authoritative of these principles are standards published by the **Financial Accounting Standards Board (FASB)**, a panel created by the **American Institute of Certified Public Accountants (AICPA)** with the cooperation of the **Securities and Exchange Commission (SEC)** to review accounting issues and promulgate GAAP standards. (In earlier times, the **Accounting Principles Board (APB)** performed a similar function, and many of its pronouncements remain valid standards to the extent that they have not been overruled by subsequent statements by the FASB.) Next in the hierarchy come other accounting standards published by AICPA, followed by general principles that pervade the practice of accounting and the accounting literature, and finally prevalent customs and usages in the practice of accounting. The SEC has legal authority to prescribe mandatory accounting standards that reporting publicly held companies must follow, but the magnitude of accounting issues has led the SEC to rely primarily on the FASB to establish principles. In other words, the accounting profession is largely self-regulated. In recent years, however, the FASB has been criticized as being too beholden to the businesses whose books they monitor, and the SEC has threatened to assume greater control. At the same time, businesses have complained that the FASB is too regulatory and disclosure-oriented in approach.

Some knowledge of the accounting process is essential for lawyers in a corporate or business practice, and indeed is useful for all lawyers without regard to the nature of their practice. Furthermore, there is an art to the process of analyzing financial statements that should be familiar to every lawyer. Law students without business or financial backgrounds may have irrational—almost primordial — fears about accounting principles and concepts. It is true that accounting can become very complex and esoteric; after all, accounting itself is a subject in which people regularly receive advanced graduate degrees and then spend productive lifetimes. On the other hand, one can readily understand the fundamental principles of accounting and learn to read and understand financial statements without becoming enmeshed in these complexities. This chapter describes the principles that underlie accounting statements. It deals with the accepted methods of treating commonly recurring accounting problems in a complex enterprise.

§6.2 The Functions of Accounting

Accounting in a large business involves two basic functions: the entering of records of transactions as they occur and the subsequent determination and reporting of results of operations on a periodic basis. In a large publicly held corporation, unaudited financial results are usually reported quarterly to the public and audited results are reported annually. Financial reports are widely publicized and are used and relied on by investors, creditors, regulatory agencies, employees, and others. The preparation of these public reports is usually described as financial accounting as contrasted with management accounting. A major goal of financial accounting is to ensure that the financial reports are prepared honestly and in accordance with GAAP so that they are comparable with earlier reports and the reports of other companies. Innumerable investment and commercial decisions are made on the premise that such reports are comparable with the same company's reports for earlier periods and with published reports of other companies in the same or different industries. Nevertheless, perfect comparability cannot be achieved, because in any complex organization numerous discretionary accounting judgments make variations in treatment inevitable.

Financial information about corporate affairs is also essential if management of a publicly held corporation is to make informed internal decisions. For internal purposes, financial results may be reported to top management and the board of directors on a weekly or even a daily basis. Financial analyses of specific business alternatives or strategies will also be prepared as the need arises. These internal reports and analyses are usually not prepared in accordance with GAAP, and they are not publicly available. Their preparation is sometimes called management accounting to distinguish this area from the publicly oriented financial accounting described in the preceding paragraph.

The routine recording and summarization of transactions is also essential to ensure that the business always has the proper inventory of raw materials and finished goods on hand. This permits the manufacturing operations of the business to continue smoothly and to actually produce what customers have ordered or are willing to buy. The two functions of accounting—keeping track and reporting—are related in that the records used in the process of recording transactions as they occur are also used as the basis for the compilation of the results of operations. Modern accounting is a continuing process that permits transactions that are numerous, large, and complex to be accounted for on a routine basis involving relatively low-paid and marginally skilled employees. Of course, the original creation of the bookkeeping process for a specific business, the oversight of that process, and decisions as to how specific significant transactions are to be accounted for within that process require the participation of persons who have a broad view of the whole accounting process.

Persons unfamiliar with the accounting process are apt to believe that accounting is a precise science, or at least that there is general acceptance of basic principles as to how transactions should be handled for financial accounting purposes. Financial accounting gives a deceptive aura of accuracy. Amounts are entered in precise dollars-and-cents figures. Accountants state that

accounting principles require a specific treatment of an item. This appearance of accuracy and specificity should not be permitted to hide the fact that there is often room for differences of opinion as to how matters should be treated and presented.

Within the accounting profession, and to a large extent in general business publications, discussions of the most appropriate treatment of specific transactions or of classes of transactions are often heated and the conclusions are controversial. For example, the seemingly arcane issue of whether the grant of stock options should be treated as an expense went on for several years and made front page news in many major papers. And a 1996 U.S. Supreme Court decision as to how a savings bank should account for the purchase of another bank resulted in an apparent increase of several billion dollars in the cost to the federal government in connection with settling certain claims by failed savings banks.

These controversies are fueled by the underlying fact that in the financial community's eyes, the success or failure of an enterprise is largely measured by its reported financial results, and any change in GAAP that significantly affects the reported results of operations of publicly held companies may have significant and wide-ranging repercussions, even though only the manner of reporting the transaction—rather than the transaction itself—has changed. In a fundamental sense, accounting is a language that (like most languages) allows considerable variation in expression; it is not a matter of right and wrong so much as what is useful and comparable and what is not.

Indeed, there is considerable disagreement as to whether the entire edifice of accounting principles described in this and the following chapters is built on quicksand and should be scrapped in favor of a discounted cash-flow analysis.

§6.3 The Basic Accounting Equation

The starting point of the whole subject of accountancy is a very simple equation:

$$\text{Equity} = \text{Assets} - \text{Liabilities}$$

Equity in this equation has nothing to do with the historical courts of equity or with notions of fairness or simple justice: It means ownership or net worth. This equation simply states that the net worth of a business is equal to its assets minus its liabilities.

A balance sheet is in many ways the most fundamental financial statement: It is simply a restatement of this fundamental equation in the form:

$$\text{Assets} = \text{Liabilities} + \text{Equity}$$

A balance sheet simply is a presentation of this equation in a chart form:

Assets:	Liabilities + Equity
_____	_____

Every balance sheet, whether it is for General Motors or the smallest retail grocery store, is based on this format. As an illustration, a hypothetical balance sheet for a large oil company is shown in Table 6-1. The basic construct should be self-evident from a casual examination of this statement, even though it is printed with the liability/equity side immediately below the asset side.

Table 6-1

	Dec. 31, 1996	Dec. 31, 1997
	(millions of dollars)	
Assets		
Current assets		
Cash	$ 2,908	$ 1,911
Marketable securities	908	620
Notes and accounts receivable, less estimated		
doubtful amounts	6,784	6,278
Inventories		
Crude oil, products and merchandise	3,603	4,200
Materials and supplies	948	972
Prepaid taxes and expenses	1,169	1,410
Total current assets	16,320	**15,391**
Investments and advances	2,778	3,822
Property, plant and equipment, at cost, less		
accumulated depreciation and depletion	49,289	53,434
Other assets, including intangibles	1,097	1,395
Total assets	$69,484	**$74,042**
Liabilities		
Current liabilities		
Notes and loans payable	$ 3,584	$ 2,864
Accounts payable and accrued liabilities	9,515	10,248
Income taxes payable	2,121	2,184
Total current liabilities	15,220	**15,296**
Long-term debt	4,294	5,021
Annuity reserves and accrued liabilities	5,121	5,902
Deferred income tax credits	10,828	11,863
Deferred income	466	560
Equity of minority shareholders in affiliated companies	1,543	1,774
Total liabilities	37,472	**40,416**
Shareholders' equity		
Capital stock without par value (authorized		
2 billion shares, 1,813 million issued)	2,822	2,822
Earnings reinvested	37,322	39,476
Cumulative foreign exchange translation adjustment	(196)	1,750
Capital stock held in treasury, at cost (378 million	(7,936)	(10,422)
shares in 1996, 434 million shares in 1987)		
Total shareholders' equity	32,012	**33,626**
Total liabilities and shareholders' equity	$69,484	**$74,042**

The asset side of a balance sheet is sometimes referred to as the left-hand side, even though it is sometimes printed above rather than to the left (as in the table). Similarly, the liability/equity side is sometimes called the right-hand side, even though it is sometimes printed below rather than to the right.

There are four fundamental premises underlying financial accounting that can readily be grasped from this simple introduction. First, financial accounting assumes that the business that is the subject of the financial statements is an entity. A person may own several different businesses; if each business maintains its own records, it will be on the assumption that each is independent from the person's other businesses. The equity referred to in that business's balance sheet will be limited to the person's investment in that single business. If a person owns two businesses that keep separate financial records, a debt that one business owes to the other will be reflected as an asset on one balance sheet and a liability on the other.

Second, all entries must be in terms of dollars (at least in the United States). All property, tangible or intangible, and obligations shown on a balance sheet must be expressed in dollars, either historical cost or fair market value or some other method of valuation. Many "assets" or "liabilities" of a business, however, are not reflected at all. A person's friendly smile may be an asset in a sense, but will not appear on a balance sheet because a dollar value is not normally given to a smile. Assets, such as a debt owed to the company or rights to a patent, on the other hand, do appear in balance sheets. On the balance sheet shown, tangible and intangible assets are combined under the entry "other assets, including intangibles." Similarly, a company may have a reputation for sharp practices or questionable dealing. Although that reputation is doubtless a liability in a sense, it is not the type of liability that appears on a balance sheet. A liability in the balance sheet sense is a recognized debt or obligation to someone else, payable either in money or in something reducible to money. Not all liabilities that in the legal or lay sense meet this test are recognized as liabilities in the accounting sense.

Third, a balance sheet must balance. The fundamental accounting equation itself states an equality: The two sides of the balance sheet restate that equality in somewhat reorganized form. A balance sheet therefore is itself an equality, and the sum of the left-hand side of the balance sheet must precisely equal the sum of the right-hand side. Indeed, when accountants are involved in auditing a complex business, they take advantage of this characteristic by running trial balances on their work to make sure that they have not inadvertently transposed or omitted figures: The mathematical equality of the two sides of the balance sheet provides a check on the accuracy of the accountant's labors. In short, if a balance sheet doesn't balance, there is a mistake somewhere.

Fourth, every transaction that a business enters into must be recorded in at least two ways if the balance sheet is to continue to balance. This last point underlies the concept of that mysterious (and somewhat illicit sounding) subject, double entry bookkeeping, and is the cornerstone on which modern accounting is built.

Assume that we have a new business that is just starting out, in which the owner has invested $10,000 in cash (for this purpose it makes no difference whether the business is going to be conducted in the form of a proprietorship,

partnership, or corporation; all that is important is that it will be accounted for as an entity separate from the owner). The opening balance sheet will look like this:

Assets:		Liabilities	-0-
Cash	10,000	Owner's Equity	10,000

Now let us assume that the owner buys a used truck for $3,000 cash. The effect of this transaction is to reduce cash by $3,000 and create a new asset on the balance sheet:

Assets:		Liabilities	-0-
Cash	7,000	Owner's Equity	10,000
Used Truck	3,000		
	10,000		10,000

Voila! The balance sheet still balances. Next, let us assume that the owner goes down to the bank and borrows an additional $1,000. This also has a dual effect: It increases cash by $1,000 (because the business is receiving the proceeds of the loan) and increases liabilities by $1,000 (because the business thereafter must repay the loan). Yet another balance sheet can be created showing the additional effect of this second transaction:

Assets:		Liabilities	
Cash	8,000	Debt to bank	1,000
Used Truck	3,000	Owner's Equity	10,000
	11,000		11,000

Further insights should be evident from these two examples: First, a balance sheet records a situation at one instant in time. It is a static concept, an equilibrium that exists at one point in time rather than a record of change from an earlier period. Put another way, every transaction potentially creates a different or new balance sheet when the transaction is recorded. Second, the bottom line of a balance sheet — $11,000 in this example — is not itself a meaningful figure, because transactions such as the bank loan that do not affect the real worth of the business to the owners may increase or decrease the bottom line.

§6.4 Accounting for Profits and Losses

The two transactions described above — the purchase of a used truck and a short-term bank loan — involve a reshuffling of assets and liabilities. From an

accounting standpoint, the owner of the business is neither richer nor poorer as a result of them. However, most transactions that a business enters into are of a different type: They involve ordinary business operations leading to a profit or loss in the current accounting period. Consider a simple example. Suppose the business described above involves hauling things in the truck for customers. Thus, the company hires a truck driver at a cost of $200 per day to drive the truck and pick up and deliver for it. During that first day the truck driver works very hard and for long hours making deliveries for which the business is paid $500. It is simple to create a profit and loss statement or income statement for the business for the one day of operation. "Profit and loss" and "income" are synonyms for this purpose. The basic formula is:

$$\text{Income} = \text{Revenues} - \text{Expenses}$$

Obviously, the business had income of $300 ($500 of revenue minus $200 of expense for the truck driver) for its first day of operation. There may have been other expenses as well that arguably should be charged to that first day of operation, but for simplicity we are ignoring that possibility.

At first glance, the income statement appears to have nothing to do with the balance sheet described in the previous section. It is possible, however, to create a new balance sheet to reflect each of these transactions.

First, the payment of the $200 to the truck driver involves a cash payment of $200 by the business; it is easy to record that. But where should the offsetting entry be? The balance sheet cannot look like this:

Assets:		Liabilities	
Cash	7,800	Debt to bank	1,000
Used Truck	3,000	Equity	10,000
	10,800		11,000

Something is obviously wrong, because this balance sheet does not balance. There must be an offsetting entry. It certainly should not be a reduction of liabilities (because the amount of the bank loan is unchanged) or an increase in value of the truck. Perhaps one could view the services as an asset something like the truck, but that does not make much sense, because the services are simply gone. One could perhaps argue that no balance sheet should be created until the payment to the truck driver is offset by whatever the driver earns during the rest of the day, but that cannot be correct either, because the balance sheet should balance after every transaction, not just at the end of a sequence of transactions. By process of elimination, the only possible solution is to reduce "owner's equity" by the payment:

Assets:		Liabilities	
Cash	7,800	Debt to bank	1,000
Used Truck	3,000	Equity	9,800
	10,800		10,800

Second, the $500 payment for the services rendered:

Assets:		Liabilities	
Cash	8,300	Debt to bank	1,000
Used Truck	3,000	Equity	10,300
	11,300		11,300

Admittedly, these two balance sheets are not very helpful in showing the relationship between the balance sheet and the income statement. What is needed is a segregation of income items within the equity account so that the permanent investment and the transient changes are shown separately. Thus, the following balance sheet at the end of the period is much more illuminating:

Assets:		Liabilities	
Cash	8,300	Debt to bank	1,000
Used Truck	3,000	Original capital	10,000
		Earnings	300
	11,300		11,300

The important point at present is that profit and loss items are reflected on the balance sheet as changes in owner's equity.

The balance sheet is a static concept showing the status of a business at a particular instant in time, while the income statement describes the results of operations over some period of time: daily, monthly, quarterly, or annually. In a sense, the balance sheet is a snapshot, and the income statement is a motion picture. The income statement also serves as the bridge between the balance sheet at the beginning of the period and the balance sheet at the end of the period, because positive income items (revenues) increase owner's equity while negative income items (expenses) reduce it.

The remainder of this chapter considers some of the practical problems of generating financial statements. Most investors and creditors look first at the (proverbial) bottom line of the income statement when evaluating financial statements. The income statement reflects the operations of the business. Thus, the balance sheet plays a lesser role in financial analysis.

The concept of profit and loss and accounting periods rests on additional fundamental postulates. First, accounting assumes the continuing existence and activity of the business enterprise as a going concern. In other words, it is assumed that the business will be around for an indefinite number of future accounting periods. If a business is in such dire straits that its continued existence is unlikely, a totally different set of accounting principles must be adopted. Second, each business must adopt a fiscal or accounting period and must report the results of operations for that period as a separate accounting unit. The unit usually chosen is a year—either a **calendar year** or a **fiscal year**. (A fiscal year is a reporting period that the business chooses that ends on a date

other than December 31 and may vary somewhat in length from a period of precisely 12 months.) Third, in determining the results of operations during an accounting period, some kind of logical relationship must be created between the revenues and expenses that are taken into account in determining profit or loss for that period. The principle usually followed is that costs allocable to the creation of revenue should be matched with that revenue. Other costs arising from the passage of time are allocated to the accounting period on the basis of that time and not the time of receipt. Fourth, some principles must be established as to when revenue is realized. Usually, the rule that is adopted is that revenues are realized when the business becomes unconditionally entitled to their receipt, not when payment is received. In the case of a contract for the sale of goods, for example, revenue may be realized when the goods are shipped, not when the contract was entered into or when payment is made. As a corollary, property of the business that may have appreciated in market value does not give rise to revenue until the gain in value is realized by sale or disposition of the property.

This concept is known as **accrual accounting**, and most businesses follow it. Indeed, most businesses of any size are required to use accrual accounting even though **cash basis accounting** might seem simpler. Most individuals use cash basis accounting for tax purposes (even if they do not know it). Accrual accounting, however, tends to give investors and creditors a better sense of the financial health of a business.

At this point, it is necessary to go back and introduce the way in which the double entry bookkeeping system is used to record transactions as they occur and to permit the development of balance sheets and income statements from those records.

§6.5 Journal Entries

The essence of double-entry bookkeeping is the systematic recordation of every transaction in the offsetting ways described above. For many centuries, the process of recordation involved the manual entry of transactions by persons wearing little green eye shades. In larger businesses, many transactions need to be entered each day. The development of the computer has automated the bookkeeping process as it has so many other areas: In most businesses today, the process involves relatively small inputs of human labor. Computerized accounting programs, however, largely follow the logic of the earlier manual system. In the following discussion, it is assumed that all transactions are entered manually so that the structure can be examined.

A business does not normally create a new balance sheet after each transaction; in any business with even minimal activity numerous entries are made each day and a balance sheet is created only periodically. The bookkeeper records each transaction in a **journal** to reflect both sides of each transaction. For example, **journal entries** to reflect the truck purchase and the bank loan transactions would look something like this:

Description of transaction	Debit	Credit
1/1/97 Cash		$3,000
Vehicles	$3,000	
To record purchase of truck		
1/2/97 Cash	$1,000	
Current Liabilities		$1,000
To record 90-day loan from bank		

There may not seem to be any relationship between these two entries and the two balance sheets previously set forth. But because of accounting conventions, they are reflections of the same transactions, and an accountant can readily go from the journal entries to the balance sheets.

First of all, a word needs to be said about the words **debit** and **credit** in the titles to the foregoing journal entries (titles, incidentally, that are so well understood that they do not usually appear on real journal pages). The word debit simply means "left hand" and the word credit means "right hand." There is widespread popular confusion over the meaning of these two terms. In a lay sense, debit is probably associated with reduction, while credit is associated with increase. Once the notion of double entry bookkeeping is introduced, however, it is clear that the words require more careful elaboration, because every transaction, in a sense, involves both an increase and a decrease. Further, all journal entries by conventional understanding are positive. The basic accounting convention that ties journal entries to balance sheet items can be simply stated but is rather confusing: A debit journal entry increases left-hand items on the balance sheet and decreases right-hand items, while a credit journal entry reduces left-hand items and increases right-hand items. Thus, in the foregoing examples, an experienced accountant looking at the two entries knows at a glance that the business reduced its cash account by $3,000 when it bought the truck and increased it by $1,000 when it entered into the bank loan. Similarly, an accountant knows at a glance that the credit reflecting the bank loan increased the business's liabilities, because "liabilities" is a right-hand account.

Because the income statement may be viewed as part of the right-hand side of the balance sheet, journal entries are also used to enter transactions involving the income statement. The basic concept is that revenue items are credits and expense items are debits. (Recall that credits increase right-hand items and debits reduce them.) Thus, the journal entries for the salary payment to the truck driver and the receipt of the fee look like this:

1/1/97		
Current salaries — expense	$200	
Cash		$200
To reflect truck driver's salary		
Cash	$500	
Fees earned — income		$500
To reflect fee for truck driver's services		

The "current salaries" account is an income statement item (an expense item that reduces earnings, as all debits must do), while the cash account to which it is joined in the journal appears only on the balance sheet; similarly the "fees earned" account is also an income statement item (a receipt item that increases earnings, as all credits must do), while the balance sheet item cash is increased.

The genius of the double entry system is that a single set of entries permits the development of both types of financial statements and provides the internal controls that are essential for any large business.

§6.6 Ledger or "T" Accounts

It is theoretically possible to develop a balance sheet and income statement directly from journal entries. In any business with a large number of transactions, however, a journal of the type described above is not very useful in determining where the business stands at any one time. Entries relating to cash and other important accounts on the balance sheet as well as income and expense items are scattered almost randomly throughout the pages of the journal. The obvious solution is to create a separate ledger or page for each important balance sheet and income statement entry. These ledger accounts are called **T accounts**, because traditionally they are kept on sheets that look like a balance sheet:

Cash	
+ entries (debits)	– entries (credits)

All debits go on the left side, and all credits on the right side. Usually, there is a separate T account for each item on the balance sheet, and as entries are made in the journal they are also entered on the appropriate T account. They may be entered simultaneously (as occurs in computerized programs), or hourly or daily, depending on the activity in the T account. In connection with the cash account, by adding each side and then subtracting the right hand side from the left hand side, one can then determine where the cash account stands at any time.

Every item on the balance sheet theoretically has its own ledger or T account. Similarly, separate ledger accounts are created for income and expense entries in much the same way as they are created for balance sheet items. T accounts can best be envisioned as subparts of the balance sheet: The "cash," "notes payable," and "retained earnings" ledgers are shown in the following diagram as a part of the balance sheet:

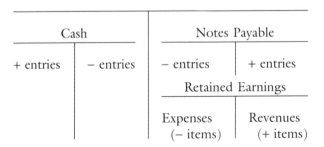

Thus, a receipt of cash is a debit to the cash account, while a payment of cash is a credit to the cash account and goes on the right-hand side of the cash account. The cash entry on a balance sheet at any time is the net difference between the debits and credits to cash. Similarly, the payment of an expense reduces the cash account (a credit) and increases the expense account (a debit). The beauty of this system is that it combines the double entry system for recording transactions with a method of developing balance sheets and income statements by following fairly simple and routine processes. If one regularly follows simple rules about recording debit and credit entries for each transaction, he or she can routinely construct balance sheets and income statements on a relatively mechanical basis as well as provide a method of recording routine transactions.

Obviously, the income statement requires its own set of ledger accounts, and many of them are extremely active in any substantial business. Depending on the nature of the business, there are whole families of increase items (e.g., receipts, sales, interest, and rent) and decrease items (e.g., salaries, cost of goods sold, depreciation, and advertising) among these new ledger accounts. These income ledger accounts differ from the balance sheet ledger accounts in one respect: Because they reflect transactions occurring during a specific time period, they must be adjusted back to zero at the beginning of each new accounting period. This is done by special journal entries at the close of the prior period that transfer the balances to the balance sheet account, usually called retained earnings. Balance sheet accounts need not be closed out after the preparation of a new balance sheet, because balance sheets reflect an instantaneous picture of the business accounts, and the balance sheet at the close of one accounting period is identical with the balance sheet at the opening of the next period.

In summary, journal entries are designed to track increases and decreases in various balance sheet and income statement items. Thus, the journal is filled with the names of various assets and liabilities and components of owner's equity (various revenues and expenses) and will reveal increases and decreases in these accounts to reflect the results of particular transactions. The vocabulary that bookkeepers use to record these transactions can be confusing because bookkeepers use the words debit and credit to mean both increase and decrease depending on which side of the balance sheet is affected.

Although debits and credits are the basic building blocks of bookkeeping, these terms do not appear in published financial statements, and most lawyers rarely need to look at a company's journals. Thus the remainder of this discussion of accounting will focus on the impact of various transactions on the balance sheet and income statement in terms of increases and decreases in assets, liabilities, and owner's equity.

§6.7 The Balance Sheet

Before turning to a discussion of some of the major issues in accounting, it is useful to present a balance sheet and income statement for a relatively complex business and briefly describe the items in each statement. The relationship of these two statements to the simple examples used in previous sections should be evident. The purpose of this exercise is primarily to familiarize the

reader with the traditional language used in financial statements and give an example of what financial statements look like.

As is customary, the balance sheet shown in Table 6-2 is as of the close of business on the last day of the accounting period covered by the income statement. The left-hand side of the balance sheet reflects the various **assets** of the business. It is usually subdivided into two categories: current assets and noncurrent assets.

Current assets consist of cash plus other assets that normally may be expected to be turned into cash within a year (or, in a few cases, in a longer period constituting the business's normal operating cycle).

Cash includes not only funds on deposit in checking accounts, but also cash equivalents. As described in earlier chapters, large sums of money are not normally left idle for even short periods of time. In most publicly held companies, temporarily excess funds are conservatively invested short-term in riskless securities that are usually not subject to swings in value. Such investments may include United States Treasury bills or notes, certificates of deposit, commercial paper, bankers' acceptances, and so-called money market accounts.

Marketable securities. Businesses may have excess or idle cash available for longer periods of time that may be temporarily invested in longer-term marketable securities. The funds may be set aside for business purposes such as long-term capital improvements or real estate acquisition, or they may simply be excess cash that the company does not want to distribute to shareholders in the form of dividends.

Accounts receivable are amounts due from customers. Accounts receivable typically arise from the sale of goods on credit. An allowance for bad debts (somtimes more elegantly referred to as an allowance for doubtful accounts) is subtracted from accounts receivable. The amount of this item is usually estimated based on the prior collection history of the business.

Inventories include several types of goods needed by the business in production of its end product: raw materials, partially finished goods in process of manufacture, and finished goods ready for shipment. The inventory of a retail operation may consist almost solely of finished goods. There are several methods of reporting inventory, and the choice of method can be controversial, as is discussed more fully below.

Noncurrent assets consist of all assets that are not classified as current and include a variety of quite different items.

Fixed assets are traditionally defined as property, plant, and equipment. Such items are usually recorded at historical cost; plant and equipment is depreciated over its expected life. Hence, the negative item, **accumulated depreciation**, appears as an offset. This negative item is the total of all prior deductions for depreciation in earlier years. The truck in

Table 6-2
ABC Incorporated
Balance Sheet as of December 31, 1997

ASSETS

Current Assets		
Cash		$ 300,000
Marketable securities at cost (market value $890,000)		460,000
Accounts receivable: 2,000,000 less $100,000 allowance for bad debt		1,900,000
Inventories		3,000,000
Total current assets		$5,660,000
Noncurrent Assets		
Fixed assets		
(property, plant, and equipment)		
Land	$ 450,000	
Building	3,600,000	
Machinery	850,000	
Office equipment	95,000	
	$4,995,000	
Less: accumulated depreciation	1,500,000	
Net fixed assets		$3,495,000
Prepayments and deferred charges		40,000
Intangible assets		
Patents and Copyrights	75,000	
Goodwill	25,000	
Other assets		100,000
		50,000
Total assets		$9,345,000

LIABILITIES

Current liabilities		
Accounts payable		$ 940,000
Notes payable		1,000,000
Accrued expenses payable		300,000
Federal income taxes payable		290,000
Total current liabilities		$2,530,000
Long-term liabilities		
5% Debentures, due 2016		2,700,000
Total liabilities		$5,230,000

STOCKHOLDERS' EQUITY

Capital stock		
Preferred stock		
($10 par value, 60,000 shares issued and oustanding)		600,000
Common stock ($5 par value, 300,000 shares issued and outstanding)		1,500,000
Additional capital paid in respect of common stock		700,000
Retained earnings		1,315,000
Total stockholders' equity		$4,115,000
Total liabilities and stockholders' equity		$9,345,000

the simple illustration used earlier to describe basic bookkeeping techniques is an example of depreciable equipment. Land is a fixed asset that is not depreciable. The reporting of fixed assets and the depreciation concept is discussed below.

Prepayments and deferred charges are also sometimes described as **prepaid charges**. They are discussed below in connection with the concept of accrual.

Intangible assets fall into various categories. Traditional intangible assets (those that are usually not controversial from the standpoint of accounting principles) include patents, trademarks, and franchises. These intangible assets are reported at acquisition or development cost. The presence of other intangible assets, particularly **goodwill**, **capitalized organizational cost**, or **capitalized research and development costs** on a balance sheet are a warning sign for careful analysis. These assets may reflect only balancing entries for prior transactions. For example, if a company buys a bundle of assets for more than the sum of their individual fair market values, the excess may be entered as "goodwill." Whether or not the purchase was desirable, not much weight can be given to goodwill as an asset. It is unclear on the face of the balance sheet what the "Goodwill — $25,000" entry represents; it is unlikely, however, that it is an asset in any realistic sense of the word.

Other assets may include a variety of interests (e.g., debts owed to the company that mature in more than one year, minority interests in other businesses, and the like).

Companies in specialized fields may include additional asset items or different breakdowns of traditional items. Energy companies, for example, present information for energy reserves separately from inventory.

Liabilities in the accounting sense are obligations that probably will need to be paid in an amount that can reasonably be estimated when the balance sheet is prepared. Material litigation or claims that do not qualify as liabilities in this sense do not appear on the balance sheet itself but should be referred to in the accompanying notes to the financial statements as contingent liabilities.

Current liabilities are those expected to be satisfied out of current assets, usually including all liabilities that will become due in the coming year. Their relationship to current assets can be an important one for evaluating the financial strength of the business. The most common current liabilities are usually broken down and listed separately.

Accounts payable are amounts owed to suppliers based on deliveries of supplies and raw materials on credit.

Notes payable are amounts due to banks and other lenders in connection with loans that mature during the following 12 months. The portion of a long-term loan payable in installments that is due to be paid within 12 months is also included within notes payable.

Accrued expenses payable is a catchall for amounts owed to other business creditors that do not fall within the categories of accounts or notes payable. It may include amounts owed to employees for wages and salaries on the date of the balance sheet; interest on open accounts not reflected as promissory notes; amounts owed to federal, state, or local governments for taxes; fees owed to attorneys; insurance premiums; required pension plan contributions; and a variety of other current liabilities. Because accountants are conservative and interested in matching costs with revenues, accrued expenses payable may include items that are not yet enforceable legal liabilities.

Long-term liabilities are liabilities due more than one year from the date of the balance sheet. The most common kinds of long-term liabilities are mortgages on real property or bonds and debentures that the company issues in order to raise working capital. The debentures shown in Table 6-2 are unsecured debt obligations of ABC carrying a 5 percent interest rate and not due for repayment for nearly 30 years. The payment date is so far in the future that such debt should realistically be viewed as part of the permanent capitalization of the company.

Stockholders' equity is the balancing factor between assets and liabilities on the balance sheet. In the case of partnerships or proprietorships, this part of the balance sheet may be titled **owners' equity**, or simply **capital** or **capital contributed by partners**. Stockholders' equity consists basically of two parts: (1) the permanent non-debt capitalization of the business, and (2) **retained earnings**. Retained earnings is the accumulated income of the business (less any distributions to owners). It is also the item that ensures that balance sheets balance.

The following formulas should clarify the relationship between the balance sheet and the income statement:

Beginning owner's equity + Net income − Dividends declared
+ Stock issued − Stock repurchased = Ending owner's equity

Beginning capital + Stock issued − Stock repurchased = Ending capital

Beginning retained earnings + Revenues − Expenses
− Dividends = Ending retained earnings

The most important concept embedded in these formulas is that the owner's equity reported on the balance sheet will increase and decrease during the year by revenues and expenses (income statement items). In other words, if instead of using journal entries, we record transactions according to the impact they have on assets, liabilities, and owner's equity, the changes to owner's equity during the year (excluding changes due to stock transactions and dividends) will be the income statement.

Preferred stock is usually a stock with a prior (but limited) claim to distributions ahead of the common shares. Preferred stock also usually has a prior (but limited) claim on liquidation. In the case of ABC, no infor-

mation is given on the balance sheet as to the **dividend preferences** or **liquidation preferences** of this preferred stock.

Common stock represents the residual ownership of the corporation. In many states, it is customary to assign a **par value** to common (and preferred) stock. Par value is an arbitrary amount, a relic of earlier corporation practices. When par value is used, the virtually universal practice is to specify a very low par value and to issue shares for a price higher than par value. Nevertheless, par value stock is entered as permanent capital on the balance sheet at its **aggregate par value**, an item that is sometimes called **stated capital**. The excess amounts that investors paid over par value when the stock was issued are shown separately as **additional capital paid in in respect of common stock** or **additional paid in capital (APIC)**. In other words, the common stock was originally sold for the total of the two amounts, $2,200,000.

§6.8 The Income Statement

The items on the income statement are relatively easier to understand than the items on the balance sheet because the entries are more self-evident. As described above, it is built on the fundamental notion that:

$$Revenues - Expenses = Net\ income$$

This relationship should be immediately apparent from even a cursory examination of the income statement shown in Table 6-3.

Table 6-3
ABC Incorporated
Income Statement for Year Ended December 31, 1997

Net sales		$10,200,000
Cost of goods sold		7,684,000
Gross margin		2,516,000
Other expenses		
Depreciation	275,000	
Selling and administrative expense	1,325,000	
		1,600,000
Operating profit		916,000
Other income		
Dividends and interest		27,000
Total income		943,000
Less interest on debentures		135,000
Income before provision for federal income tax		808,000
Provision for federal income tax		365,000
Net profit for year before extraordinary times		443,000
Extraordinary gain—settlement of legal action	123,000	
Less applicable taxes	55,000	68,000
Net income for year		$511,000

The income statement set forth here is for a business primarily involved in manufacturing and selling some sort of tangible product. (In the case of a business not involved primarily in selling goods, the revenue side may be titled operating revenues and the expense side not broken down between costs of goods sold and other expenses.) It should be noted that there are six "bottom lines" in this rather elaborate income statement: (1) sales minus **cost of goods sold** equals **gross margin**; (2) gross margin minus **operating expenses** (expenses not allocable directly to the goods sold) equals **operating profit**; (3) operating profit plus other income (e.g., income from dividends, interest, or rent not connected with the entity's principal business) equals **total income**; (4) total income less interest on long-term debentures equals **income before provision for income tax**; (5) income before provision for income tax minus income tax equals **net income for year before extraordinary items**; and finally, (6) net income takes into account the extraordinary gain from the settlement of litigation, which is the bottom bottom line. The net income for year before extraordinary items is normally used to compare results with previous years or with other companies. Not all published income statements contain this degree of breakdown: For example, gross margin is primarily useful for internal control and projections by management and is not ordinarily separated out. Similarly, interest on bonds or debentures is often not separated out but included as a part of operating expenses as a single item interest expense, so that the distinction between total income and income before provision for federal income tax disappears.

Net sales means gross sales minus returns. One of the expenses deducted as other expenses from net sales is **depreciation**. This reflects the portion of the original purchase price of each depreciable asset that is allocated to the current year as the cost of gradually using up that asset, and should be distinguished from the **accumulated depreciation** item on the balance sheet, which represents all prior deductions for depreciation of all depreciable property in the asset account.

Extraordinary items are nonrecurring items that materially affect the operating results. Such items are usually separated out and shown at the very bottom of the income statement after calculating the operating profit, which represents the earnings capacity typical of the firm. Then, an estimate of the taxes that would be due on that profit is determined. Extraordinary items may or may not give rise to accompanying income tax adjustments. For example, an extraordinary item involving the writing off of assets no longer needed in business operations may not be deductible from federal income taxes. When an extraordinary loss item is deductible for tax purposes in the year in question, the extraordinary loss is shown below the net profit from operations line, reduced by the accompanying tax saving. As a result, taxes payable on regular operations are shown separately from those arising from the extraordinary item, for example:

Extraordinary loss from confiscation of Iran Properties	$6,000,000
Less tax saving	$2,800,000
Net extraordinary loss	$3,200,000

§6.9 The Concept of Accrual

Most individuals and households keep their accounts (such as they are) on a **cash basis**. Salaries and other income are entered into the checkbook when they are received; payments are entered when they are made. For most people, this method of accounting for personal income and expenses is reasonably satisfactory. Most businesses, however, find this method of accounting inadequate, and operate on an **accrual basis**. Indeed, accrual accounting is required by GAAP and by the Internal Revenue Service (IRS) for most businesses that sell goods.

The basic difference between the accrual and cash methods of accounting lies in the answer to the question, when should transactions be recognized? The cash method of accounting is based on the convention that transactions should be recognized when cash comes in or goes out. That system, however, is likely to lead to very erratic results and be subject to manipulation in businesses that maintain an inventory of goods. A large purchase of inventory at a very favorable price in one year should not be treated as an expense for that period. To do so may result in the business showing a loss for the accounting period for that year even though the purchase permitted the business to enjoy high profits in later years. If the accounting process is to reflect what is really happening, that inventory should be treated as an asset and taken into expense only when sales are made from it. Hence, the development of **accrual accounting**.

Second, emphasis on cash payments or receipts ignores the most significant event in the transaction, namely doing the work or committing oneself to pay for something that is used immediately but paid for later.

Third, it is relatively easy to manipulate accounting results if a transaction enters the accounting system only when cash comes in or goes out. One can defer receipt or put off paying, whichever happens to be in the interest of the management of the business. (This should not be construed as indicating that manipulation is not possible in the accrual system. It is, but it is not as easy.) Businesses in which inventories of physical goods are an important aspect of the operation almost universally operate on the accrual system to avoid distortions of income and expense caused by the timing of raw material purchases and sales on cash or credit. It is for this reason that the Internal Revenue Code requires accrual tax accounting for such businesses.

In any event, the accrual system assumes that transactions should be recognized and taken into account when they have their primary economic impact, not necessarily when cash is received or disbursed. On the revenue side, that time is usually the rendering of service or the sale of goods. In the case of revenue items dependent on the passage of time — say, rent or interest — the critical event is simply the passage of time. As a practical matter, that means such items are taken into account at the end of specific time periods: weekly, monthly, quarterly, or annually. Thus, revenue items may, and often do, accrue even though they have not been billed and even though there is no right to immediate payment.

Under the accrual system, costs or expenses are taken into account when the benefit occurs, which is typically when the revenues to which they relate are earned. In short, the goal of the accrual system is the matching of expenses with corresponding revenues wherever possible. However, a variety of indirect ex-

penses cannot be allocated to specific revenues; these items are accrued over time and independent of revenues. Examples of indirect expenses are interest on borrowed funds or rent that must be paid on land.

Cash receipts or payments that relate to income or expenses for accounting periods other than the current period are viewed as creating assets or liabilities on the balance sheet; these assets or liabilities are **parked** on the balance sheet and **written off** (i.e., taken as expenses) in the year in which they are recognized for accounting purposes. A few examples of the accrual concept may be useful. In the following examples, assume that the business's accounting period closes on December 31.

(a) The business purchases inventory (goods for resale) on 12/15, paying $500 in cash. This transaction affects only the balance sheet, increasing inventory by $500 and reducing cash by the same amount. Although it should go without saying that assets generally equal liabilities plus owner's equity, it is important to understand that this equation holds true for every individual transaction. In other words, the balance sheet must remain in balance at all times. If an asset is increased, either another asset must be decreased or liabilities or owner's equity must be increased. Thus, a particular transaction may affect just one side of the balance sheet in offsetting ways, or it may affect both sides of the balance sheet by the same amount. If an increase in an asset is not offset by a decrease in another asset or an equal increase in a liability, then it must generate an increase in owner's equity. If there is an increase in owner's equity, it must be because the business made a profit. Profits must, of course, be reflected on the income statement, and accordingly it may take more than one set of journal entries to account for such a transaction. Nevertheless, the relationship between the balance sheet and the income statement can be appreciated if one simply keeps in mind that every transaction must leave the balance sheet in balance and that any net increase or decrease in assets or liabilities must affect owner's equity and must thus somehow be reflected on the income statement. Finally, it should also be clear that there are many transactions that involve cash flows that do not affect the income statement. Indeed, the above purchase of inventory for cash is just such a transaction.

(b) On 1/6, the business sells to a retail customer from inventory goods that cost $300; the sales price for the goods is $600, to be paid within 90 days. This transaction decreases inventory by $300 (the cost of the goods sold) and increases accounts receivable by $600 (the sales price that is now owed to the business). The $300 difference is the profit on the transaction and it increases retained earnings, which of course is a component of owner's equity. When the increase in retained earnings is reported on the income statement, it has two components: sales revenue ($600) and cost of goods sold ($300).

(c) On 3/9, the customer pays her $600 bill. Cash is increased by this amount and accounts receivable are reduced. Again, the transaction affects only the asset side of the balance sheet and thus has no impact on earnings, although it clearly constitutes cash flow.

The effect of these various transactions is that the sale of goods is taken into income in January when the sale takes place; the earlier purchase of inventory is parked in the inventory account on the balance sheet until the sale occurs, and then it is moved into the income statement as part of cost of goods sold. The corporation's income accounts would not be affected if the payment

of the account had occurred in the following year, whether the transaction was a cash rather than a credit sale, or whether the customer had made a series of layaway payments in the prior year. In each event, the income statement would reflect the sales revenue of $600, in the year in which the sale itself was made.

(d) The business opens a new store on 12/1 and is required by its new landlord to pay two years of rent in advance. Transactions of this type require the creation of a new balance sheet asset account, "prepaid rent." At the end of one month, $500 is deducted from the prepaid rent account, thus decreasing owners' equity by the same amount. When the decrease in retained earnings is recorded on the income statement, it is called "rent expense." During each month of the following year, the appropriate amount of rent is deducted from prepaid rent and retained earnings are reduced. The effect of this treatment is that the prepayment of rent is actually allocated to each time period during which the business has the use of the rented property for income statement purposes. Prepaid expenses are assets, while the receipt of prepaid income creates a liability.

(e) The business owns an apartment house. It rents an apartment to X, who is required to pay the first and last month's rent of $800 (for a total of $1600) when he enters into the lease on the first day of the tenancy. A new balance sheet liability, "unearned rent," is created to reflect the receipt of the rent for which services have not yet been provided. At the end of the first month, rental income is recognized for the first month's rent. Liabilities are reduced by $800, which means that retained earnings must increase by $800 in order for the balance sheet to remain in balance. When the increase in retained earnings is reported on the income statement, it is called "rental income." The unearned rent liability remains on the books of the business until the last month of the rental. It is eliminated when the last month's rent has been earned.

There is a common theme in all of these examples: Because revenue is not accounted for until the transaction occurs (or time passes, in the case of rental income), any receipts or payments of cash allocable to other accounting periods are treated purely as balance sheet entries. Prepaid expenses are treated as assets and unearned receipts are treated as liabilities. Although some people sometimes find it difficult to accept that the prepayment of an expense item creates an asset while the receipt of unearned income creates a liability, this treatment may be appreciated intuitively by noting that the prepayment of an expense is indistinguishable in principle from the purchase of an asset such as a truck. Indeed, in one sense, all assets on a balance sheet other than cash are expenses waiting to be written off (used up) in an appropriate future accounting period.

It should also be noted that in accrual accounting, income and expense items are not adjusted for many transactions that intuitively seem to be income-generating or expense-generating unless gain or loss is recognized. For example, no income is recognized upon the receipt of prepaid rent; that rent can be earned only by the passage of time.

§6.10 Accrual Accounting for Long Lead-Time Businesses

The simple accrual system works best for businesses that have large numbers of profit-making or loss-creating transactions during each accounting pe-

riod. In other types of businesses, however, traditional accrual accounting results in the bunching of income, making accounting results incomparable from one year to the next.

A classic example of this latter type of business is an airplane manufacturer with a contract that involves two years of design and construction work before the first plane is delivered. If the contract involves, say, a $60,000,000 payment when each plane is delivered, the airplane manufacturer, if it follows simple accrual accounting principles, will show no income during the two-year development phase and will record its first revenue with the sale of the first plane in the third year of the contract. If the airplane manufacturer follows conventional accrual principles, it will capitalize development expenses (i.e., treat them as an asset rather than as expenses) and will show zero income for the first two years, followed by profits in the years during which the planes are sold. However, if it appears likely from the outset that the project will be profitable, it is more realistic to allocate a portion of the ultimate profit to each of the two developmental years in which much of the work is done rather than show an erratic and unrealistic zero-profit income statement for two years, followed by years of high income when the airplanes are sold. Much the same pattern may be present in the development of software for computers, the production of motion pictures, heavy construction projects, and other business activities that involve development periods of more than one year.

The application of an accrual accounting system to such businesses is not without controversy. The accountant takes pride in treating recognition issues conservatively, and refusing to recognize income unless it is certain to be earned. The difficulty with our hypothetical airplane manufacturer is that it is usually not possible to determine that the airplane being developed will in fact be salable until after sales begin.

Accounting on a basis other than traditional accrual principles is nevertheless well accepted in some industries. For example, many companies engaged in commercial construction report income on a percentage-of-contract-completion basis that spreads anticipated profits over the lifetime of the contract. Sellers of large consumer or commercial equipment on credit may report income on the installment basis rather than using the point of sale as the time of realization of income. Deciding what is the most appropriate time for revenue recognition is often a matter of judgment.

§6.11 Depreciation, Depletion, and Amortization

Depreciation, **depletion**, and **amortization** all refer to the allocation of the cost of a long-lived asset to consecutive accounting periods as expenses to reflect the gradual using up of the asset. Depreciation is associated with the process of writing off plant and equipment; depletion refers to the gradual exhaustion of natural resources. Amortization is used with intangible assets (such as copyrights or patents) and deferred charges (such as organizational expenses, research and development costs, or dry holes in oil and gas exploration). In a sense, the writing off or **expensing** of long-lived assets is similar to any prepayment of future expenses: The purchase of a truck, for example, can

be seen as a prepayment to ensure the availability of the truck over the balance of its useful life in much the same way that the advance payment of two years' rent creates an asset — prepaid expenses.

One of the transactions discussed in this chapter was the purchase of a used truck for $3,000. This purchase led to an increase in the asset "truck" of $3,000, the truck's purchase price (historical cost). The following steps are required to calculate the depreciation of this asset following its acquisition: Someone (presumably an accountant) estimates (1) the useful life of the truck and (2) the scrap or resale value of the truck, if any, at the end of that period. Assuming that **straight line depreciation** is being followed, the difference between the original cost and the **scrap value** (or **salvage value**) is then divided by the number of years of the truck's estimated useful life. That amount is treated as the annual expense of using up the truck. For example, if the useful life of the truck is estimated to be five years, and the resale value of the truck at the end of that period is estimated to be zero, straight line depreciation accounting requires that the business include as an expense, in each of the next five years, ($3,000 – 0) / 5, or $600 per year. In each of those years, the asset truck will decrease by $600 and there will be a corresponding $600 decrease in retained earnings. When reported on the income statement, this decrease in retained earnings will be called **depreciation expense**. Often, a special account called a **contra account** will be added to the balance sheet to record the cumulative decrease in the depreciable asset. After two years of depreciation have been expensed, the balance sheet entry will look like this:

Equipment (truck)	$3,000	
Less: Accumulated depreciation	$1,200	
		$1,800

There are several important points to make about this simple example. First, the balance sheet item **accumulated depreciation** is purely a bookkeeping item. There is no separate fund or separate account in the corporation's assets marked "depreciation account" or "depreciation reserve" that contains $1,200, and there are no funds set aside to help pay for the truck's replacement when it wears out. Rather, the $1,200 is simply the sum of two $600 items taken as expenses. Thus, in the example, instead of reducing the asset "truck" by $600, the contra account, "accumulated depreciation" would be increased by that amount. The offsetting charge to retained earnings remains the same.

Second, the truck will gradually wear out, and will presumably need to be replaced. Depreciation deductions do not affect this process in a direct way. The only real effect of depreciation expense is that it (1) reduces reported earnings without being a drain on the business's current cash flow, and (2) reduces the business's tax bill (assuming that the Internal Revenue Code permits the particular depreciation deduction to be calculated and claimed in the way proposed). This tax consequence arises because depreciation is a deductible expense for tax purposes, and larger depreciation deductions mean lower income subject to tax. Arguments for faster depreciation deductions are usually motivated to some extent by the prospect of larger tax deductions.

Third, after two years, the $3,000 amount reported for the truck has been

reduced to $1,800 on the books of the business through two depreciation deductions of $600 each. This $1,800 figure is called the **book value** of the truck (because it is the value of the truck as shown on the books of the business). Is there any relationship between this book value and what the truck is actually worth after two years? Probably not. If the current market value of the truck is in fact $1,800, it is purely by chance. Trucks do not usually decline in value at a steady rate precisely equal to that originally estimated by an accountant. Furthermore, the starting value for the depreciation calculation was the cost of the truck two years ago. What has happened to the used truck market in the meantime? Indeed, there is no reason to believe that the business originally paid the truck's fair market value when it bought the truck: It could have paid too much or too little. For accounting purposes, however, the value of the truck when it is purchased is its cost. Certainly, the depreciation calculation takes none of these factors into account. When the business sells the truck, it probably will be at a price different from its book value; the gain or loss on that transaction is reflected in income or retained earnings at that time.

Fourth, does the truck disappear after it has been reduced to zero on the books of the business? Of course not. If the truck still has economic value it may continue to be used in the business. In this case, the original estimate of the truck's useful life was too conservative — the truck was written off more quickly than its useful life actually warranted. Once the truck has been fully depreciated (i.e., reduced to its estimated scrap or resale value) no further depreciation deductions are available to the business for that truck if it continues to be used in the business thereafter. But if the truck is sold to another business, it may be depreciated all over again to the extent of the sale price.

This traditional way of handling depreciation has one justification: It requires that costs of certain assets be allocated in an orderly and verifiable fashion to different accounting periods. Whether or not the specific allocations to specific periods are accurate may be less important than that they be done on a systematic basis that approximates the useful life span of the asset.

The foregoing discussion has assumed that annual depreciation deductions would be calculated by dividing the depreciable value of the property by its expected life. This type of depreciation is usually called **straight line depreciation**, because the amount of the deduction for depreciation each year is constant over the life of the asset. That is, a graph of the book value of the asset over time would be a downward sloping straight line.

Accelerated depreciation systems involve placing relatively larger amounts of the depreciation deductions in the early years of the asset's life. These systems are to a large extent tax-oriented, because the increased deductions that these systems generate in the early years of the life of the asset, if accepted for federal income tax purposes, create significant tax benefits. In some circumstances, however, these systems may be independently justified from an accounting standpoint, because taking most of the depreciation charges in the early years of the asset's life more closely approximates actual market values for assets such as automobiles or trucks, which typically depreciate in value very rapidly during their early years of use.

Perhaps the most popular accelerated depreciation system is the **sum of the digits method**. In this method, the depreciation deduction is calculated

each year by creating a fraction, in which the numerator equals the number of years of useful life remaining and the denominator equals the sum of all the useful years of life of the asset. For example, for the truck with a five-year useful life expectancy, the denominator is 5 + 4 + 3 + 2 + 1, or 15. In the first year, the numerator is five (and the fraction is 5/15 or 1/3); in the second year, the numerator is 4 (and the fraction is 4/15); in the third year, the numerator is 3 (and the fraction is 3/15 or 1/5), and so forth. The logic of this system is not as important as the accelerated pattern of deductions that it creates.

Another popular accelerated depreciation system is the **declining balance method**. In this method, a stable fraction or percentage is applied to the current book value of the asset (historical cost minus previous depreciation deductions), rather than to original cost less salvage value. (Salvage value is not considered when applying the declining balance method.) The fraction or percentage is usually a multiple of the straight line depreciation rate. Thus, if the asset has a five-year life, the straight line depreciation rate is 20 percent per year. The double declining balance method applies twice the 20 percent rate, or 40 percent per year. For example, a $3,000 truck depreciated over five years by the double declining balance method would lead to the following depreciation deductions in the first five years:

Cost less depreciation	Rate	Depreciation deduction
$3,000	40%	$1,200
(3,000 − 1,200) = 1,800	40%	$720
(1,800 − 720) = 1,080	40%	$432
(1,080 − 432) = 638	40%	$259.20
(638 − 259.20) = 378.80	40%	$151.52

The **150 percent declining balance method** would entail the use of a 30 percent rate on a five-year asset. The declining balance method, like the sum of the digits method, results in very substantial deductions in early years. In the above example, the double declining balance method results in a write-off of 40 percent of the cost of the truck in the first year, compared with the 33 percent maximum write-off obtainable under the sum of the digits method.

Between 1981 and 1986, the Internal Revenue Code permitted the use of the **accelerated cost recovery system (ACRS)**. This depreciation system permitted accelerated depreciation by allowing the adoption of useful lives that are significantly shorter than the useful lives usually adopted for depreciation purposes. Under the ACRS, property was divided into four principal categories: 3-year, 5-year, 10-year, and 15-year property. In each instance, the actual useful lives of the assets were significantly longer than the depreciation period. For example, physical plant (buildings and the like) is usually written off over 30 or 40 years under traditional cost accounting: Under the ACRS, these assets fell within the 15-year category. The Tax Reform Act of 1986 generally extended the mandatory lives of assets and repealed the ACRS, but still retains a separate set of depreciation schedules that must be used for tax purposes. The result of different depreciation schedules for tax and for general accounting purposes is that businesses must calculate income for tax purposes on a different basis than income for the purpose of reporting results of operations to shareholders and

the public. Over the years, the divergence between these two methods of accounting have increased. Thus, the 1986 amendments to the Internal Revenue Code imposed an alternative minimum tax that in effect taxes a portion of accounting income as opposed to "taxable" income.

Depletion. The calculation of depletion of natural resources is usually made on the basis of estimates of the total recoverable resources in the property in question. The original purchase price or cost of the asset is divided by the estimated recoverable resources in the oil field, ore body, timber reserve, or other property to determine the cost per unit. Then, as each unit is captured and recovered, the cost is shown less accumulated depletion much the same way as depreciation is shown. In effect, depletion allocates the investment's initial cost in accordance with the recovery from the asset itself rather than over an arbitrary period of years, as is done with depreciation. If the field or ore body contains more resources than estimated, recovery after full depletion of the original cost results in a zero deduction for depletion of the additional units. For many years, depletion of oil or gas reserves was on an income rather than cost basis. That is, a fixed percentage of income (depending on the nature of the asset) was written off as cost. However, that is now permitted only for smaller unintegrated firms.

Amortization. The amortization of intangible assets and deferred charges follows a similar pattern, though the issues are considerably more controversial. Relatively few problems are created by traditional intangible assets such as patents, copyrights, and trade names that are purchased or developed internally so that the cost of acquisition or development can be readily established. Serious problems, however, are created by the capitalization and amortization of **research and development (R&D) costs**—the drilling of dry holes in connection with the successful exploration of oil and gas, and start-up expenses for a variety of new businesses or enterprises. If a firm expends funds for R&D, for example, it generally must treat the expenditures as expenses in the year incurred unless it can show that the expenditures will lead to marketable products. If the firm can prove this connection, it may capitalize the expenditures and write them off in future years against those products. Although R&D expenditures directed toward a specific product or project probably should be capitalized, basic or general research often cannot be allocated with any precision, and it is usually **expensed** when incurred. The variety of treatment of R&D expenses among publicly reporting companies was so great that GAAP was revised in 1974 to require that most R&D expenditures be expensed currently. Although this treatment is not entirely consistent with the basic notion that expenses should be recognized when the revenue to which they relate is recognized, the possibility of manipulation and foul play in financial statements was so great that an objective and relatively bright-line rule was thought appropriate.

The same basic issue is involved in the treatment of "dry holes" in petroleum exploration. A certain number of dry holes may be necessary for the exploration and development of a productive field. Many smaller oil companies capitalize the cost of the dry holes; these companies are known as full-cost companies, because the reported costs of their reserves include the cost of

drilling unsuccessful wells as well as successful ones. Larger companies usually expense the dry holes immediately; these companies are known as successful efforts companies because the reported costs of reserves include only costs of drilling successful wells. The financial statement set forth in Table 6-1 is an example of the reporting of costs by a successful efforts company. Its income statement simply sets forth as an expense: "Exploration expenses, including dry holes." At the present time, firms may use either accounting system but must disclose the extent of their reserves.

Prior to 1993, few intangible assets qualified for amortization for tax purposes. Only intangible assets distinct from goodwill or going concern value that had an ascertainable useful life were eligible to be amortized. Thus, a business that purchased another business for more than the fair market value of the tangible assets (which was and is often the case) could seldom write off the excess for tax purposes. Because of the large number of cases in which taxpayers sought to demonstrate that a particular asset qualified (and the concomitant strain of IRS resources), the Omnibus Budget Reconciliation Act of 1993 changed the rule and now allows most intangible assets to be amortized ratably over a 15-year period regardless of actual useful life. Certain assets, such as stock and financial instruments, copyrights, and sports franchises, do not qualify for amortization of Section 197 of the Internal Revenue Code, and assets acquired in certain transactions, most notably with related parties, are also excluded. Nevertheless, Section 197 is an important benefit for any business that acquires another business in a taxable transaction where (as is typical) the purchase price exceeds the tangible asset value.

§6.12 An Introduction to Inflation Accounting

Inflation creates several problems for the accounting system. For one thing, accounting assumes that each dollar is worth the same amount. During periods of **inflation**, this is not true: A dollar next year will buy less than a dollar this year. Second, artificial profits occur simply when assets are held during inflationary periods. These artificial profits should be distinguished from real profits occurring because of productive activity. Third, in determining the real costs of operation, it may be argued, one should view the business over an entire productive plant replacement cycle. In effect, one should view expenses as including all expenditures necessary to keep the productive plant in good order. Income should consist only of the amount by which revenues exceed the expenses so measured.

Most attention has been focused on the third problem, which naturally leads to a consideration of the use of replacement cost rather than historical cost in determining depreciation deductions. Replacement cost is the estimated cost of replacing the asset when it is used up or worn out. It seems clear that depreciation deductions based on historical cost are unrealistically low during periods of inflation if replacement cost is the standard. If depreciation deductions are too low, it follows that some portion of reported earnings represents the cost of replacing capital assets rather than income. On the other hand, depreciation accounting does not prevent a business from planning for future

price increases for capital equipment in the sense that it can set aside funds in a reserve for future capital equipment acquisitions. The business cannot, however, treat transfers to this reserve account as expenses that reduce income for accounting or tax purposes. Moreover, inflation may make it easier for the business to pay off existing debts that may even have been incurred to purchase the assets that are being depreciated too slowly. In other words, it may all come out in the wash. In any case, it is important to remember that the issue for accounting purposes is simply whether the income that the business reports is overstated because of inflation and, if so, whether a more realistic measure of income can be developed.

During the late 1970s and early 1980s, when the inflation rate was relatively high, attempts were made to devise a system of inflation accounting that would more adequately reflect the cost of capital asset replacement. The effort revealed that inflation accounting involved practical problems and was confusing to users of financial statements. Companies were required by the Securities and Exchange Commission to create alternative income statements on the basis of **current replacement costs** (i.e., replacement cost measured as of the time the financial statements were prepared without regard to the anticipated future life of the capital asset) rather than historical costs in calculating depreciation deductions. Current replacement cost, of course, comes much closer to the current value of the business's productive plant if it were to sell its assets today than do the historical cost figures.

On the other hand, there are conceptual problems inherent in the use of current replacement cost. For one thing, few businesses have real plans to sell off or replicate productive plant. Yet, this is what the use of current replacement cost assumes. Thus, the proposal can be criticized at the outset for attempting to measure a hypothetical scenario. Also, current replacement cost does not fully meet the theoretical objections to traditional depreciation accounting. A true replacement cost theory would require depreciation to be calculated on the basis of estimated replacement cost at the time when replacement is likely to occur.

The experiment with replacement cost accounting also revealed formidable practical problems in preparing alternative inflation statements. The most serious problem was that determinations of current replacement cost must involve estimates as to the current market value of many individual assets. Yet, there were no market quotations for many assets, and in the case of land or other unique assets, the comparability may be uncertain. Further, the introduction of soft numbers that cannot be objectively ascertained opens the way to fraud or "cooking the books." One major advantage of historical cost depreciation accounting is that the numbers used are more difficult to manipulate, because they are readily verifiable and represent real economic events in the past. Books based on historical cost also provide a complete historical record relating to each particular asset. Of course, the use of historical cost is hardly a guarantee against cooking the books, but current replacement cost accounting may be so easily subject to manipulation as to invite it. Indeed, the problem is even more serious if ultimate replacement cost estimates are used. Such estimates may need to be made years before replacement actually occurs, and some manner of handling erroneous asset life expectancies and unanticipated price changes

would need to be created. Such calculations would involve numerous assumptions about future price trends, times of replacement, and future changes in technology, and the resulting system would be even more subjective and open to abuse than the experimental current replacement cost standard.

In the 1990s, less attention has been given to the fundamental accounting issues created by inflation, in part because inflation pressures have eased. To the extent inflation is relevant to accounting's goals, the problems are not limited to asset valuations and depreciation deductions. All income figures are inflated to some degree if prices increase generally across the economy. For example, if we assume a 10 percent increase during one year because of inflation, the business's reported earnings will presumably also increase by about 10 percent as sales receipts and expenses both reflect the same percentage increases. It is doubtful, however, whether the owners of the business will feel 10 percent better off even though reported earnings are up by 10 percent. A plausible solution to this inflation problem might be to require all businesses to reduce current earnings by an appropriate inflation index. Then historical comparisons might be more meaningful, because all results would be stated in constant dollars.

These problems of inflation accounting suggest some final observations about the traditional accounting system. Earlier chapters of this book addressed the time value of money, and the importance of reducing future payments to current values. Traditional accounting practice is unrealistic in that it does not take into account the time value of money. Debentures carrying low or zero interest rates due in 30 years are reported as liabilities today on the balance sheet at their ultimate face value and no attempt is made to report these obligations at the current value of the future payments. In addition, the accounting system takes no account of past inflation; 1950 dollar amounts and current dollar amounts are sometimes added together within a single account without any recognition that 1950 dollars purchased a lot more than today's dollars do. These anomalies can be traced back to the use of historical cost as the core concept underlying modern accounting systems.

§6.13 Accounting for Inventory

Inventory includes (1) **finished goods** awaiting sale, (2) goods in various stages of production including raw materials (**work-in-process**), and (3) goods on hand that are ultimately consumed in the production of goods (**raw materials**). Accounting for inventory is complex primarily because there is tremendous variation from business to business as to the nature and variety of items maintained in inventory.

Control of inventory costs is a major component in determining whether a business is successful. Problems of pilferage or shortages are most likely to involve inventory. Unaccountable losses of inventory—whether due to pilferage, failure to maintain adequate records, spoilage, or other causes—are also called, somewhat charitably, **shrinkage**.

Goods that are manufactured or purchased are usually stored (or parked) in the inventory account on the balance sheet until they are taken into the

expense account of the income statement. Practical considerations, however, require most businesses to adopt artificial conventions for estimating inventory costs, because it is not practical for most businesses to keep track of each inventory item as it wends its way through the manufacturing process.

The most widely used inventory systems require businesses to record additions to inventory as they occur on the balance sheet, but to determine the cost of goods sold only at the end of each accounting period. The cost of goods sold for a period is determined at the close of the period by the following basic formula:

(1) Cost of goods sold = Opening inventory
+ Additions to inventory – Closing inventory

Both the opening inventory and the closing inventory are determined by taking physical counts of what is on hand at the end of an accounting period and then assigning it a dollar amount. In other words, an essential part of the year-end auditing process is a physical count of inventory. (The inventory amount at the end of one period (the **closing inventory**) is the inventory amount at the beginning of the next period (the **opening inventory**) so that only one physical count per year is necessary.) The manner of placing dollar amounts on the items counted when inventory additions occur at varying prices is the subject of the remainder of this section. Before turning to this question, however, a second formula should be introduced to make clear the importance of the physical inventory count and the manner of reporting that inventory in determining the profitability of the business:

(2) Gross profit = Net sales – Cost of goods sold

This formula reveals that every change in the number of dollars attributed to **cost of goods sold** leads to a dollar-for-dollar increase or reduction in the gross profit of the business. Further, these two formulas are obviously interrelated; one can substitute formula (1) into formula (2) to yield this:

(3) Gross profit = Net sales – Value of opening inventory
– Additions to inventory + Value of closing inventory

(Remember the effect of minus signs on other minus signs.) The implications to be drawn from formula (3) are these: First, every change in the number of dollars attributed to closing inventory also means a dollar-for-dollar change in gross profit. Second, the higher the closing inventory, the lower the cost of goods sold and the higher the gross profit. Correspondingly, the lower the closing inventory, the higher the cost of goods sold and the lower the gross profit.

That the closing inventory affects cost of goods sold is a result of the use of a formula to calculate the costs of goods sold: The calculation does not attempt to trace what specific inventory items were actually consumed during the period in question, but simply subtracts closing inventory from all inventory available to the business during the period (opening inventory plus additions

to inventory for the period). Because the increase of closing inventory by one dollar increases gross profit by one dollar, while the decrease of closing inventory by one dollar decreases gross profit by that amount, the manner of assigning dollar amounts to closing inventory significantly affects reported earnings.

Before turning to methods of measuring closing inventory, it may be helpful to consider the nature of the inventory of three prototype businesses. To take the simplest case first, assume that the business involves only the retail sale of new automobiles. The number of inventory items is relatively small and each inventory item — each new car — is clearly identifiable by serial number, and the cost of each item in inventory is readily known. In effect, each inventory item can be "tagged" with its applicable cost, and the process of determining the value of the closing inventory for such a business involves merely identifying which cars are on hand at the close of the period and adding up their costs.

Second, consider a corn oil manufacturer whose inventory consists of raw corn to be crushed for oil. The corn is stored in a large bin. From time to time, additional corn is added, always to the top of the bin. Raw corn varies in price from day to day, although the amount and cost of all the raw corn added to the top of the bin can be readily calculated. When the manufacturing process needs more raw material, there are two alternatives: Either someone opens a valve and corn pours out of the bottom or someone opens a trap door and shovels some corn out from the top of the bin. Although one must question whether the use of corn from the bottom or from the top of the bin should be decisive in determining the value of closing inventory, there is clearly no way that the corn oil producer can physically tag raw corn and determine the cost of the raw materials on hand at the end of the accounting period. It must adopt a more general system.

Third, consider a large retail clothing store. It has on hand at any one time thousands of products in hundreds of sizes, styles, and colors. The number of units of each specific type, size, and style of product retained in inventory is relatively small for most items. Again, prices of individual items may vary over time so that, for example, two indistinguishable hats lying side by side may have originally cost different amounts. Although it may be theoretically possible to tag each item and determine its actual cost in closing inventory within the store, such a system is not very practical or cost-justified. With the development of computerized sales recording and reordering systems for many retail operations, tagging may become more feasible, but it is unlikely to supplant existing accounting methods of measuring closing inventory.

These last two prototypes are much more typical of the average inventory problems that businesses face than is the tagged inventory of the retail new car business. Indeed, when one considers the problems of the service department of the hypothetical retail new car business with an inventory consisting of replacement parts, boxes of spark plugs, bins of screws and bolts, barrels of motor oil or transmission fluid, and the like, it should be apparent that even a new car dealer must adopt generalized accounting procedures for much of its inventory.

Specific identification inventory method. Intuitively, the simplest method of assigning dollar amounts to closing inventory is to keep track of the cost of individual items. The new car inventory of the automobile dealer is a

Table 6-4

| Date | Purchases | | Sales |
	No. units	Cost	No. units
On hand	200	$5	
3/1	100	$6	
3/15			200
6/15	400	$7	
7/15			300
8/15	200	$8	
12/10			300
12/15	300	$9	
Close	400	?	

good illustration. This system, however, has basic problems. Assume that the information in Table 6-4 about one inventory item (all of which items are identical) is available. As in other examples used throughout this chapter, only a skeletal number of transactions is set forth to illustrate the basic principles.

If one can establish, by examining the "tags," that the 400 units on hand at the end of the accounting period consisted of (a) 200 units purchased on 8/15, (b) 100 units purchased on 3/1, and (c) 100 units carried over from the start of the year, one can determine the value of the closing inventory:

$$200 \times 8 + 100 \times 6 + 100 \times 5 = \$2,700$$

Of course, from this number, one can determine the cost of goods sold and the gross profit of the business from the formulas set forth earlier in this section.

One immediate problem with this method of measuring closing inventory is that it may encourage management to behave opportunistically. Management can increase or decrease gross profit by selecting which units are sold and which units are carried over into closing inventory. For example, if it wished to increase gross profit, management might sell all the cheaper items and keep in inventory only the items purchased on 8/15 and 12/15, so that the closing inventory value would be:

$$300 \times 9 + 100 \times 8 = \$3,500$$

Similarly if management wished to reduce gross profit, possibly to defer the profit to the next accounting period, it could sell the most expensive items and preserve the cheaper ones in closing inventory. It should be emphasized that even though gross profit may be manipulated in this fashion, the real worth of the business is unchanged.

Weighted average method. This method determines the weighted average price of every unit of inventory on hand at any time during the accounting period and assigns that average value to every unit. It is a "weighted" average because the number of units at each price is taken into account:

$$\frac{200 \times 5 + 100 \times 6 + 400 \times 7 + 200 \times 8 + 300 \times 9}{1,200 \text{ (the total number of units)}} = \frac{8,700}{1,200} = \$7.25 \text{ per unit}$$

The average cost per unit in the above example is $7.25; the value of closing inventory is then $400 \times 7.25 = \$2,900$, and the cost of goods sold is $800 \times 7.25 = \$5,800$.

This method is not widely used in part because of its complexity in other than the simplest situations, and in part because the system creates its own anomalies. For example, the purchase of 300 units on 12/15 in the foregoing example increased the cost of all goods sold during the year even though all the actual sales of goods occurred before this final purchase.

First-in first-out method. One widely used method of computing closing inventory is to assume that the earliest items in inventory are always sold first. In the foregoing example, the sale of 800 units during the year is assumed to be composed of the earliest items acquired; the 200 items carried over from the prior accounting period and the purchases on 3/1, 6/15, and, in part, on 8/15. Closing inventory would then consist of 300 units at $9 and 100 units at $8, for a total of $3,500. This method of computing inventory is universally known as **FIFO**, which stands for first-in first-out.

FIFO has certain advantages. For one thing, it actually conforms with the physical inventory practices of many businesses, which follow the principle that because of spoilage, staleness, or obsolescence, the oldest items should always be sold first. That would be true, for example, for our corn oil producer if the corn was always poured from the bottom. Second, FIFO is relatively easy to administer. Third, it eliminates the possible manipulation of gross profit by management that is inherent in any system of assigning varying costs to specific inventory units. Under FIFO, it makes no difference whether the corn is taken from the bottom or from the top; in either case it is presumed that the oldest corn is used first. Finally, because inventory is always composed of the last-acquired items, the amount of closing inventory on the balance sheet is likely to reflect closely the current market value of inventory items. In this sense, FIFO improves the reliability of the balance sheet because the important inventory item reflects the most current prices at which inventory was actually purchased. But, as will be seen, it has the opposite effect on the income statement.

Last-in first-out method. The major alternative to FIFO proceeds on the opposite assumption, namely that the last items are always sold first, hence the acronym **LIFO**, which stands for last-in first-out. (When comparing LIFO with FIFO, it may be helpful to think of LIFO as FISH — first-in still-here.) In the foregoing example, the 400 units of closing inventory is assumed to consist of 200 units at $5, 100 units at $6, and 100 units at $7, for a total value of $2,300. No account is taken of the sequence of actual subtractions from inventory in applying either FIFO or LIFO. If one chooses LIFO, it is assumed that corn is always taken from the top of the bin no matter what the actual practice is.

The advantages of LIFO over FIFO arise because of inflation. By generally increasing inventory replacement costs consistent with inflation, LIFO tends to decrease the value of closing inventories, thereby reducing reported income and federal income tax liability. (Since 1939, businesses have generally been permitted to use LIFO in calculating federal income tax.) Indeed, if one assumes that inventory costs increase steadily, FIFO maximizes the business's taxes, while

LIFO minimizes them. Arguably, every business should shift from FIFO to LIFO simply because of this tax saving. Paradoxically, however, some companies continue to use FIFO despite the virtually universal view of accountants and financial management strategists that most companies would obtain significant tax benefits from adopting LIFO. One argument that is sometimes made for FIFO is that the stock market would react negatively to lower earnings figures. But studies of securities prices of businesses that shift from FIFO to LIFO indicate that the market does not reduce securities prices to reflect the reduced earnings caused by the shift to LIFO. In other words, markets apparently understand that the reduction in earnings caused by a change in accounting for inventory is not a real change in earnings.

The tax savings arising from LIFO are permanent as a practical matter. Theoretically, tax savings arising from LIFO will be lost when the low-cost LIFO inventory is liquidated. Indeed, when inventory is totally liquidated, FIFO and LIFO should have led to the same total cost of goods sold. This, however, ignores the time value of money: The immediate reduction of taxes through LIFO is worth much more than the future increase in taxes when the LIFO inventory is consumed. Moreover, most companies go on for years or centuries without totally liquidating inventory. Thus, practically speaking, the tax benefits of the LIFO election are not only immediate, but they are also permanent.

A second advantage of LIFO is that it tends to cause reported earnings to reflect the cost of goods sold more accurately. LIFO uses more current inventory costs. FIFO tends to make the inventory number shown on the balance sheet relatively current, but it overstates earnings. LIFO emphasizes the accuracy of the income statement over that of the balance sheet — consistent with modern thinking about the relative roles of the two statements. The major disadvantage of LIFO is that the cost of inventory as shown on the balance sheet tends to become increasingly obsolete if, as is usually the case, the business maintains a stable or increasing inventory over several years. If a stable inventory is assumed, the LIFO inventory will always be reported at the cost it had as of the date on which the LIFO election was made. In other words, it is quite possible that a current balance sheet reflects inventory costs based on, say, 1950 product prices.

A second major problem with LIFO arises when, by reason of a strike or shortage, for example, a LIFO inventory must be partially consumed to keep up current production or sales. The inventory so consumed, which is carried on the books at an artificially low price, causes earnings to be inflated solely because of the method of accounting for inventory costs.

A final observation may be made about the choice between FIFO and LIFO in inflationary periods. Irrespective of the inventory accounting system adopted, profits are going to be inflated during inflationary periods simply from price increases occurring during the period between the time of purchasing inventory and the time of recording it as an expense. The profit that the business records is in part its normal operating profit from whatever business it is in and in part an abnormal trading profit caused by price increases during the manufacturing or resale process. LIFO tends to minimize the amount of this artificial profit, but does not eliminate it entirely. Elimination would require a radical

shift to a current value system for reporting inventory consumed during the accounting period similar to that discussed in the previous section relating to depreciable plant and equipment. For example, one might imagine a system based on a next-in first-out (NIFO) convention. Such a proposal has never been adopted. But LIFO is more sensitive to the effect of inflation on income statements than is FIFO.

Of course, not all goods appreciate in value over time, even during inflationary periods. Changes in technology may lead to price reductions even though prices generally have increased. A good example is the modern personal computer industry, which over the last decade has seen product prices decline as product quality and sophistication have improved steadily. Firms in such an industry have little or no tax reason to adopt LIFO accounting.

§6.14 Why Does the Accountant Use Historical Cost?

Historical cost has little or nothing to do with value. Value usually means the price established by transactions between willing buyers and sellers in a market. It might also mean the value of the asset to the user, or the cost of reproducing or replacing the asset. Usually, the one thing it most certainly does not mean is what the asset cost, perhaps years earlier. Yet, that is precisely the number from which most financial statements under GAAP are derived. The use of historical cost as the basis for accounting can be justified on several pragmatic grounds. It fits in easily with the intricate systems of accounts created under principles of double entry bookkeeping. It is also objective and easily verifiable. Indeed, the use of historical cost is so basic to the modern accounting system that even assets whose current market values may be determined without difficulty are nevertheless recorded at cost. The value of a portfolio of marketable securities, for example, may be determined by a single telephone call to a securities broker. Yet, such securities are always shown at cost on the financial statements though it is customary to show current market values as a parenthetical addition to the balance sheet as part of the description of the account:

> "Marketable securities at cost (market
>   value 12/31/87, $3,500,000) $2,800,000."

A corollary of the basic historical cost principle is that a business should not record appreciation in the value of assets until that appreciation has been realized by sale or disposition of the asset.

Theoretically, one could develop an alternative accounting system that immediately recorded unrealized appreciation. Abstractly, such a system is neither right nor wrong. However, such a system would be risky, because asset values that go up can also go down, as was vividly demonstrated by the Great Depression and more recently by the thrift crisis. Moreover, there is a serious risk that such asset values might be intentionally overstated.

A couple of important qualifications to the historical cost principle are contained in GAAP. One qualification is that GAAP assumes that the business is a **going concern**. If an auditor concludes that the business is contemplating

liquidation or is otherwise unlikely to survive, he or she should insist that the basis for reporting values be changed from historical cost to liquidation values. As a practical matter, that change usually results in a significant mark-down in reported amounts and the elimination of many assets from the balance sheet. For example, organizational expenses may be capitalized and viewed as an asset only if the business is a going concern: It is clear that these expenses have little or no inherent market value if the business is to be liquidated.

Another major qualification is embodied in the principle that assets the firm holds for resale should be reported at the **lower of cost or market**. In other words, if the market value of inventory or marketable securities is less than their original cost, those assets should be immediately written down to current market value. In connection with inventory, this devaluation of assets may be made either on an item-by-item basis, or by classes of products. With respect to securities, it is customary to net appreciation and depreciation in value of all marketable securities, and to make the write-down only if the balance is negative.

The principles outlined in this section are sometimes cited as illustrating the conservatism of the accounting profession. Accountants may in fact be conservative, but it should be recognized that historical cost can just as easily overstate current value as understate it. To be sure, it seems likely that using historical cost understates assets more often than it overstates them. But although the accountant's conservatism is likely to hurt (say) sellers of shares, it is equally likely to help buyers of shares, assuming, of course, that either takes financial statements at face value.

§6.15 Current Value Accounting and Other Issues

The issue of historical cost versus current value accounting arose in connection with the savings and loan and banking industry problems in the late 1980s and early 1990s. By using historical cost figures, many insolvent financial institutions were able to hide their true condition. To a significant extent, accounting rules have been revised to require financial institutions to mark the book value of assets down to market. In 1993, the FASB required such mark-downs for bonds held for resale. Similar action is required (at least in footnote form) for loans for which the bank has had to renegotiate the terms in order to avoid foreclosure. And foreclosed property must be reflected at current market value rather than at the price bid at the foreclosure sale.

Some major insurers, recognizing that the book values of major commercial real estate investments exceed their market values, have created reserves to cover potential losses to be realized when the properties are sold. These reserves involve a debit against current income and a credit to a reserve for losses. This practice has been limited to the very largest insurance companies, and the amounts involved do not significantly reduce reported earnings.

In December 1991, the FASB issued Statement of Financial Accounting Standards (SFAS) No. 107, which requires all reporting entities to disclose the fair value of virtually all financial instruments owned by the entity. SFAS 107 is a disclosure requirement, not a change in accounting principles, so that disclo-

sure may be made either in the body of the financial statements or in notes to the statements. In 1996, the FASB formally proposed that derivatives and other hedging instruments be shown at fair market value rather than historical cost.

The FASB also has acted in two other areas that have proved to be highly controversial. A regulation approved in 1991 requires corporations to book today their estimate of the costs of health care for retired employees and their dependents. This requirement caused a number of corporations to report material reductions in earnings and doubtless has encouraged the trend toward shifting the cost of retired health care to the retirees themselves.

In 1993, the FASB proposed a highly controversial rule that would have required issuing companies to subtract the value of executive stock options from current earnings. Ultimately, the FASB declined to adopt the rule, but instead adopted a rule that requires that a footnote state what the charge against earnings would have been if the estimated value of the options were treated as an expense.

§6.16 Accumulated Retained Earnings and Statement of Source and Application of Funds

The previous discussion has focused exclusively on the balance sheet and the income statement, the most fundamental accounting statements. These statements are usually accompanied by two additional statements, which are described briefly in this section.

The first, the **Accumulated Retained Earnings Statement** (or **Statements of Changes in Retained Earnings**, as it is often titled) makes explicit the direct link between the income statement and the balance sheet. Table 6-5 provides an illustration.

Table 6-5 is based on the following self-evident formula:

Retained earnings at beginning of period + Income for period
− Dividends declared = Retained earnings at end of period

This formula makes explicit the common sense notion that earnings for the accounting period in question should be reduced by dividends declared during

Table 6-5
ABC Incorporated
Accumulated Retained Earnings Statement
for Year Ended December 31, 1997

Balance January 1	$1,022,000
Net income for year	511,000
Total	1,533,000
Less: Dividends paid	
On preferred stock	30,000
On common stock	188,000
Balance December 31	1,315,000

Table 6-6
ABC Incorporated
Statement of Source and Application of Working Capital
1997

Sources of working capital		
Operations		
Net income	$511,000	
Depreciation	275,000	
Amount borrowed from bank	100,000	
Total sources of working capital		886,000
Applications of working capital		
Cash dividends		
Preferred stock	30,000	
Common stock	188,000	
Purchases of plant and equipment	305,000	
Increase (decrease) in other assets	(10,000)	
Total applications of working capital		513,000
Net increase in working capital		$373,000

the period in computing the increment to retained earnings from the start of the period. If new permanent capital is raised during the accounting period or shares are issued pursuant to the exercise of conversion rights or options, this information may also appear in the Accumulated Retained Earnings Statement, or it may be described in yet another table usually entitled **Statement of Changes in Owners' Equity Accounts**.

The second table, usually entitled **Statement of Changes in Financial Position** or **Statement of Source and Application of Funds** (or **Statement of Source and Application of Working Capital**) is a reclassification of items that appear in the balance sheet and income statement. It concentrates on the flow of funds or working capital during the accounting period—how a company acquired working capital and what it did with it. A typical funds statement is shown in Table 6-6.

The logic underlying this statement is curious. In effect it begins with the assumption that income is equivalent to cash and then proceeds to list all the ways in which it is not and to add or subtract appropriate amounts to arrive at a number equal to the change in working capital.

There is a considerably greater degree of variation or diversity in this statement than in other GAAP statements. There is little agreement on what is meant by **funds**. Indeed, in some cases the concept of funds does not include cash. About half of large publicly held corporations use a working-capital concept of funds, something like that appearing in Table 6-6. The other half may use cash, cash and equivalents, or cash and marketable securities. This definition of funds is probably the result of efforts to use the sources and applications statement as a cash-flow statement, that is, as a way of reporting the company's liquidity. The problem is that cash flows in many ways that do not necessarily result in changes in balance sheet amounts year to year. Thus, no matter how one tries to patch it up, the statement fails to disclose vital cash-flow information that many users of financial statements want and need. In the

end, there is no substitute for doing one's own analysis. This diversity sharply limits the comparability and usefulness of these statements. The variation in and questionable usefulness of these statements may be a result of accounting preoccupation with the profit and loss statement at the cost of more complete information about actual cash flows. It has been suggested that the funds statement should be standardized and made into a true cash-flow statement.

CHAPTER 7

HOW TO READ AND USE FINANCIAL STATEMENTS

§7.1 Introduction

The analysis of financial statements is usually the responsibility of accountants and other experts specifically trained in that field. Nevertheless, corporate lawyers are often expected to examine and analyze unfamiliar financial statements on behalf of clients with or without the assistance of outside experts. Moreover, in the routine representation of business clients, lawyers are involved in transactions in which the financial position of another entity is important. As a result, lawyers must have some knowledge of financial statements and must be familiar with the way financial statements are prepared, how useful information can be squeezed from them, and how to recognize the signs of trouble. This chapter provides an introduction to this arcane art.

§7.2 Uses of Financial Statements

When examining financial statements, one must always keep in mind the examination's purpose. What is the client proposing to do? The client may be considering (1) lending money to a business; (2) buying from, selling to, or

otherwise dealing with a business; (3) making an investment in a business; or (4) buying a business outright. The attitude one takes toward financial statements depends on the nature of the proposed transaction and the client's exposure to loss should the other party run into unexpected financial difficulties or be unable to perform as contemplated.

If the proposed transaction involves lending money to or entering into commercial transactions with the business on a relatively short-term basis, an extended analysis of financial statements is seldom required. The question usually is simply whether the business is likely to be able to repay the loan or pay for the goods or services being provided. For this purpose, a credit check through one of the commercial credit reporting agencies may provide information about the bill-paying history of the business that is more useful than information garnered from financial statements. In addition, useful information about specific companies may be obtained from a variety of publications such as Standard & Poor's Corporation Records, Moody's Industrial Manual, and the Value Line Industrial Survey.

The risk of nonpayment may also be reduced or eliminated by simple protective measures: obtaining a lien or security interest in the debtor's property, requiring the principal shareholders of the debtor to guarantee personally the payment of the debt, or requiring the debtor to provide a letter of credit from a responsible financial institution that assures that payment will be made when required. If a personal guarantee is sought, it is essential to obtain financial statements of both the guarantors and the principal debtor.

In assessing the risk of nonpayment, the debtor's financial statements may be examined to determine whether the transaction is of such a magnitude that it may strain the debtor's normal resources. If so, a short-range cash-flow analysis may be done in order to determine how the debtor contemplates obtaining the necessary funds to complete the transaction. When the risk appears to be substantial, a client may structure the transaction in order to limit risk (e.g., by providing that performance may be suspended if payments are not made at specified intervals).

Decisions concerning long-term investment in another business (either of debt or equity) are almost always preceded by an investigation into the nature and quality of the business. Expert analysis of the financial statements (often referred to simply as financials) is generally a part of this investigation. Earning potential or longer-term cash flows should be evaluated. Financial statements, prepared on the basis of generally accepted accounting principles (GAAP) or otherwise, may be the principal source of information for this analysis.

In this situation, one must always be alert for danger signals indicating that the business is not as healthy as the financial statements might indicate. In making a financial analysis, one should always try to obtain financial statements for at least the last five years to study trends not apparent from current financial statements only. A declining rate of growth or a rate of growth smaller than the industry as a whole are signs of possible trouble. Many danger signals, however, cannot be detected solely from the financial statements themselves. They include unusual turnover of key personnel, changes in auditors, and a gradual slowdown in the rate of payment of liabilities. Additional factors are described in subsequent sections.

If a client proposes to acquire control of the business, a basic question is whether the client wants to acquire specific assets or the entire business. Matters of concern are whether the book value of assets significantly overstates their market value, whether the cash flows of the business appear to be sufficient to finance future growth, and whether the business has undisclosed or contingent or **off-book liabilities**, such as pending litigation, the probability of future product liability claims, tax claims, and the like. Obviously, whether such liabilities exist cannot be discovered solely from examining the financial statements.

When a business is purchased, risk can be reduced in various ways. For example, one may require the seller to warrant the accuracy of the financial statements and to represent that there are no material off-book liabilities. A right to rescind the entire transaction may be negotiated if these warranties and representations turn out to be false after the transaction is closed. It also may be possible to structure the transaction as an asset-purchase transaction that does not involve the assumption of contingent or undisclosed liabilities rather than as a stock-purchase transaction that leaves the purchased business subject to these liabilities. As a general rule, a purchaser of assets alone for fair value is not obligated to assume liabilities (unless, of course, the purchaser expressly agrees to do so). However, in some situations courts have ruled that an asset-purchaser must also take responsibility, for example, for product liability claims, despite express provisions that the purchaser does not assume such liabilities. And some claims, such as those for environmental harms, must effectively be assumed as a matter of statutory law no matter how the transaction is structured. When shares of stock in a corporation are acquired by purchase or the corporation itself is acquired by a merger, the business acquired (and quite possibly the acquirer as well) remains liable on preacquisition liabilities.

Negative factors, such as the existence of undisclosed or contingent liabilities, may affect only the amount of consideration being paid for the business. In some circumstances, however, the problems discovered may be so significant as to call into question the soundness of the entire transaction.

§7.3 GAAP and Non-GAAP Financial Statements

Publicly held corporations (i.e., corporations registered under the Securities Exchange Act of 1934), are required to prepare public financial statements in accordance with GAAP. A major purpose of these mandatory principles is to ensure comparability of public financial statements. In addition, there are standards for auditor independence and the conduct of audits that permit a user to deal with such financial statements with some confidence. However, one should not overstate the degree of reliability of financial statements on the basis of an unqualified or "clean" opinion by an outside auditor.

Even though GAAP is designed to ensure that operating results that different publicly held businesses report have a large degree of comparability, it is important to recognize that GAAP, like accounting generally, is not a set of precise mathematical rules. Rather, it is a set of principles intended to make financial statements useful to persons who use them. There is considerable

discretion as to how certain transactions are treated for accounting purposes. When transactions are material, a reference to the way they are treated should appear either in the auditor's statement or in the notes to the financial statements. Management, rather than the outside auditor, usually makes these discretionary decisions, though the outside auditor has a voice in the matter, and that voice may sometimes be decisive as discussed more fully below. Significant disagreements between a business and its outside auditors as to how a transaction should be treated under GAAP do not occur often, but the fact that they occur at all reveals that even fundamental accounting notions may be subject to challenge and that accounting principles are neither right nor wrong in any absolute sense. Like legal principles generally, the application of GAAP in a specific situation involves exercise of judgment.

Properly read and understood, financial statements created in accordance with GAAP can be used with some confidence. In any event, GAAP statements are the most that normally can be expected. The following sections of this chapter describe more or less standard methods of analysis of financial statements assuming the basic accuracy and comparability of the published figures. These methods of analysis usually may be applied to GAAP financial statements with relative confidence without making an extensive inquiry into what lies behind the figures.

Many smaller businesses and closely held corporations use professional accounting services but do not prepare financial statements on the basis of GAAP. Rather, such statements may incorporate GAAP treatment of some assets or transactions but depart from GAAP in other respects. Such statements may also be useful for analysis; indeed, there is no one right way to present the results of operations of a complex business. Statements that depart from GAAP, however, must be used with caution. Material adjustments may be necessary in a number of areas in order to reflect income accurately or to allow for comparison with businesses that follow GAAP. Of course, considerable variation also exists within GAAP statements in these respects as well.

It should not be assumed that there is a consistent bias in the direction of overstating assets or income in non-GAAP statements. Closely held corporations often adopt accounting principles in an effort to minimize income rather than to maximize it. For example, many closely held corporations follow a policy of "expensing" as many asset acquisitions as possible in order to reduce stated income and federal income taxes. Excessive salaries payable to the major equity owners of the business who control day-to-day operations may appear as expenses even though these salary payments should be treated as dividends. Similarly, expense accounts may reflect hidden compensation. In these instances, the reported earnings of the closely held corporation may be significantly understated. Moreover, even the assumption that a single accounting system has been consistently applied by a closely held corporation is open to question.

Finally, it is important to recognize that all accounting principles, whether or not GAAP, involve not only flexibility and discretion, but also conventions and assumptions about honesty and good faith. Financial statements are usually prepared to put the best possible face on management's performance, and, as discussed more fully below, management has considerable discretion as to which accounting conventions are adopted. No accounting system provides protection

against outright fraud or theft. There are many dishonest ways to cook the books even if they are nominally kept on a GAAP basis. One major fraud, for example, was based on rigging the inventory count at the end of the accounting period by counting four boxes of sutures as 44, three boxes of gauze pads as 33, and so forth. Even though the auditor participated in the physical count of inventory, it did not notice these discrepancies. By overstating the closing inventory, the perpetrators sought to overstate gross profit. Thereafter, the scheme was to "destroy" the nonexistent inventory thus created. Because one of the conspirators went to the Securities and Exchange Commission (SEC) in an effort to avoid prosecution, the scheme collapsed. Obviously, even the finest GAAP financial statements cannot guarantee the honesty and probity of their creation.

Although the idea that a business might keep multiple sets of books may sound vaguely criminal, there are very good reasons for doing so, and the practice is indeed common. For most purposes, the books of a business should be kept according to GAAP. Tax accounting, as dictated by the Internal Revenue Code (IRC) and regulations and practices thereunder, may differ significantly from GAAP. For example, under tax law, depreciation and depletion allowances may be able to be taken at a faster rate than is economically realistic for a particular business. Thus, taxes may legitimately be reduced. (The discrepancy is what gives rise to the **deferred tax** account one sometimes sees on a GAAP balance sheet.) Yet another situation that might call for a third set of books arises because corporation law often allows distributions to be made to shareholders on the basis of accounting principles set down as a matter of state statute. Although a few states expressly incorporate GAAP into their corporation laws, most do not. On the other hand, most states afford corporate boards of directors the ability to rely on financial statements rendered by trusted accounting professionals. Thus, in practice many boards of directors find it desirable to forgo whatever flexibility may be available by following statutory accounting principles. Finally, for purposes of negotiations in connection with mergers and acquisitions and in many valuation proceedings, yet another method of accounting involving the calculation of cash flow, as opposed to accounting income, is generally followed.

§7.4 Cash-Flow Financial Projections

In recent years, an alternative method of analysis — a study of expected cash flows — has become popular. Many persons believe that cash-flow analysis is inherently more reliable than GAAP financial statements in estimating the risks presented by specific investments. This is particularly true with short-term extensions of credit where repayment is not dependent on long-term profitability.

Cash-flow statements are usually specific projections of what funds are likely to be available to the business in the future. GAAP statements, of course, reflect what happened in the past, and projections of earnings trends into the future must be provided by the user of the financial statements.

When one encounters a financial statement or financial analysis that in-

cludes projections or cash-flow analysis, they should be examined with care, particularly the bases or assumptions on which projections of cash flow are made. It is very easy to project continued growth and continued improvement in sales, rents, or fees indefinitely into the future, but these projections are rarely realistic. Cash-flow projections that extend far into the future are obviously less reliable than short-term cash-flow projections based on results of operations in the recent past and indeed may be inherently unreliable. Since the early 1980s, the SEC has permitted good-faith projections and estimates of future cash flow to appear in disclosure documents, but good faith is no guarantee of accuracy.

Cash-flow analysis is not always focused on the future. In some cases, a lender or other investor will want to know whether a profitable company in fact generates enough cash to pay back a loan or otherwise make good on an obligation or investment. After all, one of the basic problems with accrual accounting is that a company may record profits and losses well before the cash actually flows. Thus, one of the more important functions of cash-flow analysis is to assess the liquidity of the company in the absence of any concern about whether the business is growing or shrinking.

As cash-flow analysis has gained popularity, techniques of estimation from traditional financial statements have become more sophisticated. Further, cash flow may itself be categorized, depending on the objective of the person making the estimate. A potential bidder for control, for example, may attempt to analyze **operating cash flow**, while an investor may analyze **free cash flow**. These concepts may be defined as follows:

$$\text{Cash flow} = \text{Net income} + \text{Depreciation} + \text{Depletion} + \text{Amortization}$$

$$\text{Operating cash flow} = \text{Cash flow} + \text{Interest expense} + \text{Income tax expense}$$

$$\text{Free cash flow} = \text{Cash flow} - \text{Capital expenditures} - \text{Dividends}.$$

The potential bidder works from operating cash flow because it plans to restructure the current capital structure of the target and eliminate income tax expense by dramatically increasing interest expense. The investor, on the other hand, is concerned with free cash flow, because the investor assumes that current operations and financial structure will remain unaffected.

For most investors, net income remains the handiest snapshot of a company's immediate future prospects. However, free cash-flow analysis may shed light on the quality of the earnings so projected: If profits appear to be improving but cash flow is not, the company's growth in earnings may be short lived.

§7.5 Who Has the Responsibility for Preparing Financial Statements?

The reliability of financial statements is to some extent dependent on their being prepared by or under the direction of independent professionals. As a result, their reliability must be viewed as seriously compromised if they are prepared by persons who are employees of, or somehow dependent on, management.

The preparation of publicly available financial statements prepared in accordance with GAAP is generally viewed as the norm. The preparation of such statements is overseen by outside and independent **certified public accountants (CPAs)**, who must certify in an auditor's report that the statements have been prepared pursuant to GAAP principles. As a practical matter, in a large and complex business, "overseen" means "spot checked" and the reality is that management largely has the responsibility for preparing the financial statements.

Most large publicly held corporations use as their outside auditors one of the **big six accounting firms** that have offices in all major cities — Price Waterhouse, Deloitte & Touche, Ernst & Young, KPMG Peat Marwick, Arthur Andersen & Co., and Coopers & Lybrand. These accounting firms are immense partnerships with hundreds or thousands of partners, though some of them have attempted to segregate out operations in each country from potential liabilities arising from activities in other countries. Smaller accounting firms may be capable of serving as auditors for huge corporations, but most of these corporations stick with the "big six."

The SEC views the selection of the auditor as an important factor in ensuring objectivity in financial statements. The SEC's regulations require the shareholders to ratify the selection of each independent auditor: The SEC has also expressed public concern over corporations that engage in **opinion shopping** by threatening to change auditors if the present auditors prove unwilling to accept the accounting treatment of transactions that management desires.

As indicated above, the actual role of outside auditors in preparing financial statements is more that of overseeing the audit than doing the audit. In a large, publicly held corporation, it is not practical for outside auditors to review all transactions or even to review a majority of them. The outside auditor's role is necessarily more limited: Typically, the outside auditors review the accounting systems used to generate the underlying data, test a sampling of the largest transactions to make sure that they are handled in an appropriate fashion, and participate to a limited extent in making physical counts of inventory, cash on hand, and other assets and liabilities. The **American Institute of Certified Public Accountants (AICPA)**, a professional society of CPAs, has established auditing standards that deal with the manner in which CPAs carry out independent examinations of the financial statements of companies. These standards are often referred to as **generally accepted auditing standards (GAAS)**. Many auditing firms have developed audit manuals to provide guidelines in various areas and for various problems. Most auditing firms also routinely use forms and checklists in connection with audits. Other mechanisms may involve the periodic rotation of audit partners or peer review, either within the large accounting firms or by outside evaluators. Nevertheless, in the final analysis, much of the compilation of data used in the outside auditor's report is actually assembled by the company's own internal accounting staff.

Under these circumstances, it is not surprising that routine outside audits often do not catch fraud or theft, particularly fraud or theft hidden by an employee who is familiar with the accounting practices followed by the company. Congress has recently required outside auditors to make greater efforts to detect fraud or theft. In early 1996, a modest provision requiring auditors of publicly traded companies to adopt procedures designed to detect illegal acts

and to report discovered acts to management and the board of directors or the SEC was adopted. It is possible that future legislation may stiffen auditing standards further. Of course, such proposals entail additional costs and greater exposure to personal liability on the part of the auditors. Auditing firms often argue that their principal function is to ensure that an acceptable system of accountability is in place and not to uncover fraud or theft. Despite this, auditing firms are often named as defendants in litigation to recover losses caused by undetected fraud or significant misrepresentations as to the prospects of the business. In these cases, the issues are whether the auditor performed its audit in accordance with accepted standards for performing audits, and if not, whether that audit would have prevented the losses if it had been performed with customary care. In many states, it is unclear whether an accountant owes a duty to exercise customary care to persons who foreseeably may rely on his or her statement, or whether claims based on failure to meet that duty are limited to those with a direct contractual relationship with the accountant.

All of the major accounting firms have been involved in litigation arising out of the collapse of numerous savings and loans institutions during the 1980s. In 1991, the major accounting firms paid out $404,000,000 (7.7 percent of accounting revenues) to litigants and their lawyers. In 1992, the amount was $477 million. During that year, a jury awarded investors $200,000,000 in damages in a case against Coopers & Lybrand arising out of major fraud by Miniscribe Corporation, a manufacturer of hard disk drives. Later in 1992, the Resolution Trust Company brought suit against Deloitte & Touche for $150 million, against Peat Marwick for $100,000,000, and against Arthur Andersen for more than $400 million. All of these suits involved earlier clean audits of failed financial institutions. Also during 1992, Ernst & Young settled all outstanding claims based on audits of financial institutions for a payment of $400,000,000. Similar settlements were made by Deloitte in 1993 ($312,000,000) and Peat Marwick in 1994 ($312,000,000). One consequence is that liability insurance for the major accounting firms has virtually dried up. Deductibles have increased from an average of $2 million in 1991 to $45,000,000 in 1993, and the maximum amount of insurance available is about $50,000,000. Although the magnitude of these amounts is unprecedented, the major accounting firms have had a long history of litigation problems arising from audits. Nevertheless, it is not surprising that accounting firms have begun to review their client lists and to drop those clients that present too great a risk of litigation.

Although it had long been the rule in federal court that others besides the primary wrongdoer in a securities fraud case could be held liable on a theory of aiding and abetting the violation—a theory that was used quite often against accounting and law firms—the Supreme Court ruled in *Central Bank v. First Interstate Bank*, 114 S. Ct. 1439 (1994), that there is no such liability in connection with a violation of Rule 10b-5, the primary federal rule under which securities fraud claims are prosecuted by private parties. Presumably the same is true in connection with violations of the Securities Act of 1933 (the 1933 Act) which deals primarily with public offerings. Liability for aiding and abetting has been restored, however, by Congress, but under the new statute it may only be asserted in an action by the SEC.

Although the trend among state courts seems to have been toward expanding accountants' liability, a California decision reaffirmed the classic case of *Ultramares Corp. v. Touche*, 255 N.Y. 170 (1931), and is likely to be quite influential nationwide. In *Bily v. Arthur Young & Co.*, 3 Cal. 4th 370 (1992), the California Supreme Court held that an auditor or accountant (in the context of an engagement to perform an audit and render a formal written report)

> owes no general duty of care regarding the conduct of an audit to persons other than the client. An auditor may, however, be held liable for negligent misrepresentations in an audit report to those persons who act in reliance upon those misrepresentations in a transaction which the auditor intended to influence. . . . [A]n auditor may also be held liable to reasonably foreseeable third persons for intentional fraud in the preparation and dissemination of an audit report.

One complicating factor in the context of auditors for publicly held corporations is that the shareholders, who are often the ones misled by erroneous financial statements, are legally speaking the owners of the company.

Further in that connection, in early 1993 the Auditing Standards Board of the AICPA issued Statement on Auditing Standards (SAS) No. 72 to provide guidance to accountants in issuing so-called **comfort letters** to underwriters and broker-dealers in connection with 1933 Act registrations. A comfort letter, sometimes also referred to as **cold comfort**, is a written representation falling short of a formal opinion, that the accountant or auditor is not aware of any adverse information. The new policy prohibits the issue of such a letter unless the requesting recipient represents that he or she has reviewed the underlying material. In other words, the policy is designed to limit the practice of using accountant comfort letters as a way for underwriters and broker-dealers to avoid due diligence as to financial statements.

As should be apparent, where publicly held corporations are concerned, the identity of the auditor is no guarantee that the financial statements accurately reflect the financial condition of the business or that a systematic examination has been made in an effort to detect fraud or misconduct. As one moves away from publicly held corporations, the relationship between auditor and corporation becomes even more critical. When considering financial statements for a small closely held corporation, one is likely to encounter financial statements prepared by local accounting firms of unknown reputation and quality. In addition, it is likely that the corporation has had close relationships with the auditor for many years, and the auditor's independence may be in serious question. In these situations, inquiry should normally be made about the auditor's local reputation as well as his or her connection with the corporation in question. Of course, one must consider whatever financial statements are available. Even financials that were prepared by a person under the control of the owner of the business are better than no financials at all. Issues of auditor independence, in other words, go only to the degree of confidence one places in the reliability of the financial statements. It is almost never practical to require a new audit, though it may be possible to request a second auditing firm to review the existing report.

§7.6 The Importance of the Auditor's Opinion

The first step in reviewing financial statements is to read carefully the auditor's opinion (i.e., the signed statement that appears immediately before the financial statements). Prior to 1989, the first paragraph of the standard **clean opinion** described the company and the financial statements being certified and concluded with this significant statement:

> Our examinations were made in accordance with generally accepted auditing standards, and, accordingly, included such tests of the accounting records and such other auditing procedures as we considered necessary in the circumstances.

The second paragraph read substantially as follows if the opinion was truly clean:

> In our opinion these financial statements present fairly the financial position of the corporation at December 31, 1987 and the results of its operations and the changes in its financial position for the year ended December 31, 1987 in conformity with generally accepted accounting principles consistently applied.

Beginning in 1989, a new form of auditor's opinion was adopted. It contains three paragraphs (rather than two) in approximately this language:

> We have audited the accompanying balance sheet of XYZ Company as of December 31, 1995 and 1996, and the related statements of income, retained earnings, and cash flows for the years then ended. These financial statements are the responsibility of the Company's management. Our responsibility is to express an opinion on these financial statements based on our audit.
>
> We conducted our audit in accordance with generally accepted auditing standards. Those standards require that we plan and perform the audit to obtain reasonable assurance whether the financial statements are free of material misstatement. An audit includes examining, on a test basis, evidence supporting the amounts and disclosures in the financial statements. An audit also includes assessing the accounting principles used and significant estimates made by management, as well as evaluating the overall financial statement presentation. We believe that our audit provides a reasonable basis for our opinion.
>
> In our opinion, the financial statements referred to above present fairly, in all material respects, the financial position of XYZ Company as of December 31, 1995 and 1996, and the results of its operations and its cash flows for the years then ended in conformity with generally accepted accounting principles.

The changes from the old format are designed to reflect more accurately the roles of management and of the auditor in preparing financial statements. One substantive change is that the language "in conformity with generally accepted accounting principles consistently applied" has been eliminated. Explanation regarding any change or variation in accounting principles must now be made in the form of exceptions in a separate paragraph. Because of the highly stylized nature of these opinion forms, any deviation from the standard language and particularly the inclusion of any additional statements in the opinion should be considered carefully and made the subject of further inquiry.

In the pre-1989 format, material changes in the treatment of one or more items were specifically referred to in the second paragraph, for example, ". . . in conformity with generally accepted accounting principles consistently applied during the period except for the change in the method of accounting for foreign currency transactions, with which we concur, described in note 1 to the Financial Statements." The method of accounting for foreign currency transactions may not sound very interesting, but it may involve hundreds of millions of dollars. Generally, if the auditor believes an item is important enough to mention in the opinion, it is important enough to be considered by users of the statements. In the new format, such changes must be explained in an additional paragraph added to the standard opinion.

The additional information referred to in an auditor's opinion is often of fundamental importance. As auditor for Texaco, Arthur Andersen was faced with the issue of what should be said about the 1985 Pennzoil judgment for $10.53 billion arising out of the struggle for Getty Oil Company. Texaco was vigorously contesting liability under the judgment, and it was therefore not reflected as a liability on the balance sheet. Arthur Andersen decided to add a third paragraph to its opinion on Texaco's 1985 financial statements referring to the Pennzoil judgment. This paragraph stated that the "ultimate outcome of this litigation is not presently determinable," and that Arthur Andersen's certification of the Texaco financial statements was therefore "subject to the effect of . . . such adjustments, if any, that might have been required had the outcome of the litigation . . . been known." That was, all would agree, an important qualification. One can imagine that Texaco was not pleased with this **qualified opinion**, but its wisdom was attested to in 1987, when the Pennzoil judgment forced Texaco to file for reorganization under Chapter 11 of the Bankruptcy Code.

In the pre-1989 format, if the auditor was unwilling to give a clean opinion, it had three choices. The auditor could give a **subject to opinion** stating that the financial statements fairly present the company's results but are subject to adjustments that are not yet known. Second, the auditor could give an **except for opinion** that indicates that the auditor was unable to audit certain areas of the company's operations and thus its opinion does not extend to those areas. Such a qualification was rarely seen outside of closely held corporations. And finally, the auditor could disclaim any opinion about the financial condition of the corporation. This was the most damaging statement of all: "Because of operating losses, no opinion is expressed as to whether the corporation will be able to continue as a going concern."

In the post-1989 format, the "subject to" opinion has been eliminated. Despite any uncertainty, the auditor must leave the third paragraph alone and conclude that the financial statements are fairly presented on the basis of the amounts recorded and the disclosures made concerning the uncertainties set forth in the footnotes. If an uncertainty is so significant that it may have a material impact on future financial statements, the auditor must red flag the item in an explanatory or emphasizing paragraph. Nevertheless, other types of qualifications to the basic opinion set forth in the third paragraph may still be made. When there is a material departure from GAAP, or when the company restricts the scope of the auditor's examination, the auditor's opinion in the

third paragraph should state that the financial statements are fairly presented "except for" the effects of the matters described in the concluding explanatory paragraph, which would describe the significance of the departures from GAAP or the restrictions on the audit's scope.

A qualification of an opinion is a serious matter and is not made lightly by the auditing firm. It may well cause the company, if it feels the qualification is unjustified, to consider changing auditing firms. On the other hand, the failure to qualify an opinion may serve as the basis for subsequent litigation against the auditor by investors or creditors. To repeat, if an auditor qualifies or withholds its opinion, a person using the financial statement should not ignore this clear warning.

§7.7 The Importance of Notes to the Financial Statements

A second source of important information about financial statements is the notes to the financial statements. Some financial statements contain the notation, "The notes are an integral part of these financial statements." Whether or not a statement of this type appears, notes should always be carefully read and their implications considered fully. This is not always easy to do, because the carefully prepared language that appears in notes to financial statements is often spare and concise, and the significance of what is being said may not always jump out at the reader. An important disclosure may be stated without any indication of its significance.

To illustrate the importance of notes, consider the following company, whose accounting period ends on December 31. The preparation of financial statements takes some time, and the statements may not actually be released until early March. A not unreasonable question is whether there were important adverse changes in the company's operations between December 31 and early March. If something important has happened after December 31—for example, the company's business has largely dried up and there is now imminent danger of insolvency — that information will not appear in the year-end financial statements themselves, but the essential facts should be set forth as the first note to the financial statements.

One problem with notes is that they are uneven: Some contain additional detail and information about the numbers, while others contain significant qualifications to the numbers. The latter is obviously more important than the former, but the notes mix the two together and do not always distinguish between them. In part this is because there is no clear line between explication and qualification. The following areas are usually covered in notes to financial statements:

1. Material adverse post-accounting period developments.

2. A summary of the discretionary accounting policies the company has elected to adopt (e.g., last-in first-out (LIFO) or first-in first-out (FIFO), depreciation schedules, and policies relating to revenue recognition and the capitalization of deferred expenses).

3. The accounting treatment of significant transactions entered into by the

company. The notes should indicate, for example, whether the obligations that the company incurred in connection with its employees' pension plan are currently funded and the extent to which the obligation appears as a liability on the balance sheet.

4. Breakdowns of reported amounts that appear as single aggregated figures in the financial statements. A one-page balance sheet often requires the consolidation of numerous accounts into single entries; the notes provide a breakdown in somewhat greater detail. Examples might include breakdowns of long-term indebtedness that the company owes and categories of fixed assets that the company owns.

5. Outstanding commitments not included as liabilities in the financial statements. Certain commitments that the company enters into may be material but not treated as liabilities under GAAP. Examples include rent obligations for future years under leases that are not cancelable, promises to redeem preferred stock at the option of the holder, and obligations to issue stock pursuant to stock options issued to employees. Material commitments of these types are all usually described in the notes to the financial statements.

6. Contingent liabilities, prospective losses, and unresolved litigation not included as liabilities in financial statements. Under GAAP, contingent items are taken into the accounts only when the outcome of the matter and the amount of the liability can be predicted with a reasonable degree of certainty. (Texaco did not show the Pennzoil judgment as a liability on its financial statements even though the trial court had entered judgment against it, because Texaco was appealing and vigorously contesting the claim.) Obviously, some contingent obligations, if they materialize, may overwhelm the company. The notes to the financial statements set forth the nature of material contingencies and an estimate of the possible range of loss. Ordinarily, the company's lawyers will be called on by the auditors to express an opinion as to the likelihood of an adverse judgment, and such inquiries can create difficult conflicts for lawyers who are bound to maintain client confidences.

7. The tax returns for specific years that have been audited by the Internal Revenue Service and the years that are currently open or in audit.

8. A 5-year or 10-year summary of operations to permit longer-term evaluations of the company.

9. Information on major lines of business and classes of products where the company is a conglomerate involved in activities in unrelated industries.

10. Information on the impact of changes in price and value (i.e., inflation accounting) by large companies. This information adjusts the financial statement's current replacement costs. It (a) restates the financial statement on a constant dollar basis to reflect changes in general price levels, and (b) reflects current replacement costs of inventory, property, plant, and equipment. Experience with inflation accounting reveals considerable divergence in approach from company to company, and many investors find this information to be confusing and complex and probably of limited value.

11. Management explanations and interpretations relating to favorable or unfavorable trends, changes in product mix, plans to acquire or dispose of major assets or lines of business, and the effect of unusual gains or losses.

§7.8 Traditional Analysis of Financial Statements

This section and the following sections describe traditional methods of analyzing financial statements once the numbers in the statements are accepted at face value (or after appropriate adjustments have been made). Adjustments to the numbers themselves that might be considered before applying the techniques described in this section are also considered briefly.

The techniques described below measure different things and are designed for different purposes. The most useful technique in a specific situation obviously depends on the transaction that is contemplated (e.g., whether it is proposed to make a loan to the business, invest in or purchase the business outrightly, sell the business, or engage in one or more commercial transactions with the business).

Most financial statements contain, either as part of the statements themselves or in the notes, historical information or summaries relating to prior accounting periods that are comparable to the information provided for the current period. Significant insights may be gained by considering trends over several accounting periods. Such analysis may show, for example, whether the company's position is improving or declining over time. Analysis of the single period covered by the most recent statements is usually enriched by historical perspective. When practicable, the ratios discussed below should be computed for several years, and changes in the ratios should be evaluated.

Of course, most clients are probably more interested in what the business is projected to do in the future than what it has done in the past. Recent historical trends must often be projected into the future, but this must be done with caution and after considering whether there have been recent changes in the business's prospects and whether there appear to be dark clouds on the horizon. The most informed projections are often those prepared by management (simply because management is most familiar with the business). Annual reports sometimes contain carefully prepared projections or predictions by management that must be evaluated. Management is often inclined to make optimistic projections, and one should always be cautious of undocumented general assertions.

There are some important situations, however, in which a client will want to know whether the financial statements are the best reflection of the past. For example, businesses are often sold at a price to be determined or adjusted on the basis of subsequent performance, often called an "earn-out." It may also be the case that some classes of stock carry dividends that must be paid if a certain level of income is achieved or if certain ratios are satisfied. And in many closely held businesses, shareholders are subject to a buy-sell agreement for their shares in which the price to be paid is determined in some fashion by the financial statements.

The balance sheet and income statement shown in Table 7-1 are the basis of the illustrations used in the following sections. To simplify the calculations in these illustrations, all numbers shown on these financial statements and used in the calculations omit six zeroes (000,000). That is, the numbers shown are in million of dollars.

Table 7-1
BALANCE SHEET—X COMPANY
December 31, 1997

ASSETS				LIABILITIES		
Current Assets				Current Liabilities		
Cash	50			Accounts payable	75	
Securities	20			Bank note	155	
Accts. rec.	100					230
Inventories	200					
		370				
				Long-term debt		250
				TOTAL LIABILITIES		480
Long-term assets						
Land	30			SHAREHOLDERS' EQUITY		
Plant/equip.	500			Common stock (800 shares)	40	
	530			Retained earnings	380	
		530				420
TOTAL ASSETS		900		TOTAL LIABILITIES/EQUITY		900

INCOME STATEMENT—X COMPANY
Year ending December 31, 1997

SALES		1000
EXPENSES		
Cost of goods sold	600	
Selling costs	170	
Depreciation	60	
Interest	16	
Operating costs		846
PRETAX INCOME		104
Income taxes		44
NET INCOME		60
Dividends		25
Retained earnings		35

§7.9 Balance Sheet Analysis

Several widely used ratios concentrate exclusively on the balance sheet. These tend to be the most traditional analytic techniques.

Net working capital. A basic question is whether a business has sufficient economic strength to continue in operation for a reasonable period. It may be recalled that current assets are those that involve cash, cash equivalents, and assets that should be reduced to cash within a year, while current liabilities are those that come due within a year. A simple measure of short-term stability of the business is to ascertain that current assets exceed current liabilities. The difference is called net working capital:

Net working capital = Current assets − Current liabilities

X Company has net working capital of $370 − $230 = $140. A negative net working capital indicates actual or potential financial difficulty in the short term. A business with negative working capital may improve its position by raising additional equity capital — selling more stock — or by borrowing long term. Of course, the purchasers of stock or long-term lenders need to assess the possibility that improved working capital will actually have a favorable effect on operational results. It may turn out that additional working capital is only a temporary expedient. If it is, the new capital investment or long-term loan should not be made. It is throwing good money after bad.

A corporation that has adopted the LIFO method of accounting for inventory almost certainly understates its current assets, because inventory is carried on the balance sheet at an historical figure that is usually less than current value. Whether or not this is material obviously depends on the circumstances.

Current ratio. A widely used measure of the adequacy of working capital is the current ratio, which is the ratio between current assets and current liabilities:

$$\text{Current ratio} = \frac{\text{current assets}}{\text{current liabilities}}$$

X Company's current ratio is 370/230, or 1.6 to 1. As a broad rule of thumb, a solid current ratio for an industrial company is 2 to 1. However, lower current ratios may be entirely adequate for many businesses. In general terms, the smaller the inventory levels required and the more easily collectible the amounts receivable, the lower the current ratio that is acceptable. Again, the election of the LIFO method of accounting for inventory may understate the current ratio and give the impression that smaller inventory levels are required than is in fact the case.

The acid test. Bankers and others considering short-term loans to a business often rely on quick asset analysis. **Quick assets** are assets that can be used to cover an immediate emergency. They differ from current assets in that they exclude inventories. Quick assets are obviously never greater than current assets.

$$\text{Quick assets} = \text{Cash} + \text{marketable securities} + \text{current receivables}$$

$$\text{Net quick assets} = \text{Quick assets} - \text{current liabilities}$$

$$\text{Quick assets ratio} = \frac{\text{quick assets}}{\text{current liabilities}}$$

The quick assets ratio is usually referred to as the acid test. X Company has quick assets of only $170 ($370 − 200); net quick assets of −$60 ($170 − $230); and a quick assets ratio of 0.74 to 1 (170/230).

A quick asset ratio of 1.0 or better shows that a company is able to meet its current liabilities without liquidating inventory. Ratios of less than 1.0 do not necessarily signify danger, however. An analysis of anticipated cash flow over

the period of the loan may show that the company is able to repay the loan without difficulty despite a ratio of less than 1.0. It all depends on how promptly liquidation or turnover of inventories occurs.

Book value. Book value is an important concept that simply means the value of net assets or owners' equity as calculated from the books of the company using the figures shown on the balance sheet. Book value does not mean market value. For example, the shares of a closely held corporation have book value even though the shares have never been bought or sold. Book value also does not mean liquidation value or "real" value, because the financial statements are constructed on historical cost rather than current market value of assets.

The book value per share of X Company's common shares is computed simply by subtracting liabilities from assets and dividing by the number of outstanding shares:

$$\text{Book value} = \frac{\text{Assets} - \text{Liabilities}}{\text{Number of shares}}$$

Book value therefore equals: ($900 − $480)/800 = $420/800 = $0.525 per share. This calculation is relatively simple in this case, because X Company has only common shares outstanding. Minor complications may arise when the company has issued more than one class of shares.

Exactly the same mathematical result may be reached in the case of X Company by adding together the capital contributed by the common shareholders and retained earnings, and dividing the sum by the number of outstanding shares: ($40 + $380)/800 = $420/800 = $0.525 per share. Indeed, this should be self-evident once it is understood how the balance sheet is constructed.

Asset coverage of debt. X Company has $250 of long-term debt. A measure of how secure the holder of this debt is can be obtained simply by subtracting current liabilities from total assets and dividing by the amount of the debt, all computed at book value:

$$\text{Asset coverage} = \frac{\text{Total assets} - \text{Current liabilities}}{\text{Long-term debt}}$$

In the case of X Company, each dollar of long-term debt is covered by $2.68 of book assets: ($900 − $230)/$250 = $670/$250 = 2.68. In this calculation, no account is taken of the interests of the holders of the common shares, because the rights of the holders of the long-term debt are senior to those of shareholders, that is, the bondholders must be paid in full before the shareholders get anything.

Debt/equity ratio. The debt/equity ratio recognizes that long-term debt is part of the permanent capitalization of the business; the ratio is computed by dividing long-term debt by the total shareholders' equity in the corporation:

$$\text{Debt/equity ratio} = \frac{\text{Long-term debt}}{\text{Total equity}}$$

In the case of X Company, the debt/equity ratio is 0.6 to 1 (250/420). The debt/equity ratio gives a picture of what proportion of the company's permanent capital is borrowed and what proportion is contributed (or internally generated as retained earnings). Because borrowed capital carries with it an obligation to pay interest, while dividends are usually discretionary, large amounts of debt in the capital structure are more risky than smaller amounts. A company with a high debt/equity ratio is said to be leveraged. A heavily leveraged corporation with most of the debt held by the corporation's shareholders is called a thin corporation or a thinly capitalized corporation.

From the standpoint of a lender, the debt/equity ratio measures the relative size of the equity "cushion" available for repayment of the debt in the case of default. A high debt/equity ratio means that a lender has a relatively small cushion and therefore an increased risk that the debt will not be fully collectible in the event of a default. Moreover, a substantial equity cushion means that the owners of the business have a stronger incentive to keep the business healthy in that they have more to lose.

Is it appropriate to consider long-term debt as a kind of capital? Debt ultimately must be repaid. Nevertheless, the treatment of debt as part of the permanent capitalization is certainly reasonable if the repayment date is far distant in the future, or sometimes even if shorter-term debt is involved. Financial statements treat debt as current only if it falls due within 12 months. Debt maturing beyond that time is considered long term within the context of the financial statement. Also, debt falling due within two or three years may reasonably be viewed as long-term capital if it is anticipated that new loans will be obtained to repay the debt when it matures, a very common phenomenon in business. This is often referred to as rolling over the debt. Shorter-term debt may be excluded from the debt/equity ratio calculation if its repayment is adequately provided for and no rollover is contemplated.

§7.10 Income Statement Analysis

For most analytic purposes, information about past earnings and prospects of future earnings is more useful than information about property and assets. An old axiom is that assets are worth only what they can earn. Assets that have no earning capacity are salable only for scrap. Hence, more reliance is usually placed on the income statement ratios described below than on the balance sheet ratios described above. Actually, it is not entirely accurate to think of the following as income statement ratios, because income statement analysis often involves ratios using items appearing on the balance sheet as well as items appearing on the income statement.

Operating margin. Perhaps the simplest analytic tool is the operating (or profit) margin, the ratio of pretax income to gross sales:

$$\text{Operating margin} = \frac{\text{Pretax income}}{\text{Gross sales}}$$

Interest on long-term debt may be added back to pretax income on the theory that this interest really represents a part of the cost of capital rather than an operating cost. In the case of X Company, the profit margin is 104/1,000 or 10 percent, if interest is included in the calculation of income, and approximately 120/1,000 or 12 percent if interest is excluded from income. The calculation is approximate, because a portion of the interest expense of $16 presumably represents interest on current liabilities.

Operating margin is a basic measure of the profitability of a business. Generally, increases in sales cause dramatic improvements in the profit margin, because some costs (e.g., rent and office expenses) are fixed and do not rise or fall in proportion to volume. Correspondingly, a decrease in sales volume may cause a disproportionately large decline in the operating margin.

Net profit ratio. The net profit ratio is simply the ratio between the bottom line and gross sales:

$$\text{Net profit ratio} = \frac{\text{Net income}}{\text{Gross sales}}$$

In the case of X company, its net profit ratio is 60/1,000 or 6 percent, not a stellar performance.

Interest coverage. Of particular interest to the holders of long-term debt is the cushion that the holders have between the interest payments on the long-term debt and the total income of the company before payment of interest or taxes. This is usually expressed as a multiple of the amount of interest due on indebtedness:

$$\text{Interest coverage} = \frac{\text{Pretax income} + \text{Interest}}{\text{Interest}}$$

In the case of X company, the interest coverage is 104 + 16 = 120/16 or 7.5 times the interest cost. The long-term debt of X Company is thus a relatively safe investment, at least as far as the payment of interest is concerned. Ratios of three times or four times the interest cost are generally viewed as acceptable for stable companies in stable industries.

Interest coverage measures the likelihood that the corporation can meet its periodic interest obligations: The asset coverage of debt measures the likelihood of repayment of principal if the debt becomes due immediately.

If X Company had outstanding an issue of preferred shares, one could measure the preferred dividend coverage in an analogous manner.

Earnings per share. Another fundamental measure of profitability that is particularly interesting to shareholders is earnings per share, computed as the net income divided by the number of shares outstanding:

$$\text{Earnings per share} = \frac{\text{Net income}}{\text{Outstanding shares}}$$

In the case of X Company, each share of common stock earned $0.075 (60/800). Earnings per share is not the same thing as dividends per share; considerably greater weight is given to earnings per share, because dividends are discretionary with the board of directors.

Earnings per share is an important ratio in the valuation of businesses. It is often assumed that earnings per share will either remain stable or increase in a predictable fashion in the future. Earnings per share should therefore be evaluated over a period of years whenever feasible.

Large publicly held corporations report earnings per share calculated two different ways. First, earnings per share is calculated on the basis of the average number of shares outstanding during the period. Second, fully diluted earnings per share is computed on the assumption that all options to purchase shares and conversion rights to convert into common shares have been exercised. Fully diluted earnings per share represents what earnings per share would have been at the worst, assuming all options and conversion rights had been exercised. The concept of dilution is discussed further in the chapter on securities.

Sales to fixed assets ratio. A ratio that helps to determine whether the capital invested in productive facilities is being used efficiently is the ratio between sales and fixed assets:

$$\text{Ratio of sales to fixed assets} = \frac{\text{Gross sales}}{\text{Long-term assets}}$$

X Company's ratio of sales to fixed assets is 1.9 (1,000/530). This ratio is particularly valuable as part of a before-and-after examination of the consequences of a significant change in productive facilities. The absolute size of this ratio largely depends on the nature of the industry in which the company is active. Lower ratios appear in heavy industry (e.g., steel or paper) and somewhat higher ratios (such as X Company's) in industries such as textiles or drugs.

Inventory turnover. In a manufacturing or retail business, an important — often critical — factor is whether the company's inventory is too large for its level of operations and whether inventory turns over quickly or is sluggish.

Inventory turnover varies widely from industry to industry, and to a lesser extent from company to company within a single industry. Inventory comparisons therefore are most useful on a historical basis for a single company or on an intercompany basis within a single industry.

The most accurate measure of inventory turnover would compare average inventory during the accounting period with cost of goods sold. However, average inventory is not usually available from financial statements, and it is therefore customary to use closing inventory. Unfortunately, the use of LIFO substantially reduces the usefulness of all ratios based on closing inventory, which is carried on the books under LIFO at an artificially low figure. The

following ratio is more useful in companies that utilize FIFO or other methods of determining cost of goods sold:

$$\text{Inventory turnover ratio} = \frac{\text{Costs of goods sold}}{\text{Closing inventory}}$$

X Company's inventory ratio is 600/200 or 3.0. A very similar ratio uses gross sales rather than cost of goods sold. This ratio is viewed as the best estimate of whether the enterprise is investing too heavily in inventory, and can also be used in connection with financial statements that do not break down cost of goods sold as a separate item.

$$\text{Ratio of sales to inventories} = \frac{\text{Gross sales}}{\text{Closing inventory}}$$

X Company's ratio of sales to inventories is 5.0 to 1 (1,000/200).

In general terms, a high or increasing ratio denotes a good quality of merchandise and accurate pricing policies, while a low or declining ratio may indicate problems (particularly for a retail sales operation), such as poor merchandising policies, a poor location, or a large amount of "stale" merchandise. High and low in this context refer to comparisons with comparable businesses, not absolute levels. In making comparisons, it is again necessary to exclude companies that have adopted LIFO from both sides of the comparison.

Another widely used ratio to estimate inventory management is inventory as a percentage of total current assets. X Company's inventory is 54 percent of its current assets (200/370). Again, this number has little inherent meaning in cross-industry comparisons but may be useful if computed across several accounting periods for a single firm or compared with other firms in the same industry.

Return on equity. Return on equity is simply the ratio of net income to net worth:

$$\text{Return on equity} = \frac{\text{Net income}}{\text{Net worth}}$$

X Company's return on equity is 15.6 percent (60/385). (Note that one must use net worth at the beginning of the year to calculate a meaningful ratio in this case.) This is one of the more widely used ratios, because it describes how much the company is earning on each dollar of shareholder investment. When applied to GAAP statements, it is also broadly comparable from company to company and from industry to industry even though it is affected to some extent by the accounting conventions adopted. It also may be subject to manipulation. Management that desires to preserve a high return on equity may decide to forgo current investments that have immediate returns smaller than the current return on equity even though the investments increase the earnings per share and have great potential for future income. These problems may sometimes be discovered by the use of operating margin and net profit ratio, as well as return

on equity, as measures of overall success of operations. Return on equity is a relatively universal measure of profitability. Information is widely available on return on equity for thousands of publicly held corporations.

Return on invested capital. Return on invested capital is analogous to return on equity but treats long-term debt as capital:

$$\text{Return on capital} = \frac{\text{Net income} + \text{Interest}}{\text{Net worth} + \text{Long-term debt}}$$

X Company's return on capital is about 12 percent $((60 + 16)/(385 + 250))$. This ratio is a broad measure of the effective use of capital assets. Like return on equity, when applied to GAAP statements it is broadly comparable from company to company and from industry to industry. Information on the return on invested capital for thousands of publicly held companies is also widely available.

Other ratios. It is possible to devise additional ratios to measure various aspects of a company's financial statements. For example, the ratio of accounts receivable to average daily sales (total sales divided by the number of selling days in the year) is a technical ratio that provides information as to the turnover rate of accounts receivable. The ratios described above, however, are the most general, the most important, and the most widely used. None of these analytic tools should be used mechanically. And even when properly used, their value depends on the quality and reliability of the financial statements to which they are applied.

§7.11 Adjusting the Numbers in Financial Statements

It is often desirable to make adjustments in financial statements before (or as part of) the analysis of them. There is nothing magical or correct about numbers simply because they are written down in an official-appearing and certified set of financial statements. And the reliability and utility of financial statements is not improved merely because they appear in an attractive format in an annual report printed in four colors and containing a glowing report from management. It is surprising how reluctant many people are to subject attractively printed financial statements to the same skeptical scrutiny they would routinely give typed or handwritten financial statements. The gift wrapping is not important: It is what is inside that counts.

When financial statements are examined, it is important to consider the basis on which they were prepared. If the statements are not GAAP statements, both that fact and the manner in which they were prepared should be revealed in the financial statements or the notes. If the contemplated analysis involves comparisons with publicly available GAAP financial statements of comparable companies, adjustments sometimes may need to be made.

In deciding what adjustments should be made even to GAAP statements, one must always keep in mind the issue that is being addressed. For example,

adjustments that entirely eliminate intangible assets such as goodwill from the balance sheet may be entirely appropriate when your client is considering the purchase of the business in order to acquire its physical assets and the question is how much to offer to pay. Similarly, if the financial statements treat as expenses amounts that should more appropriately be viewed as distributions to the shareholders, income should be increased and expenses decreased appropriately if one is using the earning capacity of the business as the basis for deciding how much to offer. Recurring types of adjustments to GAAP financial statements are described below.

Current market value. Assume that you are considering financial statements of a company that has been continuously in existence since 1923. On its balance sheet is the enigmatic entry "Land . . . . $300,000." Such an entry should be a red flag for further investigation and possible adjustment, because that $300,000 is a cost figure, and it may reflect either a purchase more than 50 years ago when land was selling for a fraction of what it is today or a purchase last week at or above current market values.

If the company owns marketable securities, the balance sheet should set forth by parenthetical notation a recent estimate of the current market value of the securities. It may be appropriate to substitute these market values for the cost figures for analytic purposes. It may also be appropriate to substitute up-to-date market values for those appearing in the parenthetical notation on the balance sheet (which states figures as of the close of the accounting period).

Other asset adjustments that should be considered include an upward adjustment in value if inventory is calculated on a LIFO basis and a readjustment of the machinery and equipment account if accelerated depreciation is used. If accelerated depreciation schedules are used, an upward adjustment to earnings may also be appropriate. On the down side, the machinery and equipment account may include obsolete assets that should be written off to zero because their usefulness is exhausted and their resale value is nonexistent. Inventory is theoretically valued at the lower of cost or market, but additional write-downs may also be appropriate for obsolete or stale items. Adjustments of these types usually require a fairly detailed investigation of specific asset accounts by a person intimately familiar with the type of business involved.

Non-asset assets. Balance sheets often contain items that have zero realizable value. The most common items of this type appear in the intangible assets account: "goodwill," "organizational expense," "capitalized promotional expense," or "capitalized development costs." It may be appropriate to eliminate these items entirely from the balance sheet, reducing retained earnings by the same amount.

The problem of non-asset assets is not limited to these intangible asset accounts. Investments in subsidiary corporations or other businesses may also have a zero realizable value. Even traditional asset accounts such as fixed assets or inventory may contain positive values for property that are unrealistic. Usually, a detailed investigation is necessary to determine the extent of overstatement in these accounts.

Off balance sheet liabilities. Most businesses have at least some material liabilities that are not reflected in the balance sheet. These items include future obligations under pension and profit-sharing plans, litigation in process, potential future product liability claims, commitments under fixed contracts such as long-term leases and employment contracts, and potential tax liabilities arising out of ongoing audits of operations of earlier years. Some of these items may be referred to in the notes to the financial statements. If not, it is usually difficult for an outsider to learn of their existence. It may be appropriate to increase book liabilities to reflect these off-book liabilities or to make an appropriate adjustment to the terms of the contemplated transaction to take account of their existence.

A separate inquiry is often made about possible future product liability claims arising from sales in earlier years. In many jurisdictions, such claims are not barred by the statute of limitations, which begins to run only when the injury occurs. The adequacy of insurance for such risks should also be investigated. Most insurance against liabilities of these types is written on a claims-made basis that may require insurance to be maintained indefinitely even if the portion of the business manufacturing the products in question is discontinued.

When a business is being purchased, it is customary to require the sellers to warrant specifically that material unknown liabilities (other than those specifically referred to in the financial statements and notes) do not exist. The absence of such liabilities may also be a condition of closing, so the purchaser may withdraw from the transaction if its investigation reveals the existence of material undisclosed liabilities.

Long-term liabilities are shown on financial statements at face value. In other words, a $10,000,000 bond issue is shown at $10,000,000 even though it may not be due to be repaid for another 20 years. Depending on the interest rate on these bonds, their market value may be significantly less than $10,000,000. See the discussion of bond pricing in Chapter 14, which discusses securities markets. If reacquisition of these bonds by market purchases is feasible, the liability item on the balance sheet may be reduced for analytic purposes to reflect the actual cost of reacquiring and retiring the bonds.

Because of the central role of the income statement in most analyses, it is important that recent changes in accounting principles or practices do not artificially inflate current earnings. For example, recent changes in the estimated lives of assets subject to amortization or depreciation might be examined for their possible effect on the income statement. Apparent reductions or deferrals of discretionary costs such as advertising or research might be reviewed, because that is a relatively easy way to preserve an earnings record despite increases in costs or declines in revenue. Of course, reduction or deferral of such items may be unwise from a longer-term perspective. Professional or expert analysis of the financial statements and the underlying accounting records is usually necessary to determine whether such changes have occurred, and whether they materially affect the results of operations.

In a closely held corporation, accounting policies are often adopted in an effort to minimize apparent income for tax or other purposes. Upward adjustments to reflect income consistent with GAAP principles may be appropriate. The most likely adjustments are to capitalize items that were treated as expenses

in the financial statements, to restore to earnings amounts distributed to the owners of the business in the form of excessive salaries or fringe benefits and to eliminate the effects of excessively rapid depreciation.

§7.12 Cooking the Books

Financial statements nominally prepared in accordance with GAAP are subject to manipulation and may involve outright fraud and misrepresentation. Fraud is often practiced by using fictitious transactions to hide thefts or by adopting non-GAAP accounting principles without disclosing them. Income statements may be blatantly overstated by rigging inventory counts, creating fictitious assets, or omitting liabilities from the balance sheet. Sales to wholly owned affiliates at attractive prices may be booked as sales to independent outside parties. Sales may be booked immediately even though goods have been shipped on approval or subject to buy-back guarantees that are likely to be exercised. Depending on the sophistication of the persons engaged in the wrongful conduct, it may be difficult or impossible to discover that the books have been cooked without tracing specific transactions. Major thefts may often be hidden in the books of a large and complex business in a way that may escape detection for long periods of time. The development of computerized accounting systems does not prevent cooking the books; it simply requires a different kind and degree of sophistication to cook the books successfully. Of course, persons who misappropriate business assets or fraudulently misrepresent the financial condition of a business usually face criminal charges if they are apprehended.

At a higher level of social acceptability are discretionary decisions that have the effect of improving the appearance of profitability. Management's goal may be to improve the market price of the stock of the company by creating the appearance of a stable history of growing earnings. Erratic earnings are not as likely to be highly capitalized by the market as steady and predictable earnings. A fair amount of smoothing out and improving of earnings may be accomplished by discretionary decisions (e.g., by booking income at an early stage of the sales process even though additional costs may later be incurred).

Another common strategy is **taking a bath** during one bad accounting period. From the standpoint of securities prices and markets it is usually desirable, if a business is going to have a bad year anyway, to take as many **write-offs** in that period as possible so that a return to predictable increases in profits becomes possible in the following year. Obviously, it is no fun to issue a press release revealing losses of hundreds of millions of dollars in a single accounting period. But memories are short, and with potential losses eliminated, the reported earnings in the following accounting periods should show dramatic improvement. For publicly held companies, taking a bath in this fashion is a widely followed strategy.

Taking a bath involves discretionary decisions to take as many losses as possible within a single accounting period. Smoothing out income involves discretionary allocations of income and expense items to specific periods to stabilize reported earnings. Many of these decisions may be consistent with

GAAP principles, because management has considerable discretion when to book transactions and when to recognize losses. For example, businesses often have assets or whole lines of business that can only be disposed of at a loss; the timing of the disposition is discretionary. Similarly, intangible assets or capitalized expenses that can never be fully recovered may be written off at a time that is to some extent at the discretion of management. Bad debts or obsolete inventory may similarly be written down or off when convenient. Whenever one reads about a company that unexpectedly announces very substantial losses despite a history of profitability, it is likely that the company is taking a bath.

Companies sometimes engage in transactions near the end of their fiscal year primarily to improve the closing figures and the various ratios described above. The company may make big shipments from inventories at bargain prices near the close of the accounting period in order to be able to book the sales. In effect, the company may be "borrowing" from next year's sales, effectively booking 13 months of sales in a single year. Manipulation of the mix of inventory between raw materials and finished products may increase closing inventory (thereby increasing gross margin) at the expense of the following year. A company that has cash-flow problems may borrow money on December 28 in order to show a large amount of cash on hand at the close of the fiscal year. Of course, that cash is only temporarily resident in the company's accounts and may disappear on January 3. These tactics are known as **window dressing** and shade off into actionable fraud or deception.

CHAPTER 8

VALUATION OF AN ONGOING BUSINESS

§8.1   Introduction

This chapter deals generally with the question of what a business is worth and what shares or interests in that business are worth. In this context "business" means any asset or group of assets that promises to produce a flow of cash or income in the future. It may include a piece of commercial real estate, a manufacturing business, a retail store, a consulting business, a barber shop, or a solo or group legal practice. The definition is broad enough to include a portfolio of marketable investment securities, but the valuation of such securities usually presents few problems, because quotations for marketable securities are readily available from brokerage firms.

The words **valuation** and **appraisal** are virtually synonymous and are used interchangeably in this chapter. In corporation law, there also exists a narrow statutory **appraisal right** or **right of dissent and appraisal** designed to protect minority shareholders against certain types of potentially abusive transactions

specifically defined in the statutes. This statutory appraisal right, described briefly in Chapter 13, which discusses mergers and acquisitions, is only incidentally involved in the issues discussed in this chapter.

Valuation of a business is a factual and business-related issue, not a legal issue on which a lawyer will ordinarily opine, although valuation may often arise as a factual issue in negotiations, transactions, and litigation. Thus, a business lawyer must be familiar with the techniques of valuation. Indeed, valuation is central to many types of calculations of damages even outside a business context.

The valuation techniques discussed in the later sections of this chapter require familiarity with concepts discussed in earlier chapters, particularly the time value of money, the valuation of real estate, and the fundamentals of accounting.

§8.2 The Standard for Valuation

There is general agreement that the fundamental goal of valuation is to determine the **fair market value (FMV)** of a business, which in turn is defined as the price that would be established by a buyer and a seller in an arm's-length negotiation for the purchase and sale of the business, with both parties ready, willing, and able to enter into the transaction, under no compulsion to enter into the transaction, and having complete information about the relevant factors.

Although this fundamental standard is relatively easy to state, it gives little guidance as a practical matter in cases in which the business is closely held by relatively few owners and there have been no recent sales of the business or a closely comparable business. Indeed, the "ready, willing, and able" test begs the question, because it gives no clue as to what techniques should be used by a hypothetical buyer and hypothetical seller in determining what price to offer and what price to accept.

In a publicly held business, there exists an active market for ownership interests — the stock market. The existence of a public market for ownership interests makes valuation of a publicly held business considerably easier than that of a closely held business, because there are always current market price quotations available. It should not be assumed, however, that there are no valuation problems in publicly held businesses.

§8.3 The Vain Search for the "Actual Value" of a Business

Those unfamiliar with the valuation process often labor under the mistaken belief that businesses have a single determinable value, and that the goal of the valuation process is to find the holy grail of true value. Valuation is not an exact science. Basically, there is no objective answer to the question, "What is this business really worth?"

Valuation issues are interesting and challenging precisely because there is no single value of a business. At best, there is a range of possible values. At worst, there are wildly varying approximations regarding value with the approxi-

mations based on different but plausible approaches as to how value should be measured. Indeed, the uncertainties of the valuation process are often so significant that high or low valuations may plausibly be asserted on the basis of the same basic technique of valuation.

A number of different adjectives may be associated with the word "value." For example, financial analysts often use **fair value, market value, book value, liquidation value**, and **replacement value**. Some of these phrases refer to specific and meaningful concepts. For example, book value, liquidation value, and replacement value all refer either to existing numbers or to a specific method of calculating a number in connection with a business. Other phrases, such as fair value, real value, true value, and actual value, have no well defined meaning at all. At best, these phrases are merely synonyms for the basic definition of value, namely the price on which a willing buyer and willing seller would agree.

Whatever the reason for the notion that a business has a single correct value, many people regularly rely on this notion when valuation issues are first discussed. One also finds traces of it in opinions of presumably sophisticated judges who argue, for example, that a transaction should be set aside because a price for shares of closely held stock was set entirely arbitrarily and did not reflect "real," "actual," or "true" value. Such reasoning is simply the assertion of a conclusion and not analysis.

The essential point is that there are many different techniques that may be used to analyze value, and each technique may yield significantly different numbers. Thus, it is considerably more accurate to envision the ultimate "value" of a business as a range than as a specific number. For the same reason, the valuation opinions of even sophisticated individuals with extensive backgrounds in valuation techniques usually may be impeached, or at least shaken, by a lawyer familiar with valuation techniques and their limitations. These various techniques are described in the following sections of this chapter.

§8.4 Expert Business Appraisers

Many individuals and firms hold themselves out as valuation or appraisal experts. These persons are retained regularly to provide opinions or recommendations or to serve as expert witnesses in litigation on valuation questions. However, valuation is not an exact science and the conclusions of even sophisticated "experts" can be suspect. Thus, although a business lawyer need not do valuations in the first instance, he or she must be familiar with techniques of valuation in order to understand the work of experts and translate it for clients and courts, and sometimes in order to challenge the work of others' experts.

It is indeed easy to be cynical when discussing valuation experts. Every person in business is familiar with stories in which valuation opinions were given primarily on the basis of what the person paying for the opinion wanted to hear. The necessary points of view are usually not conveyed by such crass statements as "I want you to come out with a high value," or "I want an opinion that this business is worth between $20,000,000 or $30,000,000," or "I want an opinion that $21 per share is a fair price for the rest of the stock." Rather, these points of view may be effectively communicated simply when the proposed

transaction or reason for the appraisal is described to the person retained to give a valuation opinion. After all, it does not take a genius to realize that sellers usually want high valuations and buyers usually want low valuations, or that minimizing taxes is the goal of an estate seeking a valuation of a closely held business. It is also not unknown for a person dissatisfied with one opinion to commission a second opinion from a different, and perhaps more sympathetic, source.

Among the many individuals and firms that consider themselves competent in business valuation matters are the following:

1. Accountants and accounting firms. These firms regularly make recommendations on valuation issues. They may prepare studies and recommendations for the benefit of management decision-making on investment or divestment issues that involve substantial valuation questions. Suppose that a company has decided to sell off a line of business on which it is currently losing money but which it believes can be turned around with different management. The price to be placed on that line may be based on a report and recommendation by the company's outside auditors. Although the company's internal accounting staff probably has essentially the same expertise as the outside auditor and may also make a study and report, or may review the outside auditor's report and make an independent recommendation, the report of an outside accounting firm may be obtained as a check on the conclusions of the inside auditors or because an internal recommendation may be viewed as subject to the domination of management.

2. Investment banking firms. These firms also regularly make valuation recommendations or give opinions relating to value, particularly with regard to transactions involving the purchase or sale of interests to the general public. The expertise of investment banking firms in the valuation area arises from their historical role of establishing prices for the sale of stock to the general public. The establishment of such public issue prices is tricky. When the offering is an initial public offering (IPO), setting the offering price involves the same difficulties faced in valuation of a closely held business. When the offering is of additional shares of a stock that is already publicly traded, the price must be low enough to attract outside capital and yet not so low as to anger existing shareholders because of the dilution caused by issuing new shares at bargain prices. Investment banking firms are also heavily involved in the takeover business, and often prepare fairness opinions on whether a proposed price for a business is a fair one. These opinions have sometimes been the subject of litigation.

3. Full-service securities brokerage firms. These firms, which provide a variety of advisory and related services in addition to the simple execution of securities transactions, offer similar valuation expertise. Such firms regularly provide investment advice that necessarily involves valuation questions, and business valuation is a natural extension of this function. In many cases, a full-service brokerage firm also maintains an investment banking operation.

4. Independent firms that describe themselves as management consulting firms. These firms, which also provide valuation services, may employ persons with experience in accounting and auditing as well as management decision-making.

5. Real estate brokerage firms or individual real estate brokers. These firms may prepare valuation or appraisals of specific income-producing properties such as commercial real estate. Persons actively engaged in buying and selling commercial real estate in the community usually have a feel for the market and are likely to be familiar with prices being paid for other commercial properties in the area and the comparability of those other properties to the property in question.

6. Auction or brokerage firms. These firms may specialize in the purchase and sale of substantial commercial assets such as heavy construction equipment, and may provide valuation opinions in some situations. These values may be liquidation values, based on the assumption that the operating assets are to be broken up and sold or auctioned off individually. For some types of second-hand equipment, there may be published blue books or catalogues used in estimating value.

7. Business brokers who specialize in listing businesses for sale and in locating persons who are interested in acquiring businesses and who have the financial resources to do so. Most businesses listed with such brokers are relatively small, but some large firms may list themselves or specific lines of business with these brokers. These brokerage firms have extensive experience with business valuation matters, although their principal interest is usually the commission upon the completion of the sale.

§8.5 Valuation Based on Asset Appraisals

Valuation based on what the assets of the business would bring if they were sold may seem to be the simplest and most intuitive method of valuation of a business. An individual who asks, "What is my financial worth?" is likely to think in terms of what the various assets he or she owns would bring if sold. For example, many individuals have had the experience of selling a used car, where value means **resale value** that can be easily approximated simply by looking it up in the "blue book," by going to several used car dealers and asking for price quotations, or by advertising the car oneself and seeing what offers come in. These are appropriate ways to measure the value of goods that are reasonably standardized and are recognized objects of trade. The problem is that businesses are rarely like used cars. They are not at all standardized, each one is unique, there is no authoritative blue book, and there is not an active market with many buyers and sellers. A value may need to be assigned to a business where there are no sales that are even remotely comparable.

A second intuitive approach toward value is to assume that value really means **liquidation value**, that is, what the assets could be sold for if the business were closed down and the assets broken up and sold. For an individual, this would be the answer to the question, "What are my worldly assets worth?" or, in more pessimistic terms, "How large would my estate be if I died today?" A business can certainly be valued in this way. However, in almost every situation, liquidation of the business is not contemplated by anyone, and what is being valued is not a mass of isolated assets but something that has value because it produced income or cash flow in the past and has (presumably) greater potential

of producing income or cash flow in years to come. The use of liquidation value in most situations is therefore illogical, because it values the business in a way that does not address the actual value-producing ability of the business.

In most circumstances, **asset valuation** is unrealistic, because neither the buyer nor the seller contemplates that the liquidation will in fact occur. Typically, what is being bought and sold is an entity that produces earnings or cash flow, not a string of individual, unrelated assets. In other words, asset valuation is often too low, because it assumes that the pieces of a business are being sold to someone other than the current owner. If the current owner is a competent manager, however, those assets should be being used in their highest and best use to produce as much income or cash flow as possible. Thus, in a sense, asset valuation assumes a sale to a second-best user and is naturally lower. It is for this reason that when a business is sold as a going concern, it is often sold for more than the value of the assets. The difference is sometimes referred to as **goodwill**, which may be thought of as a number that represents the intangible capacity of well-managed assets to generate more in income than the assets are worth separately.

Asset valuations nevertheless may enter into the calculation of the value of a business in many circumstances. The most obvious situation is one in which the purchaser's goal is in fact to liquidate the business—a **bust-up transaction**, as it is sometimes called. Bust-up transactions occur in publicly held corporations when the corporation's securities are depressed in price and the liquidation value of its assets exceeds its value as a going business as measured in the securities markets. Similar transactions may also occur in closely held corporations if the incumbent owners fail to recognize that the corporation is worth more liquidated than as a going entity.

Another situation in which liquidation values may enter into the valuation of a business arises when the purchaser's basic goal is to obtain the use of one asset or line of business and to dispose of the other assets after the sale is completed. In this situation, the buyer is likely to value the business by determining the value of the desired asset or line of business (based on its contemplated cash flow or income) and adding to it an estimate of the liquidation value of the remaining assets.

If the business being acquired has assets that the purchaser believes to be unnecessary for the successful continuation of the business (or if the assets duplicate underutilized property that the purchaser currently owns), the purchaser may again simply add the liquidation value of these assets to the value based on earnings to determine the total price he or she is willing to offer. Similarly, if the company being valued has cash or marketable securities in excess of its needs, the buyer may increase the price by the amount of the excess cash or cash equivalents, which, if the purchase is successful, may be withdrawn without adversely affecting the operation of the acquired business. In effect, the buyer pays cash for cash or cash equivalents. In many of these situations, the seller may be aware of the existence of the excess assets and will exclude them from the sale (or distribute them as dividends to the owners of the business before the sale takes place).

The calculation of liquidation value becomes very difficult on an asset-by-asset basis for any substantial business. In such situations, estimates of net asset

value are usually made by using book values and making adjustments for assets such as land, marketable securities, and last-in first-out (LIFO) inventories. When lines of business are salable as units, income or cash-flow analysis may be applied to these lines with the resulting value being treated as net asset values for each particular line.

Assets may also be valued on the basis of what it would cost to replicate or replace the plant and operations of the business, rather than what the assets of the corporation would bring upon dissolution. **Replacement cost** is often used when a business is contemplating expanding into a new area of operation and is choosing between building a plant from scratch or buying an existing company. However, replacement cost, like liquidation value, is generally not an appropriate way to measure the value of an ongoing business, because the purchaser normally would not view the business as equal in value to what a brand-new plant created from scratch would cost. Indeed, in the case of many mature businesses, the replacement cost of a plant greatly exceeds the value based on future cash flow, which ultimately is the only reliable indication of value.

§8.6 Valuation Based on Book Value

Book value means **net worth** or **owners' equity** according to the financial records of the business. It is the amount that remains after subtracting liabilities from assets. Thus, book value is an accounting concept rather than a true measure of value. Financial records are normally kept on the basis of historical cost, and book value therefore usually does not reflect either the earning capacity of the business or the current value of its inventory and capital assets.

Despite these deficiencies, book value is almost always calculated as part of the valuation process. There are several reasons. First, it is always easy to calculate book value from the financial records of the business; second, book value tends to increase with the success of the business so that it is not automatically made obsolete simply by the passage of time; third, shareholders may view book value as a floor under the price for shares and resist proposed sales for less than book value. On the securities markets, a stock that is selling for less than book value is often viewed, somewhat irrationally, as a questionable investment. Even though these attitudes are not strictly logical, they do reveal that book value, based as it is on historical cost, is given some weight in the valuation process.

One problem with book value is that it may be significantly affected by accounting conventions that do not themselves affect the earning capacity or assets of the business. For example, if there are two identical companies, one using LIFO and the other using first-in first-out (FIFO) to reflect inventory costs, the book value of the FIFO company will usually be higher than the book value of the LIFO company. Thus, if book value is relied on, adjustments may be necessary to offset the use of these accounting conventions.

Another problem with book value is that a company that pays generous dividends will have a smaller book value, other things equal, than a company that retains more cash, even though the two companies may have identical

earning power. Moreover, although the payment of a dividend reduces owners equity, the payment of a dividend is also the basic way in which investors receive their financial return (short of selling their stock or interest or of the company liquidating). Thus, book value may significantly understate the true value of a company that has adopted a policy of paying substantial dividends.

§8.7 Valuation Based on Cash Flow or Income

Usually, a business's value lies in its ability to provide a future stream of net cash. The most direct way of measuring value, therefore, is to estimate what this stream will be in the future and assign a value to it, using the techniques described in earlier chapters on discounting future payments to present value. Usually, reliable estimates of future cash flows will not be available, and the only available information will be conventionally prepared income statements for prior accounting periods. Estimates of future income flows, based on conventional income statements, are widely used instead of estimates of cash flows, simply because income numbers are usually easy to obtain directly from accounting statements. Indeed, this method of valuation is usually described as the **capitalization of income** or **capitalization of earnings**. It is a well-established method of estimating value.

As should be apparent from earlier chapters, however, income as determined by accountants is subject to numerous rules and discretionary choices in presentation that may cause the bottom line of income to diverge significantly from the amount of cash that is in fact available to the owner (even after setting aside realistic amounts for the replacement of aging plant and equipment and taking taxes into consideration). The amount available to the owner is sometimes referred to as **free cash flow** and may be thought of as a firm's capacity to make distributions. An investor is primarily (and often only) interested in the cash return that a business will generate. Thus, although accounting income may come quite close to cash flow over the long haul, it is cash flow and not accounting income that is ultimately most important to investors. Although it is tempting to use the terms cash flow and income (or earnings) interchangeably, it should always be kept in mind that these terms have distinct meanings and that cash flow should be the focus of any rigorous valuation.

It will be recalled that the valuation of an annuity or a stream of cash payments in the future requires knowledge of two variables: the size of the payments each year and the appropriate discount or interest rate by which the future payments can be discounted to present value. This rate in turn is a function of two variables: the market interest rate for riskless loans and a **risk premium**, that is, an additional amount of interest dependent on the degree of risk presented by the specific transaction. When constant perpetual payments are involved — that is, the stream of payments is assumed to remain fixed in amount and continue permanently in the future — the present value of the stream is equal to the reciprocal of the interest rate multiplied by the payment:

$$\text{Present value} = \text{Payment} \times \frac{1}{\text{Discount rate}}$$

Table 8-1

Discount rate	Capitalization factor
100%	1
50%	2
33.33%	3
25%	4
20%	5
16.66%	6
12.5%	8
10%	10
8%	12.5
7%	14
6%	16.7
5%	20

The reciprocal of the **discount rate** (1/interest rate) is often called the **multiplier** or **capitalization factor**. Table 8-1 shows how one can quickly develop a table of reciprocals that show what the multiplier is for a variety of discount rates.

In the context of a going business, a value can be obtained simply by estimating the future income or cash flow of the business, selecting a discount rate, and multiplying by the reciprocal set forth in Table 8-1. Thus, if a business's estimated future cash flow is $120,000 per year, and it is determined that an appropriate discount rate is 10 percent, that business is worth 10 × $120,000, or $1,200,000. If the estimated future cash flow is $90,000 per year, the value would be $900,000. If the business is considerably riskier and the appropriate discount rate is 20 percent, the company would be worth precisely half as much: 5 × $100,000 or $500,000. The riskier the business, the higher the discount rate, the smaller the multiplier, and the lower the value placed on the cash flow (or income). It is apparent that accurate assessments of both anticipated cash flow (or income) and discount rate are essential if the valuation so obtained is to be reliable. In real life, however, accurate information about both variables is difficult to find.

§8.8 Estimating the Amount of Cash Flow or Income

For some businesses, future cash flows can be estimated with a fair degree of reliability. For example, the rental income of a shopping center may be based on long-term leases that provide a reasonable basis for estimating future returns (though the standard practice of charging rent based in part on a percentage of gross sales may be a complicating factor). Much the same thing may be true of a hotel or an apartment house in which vacancy rates can be estimated based on experience or historic patterns. The more common situation, however, is that future cash flows or income are highly erratic, uncertain and problematic.

As described in the chapters on accounting, in some instances projections of future income or cash flow prepared by management may be available. These

Table 8-2

Year	Net income after taxes
Year 1	$100,000
Year 2	$120,000
Year 3	$180,000
Year 4	$210,000
Year 5	$160,000

estimates may be used as the projection of earnings into the future; there is a risk, however, that these estimates may be overly optimistic.

For most businesses, historical information is available as to how the business fared in the recent past. Table 8-2 is an example of information that may be available as to income for the previous five years.

Again a caveat is necessary: These are **book earnings** taken directly from the company's financial statements. Adjustments may be necessary to reflect the true capacity of the company to generate cash flow or income as discussed more fully in Chapter 7, which discussed the analysis of financial statements. For example, in the case of many small businesses, the earnings of the business may or may not include compensation to the owner. If the business is unincorporated and therefore not required to file a tax return that is separate from that of the owner, it may well be that the owner has viewed the income of the business and his or her personal income as one in the same. This may mask the fact that if the business needed to hire a manager, the investment return of the business would be somewhat smaller than the income figures indicate.

Another important consideration that may apply even in the case of relatively large and incorporated businesses is that income may reflect the way the business has been financed and the accounting choices that have been made in calculating the income. In many closely held businesses, the owners choose to lend significant sums of money to the business instead of investing it permanently in the company as part of its capital. The reason is that interest payments on debt are deductible by the corporation, and thus reduce corporate income for tax purposes. Moreover, lending money to the corporation, rather than contributing it in exchange for stock, may create additional protections on bankruptcy, permit control to be divided up in a different way from financial participation, and allow some investors to enjoy leveraged returns (though the same investor cannot leverage his or her own return by lending his or her own money to the business). In any event, it is quite common for stockholders in closely held corporations also to be creditors of the corporation, and such arrangements are generally respected for tax and other purposes as long as the amount of stockholder debt is not excessive in comparison to equity.

The point for present purposes is that when the income of a business is determined for valuation purposes, it is usually best to calculate **earnings before interest and taxes (EBIT)**, because deductible interest may in fact be an element of return to the owner and its deduction reduces the amount of tax owed. Some analysts extend the concept of EBIT also to exclude depreciation and amortization (**EBITDA**). EBITDA is, however, really an effort to combine cash-flow analysis with adjustments for interest and taxes. The problem is that

these two adjustments are conceptually very different and any effort to perform both at the same time may lead to confusion and even double counting. Moreover, there is more to cash-flow analysis than adding back depreciation and amortization. (Indeed, it is not entirely realistic to ignore these noncash expenses unless one in fact has no plans to replace aging assets.)

Assuming, however, that the income stream has already been suitably adjusted, can one draw an inference about what future income will be from this historical data? Referring back to Table 8-2, one might take the average earnings over these five years ($154,000) and conclude that this number is a reasonable estimate of the average earnings of the business in the future. One can then choose an appropriate discount rate and calculate the business's value. For example, at 12.5 percent, the multiplier would be 8 and the value of the business would be $1,232,000.

It is easy to raise objections to the reliability of this process. First of all, is it realistic to assume that the earnings will average $154,000 per year forever? What about the period beginning three years from now? Ten years from now? Certainly, as the time frame lengthens, the uncertainties and inaccuracies of present predictions must also increase. On the other hand, as pointed out in an earlier chapter, because of the time value of money, the contribution to value made by these later years is relatively small in contrast to the contribution of the next few years, where the estimate presumably is more reliable. In other words, most of the overall value is represented by the next five, more reliable years, and a relatively small amount is represented by the assumption that earnings will average $154,000 thereafter. Hence, one might conclude that the calculation should not be materially changed if the $154,000 assumption were extended to the infinite future or, alternatively, that a different assumption were made about the income in these later years. Moreover, although it is true that uncertainties increase further into the future, it also is as likely that the current estimate will understate future earnings as it is that it will overstate them. If the probability of upside error and downside error are roughly equal, the current estimate will not be materially changed. We are clearly engaged in an impressionistic and not a scientific inquiry, and there is a gamble in it from the perspective of both sides.

The seller of the contemplated business (who obviously wants a high valuation) might legitimately complain that the $154,000 average figure gives undue weight to the first two years, which are the most remote from the present. After all, in the last three years of the five-year period, earnings never were below $160,000 and yet future earnings are estimated at only $154,000. It is more reasonable, it might be argued, to use only the average earnings of the last three years, which places the estimated earnings at $183,333 per year. The overall value of the business, using a 12.5 percent discount rate, would then be $1,466,664. In response, it might be argued that the significant decline in earnings in the last year is a warning that conditions giving rise to the steady increase in earnings in prior years may have changed, and that the average earnings in the future should in no event be viewed as being greater than those in the last year ($160,000). Along the same line, earnings arguably should be less than $160,000 if the downward trend can be expected to continue. Obviously, analysis of causes of the decline is of central importance in this debate.

Let us assume a somewhat different pattern of earnings with no change in average earnings for the period:

Year 1	$100,000
Year 2	$120,000
Year 3	$160,000
Year 4	$180,000
Year 5	$210,000

This rather minor adjustment gives a dramatically different appearance to the business's future. The seller might well argue that the estimate of average income in the future should build in a growth factor. For example, the seller might argue that the trend of growth in current earnings should be extrapolated into the future, for example:

Year 5 (actual)	$210,000
Year 6 (estimate)	$240,000
Year 7 (estimate)	$270,000
Year 8 (estimate)	$300,000

If this analysis is accepted, and the average of these four projections ($255,000) is taken as the anticipated income or cash-flow stream, the value of this business at a 12.5 percent discount factor becomes $2,040,000. At the very least, the trend might justify the use of the results for the most recent year ($210,000) as estimated future income. If the 12.5 percent discount rate is applied to this figure, the value of the business is $1,680,000.

§8.9 Valuation With Growth

When a constant rate of growth can be anticipated, a useful formula is:

$$\text{Value} = \frac{\text{Income}}{\text{Capitalization rate} - \text{Growth rate}}$$

For example, consider a business with income of $200,000 in the most recent year. This business is expected to grow at an annual rate of 10 percent. In other words, the income is expected to be $240,000 in the next year and $288,000 in the year after that, and so on. If the appropriate capitalization rate before growth is 12.5 percent, the value of the business would be:

$$\$200,000 \, / \, (.125 - .10) \text{ or } 200,000 \, / \, .025$$

Because of the extremely low (net) capitalization rate, the value of the business works out to a whopping $8,000,000 rather than a modest $1.6 million for the same business without growth.

It is extremely important in considering the effect of growth on valuation to think clearly about the source of the growth. How would a company with income of $200,000 per year that is capitalized at 12.5 percent and therefore

worth $1.6 million make itself grow at 10 percent per year? Although it is possible that the company has happened onto a growth opportunity that requires little or no new investment, such opportunities will usually be subject to intense competition. It is much more likely that the business will grow by investing more in its current line of business. Assume that the company decides to plow back half of its income into investment in expanded facilities in order to make the company grow. Assuming that the $100,000 will generate a return of 12.5 percent (which is the current return on the $1.6 million in value that investors currently have invested), the increase in earnings will be $12,500 or 6.25 percent. How much will the company now be worth according to the valuation with growth formula? Plugging the numbers into the formula:

$$\$200,000 - \$100,000 \;/\; (.125 - .0625) = \$100,000 \;/\; .0625 = \$1,600,000$$

In other words, the company is worth exactly what it was worth without growth. The reason is that one must subtract the amount that is reinvested in growth, because such funds are not in fact free cash flow available for distribution to the owners. To be sure, reinvested funds still belong to the owners and have the effect of increasing the value of the company's assets. And the funds could be used to pay dividends instead of financing growth. But to count the funds as available for distribution when they are being committed to the generation of more income in the future, and then to count the increased future income as well, is to count the same money twice. (Indeed, counting both has the effect of mixing asset valuation with going-concern valuation.)

In the real world, many companies continue to pay dividends and borrow to finance new growth. But borrowing creates a dollar-for-dollar increase in liabilities that cancels out the increase from growth unless the company can borrow at interest rates lower than its capitalization rate. The resulting growth is as much a result of an increase in leverage as it is of the discovery of a new opportunity for extraordinary profits.

The most important point about valuation with growth is that the value of the company turns out to be the same as without growth if one assumes that the rate of return on new investment is the same as the rate of return on existing business. The value of an additional $12,500 in income capitalized at 12.5 percent is $100,000, exactly the same as the amount invested.

How realistic is the assumption that new business will generate income at the existing capitalization rate? Quite. Clearly a business should never invest in new business with a rate of return less than its capitalization rate. To do so will depress the value of the business as a whole. (If the new business is significantly less risky than the existing business, however, investors may capitalize the new business at a lower rate, thus placing a higher value on smaller chunks of income and keeping the value of the business steady. That is why a business that retains some of its income in money market funds or government securities rather than using every last penny to pay dividends is generally not penalized in terms of market value.) On the other hand, if the business can find new business with a rate of return that exceeds its capitalization rate, then undertaking that business will generate more return percentagewise than existing business and will increase the value of the company in the aggregate. But how likely is it that such op-

portunities will regularly be found? Not very. If the business operates in a competitive environment, as many businesses do, everyone will seek valuable opportunities and competition for the business will have the effect of reducing the return on it to the bare minimum necessary to make it worth undertaking. To be sure, there may be situations in which new business carries a higher rate of return. For example, the business may be able to take advantage of economies of scale. The business may have unused production capacity that can be exploited simply by investing in a few new salespeople. Needless to say, such opportunities tend to be exploited quickly and are thus not likely to be a permanent trait of the business. Still, it is crucial in doing a valuation to have some sense of where a business is in its life cycle.

One important implication of this discussion is that it is crucial for financial managers within a company to have a good sense of the company's capitalization rate. Indeed, it may be more important for those within the company than for anyone else. Management may otherwise be tempted to take on new business that will cause the value of the company to fall, possibly exposing the company to the threat of takeover. As discussed in Chapter 2, which covered present value, for any new business under consideration, management will typically calculate an **internal rate of return (IRR)** based on projected cash flows of the new business. If the IRR equals or exceeds the capitalization rate, then the new business is worth considering further. In practice, financial managers actually do use the capitalization rate (often referring to it as the cost of capital) to set goals in terms of the required rate of return that must be generated by any new business being considered.

The fact that the value of a business tends to be the same with or without growth makes the valuation process much easier in a way. It means that as long as one is careful to calculate the maximum amount that the business can distribute without compromising its ability to keep generating cash to make such distributions indefinitely into the future, it is unimportant to consider what the company is in fact doing with its money as long as one is generally confident that the company is well managed. Thus, the exercise of calculating value with growth is a powerful argument for cash-flow analysis, because the central goal of the valuation process becomes a determination the maximum return that the business could in fact pay to its owners indefinitely. The relationship between valuation without growth and valuation with growth makes it clear that one should focus on cash flow.

Although the previous example involves much guesswork, it gives a flavor of the process. In real life, a cash-flow valuation will often involve the assessment of likely future cash-flow outcomes, the assignment of probabilities to each outcome, and the weighting of all possible results with the probability that that result will occur. The end result of this process is a single number that represents the value of the probable outcome given the uncertainties worked into the analysis. This analysis is often presented in the form of a **decision tree** that may help in making sure that major contingencies are not overlooked. The process is sometimes also called **scenario analysis**.

Consider the following simple example. In arriving at the above estimate that earnings for Year 6 would be $240,000, an analyst might attempt to predict results under a best case, average case, and worst case. (What constitutes each

case could be any conceivable factor that is important to the business's success, ranging from interest rates, to corn prices, to ski conditions. And in most businesses there will be many such factors to be considered.) The analyst has come up with the following outcomes and probabilities (with the probabilities expressed as decimals):

	Outcome	Probability	Expected Return
Best Case:	$300,000	(.25)	$ 75,000
Average Case:	$230,000	(.50)	$115,000
Worst Case:	$200,000	(.25)	$ 50,000
Total (Weighted Average):			$240,000

The expected return column shows the product of the outcome multiplied by the probability of that outcome. In essence, each possible payoff is multiplied by the odds that it will happen to determine how much the bet is worth. By adding up the values of each of the outcomes, one can place a value on all of the outcomes in the aggregate. Such a **weighted average** is usually more accurate than an effort simply to choose a most likely outcome, because a weighted average values all outcomes in proportion to their likelihood. Indeed, it bears noting that in the above example, there is no situation in which the analyst really expects earnings to be $240,000, even though that turns out to be the best guess if one calculates a weighted average of possible outcomes.

Using a weighted average also allows for the quantification of risk. Consider the following, which is a different estimate of probable outcomes:

	Outcome	Probability	Expected Return
Best Case:	$400,000	(.25)	$100,000
Average Case:	$230,000	(.50)	$115,000
Worst Case:	$100,000	(.25)	$ 25,000
Total (Weighted Average):			$240,000

The expected return for this period is the same as in the earlier example. But are the two investments worth the same? Clearly not. The first is worth more because the dispersion of expected returns is narrower and therefore less risky than the second. The return is less volatile. (**Risk, dispersion**, and **volatility of returns** are all the same thing.) To be sure, there is always the chance with the second investment that one would receive $400,000. But there is an equal chance that one would receive only $100,000. The potential gain on the upside is thus precisely offset by a potential loss on the downside. Yet, the same expected return is available in the first investment without wild swings in outcome. Intuitively, other things equal, the first investment is better because it is less risky. Although it is difficult to quantify the difference, it seems clear that if both investments were offered at the same price, that is, if both required a commitment of the same amount of capital, investors should choose to put their money in the first before turning to the second. In order to make the second investment equally attractive to investors, it must be offered at a lower price. For example, if the first opportunity could be sold to an informed investor for $2,400,000 (to generate a 10 percent return), the second investment might

need to be offered at $2,000,000 (to generate a 12 percent return). A rational investor demands more return if he or she takes more risk.

By using a weighted average approach to valuation, it is possible to quantify to some extent the risk of the two investments. The traditional method of quantifying dispersion of outcomes is by calculating a **standard deviation**. (A standard deviation is the square root of the sum of the squares of the differences between the average outcome and each individual outcome each multiplied by the probability of that outcome.) Without belaboring the process here, the standard deviation of the first investment is about $37,000, whereas the standard deviation of the second is about $107,000. Note that the standard deviation is expressed in the same terms (dollars) as the outcomes. The chances are about two out of three that the actual outcome will be within one standard deviation of the mean, and about 95 percent that it will be within two standard deviations. Although the standard deviation gives some sense of risk, it is not especially useful in comparing different investments, because it varies in proportion to the amounts in question. In the examples given, this is no problem, because the average return is the same for both investments, and the two standard deviations may thus be directly compared. But an investor is often faced with two or more possible investments with very different weighted average returns. The solution to this problem is to calculate a **coefficient of variation (COV)**, which is the standard deviation divided by the mean. The COV for the first investment is 37,000/240,000 or about 15 percent, while the COV for the second investment is 107,000/240,000 or about 45 percent. One can also think of the COV as an expression of units of risk per dollar of return that allows different investments to be compared to each other.

The isolation of possible outcomes and the assignment of specific probabilities to each outcome gives a satisfying specificity to the entire operation. However, even if all major contingencies are isolated in the decision tree analysis (itself a dubious assumption), the assignment of probabilities to them usually involves so much guesswork and is so uncertain that it is doubtful that this technique's use in real life situations provides a materially improved estimate of future events than the much more impressionistic analysis based on a mixture of historical results and generalized predictions about future trends set forth above. And the danger of assigning hard numbers to estimates is that the conclusion may appear to be more specific, and therefore more reliable, than it actually is.

§8.10 Capitalization Rates

Recall that the interest rate used to discount future payments back to present values in effect describes a measure of the risk that the payments will not occur. The same process applies in connection with valuation of a going concern. Typically, the terms **capitalization rate** or **multiplier** are used in this context rather than **discount rate** or **interest rate**. The capitalization rate is the **rate of return** that an investor would demand in exchange for making the investment in question given other available investment opportunities. The multiplier is the reciprocal of the capitalization rate. Because investors demand more return when they take more risk, the capitalization rate varies directly with

the riskiness of the venture. The higher the risk, the higher the capitalization rate, and the smaller the multiplier.

The determination of which capitalization rate or multiplier to use in valuing a business appears at first glance to involve variables even more uncertain than the determination of the anticipated income or cash flow of the business. Indeed, one might argue that the multiplication of one gross approximation by an even grosser approximation is a classic example of garbage in garbage out and results in a figure that is so unreliable that it should not be used at all.

Usually the capitalization rate or multiplier used in valuing a business is established from the actual relationships between average earnings and sales prices of similar businesses in the recent past, rather than from a market interest rate plus additional risk assessment. Persons familiar with the purchase and sale of businesses usually are also generally familiar with actual sales prices of businesses that have been sold in the recent past and the estimated earnings used in the negotiations leading to these sales. Statements such as "Companies in which the personal services of the owners are an important income-producing factor generally sell at two times earnings, or less," or "Steel companies generally sell for about eight times earnings," or "Companies developing computer software that have marketed at least one successful product generally sell for at least 15 times earnings," are all meaningful statements that provide useful signposts for the selection of an appropriate capitalization factor for a roughly comparable business in the same or related industry.

In addition, for publicly traded securities there is readily available information about **price/earnings (P/E) ratios**. The P/E ratio is the ratio between the market price per share and the earnings per share of the publicly held stock for the last available accounting period.

The P/E ratios for individual companies (and indeed for industry groups) can be highly misleading. Because the published P/E ratio is (necessarily) based on the previous year's income, it does not convey a sense of what investors expect in the future. Ultimately investors care only about the future. Thus, a company that had a loss in the most recent year will nevertheless have a positive stock price and therefore will have a P/E ratio of infinity (because the denominator—that is, the figure representing earnings—is less than zero). Clearly, no one should be misled by a P/E ratio of infinity, but a similar effect arises if a company has substantial prospects but only barely positive earnings in the past year. If a company had earnings of (say) 10 cents per share last year and a current stock price of $20, the P/E is 200. But it may be that the previous year was a transition year and investors expect earnings of $2 per share in coming years. If so, the multiplier should be seen as 10, not 200. Most newspapers do not publish P/E ratios of 100 or more, although clearly a P/E of 60 or 70 is likely to be as misleading. In any event, one should be careful in using the P/E ratio of a single stock for purposes of valuation. If the P/E ratio is not extremely high and has been reasonably stable over the last few years, it is probably a reliable indicator of the appropriate capitalization rate. In most industries, using an industry average will control for the differing fortunes of individual companies, though it is possible that even an industry average will be misleading if the entire industry had an unusually good or bad year.

Yet another reason why the P/E ratio is not a precise indicator of the

appropriate capitalization rate or multiplier is because the P/E ratio of a publicly traded stock reflects a multitude of investment decisions for small blocks of stock not affecting the control of the business, while the capitalization rate or multiplier should reflect the fact that control of the business is being bought and sold. In other words, the P/E ratio of publicly held companies, as usually computed, reflects only the investment value of securities and not any premium that represents control. If takeover bids are any indication, control premiums average about 50 percent higher and may be as high as 100 percent above the market price. Use of P/E ratios as the capitalization factor for valuation purposes for closely held businesses therefore may considerably underestimate the value of the company being appraised.

In the end, however, the uncertainties inherent in the valuation of a closely held business may outweigh uncertainties about the accuracy of P/E ratios for publicly held businesses. Clearly, the two are closely related, and P/E ratios (with appropriate adjustments) are routinely used as estimates of capitalization rates.

In an ideal situation, one may be able to find a publicly held corporation that is similar in most important respects to the closely held business being valued. If the two businesses are roughly comparable, then the P/E ratio of the publicly held stock can be applied as a ballpark estimate of the appropriate capitalization rate for the closely held company being valued. Again, it must be remembered that we are not dealing here with precise scientific data but with an impressionistic analysis establishing a **range of values**.

Unfortunately, however, there is often no publicly held corporation that is a close match for the company being valued. The most common problem of noncomparability is that the publicly held corporation has substantial business operations in several different industries, while the closely held corporation being valued is active in only a single industry. In this situation, one may use a composite P/E ratio for all the publicly held companies in the industry, if that is available. That composite ratio may be an appropriate capitalization factor for a business active only in the same industry on the theory that the averaging of P/E ratios for different publicly held companies tends to cancel out the effect of different multiple operations in different industries. If the notes to the financial statements of one or more of the publicly held corporations contain sufficient breakdowns and information on the results of operations in the industry in question, it may be possible to derive an estimate of a separate P/E ratio for those operations alone.

In selecting an appropriate capitalization rate, it may be appropriate to adjust an industrywide P/E ratio to reflect unique aspects of the company in question. For example, if the company appears to have a more obsolete plant than the comparable company or the industry average, it may be appropriate to reduce the capitalization rate. There are two problems with such an adjustment, however. First, it is relatively easy to say that an "appropriate" adjustment should be made, but there is usually no criterion for determining what that adjustment should be. If the base rate is 9 times earnings, should the appropriate capitalization rate for the corporation with a somewhat obsolete plant be 8 times earnings? 8.5 times? 8.75 times? Such differences in the capitalization rate may have substantial effects on the business's overall value. The difference between

8.5 and 8 times earnings may easily involve millions of dollars. The second problem is the risk of double counting a negative factor. If the obsolete plant is used first to justify a reduction of anticipated future earnings or cash flow, and a second time to reduce the appropriate capitalization rate, it is likely that the double use of the same negative factor will overstate its importance.

Logically, an adjustment of this nature probably should be made in the expected cash flow or income determination rather than the discount rate, because changes in the capitalization rate affect all elements of cash flow and not just reductions that may be entailed by replacing an outdated plant.

§8.11 Capitalization Rates Calculated From Scratch

Although it is clearly easier to refer to sales of comparable companies or to P/E ratios, it should always be kept in mind that both are short cuts for the process of assigning a capitalization rate. Again, the capitalization rate is the rate of return that a rational investor would demand in exchange for making the investment in question given other investment opportunities available. Because investors demand more return when they take more risk, capitalization rates must vary directly with the riskiness of the venture. The higher the risk, the higher the capitalization rate. The capitalization rate may be estimated by taking the prevailing **riskless rate of return** and adding a premium for the riskiness of the venture in question. Thus, if the riskless rate of return is 6 percent and because of the risk involved in a given venture an investor would require an additional 12 percent, the capitalization rate should be 18 percent, which translates into a multiplier of about 5.6.

The beginning point for choosing a capitalization rate from scratch is the riskless rate of return, that is, the rate of return available on long-term government securities. (When valuing a business, it is usually appropriate to use the rate on long-term securities as a benchmark, because such securities will only mature in the distant future and thus come closest to matching the typical business situation in which no liquidation is contemplated.) In some cases, however, the riskless rate of return may in fact be too high, because some portion of it is attributable to inflation. Creditors, after all, understand that repayment in inflated dollars reduces the effective return. The riskless rate of return actually has two elements: the so-called **real interest rate** and an inflation factor. In some cases, it may be appropriate to base a going-concern valuation on the real interest rate without an inflation factor. A good example is a business that is largely immune to the effects of inflation because the price of its product may be easily increased with inflation. (Indeed, such a business may make money from inflation to the extent that its inventory increases in value simply from the passage of time.)

Finding the appropriate **risk premium** is considerably more difficult than finding the appropriate base rate, but again it helps to keep in mind that the goal of the process is to determine the required rate of return. If one has estimated the cash flow or income from the business on the basis of a weighted average calculation, then to some extent risk can be quantified in at least relative terms by calculating the COV. The COV may then be compared with other

investments of varying risk to get a sense of how much additional return is needed to compensate for additional risk.

Charts and tables that suggest risk premiums for various types of businesses are also available in business publications. One author suggests that risk premiums should range from 6 to 10 percent for established businesses with a large share of the relevant market, strong financing, stable earnings history, and depth of management to 26 to 30 percent for a one-person firm in a personal services business. With regard to larger businesses, it bears noting that research based on stock market prices does seem to indicate that the premium over the riskless rate is about 6 percent on the average. Stock prices, however, do not include dividend payments, which average at about 3 percent for publicly traded common stocks, suggesting that the true minimum risk premium for equity is closer to 9 percent.

What then should be said about capitalization of earnings or cash flow as a valuation method? It is the most popular method of valuation of closely held businesses that are being purchased because of their potential earnings or cash flow. It is also widely used in valuation disputes generally, such as those relating to the value of stock in a closely held business for gift and estate tax purposes. Indeed, despite its drawbacks, the capitalization of earnings or cash flow is generally believed to be the most reliable method of estimating the value of a business anticipated to be in existence indefinitely.

§8.12 Valuation Based on Prior Purchases and Sales

This section considers the relevance of prior sales of the business, or more commonly, prior sales of shares of stock or other interests in the business, in determining the value of the business. This discussion sharply distinguishes between a closely held business, where there is no regular market for the shares of the business, and businesses whose shares are publicly traded. The distinction between these two is discussed more fully in Chapter 10, which discusses forms of organization.

When valuing a business, one sometimes discovers that a negotiated sale of the entire business occurred at some earlier time. A sale of the entire business in the fairly recent past, in an arm's-length transaction between sophisticated individuals, is considered practically conclusive evidence of value as of the time of the sale. Indeed, when a retrospective valuation is involved, such as for tax purposes in connection with a gift made several years ago, an arm's-length sale occurring years after the gift will usually be seen as providing a reliable basis for going back and estimating the business's value at the earlier time. Adjustments made to that negotiated sales price are limited to changes that occurred in the business between the time the sale took place and the earlier or later date on which the value is to be ascertained.

More commonly, prior transactions involve purchases and sales of shares of voting stock of the company rather than a sale of the entire company. At this point, the difference between a closely held corporation and a publicly held corporation becomes critical. In the case of a publicly held company, purchases and sales of stock usually occur daily. Professional analysts keep up with the

company and make recommendations about the stock. In closely held corporations, on the other hand, the sales are almost by definition isolated, infrequent, and few in number. Furthermore, transactions in shares in closely held corporations are usually made without skilled investment advice, and under circumstances in which one party to the transaction is under financial compulsion to sell while the other party may be under little or no compulsion to buy.

Because the abstract test of fair market value is a price established by negotiation between hypothetical buyers and sellers, it should not be surprising that actual sales of small portions of a business are given great weight in the process of making a valuation of the whole business when it seems clear that the earlier transactions were in fact at arm's length. Obviously, more recent transactions should be given more weight than older ones. However, in every case the circumstances surrounding a specific sale need to be examined to determine how closely the transaction reflects the abstract ideal of the **arm's length transaction**.

In a closely held corporation, minority interests in the corporation are unlikely to be salable to outside investors at prices that reflect their allocable portion of the value of the business if sold as a unit. One reason for this is that closely held corporations rarely pay dividends; rather, they tend to disguise distributions as salary expenses and similar payments to shareholders. A minority shareholder, therefore, has no assurance of any return from his or her investment unless the majority shareholders permit the minority shareholder to be an employee of the corporation at a salary that is comparable with the salaries of other shareholder-employees. Because the minority shareholder cannot assure an outsider of employment with the corporation, even if the outsider would be interested in the job, it is unusual for a nonshareholder to negotiate independently with a minority shareholder to acquire a minority interest. When such negotiations occur, the nonshareholder is apt to demand a significant discount to reflect the lack of liquidity of the investment and the risk that the anticipated return may not be forthcoming.

Shares of closely held corporations are usually subject to **share transfer restrictions** or **buy/sell agreements** that require a shareholder who dies or who desires to dispose of his or her shares to offer (or sell) the shares to the corporation or to the other shareholders at a fixed or readily determinable price. A very popular price used in these agreements is book value. An option agreement commits the shareholder to sell but does not commit the corporation or other shareholders to purchase; a buy/sell agreement commits the purchaser as well as the seller to the transaction. Binding agreements of these types set a cap on the value that may be placed on the shares for most purposes. If the agreement is a buy/sell agreement that binds the purchaser as well as the seller, the shares are usually valued at the contract price (assuming that the purchaser is capable of making the purchase); if it is an option agreement in which the purchaser has the power to purchase at a designated price but is not committed to do so, the shares may be valued at or below the agreed upon price.

In the absence of a binding option or buy/sell agreement, a minority shareholder desiring to sell his or her shares usually cannot compel the corporation or other shareholders to purchase. The shareholder who desires to sell must instead seek voluntary transactions either with the corporation or with

one or more other shareholders. In most cases, such sales will be negotiated with the corporation itself, rather than individual shareholders, because a purchase by the corporation does not affect the relative holdings of the remaining shareholders. Moreover, neither majority nor minority shareholders have a strong incentive to offer the selling shareholder a generous price: Other minority shareholders do not generally improve their position significantly vis-à-vis each other or the majority shareholder by becoming larger minority shareholders. The majority shareholder, on the other hand, by hypothesis already has a controlling position and does not need the additional minority shares to cement or preserve that control. However, the other shareholders collectively, and the majority shareholder individually, usually do desire to eliminate minority interests if they can do so on an acceptable basis: Minority shareholders are therefore usually able to liquidate their holdings by selling to the corporation or to the majority shareholder if they are willing to accept a low enough price. Even though the situation is not hopeless in terms of finding a buyer, it is certainly not the traditional willing buyer and willing seller exchange.

When three or more factions exist, and none of these factions individually has a majority of the outstanding shares, the dynamics are quite different. If the balance of power is represented by the shares owned by the shareholder who wishes to sell, spirited bidding by the remaining factions may occur as each seeks to obtain the **swing shares** necessary to acquire the controlling interest in the management of the business. The per-share value of the swing block may overstate the aggregate per share value of the business in this situation.

Although it is clear that when a minority shareholder desires to sell out, he or she must often accept a lesser price, it does not necessarily follow that the majority shareholder can take advantage of the differential by (say) arranging to have the corporation repurchase his own shares at a higher price than might be offered to the minority. The courts quite routinely enjoin transactions in which the majority seeks to use its power over the corporation to obtain favored treatment, though the courts also recognize that there are some situations (e.g., where a majority shareholder desires to retire) in which the minority may not be entitled to strictly identical treatment. Similarly, the courts have been quite ready to review actions made by majority shareholders to remove minority shareholders from offices or jobs with the corporation. Although the courts recognize that one faction must sometimes prevail over another when there are genuine differences of opinion as to how to run the business, the courts also recognize that the power of the majority to eliminate the primary form of a return enjoyed by most shareholders in closely held businesses (a paying job) can be used as a way of pressuring the minority shareholder to sell out to the majority at a bargain price.

When shares of a closely held business are subject to a buy/sell agreement or when the transaction in question is such that the majority would be precluded from using its power to exact favorable treatment from the corporation, it is arguable that neither a control premium nor a minority discount should be applied. Nevertheless, the Internal Revenue Service, always on the lookout for ways to maximize tax dollars, often argues for estate tax purposes that control shares should be valued more highly even though the corporation or other shareholders are contractually entitled to purchase such shares at the same price

at which the minority would be required to sell their shares. Moreover, as a matter of logic, any control premium assigned to one block of shares should be matched by a comparable minority discount for other blocks of shares. After all, the business as a business is only worth so much. Nevertheless, in matters of estate tax, as well as other areas of the real world, things do not always work out so neatly.

When valuing the overall business, what weight, if any, should be given to a sale of a minority interest — say, a 10 percent interest — that does not involve control considerations by a minority shareholder? This question has no fixed answer: It depends entirely on the circumstances. Such sales should be investigated to determine how closely they meet the valuation ideal (a ready buyer, ready seller, and the like). Thus, a sale between family members under circumstances indicating that a motive for the transaction may have been partially to make a gift is given little or no weight. A sale to the corporation, to the majority shareholder, to another minority shareholder, or conceivably to an outsider, that appears to be at arm's length and not entered into by the seller under financial exigency or pressure, may be presumptively accepted as an accurate valuation of at least a minority interest at the time of the sale. When the purchaser is the corporation or the majority shareholder, however, it is likely that the minority shareholder was under considerably greater compulsion to sell than the purchaser was to buy. Thus, the circumstances underlying each specific sale must be examined carefully.

For example, an arm's-length sale by a 10 percent shareholder to the majority shareholder at a price that was clearly bargained over would be given some weight even though it might appear that the seller was in some financial distress and needed cash for personal reasons. Absolute perfection in the bargaining process is not required. On the other hand, if it appears that in a similar transaction (1) there were unsuccessful attempts by the seller to find other potential purchasers, (2) the seller needed cash urgently for personal reasons or to avoid bankruptcy, or (3) the sale took place at a price set by the buyer on a take-it-or-leave-it basis, the sale is not a reliable indication of value. It all depends on an estimate of how close the actual transaction came to the theoretical ideal. In many other contexts, a price negotiated at arm's length is given some weight in assessing the fair market value of an asset even though defects exist in the negotiation process. One need only think of transactions taking place at rug bazaars, at country auctions, and in a host of everyday transactions in which it is unlikely that the ideal conditions of perfect knowledge and lack of compulsion are present. The same thing is true of isolated arm's-length sales of closely held securities to outsiders, to the corporation, to other minority shareholders, or to the majority shareholder.

When the value of an entire business is estimated from isolated sales of minority shares, an appropriate adjustment should be made to reflect the discounts normally applied to such shares for lack of marketability and the minority status of such shares. This subject is discussed more fully below.

Prior sales of controlling interests in closely held businesses, unlike sales of minority interests, are usually viewed as reliable indicators of value. The majority shareholder usually is reasonably sophisticated and knowledgeable about his or her business and is in a position to negotiate effectively. Further, controlling

interests are more salable to outside persons than minority interests, because the purchaser obtains the power to manage the business rather than becoming a passive investor subject to the whim of the majority. As a result, a majority block of shares commands a significantly higher price per share than a minority block, even though the shares are formally indistinguishable. The majority shares are referred to as **control shares**. Minority shares that are not part of the control block sell at significant discounts from the price that control shares command, when they sell at all. It is not uncommon for a person seeking to buy all of the outstanding shares of a closely held corporation to offer a significantly lower price per share for the minority shares than for the control shares on a per-share basis. In the closely held corporation, this distinction between control shares and minority shares is easy to visualize, because ordinarily it is permanent: It is not physically possible for minority blocks of shares aggregating 40 percent of the stock, say, ever to outvote the majority's 60 percent block.

When the common stock of a company is publicly traded on an exchange or in the over-the-counter market, the market price usually establishes the value of all noncontrol blocks of stock on that date. Indeed, in widely traded stocks, the textbook methods of determining value are to use either the closing price on that date or the mean between the bid and asked offers at the closing.

Many smaller companies are publicly traded on the over-the-counter market, but by reason of their size or the number of shareholders, the volume of trading does not approach that of companies listed on the major exchanges. These publicly held stocks are referred to as being **thinly traded** or having **thin markets**. Prices of trades in thin markets may need to be individually examined, because some thinly traded stocks may have more characteristics of closely held corporations than of publicly held corporations.

Even when a publicly traded stock has a broad market with numerous transactions each hour, it does not necessarily follow that the total value of the business, if it were sold as a single entity, equals the current market price per share multiplied by the total number of shares outstanding. To be sure, the outstanding shares represent the aggregate equity ownership interest in the corporation, and the common stock usually possesses the entire voting power to elect directors. Under these circumstances, it is tempting to view each transaction in a publicly traded common stock as a trade that represents the value of the underlying business in microcosm. If this conclusion were correct, valuation of publicly held corporations would be relatively easy, because one could obtain the current value of the entire business simply by adding up the current market values of all outstanding shares. Many persons do, in fact, use this market value as a measure of the corporation's value under present management and in current circumstances. Academic writers in the field of law and economics often make this assumption.

The premiums typically paid to shareholders in corporate takeovers, however, demonstrate that the value placed on a business by the securities markets is usually significantly lower than the amount a purchaser is willing to pay for the entire business (or all the outstanding stock) if it were in fact put up for sale. In other words, the public market for stock often appears to significantly understate the value of the entire company when it is put up for sale as an entity.

This phenomenon has been the subject of considerable speculation, because there is a great deal of evidence in other contexts that the public securities markets are efficient in the sense that the price reflects all currently available public information about the stock. The efficient market theory is discussed in more detail in Chapter 14, which covers securities markets. Of course, it may be that the market is not efficient, or that it is efficient only in the sense that it processes information efficiently even though some or much of the information may be false or somehow misconstrued. Nevertheless, the fact that investors and many others rely on the market not only to set prices, but also as a reliable indicator of value for innumerable other purposes, suggests that it is widely believed that the market is basically efficient.

One plausible explanation for the price variation in some takeovers (but not in others) is that the securities markets value the business only on the assumption that current management will remain in office, while bidders in takeovers set a higher value, because they plan to replace incumbent management with more effective management that justifies a higher price per share.

Another explanation is that the trading markets for securities are primarily markets for investments, not markets for controlling interests in companies. Almost all transactions on public securities markets involve minute fractions of the total outstanding shares of companies, and these transactions individually do not carry with them any meaningful opportunity to affect the company's business policies. However, where the transactions increase in size so that control of the company may be involved, the purchasers are willing to pay more — usually significantly more — than the prices for smaller blocks of shares that are traded solely as investments. Of course, if one person buys enough small blocks in a publicly held corporation, he or she will ultimately end up with a big block, and conceivably a majority block. But that is not the way things usually work, because only a few persons have the financial resources to assemble such a block of shares, and federal law requires public disclosure of a person who accumulates more than 5 percent of any public corporation's stock. The result is that the market for the whole corporation — the takeover market or market for control, as it is sometimes called — arguably is different from the regular market for investment securities.

Yet a third explanation is that the price offered for a controlling interest of publicly held corporations is dictated more by the availability of risk capital to finance the acquisition than considerations of value. Many acquisitions of publicly held corporations involve the extensive use of debt to finance the purchase. Usually, the business being purchased becomes the ultimate debtor whose cash flow is expected to discharge the debts incurred in the takeover. This type of acquisition is called a **bootstrap acquisition** (because the company is in effect purchased with its own assets) or a **leveraged buyout** (if incumbent management and outside financiers end up as the ultimate owners of the business). How is the price to be offered for such a transaction ascertained? Clearly, it must be set significantly higher than the current market price in order to be attractive to investors and to close out possible competitive offers from other sources. The decision as to whether such a transaction is feasible may be based on (1) a cash-flow analysis indicating the maximum amount of debt the business can possibly carry and (2) estimates of the amounts for which nonessential assets

or peripheral lines of business can be sold for. In the most extreme case, most of the business's assets may be sold off to raise funds to reduce the outstanding indebtedness incurred to finance the purchase price: a **bust-up acquisition** in the true sense of the word. Although this description may seem to have little to do with the value of the target company, the fact that borrowed money is used to purchase target stock may mean that the potential cash flow of the target is higher than the market perceives or that the capitalization rate applied by the market is too high. This explanation is consistent with the facts that valuation is an art, that varying estimates and assumptions made by an appraiser may lead to very different results, and that valuation studies may lead to the discovery of important business opportunities.

There are other theories regarding why publicly traded companies are routinely bought and sold for more than the aggregate market value of their shares and how takeover premiums can be reconciled with the idea that the securities market is efficient. It is possible that bidders simply overpay for many target companies. It is also possible that investors disfavor diversified or under-leveraged companies. And it may be that the market is not perfectly efficient — that market prices are determined by a range of investor perceptions and tend to change with the changing supply of stock or in reaction to fluctuations in trading by successive groups of investors who see a stock as overpriced or underpriced as a result of trading by other investors with other opinions or pursuant to other strategies. In the end, there may be truth in all of these explanations. These forces, either individually or working together, may drive market prices for individual companies away from the value that would be set by a perfectly efficient securities market. The resulting fluctuations in market prices are sometimes called **market noise**.

§8.13 Valuation Based on Subsequent Performance of the Business

When a business is being sold for cash to an independent purchaser, differing valuations of the business may create an impasse. The gap between the lowest price the seller is willing to accept and the highest price the buyer is willing to offer may be unbridgeable by negotiation. This gap is usually traceable to differing assumptions about what the future holds for the business. The parties agree that the price should be 10 times future earnings but they disagree on what the future earnings are likely to be: The seller sees a high probability of continuing improvement in earnings or cash flow with relatively little risk, while the buyer, naturally more cautious, sees cloudier skies with greater prob-ability of disappointing results. This impasse threatens to kill the deal entirely, and yet it involves the valuation issue exclusively.

Devices exist that may enable the parties to bridge the gap between these inconsistent expectations and forecasts. These devices basically set the initial contract price at the buyer's price but defer the final determination of the sales price until after the post-sale operations of the business can be evaluated. The buyer commits to the conservative price he or she is willing to pay and agrees to pay an additional amount at the end of one or two years if earnings exceed

an amount stated in the agreement (basically the buyer's conservative prediction). If the operations are more profitable than this stated amount, the seller is entitled to an addition to the purchase price computed on the actual post-sale earnings. This contingent payment based on actual post-sale results largely eliminates the impasse over valuation. If the buyer's more pessimistic forecasts turn out to be accurate, no further payment is due, while if the business is as profitable as the seller expects, the ultimate purchase price will be based on the seller's estimate. These devices are sometimes called **earnout agreements** or **workout agreements**, because a portion of the purchase price is earned or worked out after the transaction is closed. (They have nothing to do with workouts of businesses on the brink of insolvency.) Agreements of this type permit transactions to close immediately without requiring consensus on the value of the company at the time of the closing. The usual period for an earnout is three years or less following the closing, although longer periods are possible.

Earnout agreements involve complex negotiation and complex drafting, particularly where the parties have no reason to trust the other side's good faith. The seller may be unwilling to accept the unsecured promise of the buyer that the additional purchase price will be paid when it becomes due a year or two after the sale has closed. The seller may request that the workout payment be placed in escrow to assure the seller that the payment will be made promptly if it is earned. The buyer may resist this proposal if he or she proposes to use the cash flow generated during the workout period to pay the additional purchase price. And, of course, an escrow arrangement ties up independent funds for a significant period of time.

There may also be detailed negotiations over the terms on which the business is to be conducted during the workout period. The seller, of course, wishes to ensure that the purchased business has a fair shot at earning whatever amount is required by the workout agreement. The two parties must decide whether the buyer or the seller is to manage the business until the workout period ends, how much additional capital the buyer must provide during the workout period (if any) and at what times and in what amounts, and a host of other business issues such as limitations on salaries, on transactions the buyer may enter into with the purchased business, and so forth. Usually, the seller proposes to run the business during the workout period: If this is acceptable to the buyer, the buyer may nevertheless seek protection against artificial changes in business operations, such as reduction of deferrable expenses, which the seller may quietly institute in order to improve earnings during the workout period and thereby earn the workout payment.

Even though the development of a workout agreement may involve difficult negotiations and complex issues, the advantage of permitting negotiations to come to a settlement without requiring either party to accept the valuation assumptions of the other is obvious.

§8.14 Valuation Based on a Mixture of Methods

When valuing a business, it is customary to make estimates of value based on different approaches or assumptions. For example, a person preparing a valuation opinion might assemble the following estimates of value:

1. Straight book value, without adjustment for accounting conventions.
2. Adjusted book value, with adjustments for such items as LIFO inventory accounting, appreciation in marketable securities, and elimination of intangible assets.
3. Capitalized earnings, assuming average performance by the business.
4. Capitalized earnings, assuming a reasonable rate of growth.
5. Capitalized cash-flow assuming the current level of debt and, in the alternative, assuming an increased level of debt if available at attractive rates.
6. Estimated resale value of assets (obtained by using balance sheet assets excluding intangible assets and making adjustments for inventory valuation, marketable securities, land, and any excess depreciation taken in earlier years).

After making these six calculations, the results may be tabulated and the degree of disagreement among the various indicated values considered. If all are within a relatively narrow range, it is likely that a value within that range is appropriate. If the numbers vary widely, it is tempting to calculate an average and view the average as the best estimate of value. This is a somewhat muddled approach. The averaging process involves combining different numbers based on different assumptions. The decision to take the arithmetic mean of book value, liquidation value, and value based on capitalized earnings estimates, for example, has little theoretical justification.

There is, however, some judicial support for averaging different estimates of value. In statutory proceedings for the appraisal of the value of shares and in other cases in which share value must be determined, some courts apply a stylized valuation technique, known as the **Delaware Block Method** to measure value based on three different approaches, and then assign weights to each approach that reflect the court's judgment as to the reliability of the factor. In *Gibbons v. Schenley Industries, Inc.*, 339 A.2d 460 (Del. Ch. 1975), for example, the court-appointed appraiser valued shares of Schenley common stock as follows:

	Value factors	Weight	Assigned value
Market	29.00	35%	10.15
Earnings value	52.78	45%	23.75
Asset value	49.83	20%	9.97
			43.87

The market value was based on actual trading of stock of Schenley. The earnings value was computed by averaging five years of earnings and applying a multiplier of 14 based on the average P/E ratio of comparable companies. The asset value was an estimate of the value of Schenley's plant, property, and equipment based on expert appraisals. On review by the Chancellor, the weight given to asset value was reduced to 0, the earnings per share were reduced by the exclusion of a nonrecurring transaction, and the multiplier was increased to $16.72. The result was that the above table was revised as follows:

	Value factors	Weight	Assigned value
Market	29.00	55%	15.95
Earnings value	39.79	45%	17.91
Asset value	49.83	0%	0.00
			33.86

This is obviously a highly stylized approach toward valuation in which the court's analysis is channeled in narrow directions. In a more recent decision, *Weinberger v. UOP, Inc.*, 457 A.2d 701 (Del. 1983), the Delaware Supreme Court rejected this long established approach toward judicial evaluation on the ground that "to the extent it excludes other generally accepted techniques used in the financial community and the courts, it is now clearly outmoded." The court adopted "a more liberal approach [which] include[s] proof of value by . . . techniques or methods which are generally considered acceptable in the financial community and otherwise admissible in court." Nevertheless, several states continue to use the Delaware Block Method of valuation.

§8.15 Discounts for Lack of Marketability and Other Factors

This section deals primarily with valuation issues pertaining to holdings of common stock, rather than to the overall value of the business itself. At the outset, it assumes that the aggregate value of the business has been established by expert opinion, prior sales transactions, analysis of net present value, or judicial decision.

Once the value of the entire business has been determined, the value per share would appear to be calculable simply by dividing the value of the business by the number of outstanding common shares. (This value per share is different from book value per share, which is obtained by dividing the net worth of the business, as ascertained from the balance sheet, by the number of outstanding shares.) Unfortunately, however, life is not that simple. When valuing share-holdings, there is no inherent reason why the value of a business must be allocated proportionately to each share. Indeed, the earlier discussion of valuation in closely held businesses should make it clear that proportional allocation is usually not realistic. The usual manner of handling these differences between otherwise identical shares is by assigning discounts and premiums that reflect such characteristics as lack of marketability or ability to control the management of the company. A discount is simply a justification for knocking off a portion of the per-share value. A premium is an additional amount added to a block of shares.

There are several justifications for discounts that are recognized in the financial community as well as in case law. The following listing is not complete, but includes most of those likely to be encountered in practice.

1. **Lack of marketability** applies to shares that are otherwise publicly traded but that are subject to significant legal restraints on transferability. (A similar discount may also be applied to closely held shares, but in most such

cases it will be called a minority interest discount.) Sometimes publicly traded stock subject to legal restraint on transferability is called letter stock or legend stock, because as a matter of law a restriction on transfer can only be enforced against a buyer if the restriction appears in writing on the share certificate or other official evidence of ownership. Stock that may be freely sold or transferred is sometimes said to be freely alienable; thus, stock that cannot be sold or transferred is sometimes said to lack alienability.

2. For the reasons discussed earlier, minority interests sell at substantial discounts from control shares. The discount from gross per share value for minority interest status may be substantial.

3. Agreements applicable to shares of publicly held corporations that require the shares to be offered first to the corporation may justify a discount from the market price of shares not subject to the restrictive agreement. The value at which the shares must be offered is likely to be accepted as the maximum value of the shares for valuation purposes without regard to other valuation techniques.

4. In connection with publicly traded stock, large blocks may be more difficult to market than smaller blocks, though mutual funds and other institutional investors routinely buy and sell thousands of shares at a time. In a thinly traded market, the dumping of a large block of shares may depress the market significantly. A discount per share for large blocks of publicly traded shares may thus be warranted. Large blocks of shares are often sold through **block positioning firms** (i.e., specialized brokerage firms that assume the risks of selling unusually large numbers of shares). These firms command high per share fees for handling such transactions, and thus large blocks of shares tend to be priced somewhat lower than shares sold in more typical quantities. Large blocks of shares may sometimes need to be sold through a costly underwriting. These costs of distribution may be viewed as an estimate of an appropriate **block discount**. Sometimes buyers of large blocks of shares agree in advance with the issuer that the issuer will at some point foot the bill for underwriting a public offering in which the buyer's shares may be sold usually in conjunction with a new issue of stock by the company. A block trading discount is limited to non-control blocks of shares. If the block of shares are control shares, normally no discount is appropriate, and a premium may indeed be justified.

There are many other examples of discounts that may be applied to reflect risk factors, including discounts for the dependence of the business on a few key individuals for success, discounts for enhanced risk because of the small size of the business or its dependence on contracts with a small number of customers or suppliers, discounts for the inability to obtain financing, discounts for the need to rely on unaudited financial statements, discounts for political risks, and so forth. In some of these cases, the discount arises because the business itself is risky, while in other cases it arises because the information on which a valuation is based is thought to be somewhat unreliable. In most of these cases, however, the discount is one that will apply to the company as a whole. Although one often hears such factors cited as reasons for imposing a discount on the valuation of the business, it is probably more appropriate and informative to reflect such uncertainties in a higher capitalization rate or lower multiplier rather than by knocking off some arbitrary dollar amount from the calculated

value of the business. After all, the capitalization rate is supposed to be the rate of return that an investor would require in exchange for assuming the risks of the investment. Thus, it makes sense to set the rate as accurately as possible. In short, the idea of a discount or premium should be reserved for valuations of blocks of shares with attributes that distinguish them from run of the mill shares of the same company.

§8.16 The Importance of Valuation in Legal Practice

Valuation is a factual and business-related issue, not a legal issue. So why might a lawyer become involved in such a question? Consider the following contexts:

1. The issue of valuation has led to litigation and you are the lead trial attorney. You must be prepared to take the deposition of a person designated as an "expert" on the valuation issue, and later to conduct a vigorous cross examination of the methods the expert used to ascertain the value he placed on the business. Other than testing his expertise (i.e., his experience and background in business appraisals), what avenues of inquiry should you pursue?

2. Your client is the sole owner of a business, and she has decided to sell it in order to retire. The issue is what asking price she should place on the business. She has hired an expert appraiser who has studied the business and has come up with a figure that she thinks is ridiculously high and will scare off possible purchasers. She asks you what she should do. The asking price obviously involves a question of strategy or tactics in a purely commercial context — clearly a pure business issue that does not lie within the expertise of a corporate lawyer. The problem is that your client has come to rely on you for your common sense business judgment as well as legal acumen. Suitable disclaimers about the appropriate roles of lawyers may be appropriate. But the client still expects you to give her sensible advice as to what price tag she should place on her business.

3. For many years you have prepared your client's tax returns and handled various tax matters as they have come up. Your client has now decided to establish a program of making annual gifts of stock in his closely held business to his three children. You are asked to advise the client on the gift tax consequences of gifts of specific numbers of shares each year, whether a gift tax return must be filed, and if so, how the gift should be reported on that return. There is an annual exemption from the gift tax for gifts of less than $10,000 per year to a single donee, and it is clearly desirable to keep the size of the gift each year within that limit for each child. The first question you ask is, "How much is the stock worth?" Your client hands you a copy of a report by the client's accountant concluding that the value is almost certainly somewhere between $10 and $30 per share, and that $25 per share seems about right. What do you do next? Unfortunately, it is not possible to obtain advance rulings from the Internal Revenue Service on factual issues such as the value of a business. Suddenly the valuation issue has become more than a purely business judgment.

4. Your client and her spouse have separated and are about to divorce. Your client has operated a successful business for several years with some assistance

from her husband. The issue of the property settlement is particularly sticky, with the value of the business being at the center of controversy. The opposing lawyer has presented a report by an expert appraiser setting a high value on the business, while it is to your client's interest to have a low valuation on the business. What do you do next? Do you get your own appraiser, attack the report of your opponent, or both? Do you try to negotiate the issue of value, and, if so, what arguments do you make? If your client is a resident of a community property state, the issues may be even more complex. In some community property states, the value of any stock that she brought to the marriage and any appreciation in that value may remain her separate property, while the income from that stock that derives from the income of the business may be regarded as community property. How do you distinguish between appreciation in value and income when the owner of a closely held business has significant say in whether the business will retain its income or pay dividends?

5. You are counsel for a closely held corporation and have been asked to draft a share transfer agreement that will obligate each shareholder (1) to sell his or her stock back to the corporation (or to the other shareholders) upon death or resignation, and (2) to offer the stock to the corporation before it is sold or transferred to any other person. The issue you face is how the price for that sale is to be determined. The price must be determinable in an objective way not dependent on the cooperation of the potential seller. (Otherwise the withdrawing shareholder or the deceased shareholder's estate could easily defeat the plan by insisting on a very high price for the shares.) What pricing mechanism should be specified in the agreement? In this instance, the lawyer drafting the agreement is creating by contract a mandatory valuation process that will later be used to determine the value of interests in the business. The valuation process, further, must be one the courts would enforce if necessary. Finally, it should lead to a reasonably fair price, because one can never tell which shareholder will be the first to die or resign. Again, knowledge about valuation techniques has moved out of the business realm and into the legal realm.

CHAPTER 9

◆ FEDERAL TAXATION

§9.1 Introduction

During most of the 20th century, federal income taxes have had a major influence on virtually all business and financial transactions. Indeed, the **Internal Revenue Code (IRC)** probably is the single most important statute ever adopted by the United States in terms of its effect on business and financial transactions, dwarfing other important statutes such as the antitrust laws, the securities acts, and the bankruptcy acts.

The federal income tax laws are administered by the **Internal Revenue**

Service (IRS), an agency within the United States **Department of the Treasury**.

This chapter, like several others in this book, deals with major legal topics that are the subject of advanced law school courses. This chapter has only a limited and modest purpose. It introduces the reader to the broadest concepts, a summary overview as it were, and tries to explain how it is that the tax laws are as complex as they are.

§9.2 The Role of Tax Law in Business and Financial Transactions

The reasons for the preeminent importance of tax law on business and financial transactions can be set forth quite simply: The purpose of business and financial transactions is to earn a profit, and the federal income tax statutes (at least since World War II) require persons who earn profits to share a substantial portion of them — indeed, at times very substantial portions of them — with the United States government. Further, the federal income tax is not, and never was, a **flat tax** imposing the same percentage tax on all income and gains (assuming that were possible), but is composed of numerous distinctions imposing different levels of taxation on different amounts of income, different types of income, and different types of taxable organizations. Different tax rates are also applicable to individuals with identical incomes depending on their marital or filing status. During the period from World War II through 1986, some dollars of income were taxed at very high rates: as high as 90 percent at some periods shortly after World War II, and as high as 70 percent as late as 1980. Tax rates at these levels provide a powerful incentive for devising techniques to avoid their full impact wherever possible. For many years, ingenious minds have been devoted to creating and perfecting such techniques. For example, at the same time that the maximum rates of 70 percent or more were in effect, the maximum tax rate on a different form of income — long-term **capital gains** arising from the sale or exchange of capital assets held for more than six months—was only 25 percent. This dramatic difference in rates created strong incentives to structure transactions or establish long-term strategies so as to transmute ordinary income into long-term capital gain in order to make the 25 percent rather than the 70 percent rate applicable.

The Tax Reform Act of 1986 (the 1986 Act) made dramatic changes in tax policy. The core ideas behind this dramatic change in tax policy were to (1) cut maximum tax rates; (2) expand the tax base; and (3) minimize or eliminate tax shelter-oriented transactions that are entered into primarily for their effect on one's tax bill. A maximum tax rate of 28 percent was applied to both ordinary income and long-term capital gain. However, because of increasing budget deficits, Congress has passed two major tax bills since 1986, increasing tax rates that partially undid the 1986 reforms. In 1990, the maximum tax rate applicable to ordinary income was increased to 31 percent, while retaining the 28 percent rate for long-term capital gains; in 1994, the maximum tax rate was increased to 36 percent with a special surtax being imposed on incomes in excess of $250,000 to increase the maximum tax rate to 39.6 percent.

There is, of course, always an incentive to structure transactions and devise strategies so as to reduce taxes no matter what the rates. Thus, the same incentive to minimize taxes exists today, although tax rates are lower today than they were 20 years ago.

§9.3 The Complexity of the Internal Revenue Code

The income tax laws (including the regulations issued by the IRS to implement these laws) are exceedingly complex and difficult to understand. Anyone attempting to read the thousand-plus page statute for the first time is almost immediately lost in numerous cross references, defined terms, and opaque and elliptical provisions that appear to form a seamless web with no beginning and no end. The regulations are in many ways even worse: they consist of multiple volumes of fine print that are, if anything, even more opaque and difficult to get through than the statute. The IRS publishes proposed regulations for comment: Such regulations are often included in commercial compilations although they have only been proposed and may be changed in substantial respects before they are finally adopted. In some instances, regulations may remain in "proposed" form for many years. The standard, multi-volume, loose-leaf tax services that are in every law library and most lawyers' offices attempt to describe and summarize the rules, but they contain even more detail than the statute and regulations. Merely using the index volume to these loose-leaf tax services may be a daunting task.

Although the tax laws have increased steadily in their complexity since World War II, this complexity has increased significantly in recent years. Beginning in about 1975, new and often fundamental concepts were introduced into the tax laws almost every year. More complexity was introduced in the 20-odd years since 1975 than in the preceding 62 years following the adoption of the Income Tax Amendment to the United States Constitution. Regrettably, the more recent tax statutes have not improved either the simplicity or clarity of these statutes. Quite the contrary. The 1986 and later statutes did not expressly eliminate or repeal; they instead added new layers of complex provisions over what was there before. This is particularly true with respect to provisions relating to tax shelters, passive losses, the deductibility of nonbusiness interest, and the alternative minimum tax (a complex set of rules designed to prevent taxpayers from using special loopholes to eliminate all or most of their tax liability). As a result the present tax laws are longer, thicker, and more difficult to understand than ever before.

Of course, many Americans are relatively unaffected by this tax complexity. Most Americans are employed and are subject to the tax-withholding mechanism that in effect requires all employers to become tax collectors for Uncle Sam. For most Americans, paying taxes involves little discretion (at least if they are honest) and usually is relatively painless. Indeed, because many taxpayers whose sole incomes are salaries or wages end up being entitled to a refund, the process is often almost pleasant. And calculation of the tax due by these taxpayers is quite simple, because a standard deduction avoids the necessity of itemizing specific deductions and special tax tables usually require no calculation

to determine the actual amount of tax due. Special tax return forms, the 1040A and 1040EZ reduce the reporting burden. Further, many low-income taxpayers today owe no federal income tax at all because the 1986 Act created much more generous personal exemptions and a larger standard deduction. Indeed, one important consequence of the 1986 Act is that many individuals at or close to the poverty line are completely exempted from all liability for federal income taxes.

§9.4 The Costs of Complexity

The natural consequence of complexity on important economic matters is the development of specialists to deal with problems and give advice. And so it has been with a vengeance in the tax area. Today, the tax laws are so complex that sometimes even tax specialists despair of understanding the entire tax structure and fear that they are becoming unable to provide prompt and accurate advice to clients without expensive study and preparation. Thirty years ago, most taxpayers filled out their own tax returns: Many lawyers who were not tax specialists advised clients on tax matters and often prepared tax returns for valued clients, either for a nominal fee or as a favor. This work is increasingly being done by accountants, "store front" commercial tax return preparers, and lawyers who specialize in tax law. The complexity of the tax laws has increased so substantially that most taxpayers today obtain professional assistance in filling out their tax returns if they involve the use of **Form 1040**, the **long form** that is required of all individuals who do not qualify for the simpler forms **1040A** or **1040EZ**. Indeed, the reputation of complexity that the IRC has leads many taxpayers who qualify for the use of these simpler forms to seek professional assistance as well.

Lawyers in general practice have become increasingly cautious about giving tax advice or preparing returns for clients. To be an effective tax lawyer today, one pretty much has to specialize in that subject. This growth of specialization is in part a result of the increased specificity of IRC provisions defining how certain transactions are to be handled. A generation ago, much tax advice involved the application of general tax principles to a specific situation. Today, there are often very specific provisions that must be located and carefully parsed in connection with each specific situation. The likelihood of overlooking relevant language or other applicable sections is obviously much greater under a very detailed statute than it is under a more general one.

§9.5 Tax Planning and Tax Evasion: The Role of Tax Advisers and Tax Attorneys

It is entirely proper to seek to minimize one's taxes by lawful means. Careful planning and judicious structuring and timing of receipts and transactions may permit the same income or gains to be taxed at much lower rates, to be deferred to a later tax year, or in some instances to escape income tax entirely. Thus the

tax attorney, tax planner, and tax adviser were born. All engage in essentially the same planning activity — to structure transactions and economic activities in a way that takes the maximum legitimate advantage of the various provisions of the IRC — to structure transactions so as to minimize taxes due to Uncle Sam. Of course, these tax specialists engage in other activities as well: They may prepare returns, represent taxpayers before the IRS in administrative proceedings or in litigation against the IRS, and so forth.

The services of the most successful tax planners are largely used only by the affluent individual taxpayer and by business. These are the only taxpayers that are regularly involved in transactions large enough to support the high fees normally charged for these services. Of course, many taxpayers engage in tax planning on a modest scale.

Every tax adviser must constantly be aware of the basic distinction between legitimate tax avoidance or **tax planning** on the one hand and improper **tax evasion** on the other. Tax planning is the structuring of transactions so as to take legitimate advantage of the provisions of the IRC and the regulations existing thereunder. Tax evasion, on the other hand, involves improper or unlawful reduction of tax liabilities by omission, misstatement, misrepresentation, or fraud. To take simple illustrations: The special tax treatment for long-term capital gains is available only for capital assets held for more than six months. Gains from the sale or exchange of capital assets held for less than six months are taxed at the relatively higher rates applicable to ordinary income. A person planning to sell a capital asset at a profit might legitimately wait until the day after the six-month period expired to make the sale. That is simple tax planning: By deferring the sale, the taxpayer takes the economic risk that the value of the capital asset may decline during that period. On the other hand, say that the same transaction is agreed on five months and twenty days after the taxpayer originally acquired the asset, possession of the asset is transferred immediately to the purchaser, and both the sale contract and the payment check are dated and delivered so that the sale appears to have occurred after the expiration of the six-month holding period. In this case, there is a significant risk that the IRS, if the circumstances become known, will treat the sale as occurring within the six-month holding period. More serious examples of improper evasion are situations involving "forgetting" to include items of income at all or claiming exemptions for six children when in fact the taxpayer only has three. If such transactions are discovered, civil fraud penalties are usually imposed, and in extreme cases, there may also be criminal prosecution.

Often, however, the distinction is not as easy or sharp as these two hypotheticals suggest. Many transactions have as their principal purpose the reduction of taxes. The IRS may attack these transactions on very broad grounds: for example, that they are **sham transactions** without **business purpose** that should be ignored entirely, that they are **step transactions** that should be viewed as a single whole rather than as a series of independent transactions, or that the effect of the transactions should be recast so as to **clearly reflect income**. In some instances, a taxpayer may be able to obtain an advance ruling as to how a specific transaction should be treated for tax purposes (a **letter ruling**, as it is usually called), but the IRS declines to give rulings in many sensitive or fact-specific areas. Tax shelters have been a major target of the

Service for many years. The tax returns of many thousands of taxpayers were ensnarled in this campaign during the late 1980s, and some are still ensnarled 10 years later.

The giving of tax advice is greatly affected by the fact that most returns are not fully audited, and the questionable treatment of a specific item may never be raised. Nevertheless, disclosure of the questionable item in the return is sensible in order to minimize the risk that the IRS may later attempt to impose a fraud penalty on the taxpayer or, conceivably, penalties on the attorney involved or on the person who prepared the return. Also, relatively high-income persons with complex or tax-planning-oriented transactions cannot rely on escaping an audit, because the probability of an audit increases substantially as the taxpayer's income increases.

§9.6 Progressive Tax Rate Structures

The pre-1986 tax rates for individuals combined high-percentage tax rates with a highly progressive rate structure. A **progressive rate** structure is one in which the rates are fixed so that as taxable income increases, the tax rate on additional dollars also increases. Under a progressive rate structure, additional or last dollars earned by a higher-income person are taxed at a higher percentage rate than the same number of additional dollars earned by a lower-income person. Current tax rates have a degree of progressivity, but are less progressive than rate structures in the pre-1986 tax law. Progressivity is illustrated below by the tax rates for the year 1980 applicable to persons filing joint returns:

Taxable income	Tax
3,400 or less	-0-
3,400–5,499	14% of income in excess of 3,400
5,500–7,599	294 plus 16% of excess over 5,500
7,600–11,899	630 plus 18% of excess over 7,600
11,900–15,999	1,404 plus 21% of excess over 11,900
16,000–20,199	2,265 plus 24% of excess over 16,000
20,200–24,599	3,273 plus 28% of excess over 20,200
24,600–29,899	4,505 plus 32% of excess over 24,600
29,900–35,199	6,201 plus 37% of excess over 29,900
35,200–45,799	8,162 plus 43% of excess over 35,200
45,800–59,999	12,720 plus 49% of excess over 45,800
60,000–85,599	19,678 plus 54% of excess over 60,000
85,600–109,399	33,502 plus 59% of excess over 85,600
109,400–162,399	47,544 plus 64% of excess over 109,400
215,400 or more	117,504 plus 70% of excess.

First, a brief description of how to read the above table might be helpful: The tax brackets are additive or cumulative. For example, a couple with a taxable income of up to $5,500 filing a joint return and paying a tax under the above schedule would owe .14 × ($5,500 − $3,400) = .14 × ($2,100) = $294. If the couple's income were $7,600, they would owe the same $294 on the first $5,500 plus 16 percent of the excess over $5,500; the tax would be .16 ×

($7,600 − $5,500) + $294 = .16 × ($2,100) + $294 = $336 + $294 = $630. As the hypothetical couple's taxable income continues to increase, the tax on the lower levels remains unaffected, but the additional income is subject to increasingly higher percentages. At the very top, the couple would owe 70 percent of each dollar of taxable income earned in excess of $215,400. Looking at this explanation of this table, it should be clear that the odd-looking numbers at the beginning of the right hand column of the table are not mysterious at all; they are simply the amount of tax determined cumulatively from the rows of the table above the row in question. The different levels of income subject to different tax rates in the above table are universally referred to as **tax brackets**. The percentage rates set forth in the above table (14 percent, 16 percent, and so on up to 70 percent) are called marginal rates because they apply only to the additional dollars earned above the previous bracket. The **marginal rate** must be distinguished from the **effective rate** of taxation, which is the percentage that the total tax is of one's total taxable income (or of one's gross income before exemptions and deductions). To illustrate, in 1980 a couple filing a joint return with precisely $35,200 dollars of taxable income was at the beginning of the 43 percent bracket. However, the amount of tax actually due on $35,200 of income was $8,162, or 23 percent of taxable income. Assuming that the person had an average amount of deductions and exemptions, that person's total income before deductions and exemptions was probably about $50,000, so that the effective tax rate on total income would have been about 16 percent. That is a large percentage to be sure, but the actual effective tax rate was nowhere near the 43 percent that a superficial examination of the tax rates might indicate to be applicable. Of course, if our hypothetical taxpayer earned additional dollars of taxable income, each of those dollars would have been taxed at the 43 percent rate until the couple reached $45,800 of taxable income, when the marginal rate would have increased from 43 percent to 49 percent.

The effective tax rate is never higher than the marginal rate (because the first dollars of income are always taxed at lower rates than the highest marginal rate), although the two tend to merge at very high incomes. For example, a couple with $300,000 of taxable income in 1980 was comfortably in the 70 percent bracket and owed $176,724 in taxes — 59 percent of taxable income. If the couple were really well off and had $10,000,000 of taxable income, their tax bill would be $6,966,724; this is an effective rate of 69.67 percent of taxable income, still lower than the marginal rate.

For tax-planning purposes, the marginal rate is usually more important than the effective rate, because most tax planning relates to specific transactions that take place "at the margin." For example, a strategy that defers tax on a transaction defers the tax that would be due if the gain from that transaction were added to all the other taxable income of the taxpayer. The bulk of the taxpayer's other income, and the tax that will be due on that income, is unaffected by that tax planning.

Under even a progressive tax rate structure with very high marginal rates, it always pays to earn another dollar (as long as the highest bracket is less than 100 percent). Some high-income taxpayers at this time indicated that "it is not worth it" to earn more money because of the tax structure. Take these remarks

with a grain of salt. Certainly, if a person earns another dollar, he or she will always keep a part of it even under a progressive tax structure. A more subtle question (which is the point the "not-worth-it" speakers may have had in mind) is whether a person will engage in risky, entrepreneurial conduct in an effort to earn an extra dollar when he or she is allowed to keep only 30 percent of it.

The high and progressive rate structure also created significant anomalies in treatment for essentially indistinguishable taxpayers. For example, one major consequence of the rate structure described above was that for higher income taxpayers, splitting income among two or more different taxpayers would often reduce the total tax due. When high progressive rates were first imposed during World War II, most families consisted of a single, male income earner and a wife who remained at home to care for the family. The first major controversy arose when married couples with a single wage earner who resided in community property states argued successfully that the nonworking spouse should report one half of the community's earnings on the theory that one-half of the earnings was hers under state law. If the couple's income was substantial, this **income-splitting** created obvious discrimination between otherwise identical families who happened to live in community property and non-community property states. This dispute was resolved by the development of different tax schedules for single individuals and for married individuals filing a joint return, with the latter entitled to use a tax schedule that in effect gave all married couples the advantage of income-splitting that community property residents were entitled to for tax purposes. The 1980 tax schedule set forth above was applicable to married couples filing joint returns. Today, there are schedules not only for married and single taxpayers but also for heads of households and married taxpayers filing separately.

With the growth in the number of working wives, the income-splitting tax schedules for families created a new type of discrimination. If one spouse within a family was the sole wage earner, the rates applicable to married taxpayers filing joint returns provided a significantly lower tax than if that same wage earner were unmarried. However, if two persons had equal amounts of income, their total tax bill was significantly higher if they were married and required to file joint returns than it would have been if they were not married and were filing separately. For example, in 1980, if two individuals living together each had precisely $25,000 of taxable income, the tax on their joint return was $14,778 if they were married. If they had remained single and each had filed separate returns as unmarried individuals, the tax would have been $5,952 each, or a total of $11,904. This results from the fact that when the two taxpayers are married, the second income is added to the first, and is taxed only at the higher brackets. When the two taxpayers are not married, each gets to take advantage of the very low marginal rates on their first dollars of income. The difference between $14,778 and $11,904 can be viewed as a **marriage penalty**, or put another way, a bonus of nearly $3,000 per year for living in sin. This discrimination against marriage even led a few married couples to divorce but continue to live together, or to divorce on December 28 and remarry on January 3, in order to save on federal income taxes. (The filing category for "married couples filing separate returns" was created to ensure that couples filing separate returns

were subject to the same tax brackets and rates as if they filed jointly; as a result the marriage penalty cannot be avoided simply by filing separate returns.)

High-income taxpayers also found it profitable from a tax standpoint to give income-producing property to infant children in order to permit the income to accumulate for college expenses at lower tax brackets than if the parent retained the property, paid tax on the income from the property, and then used the remainder to pay for college. Indeed, a number of tax-oriented trust and custodial devices were invented in order to enable high-income taxpayers to minimize the effect of the sharp progressivism of rates. This strategy was largely foreclosed in the 1986 Act by enactment of a provision that basically requires the **unearned income** of children under the age of 14 to be taxed at their parent's top rates (except for the first $500 of income). This change has greatly complicated the tax structure, requiring many children to obtain social security numbers and file returns; it has also created potential complications and anomalies when the minor child works for all or, more likely, part of the year.

The progressive structure of rates also has one other significant effect. It caused tax revenues to increase automatically during periods of inflation. Whatever was happening at the high-income level of the spectrum, millions of taxpayers whose sole income was from wages and salary were paying taxes under a progressive tax structure that built in progressivism at a relatively low level. During periods of inflation, as individual incomes increased along with price increases, taxpayers were pushed into higher marginal brackets, and the revenues of the United States government increased dramatically, although the taxpayers were probably not better off economically from the increased wages. The large number of brackets at relatively low levels of income reflect the brackets originally established when income levels were perhaps one-third of what they were in 1981. As inflation continued, the progressive income tax rates became an effective money machine for government. Perhaps no feature of the progressive tax structure infuriated the Reagan administration more than this automatic increase in governmental revenues due purely to the interaction between inflation and progressive tax rates.

§9.7 Attacks on Progressivity and High Tax Rates

The sharply progressive tax structure and relatively high marginal rates illustrated by the 1980 tax rates was a basic philosophical underpinning of tax policy for more than 50 years. The notion that a person who makes more could afford to, and should be required to, pay a higher portion of the extra dollars earned seemed so obvious as not to require extended discussion. The resulting anomalies that were necessarily created between married and cohabiting taxpayers, or between single and married one-income taxpayers, were viewed as an inevitable cost of a progressive system. However, as early as the 1950s, and increasingly during the 1960s and 1970s, serious criticism of the theory underlying high tax rates and a progressive rate structure in the IRC surfaced. The first tangible product of this discontent was the enactment of the 1986 Act, which basically established a maximum 28 percent marginal rate, but as indi-

cated above, progressivity and higher tax rates for high-income taxpayers have gradually found their way back into the current tax structure. Today, the maximum marginal rate is 39.6 percent. As a result, criticism of the present tax structure continues to be widespread, and sometimes vitriolic. A good example are comments by Representative Phil Crane, Republican of Illinois, in 1996:

> The U.S. Internal Revenue Code (the Code) is the modern-day manifestation of the power to destroy. Our tax system does harm to the principle of sound money management. The Code further injures the capitalist system on which our nation's economy is based. . . . Although Congress has attempted to make taxes fair by making the Code progressive, it is in fact the progressivity that has added to the complexity and inequity of the Code. While I agree that one's ability to pay ought to be considered with regard to one's tax burden, progressivity, as practiced by Washington social engineers, is more appropriately described as a vendetta to soak the rich. What appears to be compassion is actually base entity. . . . [C]onstant tinkering with federal taxes, instead of improving the Code, has actually injured America's prosperity.

Given these strongly held views, it is not surprising that various proposals have been put forward, suggesting either a different income tax rate structure or, more radically, the abandonment of the income tax entirely for a national sales tax, value added tax, or other tax structure.

It is important to recognize that some arguments against progressivity and the present federal tax structure are based on profound dissatisfaction with government in general, and the federal government in particular. Many people believe the federal government is too large, too heavily oriented toward ill-conceived welfare schemes, and too intrusive on individual citizens and local governments. One way to attack big government is based on the quite errone-ous belief that reduction of tax revenues will automatically lead to a reduction in growth of governmental operations. In fact, reductions in the growth of tax revenues, when they did occur following the 1986 tax changes, did not produce a corresponding change in governmental activities, but rather simply inflated the federal deficit. A second, and somewhat inconsistent conservative argument is that high taxes and high tax rates are undesirable because they have adverse effects on the economy. Lower tax rates, it is argued, spur economic activity and increase national wealth. Whether this is true is debatable from an historical standpoint.

A third argument attacks the basic premise of progressivity that it is fair to tax higher incomes at a higher rate than lower incomes. Fairness, it may be argued, requires a flat tax, with the same rate applicable to everyone. Rather inconsistently, proponents of a flat tax argue that a fair amount of proportion-ality is created automatically if there is a rather high basic exemption before any tax is imposed.

A more pragmatic argument is that the high and progressive rate structure prompts inexorable political pressure by interest groups for special deductions, special exceptions, and special credits for favored activity. By 1980, the IRC, it may be argued, had become so riddled with special interest provisions that it had actually ceased to be a fair and progressive structure. One perverse result

of this constant pressure was that the tax system enabled many high-income individuals quite legally to avoid paying taxes entirely or to pay only very small amounts — often less than a middle-class wage earner. Also, it quickly became clear that the tax changes made in 1981 to encourage and assist business to recover from the deep recession of that period had virtually eliminated the corporate income tax as a factor in raising revenue: Many very large companies ended up owing no tax or even being entitled to refunds of tax from earlier years despite the fact that they were reporting substantial earnings to their investors. What appears on the surface to be a progressive tax system may in fact hide a system of special benefits for the sophisticated and wealthy so that the tax burden falls disproportionally on the average wage earner who has no special benefits.

In addition, high progressive tax rates and complex rules tend to lead to the development of sophisticated planning techniques by affluent taxpayers. Congress has responded to many of these techniques over the years by special provisions designed to close off specific techniques. This, however, increased the IRC's complexity and did not solve the underlying problem, which was the motivation to create new techniques caused by the high and progressive rates. New tax-planning devices were created about as rapidly as older ones were closed off.

Finally, there is the belief that the special tax treatment of long-term capital gains gives unwarranted tax benefits to high-income taxpayers who use complex strategies to transmute ordinary income into capital gains and who use capital gains treatment as the device ultimately to bail out of tax shelters. At the other extreme, arguments are made that a reduction of the tax on capital gains would free up many transactions that would lead to a higher level of economic activity.

Although complaints about the current tax structure are numerous and there are many suggestions for radical change, there is no consensus about what should be done. With the Republican electoral victory in 1994, the possibility of a truly radical change in the federal income tax system became at least conceivable. Prior to that time, proposals to replace the current income tax structure with a variety of consumption taxes, sales taxes, value added taxes (VATs), flat tax systems, or some combination of these alternatives were viewed as about as plausible as proposals to create a settlement on the planet Mars. Although it is still unlikely to occur, radical tax change is now at least conceivable.

Most of these radical new tax proposals would change the basis of federal taxation away from using income or earnings as the measure of taxation to using consumption or some related kind of measurement. The following alternative tax structures have been seriously discussed.

1. A **national sales tax**. Such a tax would be a tax based purely on consumption. The tax would be imposed at the final point of sale as an add-on to the base price. A rate of perhaps 20 percent would be necessary to approach the current level of revenue provided by the federal income tax. Such a tax would be highly regressive, hitting families with the lowest income hardest, and would presumably be paired with some device to reduce the regressive nature of the tax. It would further create serious intergenerational transition problems. Consider, for example, a family that has saved successfully for retirement largely with after-tax dollars. As that family expends these dollars for living expenses

during their retirement years, they will be subject to the hefty consumption or USA tax (discussed below), in effect taxing the same dollars a second time.

2. A **VAT**. A VAT is a sales tax imposed successively at each level of production, with the tax being incorporated into the price at each level of sale. In the VAT system, taxes are imposed on the basis of adding economic value to the product involved. VATs are widely used in European countries. Goods that are exported are not subject to the VAT and most tourists in Europe are familiar with the complex refund procedures they must follow in order to obtain a refund of the VAT. The VAT is also a consumption tax. Its principal advantage over a direct national sales tax is that it is much less visible, being incorporated in the price of the product.

3. The **USA tax**. The so-called USA Tax is a disguised consumption tax. It would apply a tax on taxable income calculated as total income minus amounts invested and amounts saved. The USA tax would require the filing of an annual return much like under the present income tax structure, but the amount of the tax would be based on consumption, not earnings. One way of looking at the USA tax is to analogize it to an immense individual retirement account (IRA) deduction. The USA tax would permit either flat or graduated tax rates, and regressivity could be reduced by providing a substantial personal exemption.

4. The **Armey flat tax**. The flat tax proposed by Congressman Dick Armey of Texas is not precisely a consumption tax nor an income tax. It would tax all businesses and individual wages, receipts, and pensions only once and at the same flat rate. Virtually all current deductions and credits would be abolished. Individual tax returns would fit neatly on a postcard. Investment income would not be taxed on the theory that it has already been taxed once. Businesses would thus be taxed on total revenues less the cost of labor, raw materials, and additions to plant and equipment. Employees would be taxed on their salaries, but all interest and dividend payments would be exempt from tax. The tax would be at a single rate for businesses and individuals alike. To lessen the regressive impact of this tax, a large personal exemption would be available for individuals. Congressman Armey's original proposal was a zero tax rate for the first $35,000 of income and a 17 percent tax on income in excess of that amount. It is doubtful that these rates would yield the United States government as much revenue as the current structure of income taxes; a flat rate of 20 or 22 percent may be necessary to do this. Nevertheless, the $35,000 exemption would reduce dramatically the shift of the tax burden that would otherwise occur from the wealthy to the lower and middle economic classes.

Although these various alternative tax proposals can be made revenue-neutral when compared with the present system, the transition problems of each of them are formidable. They will have disproportionate effects on various industries. Compared with domestically oriented firms, exporting firms are benefited by the consumption tax proposals. Labor intensive and capital intensive industries may have dramatically different tax obligations under the flat tax proposal than they now do. Debt-intensive industries that are viable today only because of the deductibility of interest may be unable to survive were this tax advantage eliminated. The loss of personal income tax deductions for mortgage interest payments might cause a massive decline in real estate values across the country. There are also difficult problems of tax avoidance, particularly in the

flat tax proposal. Although a 17 or 22 percent is more attractive than the current 36 or 39.6 percent rates, the same incentive to minimize taxes is still present, and it is impossible to foresee all possible avoidance techniques. Salary payments for high-level executives might be eliminated in favor of stock options or rights, for example.

Although dislike of the present income tax system is certainly great, the actual enactment of a radical system is problematic. Certainly, adoption of any of these alternative systems of taxation would be such an epochal change in the United States that it is difficult to imagine what this brave new world would look like.

§9.8 Individual Income Taxes

This and the following sections give a broad and somewhat cursory analysis of the present-day individual income tax. The discussion below assumes that the individual in question files Form 1040, the standard full-length individual income tax return, and not one of the short forms, 1040A or 1040EZ, that are available to lower-income taxpayers.

The current federal income tax is a tax on **income**, not **gross receipts**. Thus, a business must subtract its costs and expenses from receipts in order to arrive at an income figure on which income taxes are calculated. An individual engaged in an individual trade or business is entitled to these deductions to the same degree as a corporation. Thus, an individual who operates a retail hardware store as a sole proprietorship may deduct the costs of inventory, rent, advertising, and the like.

In addition to business expenses, individual taxpayers are entitled to a number of credits or deductions in the calculation of the amount of tax due in addition to the deduction of trade or business expenses. The process by which a taxpayer who receives salary or wages moves from his or her gross receipts to the amount of income subject to tax (or **taxable income**) involves a series of discrete steps. These steps are set forth on Form 1040 (a copy of which is reproduced as Figure 9-1). The steps involved are as follows:

1. One starts with gross receipts and subtracts trade and business expenses and expenses directly connected with other gainful, nonemployment activity in order to determine total income.
2. From total income, one subtracts "adjustments to income" (employee business and moving expenses, pension plan deductions, and alimony) in order to determine **adjusted gross income**.
3. From adjusted gross income, one subtracts allowable itemized personal deductions (or the **standard deduction** if one does not itemize) minus an allowance for **personal exemptions** based on the number of individuals in the household, which equals **taxable income**.
4. One calculates the tax due on the taxable income reflected in the return either from tax tables (if taxable income is less than $50,000) or by a calculation using formulas described below. This is the amount of tax due.
5. Following the calculation of the amount of tax due, one goes through another set of calculations to determine the amount that should actually

Figure 9-1

Tax Compu- tation	32	Amount from line 31 (adjusted gross income)	32	
	33a	Check if: ☐ **You** were 65 or older, ☐ Blind; ☐ **Spouse** was 65 or older, ☐ Blind. Add the number of boxes checked above and enter the total here . . . . ▶ **33a**		
	b	If you are married filing separately and your spouse itemizes deductions or you were a dual-status alien, see instructions and check here . . . . . ▶ **33b** ☐		
	34	Enter the **larger** of your: { **Itemized deductions** from Schedule A, line 28, **OR** **Standard deduction** shown below for your filing status. **But see the** instructions if you checked any box on line 33a or b **or** someone can claim you as a dependent. • Single—$4,000 • Married filing jointly or Qualifying widow(er)—$6,700 • Head of household—$5,900 • Married filing separately—$3,350	34	
	35	Subtract line 34 from line 32	35	
If you want the IRS to figure your tax, see the instructions for line 37.	36	If line 32 is $88,475 or less, multiply $2,550 by the total number of exemptions claimed on line 6d. If line 32 is over $88,475, see the worksheet in the inst. for the amount to enter .	36	
	37	**Taxable income.** Subtract line 36 from line 35. If line 36 is more than line 35, enter -0-	37	
	38	**Tax.** See instructions. Check if total includes any tax from **a** ☐ Form(s) 8814 **b** ☐ Form 4972 . . . . ▶	38	
Credits	39	Credit for child and dependent care expenses. Attach Form 2441	**39**			
	40	Credit for the elderly or the disabled. Attach Schedule R . .	**40**			
	41	Foreign tax credit. Attach Form 1116	**41**			
	42	Other. Check if from **a** ☐ Form 3800 **b** ☐ Form 8396 **c** ☐ Form 8801 **d** ☐ Form (specify) _____	**42**			
	43	Add lines 39 through 42	43	
	44	Subtract line 43 from line 38. If line 43 is more than line 38, enter -0- . . . . . ▶	44	
Other Taxes	45	Self-employment tax. Attach Schedule SE	45	
	46	Alternative minimum tax. Attach Form 6251	46	
	47	Social security and Medicare tax on tip income not reported to employer. Attach Form 4137	47	
	48	Tax on qualified retirement plans, including IRAs. If required, attach Form 5329 . . .	48	
	49	Advance earned income credit payments from Form(s) W-2	49	
	50	Household employment taxes. Attach Schedule H	50	
	51	Add lines 44 through 50. This is your **total tax** . . . . ▶	51	
Payments	52	Federal income tax withheld from Forms W-2 and 1099 .	**52**			
	53	1996 estimated tax payments and amount applied from 1995 return .	**53**			
	54	**Earned income credit.** Attach Schedule EIC if you have a qualifying child. Nontaxable earned income: amount ▶ [ ] and type ▶	**54**			
Attach Forms W-2, W-2G, and 1099-R on the front.	55	Amount paid with Form 4868 (request for extension) . . .	**55**			
	56	Excess social security and RRTA tax withheld (see inst.) . .	**56**			
	57	Other payments. Check if from **a** ☐ Form 2439 **b** ☐ Form 4136	**57**			
	58	Add lines 52 through 57. These are your **total payments** . . . . ▶	58	
Refund **Have it sent directly to your bank account! See inst. and fill in 60b, c, and d.**	59	If line 58 is more than line 51, subtract line 51 from line 58. This is the amount you **OVERPAID**	59	
	60a	Amount of line 59 you want **REFUNDED TO YOU** . . . . ▶	60a	
	▶ b	Routing number [ ] **c** Type: ☐ Checking ☐ Savings		
	▶ d	Account number [ ]		
	61	Amount of line 59 you want **APPLIED TO YOUR 1997 ESTIMATED TAX** ▶	**61**		
Amount You Owe	62	If line 51 is more than line 58, subtract line 58 from line 51. This is the **AMOUNT YOU OWE.** For details on how to pay and use **Form 1040-V**, see instructions . . . . . . ▶	62	
	63	Estimated tax penalty. Also include on line 62	**63**		

Sign Here

Keep a copy of this return for your records.

Under penalties of perjury, I declare that I have examined this return and accompanying schedules and statements, and to the best of my knowledge and belief, they are true, correct, and complete. Declaration of preparer (other than taxpayer) is based on all information of which preparer has any knowledge.

Your signature	Date	Your occupation
Spouse's signature. If a joint return, BOTH must sign.	Date	Spouse's occupation

Paid Preparer's Use Only

Preparer's signature	Date	Check if self-employed ☐	Preparer's social security no.
Firm's name (or yours if self-employed) and address		EIN	
		ZIP code	

Figure 9-1 (*cont.*)

239

be paid with the return. The amount of tax due is then reduced by certain allowable credits that may be treated as payments of tax and by payments made under the "pay as you go" system of tax collection described below. This system involves withholding by employees or quarterly payments of estimated tax by persons who have taxable income that is not subject to withholding. The net result is the amount of the additional payment that is due from the taxpayer or the amount of refund the United States pays to the taxpayer. The system is structured so that most taxpayers — particularly those whose income is derived solely from wages or salaries subject to withholding — are entitled to receive a refund from the government.

In this calculation of income tax liability, a sharp distinction must be drawn between **deductions**, which are subtracted from gross income to determine taxable income, and **credits**, which are treated as payments of tax itself. There is a large amount of background and nuance in this structure that is described in the following sections.

§9.9 Calculation of Trade or Business Income

An individual who is the owner of a business is, of course, entitled to deduct the costs and expenses of the business from its receipts. These expenses are deductible on a separate schedule, **Schedule C**, that is similar to a profit and loss statement for any business. After deducting these expenses, only the net amount of income is transferred forward to the Form 1040. Much the same pattern of deduction of business expenses from gross receipts before the calculation of total income also appears in **Schedule E** (income from "rents, royalties, partnerships, trusts, etc.") and **Schedule F** (farm income). In effect, Schedules C, E, and F permit deduction of trade and business expenses before the calculation of total income. The test for whether specific trade or business, rental, or farming expenses are deductible is whether they are "ordinary and necessary" for the business and "paid or incurred" during the taxable year in question. Expenses that provide a benefit over several taxable years, (e.g., the purchase of a truck) must be capitalized and depreciated (or amortized) over the useful life of the asset. Depreciation schedules for most major assets are set by the statute rather than by individualistic estimates of useful life.

The 1986 Act added a major wrinkle to the deductibility of business expenses when it created three classes of income: **active business income**, **investment income**, and **passive income**, and limited the deductibility of expenses to that from the last two categories.

§9.10 Calculation of Adjusted Gross Income

A second category of business-related expenses that are treated differently from trade or business expenses involves **employee business expenses, expenses for the production of income**, and a limited number of other deductions that share one common characteristic: Congress has decreed that these

expenses shall be deducted before the calculation of **adjusted gross income**. These expenses fall into several categories:

1. Expenses relating to the production of income or wages by an employee not directly related to a trade or business: unreimbursed moving expenses and employee business expenses such as union dues, uniforms (where required by the employer), unreimbursed travel expense, the expense of maintaining an office in the home, and unreimbursed entertainment expense. Many expenses that in a sense relate to a job, however, are viewed as personal and not deductible: for example, commuting expenses are not deductible, because they are viewed as arising from the employee's personal choice as to where to live. Educational expenses designed to improve the employee's job status also are not deductible, because they are not required for the employee's job. Also, many items deducted from the employee's salary check, such as payments on account of federal income taxes, social security, and health benefits, are also not deductible as expenses for the production of income, although some may be deductible on some other basis.

2. Expenses for the production of income, including rental fees for safe deposit boxes, accountants' fees for keeping books of income-producing property, insurance charges to protect merchandise held by the taxpayer for resale as an investment, investment advisers, and the like. These income-generating expenses are deductible only to the extent that they exceed 2 percent of total income. This calculation appears on Form 2106 rather than on the Form 1040. In other words, the amount entered on the Form 1040 has already been reduced by 2 percent of the amount shown on line 22. There are two justifications for this 2 percent "floor." First, concern about revenue loss arises, because many of the expenses in this category historically have been subject to abuse in the sense that taxpayers have claimed deductions to which they are arguably not entitled. These deductions are also claimed by millions of lower- and middle-income taxpayers so that widespread cheating entails a very substantial revenue loss. Second, the floor also simplifies the preparation of returns for many lower-income taxpayers whose deductions are likely to be less than the floor. On the other hand (and this illustrates that many simplifying changes may cause increased complexity in individual returns), in the case of a joint return, this 2 percent floor is calculated on the combined income of husband and wife; where both spouses have income but only one has expenses subject to the floor, the filing of separate returns may yield a lower tax because the 2 percent floor is then calculated only on the income of the spouse that has the expenses subject to the floor.

3. IRA and Keogh plan contributions.

4. Penalties on early withdrawal of savings from retirement plans.

5. Alimony.

These last three deductions (and a very small number of other itemized deductions) are not subject to the 2 percent floor.

§9.11 Deductions and Exemptions

In addition to business or income-oriented expenses, the IRC has always allowed, as a matter of policy, the deduction of certain classes or types of

personal expenses. Historically, the most important of these were state income, property and sales taxes, interest on personal debts and on real estate mortgages, medical and dental expenses, charitable contributions, and casualty losses. The reasons underlying these deductions obviously vary: encouraging charitable contributions, lessening the financial burden on the unfortunate family struck by a major casualty loss or catastrophic medical expenses, and so forth.

The policies underlying some of these deductions have often been viewed as suspect by tax theorists, because they involve personal rather than business expenditures. From a political standpoint, however, some of them are immensely popular. These personal expenses have also involved a fair amount of petty cheating by large numbers of taxpayers. In 1986, Congress took several steps to limit the widespread use and misuse of these deductions. The most important substantive changes were that it limited the deduction of state taxes to income and real estate taxes, excluding state sales taxes, and limited the deduction of interest on nonbusiness loans basically to those arising from the purchase of residential real estate or, to a limited extent, loans secured by liens on such real estate.

The IRC has adopted several devices to limit the availability of personal deductions. First, the most important device is the availability to all taxpayers of the **standard deduction** that may be used in lieu of the **itemization** of all **personal deductions**. The size of the standard deduction varies with the filing status of the taxpayer discussed below and is indexed for inflation. In 1996 the amounts were as follows:

> Single persons: $4,000;
> Heads of households: $5,900
> Married persons filing jointly: $6,700
> Married persons filing separately: $3,350

The standard deduction applies only to personal deductions: It does not affect the deductibility of employee business expenses or expenses incurred in the production of income. Also, as indicated above, the standard deduction is not a floor (like that applied to employee business expenses). Instead, it is an amount that is available to and may be claimed by every taxpayer as an alternative to itemization. If the standard deduction is generous enough, most persons, of course, do not itemize but simply elect to take the standard deduction. This has multiple advantages from the standpoint of the system: It eliminates petty cheating, it simplifies the preparation of returns for many taxpayers, and it improves inter-taxpayer general equity, because more taxpayers compute their taxes on precisely the same basis.

The second important device designed to limit personal deductions to extraordinary or unusual situations (and possibly also to prevent petty cheating) is the imposition of a floor on specific types of expenses similar to that imposed on employee business expenses. The oldest such floor is on medical expenses, where Congress originally attempted to distinguish between ordinary medical expenses and extraordinary ones by limiting their aggregate deductibility to medical expenses that exceed 3 percent of adjusted gross income. This floor was raised to 7.5 percent in the 1986 Act, thereby eliminating deductions in all but extraordinary situations given the amount of available income. A similar floor

was placed on casualty losses in the 1960s because of perceived abuses of claimed losses that were minor in character and often not of the true "casualty" type. Currently, any claimed casualty loss must be reduced by (a) $100, and (b) 10 percent of adjusted gross income, and only the excess is deductible. Again the policy of limiting the deduction to extraordinary losses given the amount of available income is clear. In both instances, only the deductible portion of medical or casualty losses is taken into account to determine whether the standard deduction is advantageous.

A final approach is to require specific documentation about claimed deductions to be filed with the return. This is required, for example, for charitable deductions claimed for contributions of noncash property, where valuation is likely to be overly optimistic.

Personal exemptions are entirely different from personal deductions. Exemptions permit the subtraction of arbitrary amounts for the taxpayer and spouse (if a joint return is filed), and for each dependent relative (defined precisely in the IRC). Additional exemptions were long provided for persons over 65 and for blind people, but the 1986 Act eliminated these exemptions in favor of a limited increase in the standard deduction for the aged and blind. The personal exemption for the 1996 tax year was $2,550 for each allowable exemption. For taxpayers reporting more than $176,950 on a joint return, the exemption is reduced in proportion to income in excess of that amount up to $299,450, at which point no deduction for exemptions is allowed. As a result of the combination of personal exemptions and the standard deduction, a family of four pays no tax if its adjusted gross income is $16,900 or less.

§9.12 The Calculation of the Tax Due on Individual Returns

Once taxable income is calculated, the next step is the calculation of the actual tax that is due. This is done either from a set of tables or by a mathematical calculation. This discussion concentrates on the formulas, which, as they applied to the 1996 tax year, are set forth in Figure 9-2.

There are four different categories of individual taxpayers with different-sized brackets depending on marital or family status. The three basic categories of taxpayers are (1) a married couple filing jointly or a surviving spouse (defined as a person whose spouse has died within the previous two years), (2) a "head of household" (defined as an unmarried person who is not a surviving spouse and who maintains a home for a dependent child or relative), and (3) a single person. The fourth category, married taxpayers filing separately, is created by simply halving every entry in the joint return category; this thereby ensures that married couples with two incomes cannot take advantage of the single person tax schedule but remain on a tax parity with families in which one spouse is the wage earner and the other is a homemaker.

In order to calculate the tax due on a given amount of taxable income, one finds the range in which the income number falls (from the first two columns), subtracts the lower number of the range from taxable income, calculates the marginal tax on the income in excess of the lower number, and

1996
Tax Rate
Schedules

Schedule X—Use if your filing status is **Single**

If the amount on Form 1040, line 37, is: Over—	But not over—	Enter on Form 1040, line 38	of the amount over—
$0	$24,000	.... 15%	$0
24,000	58,150	$3,600.00 + 28%	24,000
58,150	121,300	13,162.00 + 31%	58,150
121,300	263,750	32,738.50 + 36%	121,300
263,750	....	84,020.50 + 39.6%	263,750

Schedule Y-1—Use if your filing status is **Married filing jointly** or **Qualifying widow(er)**

If the amount on Form 1040, line 37, is: Over—	But not over—	Enter on Form 1040, line 38	of the amount over—
$0	$40,100	.... 15%	$0
40,100	96,900	$6,015.00 + 28%	40,100
96,900	147,700	21,919.00 + 31%	96,900
147,700	263,750	37,667.00 + 36%	147,700
263,750	....	79,445.00 + 39.6%	263,750

Schedule Y-2—Use if your filing status is **Married filing separately**

If the amount on Form 1040, line 37, is: Over—	But not over—	Enter on Form 1040, line 38	of the amount over—
$0	$20,050	.... 15%	$0
20,050	48,450	$3,007.50 + 28%	20,050
48,450	73,850	10,959.50 + 31%	48,450
73,850	131,875	18,833.50 + 36%	73,850
131,875	....	39,722.50 + 39.6%	131,875

Schedule Z—Use if your filing status is **Head of household**

If the amount on Form 1040, line 37, is: Over—	But not over—	Enter on Form 1040, line 38	of the amount over—
$0	$32,150	.... 15%	$0
32,150	83,050	$4,822.50 + 28%	32,150
83,050	134,500	19,074.50 + 31%	83,050
134,500	263,750	35,024.00 + 36%	134,500
263,750	....	81,554.00 + 39.6%	263,750

Figure 9-2

244

adds to that the base amount of tax, which gives the total tax. Thus, for a single taxpayer with taxable income of $100,000, the taxpayer would subtract $58,150 from $100,000, which leaves $41,850. The tax on $41,850 at 31 percent is $12,974, which when added to the base amount of tax of $13,162 indicates a total tax of $26,136. Therefore, one might say that the effective tax rate on $100,000 of income for a single taxpayer is about 26 percent even though the marginal tax rate (i.e., the rate on each next dollar of income up to $121,300) is 31 percent.

§9.13 Limitations on the Deductibility of Passive Losses and Investment Interest

The 1986 Act develops a classification of interest and passive loss deductions primarily to eliminate excessive deductions from tax shelters. Unfortunately, in doing so, Congress again significantly increased the complexity of the individual income tax system.

The basic idea is not very complicated. **Investment interest**, for example, is interest on obligations incurred to buy or carry investment property. That interest is to be deductible only to the extent the taxpayer has income from the investments. The purpose of this provision is to prevent a taxpayer from borrowing funds to acquire deferred income investments and deducting the interest immediately, thereby sheltering other current income from tax. If one does incur interest in a year when it is not deductible because of the absence of investment income, that deduction is not lost but may be carried over indefinitely and deducted in a later year when the taxpayer does have available investment income in excess of investment interest.

The 1986 Act also establishes a similar pattern by creating a class of losses and credits called **passive losses**, which can be deducted only to the extent that there is income from passive activities. Passive activities are defined to include essentially all rental activities and trade or business activities in which the taxpayer does not materially participate. Investment activity is not passive activity. The ownership and rental of commercial or residential property is expressly included in the definition of passive activities, and participation by owners in decisions on such matters as who should be tenants does not take the activity out of the passive category. Virtually the only nonpassive commercial real estate activity is owning and operating a hotel. The purpose of this provision is to eliminate most tax shelters, particularly tax shelters involving the direct ownership of commercial or rental residential real estate. However, there are exceptions to this rigid treatment of passive activity, including the right to deduct up to $25,000 of passive losses for taxpayers with adjusted gross incomes of up to $100,000; this deduction is itself gradually phased out at higher incomes until all deduction is prohibited for taxpayers with adjusted gross incomes in excess of $150,000. Passive losses that cannot be taken advantage of in any year because of the lack of passive income also do not disappear but may be carried over to later years in which there is passive income in excess of passive losses.

Losses and credits arising from a trade or business in which the taxpayer materially participates are fully deductible. Materially means that the taxpayer

is involved in the operations of the activity on a regular, continuous, and substantial basis. If the activity is not material, the business becomes a passive activity. Thus, there is a threefold classification of individual profit-making activity that is designed to eliminate tax shelters and related activities. Except for real estate activities that are clearly defined as passive activities, difficult problems of classification at or near the boundaries between these three categories are sure to arise. Indeed, the mere reporting of activities in each category significantly increases the complexity of the schedules to Form 1040.

§9.14 The Alternative Minimum Tax

The **alternative minimum tax** attacks the proliferation of preferential provisions in the IRC and limits the ability of a taxpayer to avoid all taxes by using these provisions, either singly or in combination. It is applicable only to taxpayers with taxable incomes in excess of $45,000. The alternative minimum tax essentially requires a second tax calculation on an entirely different set of computational rules. If the alternative minimum tax is greater than the tax computed in the normal manner, then the taxpayer's tax liability is based on the alternative minimum tax rather than on the normal computation of tax.

The alternative minimum tax is figured on an amount computed as follows: One starts with the adjusted gross income of the taxpayer computed on the normal basis, and adds back in specific **tax preference items** claimed by the taxpayer in the calculation of adjusted gross income. From this amount, one subtracts (1) $45,000, and (2) allowable deductions for charitable contributions, interest on mortgages on the personal residence of the taxpayers, and investment interest. The alternative minimum tax is 26 percent of the amount so computed up to $175,000, and it is 28 percent thereafter.

The tax preference items that must be added back into income for the computation of the amount subject to the alternative minimum tax include accelerated depreciation on property, capital gains deductions, portions of incentive stock options excluded from income, and percentage depletion.

The alternative minimum tax provision is an effort to overcome the deficiencies of the normal income tax structure by overlaying a separate tax schedule on most loopholes. The alternative minimum tax obviously complicates the tax returns of all high-income taxpayers.

§9.15 The Collection Process

The IRS has the responsibility for collection of federal income, gift, estate, and excise taxes. The discussion here is limited to the process of collection of income taxes.

Income taxes are collected on a highly efficient "pay as you go" basis. For most Americans, the "pay as you go" system means simply that employers must withhold from each paycheck an amount that approximately covers the employee's tax liability by the end of the year. Probably every reader has had some contact with this **withholding** system, involving the filing of a Form W-4 with one's employer declaring the number of exemptions claimed, and the receipt

from the employer each January of a W-2 Form that shows the amounts actually withheld during the previous calendar year. The withholding schedules and tax rates are structured so that if a person accurately declares the number of exemptions and uses the standard deduction, he or she ends up having more deducted from paychecks than the amount of tax actually due. Most taxpayers therefore receive refunds every year. Of course, these refunds are paid in effect from funds painlessly collected from the taxpayer by his or her employer over the course of the preceding year without interest. The fact that most people are entitled to refunds each year materially increases the political acceptability of the system. The arrangement is attractive to the federal government as well: The collection process is painless and does not give rise to large amounts of resentment, the government has the interest-free use of funds for nearly a year, and tax collections are spread around the year and not bunched in a single month.

The employer is required to pay over to the IRS the amount withheld from employees at the end of each calendar quarter. Although the IRC requires that these withheld funds be placed in a separate account, most employers do not segregate the funds but simply use them as part of general working capital until the check is written to the IRS. Of course, from time to time a business may become insolvent without having forwarded the money withheld from employees to the IRS. There is a 100 percent penalty against an individual with the responsibility for these funds who fails to pay them over to the IRS. In other words, the corporate treasurer or individual with analogous responsibilities is personally liable for the amount withheld if it is not in fact paid over. Like other claims arising under the IRC, this liability is not discharged in bankruptcy. Whether or not the Service successfully collects the withheld taxes from the employer, however, the employee is entitled to credit against his or her taxes of the amounts shown as withheld on statements reported to the IRS.

If persons have income or gains not subject to withholding, they may be required to file quarterly declarations of **estimated tax**, which are intended to provide a "pay as you go" system to taxpayers with substantial amounts of self-employment activity, personal investments, and other sources of nonwithheld income, such as gambling or stock market trading. Quarterly declarations are due April 15, June 15, September 15, and January 15, and must be accompanied by a proportional amount of the estimated tax that is shown to be due on the estimate. A person subject to withholding is theoretically required to file a quarterly declaration whenever taxes withheld are less than 90 percent of taxes due, but such persons may avoid this filing if they increase the amount of withholding so that the estimated tax for that quarter is shown to be zero. The obligation to file quarterly declarations of estimated tax, and to pay the proportional amount of tax due, is enforced by penalties applied when the final return is filed for the year showing substantial underpayment of tax. What is substantial in this context is very specifically defined in the IRC: if the amount paid by withholding and quarterly estimates is less than 90 percent of the actual tax shown to be due on the return. The 1986 Act imposes a stiff penalty if the total "pay as you go" payments fail to equal 90 percent of the actual tax; in earlier years, a smaller penalty was due only if the payments were less than 80 percent of the actual tax due. There are also other bases on which this penalty may be avoided.

§9.16 Tax Accounting

The IRC obviously requires the use of accounting concepts for determining in which years items of income and deduction should be reported. Tax accounting differs materially from traditional income accounting in numerous specific respects. Tax returns are not prepared on generally accepted accounting practices (GAAP) principles, so income for tax purposes and income for accounting purposes may vary substantially.

Most individual taxpayers are on the **cash basis**, that is, they report income when it is received rather than when it is earned and take advantage of deductions when they are paid rather than when they are incurred or when they are due. This permits some income and deduction shifting from one year to another. For example, a doctor who does not bill for November or December services until January takes the income arising from these services into his or her tax return for the second year, not the first. It is almost always advantageous to defer taxes even if tax rates are identical, because of the time value of a deferred payment. Sometimes, year-end planning may also permit a taxpayer to shift income from a high-income year to a lower-income year so that it is taxed at lower marginal rates. Similarly, a taxpayer may be able to shift two years' real estate property taxes into a single year by paying one year's taxes in January and prepaying the next year's taxes in December of the same year. Combining two years' taxes into a single year may be advantageous if the standard deduction is claimed for the year in which no payments of real estate tax are made. Strategies of this type do offer some modest degree of tax saving and tax avoidance for individuals.

There are some exceptions to the straight cash basis of individual taxpayer accounting. The doctrine of **constructive receipt** does not permit a taxpayer to defer reporting income items that are within his or her immediate control. An income item, for example, cannot be deferred merely by not depositing a check until the following year. There are also special rules relating to receipt of interest. Interest on financial instruments such as zero coupon bonds purchased at a discount from face value (**original issue discount** or **OID**) must be reported as it is earned rather than being deferred until the instrument is paid. (Zero coupon bonds and other similar instruments are discussed in Chapters 14 and 15, which discuss trading markets and investment strategies.) Similarly, interest that a taxpayer pays in a lump sum to cover several accounting periods cannot be deducted in the year of payment but must be deducted ratably over the relevant periods, although it is paid in a single year. Restrictions are also imposed on the deductibility of prepaid amounts. These various qualifications to the general cash method of accounting reflect pragmatic judgments designed to limit revenue loss from tax-minimizing transactions.

It has long been a fact of corporate life that many publicly held corporations reflect substantial earnings in their financial statements and reports to shareholders but pay little or no federal income tax. Undoubtedly, much of this difference is due to tax benefits intentionally given to business, such as the **accelerated cost recovery system (ACRS)** for calculating depreciation deductions and **investment tax credits**. However, the difference is partly due to differences in accounting principles.

Financial accounting for publicly held corporations must comply with

GAAP, which does not permit the use of cash accounting for most businesses. The IRC similarly prohibits corporations and specified other types of businesses from adopting a cash basis of accounting for tax purposes. However, tax accounting and GAAP are designed for different purposes, and as a result there are many differences in detail and the way specific transactions are handled. The primary goal of financial accounting is to provide useful information to management, shareholders, creditors, and others who are properly interested in the business. The primary goal of the income tax system, on the other hand, is to protect the public **fisc**. The general principle of tax accounting is that the method used must clearly reflect income. The tax system, for example, may require that receipts of cash be included in income immediately, while GAAP requires that they be taken into income only when the services have been performed or the goods delivered. Similarly, GAAP may call for the creation of reserves for losses and the treatment of amounts allocated to them as expenses reducing earnings. Such expenses are often not recognized as deductions for income tax purposes.

The differences between tax accounting and financial accounting is a specialized area of interest primarily to accountants and attorneys who represent businesses in tax matters. They are the outgrowth of basic differences in the purposes of the two accounting systems. Because the systems are different, businesses must usually keep tax books and financial books separately.

In 1986, a controversial and novel accounting-related concept was introduced into the tax accounting system. It requires corporations to include a fraction of the difference between their taxable income and their net book income as reported to shareholders in the calculation of the alternative minimum tax for corporations. The purpose of this provision is to ensure that corporations that show substantial book earnings in reports to shareholders also pay a reasonable amount of tax. However, it is uncertain how important this provision is in practice, because the manner of calculating a corporation's alternative minimum taxable income already takes into account the impact of some of the most important corporate tax preferences, such as ACRS.

§9.17 Sales and Exchanges of Property in General

A major area of tax law deals with gains and losses from the sale or exchange of property. At the most basic level, a sale or exchange of property gives rise to taxable income. Say that a farmer swaps a side of beef for a bolt of cloth from the local dry goods store. The exchange is a taxable transaction, and each participant should report gain or loss from the transaction on his or her federal income tax return. Obviously, in the **barter economy** that quietly exists in many communities, a lot of tax evading goes on, because it is likely that few, if any, transactions of this type are reported.

Of course, in the barter of the beef for the cloth, both parties are swapping goods that involve their trade or business. But that is not essential. If you sell your secondhand car at a profit, the gain should be reported to the IRS as income. Similarly, if you swap your car for a motorcycle or a used computer, the gain should be reported. (Losses from such personal transactions are not deductible at all, and hence need not be reported.)

The calculation of the amount of the gain from sales or exchanges involves the use of technical language that is fundamental to any understanding of the tax laws:

1. **Basis** is the investment the seller of the property has in the property. It is the cost or purchase price of the property that the seller pays or incurrs in acquiring the property. In the case of property acquired by gift, the basis in the hands of the donee is usually the same as the basis in the hands of the donor (a **substituted basis**); in the case of property acquired by inheritance, it is generally the fair market value of the assets on the death of decedent (a **stepped-up basis**).

2. **Adjusted basis** is the basis of the property (1) plus capital improvements made by the seller, commissions originally paid by the seller, legal costs for defending or perfecting title, and so forth, and (2) minus returns of capital, particularly **depreciation** claimed as tax deductions, **depletion**, deducted **casualty losses**, insurance reimbursements, and the like.

3. The **amount realized** includes the cash received for the property on a sale or the fair market value of the property received in exchange for the property. Selling expenses, including brokerage commissions that the seller pays, reduce the amount realized. In the case of property subject to a mortgage, the amount realized also includes the amount of mortgage debt that the seller is relieved from paying as a result of the sale. For example, if an owner of real estate who is encumbered by a $50,000 mortgage sells the property for $10,000 cash over and above the mortgage, which the buyer agrees to assume and pay, the amount realized from the sale is $60,000, not $10,000. If the property is sold with the seller giving the buyer $5,000 for assuming the mortgage of $50,000, the amount realized is $45,000.

4. **Gain** on a transaction equals the amount realized minus the adjusted basis. If the adjusted basis is greater than the amount realized, the difference is the loss.

§9.18 The Concept of "Recognition" of Gain or Loss

In order to be taxable, a gain or loss must be **recognized** as well as **realized**. Realized means that the transaction is closed and the sale or exchange has occurred. Recognized means that the gain or loss is also to be taken into account as a taxable transaction. If a realized gain or loss is not recognized, it is deferred to a later year.

Generally, gain or loss is recognized whenever property is sold or exchanged, but there are significant exceptions: **like kind exchanges** of property, **involuntary conversions** of property, sales of residences followed by a **rollover** of the purchase price into a new residence, sales between related persons, and many transactions made by a corporation involving its own stock.

A gain on the sale or exchange of the property may be recognized, although a loss on the sale of the same property is not deductible. This includes, for example, a sale of personal assets such as the family home. The loss is not recognized in the case of personal assets, because it is considered a result of the personal consumption involved in living in a home rather than an economic loss.

The recognition concept is particularly important in connection with trans-

actions relating to the formation and reorganizations of corporations. Many corporate transactions would be economically impractical if gains or losses from the transaction were recognized. For example, consider the problem of investors in a new corporation planning to contribute not cash but property in exchange for its stock. Assume further that the property has a fair market value today of $25,000 and a basis in the hands of the investor of $16,000. The stock being received also has a fair market value of $25,000. In the absence of a nonrecognition provision, the exchange of the real estate for the stock would result in the realization of gain in the amount of $9,000 (the difference between the fair market value of the property being received in the exchange and the basis of the property being exchanged). The result would be that the investor would owe some $3,000 in tax as a result of making the investment. Fortunately, the IRC permits the transfer of assets to a corporation controlled by the transferor (or a group of which he or she is a member) without recognition of gain if the investors in the corporation are in **control** of the corporation after the transaction. In this context, control means ownership of at least 80 percent of the voting stock of the corporation and at least 80 percent of all other classes of stock. If this provision applies, the investor does not recognize any gain from the exchange of stock for property, and the basis of the stock received is $16,000, the basis of the property exchanged.

Gain may be recognized, however, if the transferor takes back cash or property other than stock, or his or her debt is assumed in the transfer. Such rebates are often called **boot**. For example, if in the above transaction, the investor is contributing real estate with a fair market value of $25,000 and a basis of $16,000 that is subject to a $19,000 lien that the corporation is to assume, the difference between the basis ($16,000) and the amount of the lien ($19,000) must be recognized as gain from the transaction. The basis of the stock received is then $19,000.

Another very important nonrecognition area in the law of corporations deals with different kinds of **reorganizations**—statutory mergers, acquisitions of all the assets of one corporation in exchange for stock of another corporation, and the like. These provisions are among the most complicated in the Code, and significantly different tax consequences may follow, depending on how the transaction is structured.

§9.19 Special Tax Treatment of Long-Term Capital Gains and Losses

The 1986 Act imposed the same tax rate on long-term capital gains and losses as on income generally. This represented a change in long-standing tax policy that was to some extent controversial at the time, and this change has not been continued. In 1990 and 1993, marginal tax rates on ordinary income were increased to as high as 39.6 percent, while the tax rate on capital gains was kept at 28 percent. As a result, the elaborate definition and classification of capital gains of the 1954 Code continue to apply today.

Prior to the 1986 Tax Act, the 1954 Code defined the term **capital asset** and provided special rules and limitations with respect to gains and losses from sales or exchanges of such assets. A capital asset is any property held by a

taxpayer other than inventory, property held primarily for sale to customers, depreciable and real property used in a trade or business, and several other less important items. A taxpayer's personal residence is thus a capital asset, but if the same property were used in a trade or business it would not be a capital asset. However, depreciable property used in a trade or business (e.g., the residence), is often entitled to special treatment that is even more favorable to the taxpayer than if it were a capital asset. Shares of stock in a corporation are capital assets; interests in a partnership are also capital assets (except for designated assets such as accounts receivable and appreciated inventory). On the other hand, an interest in a proprietorship is not a capital asset but a composite of individual assets.

A **capital gain** or **capital loss** arises from the **sale or exchange** of a capital asset. A distinction is also made between long-term and short-term capital gains and losses; the dividing line historically was a holding period of six months in order for the gain or loss to be long term; today, the holding period is one year. **Long-term capital gains** were subject to special treatment that in effect imposed a maximum tax of 25 percent on them when other income was being taxed at progressive rates up to 70 percent. Long-term capital losses were also subject to special treatment, but that treatment was usually disadvantageous to the taxpayer, because long-term losses were deductible against ordinary income only to a limited extent and in many years not on a dollar-for-dollar basis.

Calculating the amount of gain or loss that qualified for long-term capital gain or loss treatment was complicated, because a single taxpayer often had both short-term and long-term gains or losses in a single tax year. Basically, the tax law required a netting of short-term gains and losses separately from long-term gains and losses, then netting the two categories. Only the ultimate difference was categorized as long-term or short-term.

If a taxpayer's return showed a net long-term capital gain, that gain was entitled to special tax treatment. The taxpayer could exclude 50 or 60 percent (depending on the year the transaction occurred) of the net long-term gain entirely from the tax computation, and only the remaining portion of the net long-term gain was included in ordinary income. Such a gain, however, could never be taxed at a higher effective rate than 25 percent.

Losses from capital assets that were for personal use (e.g., a residence or an automobile) were not deductible at all. Other long-term capital losses (after the netting process described above) were deductible against ordinary income only up to the amount of $3,000, and long-term capital losses counted for only one half, so that $6,000 of long-term losses were needed to obtain a $3,000 deduction. The precise treatment of net capital losses varied somewhat depending on the year in question. Short-term capital gains (after the netting process described above) were includable in ordinary income in their entirety, while short-term capital losses were deductible in full against ordinary income. In these pre-1986 years, it was generally desirable to structure sales and exchanges so that the taxpayer showed either a net long-term capital gain or a short-term capital loss, or even better, an ordinary loss.

To complicate matters further, the sale of depreciable properties used in a trade or business that did not fall within the definition of capital asset was nevertheless entitled to the best of both worlds: to long-term capital gain treatment in the case of a gain and ordinary loss treatment in the event of a

loss. Such gain, however, in some circumstances might be recaptured and subject to ordinary income treatment. Similarly, other capital asset transactions were made subject to other complex recapture provisions, all designed to limit the ability of taxpayers to transmute ordinary income into long-term capital gain. Again the precise rules that apply to these situations vary somewhat, depending on the year in which the transaction occurred.

The 1986 Tax Act eliminated all special treatment of long-term capital gains after 1987, at least in terms of allowing any portion of gain to be excluded from income. The application of the $3,000 maximum deduction for long-term capital losses nevertheless continues to apply after 1987, but the old two-for-one rule is eliminated. However, the complex of rules about netting long- and short-term gains remains in effect.

The special tax treatment for long-term capital gains was restored to the tax laws because of concern that complete elimination of any difference in treatment might lead investors to stress current income at the expense of risk-taking in new ventures promising higher growth returns in the future. It is difficult to assess whether these concerns are justified. However, most industrial countries tax long-term capital gains at low rates or not at all.

§9.20 Corporations and Other Business Forms

Corporations are generally treated as separate taxable entities under the IRC with their own sets of rules and their own tax schedules. Unincorporated business entities, including partnerships, limited partnerships, and limited liability companies, on the other hand, are not treated as separate taxable entities. Rather, unincorporated businesses file information returns showing the results of operations and allocating the profit or loss among the owners, who then must include the income or loss in their own personal returns, whether or not any monies are in fact distributed to them. This method of taxation is usually called **pass through** or **conduit taxation**. (The limitations on deductions of passive losses and investment interest discussed earlier are, however, applicable to losses incurred through an unincorporated business.) Because corporation income is taxed at the corporate level and again at the individual level if there is a distribution to the shareholders, it is sometimes said that corporations are subject to **double taxation**. It is possible, however, for smaller corporations (with 75 or fewer shareholders and meeting certain other requirements) to elect to be treated as an **S Corporation**, which status allows many but not all of the benefits of pass through taxation. The differences between these ways of taxing business income (as well as various planning strategies designed to minimize the differences) are discussed more fully in Chapter 10.

Corporations are currently subject to tax on income at these rates:

Taxable income	Tax rate
Not over $50,000	15%
Over $50,000, under $75,000	25%
Over $75,000, under $10,000,000	34%
Over $10,000,000	35%

In addition, there is an alternative minimum tax for corporations that taxes a corporation's alternative minimum taxable income at a flat 20 percent. This income is computed by taking the corporation's regular taxable income and increasing it by specified tax preferences: accelerated depreciation on real and personal property, rapid amortization, and (in a novel provision described above) 75 percent of the difference between the taxpayer's adjusted net book income and its alternative minimum taxable income.

§9.21 Taxation of Trusts and Estates

Trusts and estates are also separate taxpayers for purposes of the federal income tax law. They must file income tax returns and must often pay income taxes. This responsibility is independent of, and different from, the possible responsibility of such entities for gift and estate taxes. Both estates and trusts, however, may largely avoid the payment of income tax by making distributions of income to beneficiaries. The beneficiaries must then include those distributions in their tax returns as income.

When a person dies, his or her representative must file a final return in the decedent's name for the period ending with death. The estate must then file an estate income tax return for the period beginning the day after the date of death and ending on a date selected by the fiduciary for the estate. Annual returns from the estate may be necessary thereafter. The income items included in the return of the estate may include investment income from assets that the estate owns, gains from the sale or exchange of estate property, and post-death income items attributable to services of the decedent, such as fees for services provided by the decedent before death if payment is received after death. These latter items are called **income in respect of a decedent**.

An important rule affecting the income tax consequences of the death of a person is the step-up in basis of property that automatically occurs upon the death of the owner. The basis of all property that the decedent owned automatically becomes its fair market value on the date of death. This principle often results in elderly or ill individuals refraining from selling or disposing of appreciated properties during the remainder of their lifetimes. The appreciation in value during the lifetime of the decedent escapes taxation entirely.

The taxation of trusts is considerably more complicated than the taxation of estates and cannot be adequately summarized in a brief comment. A taxpayer may create numerous trusts, and each will be a separate taxpayer unless the IRS determines that tax avoidance was a principal factor in their creation and the beneficiaries are substantially identical. In addition, trusts may be created in which the trustee has authority to distribute income or accumulate it for long periods. Further, a grantor of a trust may reserve substantial powers of management and control, and may also retain a reversionary interest in the trust. Certain **revocable trusts** and short-term trusts are not recognized as separate taxpayers. The income from such trusts is taxed directly to the creator.

IV

BUSINESS FORMS

CHAPTER 10

A SURVEY OF BUSINESS FORMS

§10.1   Publicly Held and Closely Held Businesses in General

This chapter is an introduction to business forms in the United States. There have been important, almost revolutionary changes in this area since 1990.

The phrase "business forms" refers to the legal relationship between a business and its owners. A traditional form of classification is between **unincorporated business forms** (e.g., proprietorships, partnerships, and limited partnerships) on the one hand and **corporations** on the other. This is a useful classification if one is to study the legal principles that apply to various business forms, but it is not a particularly useful economic classification, because the corporate form is suitable for businesses of all sizes.

A second approach is to classify businesses by size (e.g., small businesses and large businesses). Businesses in the United States, however, range from the very small start-up business, perhaps as small as a lemonade stand on a front lawn in the summer, to immense corporations such as General Motors Corporation, with sales in the billions of dollars each year. There is a continuum of business sizes: For any specific business, it is always possible to find another that is either slightly bigger or slightly smaller. Lines drawn based solely on size are therefore necessarily arbitrary.

A third approach, and the one adopted here, is to classify businesses on the basis of whether they are closely held or publicly held. A **closely held business** is one for which there is no established public market for the ownership interests in the business. Usually closely held businesses are small and owned by a few persons. However, some closely held businesses are very large. For example,

Brown & Root, Inc., a major construction company, is a wholly owned subsidiary of Halliburton, Inc. Brown & Root has one owner and is therefore closely held; its owner, Halliburton, is publicly held. Its stock is actively traded on the **New York Stock Exchange (NYSE)**. What all closely held businesses have in common is that there is no established way for an outside investor to invest in the business and no assurance that current owners can sell their ownership interests and exit from the business. Of course, negotiated purchases or sales of interests in closely held businesses are always possible and occur all the time, but there is no established trading market.

Publicly held businesses are those in which a public market exists for ownership interests. The NYSE is the best-known market for shares of stock; the second major market today is the over the counter market known as the **National Association of Securities Dealers Automated Quotation (NASDAQ)** system. In addition to these two national markets and the **American Stock Exchange (AMEX)**, several regional markets exist as well as several privately owned trading systems that only very large investors use.

In some other contexts, public businesses may refer to government-owned businesses, which are quite different from the meaning of publicly held business used here. As used here, public businesses means private businesses owned in whole or in part by members of the general public. Virtually all publicly held businesses are corporations (though a few have adopted other business forms), and many of them are huge enterprises, with billions of dollars in assets and sales. Because almost all publicly held businesses are corporations, it is customary to refer to them also as publicly held corporations.

§10.2 Availability of Information About Businesses

Closely held and publicly held businesses differ dramatically in the availability of information about their businesses and affairs. Closely held businesses are essentially private operations. There is usually little publicly available information about them. The only real sources of information are collected by credit reporting agencies and to a lesser extent by compilations of information done by Dunn & Bradstreet and similar organizations that rely on voluntary disclosures. In contrast, publicly held corporations operate in a virtual goldfish bowl: Each publicly held corporation must periodically file information with the Securities and Exchange Commission (SEC) and that information is immediately made available to the public through electronic and other means. If the corporation's shares are traded on a national or regional securities exchange, the corporation must also make public announcements about its affairs. Should someone want to know the compensation of the chief executive officer of General Motors Corporation the previous year, that is public information available for the asking. However, if someone wants to know the compensation of the president of a closely held corporation, there is usually no way to find out if the business does not want that information known.

It may be noted in passing that the availability of information with respect to publicly held corporations is not directly tied to the presence of an active public market for shares. If a business has made a **public offering** of its

ownership interests, it becomes subject to the disclosure requirements outlined above, whether or not a public market for those ownership interests develops. It is quite possible that a relatively small public offering of ownership interests may not lead to the development of an active trading market for shares. Although a market of sorts usually arises following a public offering for shares, that is not necessarily the case, and if a market does develop, it may involve relatively few transactions. The shares are said to be **illiquid**. (A **liquid market** is one in which there is a large amount of trading interest and prices are set by numerous transactions.) An example of an illiquid or nonexistent market that arose following a public offering was the sale of interests in limited partnerships investing in real estate in the 1980s.

§10.3 The Significance of a Public Market for Ownership Interests

The absence of a public market for ownership interests in closely held businesses creates problems that do not exist in publicly held corporations. For one thing, there is no easy way to determine how much such an ownership interest is worth. A public market is marked by the presence of buyers and sellers ready, willing, and able to buy and sell. The prices struck in a market are the best guide for what an interest is worth. In a closely held business, one may infer or estimate the value based on techniques described elsewhere in this book, but these values are estimates of what an interest would be worth if there were an active trading market.

For a similar reason it may be difficult or impossible to sell an ownership interest in a closely held business. First one needs to find someone who is interested in making an investment in the business. And, if the present owner is having difficulty finding somebody who is interested in buying, any potential purchasers should realize that they may also have a problem of disposing of the interest if they buy and then later decide to sell. In many situations, the only persons interested in buying will be those who already own an interest in the business, and these buyers may not be willing to offer very much for the interest. This lack of power to exit is to some extent a function of the business form chosen for the closely held business; in some instances, a participant in a closely held business may have the power to compel the business to purchase his or her interest or to liquidate the business. Also, the lack of power to exit may be a function of lack of advance planning. Because of the absence of an established market, it is only prudent for a potential purchaser to obtain a contractual commitment from the business or other owners of the business that they will buy the interest when the purchaser desires to exit.

Yet another facet of the closely held business is that if there is more than one owner, it is possible that one or more persons owning minority interests in the business may be locked in to the business and yet be excluded from any financial participation in the benefits of the business. Minority owners of a closely held business may find that whatever financial rights they have can be granted or withheld by the controlling owner. Where a controlling owner possesses this power, the other owners may be **frozen out** or **squeezed out**.

One recurring issue in the law of closely held businesses is the extent to which the legal system should protect minority owners in this situation when there is no contractual obligation by someone to buy that minority interest.

In contrast, investors in a publicly held corporation usually have the power to exit at any time: They can eliminate their investment simply by calling their broker and directing the broker to sell the interest at whatever the current market price is. On the other hand, there are some instances (1) in which very large shareholders of publicly held corporations may find it difficult to sell their interests because of the size of the holdings, and (2) in which SEC regulations prohibit certain owners of shares from reselling them during certain periods.

The balance of this chapter is devoted to a consideration of the various types of business forms that are currently in general use in the United States. Much of this discussion relates to closely held business forms. In the chapters that follow on securities, dividends, and markets, the emphasis is on publicly held corporations.

The radical changes that have occurred since 1990 all involve closely held businesses. They include the development of novel business forms that provide limited liability for owners, specifically, limited liability companies (LLCs) and limited liability partnerships (LLPs), and the promulgation by the Internal Revenue Service (IRS) of regulations, called **check-the-box regulations**, that greatly simplify the system of taxation to which a closely held business will be subject.

§10.4 Proprietorships

Consider first a business that is to be operated by a single person. Perhaps it is a service business, (e.g., an accountant going into business on her own, an attorney hanging out a shingle, or a person good with his hands putting up a sign offering to do odd repair jobs). In these simple situations, it is almost always convenient to conduct the business as a proprietorship. A proprietorship is simply a business individually owned by a single person.

A business that a single person owns may also be conducted as a corporation. In many states, such a business may also be conducted as a one-person LLC. However, this section is limited to the proprietorship in which no alternative business form is elected.

A proprietor can simply go into business without any concern about business forms. In the very simplest cases, there may be little or no distinction between the affairs of the business and the affairs of the individual owner. However, most proprietors find it necessary or desirable to keep a fair degree of separation between the business and the owner for accounting and record-keeping purposes. At the very least, a set of books is maintained independent of the personal accounts of the individual owner. This simplifies the preparation of tax returns and permits the owner to identify the profitability of his or her endeavors. It also permits ready identification of property that is formally devoted to the business. Today, a proprietorship also normally has its own bank account, stationery, and other distinguishing characteristics that indicate the separation of business transactions from personal ones.

Whether the degree of separation between the owner's personal and business affairs is large or small, it is useful to discuss the owner (the proprietor) and the business (the proprietorship) as though they were separate entities.

Proprietors may conduct business either in their own name or in a trade or assumed name. Many states have **assumed name statutes** that require a public disclosure of the identity of persons conducting business in a name other than their own, but that is a simple and straightforward process. Proprietorships often do business and enter into contracts in the form Joan Jones dba Jones Construction Company. The **dba** (or **d/b/a**) stands for "doing business as." In this way, both the proprietor and the trade name under which the proprietor is conducting business appear on most business transactions. There are few restrictions on the use of trade or assumed names: As long as the name is not misleadingly similar to the name of a competing business or otherwise used in a fraudulent or deceptive manner, a person may conduct business in any name he or she wishes. However, a few words, such as **Corporation, Incorporated**, or **Inc.** may not be used because they falsely imply that the business is incorporated. The word **company** does not carry this implication.

The owner of a proprietorship may act individually or employ one or more agents, employees, or managers to act on his or her behalf. As a result, the proprietor can delegate business-related activity and decisions freely to subordinates or employees. Thus, the benefits of efficiency and flexibility that arise from specialization and separation of functions are as readily available in a proprietorship as they are in other forms of business enterprise.

A proprietorship's owner is entitled to the fruits of the business, that is, its income and cash flow (after making due provision for its debts), without any formality or difficulty. For example, a proprietor may simply empty the cash drawer of the business to pay for his or her personal vacation if that does not disrupt business operations and if appropriate records are maintained.

For legal purposes, a proprietorship is not a separate entity. For example, the owner of a proprietorship is liable for all business debts. A proprietor of a business may borrow money on his or her personal credit either for personal use (e.g., a family vacation) or for use in the business. If such a loan is unsecured, the creditor may levy upon either personal or business assets if there is a default without regard to whether the loan was originally used for business or personal purposes. Loans may also be obtained solely in the name of, and on the credit of, the proprietorship, but proprietors are individually liable on such loans whether or not their name appears on the note or whether they actually negotiated the loan and signed the note. Often a proprietorship purchases inventory, supplies, or machinery in its assumed name on credit secured by a lien or security interest in the property being purchased. The owner of the business is personally liable on these obligations as well, though the creditor in these situations may as a practical matter look only to the property securing the loan or to the assets of the business itself in determining whether to extend credit.

Similarly, if the business becomes involved in litigation, the proprietor is the appropriate plaintiff; if the business is sued, the proprietor is the proper defendant. In litigation involving a proprietorship, it is customary in many jurisdictions to use the dba designation when describing the party suing or being sued.

A proprietorship is not a separate taxable entity and no separate federal income tax return is filed, though proprietors must file a **Schedule C** with their personal return showing revenues and expenses of the business. Proprietors must also obtain an employer's identification number from the IRS. The business may also need to obtain local permits to engage in specific businesses or occupy space for commercial purposes. Again, these permits are usually issued in the dba form. If it is a law, medical, or accounting practice, of course, the owner must be a licensed professional.

If the proprietorship opens an office in a different state, there are no additional formalities or consents required other than those applicable to anyone engaging in that business in the new state.

A. PARTNERSHIPS AND LIMITED PARTNERSHIPS

§10.5 General Partnerships

General partnerships have a long history. Enterprises in Babylonian times had many characteristics of a modern partnership, and partnerships were well known in England in medieval times.

A partnership is a logical extension of a proprietorship when there is more than one owner. A partnership (sometimes called a **general partnership** to distinguish it from the **limited partnership**, discussed below) is the operation of a business by co-owners. It can be formed simply by a handshake. There is generally no need for a written agreement and no public filing of any document other than an assumed name certificate that may be required if the business is conducted under a trade name and not the names of the partners. With respect to local permits and qualifications, interstate operations and the like, generally the same rules apply to partnerships as to proprietorships.

Some additional complexity is created, of course, simply because there is more than one owner. In a proprietorship, the owner calls all the shots. In a partnership, there is more than one owner, and ground rules are needed for determining how decisions are to be made and how the rights of individual partners are to be ascertained.

§10.6 Sources of Partnership Law

The law of partnership was largely codified in the **Uniform Partnership Act** (**UPA**), approved in 1914, that was adopted by virtually every state without significant change. In the 1980s, interest in partnership law increased dramatically as a result of changes in federal income tax law, and some states adopted significant revisions to their uniform acts. These changes, in turn, led to a revision of the UPA in 1994. However, although some smaller states have adopted the **Revised Uniform Partnership Act** (**RUPA**) without change, many states have not. Further, some states made significant revisions to the

1994 version, with the result that statutory partnership law in the United States is now not at all uniform. In addition, some areas of partnership law are still governed by common law principles. Although significant variations in partnership law exist, there is, as in many areas of law, a common core of principles and understanding.

The primary source of law relating to a specific partnership is the partnership agreement. Partnership agreements may be written or oral, but there is a strong trend toward written agreements, at least for larger partnerships. Partners are able to structure their relationships by appropriate provisions in the partnership agreement to a considerably greater extent than participants in other forms of business enterprise. The partnership agreement is called the law of that particular partnership. The RUPA departs from this consensual model in two important respects:

1. RUPA includes a variety of **default provisions** that govern aspects of the partnership relation in the absence of express agreement. These default provisions are most likely to be applicable to handshake partnerships without formal written partnership agreements and partnership arrangements entered into by nonlawyers without legal assistance. However, even carefully drafted partnership agreements sometimes do not cover all matters. These default provisions may not always be the provisions that would have been selected by the partners for the specific situation if the possibility of that situation arising had been brought to their attention at the time the partnership agreement was being negotiated. It is generally desirable to agree explicitly on basic rights, powers, and duties rather than to rely on these default provisions.

2. The RUPA contains a list of provisions governing the relationships among partners that cannot be varied by the agreement among partners except to the extent specifically authorized by the statute. These mandatory provisions include the power of every partner to dissolve the partnership by his or her express will at any time, the unlimited liability of every partner for partnership obligations, and the apparent authority of partners to bind the partnership to obligations within the apparent scope of the corporate business. These mandatory provisions largely codify fundamental common law partnership principles.

§10.7 Control and Management

In the absence of an agreement to the contrary, the partners in a partnership have equal rights to participate in the management of the business, which can be conducted with whatever degree of informality the partners desire. The default rule is that if a vote is taken on specific matters, each partner has one vote and the majority decision controls in the absence of an agreement to the contrary. There is no specification, however, of the required quorum. When financial contributions are unequal, the normal assumption is that votes should be weighted in accordance with relative financial interests rather than being on a per capita basis, but this is not the case unless the partners so agree.

The partnership agreement may create classes of partners with different voting and financial rights. For example, classes of junior or senior partners may be created, or a managing partner or management committee with designated

rights and responsibilities may be established. Many law firms use classes of partners to ensure that senior partners have power to govern the affairs of the partnership and share in the returns of the partnership in a manner different from more junior partners. Some law firms distinguish between income partners and equity partners. Depending upon the terms of the specific partnership agreement, an income partner may be virtually indistinguishable from an associate in the law firm.

Partners also have apparent and actual authority to bind the partnership to obligations relating to the business of the partnership. Thus, a partner may bind the partnership on obligations he or she was not authorized to create. The partner so acting is presumably in breach of his or her obligations under the partnership agreement, but the partnership is nevertheless bound by the commitment entered into by the partner.

§10.8 Financial Provisions

Partners may share profits and losses in any way they agree, and they may agree to share losses in a different way than they share profits. Profits may be shared on a flat percentage basis, in proportion to the relative financial investments in the partnership, on a sliding scale based on receipts attributable to each partner's efforts, or on some other basis. One or more partners may be paid a fixed salary that the agreement requires to be viewed as an expense of the business (i.e., deducted from revenues before calculating distributable income). Alternatively, the agreement may provide that the salary is to be charged against the partner's distributive share with the proviso that no refund is required in any year in which the salary exceeds that partner's distributive share for the year. This arrangement is called a **guaranteed payment**. In the absence of an agreement about how profits are to be shared, the default rule under both the UPA and the RUPA is that partners share profits equally, and that losses are shared in the same proportion as profits are shared.

Because profits are determined on an annual basis, **drawing accounts** or advances may be authorized so that each partner may draw specified amounts monthly or weekly against the ultimate distribution of profits. Many partnership agreements provide for different ownership accounts for each partner: a **capital account**, reflecting amounts invested by each partner in the business, an **income account** to which is credited income as it is ascertained and allocated among the partners, and the drawing account described above. The drawing account is usually closed out against the income account on an annual basis. Income earned in excess of distributions may be paid to each partner in a lump sum shortly after the close of the accounting period, or may be added to the capital account in whole or in part to be retained by the partnership or withdrawn by the partner at a later time.

Partnerships must retain a separate set of tax books to reflect the tax obligations of each partner. The central account in the tax records is the capital account of each partner. The capital account is the amount each partner has invested in the partnership; it is increased by earnings and decreased by distributions or losses. In partnership practice, a distinction is drawn between allo-

cations of **income** and allocations of **cash available for distribution**. Allocations of income determine tax liability, while allocations of cash determine how much a partner can withdraw and is based on the cash flow within the partnership.

Each partner is unlimitedly liable for the debts of the partnership. This unlimited liability is ultimately independent of whatever agreement exists among the partners as to how losses should be shared. In other words, any partner may be called on by a creditor at any time to pay a specific partnership debt. But there are significant procedural hurdles in many states that effectively require the plaintiff to pursue the partnership first. Moreover, under the RUPA, the plaintiff must do so. If a partner pays a debt on behalf of the partnership, that partner then has a right to reimbursement from the partnership or from the other partners in accordance with the agreed-on loss-sharing ratio. If one or more partners is insolvent or unable to pay the agreed share of partnership losses, the solvent partners must do so. In the 1990s, a major variation of the general partnership, an LLP, described below, has been created that dramatically modifies these rules of unlimited personal liability for each partner.

A distinction is made in partnership law between **partnership obligations** and **nonpartnership obligations** of individual partners. The distinction is basically between business debts of the partnership and personal or individual debts of a partner. A personal creditor of a partner cannot attach or seize partnership assets: Such a creditor must proceed against the interest of the partner in the partnership through the device of a **charging order**. The protection of partnership assets against seizure by individual creditors reflects the fact that all partners have interests in partnership assets and that a partnership business should not be disrupted because of the financial problems of an individual partner.

§10.9 Contributions of Property or Services

The contributions of one partner to a partnership may differ from the contributions of other partners either in amount or in kind. For example, it is very common for one partner to contribute his or her services, primarily or exclusively, while one or more other partners contribute capital or property, primarily or exclusively. Both service and capital partners may therefore participate in the management of the business financed by the capital-contributing partners.

In negotiating a partnership agreement that involves dissimilar contributions, interests may conflict; a single lawyer should be very cautious about agreeing to represent different interests simultaneously in such a situation. Each partner should be encouraged to have individual legal representation.

When one partner is contributing services over a period of time for a partnership interest, and another partner is contributing capital immediately, difficult issues may arise as to when the service partner should be deemed to have earned his or her interest, what the value of the contributed services is, and what the responsibilities of the respective partners are if the partnership incurs losses. The default provisions of the UPA and the RUPA are unhelpful

in this regard because they simply provide that in the absence of agreement, (a) partners are not entitled to compensation for services rendered on behalf of the partnership and (b) as among themselves, each partner must contribute toward losses in accordance with his or her share of the profits.

In law partnerships, when an associate is made a partner, provision may be made for the new partner to make a capital contribution to the partnership; as a practical matter this contribution is often in the form of reduced cash distributions for a limited period of time.

§10.10 Dissolution, Winding up, and Continuation of the Business

A partnership is dissolved in a variety of circumstances set forth in the UPA, including, for example, the death or bankruptcy of a partner, but the unique feature of partnership law that distinguishes it from corporation law is that each partner has the power to dissolve the relationship at any time. The word "**dissolution**" is used in an unusual way in the UPA; it refers to the termination of the legal relationship among the partners, not to the **winding up** and disposition of the partnership business. In the RUPA, the term "**dissociation**" is used to refer to the termination of the legal relationship; dissolution refers to the winding up of the business. In this section, dissolution is used in the UPA sense to refer to the legal relationship.

Exercise of the power to dissolve a partnership at any time may lead to adverse consequences, because any partner may exercise this power to advance his or her own personal interests. These problems may be avoided somewhat if the partnership agreement provides that the partnership is to continue for a specified term or until the occurrence of a specified event. If so, early dissolution by a partner is a breach of the partnership agreement and opens the dissolving party to liability for breach of contract. On the other hand, if the partnership agreement is silent and does not set forth a specified term, a **partnership at will** has been created that may be dissolved at any time without liability. Informal partnerships are almost always partnerships at will. A partnership that is to continue for a specified term or until the occurrence of a specified event is usually called a **partnership for a term**.

Partnership agreements often provide that upon the death or withdrawal of a partner, the partnership continues and the withdrawing partner is entitled to receive the value of the partnership interest as specified in the agreement. The agreement often specifies how the value is to be calculated and the period over which it is to be paid. Provisions of this nature are binding on the withdrawing partner in accordance with the general principle that the partnership agreement is the law of that partnership. In the absence of an agreement, the statutory default provisions of the original UPA provide that upon the dissolution of a partnership, the withdrawing partner may compel the partnership business to be wound up and liquidated or may permit the partnership business to continue and instead to receive the value of the partnership interest at the time of dissolution plus, at the election of the withdrawing partner, either interest or a continuing share of the profits until payment is made. The RUPA

changes this pattern by giving the remaining partners an option to continue the partnership, if they wish, by paying the withdrawing partner the value of his or her partnership share plus interest. The option to receive either interest or profits was eliminated at the same time.

When the partnership continues, a question sometimes arises as to whether a new partnership has been created following the dissolution of the old, or whether the old partnership continues, at least with respect to the partners who remain in the business. This appears to be purely a conceptual question on which no substantive issue turns.

§10.11 Fiduciary Duties

The relation among partners is one of trust and confidence. This follows necessarily from the agency powers of each partner to bind the partnership to obligations as well as the concept of cooperative enterprise inherent in a partnership. The relation of trust and confidence is enforced judicially through the recognition of a broad fiduciary duty each partner owes to the other in connection with all matters relating to the partnership. This duty may require voluntary disclosure of relevant information. It continues to exist even though the partners are antagonistic to each other and are in the process of dissolving their relationship; it also covers all activities relating to the use and distribution of partnership property. In many states, this fiduciary duty is vigorously enforced.

§10.12 The Partnership as an Entity

A long and rather sterile debate exists as to whether a partnership should be viewed as a separate legal entity or whether it is, like a proprietorship, simply an extension of the individual partners without separate legal status. The distinction is usually phrased in terms of whether a partnership is an **entity** or an **aggregate** of the partners. The UPA contains internal evidence of both theories: Much of the early case law adopts the aggregate theory, but the RUPA and modern case law almost uniformly view the partnership as a separate legal entity. The characterization may be important when analyzing issues not specifically addressed in the UPA.

A partnership is not an entity for purposes of most state statutes requiring foreign entities to register if they transact business in the state. It is usually viewed as an entity for purposes of litigation (though rules differ from state to state). In many states, for example, it is possible to sue a partnership without suing any of the partners individually, and partners may be held individually liable only if the complaint or other process expressly states that recovery is being sought from their individual assets. These rules about procedure and civil process, of course, do not affect the basic responsibility of each partner for the debts of the partnership if they are made defendants in the litigation.

§10.13 Federal Income Taxation of a Partnership

A partnership is not a separate taxable entity under the Internal Revenue Code (IRC). Under the IRC, a partnership must prepare an **information return** each year that shows partnership income and expenses, and allocates the income or loss of the partnership to the individual partners in accordance with the partnership agreement. Each individual partner must then include in his or her personal income tax return the amount of the income or loss so allocated. A positive allocation of income to a specific partner for tax purposes may occur even though the partnership may not in fact make any distributions of cash or property to that partner with respect to the year in question. Similarly, a partnership may have a loss for tax purposes in one or more years even though it makes substantial capital distributions during those years to the partners.

The provisions of the IRC and the regulations issued thereunder are exceptionally complex. This complexity is doubtless a deterrent to the use of partnership forms in some instances, even though under the tax rules in effect in 1997, the partnership form of taxation usually minimizes the aggregate tax obligations of the business and owners. Partnership taxation and how it differs from the taxation of corporations is discussed in more detail later in this chapter.

§10.14 Miscellaneous

A general partnership, unlike many other forms of business, does not make a public filing in order to be legally formed. When a partnership has offices in more than one state (as many law firms do), which state law governs that partnership? When the UPA (1914) was in effect in virtually all states, this question was not as important as it is today with the numerous differences in the state law of partnership that have developed. The RUPA refers to the home office of a partnership, but does not define it. Presumably, each partnership is free to designate which office is its home office.

It is highly desirable not only to have an agreement dealing with the various rights of partners but also to have it reduced to writing so that rights and duties are explicitly defined and known not only to the partners themselves but also to their heirs and assignees. The preparation of such an agreement usually requires the services of a lawyer and thus increases the costs of formation. Even in situations in which cost is no problem, a surprisingly large number of partnerships, including some law partnerships, operate successfully for many years without a written agreement. Of course, the partners may have verbal or implicit understandings as to how the business should be conducted. Major problems are likely to arise, however, if there is a falling out between partners and upon a partner's death or retirement.

Whether or not there is a formal written agreement, a partnership is inherently a more complex and expensive manner of conducting business than a single person running a proprietorship. Nevertheless, it is usually less expensive than alternative forms of business operation involving several owners, and is often the most convenient form of operation for many small businesses if the

unlimited liability of each partner for partnership obligations is not a matter of serious concern to any partner.

§10.15 Joint Ventures

Many cases involving partnership-like relations describe the relationship as a **joint venture** rather than a partnership. If there is any difference, it is that a joint venture involves a more limited business purpose than a partnership — perhaps a partnership for a single transaction. Most partnership rules are applicable to joint ventures; the major difference is the scope of the actual and apparent authority that each joint venturer possesses to bind the venture.

There is some tendency for courts to accept the categorization of the agreement itself. However, there appear to be relatively few practical differences in the legal principles applicable to a partnership and to a joint venture.

The phrase "joint venture" may also be used in a broader sense to refer to any cooperative enterprise, no matter what form of business the enterprise takes. For example, in 1943, when Dow Chemical Company and Corning Glass Works, Inc. decided to form a joint venture to develop the commercial and military use of silicones, the two companies actually formed a third corporation, Dow Corning, Inc., with each company owning 50 percent of the stock of Dow Corning. A more appropriate phrase for this type of enterprise might be a joint venture corporation.

Joint venture arrangements today may also take the form of an LLC.

§10.16 Limited Partnerships

A limited partnership differs from a general partnership in that there are two classes of partners, one or more **general partners**, and one or more **limited partners**, who are not personally liable for the debts of the partnership and who are not expected to participate in the partnership's day-to-day affairs. In effect, limited partners are passive investors who stand to lose what they have invested in the enterprise but no more. Partners who are not specifically identified as limited partners are general partners and are unlimitedly liable for the debts of the business.

Limited partnerships were attractive in the 1970s and 1980s, because they provided a combination of factors that were not then obtainable in any other business form at the time: partnership type taxation for federal income tax purposes and limited liability for investors. The 1970s were the heyday of the **tax shelter** and most of these shelters were created as limited partnerships in real estate, race horses, railway freight cars, cable television companies, and a variety of other investments that promised to generate tax deductions in excess of the amount contributed. Many had hundreds or thousands of limited partners. Even after the Tax Reform Act of 1986 closed off the most egregious tax shelters, the limited partnership continued to be widely used for many types of real estate ventures in which this combination of income tax treatment and limited liability was attractive. Many of these limited partnerships continue to exist today. Unfortunately, most of them have turned out very badly for inves-

tors, and special legislation was enacted in 1990 in an effort to give these investors greater protection.

The development of the LLC in the early 1990s, discussed below, probably signals the end of the popularity of the limited partnership form of business. The LLC not only combines limited liability for all investors with federal partnership-type taxation but also avoids technical problems associated with the management roles of limited partners in a limited partnership. Although existing limited partnerships will remain with us for some time, the popularity of this business form appears to be declining rapidly as more and more new enterprises opt to become LLCs rather than limited partnerships.

§10.17 Corporate General Partners

The tax shelter era shaped another development that continues to affect all unincorporated business forms — the use of a corporate general partner or corporate manager to manage the business and affairs of the unincorporated business. Until the middle of the 20th century, doubt existed whether a corporation could be a general partner in a partnership. But the modern view, accepted today apparently in all states, is that corporations may act as general partners to the same extent as individuals can.

Tax shelter limited partnerships created during the 1970s and 1980s typically had only one general partner, a corporation. There might be hundreds or thousands of limited partners whose sole function was to provide the capital needed for the enterprise, and who hoped to obtain tax benefits in the form of deductible losses exceeding the capital invested. Later, in the 1980s, investors in limited partnerships hoped to obtain tax-sheltered income rather than tax losses.

The use of a corporate general partner results in a partnership in which no individual may be personally liable for the partnership obligations. The IRS recognized these organizations as eligible for partnership taxation as long as the corporate general partner had substantial assets invested in the partnership. Today, under the check-the-box regulations, a limited partnership with a nominally financed corporate general partner may simply elect partnership taxation.

A major disadvantage of the limited partnership as a tax-oriented investment vehicle is that the provisions relating to distributions and allocations of income, loss, and excess cash flow in partnerships are extremely complex. This was particularly true of tax shelter limited partnership agreements, which usually provided for the allocation of income or loss on one basis and the allocation of excess cash on a different basis. These ratios might shift after the limited partners received the return of their cash investments in order to increase the shares allocable to the corporate general partner that was owned by the original promoters.

§10.18 Master Limited Partnerships

In 1986, Congress amended the IRC to discourage tax shelters and to reduce marginal tax rates applicable to individuals and to corporations. One

inadvertent consequence of these tax rate changes was to make partnership-type taxation much more attractive than corporate-type taxation for profitable businesses.

It did not take long for entrepreneurs to recognize that there was a tax advantage of creating publicly traded limited partnerships. These organizations created limited partnership interests that were readily marketable and traded either over-the-counter or on securities exchanges much as though they were shares of stock. This public trading was technically trading in the form of depository receipts for limited partnership interests rather than in the interests themselves. These organizations were known as **master limited partnerships**.

Most master limited partnerships were concentrated in certain types of businesses (e.g., extraction of natural resources), but the tax benefits were potentially available in many areas. As the use of master limited partnerships spread to new kinds of business, Congress was faced with the threatened disincorporation of publicly held businesses. A statute hurriedly enacted in 1987 closed off this approach by requiring that entities with publicly traded ownership interests must be taxed as corporations without regard to the business form adopted. However, master limited partnerships created prior to the effective date of this legislation were phased out, and some of these organizations were permitted to continue indefinitely. With these exceptions, all business entities that have or develop a public market for ownership interests must be taxed as corporations.

B. CORPORATIONS

§10.19 Corporations

A corporation is a relatively complex form of business that plays a vital role in American society. Aspects of financial concepts relating to corporations and trading in securities of corporations are discussed at length in subsequent chapters. This introductory discussion presents the most fundamental aspects of corporateness, primarily in the context of closely held businesses.

§10.20 What Is a Corporation?

A corporation is usually viewed as a fictitious legal entity separate from its owners, the shareholders. The fictitious entity is created by a public filing with the secretary of state (or other designated public official in the state) and the payment of a filing fee. In comparison to proprietorships and general partnerships, this is a relatively expensive form of business organization, because legal assistance is usually involved not only in its creation but also in its continued operation. Operational costs at the state level are relatively high because all states

impose annual franchise or stock taxes on corporations. Further, a corporation engaged in business in several states may need to qualify to transact business in each state and may thereby become subject to taxes in each state.

The nature of the corporation has never been precisely defined. A corporation can be envisioned as an artificial person having most of the same powers, rights, and duties of an individual. This artificial person has no flesh, no blood, no eyes, or mouth, but it may nevertheless do many things that real people do: it may sue and be sued, enter into contracts, purchase property, run a business, and so forth. It may also be viewed as a "nexus of contracts" among the participants, or as a contract between the state and the participants, or between the state and the corporation. Or, it may be viewed as a process, a form of management organization, and not as a thing at all.

In considering what it really means to conduct business in the corporate form, it is useful to consider the one-person corporation, (i.e., a corporation in which one single individual owns all the outstanding shares of the corporation). In effect, the business is an incorporated proprietorship. One should understand precisely what the notion of a fictitious entity means in this situation. In practical and economic effect, the shareholder runs the business much as though it were a proprietorship. The shareholder decides what business the corporation should be in, whether it should enter into specific contracts, what price to charge for its products, and so forth. The shareholder in a sense also owns the entire corporation, because she owns all the outstanding shares. Indeed, the combination of total ownership and total control in this situation often leads the shareholder to believe that he or she owns the corporation's business and property much as though the business were conducted in the form of an unincorporated proprietorship. I own this business, the shareholder may proudly say. Although this is true in an economic sense, in the legal sense it is not at all true. If a business is incorporated, the business's assets are owned by the corporation, not by the person who owns the shares in the corporation. The shares are property, but they are not the corporate assets. Further, the shareholder exercises control over corporation activities not through ownership of business assets but by serving the corporation basically as its sole agent. Then again, a fictitious entity can only act through agents. Assume that a sole shareholder decides she wants to be employed by the corporation and receive a salary. Acting as agent on behalf of the corporation, she offers herself employment with the corporation at a salary in a specified amount, and acting as an individual she may then accept the corporation's offer. This is not a sham transaction for most purposes: the IRS, for example, unhesitatingly recognizes the validity of such transactions if the compensation is reasonable in amount, giving the corporation a deduction for salaries paid, requiring the corporation to withhold for federal income taxes, FICA, and the like, and requiring the shareholder to include as wages the amount paid to her under this arrangement.

Where does the sole shareholder in this example obtain the authority from the fictitious entity to act as its agent and offer herself the employment contract? That is the subject of corporation law: The corporation's affairs are managed by a board of directors elected by the shareholders; the sole shareholder thus elects the board of directors (which may consist of only herself in most states), and the board of directors then appoints a president or other officer (who again

may be the sole shareholder) to negotiate the employment contract on behalf of the corporation. It is all a bit incestuous.

The corporation provides limited liability for the shareholders, because all obligations are entered into in the name of the corporation rather than in the names of the individual owners, and the corporation is a separate legal entity. Further, an agent (who may or may not be a shareholder) who commits the corporation to a transaction giving rise to liability is not personally liable on obligations negotiated on the principal's — the corporation's — behalf under accepted agency principles. The result is that a corporation, unlike a general partnership, provides (at least in theory) limited liability for its owners, and, unlike the limited partnership, the persons with limited liability in a corporation may participate freely in its management and control as long as they stay in their proper role as agents of the fictitious entity. Of course, sophisticated creditors are unlikely to be willing to deal with a small corporation with limited assets unless the shareholders agree to give personal guarantees to pay the corporate debt. Thus, as a practical matter, in the very small corporation, the protection against unlimited liability provided by the corporate form is not as important as might first appear.

There is obviously an element of play-acting in closely held corporations, because the formalities that must be followed do not reflect the reality that the business is actually owned and operated by individuals; the theory assumes that the same individuals assume different roles as shareholders, directors, or agents, and act according to the appropriate role. But there is a serious aspect to these formalities. A failure to follow them may result in the court **piercing the corporate veil** — and holding shareholders personally liable on corporation debts.

Because a corporation can have only one shareholder, a sole proprietor may decide to incorporate his or her business without losing control and without having to cut other people in on the action.

§10.21 Sources of Corporation Law

The major source of corporation law is state corporation statutes, the provisions of which vary from state to state. The variation is considerably wider than the statutes relating to partnerships or limited partnerships, although there is a surprising core of uniformity in these statutes. Part of this uniformity may be traced to the Model Business Corporation Act drafted by a committee of the American Bar Association, and part may be traced to the leadership of the state of Delaware in developing significant principles of corporation law. Part may be traced to the natural tendency of one state to copy statutes that embody good ideas that other states develop.

State corporation statutes deal with issues of formation, corporate purposes and powers, internal organization (the roles of shareholders, directors, and officers), permissible securities that corporations may issue in order to raise capital, mergers and consolidations of corporations, foreign corporations, and dissolution. In addition, states may require annual reports as well as franchise tax returns and other reporting requirements. These state statutes thus largely

deal with the internal relationships within a corporation, but they also may affect other important aspects of corporation behavior. State corporation statutes are largely technical in nature and generally not the subject of extensive debate in state legislatures. Committees of the state bar association develop many proposed changes in corporation statutes, although these provisions must run the same legislative gauntlet as any other proposed legislation.

In the United States, there is no federal or national corporation statute. Every domestic corporation, no matter how large, is incorporated under the statute of some state—usually Delaware in the case of the largest corporations. Two New Deal federal statutes—the Securities Act of 1933 and the Securities Exchange Act of 1934 — provide a substantial degree of federal regulation, particularly for large corporations with more than 500 shareholders.

In addition to state corporation statutes, all states have adopted **blue sky laws** that regulate the public sale of corporate securities within the state. In 1996, Congress enacted a statute that greatly reduces the role of states in regulating securities transactions of corporations that are subject to federal regulation under the Securities Exchange Act.

§10.22 The Internal Structure of a Corporation

The internal organization of a corporation consists of three levels or tiers: shareholders, directors, and officers.

Shareholders are persons who own shares in a corporation. Shares represent the ultimate ownership interests in the corporation. Shares may be divided into two or more different classes with different financial and voting rights. As described above, one individual may own all the shares of a corporation; at the other extreme, there is no limit on the number of shareholders or the number of shares that a corporation may issue, so that a corporation may have thousands or even millions of shareholders. Despite the wide gulf between a corporation that one person owns and a corporation with hundreds of thousands of shareholders, the two corporations are largely governed by the same theoretical organizational structure.

The board of directors has the responsibility of managing, or overseeing the management of, the corporation's business. Historically, the traditional statute required a board of directors to consist of at least three directors; today, in most states, a board of directors may consist of a single director, though in some states the privilege of having a board of one or two members is limited to corporations with one or two shareholders. In a few states, three directors are still required; in these states, sole proprietors planning to incorporate their business must find two loyal persons to serve as directors with them.

The board of directors selects corporate officers to execute the decisions of the board and conduct the business on a day-to-day basis. Traditional officers are a president, one or more vice presidents, a secretary, and a treasurer, though many modern statutes do not require designated offices. Most modern statutes also permit a single person to hold more than one office simultaneously, though a fair number of statutes require the corporate president and secretary to be different persons. Corporate officers may also have discretion to appoint addi-

tional assistant officers and employees. In large, publicly held corporations, the corporate officers — often collectively referred to as management — may have the broadest discretion in fact on both routine and extraordinary matters. The theory, however, is that the ultimate power of management and control rests in the board of directors, not the officers of the corporation.

There is no requirement that officers or directors also be shareholders, though such a requirement may be imposed voluntarily by appropriate provisions in the corporation's governing documents. In some states, special close corporation statutes give small corporations the option of adopting management principles much as though they were general partnerships.

§10.23 The Documents Governing Internal Corporate Matters

The two basic documents within every corporation are the **articles of incorporation** and the **bylaws**. The articles of incorporation are filed with the appropriate state agency to form the corporation and are the basic constitution of that particular corporation. Terminology in this respect is not uniform from one state to another: In some states this basic constitutional document is known as the **charter** or the **certificate of incorporation** or by other names. In many states, the filing authority issues a certificate of incorporation to reflect that articles of incorporation have been filed and approved. Amendment of articles of incorporation generally requires approval by a specified vote of the shareholders as well as approval by the board of directors.

The bylaws constitute an internal set of rules for the governance of a corporation. They deal with such matters as elections, notices, size of board of directors, restrictions on the transfer of shares, and similar matters. The bylaws may usually be amended by the board of directors acting alone, or by the shareholders.

Many provisions relating to the corporation's internal affairs may be placed either in the articles of incorporation or the bylaws, at the option of the management of the corporation. Provisions placed in the articles of incorporation become a matter of public record: Where the number of shareholders is large, they may be more difficult to amend. Many lawyers prefer that important and unusual governance provisions appear in the articles of incorporation rather than the bylaws, because the provisions are then a matter of public record.

§10.24 A Taxonomy of Corporations

It is sometimes not fully appreciated that even though closely held and publicly held corporations differ widely in form and structure, they are all cast from the single mold of the state corporation statutes. Thus, both have the same internal tripartite structure described above: shareholders, a board of directors, and corporate officers. As a result, they share a common core of legal principles

despite the very different — indeed, radically different — economic and social environments in which they operate.

Nearly half of all publicly held corporations are incorporated in the state of Delaware. The General Corporation Law of that state is therefore virtually a national code for publicly held corporations. Many corporations change their state of incorporation to Delaware when they plan to become publicly held.

Many publicly held companies are quite large. The so-called Fortune 500 — the 500 largest corporations as determined by *Fortune* magazine — is comprised almost entirely of publicly held companies. These companies each have billions of dollars of assets and annual sales, thousands of employees, and usually tens or hundreds of thousands of shareholders. These corporations possess tremendous economic and political power merely from their size and their importance to the economy of communities, cities, and indeed, whole states.

Most corporations in the United States, however, are very small and closely held. In 1993, the IRS received about 3,965,000 corporate federal income tax returns. Of these returns, 3,278,000 reflected receipts of less than $1,000,000. It is unlikely that very many, if any, of these corporations had more than a handful of shareholders.

There were 687,000 corporations in 1993 that had annual receipts of more than $1,000,000. They constituted about 17 percent of all corporations filing tax returns in 1993. However, the economic importance of these 687,000 corporations dwarfs the other 3,278,000. The receipts of these 687,000 corporations constituted 94 percent of all business receipts reported by the 3,965,000 filing corporations.

The American Law Institute's Corporate Governance Project in 1984 estimated that there were between 1,500 and 2,000 corporations with more than 2,000 shareholders and $100,000,000 of assets, and that there were between 5,500 and 6,000 corporations with more than 500 shareholders and $3,000,000 of assets. These figures, which are unlikely to have changed materially in the decade after 1984, indicate that most of the 687,000 corporations with more than $1,000,000 of business receipts are themselves relatively small when compared, for example, with the 30 corporations that compose the Dow Jones Industrial Average.

§10.25 The Registration of Public Offerings of Securities

Corporations with more than $10 million of assets and an outstanding class of securities held by more than 500 shareholders of record are subject to special regulation under the federal **Securities Exchange Act of 1934 (the 1934 Act)**, including requirements that the corporation register with the SEC and make public periodic financial information. Corporations with securities registered under the 1934 Act (often called, not surprisingly, registered corporations) are all publicly held corporations.

Corporations usually do not gradually grow in size and the number of shareholders until they become subject to the disclosure requirements of the 1934 Act. They instead first become subject to SEC regulation when they make

an **initial public offering** (**IPO**) of their shares. The important point here is that a different federal statute, the federal **Securities Act of 1933** (**the 1933 Act**) requires that a corporation planning to make an initial public offering must have in effect a 1933 Act registration statement before it may sell securities to the public. The 1933 Act registration is an important and often difficult step for an unregistered corporation that is planning to make its IPO. Full disclosure of a wide variety of matters is required; sophisticated assistance is required to meet these disclosure requirements. In addition, it is often advisable to amend articles of incorporation and bylaws to make sure the corporation can operate effectively as a publicly held corporation. Usually, an unregistered corporation that makes its first public offering files a 1934 Act registration shortly after the public distribution is completed.

An offering to a very small number of unsophisticated potential investors may be a public offering under the 1933 Act, and as a result it is important that closely held corporations raising capital through the sale of securities make sure that an exemption from registration under the 1933 Act is available. As a result, the 1933 Act (and similar registration requirements under state **blue sky laws**) affect even small, closely held enterprises.

Corporations that have registered a class of securities under the 1934 Act may thereafter raise additional capital by a public offering under the 1933 Act. Registration of the new public offering under the 1933 Act is technically required, but that is usually relatively simple to do, because under the SEC's **integrated disclosure system**, most corporations may incorporate by reference their 1934 Act filings in a 1933 Act registration.

Although the vast majority of businesses affected by federal securities law are corporations, these statutes apply to any business, no matter what the form, that makes a public offering or that meets the $10 million in assets and 500 investor standard.

§10.26 Closely Held Corporations

Typically a closely held corporation is one in which (1) the number of shareholders is small, (2) there is no outside market for its shares, (3) all or most of the principal shareholders participate in its management, and (4) the free transferability of shares is restricted by agreement. A closely held corporation is almost always one that has never made a successful IPO of securities and is not registered with the SEC under the 1934 Act. A publicly held corporation that is reducing its number of shareholders may withdraw from registration under the 1934 Act when it has fewer than 300 shareholders.

Because there is no market for shares of a closely held corporation, there is a substantial risk that minority shareholders may be locked in with no avenue to sell their shares if they become alienated from the majority shareholders. As a result, outside investors are usually reluctant to make equity investments in closely held corporations, and do so only if contractual commitments are entered into under which the shares of minority shareholders will be purchased by the corporation, or more rarely, by other shareholders under specified circumstances. Where a closely held corporation is involved, one should never

assume that a market for the shares exists or that a dissatisfied minority share-holder has the option of selling his or her shares at a fair price.

§10.27 Management of Corporations

The corporate model that appears in state incorporation statutes assumes that shareholders are the ultimate owners of the enterprise and that they elect directors to manage the affairs of the corporation. The directors in turn select officers to implement the board's policies. This is an idealized model that is not tailored specifically either for the closely held corporation or for the publicly held corporation. It is a model that is sufficiently broad and generalized that large portions of it are appropriate for both the very large and the very small. Despite this common core of legal principles, managements of publicly held and closely held corporations usually have little in common.

In a closely held corporation, the principal shareholders in the corporation are usually actively involved in management. Decisions are apt to be made without formal meetings or votes. If there is a single person who owns a majority of the shares, he or she will effectively make business decisions for the corpo-ration. In closely held corporations that are taxed as C corporations, it is unusual for the corporation to pay dividends. Rather, most of the earnings will be distributed in the form of salaries, interest, or rent to specific shareholders rather than distributed to the shareholders, generally in the form of dividends. A minority shareholder may easily be frozen out from financial participation merely by the controlling shareholders' refusing to allow the shareholder to participate in management decisions or to receive salary or other payments from the corporation. About 18 states have supplemented their general corporation statutes with optional special statutes designed to provide relaxed rules of management for closely held corporations.

In a publicly held corporation, the management structure is usually entirely different. There are many disorganized and diffuse shareholders; usually no individual or group owns a majority of the voting shares. Management usually comprises professional managers who own relatively small interests in the cor-poration, often less than one percent. Shareholders usually have little role in deciding who should be the managers of the corporation. Consider, for exam-ple, the role of the small shareholder in selecting directors in a publicly held corporation. He is presented with a list of candidates selected and recommended by the corporation's current managers. The shareholder may vote for them or withhold his vote; rarely does he have a choice among competing directorial candidates. Further, because the overwhelming majority of the shareholders are going to vote in favor of the persons proposed by management, it really does not make much difference whether the small shareholder casts his votes or pitches the proxy form into the nearest trash basket.

For purposes of locating the real source of selection of directors, one must usually look not to the election process, but to some earlier point where a decision was made as to which names should be presented to the shareholders as the management's candidates. For many years, this decision was made by the chief executive officer (CEO) individually; today, it is increasingly made by a

committee comprising members of the board of directors. The extent to which this critical committee is influenced by the CEO's wishes varies from corporation to corporation. The important point, however, is that the actual selection of directors occurs not at the level of the shareholders but at the level of the chief executive officer or the board of directors. The role of shareholders in publicly held corporations is merely to ratify this selection.

Another reason for the seeming passivity of shareholders is that there tends to be self-selection by shareholders. The presence of an active market in shares means that shareholders dissatisfied with the management of a corporation may exercise the Wall Street option (i.e., sell their shares and invest the proceeds elsewhere) rather than fight incumbent management. Thus, by a process of self-elimination, shareholders who are unhappy with management tend to disappear, and the remaining shareholders tend to be pro-management, or at least not anti-management. Of course, the exercise of the Wall Street option is, in a sense, a vote. A poor operating performance by management results in depressed share prices and may lead indirectly to the ouster of management.

Another factor that limits the power of management is that the nature of shareholdings has changed dramatically in the last 50 years. Before World War II, the predominant view was that share ownership of publicly held corporations was almost atomistic, and that as a result management had virtually a free hand. Ownership had become separated from control. This was the position put forth by A. Berle and G. Means in their influential 1932 book, *The Modern Corporation and Private Property*, and was not seriously questioned until relatively recently.

Although it is doubtful that the Berle and Means view was ever entirely correct, more recent developments have created quite different share ownership patterns. A new type of public investor has grown tremendously in importance—the institutional investor. Institutional investors mainly collect and invest other people's money. They include life insurance companies, retirement funds, investment companies (mutual funds), bank trust departments, university endowments, and similar organizations. These institutional investors invest only in publicly held corporations, and often only in the largest and most widely traded companies. Overall, they invest huge amounts of capital in a large variety of securities traded on the major securities exchanges. As a group, they are now the largest single owner of publicly held corporations; their holdings in the aggregate are in excess of 40 percent of all the outstanding shares of listed publicly held corporations, and, in specific corporations, the percentage is well over 50 percent.

Funds invested by institutional investors ultimately belong to members of the general public in the form of pensions, life insurance proceeds, savings, or financial investments. In a sense, therefore, their growth has increased the broad base of ownership of the means of production. However, in terms of power and potential control, the growth of institutional investors represents a concentration of the base. Now only a relatively few persons—the managers of and investment advisers for the institutional investors—determine where huge investments are to be placed and how large blocks of shares are to be voted.

Institutional investors often have the power, if they band together, to dominate and control many large publicly held corporations. Until relatively

recently, however, they have not done so. Most institutional investors have viewed their role as passive investors and have eschewed any interest in managing or exercising control over the business and affairs of corporations. In part, this view was based on perceived problems with respect to cooperative efforts by institutional investors. The SEC has long had rules that require persons soliciting proxies to disclose basic information and that make solicitations not conforming to these rules unlawful. There was concern that cooperative effort by institutional investors might violate these rules. This problem was resolved in 1992, when the SEC changed its regulations expressly allowing for communications among institutional investors as long as the communication does not solicit proxy votes or urge recipients to vote in a specific way.

It is difficult to evaluate the overall impact of institutional investors on corporate governance. There is anecdotal evidence about situations in which institutional investors have sought to replace ineffective managers. This is often done by communication with nonmanagement directors on the corporation's board of directors. However, there has been no systematic evaluation of the effectiveness of this development.

Even though institutional investors view themselves as predominantly ordinary investors, their sheer size raises unique market problems. For example, if an institutional investor decides to exercise its Wall Street option and sell its shares, the block may be so large that only other institutional investors have the capacity to absorb the shares. Large institutional holdings may therefore increase the volatility of share prices, because an independent decision by several large institutional investors to dispose of their shares might markedly depress short-run prices because there is not enough demand to absorb the shares being dumped on the market.

Institutional investors usually owe fiduciary duties to pension beneficiaries or beneficial owners of investment company shares. These duties may be construed as requiring that the institutional investor maximize its short-run market gains. It has been feared that this concern for short-run return by the largest and most important shareholders may in turn compel corporate management to concentrate on maximizing its short-term earnings to the possible detriment of longer-range profitability. Whether this fear is justified is uncertain.

C. LLCs AND OTHER FORMS OF ORGANIZATION

§10.28 Limited Liability Companies

The most astonishing development in the area of business forms in the 1990s has been the growth and spread of a novel business form, the **limited liability company** (**LLC**). The attractiveness of this hybrid business form basically arises from its combination of desirable tax and business features: (1) limited liability for all of its owners, (2) the pass-through tax treatment and capital structure of a partnership, and (3) almost complete internal flexibility in terms of management and control. This internal flexibility leaves the parties free to develop their own organizational and management structure, and, at least to

some extent, their own governing rules and principles. The default rules for LLCs are drawn in part from corporation law, from general partnership law, and from limited partnership law. In short, the LLC is an eclectic mixture of features drawn from several different traditional business forms that create an attractive package for many enterprises.

LLCs bear a close resemblance to corporations in many aspects, because they have many corporate characteristics. However, they lack the fundamental corporate characteristic that determines the federal tax classification of the entity— they do not receive a "franchise" or "charter" from the state of incorporation. An LLC may also be analogized either to a limited partnership that comprises only limited partners or to a general partnership in which there is no personal liability to creditors. Neither of these analogies is entirely apt; an LLC is a limited liability business form that is neither a corporation nor a limited partnership.

Because LLCs have been in existence for only a brief period and the rules have evolved from varied sources, considerable diversity exists among the state LLC statutes. However, the **National Conference of Commissioners on Uniform State Laws** (**NCCUSL**) approved a **Uniform Limited Liability Company Act** (**ULLCA**) in 1995. A couple of years earlier, the ABA developed a prototype statute that differs in many respects from the ULLCA. Because virtually all states had adopted their own LLC statutes prior to the ULLCA, it remains to be seen whether the ULLCA will be generally followed. At this point, it appears likely that variations in LLC statutes that are much greater than those that exist among state statutes relating to the traditional corporation, general partnership, and limited partnership will remain. These variations are likely to be important only when an LLC formed in one state plans to conduct business in other states.

LLCs are used primarily for closely held enterprises. There is no inherent reason why an LLC could not have hundreds or thousands of members and be publicly held. However, once ownership interests become publicly traded, the entity becomes subject to C corporation tax treatment under the master limited partnership provisions of the IRC and the major advantage of the LLC is therefore lost.

§10.29 The Development of LLCs in the United States

Business entities similar to LLCs exist in many foreign countries. Examples include the German **GmbH**, the **limitadas** that exist in Latin American countries (including the **sociedad de responsabilidad limitada** (**S.de R.L.**) of Mexico), and the Portuguese **sociedate por quotas responsibilitidade limitada**. Similar entities also exist in countries in the common law tradition. Perhaps the closest ancestor in the English tradition is the unincorporated **joint stock company** that developed in England as a commercial substitute for the royal corporate charters that created the City of London and the universities of Oxford and Cambridge. The American colonies were well acquainted with these joint stock companies and by and large detested them, because they had been given monopolies to trade with major portions of the New World.

The LLC also bears resemblance to partnership associations or **limited partnership associations** created in Pennsylvania, Michigan, New Jersey, Ohio, and Virginia in the late 1870s. These variant partnership forms, however, are apparently only of historic interest and have not been used during the 20th century.

Whatever its origins, the LLC is a distinctly modern creation in the United States. It can be traced to the attempt by the Hamilton Brothers Oil Company of Denver in the 1970s to form an entity in the United States similar to the limitada with which it was familiar in Central America. It chose Wyoming as the focus of its legislative effort. The Wyoming legislature adopted an LLC statute apparently on the belief if that was what a major business wanted, they should have it. The Hamilton Brothers company eventually did obtain a tax ruling that it should be classified as a partnership for tax purposes. However, in 1980 the IRS proposed new regulations that took the uncompromising position that an entity must be classified as a corporation for tax purposes if no investor is personally liable for its obligations. These proposed regulations were highly controversial and were ultimately withdrawn without ever having been promulgated, but they did delay the recognition of the LLC for nearly a decade.

The IRS recognized that an LLC was entitled to partnership-type tax treatment in 1988. This ruling opened the flood gates. Within six years, 47 states had adopted LLC statutes, and the remaining handful of states followed shortly thereafter.

Statistics on the number of business formations are maintained in many states by filing authorities. In many states, the number of LLC formations has risen dramatically so that it rivals the number of new incorporations. In these states, the number of limited partnership formations has declined precipitously, and it seems clear that the LLC is largely responsible for this decline. In 1997, one commentator estimated that by the end of 1995, more than 210,000 LLCs had been created in the United States.

§10.30 Comparison With Other Business Forms

An LLC has organizational features that are part limited partnership and part corporation.

Comparison With a Corporation. An LLC is superficially similar to a corporation. It is a separate legal entity that is formed by filing articles of organization with the secretary of state (or other designated state official) and paying a filing fee. It may be formed for any lawful purpose, subject to exceptions for certain kinds of business such as banking and insurance. However, most state statutes do not require that an LLC be formed as a business for profit and there seems to be no inherent reason why an LLC should not be used in lieu of a not-for-profit corporation.

The relationship between the corporate statutes and LLC statutes is made vivid by contrasting statutory language. One speaks of articles of incorporation in a corporation and articles of organization in an LLC. Rather than having bylaws, an LLC has regulations or an operating agreement. The owners are

called members rather than shareholders. Rather than having directors, LLCs may have managers. The managers may be chosen by the members in a manner similar to the way shareholders choose directors in a corporation. An LLC may have officers selected by the board of managers. Managers and officers need not be members unless the operative documents provide otherwise. LLC statutory provisions relating to purposes and powers are also closely modeled after similar provisions in state corporation statutes. LLC statutes authorize the merger or consolidation of LLCs with other LLCs or with other forms of business in language modeled directly on the language of corporation statutes. Some state LLC statutes provide expressly that a piercing the corporate veil principle applies to LLCs. The duties of managers of an LLC may be described by language directly taken from the corporation statutes relating to the duties of directors. Some states provide for dissenters rights in LLCs analogous to such rights in corporations.

In some respects, of course, the LLC does not resemble a corporation. An LLC may be member managed, in which event management principles are drawn from a general partnership model. The LLC statutes of most states provide flexibility with respect to the internal organization of an LLC; there are few mandatory statutory requirements, and internal relationships are largely governed by contract rather than by mandatory statutory provision. In contrast, corporation statutes are notoriously specific. They provide detailed rules for the financing and management of corporations that may be binding on all corporations. Most state corporation statutes have complex provisions regarding the issuance of securities and maintenance of capital; although LLCs may adopt similar provisions, they are free to construct simpler financial structures, such as those that typically appear in partnerships.

One important theoretical difference is that in a corporation the articles of incorporation control over bylaws or contractual obligations in case of a conflict; an LLC is based on the theory that it is a contract among the members, and thus the terms of the operating agreement control over the articles of organization in case of conflict.

As LLCs have proliferated, courts have been compelled to consider whether corporation or partnership principles should be applied when the LLC statute is silent. The limited number of reported cases indicates that courts will turn to corporation law for guidance. A lower court opinion in Delaware, for example, involved the question whether an LLC, like a corporation, may only appear in court through an attorney, or whether an officer or manager of the LLC who is not a lawyer may appear on behalf of the entity (much the way a partner may appear and represent a partnership in court). Without finding any governing or even relevant authority one way or the other, the court concluded that the corporate analogy should be applied, because the underlying purpose of the rule prohibiting the appearance of a corporation by anyone other than a member of the Delaware Bar also applied to the representation of LLCs.

Even though an LLC is not a corporation, some states subject it to corporate tax treatment. This is true, for example, in Florida, Pennsylvania, and Texas. The reasons that states insist that LLCs be taxed as corporations is apparently based not so much on the corporate characteristics of an LLC as on the fear that otherwise state revenues will decline as firms change their business

form to LLCs, and as new businesses elect to be LLCs from the outset. One consequence of this treatment is that the LLC is less attractive in these states.

Comparison With a Partnership. LLCs also have strong antecedents in the law of partnership. This is particularly true in the ULLCA, which draws from the partnership model in many respects. An LLC may elect to assume a management structure that is virtually identical to that of a general partnership (with the sole exception of avoidance of unlimited liability). The operating agreement in many LLCs more closely approximates a partnership agreement than corporate bylaws. Some states permit LLC operating agreements to be oral rather than written, an option not available for corporate bylaws. Membership interests in an LLC also have significant partnership characteristics. Under some statutes, for example, transferees of membership interests may be admitted only with the unanimous consent of the members. The death, bankruptcy, or retirement of a member may constitute a dissolution (or dissociation) of the LLC unless a majority in interest of the remaining members votes to continue the LLC. These provisions are clearly based on the general partnership model. Under other statutes, partnership rules may be applicable unless the operating agreement provides to the contrary. Voting in an LLC may be on a per capita basis (though the default rule for voting in LLCs is usually the corporate default rule of voting by percentage of interest). An LLC, in short, is, or may elect to become, quite partnership-like without sacrificing the benefit of limited liability.

Statutes defining member-managed limited liability companies follow the partnership model. They provide that each member is an agent of the LLC for the purpose of its business, that each member has the right to possess LLC property for business purposes, and so forth. These statutes may also provide for partnership-type duties of care and loyalty.

Some state statutes provide that the default rule for an LLC is member-management rather than manager-management. Other statutes adopt the opposite default rule, presuming that all LLCs will be manager-managed unless specific provision to the contrary is made in the controlling documents. Pennsylvania adopts yet another approach, applying the management provisions of its limited partnership statute to manager-managed limited liability companies.

Comparison With a Limited Partnership. The LLC differs from a limited partnership in that all participants may actively take part in control of the business without restriction and without fear of personal liability for the business obligations. A member-managed LLC is similar to a general partnership, minus the personal liability of partners for partnership obligations.

The source of limited liability provided by an LLC is analogous to that provided by limited partnership statutes for limited partners. A limited partnership files a certificate with the designated state official, and the limited partners thereby obtain the shield of limited liability. Similarly, an LLC files articles of organization with a designated state official, and the members of the LLC thereby obtain the shield of limited liability. In this respect, an LLC resembles a limited partnership more than a corporation, which obtains limited liability through the fiction that a charter has been issued so that a separate legal entity has been created. A formal difference of this nature should make no practical

difference. The fact that obtaining limited liability by incorporating leads immediately to classification as a corporation for income tax purposes (while obtaining limited liability by forming an LLC does not) illustrates the IRC's formalistic character in this respect.

§10.31 Default Rules for LLCs

The flexibility in management structure may create practical problems for LLCs when they enter into transactions with third persons, particularly when the third person is not familiar with the LLC concept. To take a simple example, when an LLC wishes to open a bank account, the bank officer must decide whether to use partnership or corporation forms, whether to require a resolution of the LLC's managers, and whether to rely on the authority of officers that the LLC designates who represent that they are authorized to act on the LLC's behalf. The answers to these questions may not be self-evident. Similarly, when an LLC wishes to borrow money, the lender may be faced with the question of whether to require personal guarantees of all members in order to replicate partnership liability for such obligations, or whether to follow the corporate model and require only a limited number of sureties. Presumably, issues of these types will gradually be worked out with increased experience and familiarity with the LLC form of business.

Other default rule problems may not be so easily resolved. The LLC draws rules from close corporation law and from partnership law. Each of these two sources of law has its own set of default rules, which are often inconsistent with each other. Individual state LLC statutes may provide for one type of default rule or another, but unfortunately some statutes are entirely silent as to which default rule should apply if the LLC itself has not made a choice in its articles of organization or operating agreement. Care should be taken in the drafting of LLC documents to make sure that rules are provided for unanticipated issues that might arise. It is undesirable to remain silent in LLC documents on basic operational questions. The default rule that the state statute provides should be specifically incorporated (if that is what is desired) and governing rules should be established if state statute specifies no default rule. Otherwise, it may not be clear which rule will be applicable. Two examples follow:

First, assume that A, a member of an LLC, assigns his entire interest to X. What does X have? In the absence of specific provision dealing with assignments, either the partnership or the corporate analogy may apply. If the partnership analogy is applied, X has all of A's financial interest but no right to participate in management. In the absence of specific provision to the contrary, A retains his management rights even though he has no financial interest in the enterprise. On the other hand, if the corporate analogy is followed, X has all of A's rights, financial and managerial, and is entitled to participate in management to the same extent as the provisions of the operating agreement permit all members to participate.

Second, to complicate the example somewhat, assume that the LLC has three members: A with 30 percent, B with 30 percent, and C with 40 percent financial interests. The agreement is silent with respect to assignments and whether management participation rights are per capita or in proportion to

financial interests. C purchases B's 30 percent interest, thereby owning a 70 percent financial interest. Does C now have a 70 percent interest in the entire LLC or a 40 percent original interest and a 30 percent assignee's interest? Does C have a 70 percent voting interest (the corporate default rule), a one-out-of-two per capita voting power (the partnership default rule), or a right to cast two votes per capita, one for the original interest and one for the assigned interest? The choice of which rule should be applicable in these instances is perhaps not as important as that the rules be readily ascertainable by members or managers who may themselves not be lawyers.

§10.32 Limited Liability Partnerships

The **limited liability partnership** (**LLP**) is essentially a new form of business enterprise. For most purposes, an LLP is a general partnership. It differs from a general partnership only because certain partners are by statute relieved of personal responsibility for certain liabilities. The earliest LLP statutes limited this immunity to liabilities created by errors, omissions, negligence, incompetence, or malpractice committed by other partners or by employees that other partners supervise. Partners involved in the wrongful or negligent acts remained personally liable; innocent partners were protected from this liability, but all partners remained personally liable for all contract liabilities. These early statutes were clearly peace of mind statutes for partners in large partnerships. Later statutes have created **full shields** for general partners and protect them from personal responsibility for all partnership obligations other than those created by their own personal misconduct. In 1996, amendments to the RUPA were promulgated recommending amendments of the full shield variety for all states, and it appears likely that all states will ultimately follow this approach.

The LLP is a new and potentially useful business form that is particularly attractive for professionals such as lawyers and accountants doing business in partnership form. However, there is no inherent reason why the LLP should be limited to professional partnerships, and under most LLP statutes, partnerships engaged in ordinary business activities may become registered LLPs. However, New York, and possibly other states as well, limits the LLP form of business to professional partnerships, broadly defined.

§10.33 LLP Contrasted With Other Business Forms

Comparison With a Limited Partnership. Even though an LLP sounds like it is similar to or a variant of a limited partnership, it is in fact quite a different animal. A limited partnership has two classes of partners — general partners and limited partners—with quite different management responsibilities and liability for partnership obligations. In a limited partnership, the limited partners are usually passive investors with virtually no powers of management and no personal liability at all for partnership obligations; a limited partner's risk of loss may not exceed his contributions of capital to the firm. In an LLP, on the other hand, all partners have the management responsibilities of partners

in a general partnership and all have the benefit of whatever shield of limited liability the particular statute provides — either a protection against malpractice claims or a full shield of protection against all liabilities except those for which they are responsible because of misconduct or negligence. In contrast, limited partners in a limited partnership have no personal responsibility for any liabilities of any nature unless they voluntarily elect to become liable.

Comparison With an LLC. There is substantial confusion between LLCs on the one hand and LLPs on the other. This confusion arises because of the similarity of the names, not any similarity of the two forms of business. The statutes under which an LLC is created are quite different from the statutes under which LLPs are created. LLC statutes embody numerous corporate concepts and provide numerous options and default regulations that give great flexibility to the LLC form of business. For example, LLC statutes permit an LLC to elect between management by the members and management by managers who have roles analogous to directors in a corporation. If management by managers is authorized, the members have only limited rights to participate in management. In contrast, LLP statutes are part of the partnership law, and management rules for partnerships govern. Although some centralization of management in a general partnership may be created by provisions in the partnership agreement itself, the flexibility in management of an LLC is not available to an LLP. LLPs are partnerships with a special rule for personal liability.

§10.34 Election of LLP Status

To become an LLP, a general partnership must file a registration statement with the secretary of state and adopt a name that includes a reference to being an LLP. Registration is usually on an annual basis and must be renewed each year if the shield of limited liability is to be maintained. In addition, in some states the partnership must also keep a specified amount of liquid assets on hand or maintain malpractice insurance in a specified amount to assure possible claimants that the firm will be reasonably able to respond to claims that the statute covers. The requirement of annual registration is apparently a revenue-raising device for individual states.

§10.35 Conflicts of Interest and the LLP Election

At first blush, the concept of providing limited liability within a general partnership does not appear to create serious problems. An LLP is simply a partnership in which no partner is personally liable unless he or she was involved in misconduct or negligence that gave rise to the liability. This concept does not appear to be significantly different than LLCs, LPs, and corporations. However, that is not the case. The LLP election creates a number of unique complexities that do not exist in the more traditional limited liability business forms. The LLP involves a confluence of legal principles that seems inevitably to lead to jockeying and opportunistic conduct whenever an LLP is faced with claims that exceed the LLP's assets.

The problem arises when some partners are required to contribute to the discharge of partnership liabilities but other partners are protected by the shield of limited liability. In a limited shield state, assume that one partner has committed a serious act of malpractice that creates a liability that exceeds the partnership's insurance and assets. The partnership also has ordinary contract obligations, including rent due on a lease and salaries owed to employees. The following principles are applicable in this situation:

1. The LLP itself is liable for both ordinary business obligations and the malpractice claim.
2. Innocent partners are personally liable only for the ordinary business obligations and they may be compelled to contribute to the LLP to permit it to discharge those obligations.
3. Innocent partners are not liable for the malpractice claim and cannot be compelled to contribute to the LLP to permit it to discharge that obligation.
4. The guilty partners are personally liable for both the malpractice claim and the ordinary business obligations and may be compelled to contribute to the LLP to permit it to discharge both types of obligations.

The interaction of these principles inevitably leads to serious conflicts in interest and opportunistic conduct as the two groups of partners seek to minimize their personal exposure to liability. The complicating factor is that the LLP's assets may be used to satisfy either general trade liabilities or the malpractice liability, or both, but the innocent partners may be compelled to contribute only to the satisfaction of the ordinary business obligations. Thus, the way the LLP's assets are used to satisfy its liabilities will inevitably affect the relative wealth of the innocent and guilty parties.

The guilty partner will prefer that the partnership expend the LLP's assets while they are held by the LLP to satisfy the malpractice claim. This may increase the amount of ordinary business obligations left unpaid when the LLP's assets are exhausted, but the innocent partners will have to contribute to satisfy these obligations, because the shield of limited liability does not protect them against such obligations.

The innocent partners, on the other hand, would prefer to use the LLP's assets to prepay rental obligations on a lease rather than to use the assets to settle the malpractice claim. Then, if there is a deficiency toward which partners must contribute, it would be based on the malpractice claim for which the innocent partners have no responsibility. The innocent partners also would always prefer that LLP assets be distributed to the partners individually rather than being retained by the LLP, because the assets distributed are removed from the LLP and cannot be used thereafter to satisfy any part of the malpractice claim. This strategy is attractive to the innocent partners, because the malpractice creditor may not recover them from the innocent partners if the remaining assets prove insufficient to satisfy the malpractice claim. If the innocent partners have received distributions after the malpractice claim arose, however, it is possible that they may be required to return them on a theory of fraudulent transfer or breach of fiduciary duty, even though they are not personally liable for the malpractice claim. Such distributions also would probably be recoverable

as preferences in a federal bankruptcy proceeding. Analogous problems also arise under a full-shield statute. Conflicts between classes of partners will occur whenever a partner is personally liable for the LLP's obligations (e.g., because the partner is guilty of malpractice or negligence) and the LLP's assets and liability insurance are, or may be, insufficient to cover both the ordinary business obligations and the tort liabilities of the LLP.

§10.36 Limited Liability Limited Partnerships

Several states authorize a combination of limited partnerships and the LLP. A **limited liability limited partnership** (**LLLP**) is a limited partnership in which the general partners have elected to become an LLP. In such an organization, the limited partners have no liability for the firm's obligations under the limited partnership statute, and the general partners, among themselves, have personal liability only to the extent provided by the LLP statute.

Although the LLLP is a logical extension of the limited partnership and registered limited liability partnership statutes, it is not clear what benefits this form of business has over a simple LLC.

§10.37 Professional Corporations

Certain professions — primarily law, medicine, and dentistry — have long been prohibited by ethical considerations from conducting business in the traditional corporation form. A **professional corporation** is a specially designed business form that enables professionals to obtain the benefits of incorporation and meet ethical requirements. The professional corporation was originally developed to take advantage of special tax rules applicable to corporations, particularly the right to create more attractive pension and profit-sharing plans than sole proprietors could provide for themselves or partnerships could create for partners. These tax advantages were eliminated in 1982, but modest fringe benefits that cannot be claimed by proprietors or provided by a partnership to its partners are still available on a before-tax basis. The continuing popularity of the professional corporation now rests primarily on the advantage of limited liability that professional corporations provide in many (but not all) states.

In many states today, a law firm may conduct business as a general partnership, an LLC, an LLP, or a professional corporation.

D. SELECTION OF BUSINESS FORM

§10.38 Selection of Business Form

In the 1950s, there were three types of business forms for closely held businesses, each combining fairly precise rules about control and governance in

their own unique ways: the partnership (or proprietorship), the limited partnership, and the corporation. These traditional businesses forms have now been supplemented by novel business forms, LLCs and LLPs, and variations thereof, that mix and match characteristics in new and challenging ways. These new business forms are so attractive and so flexible that it is quite possible that they will eventually become the dominant business forms for closely held enterprises. As far as publicly held businesses are concerned, virtually all are corporations, and, given the present tax rules, there is no incentive to use any of the newly developed business forms for publicly held enterprises.

The following are the most significant factors in the selection of a business form:

1. Considerations of internal efficiency, operational cost, and organizational convenience;
2. Considerations of limited liability and the responsibility of the owners of a business for its debts;
3. The minimization of federal income taxation;
4. The minimization of state income and franchise tax obligations;
5. Legal restrictions on the ability of certain businesses (e.g., law firms) to select specific business forms; and
6. Considerations relating to the ease of raising capital in the future.

Traditional legal texts often analyze the differences among the forms of business organization in terms of legal differences: continuity of life, centralization of management, and free transferability of interest. These factors are also discussed below; they are not truly unique characteristics of a specific form of business enterprise. By suitable advance planning, a considerable degree of continuity of life, centralization of management, and free transferability of interest may be granted to, or withheld from, any form of business organization. At one time, these factors were of central importance in determining the federal income tax regime applicable to a specific business. However, because these factors were manipulable, the selection of applicable tax regime also became manipulable. Ultimately, the IRS recognized this fact, and made selection of tax regime completely elective in late 1996 when it adopted its check-the-box regulations.

§10.39 Limited Liability

As one reflects on the importance of limited liability, the first reaction of law students is usually that protection against unlimited liability is of great significance, and that in terms of selecting an appropriate business form, one should always opt for this protection. Of course, there is clearly some value in protection against unexpected liability, but one should not overstate its significance.

Sophisticated creditors often decline to deal with small limited liability enterprises unless the owners (or some of them) voluntarily agree to guarantee the payment of the obligations by the enterprise. These creditors understand that limited liability means that the creditor can only look to the assets of the

business: They may (and usually do) decline to do business with a limited liability enterprise without substantial assets unless the owners voluntarily guarantee repayment of the debt. When owners are called on to make personal guarantees, the value of limited liability is obviously significantly diminished.

There are, however, some significant kinds of contract claims in which it is not customary or practical for the creditor to require the owners to give personal guarantees of the payment of the debt. An obvious example is employee wage and salary claims. Usually, the economic bargaining power of employees is such that they are in no position to ask for or obtain such guarantees. Small creditors also may not request guarantees, simply because the cost of requesting and obtaining them exceeds the amount of the credit they expect to extend. Other creditors may be satisfied with a purchase money security interest or other type of lien, and may not request personal guarantees. Thus, the protection of limited liability in these areas may have some favorable practical consequences from the standpoint of owners.

As for tort liabilities, in very small businesses the owner or owners will often be personally involved in the activities giving rise to the judgment and thus will be individually liable irrespective of limited liability. In somewhat larger businesses, the owners usually have more wealth at stake and have a strong incentive to make sure that employees take due care in doing the work of the business. Thus limited liability is of limited value even on the tort side. Moreover, even limited liability enterprises purchase liability insurance to protect their assets from being consumed by a tort judgment. This insurance normally protects the owners of the business as well as the business's assets from tort claims. It is possible, of course, for a tort judgment to exceed the amount of liability insurance available, but that is at best a remote risk. One can also purchase insurance against excess liability — so-called umbrella policies — which is relatively inexpensive. The difference in annual cost between $100,000 of coverage and $10,000,000 of coverage, for example, is usually not very great.

There are some tort claims for which insurance protection is simply not available. Intentional torts fall into this category. However, the probability of such liability actually arising in a commercial context is quite small for most businesses. Further, where true intentional torts are involved, there is a fairly high possibility of liability being imposed through direct participation by the owners, by agency principles, or by piercing the veil of limited liability by a court.

There are other types of claims not falling clearly into either the contract or tort category that also may be affected by limited liability. Some tax claims, for example, may only be the responsibility of the limited liability entity; presumably owners of the business are not personally liable for such claims.

If one weighs the advantages and costs of limited liability from a realistic perspective, a fair conclusion is that limited liability is a definite but limited benefit from the standpoint of the owners. Its advantages are not so overwhelming that it should be insisted on in every case. For this reason, many law firms continue to conduct their business as general partnerships despite the availability of the LLP business form. Obviously, some individuals are more risk-averse than others: The more risk-averse, the more important limited liability is apt to appear.

§10.40 Federal Income Taxation of Business Entities

It is essential to understand the alternative tax regimes that are available to businesses with more than a single owner. There are three different tax regimes for businesses: C corporation taxation, S corporation taxation, and partnership taxation. Under the check-the-box regulations adopted in 1996, a closely held unincorporated business may simply elect the tax regime that will apply to it at the time of formation. Once made, however, the election is not easily changed.

§10.41 Corporate Taxation in General

The check-the-box regulations make clear that a corporation is not eligible to elect partnership taxation. A corporation formed under state law is a corporation for tax purposes and is limited to the choices discussed in this and the following sections.

The starting point for corporate taxation is that the corporation is a separate taxable entity independent of its shareholders. The IRC imposes a tax on both the corporation and the individual shareholder. Thus, the earnings of a corporation may be subject to federal income taxation at two different levels: at the corporate level on the corporation's taxable income and a second time, at the shareholder level when the corporation distributes assets to the shareholders. Of course, a corporation is not required to make distributions to its shareholders, and no tax is due at the shareholder level until distributions are made. If the corporation is profitable but distributions are not made, the value of the corporation's assets will increase. Shareholders may be able to capture this increase in value by selling their stock. The gain from such a sale will usually be taxed as a long-term capital gain subject to tax at a rate usually somewhat lower than the rate applicable to ordinary income.

Federal income taxation of corporations is not monolithic. In 1957, Congress created a special tax election for certain corporations—the S corporation election—that now permits most corporations with fewer than 75 shareholders to elect to be taxed in a manner that generally permits income to be passed through the corporation and to be taxed directly to shareholders.

Subchapter S tax treatment is similar to (but in some respects significantly different from) pass-through tax treatment applicable to partnerships. A corporation that has elected to be taxed under subchapter S is called, not surprisingly, an S corporation. A corporation that has not elected to be an S corporation is called a C corporation, because the corporate income tax is imposed by Subchapter C of the IRC. Because the S corporation election is available only for corporations with fewer than 75 shareholders, large publicly held corporations have no choice but to be C corporations. In addition, many smaller corporations may be ineligible for S corporation treatment, or may not elect such treatment if it is available, so that C corporations include many small, closely held businesses.

§10.42 C Corporations and Double Taxation

A C corporation is a separate taxpayer that must pay taxes on its income according to a tax rate schedule set forth in the IRC that is different from the schedules applicable to individuals. As of 1996, the corporate tax schedule begins at 15 percent (on the first $50,000 of income) and goes up to a maximum tax of 35 percent applicable to corporate income in excess of $10 million. C corporation taxation involves double taxation in this sense: The corporation is first taxed directly on its income calculated using this corporate rate schedule. If it then makes distributions to its shareholders, the amount of those distributions is subject to a second tax at the shareholder level to the extent the corporation has earnings and profits. From the prism of a shareholder in a closely held corporation who must have distributions in order to meet ordinary living expenses, this double taxation has long been viewed as unfair, as a needless penalty on the use of the corporate form of business, and as the imposition of an unreasonably high tax on corporate earnings.

The extent of the penalty caused by this double tax depends not only on the tax rates that apply to corporations but also the rates applicable to individual shareholders. The effect of the double tax at 1996 rate levels is a good illustration. If a corporation has $100,000 of taxable income in 1996, it will pay a tax of $22,250, reducing the income available for distribution to $77,750. The tax due on this distribution depends on the shareholder's other income, deductions, and marital status. If we assume that there is only one shareholder (a married person filing a joint return, with $140,000 of taxable income from salaries and other sources), the shareholder is in the 36 percent bracket, and the distribution of the extra $77,750 will increase the shareholder's tax bill by $27,990 ($77,750 × .36 = $27,990). Of the $100,000 of taxable income originally received by the corporation, the shareholder will be able to retain $49,760 ($77,750 − $27,990 = $49,760) after all taxes have been paid. Even though the effective corporate rate was 34 percent and the effective personal rate was 35 percent, the effective tax rate on the corporation and shareholder combined is 50.24 percent.

If the same business had been operated in a form that provided for conduit tax treatment, the shareholder's total income would have been increased from $140,000 to $240,000 by the inclusion of the corporation's income in the shareholder's tax return. The additional income would have been taxed at the 36 percent rate, and the couple's tax bill would thereby have been increased by exactly $36,000. In this scenario, the couple would have retained $64,000 from the corporation after tax. In other words, permitting the income to be taxed twice in the C corporation creates a minor disaster, costing the shareholder an additional $13,760 ($49,760 − $36,000 = $13,760) in unnecessary taxes in a single year.

Corporate earnings of C corporations are subject to the double tax only to the extent earnings are distributed to the shareholders. If they are retained in the business, they are taxed only once, at the applicable corporate rate. Of course, the shareholders then do not have the direct use of those earnings, because they are technically owned by the corporation and not by the shareholders. However, it is usually possible to structure the contractual relationships

between the corporation and the shareholder in such a way that most of the distribution to the shareholder is deductible by the corporation as salary, rent, interest, or other deductible payment. Other possibilities might include having the corporation lease an automobile for the use of the shareholder that qualifies as an ordinary and necessary expense from the standpoint of the corporation, provide a country club membership for the shareholder if business is extensively conducted at that location, and so forth. If these are ordinary and necessary expenses of the corporation, they are deductible by it and are not income taxable to the shareholder. Of course, claiming deductions of this nature may trigger an audit of the corporation's tax returns, and if such amounts are disallowed, the IRS will view the payments to the automobile leasing company or country club as constructive dividends to the shareholder as well as disallowing their deduction by the corporation.

In some situations, it may be attractive to allow earnings to accumulate in the corporation. Of course, earnings will need to be withdrawn at some point, so the second tax at the shareholder level is deferred but not eliminated. The simplest way of withdrawing the earnings is by selling shares. At that point, the shareholders will realize gain equal to the difference between their basis for the shares and the sales price. This gain, which presumably incorporates the accumulated earnings, however, will usually be taxable as a long-term capital gain rather than as ordinary income, which reduces the second tax bite somewhat. In an earlier era, the individual income tax rates for ordinary income were very high (as high as 90 percent immediately after World War II), while capital gains rates were capped at 25 percent. Under this tax regime, the strategy of accumulation followed by sale of the stock was so common that it has its own name: the accumulate and bail out strategy. Today, the accumulate and bail out strategy is less attractive, because the maximum capital gains tax rate is 28 per cent, while the maximum individual income tax rate is 39.6 per cent, a significant but not massive difference. For persons in the 39.6 percent bracket, the accumulate and bail out strategy may yield a better tax result than the S corporation election or a strategy of zeroing out corporate income by tax-deductible payments to shareholders.

The accumulate and bail out strategy is most attractive for elderly shareholders who do not need current distributions for living expenses. When a shareholder dies owning the appreciated shares, the tax law provides a stepped up basis for the deceased's property equal to the fair market value of the property at the date of death, and the increase in basis is never subject to income tax by anyone. This yields the best income tax result; however, the fair value of the shares may be subject to estate taxation.

A final alternative is to give shares to children or grandchildren in relatively small amounts that avoid gift taxes. However, the so-called kiddy tax greatly reduces the attractiveness of gifts to children or grandchildren under the age of 14, because it taxes income to the children at the marginal rate that applies to the donor. The gift of shares also results in a transfer of the donor's tax basis to the donee, so the children or grandchildren would need to pay income tax on any resale of the shares. Prior to 1986, it was possible to extract some gain through voluntary dissolution, because unrealized appreciation of corporate assets escaped income taxation under the *General Utilities* doctrine. The Tax

Reform Act of 1986 repealed this doctrine, thereby also greatly complicating conversions of corporations into other business forms.

The double taxation problem is of concern primarily for shareholders who are individuals. It is not generally a problem for shareholders who are corporations, because a **dividends received deduction** is available for corporate shareholders. This deduction ranges from a 100 percent deduction for dividends paid to an affiliated corporation that owns 80 percent or more of the voting power and value of the payer's stock to a 70 percent deduction for dividends paid to corporations owning less than 20 percent of the payer's stock. The reason for the deduction is that to tax dividends between corporations would effectively add a third level of taxation, thus practically precluding intercorporate investments.

From an economic standpoint, the double tax structure applicable to corporations has serious economic costs. For example, it encourages indirect distributions that the corporation claims as tax deductions. The corporate tax treatment also imposes tax at the corporate level without regard to shareholder characteristics, arguably overtaxing low bracket or tax-exempt shareholders. It encourages the excessive use of debt, because interest payments are tax deductible, while dividend payments are not. It leads corporations to adopt a policy of retaining excess earnings within the corporation rather than distributing them promptly to shareholders who may reinvest them. It therefore encourages over-investment at the corporate level and a misallocation of limited capital resources. Finally, it deters the use of the corporate form of business for closely held businesses and encourages the development of new business forms whose principal advantage is tax savings. Arguably none of these practices are in the best interest of society generally.

The United States is unique among industrialized nations in imposing a double tax burden on corporate distributions. As a result, there have been numerous proposals to amend the tax law to eliminate the double tax. Tax academics generally support the view that an individual should be taxed only on accretion of wealth and that no source-based rules should be imposed. Although this ideal is easy to state, and there is no shortage of suggestions as to how integration may be achieved, there are serious problems in implementation.

The double taxation problem might be eliminated by the outright repeal of the corporate income tax or by permitting corporations to deduct dividend payments the way they now deduct interest payments. Shareholders might be permitted to exclude all or a substantial portion of dividend distributions from their adjusted gross income or to treat corporate tax payments as a credit against their own tax bill in much the same way as an employer creates credits for individual taxpayers by withholding income taxes. Plans to eliminate the double tax are generally referred to as **integration** proposals.

Enactment of an integration proposal requires recognition of certain political realities and numerous conflicting claims of equity. The simple fact is that the present law has developed a morass of tax preferences, rules of deductibility, and special tax rates for certain types of income and for certain types of taxpayers. Integration is difficult because it reopens many controversial and difficult issues over which figurative blood has been shed in the past.

Although amendments to the IRC eliminating the double taxation of dividends are possible, it does not appear to have very high priority. In part, this may be because the development of the LLC and the check-the-box regulations permit businesses with relatively few owners to obtain the desired benefits of incorporation combined with true conduit or pass-through taxation.

§10.43 Partnership Taxation

The method of taxation that applies to a partnership is usually referred to as **pass-through taxation** or **conduit taxation**. A partnership must prepare an information return each year that shows partnership income and expenses, but it does not itself pay any tax. Rather, the partnership then allocates its income or loss among the individual partners in accordance with the partnership agreement. Each partner must then include in his or her personal income tax return the amount of each item so allocated.

Tax treatment as a partnership is also attractive for technical reasons unrelated to the double tax issue. These technical benefits include flexibility in allowing special allocations of a partnership's profit and loss to individual partners (as long as the allocations have substantial economic effect outside of the tax consequences) and nonrecognition of gain upon the distribution in kind of appreciated property to partners. The detailed tax rules that apply to general partnerships are quite complex and certainly this complexity is a negative feature of this tax regime. Advice by tax counsel is virtually essential whenever a complex business is conducted as a partnership. (The discussion that follows is intended to convey a general sense of the complex issues that arise in connection with partnership taxation and to serve as a basis for distinguishing S corporation tax treatment in the next section. Readers who are more interested in nontax aspects of partnership may safely skip this material.)

Taxation is determined by the allocation of income to the partners, not by actual distributions to the partner. This allocation is referred to as the partner's **distributive share**. The partners must include their distributive shares of profit in their personal tax returns as income and pay tax on these amounts, even though they may not receive any cash from the partnership and indeed may never receive any cash from the partnership. If there is an allocation of income to a partner but no distributions are made, that partner will have to use personal funds to pay the additional tax that arises from including the share of partnership income in the partner's tax return. When accumulations of capital are contemplated, partnership agreements may provide that the partnership must distribute each year an amount equal to the profit allocated to each partner multiplied by the highest federal income tax rate. This ensures that the partner will have funds available to pay the tax that is due. These payments are often called **tax distributions**.

The allocations of the partnership may include not only the distributive share of ordinary income but also short- or long-term capital gains, charitable contributions, foreign taxes, and other items that are subject to special tax treatment under the IRC. In general terms, these special tax items must be separately identified and allocated to the partners and they retain the same

character as if the taxpayer had directly realized or incurred them. These special allocations are also determined by the partnership or by the partnership agreement. The IRS will accept the partnership's allocations if the capital accounts are maintained in accordance with detailed tax regulations. In effect, these regulations create a safe harbor that protects partners from possible attacks on the allocations of tax items if the capital accounts are maintained in accordance with the regulations. As a result, the provisions relating to the capital accounts in partnership agreements are usually tied closely to the tax regulations, often using concepts defined in the regulations and making specific reference to sections or subsections of the regulations when dealing with such matters as the handling of nonrecourse loans or the assumption of indebtedness by the partnership. To a person not familiar with these detailed regulations, the provisions in the partnership agreement may seem arcane at best or incomprehensible at worst. Further, because of the potential complexity of partnership transactions, it is not practical to provide rules that cover every possible transaction. Partnership agreements therefore also usually grant the managing partners (or a majority of the partners) authority to determine how specific transactions should be reflected in the capital accounts in order to ensure compliance with the detailed tax regulations, usually with an exception to prohibit changes to be made in the amount of distributions that each partner is to receive.

Basis in tax law means the amount that a taxpayer invests in an asset for tax purposes. In calculating the gain from sale of an asset, one begins with the sale price and subtracts the basis of the asset. Basis may include initial purchase price, the cost of subsequent improvements, and reductions arising from distributions. At first blush, the basis of a partnership's interest would appear to be similar to the amount in the capital account. Both record the history of the partner's transactions with the partnership. The capital account, however, reflects economic relationships; transactions are recorded in that account at their market values. Basis reflects only amounts for which tax liabilities have been previously settled and excludes unrecognized gains and losses that affect market value.

The tax basis of a partnership interest operates similarly to the partner's capital account. Contributions of property to the partnership increases basis as does the allocation of taxable income to the partner. Basis is reduced by losses and by distributions to the partner. When a loss is allocated to a partner, he or she includes the amount of that loss as a deduction against other income and his or her basis is reduced by that amount. However, losses are not recognized to the extent they would reduce the tax basis of the partnership interest below zero. If the partner's tax basis is zero, any distribution to the partner creates taxable income.

Section 754 of the IRC permits a partnership to step up the basis in partnership assets to reflect the basis of the partner's interest in the partnership following a transaction in which a partner's interest in the partnership is redeemed or liquidated.

The contribution of property rather than cash to a partnership also creates considerable complexity and usually leads immediately to a divergence between business accounting and tax accounting. In general terms, for accounting purposes a valuation must be placed on all property contributions in order to establish the capital accounts of the partners. Parity of economic treatment in

the future can be ensured only if all contributions are entered in the capital accounts of the partnership at their fair market values. For example, if a partner contributes property with a fair market value of $100 and a tax basis in his hands of $50, while the other partner contributes $100 in cash, each partner's capital contribution must be reflected as $100 in the capital accounts to ensure economic parity of treatment in the future. However, the contribution of appreciated property does not result in the recognition of gain to the contributing partner. ("Recognition" in tax law means that a person is to be taxed on the appreciation of property; thus, a partner who contributes the appreciated property is not immediately taxed on that appreciation when the property is contributed to the partnership.) Rather, the basis of the contributed property is simply transferred to the partnership. At this point, the tax basis of the partner's interest in the partnership reflects the tax basis of the contributed property and not its fair market value. In the above example, each partner has an economic interest in the partnership of $100 as reflected by its capital accounts, but the tax basis of the partnership interest of the partner contributing cash will be $100, while the tax basis of the partner contributing the property will be $50. The basis of the property in the hands of the partnership is also $50. Unrealized gain that is in existence when the property is contributed to the partnership is called **built-in gain**.

The traditional treatment of gain from the sale of property with built-in gain is that the gain should be allocated entirely to the partner contributing the appreciated property. The purpose of this rule is to prevent the use of the partnership form to shift the responsibility for the tax payable on the gain. Thus, under the traditional rule, if the property is subsequently sold for $120, the built-in gain of $50 would be allocated to the partner contributing the property and the additional gain of $20 would be allocated among all the partners in accordance with their profit-sharing ratios. Thus, the entire built-in gain on the sale of the appreciated property ultimately is attributable to the contributing partner. If the property were sold for $80, there would be a gain from the tax standpoint but a loss from the economic standpoint. Presumably, the taxable gain would be allocated entirely to the partner contributing the property and the entire loss allocated in proportion to the profit-sharing ratios. The current regulations permit some deviation from this traditional approach, but the IRS accepts alternative allocations of built-in gain only if they reflect the substantial economic effect of the transaction.

If the property is depreciable, the calculation becomes even more complicated. If it is assumed that the property is depreciable on a straight-line basis over 10 years, 10 percent of the fair market value would be viewed as an expense of the partnership each year for purposes of calculating income or loss, but the tax deduction for depreciation each year would be based on 10 percent of the basis of the property.

§10.44 The S Corporation Election in General

As indicated above, the major alternative to C corporation tax treatment is the S corporation election. The effect of this election is that the corporation has many of the tax characteristics of a conduit entity, with corporate income

or loss being allocated directly to the shareholders. This election is available only in limited circumstances: (1) the corporation must have no more than 75 shareholders; (2) all shareholders must be individuals, estates of decedents, certain trusts, or charitable organizations; (3) no shareholder may be a nonresident alien; and (4) the corporation must have only one class of stock. There is no size limitation on corporations eligible for the S corporation election, though most eligible business are relatively small.

An S corporation election can be made by filing a relatively simple form, together with written consents by all persons who are shareholders on the day the election is made. Once made, the election continues indefinitely. It may be terminated by a voluntary revocation by a majority of all the shareholders, by the failure of the corporation to satisfy any of the requirements for qualification, or in certain other circumstances. Generally, a corporation can move from being an S corporation to a C corporation at any time, but if it does so, it cannot again elect to return to being an S corporation for five years unless the IRS consents.

One undesirable feature of the S corporation election is that these technical rules about disqualification make it relatively easy for a single shareholder in an S corporation to commit some act that effectively revokes that election (e.g., by selling some shares so that there are more than 75 shareholders). In some instances in which there is conflict within the corporation, the threat by a minority shareholder to commit such an act carries some weight, even though the consequences probably will be to create financial injury in the form of increased tax liabilities for all shareholders. In order to prevent this tactic, share transfer restrictions may be imposed that effectively prohibit the minority shareholder from transferring his or her shares. In the absence of advance planning, however, the S corporation election itself may well become a bargaining chit in resolving intracorporate conflict.

S corporation tax treatment is often described as pass-through or partnership-type tax treatment. Although the S corporation election makes partnership-type taxation generally available to small corporations, there are significant differences in detail between the tax treatment of an S corporation and the tax treatment of a proprietorship or partnership. These differences greatly reduce the attractiveness of the S corporation alternative, and together with the procedural requirements for making and revoking the S corporation election, doubtless have encouraged the development of the LLC and related limited liability pass-through entities. In other words, an LLC, if properly structured, is treated as a true partnership for tax purposes and not as an S corporation. When reference is made to partnership tax treatment in the following discussion, the business under discussion is subject to true partnership taxation. (Again, the discussion that follows is somewhat technical and may safely be skipped by readers who are less interested in the finer distinctions between S corporation taxation and partnership taxation.)

In most respects, the taxation of income of an S corporation is similar to that of a partnership. As in partnerships, a basic distinction is made between distributions and allocations. A shareholder of an S corporation must include in taxable income the amount of the income of the S corporation based on proportional share ownership in the corporation without regard to the amount

distributed. The tax rules that apply to partnerships give the business some discretion as to how income or loss are to be allocated among the participants, allocations that may produce a net tax saving. There is no similar flexibility in an S corporation; allocations of profit or loss in an S corporation must be exclusively and strictly on the basis of stock ownership. This lack of flexibility is certainly a major disadvantage of S corporation tax treatment as compared with partnership tax treatment.

As in a partnership, allocations of income in an S corporation increase the basis of the shareholder's interest in the corporation and distributions by the S corporation reduce that basis. For example, if X is a 50 percent shareholder in an S corporation with a tax basis in his stock of $20,000, and the corporation has earnings of $50,000 and distributes $12,500 to each of the shareholders, X must include $25,000 as his allocation of income in his personal tax return. This increases his basis by the same amount but the distribution reduces it, so that X's new basis is $20,000 + $25,000 − $12,500 = $32,500. As in a partnership, losses by the corporation reduce the taxable income of the shareholder and basis in the stock as long as the shareholder has a positive basis in the stock. In the above example, if the corporation has a loss of $30,000 in the following year, X may claim a deductible loss of $15,000 and basis will be reduced from $32,500 to $17,500. If the corporation distributes an additional $10,000 to him, that distribution does not affect X's taxable income, but reduces basis in the stock to $7,500. If the corporation distributes cash or property to a shareholder in excess of the shareholder's basis, the excess is taxable income.

S corporation and partnership tax treatment also differ in the manner in which gain is recognized if a participant in the business contributes appreciated property to the business. In a partnership, gain from any sale of the property within two years must be allocated back to the contributing partner. In an S corporation, however, the gain must be allocated strictly in accordance with ownership interests. For example, assume that A contributes $10,000 in cash and B contributes a piece of real estate having a tax basis of $4,000 and a fair market of $10,000. Each has a 50 percent interest in the business. There is built-in gain of $6,000. Shortly thereafter, the business sells the real estate for $10,000. If the business is subject to partnership tax treatment, the $6,000 gain must be allocated to B. B must pay tax on this gain (presumably as a capital gain) and his basis in the partnership becomes $10,000. If the business is subject to S corporation tax treatment, on the other hand, $3,000 of the gain must be allocated to A and $3,000 to B. A in effect will be taxed on a portion of the gain attributable to B's contribution of property, and the tax basis of A's and B's interests in the corporation will not be equal even though each contributed property of equal value. Depending on the tax brackets of A and B, this may be advantageous or disadvantageous.

Another difference in tax treatment arises if an S corporation owns property that has appreciated in value while owned by the business, and distributes that property to its shareholders. In the case of a partnership, no gain is recognized on such a transaction and the basis of each partner in the property is carried over from the partnership's basis. In an S corporation, on the other hand, the distribution of appreciated property results in the immediate recognition of

gain, its allocation to the shareholders, and a tax on the gain being due even if the appreciated property has not been sold to third parties.

Yet another significant difference between S corporation and partnership tax treatment relates to adjustments to basis for liabilities that the business incurs itself. Losses are deductible by partners and S corporation shareholders only to the extent of the tax basis of their interest in the firm. If a partnership borrows money for purposes of its business, the tax basis of each partner's interest in the partnership is increased by his or her proportionate share of the new liability. The rules for an S corporation, however, are different. If money is borrowed by the shareholder and contributed to the corporation, the shareholder's basis is increased by the amount of the loan. However, if the S corporation directly incurs the indebtedness, there is no adjustment in the shareholders' basis in the stock and a valuable tax attribute is lost. This may be a trap for the unwary, because it is always advantageous to increase one's basis in S corporation shares, and the shareholders may obtain an increase in basis if they borrow the funds that the corporation needs and turn the proceeds over to the corporation. However, if the corporation simply enters into the transaction directly, which is certainly the normal and sensible thing to do in most circumstances (absent the tax problem), the increase in basis is lost forever. Of course, the shareholders must incur personal liability on the loan if they wish to obtain the increase in basis. This rule makes it difficult for real estate ventures to be conducted in the form of S corporations, because most loans must be secured by a lien on the real estate involved, and the shareholder is not able to grant such a lien on his own.

An S corporation differs from a partnership in one other important respect. Section 754 of the IRC permits a step-up of basis in partnership assets to reflect the partners' basis in the partnership whenever a partner's interest is redeemed or liquidated. An S corporation does not have this privilege, with the result that valuable tax benefits may be lost in the S corporation.

Although these differences between partnership and S corporation taxation may appear to be technical, they involve real dollars in the real world. Because virtually all of the rule differences favor the partnership form of taxation over the S corporation, practitioners have naturally gravitated toward the LLC in preference to the S corporation. In effect, the LLC constitutes an end run around the S corporation restrictions.

The decision as to whether an eligible corporation should elect S corporation treatment depends on three basic variables: (1) the relative tax rates applicable to the corporation and to individual shareholders; (2) the probable distribution pattern that the corporation will follow in the future; and (3) whether the corporation may have losses for tax purposes in the near future.

Before 1980, the individual marginal income tax rates for upper-income taxpayers were considerably higher than marginal rates for corporations. In this environment, the pass-through feature of the S corporation was usually a detriment rather than a benefit to high-income shareholders. If shareholders were in high tax brackets and the corporation was profitable, the S corporation election almost never the most tax-efficient solution. Rather, most profitable closely held corporations operated as C corporations and adopted the accumu-

late and bail out strategy discussed earlier. Dividends and distributions were minimized, and the ultimate resolution involved either a sale of the stock of the corporation at favorable long-term capital gain rates, a dissolution of the corporation, or the death of shareholders with a subsequent step-up in basis on death.

In this pre-1980 tax environment, an entirely different set of minimization principles applied to a corporation that expected temporary operating losses. If the corporation had high bracket shareholders, the S corporation election permitted the shareholders to use the corporate losses to shield other taxable income from rates as high as 75 percent. When the corporation became profitable, the S corporation election was terminated. This sequence was so common as to be almost routine. During this period, the number of corporations electing S corporation treatment was relatively small, presumably reflecting the fact that the election was attractive only for loss corporations.

The very high individual tax rates of the pre-1980s were steadily reduced during the 1980s. The lowest point of individual tax rates in the modern era were established by the Tax Reform Act of 1986, a statute that made sweeping changes in tax rules. The basic purposes of this statute were (1) to reduce maximum tax rates; (2) to expand the tax base; and (3) to eliminate or minimize tax avoidance and tax shelter transactions. This act reversed the historic relationship between the maximum personal and corporate tax rates: the maximum individual tax rate was reduced to 28 percent, while the maximum corporate rate was reduced only to 34 percent. Further, the special treatment of long-term capital gains was eliminated. These changes in basic structure suddenly made partnership-type taxation much more attractive than the two-tiered taxation of corporations, and the number of S corporation elections soared. Indeed, this was the period during which master limited partnerships were created, and there was concern that the changes in tax rates might lead to widespread disincorporation.

Subsequent tax statutes have partially reversed the pattern of tax rates that the Tax Reform Act of 1986 established. The maximum individual rate was gradually increased to 39.6 percent in 1994, while at the same time the maximum corporate rate was increased to 35 percent. These changes in the relative tax rates applicable to individuals and corporations have caused further changes in the use of the S corporation election and distribution policy by closely held corporations as shareholders have continued to adopt corporate and individual strategies that minimize their total tax bills. The tax rates discussed here are the maximum marginal rates. Lower marginal rates apply to individuals and corporations with smaller incomes. Both corporate and individual rate schedules have special surtaxes designed to recapture the benefit of lower brackets and of personal deductions so that at specified brackets the marginal tax rates may be even higher than the "maximum."

In today's relatively even tax bracket environment, the choice between C corporations and S corporations depends even more on the specific circumstances. The single tax structure applicable to partnerships or S corporations is certainly to be preferred to a C corporation that distributes most of its income in the form of nondeductible dividends. Also, a partnership or S corporation

election is preferable if the business expects to show losses for a period of time. However, there are several situations where C corporation tax treatment may be attractive.

Because the maximum corporate rate is somewhat lower than the individual rate, a corporation that plans to reinvest substantially all of its earnings in plant and equipment reduces taxes by electing to remain a C corporation. Moreover, it is always possible to make some distributions in a form that is tax deductible by the corporation. Another situation in which C corporation tax treatment may be preferred involves elderly shareholders who expect to retain shares indefinitely so that it is likely that their shares will receive a tax free step-up in basis on their death.

Even when C corporation tax treatment is attractive, an LLC may in effect achieve that result by electing to be taxed as a corporation and not making an S corporation election. However, an LLC that has made this election may find that it is uneconomic to revoke the election.

CHAPTER 11
◆ CORPORATE SECURITIES

§11.1 Introduction

Perhaps no other area of corporation law is more confusing to persons without prior business backgrounds than corporate securities such as stock, bonds, and debentures. The language is new and unfamiliar, the concepts seem mysterious and sometimes illogical, and everything seems to build on historical concepts that today are of dubious relevance. This chapter should help to dispel the mystery.

This chapter focuses on publicly traded securities that large, publicly held corporations issue. It therefore provides important background for the following chapters of this book dealing with dividend policies, takeovers, securities markets, and investment strategies.

§11.2 Common Shares

Shares of **common stock** are the fundamental units into which the proprietary interest of the corporation is divided. If a corporation issues only one class of shares, they may be referred to by a variety of similar names: common shares, common stock, capital stock, or possibly simply shares or stock. Whatever the name, they are the basic proprietary units of ownership and are referred to here as common shares or common stock.

The two fundamental characteristics of common shares are (1) they are entitled to vote for the election of directors and on other matters coming before the shareholders and (2) they are entitled to the net assets of the corporation (after making allowance for debts and senior securities) when distributions are to be made, either during the life of the corporation or upon its dissolution.

The fundamental incorporating document of every corporation must state the number of shares of common stock the corporation is authorized to issue. This number is known as the corporation's **authorized shares**. In states with older statutes, that document must also set forth the **par value** of the authorized shares or a statement that the shares are without par value. Par value is an arbitrary number without economic significance that, in older statutes, determines the amount of permanent capital and capital surplus in the original capitalization of the corporation.

Corporations usually authorize more common shares than they currently plan to issue. Additional authorized shares may be useful if it is decided, for example, to raise capital in the future by selling additional shares, to provide economic incentives to executives or key employees by granting them options to purchase shares at favorable prices, to create an **employee stock ownership plan (ESOP)** for all employees, or to issue debt or senior classes of securities that may be converted into common shares.

The capitalization of a corporation is based on the number of shares actually issued and the consideration received for them, not on the number of authorized shares. Capital received in exchange for shares is usually referred to as the corporation's invested capital (or sometimes its contributed capital), and from an accounting standpoint it is viewed as being invested in the corporation permanently or indefinitely.

§11.3 Reporting of Earnings per Share

Publicly held corporations report publicly their earnings each year on an aggregate basis and on a per-share basis. **Earnings per share** equal net earnings divided by the number of shares outstanding. Publicly held corporations almost always have outstanding commitments to issue, or have granted rights in third persons to acquire additional shares either by purchase, option exercise, or conversion of convertible securities. These are potential shares, because the privilege of acquiring the shares has not yet been exercised. The number of potential shares may be large in comparison with the number of actually issued and outstanding shares. The question then arises, what should be done about

potential shares when reporting earnings? Should earnings per share be calculated on shares actually outstanding or on shares potentially outstanding? The solution that the Securities and Exchange Commission (the SEC) adopted is very sensible. When the number of potential shares is material, earnings per share must be reported on both an actual share basis and a **fully diluted** basis, that is on the assumption that all options and rights to acquire additional shares have been exercised. Table 11-1 is an example of such reporting for the quarterly earnings of several publicly traded corporations.

§11.4 Preferred Shares

Preferred shares differ from common shares in that (1) they usually have limited rights and (2) one or more of those rights has a preference over the rights of common shares. Preferential rights are almost always financial in character. Most preferred shares have preferential rights over common shares both in connection with the payment of dividends and in connection with distributions of assets in voluntary or involuntary dissolution of the corporation. A **dividend preference** means that the preferred shares are entitled to receive a specified dividend before any dividend may be paid on the common shares; a **liquidation preference** means that the preferred shares are entitled to receive a specified distribution from corporate assets in liquidation (after provision has been made for corporate debts) before the common shares are entitled to receive anything. However, some preferred shares may have only a dividend preference and no liquidation preference, or vice versa.

The rights of preferred shareholders are defined in the corporation's articles of incorporation (or other incorporating document), bylaws, or directors' resolutions filed with the articles of incorporation (in the case of series of preferred shares). If an existing corporation wishes to create a new class of preferred shares, it must usually formally amend its articles of incorporation. Collectively the provisions in these basic corporate documents describing and defining the terms and rights of preferred shareholders constitute the preferred shareholders' contract with the corporation. Preferred shareholders are generally limited to the rights set forth in these documents and have relatively few rights outside of those expressly set forth.

A single corporation may have outstanding several different classes of preferred shares with varying rights and preferences. Although a specific class of preferred may have rights subordinate to another class of preferred, both are still preferred shares, because both have preferences over the common shares. The dividend preference may be described either in terms of dollars per share ("$3.20 preferred") or as a percentage of par or stated value (the "5 percent preferred"). A dividend preference does not mean that the preferred is entitled to payment in the same way that a creditor is entitled to payment. A preferred dividend is still a dividend and may be paid only if the corporation has available surplus. Further, even if there are funds legally available from which a preferred dividend may be paid, the directors may decide to omit dividends. The incentive to pay a preferred dividend is that if it is omitted all dividends on the common shares must also be omitted.

Table 11-1

DIGEST OF EARNINGS REPORTS

ABBREVIATIONS

A partial list of frequently used abbreviations: Acctg adj (Cumulative effect of an accounting change); Extrd chg (Extraordinary charge); Extrd cred (Extraordinary credit); Inco cnt op (Income from continuing operations); Inco dis op (Income from discontinued operations). Footnotes: p-pro forma; r-restated.

BIOSOURCE INTERNATIONL (Nq)

Quar Sept 30:	1997	1996
Sales	$5,182,450	$5,039,529
Net income	855,401	806,380
Avg shares	8,889,485	8,450,000
Shr earns:		
Net income	.10	.10
9 months:		
Sales	15,675,306	10,820,724
Net income	2,489,991	1,917,028
Avg shares	9,004,972	7,130,000
Shr earns:		
Net income	.28	.27

BONDED MOTORS INC. (Nq)

Quar Sept 30:	1997	1996
Sales	$6,576,528	$4,993,029
Net income	212,373	618,895
Avg shares	3,117,000	3,044,000
Shr earns (com & com equiv):		
Net income	.07	.20
9 months:		
Sales	17,924,622	14,225,703
Net income	923,753	1,220,088
Avg shares	3,113,000	2,696,000
Shr earns (com & com equiv):		
Net income	.30	.45

BOSTON CHICKEN INC. (Nq)

12 wk Oct 5:	1997	1996
Revenues	$110,826,000	$74,310,000
Net income	10,964,000	17,300,000
Avg shares	69,562,000	67,416,000
Shr earns (com & com equiv):		
Net income	.16	.26
40 weeks:		
Revenues	344,186,000	186,218,000
Net income	a49,650,000	48,865,000
Avg shares	68,294,000	66,091,000
Shr earns (com & com equiv):		
Net income	.73	.74

a-Includes net nonrecurring charges of $2,440,000.

BRISTOL HOTEL CO. (N) ♣

Quar Sept 30:	1997	1996
Revenues	$163,005,000	$58,571,000
Net income	12,066,000	c6,835,000
Avg shares	44,643,000	a25,529,000
Shr earns:		
Net income	.27	a.27
9 months:		
Revenues	352,882,000	159,485,000
Income	b26,098,000	c15,073,000
Extrd chg	(1,338,000)	....
Net income	24,760,000	15,073,000
Avg shares	36,213,000	a25,524,000
Shr earns:		
Income	.72	a.59
Net income	.68	a.59

a-Adjusted for a three-for-two stock split paid in July 1997. b-Includes a nonrecurring net charge of $1,860,000 in the nine months of 1997. c-Includes net gains of $569,000 from settlement of litigation in the quarter and nine months and $268,000 from sale of securities in the nine months.

CELLNET DATA SYSTEMS (Nq)

Quar Sept 30:	1997	1996
Revenues	$1,533,000	$515,000
Income	(25,208,000)	(20,454,000)
Extrd chg	(11,417,000)	....
Net income	(36,625,000)	(20,454,000)
Avg shares	41,614,000	34,345,000
Shr earns:		
Income	(.62)	(.60)
Net income	(.89)	(.60)
9 months:		
Revenues	4,026,000	935,000
Income	(71,134,000)	(52,767,000)
Extrd chg	(11,417,000)	....
Net income	(82,551,000)	(52,767,000)
Avg shares	40,157,000	33,952,000
Shr earns:		
Income	(1.78)	(1.55)
Net income	(2.05)	(1.55)

CELLPRO INC. (Nq)

Quar Sept 30:	1997	1996
Revenues	$2,540,062	$1,929,224
Net income	(6,084,322)	(5,110,915)
Avg shares	14,514,390	14,393,595
Shr earns:		
Net income	(.42)	(.36)
6 months:		
Revenues	5,092,981	3,935,037
Net income	(11,166,267)	(9,719,108)
Avg shares	14,507,064	14,384,069
Shr earns:		
Net income	(.77)	(.68)

CENTRAL LOUISIANA ELEC (N)

Quar Sept 30:	1997	1996
Revenues	$138,099,000	$130,477,000
Net income	22,888,000	20,900,000
Shr earns (primary):		
Net income	1.00	.91
Shr earns (fully diluted):		
Net income	.95	.87
12 months:		
Revenues	435,800,000	433,829,000
Net income	a48,345,000	51,013,000
Shr earns (primary):		
Net income	2.06	2.18
Shr earns (fully diluted):		
Net income	2.01	2.12

a-Includes a charge of $1,900,000 related to reorganization.

CENTURA SOFTWARE CORP. (Nq)

Quar Sept 30:	1997	1996
Revenues	$13,698,000	$14,610,000
Net income	a110,000	97,000
Avg shares	15,464,000	12,760,000
Shr earns (com & com equiv):		
Net income	.01	.01
9 months:		
Revenues	43,402,000	45,649,000
Net income	a(1,679,000)	841,000
Avg shares	15,327,000	12,720,000
Shr earns (com & com equiv):		
Net income	(.11)	.07

a-Includes non-recurring charges of $563,000 in the quarter and $1,094,000 in the nine months.

CHICAGO BRIDGE & IRON (N)

Quar Sept 30:	1997	1996
Revenues	$166,755,000	$183,021,000
Net income	1,112,000	5,373,000
Shr earns:		
Net income	.09	....
9 months:		
Revenues	477,500,000	483,531,000
Net income	a(1,089,000)	10,930,000
Shr earns:		
Net income	(.09)	....

a-Includes nonrecurring net charge of $10,064,000.

CONCENTRIC NETWORK (Nq)

Quar Sept 30:	1997	1996
Revenues	$11,824,000	$4,193,000
Net income	(14,218,000)	(14,473,000)
Avg shares	9,733,000	p5,820,000
Shr earns:		
Net income	(1.46)	p(2.49)
9 months:		
Revenues	31,792,000	8,215,000
Net income	(41,803,000)	(40,273,000)
pAvg shares	8,939,000	4,980,000
pShr earns:		
Net income	(4.68)	(8.09)

CONGOLEUM CORP. (N)

Quar Sept 30:	1997	1996
Sales	$69,526,000	$71,900,000
Net income	2,198,000	4,392,000
Avg shares	9,823,000	9,997,000
Shr earns (com & com equiv):		
Net income	.22	.44
9 months:		
Sales	195,518,000	200,398,000
Net income	5,315,000	8,198,000
Avg shares	9,934,000	9,999,000
Shr earns (com & com equiv):		
Net income	.54	.82

CONSOLIDATED GRAPHICS (N)

Quar Sept 30:	1997	1996
Sales	$53,363,000	$34,451,000
Net income	4,275,000	2,432,000
Avg shares	13,029,000	a12,233,000
Shr earns:		
Net income	.33	a.20
6 months:		
Sales	104,038,000	62,709,000
Net income	8,135,000	4,105,000
Avg shares	12,963,000	a12,048,000
Shr earns:		
Net income	.63	a.34

a-Adjusted for a two-for-one stock split paid in January 1997.

CONSOLIDATED NAT GAS (N)

Quar Sept 30:	1997	1996
Revenues	$1,130,477,000	$595,057,000
Net income	4,538,000	(5,118,000)
Avg shares	95,366,000	94,637,000
Shr earns:		
Net income	.05	(.05)
9 months:		
Revenues	3,859,930,000	2,565,091,000
Net income	215,014,000	210,299,000
Avg shares	95,121,000	94,284,000
Shr earns:		
Net income	2.26	2.23

CORE INC. (Nq)

Quar Sept 30:	1997	1996
Revenues	$10,531,319	$7,460,262
Net income	1,108,405	a(1,257,138)
Avg shares	7,970,000	6,072,000
Shr earns (com & com equiv):		
Net income	.14	(.21)
9 months:		
Revenues	27,629,939	20,603,169
Net income	1,931,815	a(220,346)
Avg shares	7,855,000	6,072,000
Shr earns (com & com equiv):		
Net income	.25	(.04)

a-Includes a charge of $2,029,555 related to a write-down.

COSMETIC CENTER INC. (Nq)

Quar Sept 26:	a1997	a1996
Sales	$45,355,000	$19,996,000
Net income	(1,319,000)	549,000
Avg shares	10,015,101	8,479,335
Shr earns:		

EINSTEIN/NOAH BAGEL (Nq)

12 wk Oct 5:	1997	1996
Revenues	$13,882,000	$10,257,000
Net income	5,364,000	3,953,000
Avg shares	34,578,000	30,377,000
Shr earns (com & com equiv):		
Net income ..	.16	.13
40 weeks:		
Revenues	43,885,000	50,842,000
Net income	15,656,000	931,000
Avg shares	34,776,000	19,225,000
Shr earns (com & com equiv):		
Net income ..	.45	.04

ELAMEX S.A. DE C.V. (Nq) ♣

13 wk Sept 28:	1997	1996
Sales	$32,872,000	$30,496,000
Net income	1,731,000	2,320,000
Avg shares	7,400,000	7,400,000
Shr earns:		
Net income ..	.23	.31
39 weeks:		
Sales	100,514,000	86,758,000
Net income	5,548,000	5,784,000
Avg shares	7,400,000	6,705,495
Shr earns:		
Net income ..	.75	.86

ELCOM INTERNATIONAL (Nq)

Quar Sept 30:	1997	1996
Sales	$198,373,000	$156,851,000
Net income	3,412,000	1,310,000
Avg shares	30,759,000	29,435,000
Shr earns:		
Net income ..	.11	.04
9 months:		
Sales	572,809,000	444,572,000
Net income	7,435,000	3,586,000
Avg shares	29,796,000	29,604,000
Shr earns:		
Net income ..	.25	.12

ELECTRONIC DESIGNS INC. (Nq)

Quar Sept 30:	1997	r1996
Revenues	$11,093,000	$13,184,000
Inco cnt op	1,125,000	1,471,000
Inco dis op	292,000	(177,000)
Net income	1,417,000	1,293,000
Avg shares	9,472,000	9,792,000
Shr earns:		
Inco cnt op ...	.13	.17
Net income ..	.16	.15
Year:		
Revenues	42,104,000	57,478,000
Inco cnt op	5,148,000	4,549,000
Inco dis op	(1,372,000)	(1,741,000)
Net income	3,776,000	2,808,000
Avg shares	9,781,000	9,795,000
Shr earns:		
Inco cnt op ...	.59	.56
Net income ..	.45	.38

EMULEX CORP. (Nq)

13 wk Sep 28:	1997	1996
Revenues	$15,007,000	$15,952,000
Net income	609,000	a(941,000)
Avg shares	6,312,000	5,998,000
Shr earns (com & com equiv):		
Net income ..	.10	(.16)

a-Includes consolidation charges of $1,280,000.

ENGINEERING ANIMATION (Nq)

Quar Sept 30:	1997	1996
Revenues	$11,086,000	$5,715,000
Net income	1,689,000	521,000
Avg shares	6,659,000	5,387,000
Shr earns:		
Net income ..	.25	.10
9 months:		
Revenues	27,564,000	13,352,000
Net income	3,515,000	1,131,000

FEATHERLITE MFG INC. (Nq)

Quar Sept 30:	1997	1996
Sales	$32,728,000	$28,384,000
Net income	a889,000	206,000
Avg shares	6,305,000	6,255,000
Shr earns:		
Net income ..	.14	.03
9 months:		
Sales	99,414,000	69,528,000
Net income	a2,259,000	271,000
Avg shares	6,309,000	6,088,000
Shr earns:		
Net income ..	.36	.04

a-Includes non-recurring gains of $275,000 in the quarter and $269,000 in the nine months.

FIDELITY NATIONAL FIN'L (N)

Quar Sept 30:	1997	1996
Net income	$15,857,000	$6,317,000
Avg shares	14,999,000	a14,321,000
Shr earns (primary):		
Net income ..	1.06	a.44
Shr earns (fully diluted):		
Net income ..	.85	a.38
9 months:		
Net income	27,985,000	18,408,000
Avg shares	14,692,000	a14,249,000
Shr earns (primary):		
Net income ..	1.90	a1.29
Shr earns (fully diluted):		
Net income ..	1.57	a1.11

a-Adjusted for a 10% stock dividend paid in January 1997.

FIRST BRANDS CORP. (N)

Quar Sept 30:	1997	1996
Sales	$269,480,000	$255,597,000
Net income	12,173,000	18,007,000
Avg shares	40,775,000	42,253,000
Shr earns (com & com equiv):		
Net income ..	.30	.43

FIRST INDUSTRIAL RLTY (N) ♣

Quar Sept 30:	1997	1996
Net income	$15,815,000	$8,660,000
Avg shares	30,257,000	24,138,000
Shr earns:		
Net income ..	.38	.32
9 months:		
Income..........	47,575,000	27,119,000
aExt chg	(12,563,000)	(821,000)
Net income	35,012,000	26,298,000
Avg shares	30,140,000	23,529,000
Shr earns:		
Income	1.33	1.03
Net income ..	.91	.99

a-From early retirement of debt.

FIRSTPLUS FINANCIAL GR (Nq)

Quar Sept 30:	1997	1996
Net income	$49,608,000	$13,378,000
Avg shares	39,061,000	a27,882,000
Shr earns (primary):		
Net income ..	1.27	a.48
Shr earns (fully diluted):		
Net income ..	1.16	a.45
Year:		
Net income	139,169,000	34,212,000
Avg shares	35,242,000	a25,358,000
Shr earns (primary):		
Net income ..	3.95	a1.35
Shr earns (fully diluted):		
Net income ..	3.52	a1.31

a-Adjusted for a two-for-one stock split paid in November 1996.

§11.5 Cumulative and Noncumulative Dividends

Preferred stock may be **cumulative**, **noncumulative**, or **partially cumu-lative**. If **cumulative dividends** are not paid in some years, they are carried forward and both they and the current year's preferred dividends must be paid in full before any common dividends may be declared. Noncumulative dividends disappear each year if they are not paid. Partially cumulative dividends are usually cumulative to the extent of earnings (i.e., the dividend is cumulative in any year only to the extent of actual earnings during that year). Unpaid cumulative dividends are not debts of the corporation, but a continued right to priority in future distributions.

An example may help to illustrate the concept of cumulative, noncumula-tive, and partially cumulative dividends. Assume that a preferred stock has a preferential right to a dividend of $5 per share per year, but the directors, as is their right, decide to omit all dividends for two consecutive years. In the third year, the directors conclude that the corporation is able to resume the payment of dividends. If the preferred shares' preferential right is cumulative, the board of directors must pay $15 on each preferred share ($5 per share for each of the two years missed plus $5 per share for the current year) before any dividend may be paid on the common shares in the third year. If the preferred shares' preferential right is noncumulative, the preferences for the two omitted years disappear entirely, and a dividend on the common shares may be paid after the $5 preferred dividend for the third year is paid. If the dividend is cumulative to the extent earned, the earnings of the corporation in each of the two years in which dividends were omitted must be examined, and the dividend is cumulative each year only to the extent the earnings cover the $5 preferred dividend: If the corporation had a loss in one of those years, the preferred dividend for that year would be lost much as though the dividend were entirely noncumulative.

In evaluating dividend policies with respect to preferred shares, one should normally start with the assumption that the board of directors, which is elected by the common shareholders, will normally maximize the dividends payable on common shares at the expense of preferred shareholders to the extent they lawfully may do so. A noncumulative preferential dividend right therefore leaves the preferred shareholders quite exposed, because the common shareholders' position is improved in the future whenever a preferred dividend is omitted. Indeed, a policy of paying dividends erratically once every few years materially improves the position of the common shares with respect to the noncumulative preferred. Such a policy, however, may be subject to legal attack as a breach of the directors' fiduciary duty to treat all classes of outstanding shares fairly.

Cumulative dividends provide preferred shareholders considerably greater protection than noncumulative or partially cumulative dividends. But cumula-tive dividends are not a complete answer either, because the board of directors may defer the payment of all dividends indefinitely in an effort to depress the price of the preferred (if it is publicly traded), which may then be acquired on the open market. On the other hand, it is customary to provide that preferred shares may elect a specified number of directors if preferred dividends have been omitted for a specified period, and the presence of one or more directors elected by the preferred shareholders may minimize the possibility of such overtly unfair strategies.

§11.6 Convertible Shares

Preferred shares may be made convertible at the option of the preferred shareholder into common shares at a specified price or a specified ratio. When **convertible shares** are converted, the original preferred shares are turned in and canceled, and new common shares are issued. The **conversion price** or ratio is fixed and defined in the preferred shareholders' contract. The **conversion ratio** is usually made adjustable for share dividends, share splits, the issuance of additional common shares, and similar transactions affecting the underlying common shares. The provisions requiring such adjustments are called **anti-dilution provisions**.

The determination of the conversion ratio (i.e., how many shares of common stock a preferred shareholder receives upon the exercise of the conversion privilege) may involve negotiation between the corporation and a potential investor before the shares are issued. Convertible preferred stock may be issued to a venture capital fund or other investor in a closely held corporation to reflect a limited equity investment in the enterprise. Publicly held corporations may also issue convertible preferred stock, which may be publicly traded. Typically, when both the common and the convertible preferred are publicly traded, the original conversion ratio is established so that the common must appreciate substantially in price before it becomes attractive to convert the preferred into common. A similar combination of risk and reward can be achieved by the sale of a preferred stock with a warrant to purchase common shares attached. Convertible preferred shares are quite common. There has been an extended and rather inconclusive theoretical discussion about why this particular security is so popular.

The conversions discussed in this section are **downstream conversions** (or downhill conversions). An **upstream conversion** (or uphill conversion) is from common shares into preferred shares (or from preferred shares to debt). Securities with upstream conversion rights are extremely rare, and may not be permitted at all under the statutes of some states.

§11.7 Redeemability of Preferred Shares

Preferred shares are usually made **redeemable** at the option of the corporation upon the payment of a fixed amount for each share. These shares may also be called **callable shares**. The **redemption price** is set in the articles of incorporation or the document creating the preferred shares and may be a matter of preissue negotiation between the corporation and an investor. Redemption prices are usually established at a level somewhat higher than the consideration that the investor originally paid for the preferred shares.

The power to redeem preferred shares usually applies only to the entire class or series of preferred as a unit. However, the preferred shareholders' contract sometimes provides that redemptions of a portion of a class or series are permitted; such provisions may also include rules for determining which shares are to be redeemed. If a convertible preferred is called for redemption, the conversion privilege typically continues after the announcement that the

shares will be called for redemption until the shares are actually redeemed. In some cases, conversion rights are triggered by a call for redemption.

§11.8 Series and Classes of Preferred Shares

Articles of incorporation may authorize preferred shares to be issued in **series**. The articles of incorporation in effect create a class of shares without any substantive terms (sometimes also called **blank check stock**) and authorize the board of directors to create series from within that class from time to time and to vary any of the substantive terms of each series. When preferred shares are to be sold by a corporation from time to time, allowing the board of directors to set financial terms simplifies financing, because the price, dividend, liquidation preference, sinking fund provision, voting rights, and other terms of each series may be tailored to then-current market conditions without incurring the expense of a proxy solicitation and the holding of a special shareholders' meeting to approve an amendment to the articles of incorporation setting forth the terms of the class. Shares of different series have identical rights except for the specified terms, which may be varied.

The power to create series of preferred shares may also be used by boards of directors of publicly held corporations to create **poison pills** without shareholder approval, as a defense against hostile takeovers. Poison pills are discussed more fully in Chapter 13.

There is little or no difference between a series or a class of shares except their manner of creation — by amendment to the articles of incorporation in the case of a class and by action of the board of directors, acting alone, in the case of a series. Indeed, the issuance of a new series of preferred usually requires that the corporation file an amendment to the articles of incorporation although no vote of the shareholders is required.

§11.9 Novel Types of Preferred Shares

The high interest rates of the early 1980s led to the development of novel financing devices, many of which involved preferred shares. For example, many corporations issued preferred shares that were redeemable at the holder's option, or that became redeemable upon the occurrence of some external event, such as a change in interest rates or the lapse of a specified period of time. Still other corporations issued preferred shares with floating or adjustable dividend rates that depended on interest rates or some similar measure. These novel preferred were designed to give corporate holders of the preferred the tax benefits of the exclusion for intercorporate dividends, while at the same time giving the holders most of the benefits of traditional debt.

§11.10 Market Price of Simple Preferred Shares

Many preferred shares are publicly traded on the major securities exchanges. Many are listed on the New York Stock Exchange. Most publicly

traded preferred shares have fixed and fully cumulative dividend rights. As a practical matter, in the case of most of these preferred shares, there is virtually no chance that a dividend will ever be omitted. In effect, these securities, like publicly traded bonds, provide a permanent cash flow in a fixed amount. The value placed on these shares in the market represents little more than the present value of this discounted future cash flow. The yields on high-quality preferred shares (the return per dollar invested in the shares) was about 8 percent in the fall of 1996. At the same time, the yield on investment quality bonds was about 7 percent. This difference in yields presumably reflects the fact that interest payments on bonds are contractually required, while dividends on preferred shares are at the discretion of the board of directors and may legally be suspended without constituting a breach of contract.

§11.11 Market Price of Convertible Preferred Shares and Arbitrage

The pricing of a **convertible** preferred is considerably more complex than the pricing of a nonconvertible preferred. Assume that a publicly held corporation has outstanding several million shares of common stock traded on the New York Stock Exchange. The current market price of the common is $20 per share, and management believes that it is likely to trade in the $20–$30 range for the indefinite future. A regular dividend of $1 per share has been paid on the common shares for the last three years, and management anticipates that this regular dividend will be continued at that rate for the indefinite future. In order to raise additional working capital, the corporation decides to make a public offering of a new class of convertible preferred shares with the following rights: It is to be entitled to a cumulative dividend of $6 per share per year and will be offered initially to the public at $54 per share in order to yield an initial investor an 11 percent return, the approximate yield of similar convertible preferred shares. There is no appreciable risk that the $6 dividend will be omitted in any year in the foreseeable future. The preferred share is convertible into two shares of common stock at any time at the option of the holder and is callable by the corporation at any time for $65 per share. It is anticipated that the preferred will also be publicly traded on the New York Stock Exchange. The basic financial characteristics described in this paragraph may be summarized:

	Preferred shares	Common shares
Market price	$54	$20
Dividend	$ 6	$ 1
Convertibility into common	2:1	N/A
Callability	$65	N/A

When the preferred is issued, it begins to trade between $52 and $60 per share. At that price, no one exercises the conversion privilege: After all, why give up something worth $52 to $60 in order to acquire two shares of stock that can be bought for $40? Similarly, the corporation probably will not give

313

serious consideration to calling the preferred at $65. If the corporation wishes to retire some preferred shares, it may buy them for $52 to $60. Why pay $65?

Now consider what happens to the price of the preferred when the price of the common begins to creep up. When it reaches $27.50 per share, the value of two shares of common has risen to $55, and the preferred must remain at or above $55 per share. If it drops to $53, traders can buy the preferred at $53 and convert it into common shares that can be immediately sold for $55, making an instant $2 profit. This type of transaction is known as **arbitrage**, a fancy term for the process of profiting on small differences in market prices of two different but equivalent securities or in the market prices of the same security in two different markets.

Assume now that the price of the common rises further to $32 per share. The floor under the preferred is now $64, and every purchaser of the initial preferred at $54 has made a tidy paper profit of at least $10 per share. (It is only a paper profit, because it has not been realized either by the sale of the preferred or by its conversion into common and the sale of the common.) More important, when the common is at $32, the preferred is no longer priced in the market as a straight preferred. Rather, its price is now directly tied to the price of the common in accordance with the conversion ratio. If the common declines in price by $1 per share, the preferred will decline by about $2 per share; if the common goes up by $3 per share to $35, the preferred will go up by about $6 per share. If the price of the common plummets falls, the preferred will follow the common down (at a $2 decline per preferred share for each $1 decline in value of the common) until the preferred reaches a price that reflects its market value as a preferred stock (plus the value of an option to buy two shares of commons at $27.50 per share); at that point, it will again trade much as a straight preferred.

Assuming that the common is trading for $32 per share, what price will the market place on the preferred? Will it be $64 or will it be even higher? At first it may seem that it must be higher than $64: if two shares of common with an aggregate $2 dividend sell for $64, a stock with the same market characteristics but with a $6 dividend is going to be worth more. How much more? One might expect it would be the present value of the stream of the $4 difference between the two dividends. It will, however, be much less than that, because it is unlikely that the difference in dividend rates will continue indefinitely. The corporation may call the preferred at some time in the future, and the $32 price may itself reflect the market anticipating an increase in the common dividend rate. It is not possible to calculate the values to be assigned to these variables mathematically and thus what the price of the preferred should be, except to conclude that it must be higher than $64—perhaps $67 or $68.

Another interesting question is this: Should a holder of the preferred convert when the common is at $32 if he believes that the price of the common will go even higher? A moment's thought should reveal that would be an unwise decision. Why give up a $6 cumulative dividend in order to obtain two common shares with a combined dividend of $2 per share? There is no risk that the expected increase in price of the common will escape the owner of the preferred, because the price of the preferred is now directly tied to the price of the common. In short, there is nothing to be gained and much to be lost by converting immediately.

§11.12 Redemption of Convertible Preferred Shares

Consider the factors relating to the corporation's power to call the preferred shares for redemption at $65 per share. A critical point is that the corporation must announce an impending redemption in advance. The privilege to convert continues after the announcement and until the redemption becomes effective.

What happens after a call for redemption is issued depends essentially on the price of the underlying common shares at the time the redemption actually occurs. If the market price of two shares of common stock is less than $65 per share, shareholders should not convert their preferred shares into common stock, but rather should permit the shares to be called at $65 per share. Thus, if the corporation calls the shares for redemption when the price of the underlying common is $32.50 or less, it should end up redeeming the entire issue for cash. On the other hand, if the market price of the common is above $32.50 per share at the time of redemption, the shareholders should exercise the conversion privilege shortly before the call becomes effective and convert the preferred into the more valuable common. For example, if the common is at $35 per share, the choice is between permitting the shares to be called for a payment of $65 or converting them into shares of common stock worth $70. Such a conversion is sometimes called a **forced conversion**, because the economics are such that a rational investor has no choice but to exercise his or her power to convert (or to sell the preferred, in which case the purchaser will convert).

In the real world, things do not work perfectly. Preferred shareholders are scattered around the country and may not be able to select the best option at the very last minute. Some must decide several days in advance of the final date, and a last-minute price movement of the common may mean that some make the wrong decision. Also, a few may simply act too late, and find that their shares were redeemed when they intended to exercise the conversion privilege. Still others may be ill, out of the country, or unaware of the pending redemption or indeed of the fact that they own the shares of preferred stock, and make no decision at all. But the great bulk of shares will be handled rationally.

Why do corporations try to compel conversions? One reason is that the substitution of two shares of common for every share of preferred causes a reduction in dividend payments from $6 to $2 for every share of preferred. This reduction in dividend payments is pure gravy, because there is no capital outflow to eliminate the more expensive preferred shares. A forced conversion may also appeal to notions of equity as between holders of common and preferred, because the preferred receives the full benefit of runups in the price of the common but enjoys three times the dividend and has some protection against price declines on the downside. Finally, the elimination of the preferred shares simplifies the capital structure of the corporation and improves the appearance of the corporation's balance sheet.

If the directors call a convertible preferred for redemption, they are required to give the holders of the preferred accurate information about the reasons for the redemption. The corporation may not withhold from the preferred shareholders information regarding developments that would affect the decision of whether to convert the shares.

§11.13 Protection of Conversion Privilege Against Dilution

In the example discussed in the last section, each share of the preferred stock is entitled to be converted into two shares of common stock. What happens if the board of directors decides to split the common shares, which are trading for $30, three-for-one—that is, the board decides to issue each shareholder two additional shares for each outstanding share so that each shareholder would have three shares instead of one? Let us further assume that the dividend rate on the new shares is one-third the rate on the old shares so that each new share sells for one-third of the price of each old share—about $10 per share if the old shares sold for approximately $30 per share before the split. What does this do to the conversion privilege of the preferred?

The black letter rule is very simple: If the drafters of the preferred shareholders' contract did not take this possibility into account, the conversion privilege is not adjusted for the share split. Each preferred share continues to be convertible into only two shares of common stock and the conversion privilege has lost two-thirds of its potential value. Provisions guarding the conversion privilege against changes of this type are called **anti-dilution provisions** and should always be included in preferred shareholders' contracts when there is a conversion privilege. Drafting an anti-dilution clause is tricky, because the courts are not going to help the draftsman out if he or she overlooks some possibility. Significant dilution may occur because of a variety of transactions, such as mergers, share dividends, executive compensation plans, and the like, and it is not always clear which issuances of new common shares the anti-dilution clause should cover. Nevertheless, the basic principle seems clear and straightforward, at least so far as shares splits are concerned: The drafters of the preferred shareholders contract should insert a clause providing that if the common stock is split, the conversion privilege should be adjusted so that each share of preferred is convertible into the number of new common shares that two shares of the old common stock became upon the split.

§11.14 Classified Common Stock

State statutes give corporations broad power to create classes of common shares with different rights or privileges. For example, the rights of two classes of shares may be identical except that one class is entitled to twice the dividend per share of the second class. Or, shares of each class may have identical financial rights per share but each class of common shares, regardless of the number of shares, is entitled to elect one director (thereby assuring equal class representation on the board of directors even though the number of shares in the two classes are unequal). Classes of shares are widely used in closely held corporations.

Publicly held corporations also use classified common shares, although their use is not widespread. The New York Stock Exchange has historically refused to list shares of a corporation if the corporation also has a class of nonvoting shares or one or more classes with fractional or multiple votes per share.

Since the 1980s, several publicly held corporations have created **dual class voting structures**. This device is often used in corporations in which a given family has long been in control but is now concerned that a takeover attempt may be in the offing. With dual class voting, special classes of shares with "super" voting rights may be issued solely to family members. The terms of these special classes may provide, for example, that family-owed shares have 10 votes per share, but their voting power declines to 1 vote per share if they are sold or conveyed to a person who is not a family member. Dual class voting permits the controlling family to retain voting control over the corporation while at the same time permitting the corporation to raise capital through the sale of common shares. In 1988, the SEC adopted Rule 19c-4, which in effect outlawed new classes of such shares for publicly traded corporations, but the courts invalidated this rule as exceeding the powers of the SEC, which basically are limited to enforcing disclosure rules.

A similar gimmick is the creation of **tenure voting** common stock, permitting shareholders who have held their shares for a specified period (e.g., for 36 months to have 5 votes per share). If shares are transferred, the new holder has 1 vote per share until his holding period exceeds 36 months, when the shareholder regains the right to 5 votes per share. Tenure voting discourages takeover attempts, because a bidder who acquires shares finds his or her voting power significantly reduced.

Both dual class and tenure voting shares have generally been upheld under state law, at least in Delaware. However, the SEC has consistently attacked these devices as being discriminatory and unfair to public shareholders. Despite the invalidation of Rule 19c-4, the SEC has persuaded the securities exchanges to keep rules that require the **delisting** of corporations that issue dual class or tenure voting shares. Delisting means that the shares of that corporation cannot thereafter be traded on that exchange.

§11.15 Transferable Warrants and Rights to Purchase Shares

Corporations may issue **warrants** or **rights** to purchase common shares. Warrants and rights are options to purchase shares at a fixed price during some defined time period. If the common shares are publicly traded, the warrants or rights may also be publicly traded.

Warrants are transferable long-term options to acquire shares from the corporation at a specified price. Warrants have many of the qualities of an equity security, because their price is a function of the market price of the underlying shares and the specified issuance price. Warrants have no voting or dividend rights. Warrants are often issued as a sweetener in connection with the distribution of a debt or preferred stock issue. They may also be issued in connection with a public exchange offer, or as compensation for handling the public distribution of other shares. Sometimes they are issued in a reorganization to holders of a class of security not otherwise recognized in the reorganization.

Rights are short-term warrants, expiring within one year. They may also

be publicly traded and listed on securities exchanges. Rights are often issued in lieu of a dividend, or in an effort to raise capital from existing shareholders.

The price relationship between a warrant or right and the underlying security is a complex one. The value of any option has two components: **intrinsic value** and **time value**. For example, if the underlying security is selling at $15 per share, and the warrant can be exercised for $12 per share, the warrant has an intrinsic value of $3; one can exercise the option and immediately sell the shares for a $3 gain. If, on the other hand, the value of the underlying security is $10 per share, one might expect that the warrant would have no value. After all, who wants a right to purchase for $12 per share something that can be bought for $10? In fact, such a warrant has some value because of the possibility that the underlying security may rise in price above $12 during the life of the warrant. This value is called the time value of the option. If the time period before expiration is relatively short, or if the exercise price is much higher than the value of the underlying security, the time value of the option is very low, perhaps only a few cents per warrant. But all options have some time value.

If the underlying security does rise above $12 per share in the above example, the market price of the warrant will also rise in value almost dollar-for-dollar. Whether it would be sensible to exercise such a warrant before its expiration depends on the income forgone on the amount paid to exercise the warrant compared with the dividends likely to be declared on the underlying security.

§11.16 Bonds and Debentures

The two types of debt instruments most commonly classed as securities are **bonds** and **debentures**. These types of securities may be publicly traded and have close economic similarities to publicly traded preferred stock.

Technically, a debenture is an unsecured corporate obligation, while a bond is secured by a lien or mortgage on specific corporate property. However, the word "bond" is often used to mean both bonds and debentures; this chapter will use it this way hereafter. The presence or absence of security in the form of a lien or mortgage for marketable debt interests is not as important as might be supposed, because if bondholders attempt to foreclose on corporate property, the corporation will obtain protection from the federal bankruptcy court and the attempt to levy upon the property will be stayed.

Debt securities are unconditional obligations to pay specific sums at a date in the future and usually to pay interest in specified amounts at specified times in the interim. They are long-term debt securities with maturities of 50 years or more in some cases, though 30 years is more common, and many bonds mature in 10 years or less.

Historically, bonds were **bearer securities**, negotiable by delivery, with interest payments represented by coupons that were periodically clipped and submitted to the issuer for payment. The Internal Revenue Code now requires virtually all new bonds to be **registered securities**, transferable only by endorsement, and as a result, bearer bonds have largely disappeared or have been made into registered securities. Registered securities are made payable to a specific

payee and interest is paid to the registered owner by check or wire transfer in much the same way as dividends are paid to the registered owner of shares of stock. A bearer instrument can be transformed into a registered security at any time. Transfer of a registered bond is effected by endorsement rather than by mere physical delivery of the piece of paper. Article 8 of the Uniform Commercial Code makes registered bonds negotiable just like any other security.

Interest payments on debt securities are usually fixed obligations expressed as a percentage of the face amount of the bond and payable irrespective of the financial performance of the issuing company. However, so-called income bonds, in which the obligation to pay interest is conditioned on adequate earnings, also exist. Somewhat rarer are so-called **participating bonds**, where the amount of interest payable on the bonds increases with earnings. These securities are known as hybrid securities because they have some characteristics of an equity security. In recent years, debt securities with variable or floating interest rates — based on market interest rates — have also been created.

Debt securities are usually subject to redemption, often at a slight premium over face value. Unlike redemption of preferred shares, individual bonds may usually be redeemed without redeeming the entire issue. Bonds selected for redemption may be chosen by lot or by some other system. Many debt securities require the corporation to create sinking funds to redeem a part of the issue each year or to accumulate to pay off the entire issue when it matures. Similar provisions are also common in connection with issues of preferred stock.

Debt securities, like preferred stock, may also be made convertible into equity securities — almost always common shares — on some predetermined ratio. The conversion privilege for bonds operates in a very similar manner to conversion privilege for preferred shares discussed above, except that with bonds the bond indenture (the instrument that sets forth the terms of the bonds) specifies some dollar amount of bonds per share of stock, because bonds are not issued in any share-like units. Like convertible preferred, the conversion ratio is usually protected against dilution by adjustments for share splits and share dividends. When convertible bonds are converted, they and the debt they represent disappear and new equity securities are issued in their place. Convertible bonds are treated as equity securities for some purposes; in calculating fully diluted earnings per share, for example, the common shares that would be issued upon conversion are taken into account in the calculation.

The interaction between the power of the corporation to call convertible debentures and the power of the holder to exercise the conversion privilege is similar to that of preferred shares. If a convertible debenture is called for redemption, the conversion privilege continues until the debentures are actually redeemed. If the value of the stock exceeds the redemption price, the conversion is forced, because it is obviously to the holders' advantage to convert following an announcement that the debentures will be called for redemption on a specified date. A conversion of bonds cleans up the balance sheet by substituting equity for debt, reducing the debt/equity ratio and otherwise appearing to improve the financial health of the business.

When debt securities mature, the issuer may borrow funds (perhaps by creating a new debt issue maturing far in the future) to pay off the maturing obligations. This process is known as **rolling over** the debt.

Although debt securities are similar in many respects to preferred stock, there are some important legal differences that may affect the value of these securities. Table 11-2 sets forth the most important similarities and differences between these two types of securities.

§11.17 Private Placements

Private placement refers to the raising of capital by the sale of securities directly to large investors. The advantages of private placement over the public sale of securities include cost savings, because registration of the issue with the SEC is unnecessary and no selling efforts are required. In addition, restrictions on the issuer's future actions are directly negotiated with the suppliers of credit and the possibility of future litigation is reduced. A significant fraction of all new issues each year—hundreds of billions of dollars of securities—are placed

Table 11-2

Characteristic	*Preferred stock*	*Bonds*
Manner of creation of new classes or issues	Amendment to articles of incorporation	Action by directors alone without shareholder approval
Maturity date	No	Yes
Voting	Usually only if dividend omitted	Rarely (prohibited in most states)
Treatment on balance sheet	Equity	Debt
Interim payments	Dividend	Interest
Amount	Fixed (usually)	Fixed (usually)
Omission of	No default; carries over if cumulative	Default
Tax effect on issuer	Not deductible	Deductible
Tax effect on recipient	Taxable, but dividend credit if receipient is corporation	Taxable
Callable	Usually	Usually
Convertible	Optional	Optional
Effect of conversion into common	Does not affect capital or debt/equity ratio; reduces dividend rates by difference between common and preferred rates; increases number of common shares	Reduces debt and increases equity; affects debt/equity ratio; eliminates interest payments; increases number of shares

privately. In recent years, pension funds have become major purchasers of privately placed securities.

§11.18 Record and Nominee Ownership of Securities

Historically, equity securities were registered in the name of the owner on the books of the issuing corporation, while debt instruments were issued in the form of bearer securities. As a consequence, the issuer knew fairly precisely who the owners of its equity securities were and could communicate with them, but it knew nothing about who owned its debt securities. The corporation could pay a dividend by check to each registered owner of shares but could make interest payments on its debt securities only when it received the interest coupons with instructions as to where to make the payment. Numerous other practical differences existed between these two forms of ownership.

In the early 1900s, practices developed that blurred the distinction between registered and bearer securities, at least in the case of stock. One practice developed by institutional investors involved using **nominees** as **record owners** of equity securities rather than registering the securities directly in their own names. This practice originally developed apparently in order to avoid onerous legal requirements that existed in many states that required fiduciaries who were designated as record owners of certificates to exhibit evidence of their authority to transfer the securities. Using a nominee (such as Abell and Company) avoided these legal requirements, because there was no evidence of fiduciary responsibility on the certificates themselves.

The second practice that blurred the distinction between registered and bearer securities was the growth of the practice of registering shares in **street name**. If a trader purchased shares of stock planning to resell them in the near future when the price rose, it was often not convenient to register the ownership in the name of the trader for the few days that he or she might hold them. Instead, shares were registered in the name of the brokerage firm handling the trade and the obligation of traders to receive or deliver securities was met simply by delivery of these street name certificates. These certificates became in effect bearer securities.

In the 1960s and 1970s, trading volume increased dramatically, and the street name system broke down in what became known as the back office crisis. The physical delivery of street name certificates simply could not keep up with the volume of trading. An entirely new system of securities ownership was created, which has become the standard for both equity and debt securities. This new system is called the **book entry** system and is quite different from the historical nominee and street name practices outlined above. Because the system has elements of nominee and street name practices, however, one sometimes sees references to securities held in book entry form as involving street name or nominee ownership.

To see how this new system works, assume that you decide to purchase 100 shares of General Motors. This transaction will be handled by a securities broker; after he purchases the shares on your behalf, you will need to provide the funds necessary to pay for the shares within three days of the transaction.

You will not, however, receive a certificate for those shares (unless you make special arrangements to do so, which may include a separate fee for providing a certificate). Rather, you will simply receive a confirmation of the transaction, and thereafter a monthly statement from your broker that shows that you own 100 shares of General Motors. When General Motors pays a dividend, the correct dividend will be added to your account (or you may arrange for the broker to send a check to you for the amount of each dividend). You will receive periodic reports, proxy statement, annual reports, and the like, all prepared by General Motors, but they will come through your broker or through a company that has a contract with your broker to forward these documents to individual shareholders. When you decide to sell your shares of General Motors, you simply call your broker and the proceeds will be added to your account three days after the sale.

This is obviously much more convenient than the old system, but to the user, it is not obvious how it works. What happens to the certificates? Today, the registered owner of the great bulk of all publicly traded securities is Cede & Company, the nominee for the Depository Trust Company (the DTC). The DTC is the principal clearing house for securities transactions in the United States. Banks, institutional investors, and securities are members of the DTC (or have affiliations with members of the DTC). Basically, certificates are immobilized in the DTC and transactions are recorded by a netting process and book entry. When you purchased the 100 shares of General Motors described above, your broker may have sold shares of General Motors owned by other customers the same day. At the end of the day, your broker reports to the DTC its net change in General Motors shares in transactions with all other members of the DTC. If it turns out that your broker had only one sale of 100 shares of General Motors and you were the sole purchaser of shares of General Motors on the day of your purchase, your broker will adjust its records to show that the seller no longer owned the 100 shares and that you now owned the shares. The movement of share ownership is reflected solely by book entry. The DTC handles net changes in ownership interests of its members in exactly the same way. If it turns out that your broker had no sales of General Motors stock on the day of your purchase, it would report to the DTC that its holdings of General Motors increased by 100 shares, while the records of some other firm would be adjusted to reflect that someone sold 100 shares of General Motors to your broker. Today, transfers of securities are reflected by book entries, not by movements of certificates.

So where is the certificate for the 100 shares of General Motors that you bought? It is most likely to be part of a jumbo certificate for millions of shares issued by General Motors in the name of Cede & Company in the vaults of the DTC. Money and shares move around from investor to investor, but the certificates remain in the DTC's vault.

If you decide you want a certificate for your shares of General Motors, your broker will contact the DTC, which in turn will arrange for General Motors to issue a certificate in your name. But that is a nuisance and many investors do not bother. If you do obtain a share certificate, you may take possession of it yourself or leave it with the brokerage firm for safekeeping. If you later decide to sell these shares, you must arrange to endorse the certificates so that they may be transferred.

The book entry system is popular with brokers not only because of its simplicity, but also because it tends to tie the customer closely to the brokerage firm. A holder of shares held in book entry can sell the shares only through the broker who has a record of the ownership. Although it is possible to transfer shares from one brokerage firm to another, an investor may be reluctant to do so and it is certainly not encouraged by brokerage firms.

The book entry system is used for both debt and equity securities. Private placements of debt securities are routinely handled in book entry form. Interest and dividend payments are made by wire transfer to brokerage firms or institutional investors. Old habits, however, sometimes die hard. Some individual investors do not trust the new system of book entry and continue to request certificates. Today, these people are in the minority.

As one reflects on this system, it is clear that the solvency and honesty of brokerage firms is an essential element of the system. It is also a potential source of weakness. A brokerage firm may own shares of General Motors in its own proprietary account as well as holding shares for its customers. SEC regulations (and the revised Article 8 of the Uniform Commercial Code) require such a firm to separate its proprietary ownership on its own records and not to sell or **hypothecate** (borrow against) its customers' securities without their consent. However, a firm that is in financial difficulty may violate these rules or simply convert customer securities to its own use. A federally chartered corporation, the **Securities Investor Protection Corporation** (the **SIPC**), protects customers against loss caused by brokerage firm failure (up to specific limits). However, it is possible that a customer may own securities that exceed the coverage that the SIPC provides, and to that extent investors are at risk of loss because of the book entry system.

The book entry system is undoubtedly an ingenious solution to the problems created by the current volume of securities transactions. The SEC has, however, long considered it to be an interim solution. Not only is there a possibility that customers may lose valuable assets through the defalcation of brokers, but also there are problems of brokerage control over securities transactions of customers and of communication between the issuers and shareholders. Communication problems arise because of the presence of at least two intermediaries between issuer and shareholder—the DTC and the customer's broker.

The long-term solution that the SEC envisions is the elimination of all share certificates and the substitution of certificate-less shares with ownership records being kept by the issuer or its transfer agent. Transfers of shares would be recorded in the books of the issuer and not of the broker. This solution would require sophisticated computer technology. Moreover, the current intermediaries are not in favor of the idea for obvious reasons. Still, the SEC has begun the first steps toward implementing this broad vision.

§11.19 Lost or Missing Certificates

An investor who permits his or her securities to be held in book entry form by a broker need not be concerned about the whereabouts of certificates for securities or bearer bonds. If, however, the investor personally wishes to main-

tain the tangible evidence of ownership and take delivery of certificates (perhaps because it affords freedom to shift among brokerage firms in order to pay the lowest commissions on trades), he or she usually rents a safe deposit box at a local bank as a secure place to keep the certificates. A safe deposit box, however, requires inconvenient and time-consuming trips to the bank whenever securities are purchased or sold. Another alternative is to leave the certificates with the broker for safekeeping. Some investors, however, use desk drawers, files in filing cabinets, and even the sock drawer as the storage place for securities. It is therefore not surprising that certificates are sometimes lost, stolen, mislaid, or inadvertently destroyed.

There is a well-established process by which certificates may be replaced. The process is time-consuming, taking from a minimum of about two weeks for share certificates to as long as four months for some bonds. During this time, the investor is "locked in" and unable to sell the securities. It is also expensive. It costs $200 to $400 to replace a certificate worth about $10,000.

When securities are lost, stolen, or misplaced, the investor's first step is to notify the issuer of the securities in writing. The investor will probably be referred to the transfer agent (for stock) or to a trustee (for a debt instrument). The agent or trustee places a "stop" on the certificate and notifies a central data base that it is missing. Brokerage firms and banks must contact this data base before buying shares or bonds from an unknown customer if the transaction involves $10,000 or more.

The investor is sent an affidavit of loss, which must be filled out and notarized. The investor must also purchase a "surety" or "indemnity" bond to protect the issuer and potential buyers in case the lost security has been negotiated. Some brokers assist customers with this paperwork, either for free or for a nominal charge, usually less than $20. The premium for the bond is usually from 2 to 4 percent of the market value of the securities. If the certificates show up within a year, some insurance companies may refund 50 percent of this premium, but others do not. Because bearer bonds are particularly susceptible to theft without discovery, some issuers require investors who lose them to buy a surety bond equal to twice the value of the lost securities.

CHAPTER 12

DIVIDENDS AND DISTRIBUTIONS

§12.1 Introduction

This chapter deals with dividends and distributions in connection with common stock. The following discussion is primarily directed to issues in publicly held corporations but considers the legality of distributions and dividends in closely held enterprises in order to give a picture of statutory regulation of distributions. The material in this chapter requires knowledge of financial statements as discussed in earlier chapters.

The word "**distribution**" in corporation law is a general term referring to any kind of payment (in cash, property, or obligations of indebtedness) by the corporation to one or more shareholders on account of the ownership of shares. The word "**dividend**" is usually understood to be a narrower term referring to a pro rata distribution to one or more classes of shareholders by the corporation usually out of its current or retained earnings. An example of a distribution that is not a dividend is a partial payment to shareholders by a solvent corporation in the process of liquidation.

Payments to a shareholder in the form of salary, interest, or rent are not normally viewed as distributions because they are on account of services rendered or property supplied to the corporation by its shareholders rather than on account of the ownership of shares. In the case of a closely held corporation, however, if the payments are so large as to bear no reasonable relationship to the value of the services or property, all or part of the payment may be viewed as a disguised or informal dividend or distribution.

Several different and superficially unrelated transactions have the effect of making distributions to shareholders. In some states with older statutes, different legal rules may apply in determining the lawfulness of a distribution depending on the type of transaction involved, but modern statutes seek to apply a single legal standard to all distributions without regard to their form.

§12.2 Distributions of Money or Property

The most common and best-known kind of distribution is a simple payment of money by the corporation to each shareholder, the amount of which is proportional to the number of shares that each shareholder owns. A corporation may also make a distribution of property other than cash, though such distributions create practical problems if the corporation has more than a handful of shareholders. Property, unlike money, is usually not readily divisible. A distribution of undivided interests in a piece of improved real estate, for example, is likely to create problems of management and control thereafter. Further, undivided interests in property may be difficult to sell except to other owners of undivided interests in the property who may be interested in reassembling the property for sale. Distributions of undivided interests in property are nevertheless sufficiently common for the corporate literature to distinguish between cash dividends and property dividends, and while most property dividends are made by closely held corporations, one sometimes encounters proposed distributions of property by publicly held corporations.

§12.3 Share Repurchases

A very important type of distributive transaction is the purchase by a corporation of its own shares. This type of transaction is often called a **share repurchase** or **share buyback.** Superficially, a purchase of shares by the corporation may not be thought of as involving a distribution at all. It appears to be the purchase of an asset rather than the making of a distribution. That analysis, however, confuses transactions in which the corporation repurchases its own shares and transactions in which it purchases shares that another corporation issues. The former is a distribution, the latter is an investment.

When a corporation buys back its own shares, it does not receive anything of value. The remaining shareholders continue to own 100 percent of the corporate assets (now reduced by the amount of the payment used to reacquire the shares). A corporation cannot treat stock in itself that it has purchased as an asset any more than it can treat its authorized but unissued shares as an asset.

One cannot own 10 percent of oneself and have one's total worth be 110 percent of the value of one's assets. Shares that another corporation issues are entirely different. Shares of Corporation B have value based on the assets that Corporation B owns; if shares of Corporation B are purchased by Corporation A, they are an asset in the hands of Corporation A.

The fact that a repurchase of shares constitutes a distribution can be most easily appreciated by considering a proportionate repurchase of stock in a closely held corporation. Assume that three persons each own 100 shares of stock in a corporation. The shareholders decide that each of them will sell 10 shares back to the corporation for $100 per share, or a total of $1,000 each. When the transaction is completed, each shareholder continues to own one-third of the corporation (now represented by 90 shares rather than 100 shares), the corporation has $3,000 less, and the shareholders each have $1,000 in cash. Clearly there has been a distribution even though the transaction was cast in the form of a repurchase of stock rather than as a dividend.

Under many state statutes, the 300 shares reacquired by the corporation in the previous example are called **treasury shares** and may be held by the corporation in a sort of twilight zone until they are either retired permanently or resold to someone else in the future. Treasury shares are not an asset, even though they may be sold at some later time. After all, exactly the same thing can be said of every share of authorized but unissued stock.

The difference between treasury shares and shares that other corporations issue is reflected in the accounting treatment of transactions in shares. When Corporation A buys shares in Corporation B, the transaction is reflected solely on the left-hand side of the balance sheet: The journal entry shows a reduction of cash and an increase in an asset account "investments in other corporations." However, when a corporation buys its own shares, the reduction of cash on the left-hand side of the balance sheet is offset by a reduction in one or more right-hand shareholders' equity accounts. A straight cash dividend is treated for accounting purposes in the same way: A reduction of the cash account on the left-hand side of the balance sheet is offset by a reduction in retained earnings or similar account on the right-hand side of the balance sheet.

A repurchase of shares by the corporation is a distribution even if the corporation purchases only shares that one shareholder owns rather than pro-portionately from each shareholder. Such a transaction is merely a dispropor-tionate distribution. The corporation has made a distribution to a single shareholder equal to the purchase price it paid for the shares. This transaction is not all bad from the standpoint of the other shareholders, however, because it simultaneously increases their percentage interest in the corporation. For example, if the corporation with three shareholders in the above example repurchased all 100 shares owned by Shareholder A for $10,000, the interests of Shareholders B and C in the corporation are each increased from 33.3 percent to 50 percent. The assets of the corporation are reduced by the $10,000 purchase price paid to Shareholder A to eliminate his or her interest in the corporation.

Distributions in the form of repurchases of shares are very common in real life. In closely held corporations, the elimination of one shareholder's interest in a corporation is almost always effected by a repurchase of shares by the

corporation. Such a transaction permits the use of corporate rather than personal assets, has favorable tax consequences, and does not affect the relative interests of the remaining shareholders.

§12.4 Share Repurchases by Publicly Held Corporations

Publicly held corporations routinely repurchase their own shares in open market transactions. The announcement of a share repurchase usually has a favorable, upward effect on share price. Indeed, it is not at all uncommon for a corporation to announce a very large possible buyback and thereafter repurchase far fewer than the maximum number of shares. In extreme cases, share buybacks may approach manipulation. One reason that is sometimes offered as to why buybacks increase the price of shares is that after the buyback, the number of outstanding shares will be reduced but the earnings of the corporation will not be significantly affected, so that earnings per share are likely to increase. There may be some truth in this explanation, but it assumes that the cash used to repurchase the shares did not generate income for the corporation.

Another reason for a share repurchase is that a publicly held corporation that has a large amount of excess liquid assets may easily become a target for takeover. Indeed, the liquid assets may be used by the bidder to pay back loans to finance part of the purchase of target shares. The alternative of paying a huge dividend may be less attractive because of federal income tax considerations: A dividend is taxable as ordinary income, while a buyback may give rise to capital gains treatment for those who sell shares back to the corporation. For those who do not sell shares, their reward is an increased value for the remaining shares.

A publicly held corporation may announce that it is buying back its own shares in order to have treasury shares available for a variety of possible uses (e.g., in compensation plans for executives or employees, or for acquisitions or other corporate purposes). It is sometimes difficult to accept these justifications at face value. More likely reasons are improvement of the market price for shares or a desire to reduce the attractiveness of the corporation as a takeover target. Nevertheless, a corporation that seeks to purchase another corporation with the purchase price being paid in shares rather than in cash may repurchase some of its own shares and offer them to the target, or it may simply issue new shares. A corporation may prefer to use repurchased shares because there is no dilutive effect on its own shareholders and because a market repurchase tends to protect or increase the market price of its own shares. In contrast, the use of new shares to purchase a target company may place downward pressure on the market price of the bidder's shares. Many of the same considerations apply to using new shares to provide incentive compensation for senior executive officers.

For the target of an unwanted takeover attempt, a common defensive tactic is to announce a major buyback in order to sop up extra cash that the corporation may have and to drive up the price of its shares to make the outside offer unattractive. Such a defense is generally tolerated by the courts because the repurchase also increases the percentage of shares that the bidder owns. Thus, a repurchase may backfire as a defensive tactic, because it increases the control value of shares that the bidder has already obtained.

§12.5 Distributions of Indebtedness

A corporation may also distribute obligations to make payments at some time in the future. The simplest way to do this is for the corporation to create instruments of indebtedness and distribute them directly to its shareholders. In closely held corporations, debt may be used to repurchase shares, because the corporation lacks ready assets to pay the full purchase price or does not want to borrow funds for this purpose or because the selling shareholder does not want to recognize all of the gain immediately for tax purposes. In any event, the use of debt means that, in effect, a portion of the agreed-on purchase price of shares is to be paid out of future cash flow.

Distributions of indebtedness are sometimes made by publicly held corporations to make the corporation unattractive as a possible takeover candidate. Often such debt will become payable in full upon any change in control. Such instruments are sometimes called **poison puts.**

§12.6 Legal Restrictions on Distributions

All state statutes contain provisions governing and restricting the power of corporations to make distributions. These statutory provisions are primarily of importance to closely held corporations, but they also apply to publicly held corporations.

These statutes are confusing, sometimes internally inconsistent or self-contradictory, and often incomplete in that they do not address some recurring issues relating to distributions. Dividend statutes contain two different types of prohibitions: (1) a capital protection provision that prohibits distributions that in some sense invade or reduce the permanent capital of the corporation, and (2) a fraudulent conveyance provision prohibiting distributions that have the effect of rendering the corporation unable to meet its obligations as they mature. The first test is usually referred to as the **balance sheet test** and the second as the **equity insolvency test.**

§12.7 The Balance Sheet Test

Statutes regulate and limit distributions by imposing restrictions on the right-hand balance sheet entries that may be debited for the payments. An oversimplified balance sheet should make this relationship clear:

Assets		Liabilities	
Cash	20,000	Bank loans	30,000
Other	40,000	Owners Equity	
		Common stock	20,000
		Earnings	
		current	3,000
		accumulated	7,000
	60,000		60,000

In the owners equity portion of the balance sheet, current earnings represent earnings of the present year, while retained earnings represent earnings from previous years not distributed in the form of dividends. The common stock entry represents what the shareholders paid for the stock when it was originally issued. Now let us assume that the corporation decides to distribute $6,000 to its shareholders. The payment of $6,000 will reduce cash by $6,000; the offsetting entry must be a reduction of some right-hand entry. The only real choices are current earnings or accumulated earnings. The legality of the distribution depends on what the state's distribution statute says about which right-hand accounts may be charged with the distribution and which may not. Because all state statutes permit the payment of dividends out of either current or retained earnings, the $6,000 payment is consistent with the balance sheet test in all states. This payment is still a dividend even though it is made in part out of earnings of prior years. The Internal Revenue Code follows the same pattern: The distribution of retained earnings is taxable as an ordinary dividend in the same manner as the distribution of current earnings. Following the payment of a dividend of $6,000, accumulated earnings available for the payment of dividends in future years would be reduced to $4,000 ($7,000 − $3,000, where $3,000 is the portion of the distribution that exceeds earnings for the year in question).

Now let us assume that the corporation wishes to distribute $15,000 to its shareholders. Can it do so? It probably can afford to in the sense that even after paying out $15,000, the corporation will have assets of $40,000 and liabilities of only $30,000. That, however, is not relevant under the balance sheet test. What is important under that test is which right-hand account or accounts are to reflect the $15,000. The earnings accounts can be reduced by $10,000 to $0 but the remaining $5,000 must be reflected as a reduction or invasion of capital. Another way of looking at this transaction is that the $15,000 payment represents a distribution of (a) $3,000 of this year's earnings, (b) $7,000 of retained earnings from previous years, and (c) $5,000 of capital. As to whether a corporation may invade or distribute capital in this manner, state statutes vary widely, with the most modern statutes permitting distributions of capital down to zero, and older statutes establishing a variety of different standards or tests on whether the distribution is permissible.

This simple example makes two critical points. First, in order to control distributions, the balance sheet test places restraints on which right-hand entries may be reduced when a distribution is made. The right-hand entries in the balance sheet serve as a kind of valve or control on distributions of assets that appear on the left-hand side of the balance sheet. Second, the balance sheet test is not directly concerned with solvency in the equity sense (i.e., the ability of the corporation to pay its bills as they become due), but rather with the preservation of capital. The balance sheet test is concerned with appearances: A corporation that says it has capital of a specified amount on its balance sheet may not make a distribution of all or a portion of that capital to shareholders. This test harks back to an early era of corporation law where the corporation's capital was viewed as a cushion or trust fund for the benefit of creditors who may be induced to extend credit in reliance on the corporation's balance sheet.

State corporation statutes have gone through at least three distinct phases

in developing balance sheet tests regulating distributions. In the earliest statutes enacted in the 19th century, provisions addressing distribution policies were primitive. Apparently proceeding on the assumption that all capital contributed to a corporation was a permanent fund for the protection of creditors, these statutes provide either that dividends can only be paid from income or, alternatively, that distributions from capital are prohibited.

In the second phase, developed during the first half of the 20th century, statutes draw a distinction between permanent capital and surplus capital (with the permanent capital usually being defined as the aggregate sum of the par values of all shares issued by the corporation). Many state dividend statutes are currently of this type. Unfortunately, these statutes can easily be evaded by the manipulation of par value principles, for example, by amending the articles of incorporation to reduce par value. As a result, they are largely ineffective in requiring minimum amounts of capital to be retained as a cushion. Indeed, these statutes give a deceptive picture of how much capital the corporation is required to maintain. Rather than providing protection to creditors, these statutes in fact become primarily rites of initiation for new corporation lawyers: When one learns how to avoid all meaningful restrictions on corporate distributions under the balance sheet test, one has proved one is a corporation lawyer.

Modern statutes, largely developed in the last decade, recognize the impracticability of defining minimum amounts of capital, and freely allow the distribution of capital as long as, after the distribution, assets exceed liabilities plus amounts payable in liquidation to holders of preferred shares. In these statutes, greater reliance is placed on the equity insolvency test described below than on the balance sheet test in order to protect creditors.

No matter what specific tests are established in these balance sheet statutes, they all suffer from one major, indeed fundamental, flaw. If you have read Chapter 6, which discusses accounting principles, it should be apparent that the distinction between capital and income is most slippery in practice. Income and capital are not self-defining but are dependent on accounting principles adequate to handle a variety of complex and subtle issues such as the allocation of income and expense items to specific periods, the principles on which assets are to be valued, depreciation schedules, the time of recognition of asset appreciation and contingent liabilities, and the like. Different accounting principles may give widely varying answers as to the corporation's income. The creation of accounting principles by legislative fiat for all corporations, large and small, is a daunting task, and no state legislature has attempted to do this. It is basically up to the courts to decide what accounting principles must be followed. The issues usually arise, furthermore, in suits to surcharge directors for approving improper dividends. That is a particularly brutal kind of litigation from the standpoint of the defendants, who are asked to restore to the corporation the amount of the distribution out of their own personal pockets, even though they may have acted in good faith in reliance on expert legal and accounting advice, and did not receive any more than the portion of the distribution their shareholdings entitled them to. It is not surprising that courts tended to find reasons to uphold the legality of distributions out of sympathy with the defendants — often people of substance in the community — who are faced with substantial liability.

At one time, most state statutes imposed a minimum absolute amount of capital that every corporation was required to have upon incorporation—usually $1,000. These provisions were also ineffective and have been repealed in most states. An arbitrary minimum ($1,000 or some other amount) suffers from the problem that it must be nominal and will afford no protection once the corporation begins business and incurs its first operating loss (if any).

The almost entire failure of elaborate balance sheet statutes in their basic purpose is also evident from the behavior of creditors, who pay no attention to the elaborate statutory provisions ostensibly designed for their protection. Instead, creditors protect themselves in different ways: (1) they rely on credit reporting agencies and similar private organizations before extending unsecured credit to businesses; (2) they obtain security interests when they sell goods on credit; and (3) in the case of larger transactions, they negotiate elaborate loan agreements with debtors by which they obtain contractual protection against unwise or improvident distributions to shareholders.

§12.8 Equity Insolvency Test

All state statutes relating to distributions impose an equity insolvency test for distributions in addition to the largely ineffective balance sheet prohibitions described above. The usual test is that a distribution to shareholders is unlawful if it makes the corporation insolvent (i.e., unable to pay its obligations as they become due in the future). At first blush, the equity insolvency test may sound like a variant of the balance sheet test for distributions. In fact, it is based on a totally different approach. The balance sheet test is based on financial statements and accounting principles. The equity insolvency test is based on an examination of estimated future cash flows after the distribution. It requires the board of directors to determine whether the corporation has or will have available funds to discharge its future obligations as they come due. This test is easily stated but requires difficult estimates and projections in practice. The board of directors must make an examination of anticipated cash flows and future cash needs arising from the maturation of debts and liabilities to determine whether, after the contemplated distribution, the corporation will be able to meet its obligations.

§12.9 Protection of Preferred Shareholders

State statutes impose restrictions on distributions to common shareholders in order to protect the liquidation preferences of preferred shareholders. Preferred shareholders are in an anomalous position with respect to dividend restrictions. On the one hand they are viewed as contributors of equity capital rather than as creditors. On the other hand, their financial interest in the corporation is usually limited, and once their dividend preference is honored in any one year, common shareholders are entitled to all future dividends and distributions during that year. From an economic standpoint, the position of the preferred shareholders' liquidation preference is closely akin to a creditor's

claim, because substantial distributions to common shareholders may effectively disable the corporation from honoring that liquidation preference. Many modern statutes require that liquidation preferences of preferred shareholders be treated as a liability for purposes of applying the restrictions on dividends.

§12.10 Suits to Compel Distributions

Deciding whether to make a distribution involves business judgment by the board of directors as to whether it is prudent to preserve earnings for future needs or whether a distribution should be made and in what amount. Courts have long recognized that this decision involves business judgments about the future cash needs both in terms of satisfying liabilities and in terms of making necessary investments in existing or new productive facilities. As a result, courts are loath to second-guess directors in connection with such decisions, and they tend to accept the decision of the board on such matters.

Directors also owe fiduciary duties to shareholders in connection with their stewardship of the corporation, and the decision to pay (or more commonly, to omit) dividends or distributions may be evaluated within these broad duties. These duties may be phrased in terms of fair treatment of minority shareholders or of all classes of shares, or in terms of not favoring a class in which members of the board of directors have substantial personal interests. There is obvious tension between these fiduciary duties and the business judgment rule described in the previous paragraph. There are, however, a large number of cases in which courts have ordered that a dividend be paid, thus illustrating that often the fiduciary duty dominates.

A compulsory dividend is most likely to be ordered when the minority shareholder can demonstrate (1) actions by the majority shareholder that may be construed as constituting antagonism or bad faith against the minority; (2) liquid assets within the corporation in excess of the apparent needs of the business and apparently available for the payment of dividends; and (3) a policy of informal distributions to favored shareholders through salaries, loans, cash advances, and the like. Still, suits to compel the payment of dividends should be viewed as a long shot even in egregious circumstances.

§12.11 Distribution Policies in Closely Held Corporations

In closely held corporations that are taxed as C corporations, distribution policies strongly tend in the direction of informal distributions in the form of tax deductible salary, rent, or interest payments rather than formally declared dividends. The principal motivation is federal income taxation: The payment of a reasonable salary to a shareholder, for example, is deductible by the corporation and to that extent avoids the double tax on income that otherwise increases the tax cost of operating as a C corporation. Such deductions are allowed only to the extent that they are "reasonable," but that standard permits considerable flexibility in distribution policy, often allowing the entire income of the corporation to be zeroed out to avoid all taxes at the corporate level.

Informal distributions of this type open the possibility of unfair treatment of minority shareholders, because they may not receive a proportionate part of the informal distribution. Even where the motive of the majority shareholder is not exclusionary, however, strict proportionality is dangerous, because it may suggest to the auditor in a subsequent tax audit that all or a portion of the corporate salary deductions should be disallowed as informal dividends.

The Internal Revenue Code contains a penalty tax against unreasonable accumulations of surplus which, if applicable, provides a strong tax incentive to pay dividends. Given current tax rates, it is unlikely that any corporation now finds it advantageous to accumulate unreasonable amounts of surplus so as to trigger the imposition of this tax.

If a corporation has elected S corporation tax treatment, corporate income is passed through to the shareholders for inclusion in their individual tax returns. There is no tax advantage in salary or other payments as a substitute for dividends. On the other hand, if the corporation fails to pay cash dividends when it has substantial taxable income, minority shareholders may find it difficult or impossible to pay their personal tax bills swollen by the inclusion of corporate income. In extreme cases, it may be necessary for minority shareholders to seek to revoke the S corporation election, if that is practical, or if it is not, to bring suit to compel the payment of dividends based on breach by the board of directors of its fiduciary duties to act in good faith and treat all shareholders equally.

§12.12 Distribution Policies in Publicly Held Corporations

Distribution policies within a publicly held corporation are quite different from the policies within a closely held corporation. In a closely held corporation, the distribution policy is likely to be viewed as primarily a tax issue: How to get corporate funds into the hands of the shareholders at the lowest tax cost.

In a publicly held company, on the other hand, the standard operating procedure is to establish an announced or regular dividend and maintain it indefinitely, or at least over several years. A regular dividend may be paid even though the corporation has suffered a loss in that year; the dividend is paid out of earnings accumulated from prior years. Most shareholders in a publicly held corporation, of course, are passive investors who come to rely on the regular dividend as part of their regular cash flow. However, the reluctance to change an announced dividend—particularly the reluctance to reduce the dividend in periods of adversity—is not based on concern about shareholders' cash flow. Rather, a change in dividend policy is widely viewed in the securities markets as a signal of management's future expectations with respect to the company. An increase in the announced dividend is viewed as signaling improved prospects. It is a strong signal, because it means that the corporate prospects have improved to the point that management thinks an increased dividend rate can be maintained indefinitely. On the other hand, a reduction in the dividend rate is a warning of rough seas ahead. The communication of bad news has a potential for serious adverse market repercussions and is not to be made prematurely or before management is reasonably certain that it is imprudent to

continue the present dividend. Certainly, such a signal should not be given because of a temporary dip in earnings.

If a corporation has an unusually good year, or has the good fortune to receive a nonrecurring windfall, management may be reluctant to announce an increase in the regular dividend, because it may be unsure that the rate can be maintained in the future. In this circumstance, management usually declares a special or nonrecurring dividend that is paid on a one-time basis and does not create an expectation that a similar payment will be forthcoming in future years. Some corporations have adopted a policy of declaring "extras" above the announced rate almost every year, but that is not the customary practice.

Rather paradoxically, some corporations as a matter of policy pay no cash dividends at all. One of the most successful enterprises of all time, Berkshire Hathaway, managed by the financier Warren Buffett, has never declared a dividend. A corporation that reinvests its cash flow productively rather than paying it out to shareholders will see a steady increase in the market price of the corporation's shares. And so it has been with Berkshire Hathaway. Similarly, a corporation that has recently gone public may have positive (and growing) earnings, but may need all available cash for internal growth purposes. In these situations a shareholder receives no immediate cash return, but he or she is rewarded by the steady increase in the market price of the stock. In effect, the market accepts and approves of the policy of deferring cash dividends to foster growth.

An extended theoretical discussion has transpired about why corporations adopt a particular dividend policy. Miller and Modigliani proved that with certain simplifying assumptions shareholders should theoretically be indifferent to the dividend policy that a corporation adopts. If the corporation fails to pay out earnings in the form of dividends, the value of the corporation's shares should rise so as to equal the amount of the dividend not paid. This irrelevance theorem suggests that shareholders in a non-dividend-paying corporation who wish current cash flow may simply sell a portion of their holdings in order to keep the value of their shares constant, and they will be as well off as if the corporation had made a distribution of current earnings. Given the present tax laws (under which dividends are taxed as ordinary income and gains on the sale of shares are taxed at lower capital gains rates), it should follow that paying dividends reduces the value of the corporation, and that no corporation should ever pay dividends. This logically correct theorem has only one problem: It does not reflect reality, because most publicly held corporations do in fact pay dividends.

A number of possible explanations have been offered to explain this dividend puzzle. The signaling idea discussed earlier may explain why dividends are paid. Another theory suggests that lower income investors are drawn to dividend-paying stocks because the tax difference is not relevant. Yet another theory is that paying dividends reduces agency costs by limiting the authority of managers in handling free cash flow. There are difficulties with each of these explanations, and it may be that securities markets and investors simply do not, on the average, have the transparency that economic theory presupposes. It is not at all clear, for example, that the market price of non-dividend-paying stocks increases rapidly enough to equal the value of the dividends not paid.

§12.13 Share Dividends

Publicly held corporations often pay share dividends or announce **share splits.** These two transactions are very similar in principle and effect, and their basic equivalence is sometimes not fully understood by investors. The following section deals specifically with splits.

A **share dividend** (or **stock dividend**) is a distribution of shares of common stock by a corporation to its shareholders in proportion to their shareholdings. Thus, a 10 percent share dividend means that the corporation issues one new share to each shareholder for every 10 shares held; a holder of 100 shares will receive 10 new shares when the distribution is made, and will then own 110 shares in all. From a purely economic or logical point of view, this is not a dividend at all, because the number of shares that each shareholder owns has been increased by exactly the same percentage, and each shareholder's proportional interest in the corporation has not been changed. In other words, a shareholder owning one percent of the outstanding shares before the share dividend is paid will own precisely one percent of the outstanding shares after it is paid. The percentage ownership has not changed even though the number of shares has increased. Despite this inescapable logic, many small shareholders welcome share dividends and many sell them shortly after they are received, perhaps not realizing (or not caring) that by doing so they have slightly reduced their (already infinitesimal) interest in the corporation. In some cases, the corporation will pay cash in lieu of fractional shares as authorized by many state statutes.

A share dividend does have one favorable consequence if the corporation also pays a regular cash dividend. It is customary to leave the regular dividend unaffected after a share dividend so that following the dividend the corporation's total dividend payout is increased (because the same rate is applied to a somewhat larger number of shares).

Why do corporations pay share dividends at all? The usual reason offered is that a share dividend is a tangible signal to shareholders that the corporation is profitable (despite the absence of a cash dividend) and is investing all available funds into the growth of the business. Although unsophisticated shareholders may view such a dividend as a little something that can be sold without reducing one's investment in the corporation, in fact it is nothing but a signal. On the other hand, a share dividend may constitute a vouch by management that even with more shares outstanding and perhaps even a larger distribution of cash thereon, things are going well enough that the stock price is likely to be maintained. In this sense, a share dividend may in fact have positive information content, particularly if management is not free to discuss publicly why prospects are rosy.

§12.14 Share Splits

A **share split** is essentially a large share dividend. In a two-for-one split, for example, a corporation with 1,000,000 shares outstanding to begin with

ends up with 2,000,000 shares outstanding after the split, and a shareholder with 100 shares before the split ends up with 200 shares after the split. True share splits are quite rare, because if the shares have par value, as most still do, the par value per share must be formally changed by amendment to the articles of incorporation so as to reflect that each outstanding share after the split represents only half as much in stated capital as before the split. Technically, in a two-for-one share split, the corporation issues two new shares for each old share that each shareholder holds. The old share is cancelled so that each shareholder now owns two shares, whereas before he or she owned only one share. Because this process is cumbersome, and because there will inevitably be some old shares that are never turned in for new shares, true share splits are very rare. Instead, in order to effect a two-for-one share split, a corporation usually issues a one-for-one share dividend of one new share for each old share and simply calls it a split.

It is customary to reduce the regular or stated dividend rate when a share split (true or otherwise) is completed; if the regular dividend is halved in connection with a two-for-one split, one would expect the market price of each new share to be approximately one-half of the market price of the pre-split shares. Often, however, the effective dividend rate is increased in connection with a share split: Thus, in a three-for-one split where the old dividend rate was 90 cents per share, the dividend rate on the split shares may be set, for example, at 35 cents, equal to a rate of $1.05 on the pre-split shares. It is difficult to square this practice with the dividend irrelevance theorem of Miller and Modigliani.

Many corporation finance officers think that there is an appropriate trading range for common shares. For example, the common stock of a corporation may have historically traded in the $20 to $30 range. If the price gradually rises to $40, the corporation may split the stock two-for-one to return the price to the lower range. One advantage of maintaining a lower trading range is that if the price of a stock rises significantly to a new plateau but the stock is not split, trading volume may decline from previous levels because most investors trade in round lots and may feel they cannot afford to invest in higher priced stocks. (Trading in round lots is discussed more fully in Chapter 14, which discusses markets.)

A split differs from a share dividend in certain minor respects relating to how the transaction is recorded for accounting purposes. These differences, however, rarely affect the shareholder.

A corporation may also "split" its stock to reduce the number of shares outstanding. This is called a **reverse stock split** and is not really a split at all. Rather, the corporation amends its articles of incorporation to reduce the number of authorized shares, and the amendment provides that each 10 (or 100 or 1,000) old shares are to be exchanged for 1 new share. Reverse stock splits often create fractional shares, and may be used to liquidate the interests of small shareholders by establishing a procedure (authorized in many state statutes) to eliminate all fractional shares for cash. Some corporations have used reverse stock splits to eliminate public shareholders by establishing the split ratio at a level sufficiently high that all nonmanagement shareholders become owners of fractional interests, which are then eliminated through a cash payment.

§12.15 Determining Who Is Entitled to a Distribution

Whenever a dividend or cash or stock distribution is contemplated, the question may arise as to who is entitled to the distribution if the shares have been sold or transferred around the time of the declaration or payment. This problem is particularly acute in publicly held corporations where many thousands of shares are traded each day among anonymous persons. The New York Stock Exchange has adopted an **ex-dividend policy** to establish whether the buyer or seller of publicly traded shares is entitled to a distribution.

Table 12-1 is taken from *The Wall Street Journal*. It is the standard chart showing dividend announcements made on the previous business day. An examination of this table reveals much about the dividend practices of publicly held corporations and the law relating to dividend declarations. First of all, the table distinguishes between various types of dividends, including regular dividends (pursuant to an announced dividend policy); irregular dividends (occasional or special payments not pursuant to an announced policy); funds, REITs, investment companies, and limited partnerships (all essentially pass through entities that distribute more or less all income); and stock dividends (as discussed above).

There are four important dates to note with respect to each dividend or distribution: (1) the date of announcement; (2) the **record date**; (3) the **payable date**; and (4) the **ex-dividend date**. The announcement date is the date of the press release that a cash or stock dividend is to be paid or a distribution is to be made. Typically, the announcement is made on the same day that the board declares the dividend. The record date determines to whom the dividend is to be paid, namely, the shareholder of record on the books of the corporation at the close of business on the record date. The payable date is the date the checks or certificates are actually mailed; a delay of one to four weeks is customary and may be necessary for the corporation to go through the mechanical process of making the distribution in the proper amounts to thousands or millions of record holders. The ex-dividend date is three business days before the record date. Ex-dividend means without the dividend. The ex-dividend date convention assigns the dividend to the buyer or seller as follows: A buyer in a transaction that occurs before the ex-dividend date is entitled to receive the dividend and the seller is not; a seller in a transaction that occurs on or after the ex-dividend date is entitled to keep the dividend. The reason for the three-day gap between the ex-dividend date and the record date is that the standard practice is settlement three business days after the transaction. On the settlement date, the buyer must pay the purchase price and the seller must deliver the shares. The ex-dividend date is a carryover from a much earlier period when securities transactions were settled by a delivery of certificates issued in the name of the seller, and endorsed to permit new certificates to be issued to the buyer. A buyer who is entitled to the certificates on or before the ex-dividend date is theoretically able to register the transfer with the corporation and become the record owner before the close of business on the record date for the dividend or distribution. The ex-dividend date is established as the last day on which that is possible. In the age of book entry registration, this may sound rather formalistic, but one must have a clear rule as to who is

entitled to the dividend or distribution, and the rule so established seems as reasonable as any.

The day a stock goes ex-dividend, its market price should decline by approximately the amount of the dividend, other things being equal, because the day before, every buyer of the stock was entitled to the dividend but on and after the ex-dividend date, buyers of the stock do not receive the dividend. Of course, this relationship may not be precise, because market conditions can change overnight.

The ex-dividend date is a convention that is not at all dependent on whether a buyer actually arranges for certificates to be issued. The ex-dividend convention does not apply to shares sold directly by one person to another not using the facilities of an exchange or the over-the-counter market. In a face-to-face transaction, the parties may make any agreement they wish regarding entitlement to declared but unpaid dividends or distributions.

Table 12-1

CORPORATE DIVIDEND NEWS

Dividends Reported October 30

Company	Period	Amt.	Payable date	Record date
REGULAR				
Aames Finl Corp	Q	.033	11−21−97	11−10
Amer Biltrite	Q	.10	1− 2−98	12−17
Anadarko Petrol	Q	.07½	12−24−97	12−10
Apple South Inc	Q	.01	11−28−97	11−14
Baltimore Gas&Elec	Q	.41	1− 2−98	12−10
Bank of Yorba Linda	Q	.05	12−15−97	11−21
Bemis Co	Q	.20	12− 1−97	11−14
BethlhmStl $2.50pf	Q	.62½	12−10−97	11−10
BethlhmStl $5.00pf	Q	1.25	12−10−97	11−10
Coca-Cola Enterp	Q	.02½	12−15−97	12− 3
Community Bks PA	Q	.21	1− 2−98	12−17
Crawford & Co clB	Q	.11	11−21−97	11− 7
Dial Corp	Q	.08	1− 6−98	12−12
DuPont $3.50pf	Q	.87½	1−24−98	1− 9
DuPont $4.50pf	Q	1.12½	1−24−98	1− 9
East Texas Finl Svcs	Q	.05	11−26−97	11−12
F&M Bancorp WI	Q	.20	12− 1−97	11−14
Genesee Corp clB	Q	.35	1− 2−98	12−15
Halliburton Co	Q	.12½	12−23−97	12− 2
Harman Intl Indus	Q	.05	11−26−97	11−12
Jannock Ltd	b.12½		1− 2−98	12− 5
Libbey Inc	Q	.07½	12− 4−97	11− 3
LILCO pfAA	Q	.49⅞	12− 1−97	11−14
Medtronic Inc	Q	.055	1−30−98	1− 9
Mid-Amer Energy Hldgs Co	Q	.30	12− 1−97	11− 7
Money Store Inc Pfd	Q	.43	12− 1−97	r11−15
Noble Affiliates	Q	.04	11−24−97	11−10
Olin Corp	Q	.30	12−10−97	11−14
Peekskill Finl Corp	Q	.09	11−28−97	11−14
Peoples Bank NC	Q	.12	12−19−97	12− 5
Providence&Worc RR	S	.06	11−28−97	11−13
Provident Cos new	Q	.10	12−10−97	11−28
Republic Sec Finl	Q	.05	12− 2−97	11−18
Ryland Group Inc	Q	.04	1−30−98	1−15
Selective Insur	Q	.28	12− 1−97	11−17
Shaw Industries	Q	.07½	11−28−97	11−14
Smucker (JM) clA	Q	.13	12− 1−97	11−17
Smucker (JM) clB	Q	.13	12− 1−97	11−17
Sthn Missouri Bcp	Q	.12½	11−28−97	11−12
Sunbeam Corp	Q	.01	12−15−97	12− 1
Tappan Zee Finl Inc	Q	.07	11−26−97	11− 6
Toledo Ed $2.365pf	Q	.59⅛	12− 1−97	11−14
Toledo Ed 8.32%pf	Q	2.08	12− 1−97	11−14
Toledo Ed 10%pf	Q	2.50	12− 1−97	11−14
UnitdFed SvgsRkyMt	Q	.06	12− 1−97	11−17
Waters Instruments	A	.04	12− 8−97	11− 7
Wendy's Intl	Q	.06	11−24−97	11−10
Westcorp Inc	Q	.10	11−24−97	11−13
IRREGULAR				
Empire Federal Bancorp	Q	.07½	11−26−97	11−12

Company	Period	Amount	Payable date	Record date
FUNDS - REITS - INVESTMENT COS - LPS				
Beacon Props	Q	.50	11−21−97	11− 7
CommonSense MuniBd	M	h.05¾	11−28−97	11−28
Hancock Pat Pfd Dv	M	.09⅝	11−28−97	11−10
Scudder Pathway Bal prtfo	Q	h.09	10−31−97	10−30
Security Cap Indus	Q	.26¾	11−25−97	11−11
VK AC USGovtC	M	h.0745	11−28−97	11−28
VK AC Strat IncoA	M	h.0825	11−28−97	11−28
VK AC CA InsTaxFreeA	M	.071	11−28−97	11−28
VK AC Corp BdB	M	h.0361	11−28−97	11−28
VK AC Corp BdC	M	h.0361	11−28−97	11−28
VK AC Corp BdA	M	h.0405	11−28−97	11−28
VK AC GlblGovtSecC	M	h.036	11−28−97	11−28
VK AC GlblGovtSecA	M	h.041	11−28−97	11−28
VK AC GlblGovtSecB	M	h.036	11−28−97	11−28
VK AC GvtSecsA	M	h.055	11−14−97	11− 3
VK AC GvtSecsB	M	h.049	11−14−97	11− 3
VK AC GvtSecsC	M	h.049	11−14−97	11− 3
VK AC HiIncoBdA	M	h.050	11−28−97	11−28
VK AC HiIncoBdB	M	h.046	11−28−97	11−28
VK AC HiYldA	M	h.07¼	11−28−97	11−28
VK AC HiYldB	M	h.0665	11−28−97	11−25
VK AC HiYldC	M	.0665	11−28−97	11−28
VK AC HiYldMuniA	M	h.06	11−28−97	11−28
VK AC HiYldMuniB	M	h.053	11−28−97	11−28
VK AC HiYldMuniC	M	h.053	11−28−97	11−28
VK AC InsdTaxFrA	M	h.08	11−28−97	11−28
VK AC InsdTaxFrB	Q	.0677	11−28−97	11−28
VK AC LtdMatGovtA	M	.05½	11−28−97	11−28
VK AC LtdMatGovtB	M	h.047	11−28−97	11−28
VK AC MuniIncoA	M	h.0705	11−28−97	11−28
VK AC MuniIncoB	M	h.061	11−28−97	11−28
VK AC PA TaxFrB	M	h.065	11−28−97	11−28
VK AC PA TaxFrA	M	h.076	11−28−97	11−28
VK AC ShtTrmGlbIncoA	M	h.039	11−28−97	11−28
VK AC Strat IncoB	M	h.0745	11−28−97	11−28
VK AC TaxFrHiIncoA	M	h.073	11−28−97	11−28
VK AC TaxFrHiIncoB	M	h.0637	11−28−97	11−28
VK AC USGovtA	M	h.0842	11−28−97	11−28
VK AC USGovtB	M	h.0745	11−28−97	11−28
VK AC USGovtIncA	M	h.04⅝	11−28−97	11−28
VK AC USGovtIncB	M	h.04⅛	11−28−97	11−28
VK AC USGovtIncC	M	h.04⅛	11−28−97	11−28
VK AC ShtTrmGlbIncoB	M	h.0342	11−28−97	11−28
STOCK				
99 Cents Only Stores			s 11−29−97	11−17
s-5-for-4 stock split.				
Abington Bancorp Inc			s 12−12−97	11−14
s-2-for-1 stock split.				
Delta & Pine Land new			s r11−20−97	r11−10
s-4-for-3 stock split.				

Company	Period	Amount	Payable date	Record date
German Amer Bncp new		5°₀	12 – 20 – 97	11 – 28
Hallmark Capital		s	11 – 24 – 97	11 – 10
s-2-for-1 stock split.				
La-Man Corp		5°₀	12 – 1 – 97	11 – 14
Mackenzie Finl		s	11 – 20 – 97	11 – 10
s-2-for-1 stock split.				
Saville Sys		s	c11 – 28 – 97	11 – 7
s-2-for-1 stock split.				
StateFed Finl Corp		s	11 – 14 – 97	10 – 31
s-2-for-1 stock split.				
World Fuel Svc		s	12 – 1 – 97	11 – 17
s-3-for-2 stock split.				

INCREASED

		--Amounts--			
		New	Old		
AmerNatlInsur Tex	Q	.67	.65	12 – 19 – 97	12 – 5
Northwest Pub Svc	Q	.24¼	.23	12 – 1 – 97	11 – 15
Poe & Brown Inc	Q	.14	.13	11 – 21 – 97	11 – 10
Poughkeepsie Finl	Q	.05	.02½	12 – 4 – 97	11 – 14
Rollins Truck Lsng	Q	.05½	.05	12 – 15 – 97	11 – 15
Sara Lee Corp	Q	.23	.21	1 – 2 – 98	12 – 1

REDUCED

		--Amounts--			
		New	Old		
Ethyl Corp	Q	.06¼	.12½	1 – 1 – 98	12 – 15

FOREIGN

Telefonica Del Peru ADS	–	†.222	12 – 10 – 97	11 – 19

INITIAL

Depuy Inc	A	.12	1 – 2 – 98	12 – 1
German Amer Bncp new	Q	.11	11 – 20 – 97	11 – 10
Hooper Holmes new	Q	.015	11 – 28 – 97	11 – 14
Oglebay Norton Co new	Q	.20	12 – 19 – 97	12 – 2
Valley Forge Corp new	Q	.04	12 – 16 – 97	12 – 5

A-Annual; b-Payable in Canadian funds; c-Corrected; h-From Income; k-From capital gains; M-Monthly; Q-Quarterly; r-Revised; S-Semi-annual; t-Approximate U.S. dollar amount per American Depositary Receipt/Share before adjustment for foreign taxes.

Stocks Ex-Dividend November 3

Company	Amount	Company	Amount
Amer Govt Inco	.03	JSB Financial	.35
Amer Govt IncoPort	.03½	LL&E Royalty Tr	.0499
Amer Muni IncoPort	.067¾	Lennar Corp	s
Amer Muni TermIII	.04¾	s-1 shr of LNR Property	
Amer Muni Term	.0542	Corp for each shr held.	
Amer Muni TermII	.0517	MinnMuniIncoPort	.067825
Amer Opport Inco	.035	MinnMuniTermII	.0492
Amer Select Port	.08½	MinnMuniTerm	.0509
AmStratIncPortII	.08¼	Pier 1 Imports	.03½
AmStratIncPortIII	.08¼	Pope & Talbot	.19
AmStratIncoPort	.08	ReinsuranceGrp new	.06
Americas Inco Tr	.05½	Sea Containers clA	.19¼
BostonFed Bancorp	.07	Sea Containers clB	.17½
Buckeye Partners	1.05	SouthCalEd 4.08%pf	.25½
Claire's Stores	.03	SouthCalEd 4.24%pf	.26½
Diagnostic Product	.12	SouthCalEd 4.78%pf	.29⅞
Downey Financial	.08	SouthCalEd 5.80%pf	.36¼
Florida Rock Indus	s	Sphere Drake Hldgs	.04
s-2-for-1 stock split.		Tektronix Inc	s
Genl Employmnt Ent	s	s-3-for-2 stock split.	
s-3-for-2 stock split.		Texaco Inc new	.45
Halter Marine Grp	s	Thermo Instrum Sys	s
s-3-for-2 stock split.		s-5-for-4 stock split.	
Heilig-Meyers	.07	Wesco Finl	.27½
Highlander Inco Fd	.088	Western Atlas Inc	s
Hudson Charter Bcp	s	s-1 shr of Unova Inc common for each shr held.	
s-3-for-2 stock split.			

341

◆ MERGERS AND ACQUISITIONS

§13.1 Introduction

Beginning in the late 1960s and continuing through the late 1980s, the business world was roiled by hostile takeovers in which one huge business acquired another. The target of a hostile takeover attempt usually fiercely resisted by using all legal, economic, and political resources at its disposal. Stories of these battles filled the newspapers and business journals, providing grist for endless discussion and speculation and leading to the development of a colorful vocabulary. For a variety of reasons, hostile takeovers had largely disappeared as of about 1990, and for a few years there were relatively few large mergers and acquisitions of any kind. By the mid 1990s, however, the **market**

for corporate control had heated up again, and the number of such transactions is probably as large as ever. The difference is that today the great majority of mergers and acquisitions are consensual (or "friendly") deals in which the board of directors of the target company negotiates on behalf of the company and its shareholders. It is by no means uncommon, however, for hostile bids to be launched, and, at any given moment, usually two or three such contests are going on.

This chapter outlines the various methods by which whole companies are bought and sold and describes the economic and financial forces that lead to such transactions. In the following discussion, the company that is the object of a takeover attempt is usually called the **target** company and the company seeking to take over the target the **bidder.** Individuals as well as corporations may act as bidders, but for simplicity it is assumed throughout this chapter that the bidder is a corporation.

§13.2 Historical Context

Before discussing the mechanics of mergers and acquisitions, it may be useful to put them into historical perspective. There have been several well-documented periods of merger movements in American history. In the late 19th century a series of acquisitions and mergers created monopolies in several basic American industries, and gave rise to the Sherman Antitrust Act. A period of similar activity before World War I led to Teddy Roosevelt's famous trust-busting activities and ultimately to the second major antitrust statute, the Clayton Act. A somewhat similar period of merger activity occurred during the 1950s, usually involving conglomeration (i.e., the assembling of a number of unrelated industries within a single corporate enterprise). The takeover movement that culminated in the 1980s was different in several significant respects from merger waves of earlier periods. Many of these takeovers involved breaking up mergers from earlier periods.

Merger movements prior to the 1960s usually involved consensual or "friendly" transactions. Management of a target corporation could have usually blocked a takeover simply by refusing to cooperate. Only when both sides agreed on the terms could one company acquire another. Thus, takeovers became a matter of negotiation over price, continuity of management, and other factors. That was not the case in the 1980s. Bidders quite regularly went over the heads of management and pitched their takeover proposals directly to shareholders of the target corporation. The pitch to shareholders, furthermore, usually involved offers of cash for stock that individual target shareholders found attractive. If the target stock was held for the benefit of others (as was very often the case, given that about half of all stock was held by large institutional investors such as mutual funds, pension plans, and insurance companies), the shareholder institution might even have felt compelled to accept the offer to avoid claims of breach of fiduciary duty owed to beneficiaries. (Indeed, as a matter of federal laws governing retirement plans, pension plans set up by the target company itself were sometimes more or less required to sell target company stock to a hostile bidder offering an attractive price.) The success or failure of a hostile

takeover thus depended on the sum total of a large number of individual decisions by shareholders rather than on a single yes-or-no decision by the managers of the target entity.

Prior to the 1960s, typical takeover transactions involved large corporations becoming larger by taking over smaller ones. In the 1980s, smaller corporations (or even individuals) successfully acquired control of publicly held corporations that sometimes had assets much larger than those of the acquirer. Rather paradoxically, many acquisitions in the 1980s involved **bust-up** transactions in which many or most portions of the acquired business were put up for sale shortly after the acquisition. Because the bidder typically borrowed funds to pay cash for target shares, the successful bidder often ended up with both the target and huge amounts of debt. Thus, the bidder was often compelled to break up and sell off components of the acquired business to raise additional cash in order to reduce the debt to manageable levels.

Local and state political forces usually viewed the threatened hostile takeover of a large local enterprise as an unmitigated disaster. They saw jobs and major industrial plants disappearing or being moved to other areas of the country if the takeover occurred. Therefore, local communities and even entire states often joined together with threatened target management to try to defeat takeover attempts.

Unlike state and local governments, the federal government has been essentially neutral with respect to takeovers. In part, this is a result of the fact that the Securities and Exchange Commission (the SEC) has been receptive to arguments based on economic analysis. The federal government does, however, have an important role in the regulation of takeover attempts. The **Williams Act** was enacted by Congress in 1968 in response to the first wave of tender offers. Technically it consists of several amendments to Sections 13 and 14 of the Securities Exchange Act of 1934 (the 1934 Act).

The purposes of the Williams Act are to create a level playing field between bidder and target and to protect shareholders from unfair or deceptive tactics. The important substantive provisions of this legislation impose disclosure requirements on bidders and targets and establish basic ground rules for the conduct of a **tender offer**. In addition, Section 14(e) of the Williams Act contains an anti-fraud provision relating to tender offers. There have been many attempts to use this provision to obtain judicial review of the tactics used by both targets and bidders. The United States Supreme Court has held, however, that an unsuccessful contestant for control does not have standing to attack the other party's actions, because the statute was intended solely to protect independent shareholders (*Piper v. Chris-Craft Industries, Inc.*, 430 U.S. 1 (1977)). Following this decision, federal courts have generally refused to consider the validity of specific tactics under federal law (although increasingly state courts do so under state law relating to duties of directors). It now appears to be accepted, at least as a matter of federal law, that the ultimate success or failure of a takeover attempt should be determined on the economic playing field rather than on the federal judicial one. Some economists argue that even the minimal degree of existing federal regulation of takeovers is too much; other persons strongly advocate greater participation by the federal government in regulating the takeover movement.

The high point of the 1980s-style leveraged transactions came in 1989, with the $25 billion buyout of RJR Nabisco by the leading takeover firm of the era, Kohlberg, Kravis, Roberts (KKR). Thereafter, the "go-go" days of takeovers abruptly ended, and the number of leveraged transactions declined to virtually zero. Although one reason for this development was a variety of legal restrictions placed on the use of junk bonds, the principal reason appears to have been financial and political rather than legal. Drexel Burnham Lambert was criminally prosecuted along with Michael Milken, its most powerful partner and the leading market-maker for junk bonds. Publicity surrounding the savings and loan crisis (which was exacerbated by a number of savings and loan associations that had made disastrous investments in junk bonds), and concern over the financial stability of the banking and insurance industries (which in many cases had made similar investments) did not help. Loan and investment policies tightened dramatically. The failure of several large leveraged buyout transactions also contributed, as the surviving entities found it impossible to make debt payments and filed for reorganization under the Bankruptcy Code. To make matters even worse, suits have been filed in these bankruptcy proceedings against banks, investment firms and advisers, controlling shareholders, and others, on the theory that the leveraged buyout itself constituted a fraudulent conveyance. These suits also doubtlessly dampened any interest in financing leveraged buyout transactions.

The market for junk bonds improved in 1992 and 1993, as yields on investment-grade securities declined, but apparently little of the cash so raised was earmarked for takeover purposes. A few large transactions occurred in 1994 and 1995, but the pace quickened thereafter. Most of these transactions are either stock-for-stock transactions or based on internally generated rather than borrowed funds. Although it is always possible that speculative, leveraged transactions may return, the frenzied activity of the 1980s appears unlikely to recur.

Aside from a lack of easy money, there were other factors that caused hostile takeovers to evolve away. First, most publicly traded companies adopted almost impermeable defenses, in particular "poison pills." These defenses effectively require any prospective bidder to gain the consent of management in connection with any takeover. However, these defensive tactics are limited by a judicially created rule that once a company is for sale it must be sold to the highest bidder after a fair auction unimpeded by the target board's favoring any particular bidder. Defensive tactics and poison pills, and the judicial limits on their use, are discussed in detail in later sections of this chapter.

In addition to target company defensive tactics, most states have adopted takeover statutes that limit the ways in which takeovers may be effected or the ability of a successful bidder to dispose of target assets after control is achieved. Undoubtedly, the most important of these statutes is the Delaware statute, which provides that unless a bidder obtains the consent of target management before acquiring 15 percent or more of target company stock (or acquires 85 percent or more of target company stock), the bidder may not buy, sell, merge, or otherwise dispose of any portion of the target company for a period of three years. The intent and effect of this statute is to make a bidder either negotiate with management or make an offer so attractive that it garners virtually all of the target shares.

Yet another possible cause for the decline of hostile takeovers may be that extraordinarily high prices in the stock market make it impractical to pay even higher cash prices for target company stock. Indeed, takeovers in the 1980s may have been motivated by the undervaluation of target companies by the stock market, while takeovers in the 1990s may be motivated by economic considerations such as gaining access to an ensured source of supply, acquiring a new product line, or securing developed expertise in a given area of business in which the bidder is weak. Intuitively, these motivations for mergers are more likely to lead to a negotiated transaction than to a hostile one.

Finally, it may be that management styles have changed as a result of the takeover wars of the 1980s. It may be that in the 1990s managers are willing to take steps voluntarily that hostile bidders threatened in the 1980s. Indeed, hardly a day goes by in the 1990s when a publicly held company does not announce that it is selling off or downsizing a division or line of business in an effort to increase efficiency and presumably its stock price. Successful bidders commonly used these tactics during the 1980s.

§13.3 Methods by Which One Corporation Can Acquire Another

There are several ways in which one corporation can combine with another either in whole or in part. The simplest method is by **merger**. In what is often called a **plain vanilla merger**, two (or more) corporations become one, and by operation of law the **surviving corporation** acquires all of the assets and liabilities of the corporations that cease to exist. In a **consolidation**, the surviving corporation is a new corporation that acquires the assets and liabilities of all of the constituent corporations. In order for a merger or consolidation to be effected, the boards of directors of the constituent corporations must agree to a plan of merger that is then submitted to a vote of the shareholders of each corporation. In most jurisdictions, the merger must be approved by the shareholders of each corporation by a majority of all the shareholders eligible to vote, although the required number may be increased in the articles of incorporation or bylaws of a corporation. (Often only a single set of proxy materials will be prepared in order to reduce the expenses of holding the vote and to minimize the possibility of discrepancies.) The shareholders of the corporation that ceases to exist may receive stock of the surviving corporation, cash, notes, or any other property that the plan of merger specifies. If the shareholders of the disappearing corporation receive stock, the merger is called a **stock-for-stock merger**; if they receive cash, it is called a **cash merger**. A shareholder who objects to a merger usually has a statutory **right of dissent and appraisal** and may demand payment in cash of the value of his or her shares as of the day before the merger.

A corporation may sell all or substantially all of its assets, with or without assignment of its liabilities, to another corporation. When a corporation seeks to sell all or substantially all of its assets, the approval process is generally the same as for a merger. The board must adopt a plan, and the shareholders must approve the proposed transaction by majority vote. It is not, however, necessary for the shareholders of the acquiring corporation to approve the transaction. In

most jurisdictions, shareholders of the selling corporation also have the right of dissent and appraisal in sale of asset transactions, although in Delaware they do not. One of the recurring issues in connections with sales of assets is what constitutes **all or substantially all** of the selling corporation's assets. Although the phrase seems clear enough, courts have ruled that the sale of the largest division or line of business (sometimes constituting less than half of the earning power of the selling corporation) may be significant enough to require a shareholder vote.

The primary advantage of a sale of assets, aside from a somewhat simpler approval process, is that the purchasing corporation may decide which liabilities it does not wish to assume. The primary disadvantage is that each individual asset and liability must be separately identified and valued in a sale of assets. Moreover, there may be complicated filing or recordation requirements for some assets (e.g., real estate) so transferred. There is also a danger that a court will deem additional liabilities to have been assumed by the purchasing corporation even though they are not expressly assumed. For example, management of a corporation facing potential products liability or environmental claims may figure that the assets can be sold for an attractive price and the corporation dissolved and the proceeds distributed to the shareholders before the claims arise. (The law generally requires a corporation that is dissolving to set aside enough to pay known claims, but that does not necessarily prevent unscrupulous managers from trying to avoid them.) Although former management of the dissolved corporation and shareholders who receive distributions in dissolution may be held liable to a limited extent, the courts often also hold the purchasing corporation liable on vague theories (e.g., that the sale of assets constituted a "de facto merger" or that the acquiring corporation was a "mere continuation" of the selling corporation). Despite this danger of **successor liability**, there is an old adage in doing deals: "Buy assets, sell stock."

In addition to mergers and sales of assets, many states also allow for a **share exchange**. In a share exchange, the purchasing corporation issues its shares directly to the target corporation shareholders. The exchange, however, is mandatory, not voluntary. The effect of the transaction is that the target becomes a wholly owned subsidiary of the purchasing company but does not go out of existence (as it would in a merger) or remain as an independent company (as it would in a sale of assets). A share exchange is generally subject to the same approval process as a merger.

There are several special forms of mergers. A **short-form merger** allows a parent company that owns 90 percent or more of the stock of a subsidiary company to effect a merger of the subsidiary into the parent without advance notice to the subsidiary company and without the need to gain the approval of the subsidiary board or hold a vote of either subsidiary or parent shareholders. Subsidiary shareholders do, however, have a right of appraisal in a short-form merger.

The words "parent" and "subsidiary" have no precise meaning. Generally speaking, a **parent company** controls a **subsidiary company** (or **sub**) by virtue of owning at least a majority of the voting stock in the subsidiary. If the parent company owns all of the subsidiary's stock, it is called a **wholly owned subsidiary**. A parent-subsidiary merger in which the subsidiary is not wholly owned

presents special problems of fiduciary duty, because the parent may theoretically dictate the terms of a merger possibly to the detriment of minority shareholders in the subsidiary. The parent company naturally desires to acquire the stock of the subsidiary it does not already own at as low a price as possible. These mergers are sometimes called **cash out mergers**, and they are subject to a heightened scrutiny by the courts under an "intrinsic fairness" test.

Another specialized merger form is the **triangular merger**. In a triangular merger, the acquiring corporation forms a new wholly owned subsidiary corporation and causes it to merge with the target corporation; the subsidiary is the surviving corporation. A triangular merger avoids a vote by the parent company shareholders and thereby the possibility that some of those shareholders may exercise their right of dissent and appraisal to force the company to buy their shares. In a **reverse triangular merger**, the subsidiary is merged into the target corporation, which survives, but the parent company ends up owning all the target company shares. A short-form merger may then be used to combine the target with the parent without any further shareholder vote.

Mergers are often used for purposes of simply reorganizing an existing enterprise. When a parent corporation merges into a subsidiary, the merger is said to be a **downstream merger**. When the subsidiary merges into the parent, the merger is said to be an **upstream merger**. For example, every state allows for mergers with corporations from other states, so-called **foreign corporations**. Indeed, if a corporation wants to change its state of incorporation, the change is usually effected by setting up a **shell corporation** in the desired state and merging the existing corporation into the new corporation; the new corporation survives and simultaneously changes its name to the name of the old corporation. In many jurisdictions it is possible for noncorporations (for example, limited partnerships and limited liability companies) also to engage in mergers either with similar or different entities. The discussion here, however, is limited to mergers in the context of corporations. A downstream merger may also be used to eliminate dividend arrearages on preferred stock by specifying in the plan of merger that the preferred stockholders receive, for example, common stock in the surviving company. As a general rule, however, if a class of shareholders will have different rights under the surviving corporation's articles of incorporation, that class may vote as a class on the merger and thus may often exact a premium price in exchange for their approval.

Most states have adopted **small scale merger** statutes that dispense with the requirement of a shareholder vote (and the right of dissent and appraisal) for the surviving corporation in a transaction in which it acquires a much smaller corporation by merger. If the number of outstanding shares of the acquiring corporation will be no more than 120 percent of the number outstanding before the merger (both in terms of voting power and in terms of unfixed financial participation), then no vote by the shareholders of the acquiring corporation is required. The idea is that such a merger has relatively little effect on the control or financial interests of the acquiring company shareholders. Therefore, the decision to acquire the target corporation is in the nature of an ordinary business decision that the board should be able to make without a shareholder vote.

A single corporation may also split itself into two or more successor corporations. Although at least one state has a statute allowing for the division

of a corporation, it is always possible for a corporation simply to form a new wholly owned subsidiary and to contribute (or **drop down**) specified assets into the new corporation. The original corporation may then distribute the shares in the subsidiary to its own shareholders with the result that the new corporation becomes effectively independent from the old. The original corporation may also elect to sell the shares to some third party buyer. One issue that arises in split-ups is whether both successor corporations are liable for all the obligations of the original corporation.

§13.4 Planning, Tax, and Accounting Considerations

Although the factors to be considered in structuring a deal are virtually innumerable, the purpose of this section is to give the reader a sense of the possibilities by discussing some common considerations that affect the ultimate terms of many mergers and acquisitions.

At the outset, it is important to understand that the form of a transaction is almost wholly a matter of choice. A sale of assets can be structured in such a way as to accomplish precisely the same outcome as a merger. For example, a target company may agree to accept survivor company stock in exchange for its assets and thereafter dissolve, distributing the stock to its shareholders. The net effect of this transaction is that the target shareholders become shareholders of the surviving company just as they would in a stock-for-stock merger.

However, significant differences often occur in the way the two transactions are taxed. Whereas a true merger is usually tax-free to both the target corporation and its shareholders, a sale of assets is generally taxable unless at least 80 percent of the consideration is stock. In many cases, the parties of course will want the transaction to be tax-free, but in some cases they may prefer it to be taxable, because the surviving corporation can then take a higher basis (a **stepped-up basis**) in the assets acquired and claim larger depreciation deductions in subsequent years. (Depreciation and basis are discussed in detail in Chapter 6 and 9, which discuss accounting and tax, respectively.)

Similar considerations may arise in connection with accounting for a merger or sale of assets. Generally speaking, a plain vanilla stock-for-stock merger is treated as a **pooling of interests** for accounting purposes. That is, the assets and liabilities of the target are simply added to the surviving company's balance sheet at the same values at which they are carried on the target's balance sheet irrespective of the fact that the stock used to "buy" the target may be worth much more than the net book value of the target. A sale of assets, on the other hand, is usually treated as a **purchase**, which, among other things, requires the purchasing company to create a goodwill asset reflecting the difference between the price paid for the target and the aggregate values assigned to individual assets and liabilities. The goodwill asset must then be amortized (see Chapter 6, which discusses accounting) and the yearly amortization expense has the effect of reducing earnings in later years under generally accepted accounting principles (GAAP). If stock is used as consideration in both cases, there is no economic difference between the two transactions, but subsequent reported earnings are higher if the transaction is a pooling than they would be if the

transaction is a purchase. Studies indicate that the stock market pays no attention to these differences in reported income and values the stock of surviving companies according to underlying fundamentals. However, many corporate managers believe their stock price will be higher in the future if the transaction is treated as a pooling transaction and per share earnings thereafter are higher than they would be if the transaction is treated as a purchase.

The accounting and tax treatment of corporate groups can be quite complex even in the absence of a formal merger or other transaction. Under both GAAP and the Internal Revenue Code (IRC), a corporation that exceeds a certain percentage ownership level is required to report earnings and pay taxes on a consolidated basis (i.e., as if the legally separate entities were one).

Reverse triangular mergers are popular, because they leave the target intact and often avoid the triggering of tax on the gain from what might be deemed to be a sale of the target's assets. A reverse triangular merger may also preserve any carryover losses that the target may have for tax purposes.

A corporation may contribute appreciated assets to a new corporation and spin off the shares as a dividend to existing shareholders who then may keep or sell the shares as they see fit. The contribution of the assets to the new corporation is a tax-free incorporation. The **spin-off** of the shares as a dividend will also be tax-free if there is a business purpose for the transaction and certain other tests are met. Although, in a sense, the recipient shareholders do not receive anything they did not have before, they do end up with more choice and therefore possibly more liquidity. In addition, the two corporations may perform better separately than they did together. In any event, tax-free spin-offs have become a major part of the deal landscape. One of the largest such deals involved the spin-off of Lucent Technologies (the former Bell Labs) from AT&T.

A spin-off or **divisive reorganization** is one of the few remaining ways to extract assets from corporate solution without triggering a tax at the corporate level because of the transaction being deemed a sale of assets by the corporation. Prior to 1986, it was possible to disincorporate tax-free under the so-called *General Utilities* doctrine. The doctrine was, however, abolished by Congress in the Tax Reform Act of 1986, although it is unclear why *incorporation* should be tax free as a mere change of the form of doing business and *disincorporation* should not be, except of course that it is a way of maximizing tax receipts because of the dual tax structure that applies to corporations.

This introduction to the complexity of planning merger and acquisition transactions should make it clear that "doing deals" generates much legal work for lawyers practicing corporation law.

§13.5 Anatomy of a Hostile Takeover

Although most mergers and acquisitions today are friendly deals, it is impossible to understand the array of laws, rules, and contractual devices governing mergers without understanding the hostile takeovers that prompted the adoption or invention of these laws, rules, and devices. In the sections that follow, a hypothetical hostile takeover attempt is discussed in detail.

Let us assume that a potential bidder has found what it believes to be a suitable target. The target is a medium-sized publicly owned corporation. From the target's SEC filings and other publicly available information, it is known that the target has 20,000,000 shares of common stock trading outstanding at about $30 per share. The market therefore currently values the target at $600,000,000. Of the 20,000,000 shares outstanding, it is estimated that 40 percent are held by some 20 or 25 institutional investors. The extent of institutional ownership is significant, because the more concentrated the stock ownership, the easier it is to make direct approaches to the holders of blocks of stock that may be decisive in a struggle for control. Like many other publicly held corporations of approximately this size, management owns an insignificant fraction of the outstanding stock: less than 100,000 shares. The target is apparently well managed and has been consistently profitable, with earnings per share of about $3 in the latest year. At a market price of $30 per share, the target's stock is selling for 10 times earnings, a rather low price/earnings (P/E) ratio for the industry. According to its latest financial statements it has about $50,000,000 of cash (or cash equivalents) on its balance sheet that appears to be in excess of its current operating requirements. The most recent annual report states that funds have been accumulated to finance needed plant expansion and acquisitions of smaller companies that complement the operations of the target corporation. The relatively low price of the target stock may be the result of the market's judgment that such expansion is unwarranted and perhaps that the available cash should be distributed as a dividend instead. In any event, the fact that the company seems to be undervalued and that it has available cash makes it an attractive takeover target.

The potential bidder is also a publicly held corporation. It has built up a "war chest" of over $300,000,000 in cash for acquisitions, and it has arranged lines of credit (usable only for takeovers) that enable it to borrow up to an additional $2,200,000,000 to finance one or more takeovers.

At the outset, the bidder knows relatively little about the target, because it does not have access to internal corporate information. Because the target is publicly held, the bidder does have available the basic data and financial information that is publicly filed with the New York Stock Exchange (the NYSE) and the SEC. It also has available private credit reports and industry and trade information about the operations of the target. It may also have the benefit of some information through hearsay, rumor, and even espionage. Although everything the bidder learns tends to confirm that it is desirable for it to attempt a takeover, this conclusion is necessarily based on incomplete and partial information, and a substantial misjudgment as to value is possible.

At this point, the bidder must decide whether to go ahead and obtain a **toehold** in the target corporation's stock. At the same time, it must make a tentative decision as to how to proceed thereafter: either by a direct appeal to the shareholders through a cash tender offer or by a negotiated transaction with target management. Both alternatives have positive and negative features. A negotiated takeover usually has the advantage of making additional information about the target's affairs available to the bidder before an irrevocable commitment is made. This additional information should permit a more accurate

estimate of the value of the target's business and minimize the danger of paying too much for the business. On the other hand, a proposal for a consensual takeover alerts the target to the threat of a direct tender offer to the shareholders and gives it an opportunity to adopt defensive tactics that might make a takeover much more difficult or even impossible. An immediate tender offer has the advantage of surprise and is more likely to succeed, even though it suffers from the disadvantage of having to proceed on less reliable information.

§13.6 Toehold Acquisitions

Once the decision to go ahead is made, the first step in practically every takeover attempt is for the bidder to purchase a substantial number of target company shares on the open market. These purchases are made at current market prices on the New York Stock Exchange or other market where the target stock is traded but are disguised. Orders may be placed with different brokers in different cities in a variety of different names. The buy orders may be executed at different times as the brokers try to acquire shares at the most favorable prices while hiding the fact that an accumulation of shares for the benefit of one entity is underway.

Under federal law, a bidder may purchase up to 5 percent of the outstanding shares of the target without disclosure. For this reason, one often reads stories about bidders acquiring 4.9 percent of the target's outstanding shares. These announcements are made because the bidder has the independent responsibility of disclosing to its own shareholders that it has made a material investment in another corporation. When ownership exceeds 5 percent, the Williams Act requires the bidder to file a statement with the SEC and to notify the target company within 10 days; but during that 10-day "window," the bidder may continue to purchase the stock. Thus, a bidder may accumulate a significant holding above 5 percent before being required to show its hand.

Assembling a block of 4.9 percent or more of the target's stock undoubtedly will drive up the price of that stock, perhaps from $30 per share to $33 or even $35 per share. If the target is at all sophisticated, it will have detected the surge of buying interest underlying this price run-up. It should suspect that a potential bidder is accumulating shares, because target management should know whether there are pending internal developments to justify the increased interest in the shares. (If there are any such developments, of course, the problem becomes one of insider trading.) Although the target may surmise that someone is accumulating its shares, it probably does not know who it is. If it has not previously adopted takeover defenses, it may hurriedly do so at this time.

The statement that must be filed with the SEC at the expiration of the 10-day window is known as a **13D statement**. The reason for this name is that the statement is required by Section 13(d) of the Securities and Exchange Act. This statement must include information about the identity of the acquirer and the reason for the accumulation of shares. If an immediate takeover attempt is planned, that must be disclosed. If the bidder wishes to keep its options open, it may state that its purpose is to make an investment and that it has no plans

to seek control at this time. If a takeover offer is made shortly thereafter, however, a legal attack may be made on the adequacy of the disclosure in the original 13D filing, and the bidder may be prohibited from voting the shares already acquired.

Let us assume that at the expiration of the 10-day window, our bidder has accumulated 8 percent of the target's stock and has moved the price of target shares to $35 per share. Thus, at the time the bidder goes public by filing its 13D statement, it has purchased 1,600,000 shares of target stock at prices ranging between $30 and $35 per share. If the average price per share was $34, the total investment of the bidder in obtaining a toehold is $54,400,000. Let us also assume that its 13D statement straightforwardly states that it has purchased these shares with a view toward obtaining control of the target.

§13.7 The Dynamics of a Cash Tender Offer

Now that the bidder has resolved to seek control of the target without negotiating with management, one way to do so is to announce a cash tender offer for 42.1 percent of the stock (42.1 percent plus 8 percent already acquired in the open market equals 50.1 percent) of the target at or about the time the 13D statement is filed. (Although such **partial offers** for a bare controlling interest in the target are perfectly legal in the United States — but not in the United Kingdom — and were quite common until the early 1980s, it became standard practice by the late 1980s to offer to purchase all of the remaining shares for cash, largely because of the ready availability of financing and because of potential competition from other bidders.) Target management may receive informal notification of the offer before it is announced, or it may receive no notification at all.

Basically, a cash tender offer is an open invitation for shareholders to submit (i.e., **tender**) shares for purchase by the bidder at a specified price. Persons desiring to accept the bidder's offer must submit their shares to a specified depository by a specified date. If enough shareholders tender their shares for purchase, the bidder has achieved its goal. If not enough do, the bidder may return all the tendered shares and not buy any of them. In this event, its investment in the target is limited to the cost of the toehold shares plus the expenses of the unsuccessful offer. If a higher bid then comes in from a third party, the bidder may tender its toehold for purchase by the new bidder, making a substantial profit.

To make a cash tender offer, the offeror must set a price, decide how many additional shares to seek, file a **14D statement** (required, not surprisingly, by section 14(d) of the 1934 Act), and publicly announce the offer. For example, in the above example, the bidder could decide to make a public offer to purchase 42.1 percent of the shares at $50 per share, with the offer to expire in 20 business days (the minimum period permitted under SEC regulation). The 14D statement must disclose, among other things, the source of financing of the purchase price and the plans the bidder has for the target if the offer is successful, as well as the precise terms of the offer.

A cash tender offer is most likely to be effective in corporations in which

management owns or controls only a small percentage or proportion of the shares. In the publicly held corporation, nonmanagement shares are held by institutional investors, brokerage firms, speculators, long-term investors, and others. Many of these shareholders may be willing to sell their shares outright at a price above the current market price (e.g., at $50 per share when the current market price is $35), even though they might hesitate to vote to oust incumbent management if they are to remain as shareholders. By offering an attractive price, the bidder appeals to the target shareholders over the head of management. The appeal is not "I can do a better job" but rather "do you want to sell at $50 per share?" If enough holders accept the offer, the offer succeeds and the bidder becomes the majority shareholder.

If the bidder acquires exactly 42.1 percent of the target stock, it will then own 50.1 percent of the target's voting stock. That is certainly sufficient to elect a majority of the target's board of directors, and is sufficient to elect the entire board of directors if the corporation does not have cumulative voting (which is likely to be the case in a publicly held corporation) or has not staggered the election of the board as a takeover defense tactic. If the bidder is able to replace a majority of the board of directors with its own people, it may thereafter replace the old target management with its own people, or it may permit that management to continue to operate the target as a subsidiary of the bidder, if the incumbent management is willing.

It is important to recognize that even if the bidder acquires over 50 percent of the outstanding shares and replaces the target's board of directors and management, it does not have a free hand with respect to the target's assets. The target is still a publicly owned company with the public owning 49.9 percent; the presence of this minority interest sharply circumscribes and limits what the bidder can do with the target's assets. For example, the bidder may not simply distribute the $50,000,000 in excess cash to itself or combine a manufacturing division owned by the target with a similar division owned by the bidder. Transactions of these types would almost certainly be viewed as in breach of the fiduciary duty new management has assumed to the former target company and would likely give rise to immediate shareholder derivative suits. Transactions between the bidder and its new partially owned subsidiary must be made at arm's length and, even then, there is a substantial opportunity for distracting litigation brought by minority shareholders of the target. Hence, there is a strong incentive for the bidder ultimately to eliminate all minority shareholders and obtain 100 percent of the stock. Once it obtains all the shares, there are no outside shareholders to complain if the bidder, for example, uses the target's $50,000,000 to defray a portion of the cost of purchasing the 8,420,000 shares (although creditors may be able to complain if the target later becomes insolvent).

Corporation law effectively allows minority shareholders to be "cashed out" involuntarily, as is discussed more fully below. The transaction to eliminate the minority shareholders is often called a **back-end merger** or **mop-up merger**. The terms of a back-end merger may be significantly less attractive than the terms of the original offer.

Say the bidder decides to make a partial offer for 42.1 percent of the target's stock: 8,420,000 shares. What price should the bidder offer? It must

be high enough above the current market price of $35 per share to attract a sufficient number of tenders to yield 8,420,000 shares of stock. It should also be high enough to discourage other possible bidders who may also be looking at the target. On the other hand, one does not want to throw money away with abandon. The bidder is offering to purchase for cash 8,420,000 shares, and the decision whether to offer $45 per share or $50 per share involves a cool $43,000,000. Average takeover premiums during the 1980s were about 50 percent over the pre-offer market price. Thus, $50 per share seems a reasonable price to offer. If this offer is successful, the bidder is committing itself to invest another $431,000,000 in addition to the $54,000,000 invested in the original toehold, in order to obtain control (50.1 percent) of the target. In terms of similar transactions during the 1980s, this nearly half-billion dollar transaction is a relatively small transaction.

Very large offers may be contingent on obtaining financing. That is not necessary in our hypothetical, because the bidder has already lined up $2,200,000,000 of cash or commitments, which is more than ample to pay for the target stock. It is common, however, to include other conditions, such as the absence of objections from the antitrust authorities. Some of these conditions may be fairly general (e.g., an absence of material changes in market conditions) so that a tender offer has some of the attributes of an option rather than of a firm offer to be accepted by individual shareholders tendering their shares. It is rare, however, for a bidder to attempt to invoke these "out" clauses to back out of a successful offer.

In a partial offer, as here, the offer is said to be over-subscribed if the total shares tendered for purchase by the deadline exceed 8,420,000 shares. In this event, the offeror (bidder) may either purchase only 8,420,000 shares or, at its option, purchase all the shares that have been tendered. Under the Williams Act and SEC rules adopted to implement it, if the bidder elects to limit its purchases to 8,420,000 shares, it must purchase shares pro rata from each tenderer; it may not purchase shares on a first-come, first-served basis. Pro rata means that if 12,000,000 shares are tendered, the bidder must purchase 8,420,000/ 12,000,000 of each individual tender. The federal prohibition against a first-come, first-served offer stems from the worry that it might cause shareholders to tender hastily without opportunity for reflection (in order to make sure that tendered shares are actually purchased) and that it tends to favor centrally located shareholders (principally in New York) at the expense of shareholders who live in more remote locations.

SEC rules under the Williams Act also provide that tendered shares may be withdrawn during the offer and after 60 days if they have not been purchased. As previously noted, the offer must remain open for at least 20 business days, and the bidder may extend it for a longer period or increase the price (e.g., in response to a competing bid at a higher price). If the bidder does increase the price, however, it must buy all shares at the higher price including shares tendered at the lower price. It is arguable, however, that **proration** discourages shareholders from tendering, and indeed it may have been a factor in the trend away from partial offers. That is, to the extent that shareholders are averse to the prospect of a partial purchase of tendered shares, a bidder who offers to buy any and all shares tendered makes a more attractive offer, other things equal,

and will presumably attract more tenders. In any event, market professionals figured out, that by tendering borrowed shares they could avoid the risk of proration, prompting the SEC to adopt a rule against **short tendering**. On the other hand, a bidder may let one offer expire and then immediately make a new offer at a higher price, thereby achieving the same result without paying everyone the increased price. SEC rules under the Williams Act also require that tender offers be made to all shareholders. That is, specific groups of shareholders may not be excluded. As long as the tender offer is open, the bidder may purchase shares only through the tender offer. The bidder may not negotiate separately with large institutional shareholders. On the other hand, immediately after the offer expires, the bidder may negotiate with shareholders and purchase their shares in private transactions. This tactic is called a street sweep and is discussed more fully below.

SEC rules also effectively prohibit lowering the price to be paid during the course of a tender offer, although theoretically a lower price may be paid if earlier tendering shareholders agree to the reduction. The **highest price rule** is apparently prompted by notions of fairness — that if some shares are worth the high price, all shares are worth the high price — though quite clearly the rule does not extend back to shares purchased in the open market on the sly to gain a toehold and, as a matter of federal law at least, does not extend forward to any cash out merger of nontendering shareholders. The highest price rule may have the effect of discouraging tender offers, because it effectively increases the price that must be paid by bidders. If bidders could make stair-step offers and were not required to pay all tendering shareholders the highest price paid to any, it would probably be cheaper to acquire control and more offers might be made. And given that many shareholders sell their shares in the open market during a tender offer (at prices affected by the pendency of the offer) rather than take the risk that the offer may fail or be over-subscribed and result in proration, many shareholders effectively opt into a stair-step bid anyway.

§13.8 Open Market Purchases as an Alternative to a Tender Offer

A few instances have occurred in which a bidder sought to obtain a majority of the outstanding shares of the target by a series of open market purchases without ever making a public tender offer. A 13D statement must be filed when the purchaser breaks the 5 percent level, but no 14D filing is required, because no public tender offer is being made. Moreover, the bidding rules do not apply. Or so the argument goes. There are problems with this approach, however. For one thing, a stream of purchases of this magnitude may drive the market price of the target stock significantly above the price that would bring forth the same number of shares if a tender offer were made. In other words, a tender offer at $50 per share — a one-shot, limited-time offer — may draw more stock out for purchase at $50 per share than could be obtained on the open market at an average price of $50 per share even if the price began at $35 per share. Second, if the bidder communicates directly with large investors while actively purchasing shares in the open market, it may be argued that the communications

constituted a tender offer (even though made only to selected persons). This is illegal under the Williams Act when it is not made to all shareholders and not made pursuant to a filed 14D statement. Curiously, the Williams Act contains no definition of what constitutes a tender offer.

§13.9 Role of Arbitrageurs and Speculators in Takeover Battles

When a cash tender offer is made for target shares, the subsequent market activity in the stock strongly influences the offer's outcome. A major run-up in price usually occurs at or shortly before the announcement of the tender offer. Major run-ups in price before the offer probably are caused by information leaks about the contemplated offer. Until recently, a large amount of trading in advance of an offer transpired. Many individuals involved in such trading have been prosecuted, and it is likely that this type of insider trading is a thing of the past. Indeed, the courts have held that information about a planned tender offer is presumed to be improperly obtained.

Leaving aside the possibility of insider trading, when a tender offer is publicly announced the market price for the target shares typically jumps almost instantly to a price nearly as high as the offer price. (The price of the bidder's shares may well decline, but that is another story as discussed more fully below.) Post-offer market activity is largely a result of trading by sophisticated speculators, known as **arbitrageurs**, who accumulate shares and plan to tender them to the bidder (or to the highest competing bidder). On the day the bidder announces its $50 bid, arbitrageurs immediately enter the market, buying target shares at whatever prices they are offered below $50 (and in some cases above $50 if they have reason to believe the bid will be increased or competing offers will be made). These transactions are not classic arbitrage, because the success of the offer is not guaranteed and therefore a degree of risk is involved. For a discussion of the traditional meaning of that term, see Chapter 11, which discusses corporate securities. One should not overstate the degree of risk. Market wisdom is that once a company is "put into play" by a tender offer, its chances of remaining an independent entity are small. In other words, arbitrageurs typically have been able to liquidate their positions in target stock at a profit. Indeed, arbitrage was so profitable in the 1980s that the financial resources of arbitrageurs increased to the point that they were a major force in takeover battles and were able to absorb billions of dollars worth of target shares as they were offered on the market.

The result of arbitrage is that upon the announcement of a bid the price of target stock is quickly driven up from the pre-offer price to a price in the neighborhood of the offered price. The precise relationship of the market price of the target's shares following the announcement to the announced tender offer price is a complex one that depends on the answers to several questions:

1. What is the probability that the offer will succeed?
2. If it does succeed (and the offer is a partial one), to what extent will it be oversubscribed?

3. If it is oversubscribed, will the offeror acquire all shares or will the offer be prorated?
4. If the offer is prorated, what are the terms of the proposed back-end or mop-up merger, if any, likely to be?
5. What are the chances that a higher offer may be forthcoming from a different source?
6. What are the chances that management will attempt a leveraged buyout or a reorganization that provides shareholders with more value than the offer?

Depending on these variables, the market price may be substantially below, slightly below, slightly above, or substantially above, the tender offer price.

Consider the position of shareholders in the target corporation when the offer is made. Upon the announcement of the offer, the shareholders see the market price of their shares advance significantly. The shareholders can choose to (1) hold their shares, hoping that the offer fails and that incumbent management remains in control or that the offer succeeds and that they will get the benefit of new and revitalized management; (2) tender their shares to the bidder pursuant to the offer, hoping that the offer succeeds and is not oversubscribed, but with the risk that they may get back some or all of their shares if the offer is prorated; or (3) sell their shares on the open market and be out of the situation entirely.

The first choice is usually unattractive, because, if the offer fails, history shows the market price of the target shares declines to levels that may be even below the pre-offer price; on the other hand, if the offer succeeds, the nontendering shareholder may be at a serious disadvantage by being remitted to whatever rights he or she may have in the subsequent back-end or mop-up transaction that is likely to occur. The second choice carries the risk that the offer may be oversubscribed and some of the shares returned with the result that the shareholder may again be remitted in part to the back-end offer. Further, tendering involves a mechanical process of complying with the terms of the tender offer and delivery of shares in advance of payment that many shareholders find complex and uncertain. The simplest thing to do is to sell the shares. One thereby obtains the benefit of most of the run-up in price with none of the problems or risks of actually making a tender. The cost of this strategy is that the selling shareholder loses any benefit of subsequent offers by third persons or the benefit of any increase in the offer price by the bidder. And, of course, the selling shareholder must pay a commission to his or her broker.

One thing is virtually certain: If shareholders of the target sell their shares during the pendency of the offer, they will be acquired by arbitrageurs and will be tendered to somebody. Open market sales are thus virtually a vote for the bidder. Put another way, arbitrageurs and bidders are natural allies in the takeover wars.

Institutional investors are under pressure to tender their shares or sell for a different reason. Many of them hold and invest funds as fiduciaries for other groups — employees, insurance policy holders, small investors, and so forth. They have fiduciary responsibilities to obtain the maximum financial return for the current beneficiaries. They may conclude that these fiduciary duties require

them to maximize short-run profit by taking advantage of the run-up in price resulting from a tender offer either by tendering shares to the bidder or by selling them during the offer.

§13.10 "Street Sweeps" Following Unsuccessful Tender Offers

As described in the previous section, when a corporation is put into play, very large market accumulations of stock are made by arbitrageurs and other speculators in anticipation of the target being taken over by another entity. Occasionally, the bidder is unexpectedly stymied by defensive techniques and thereby compelled to withdraw its offer. At that point, there is a risk that there will be no takeover at all and arbitrageurs face massive losses, because they have paid high prices for shares that will now decline dramatically in price when the takeover threat disappears.

Even in this situation, arbitrageurs have usually avoided substantial losses. Despite the withdrawal of the tender offer, the target remains in a very precarious situation because of the concentration of share ownership in the hands of arbitrageurs and other speculators who are anxious to sell. The percentage ownership of target shares by this relatively small group may approach or exceed 50 percent of the outstanding shares. The target is even more ripe for a takeover than it was before the offer was originally made because of this concentration of ownership in the hands of persons who have no loyalty to the target and who are interested only in an immediate financial return. It is easy for either the bidder that withdrew its recent offer or an opportunistic third person to contact the arbitrageurs directly and offer to buy their holdings of target shares. The price offered for the shares may be somewhat below the price previously offered in the withdrawn tender offer but certainly above the pre-offer price, because the shares being purchased may determine who has working control of the target enterprise. This practice of purchasing shares directly from arbitrageurs and speculators immediately after an unsuccessful tender offer has come to be known as a **street sweep** (the street being Wall Street).

The SEC unsuccessfully challenged street sweeps as violations of the Williams Act and as being unfair to smaller shareholders who are not offered the opportunity to sell their shares in the sweep. The SEC proposed a rule that would make all street sweeps within 10 days after an offer is withdrawn subject to the Williams Act, but the rule was never adopted.

§13.11 Back-End Transactions

As described above, most bidders ultimately desire to acquire 100 percent of the outstanding shares of the target. However, it is not possible as a practical matter to acquire 100 percent of the shares of a publicly held corporation by a tender offer. Even in an irresistibly attractive tender offer for all shares, a few shareholders always fail to tender by reason of inadvertence or inattention, and there always are a few small shareholders who hold out and refuse to accept an

offer at any price. A follow-up transaction to eliminate the remaining public shareholders is an essential step when 100 percent ownership is desired. These follow-up transactions, often called back-end or mop-up transactions, are statutory mergers. A back-end transaction is not necessary if the bidder is willing to accept the status of a majority shareholder in a publicly held corporation with minority shareholders.

In a public cash tender offer, the bidder may make the back-end transaction an affirmative weapon. The bidder may make a partial tender offer, seeking to acquire a controlling interest but less than all of the target's outstanding shares, and at the same time announce, as part of its takeover strategy, the terms of the back-end merger that will eliminate all of the remaining outstanding shares if the original partial offer is successful. Such an offer is known as a **two-step offer** or **two-tier offer**. The terms of the back-end part of the two-step offer, moreover, may be less attractive than the terms of the original cash tender offer, thereby encouraging (or coercing) all shareholders to tender promptly to avoid the less attractive terms of the follow-up transaction. Such an offer is known as a **front-end loaded offer** and is sometimes referred to as a **coercive offer** (although coercion comes in many forms). Many states have enacted statutes restricting back-end transactions.

Assume (as in the foregoing hypothetical) that the bidder has acquired 50.1 percent of the outstanding shares of the target for a total consideration of $485 million. It has decided to force out the remaining 49.1 percent of the shares at $50 per share. The bidder creates a wholly owned subsidiary and transfers to that subsidiary cash and notes to enable the subsidiary to pay the holders of the 49.1 percent of the target shares the bidder does not own. The bidder then proposes a merger of the target corporation into the subsidiary (i.e., a merger in which the surviving corporation is the subsidiary) under the terms of which the holders of the 49.1 percent minority shares are to receive a consideration of $50 in cash and notes for each of their shares in the target. Although the bidder as the majority shareholder of the target is technically entitled to receive the same consideration as the minority shareholders, as the sole shareholder of the surviving subsidiary, the bidder need not bother to pay itself. Approval of this transaction is no problem: The bidder already owns all the stock of one party to the transaction (its subsidiary) and 50.1 percent of the stock of the other (the target), and because a simple majority of the outstanding shares of each constituent corporation is all that is required to approve the merger, the result of the vote is a foregone conclusion. When the transaction is closed, each minority shareholder receives $50 per share. All shares of the target are cancelled; because the wholly owned subsidiary is the surviving corporation in the merger, it ends up with the property and business of the target and the bidder is the owner of 100 percent of the outstanding shares of that corporation. The net effect of this merger is that the remaining shareholders of the target are forced to accept cash and notes for their shares, while the bidder keeps the business as the sole shareholder of the surviving company.

Seemingly, the minority shareholders of the target must be satisfied with whatever pittance the bidder—the new majority shareholder—decides to give them. There are, however, several important protections for minority shareholder interests. The first is the statutory right of **dissent and appraisal** that

permits any minority shareholder dissatisfied with the proffered terms (1) to reject them; (2) to obtain an independent judicial appraisal of the value of his or her shares; and (3) to receive that value in cash in lieu of the consideration offered in the cash merger transaction. This alternative is not really as attractive as it might first appear. There are major practical problems with appraisal rights from the standpoint of small shareholders: the cost of maintaining any judicial proceeding, delays (during which the shareholder loses the use of money), and the uncertainty in outcome inherent in any judicial proceeding. Moreover, the courts of some states adhere to the view that if the stock in question is publicly traded, the market price is presumed to be fair, despite the fact that bidders invariably must offer a substantial premium over the market price in order to induce sufficient tenders to gain control. Indeed, in certain circumstances, some states deny dissenters rights for certain types of transactions involving publicly traded companies. Delaware even denies dissenters' rights in connection with transactions structured as sales of assets rather than mergers. Nevertheless, if the new majority shareholder is too stingy with the minority, it will find itself involved in litigation with unhappy minority shareholders over the value of the minority shares, with a contingent obligation to pay the dissenting shareholders immediately in cash whatever amount the court ultimately determines to be the fair value of the minority shares. Thus, bidders have a strong incentive to offer back-end consideration that will minimize the number of dissenters.

A second major safety valve is the recognition by the Delaware Supreme Court that the majority shareholder, when it decides to vote its 50.1 percent of the target's stock to approve the transaction, is engaged in a self-dealing transaction that must meet a standard of **intrinsic fairness**. *See Weinberger v. UOP, Inc.*, 457 A.2d 701 (1983). Intrinsic fairness requires fair dealing (including full disclosure of all relevant facts as well as a fair opportunity for some type of negotiation on behalf of the minority) and fair price, with the bidder having the burden of proof in any lawsuit brought by the minority that the standard of fairness has been met. This burden may be shifted to the plaintiff shareholders, however, if the transaction is approved after full disclosure by the minority shareholders voting separately — a majority of the minority vote, so to speak. Although such a minority vote is not required under the merger statute, approval by the minority may, as a practical matter, be necessary if the merger is to withstand judicial scrutiny. Although the majority of the minority vote is a court-created protection under Delaware law, the Model Business Corporation Act of 1984 and several of the states that follow it closely have adopted the device as a matter of statute.

A third safety valve is that Delaware case law permits more powerful defensive tactics by a target against a proposed takeover bid if the target reasonably believes that the proposed back-end transaction makes the entire transaction inadequate or coercive to minority shareholders.

If a bidder announces a two-tier offer in which the amount offered for the back end of the offer is openly stated to be less than the amount offered in the front-end offer, the offer is called a "front-end loaded" tender offer. In one famous case involving the takeover of Marathon Oil by United States Steel in 1981, the bidder, United States Steel, announced a tender offer at $125 per share for 51 percent of the shares and also announced that if the first offer were

successful a back-end transaction would be proposed eliminating the unpurchased shares for a consideration to be paid in the form of bonds worth approximately $76 per share. (The eventually successful offer was arranged in cooperation with the target, because of an earlier unwelcome offer by Mobil Oil.) Such an offer places economic pressure on all shareholders to tender into the original offer in order to take advantage of the front-end price and avoid the lower back-end price. As a result, a transaction structured in this way is generally viewed as highly coercive, though its use has been defended on abstract grounds by some economists. Their argument is that the true price being offered for the target company is the **blended price** obtained by averaging the front-end and back-end prices. If this blended price is above the pre-offer market price, the transaction still creates value for the target shareholders as a whole. This argument assumes implicitly that all shareholders will tender into the front-end offer, as they rationally should do. The shareholders then sustain no harm, because they all will effectively obtain the blended price (because all will share proportionately in both the front-end and back-end prices when the oversubscribed offer is prorated). However, these arguments mask a considerable potential for unfairness to individual shareholders, not all of whom may be aware that a rational decision is required or be able to act on a timely basis to accept the front-end offer. Devices such as short tendering also exist; these devices allow sophisticated shareholders to obtain the purchase of a larger percentage of their shares at the front-end price than other shareholders.

A second approach toward front-end loaded offers is illustrated by the offer of Mesa Petroleum for Unocal Corporation. Mesa offered $54 per share in a tender offer for enough shares (an additional 37 percent) to raise its holdings to just over 50 percent of Unocal, and in the back-end offer, proposed a consideration of "highly subordinated" Unocal debt securities "with a market value of $54." Presumably the "subordination" referred to new bank loans to be obtained by Unocal to assist Mesa in financing the original purchase of the 37 percent of Unocal. Unocal vigorously opposed this transaction, pejoratively describing the debt securities that Mesa proposed as "junk bonds," and proposing an exchange offer to all of its remaining shareholders — except Mesa — that would have provided each shareholder with a substantial amount of senior Unocal debt. This discriminatory offer was upheld by the Delaware Supreme Court in *Unocal v. Mesa Petroleum Co.*, 493 A.2d 946 (Del. 1985), and ultimately Mesa's offer was defeated. Following the Unocal opinion, the Securities and Exchange Commission adopted an **all holders rule** to prohibit the kind of discriminatory offer that Unocal made in this case.

As a general proposition, it is difficult to quarrel with the Delaware Supreme Court's categorization of Mesa's offer for Unocal. An all-cash $54 offer is more attractive than an offer of debt and securities "with a market value of" $54, because of the uncertainties of valuation and the possibility that the market may value the debt securities at a lower price than what the offeror optimistically estimates. Further, the ready marketability of the debt may be doubtful, particularly for large holders. Hence, this type of offer appears also to be a type of front-end loaded offer, though perhaps not as blatant as a dual-price cash offer.

Front-end loaded offers declined dramatically after 1985. The most common pattern became to announce that in the back-end offer the same amount

of cash would be paid as in the front-end offer (or to state that no plans for a back-end offer existed). Several factors caused the apparent abandonment of the front-end loaded offer. A number of corporations adopted **fair price amendments** to their articles of incorporation requiring back-end transactions to be made at prices at least as favorable as the front-end offer price. Several states imposed similar fair price requirements for such mergers by statute: Maryland was the first state to adopt this type of statute. (But neither fair price amendments nor fair price statutes dealt with the possibility that the bidder might simply decline to do a back-end merger and leave the minority shareholders frozen into their investment in a controlled corporation.) Judicial antagonism to front-end loaded offers, epitomized by the Delaware Supreme Court's categorization of Mesa's offer for Unocal as an "inadequate and coercive two-tier tender offer," indicated a willingness by courts to permit extreme defensive measures to defeat such offers. Finally, because a noncoercive all cash offer is more attractive to target shareholders, competition from other bidders tended to force serious initial bidders to make all cash **any-or-all offers** in the first place, in part because it became quite easy to raise larger amounts of cash through junk bonds. Nevertheless, a two-tier offer prevailed in the 1994 Viacom bid for Paramount, suggesting either that target shareholders had forgotten what they learned earlier or that the terms of offers may change over time much as fashions do.

§13.12 The Proxy Fight

The oldest type of nonconsensual takeover technique, long antedating the development of the cash tender offer, is the proxy fight. In a **proxy fight**, the bidder solicits the target's shareholders with a proposal that they vote for an alternative slate of directors. If holders of a majority of the shares vote for the alternative slate, the bidder obtains control of the board of directors of the target. Thereafter, a cash-out merger with the bidder may be negotiated or the target may remain in business as a separate entity indefinitely under the new management. The proxy fight is much more akin to a traditional political campaign than a tender offer; shareholders who vote in favor of the bidder generally remain shareholders after the change in management occurs. Proxy fights are subject to significant regulation under the proxy rules adopted by the SEC. These rules basically require full and open disclosure of objectives and plans.

The proxy fight has not been a popular device in the recent past primarily because the probability of its success is relatively low and because cash is usually available to buy control directly through a cash tender offer. The reason for the low probability of success is that it is difficult to persuade shareholders to vote out incumbent management when they will remain as shareholders in the target corporation after the change in management occurs. Nevertheless, a handful of attempts have taken place during the recent takeover movement to use the proxy fight as an auxiliary device to place additional pressure on the target short of making an outright offer to purchase control. This usually occurs when it appears the target is so large, or its defenses seem so impregnable, that it is impractical for the bidder to mount a cash tender offer.

With the development of powerful takeover defenses by corporations and the enactment of statutes by Delaware and other states that make takeovers more difficult, it is possible that proxy fights may be more widely used in the future than in the past.

§13.13 Exchange Offers

A few takeover offers have been based not on offers of cash for target securities but on offers of exchanges of bidder debt for shares of the target. Ted Turner once unsuccessfully attempted to acquire a controlling interest in rival CBS, Inc. by an offer to swap a variety of debt instruments, including several zero coupon notes, for CBS stock. The offer did not succeed, in part because CBS installed substantial takeover defenses that probably would have made it impractical for Turner to use CBS assets or cash flow to service any of the additional debt.

Transactions are cast in the form of exchange offers when the bidder finds it impractical to raise sufficient cash to mount a straight tender offer. Exchange offers suffer from problems of uncertainty over the market value of the proffered debt securities and concerns over the potential lack of marketability of large blocks of those securities. In addition, a substantial risk of default may take place: The bidder may be unable to satisfy the obligations set forth in the debt securities it is offering, and the market may discount the securities accordingly. These securities are sometimes called "funny money," a phrase that reflects the skepticism of the market about this type of transaction.

An offer of bidder-issued debt for stock in the target in a sense proposes that the shareholders of the target themselves finance the takeover of their own company. Rather than the bidder borrowing money from third parties by issuing debt and using the money to purchase shares, the bidder offers the debt directly to the target shareholders. On the other hand, one could think of such an offer as a firm commitment to cause the target company to make generous distributions, and indeed many offers have been prompted by the target company's stinginess in making distributions and its decision to invest extra cash in questionable ways. Nevertheless, it is not surprising that offers of funny money have not proved to be attractive.

§13.14 Defensive Tactics in General

When the first cash tender offers were made, the targets were virtually defenseless. They were often unprepared for the offer, and a successful purchase of the majority of the outstanding shares often occurred before the simplest defensive measures could be taken. The Williams Act sharply cut down the advantage of surprise by its disclosure requirements and the provision that all tender offers must remain open for at least 20 business days, thereby eliminating pressure on shareholders to tender immediately or lose out.

Today, **defensive tactics** are well understood and practically every publicly held corporation has erected a shield consisting of a number of different types of defenses. Defenses may be classified into two basic types: (1) those put into

place before any tender offer is made and designed to discourage the approach in the first place and (2) those instituted after a cash tender offer has been launched in an effort to defeat that particular offer.

The simplest types of pre-offer defenses involve the use of devices long provided for in corporation statutes that make it difficult to obtain working control of the target even if the bidder obtains a majority of its outstanding voting shares. These provisions, known as **shark repellants** or **porcupine provisions**, may either make the process by which the board of directors is replaced by a new majority shareholder more difficult or impose additional costs on the corporation in the event of a successful takeover.

A popular defense is to stagger the election of directors so that directors have three-year terms and only one-third of the board is elected each year. At the same time, it is necessary to provide that directors may only be removed for "cause" in order to prevent a new majority shareholder from calling a meeting of shareholders and simply removing all the directors without cause, as is permitted under most state corporation statutes. The theory of these provisions is that it may take the bidder two years after obtaining a majority of the shares before it is able to replace a majority of the board of directors with its own designees.

Another popular provision limits the power of shareholders to call special meetings on the theory that the new majority shareholder may be unable to act except at a meeting. In states that permit the shareholders to act by majority consent informally without a meeting (an option that is available in Delaware and a limited number of other states), bylaw or charter provisions may also be adopted defining and circumscribing that power, again making it difficult for a new majority shareholder to translate its shareholdings into operating control of the target.

Pre-offer defensive tactics may also involve economic changes designed to make the corporation less attractive as a target. This is a second line of defense independent of the internal corporate changes described above. For example, corporations may grant officers and mid-level employees **golden parachutes** or **tin parachutes** triggered by a takeover of the management of the corporation over the objection of incumbent management. Golden parachutes are lucrative severance contracts for top management whose employment with the corporation may be terminated upon a successful takeover. Tin parachutes are smaller severance contracts for middle-level management. The total payments required under individual contracts may run into the tens of millions of dollars for high-level individual officers. Aggregate payments may be several times larger. Even with large payments, however, it is unlikely that they will seriously deter a bidder who is already contemplating a transaction running into the hundreds of millions or billions of dollars. Moreover, it is arguable that golden parachutes allow management to serve the corporation during the pendency of a takeover bid without concern about their personal economic futures and encourage management to consider the interests of the target shareholders seriously.

Another type of economic defense against unwanted takeover attempts involves restructuring the corporation to reduce its attractiveness as a takeover target. Many corporations, for example, have distributed excess cash to shareholders either in the form of an extraordinary dividend, or, more commonly, in

the form of open market share repurchases. A major share repurchase plan (1) reduces the number of outstanding shares; (2) leaves total earnings per share virtually unchanged or may indeed increase earnings per share (because the cash used is excess and not essential for the operation of the target's business and because of the reduced number of shares); and (3) increases the market price of the target shares through simple reduction in supply.

The business may also be recapitalized by the sale of nonessential lines of business and distribution of the proceeds to the shareholders in the form of extraordinary distributions or a share repurchase program. Large amounts may also be borrowed in order to leverage up the target and increase its debt/equity ratio; the cash is again distributed to shareholders. Such a transaction is often called a **leveraged recapitalization**. This makes the target "leaner and meaner" and basically does what a successful bidder would be likely to do if it obtained working control of the target. Whether these transactions are desirable from the standpoint of the economic well-being of the target may be questionable.

Yet another popular defensive tactic is to make it difficult for a successful bidder to obtain approval of back-end merger transactions. These provisions may no longer be necessary in Delaware corporations (and corporations formed in states with statutes similar to Delaware's), because a statute now limits such transactions. Corporations formed in other states may adopt super-majority provisions that require approval by more than a majority vote of the shareholders: a two-thirds or even higher percentage vote of the shareholders may be required for approval of transactions between the target corporation and the bidder or a corporation that the bidder controls. To avoid imposing impossible restraints on desired transactions with major shareholders, the super-majority provision may be made waivable by the board of directors or applicable only to transactions with a person who recently acquired a substantial interest in the target's stock. A more radical type of provision grants rights of redemption to minority shareholders at the same price paid by a bidder who acquires a majority of the outstanding shares. Another provision limits the power of a bidder to impose a back-end transaction on terms less favorable than the terms on which the bidder obtained its controlling interest. Other pre-offer defenses are poison pills and control share acquisition plans, both of which are discussed below.

Once an offer is made, the nature of defensive tactics changes materially. The object is to defeat the offer by any fair (or not so fair) means. The following are typical (though the list is not exhaustive):

1. Acquiring another corporation that creates antitrust problems for the bidder if it completes the purchase of the target company.
2. Attacking the funding of the offer, usually by direct approaches to the financial institutions named in the bidder's 14D statement.
3. Driving up the price of target stock so that it is above the tender offer price. This may be accomplished by making a major distribution (a type of restructuring or recapitalizing), or by a large share repurchase plan that may reduce the number of outstanding shares by 20 percent or more.
4. Disposing of desirable assets—**crown jewels**—to friendly entities on terms that are less than favorable to the target. The object of these

transactions is to make the target less attractive as a target. At the most extreme, the target may destroy itself as a viable economic entity to avoid capture. This is a **scorched earth** tactic.

5. Granting **lock up** options or rights to friendly interests to purchase additional shares of target stock at bargain prices. Such transactions increase the number of shares needed to be purchased by the bidder.

6. Making a competing tender offer for the bidder's stock. Often referred to as the **pac man defense**, this strategy may lead to the bizarre situation in which each corporation has acquired a majority of the outstanding shares of the other corporation. This strategy has only rarely been attempted.

7. Finding a more congenial suitor — a **white knight** — and arranging a consensual transaction.

8. Arranging a **leveraged buyout** with a new entity in which incumbent management participates.

9. Adopting poison pill or control share acquisition provisions (discussed in the two following sections).

10. Changing the state of incorporation to take advantage of more favorable state laws or seeking changes in home-state corporation laws, which in some cases may be easier, cheaper, and quicker than amending the corporation's articles or bylaws.

Some of these defensive tactics may lead to the defeat of the takeover attempt outright, while others tend to encourage bidding contests by introducing new contestants for control of the target.

§13.15 Poison Pills

A **poison pill** is a special type of preferred stock or debt issued by a potential target corporation with rights that are designed to make a hostile takeover attempt difficult, impractical, or impossible. Poison pills were invented in the early 1980s and have become one of the most popular takeover defenses; hundreds of publicly held corporations have adopted them. The phrases "poison pill" and "poison pill preferred" are virtually synonymous, because almost all poison pills are created using preferred stock as the vehicle.

The board of directors acting alone usually creates poison pills without shareholder vote pursuant to the statutory power to create series of preferred shares (if authorized to do so in the articles of incorporation). Although a poison pill theoretically could be created by shareholder action, boards of directors usually prefer not to submit such a controversial issue to the shareholders. Because shareholder approval is not obtained, it has been argued that poison pills are intended primarily to entrench incumbent management and that their adoption is in violation of duties owed to the corporation and its shareholders. The Supreme Court of Delaware has held, however, that a poison pill adopted in advance of any takeover threat is not illegal if the pill is fashioned so as not to prevent all takeovers. The decision of whether to adopt such a pill thus becomes a matter of business judgment. *See Moran v. Household International, Inc.*, 500 A.2d 1346 (1985).

The unique characteristic of a poison pill is that additional rights are granted to shareholders when a bidder makes a public tender offer for target shares or acquires a specified percentage of the target shares. Typical triggering events are either a tender offer for 30 percent of the target's shares or the acquisition of 20 percent or more of target shares. The additional rights may consist of increased voting rights for shareholders other than the bidder. For example, shareholders other than the bidder or potential bidder may become entitled to 10 votes per share when the pill is triggered, while the voting rights of the bidder are unchanged. A poison pill may also grant additional financial rights in the target such as the right to acquire additional shares or indebtedness issued by the target corporation at a bargain price if the poison pill is triggered (a **flip-in plan**), or rights to purchase bidder shares at bargain prices in the event of a back-end merger, such as the right to purchase $200 worth of the common shares of the tender offeror for $100 in the merger (a **flip-over plan**). Typically, management may disarm these potent devices by redeeming the poison pill preferred at a nominal price before its rights become vested.

Voting rights poison pills have been invalidated in two cases (arising under New Jersey law) on the ground that the corporation statute of that state does not contemplate that differential voting rights may be created for some common shares while being withheld from others. Because these decisions do not appear to be based on unique New Jersey law, many companies avoid voting rights poison pills.

In practice, poison pills turn out to be negotiating devices more than deterrents. They tend to compel potential bidders to negotiate with incumbent management for a takeover and are rarely actually triggered by a tender offer. Poison pills are not foolproof defenses; they may be neutralized in the context of an unwanted tender offer in several ways. For example, the bidder may make a tender offer on condition that the board redeems the poison pill preferred, or the bidder may tender for both shares and rights under the poison pill preferred, or it may tender and simultaneously solicit consents to replace the board and redeem the rights, or it may acquire over 50 percent of the target shares and then cause the target to self-tender for the rights.

Litigation may also be possible on the premise that the target board of directors may not arbitrarily reject a tender offer or refuse to redeem rights in order to preserve their positions within the corporation.

Section 203 of the Delaware General Corporation Law, which requires in effect 85 percent ownership of target stock before any back-end merger may be effected, may largely duplicate the protection that poison pills provide, but as a practical matter it is likely that corporations with poison pill defenses already in place will simply retain them. Section 203 is discussed in more detail below.

A closely related preemptive defensive tactic is a **dual class recapitalization**. Hostile takeovers depend on the bidder's ability to amass voting stock. One way for a potential target to avoid takeover is to eliminate voting stock in the hands of the public. A dual class recapitalization is a transaction in which the potential target firm offers shares of nonvoting common stock in exchange for shares of voting stock. Assuming that two shares of nonvoting stock are issued for each share of voting stock and both classes have equal financial rights, the trade appears to be attractive from the point of view of the shareholder

whose vote likely counts for little anyway. Assume, however, that management owns 10,000,000 shares before the exchange and that 90,000,000 shares are owned by scattered public shareholders. If all of the shareholders other than management accept the exchange, there will be 190,000,000 shares outstanding and the public shareholders will have 180,000,000 nonvoting shares. In other words, their aggregate ownership interest will have increased from 90 percent to just 94.7 percent, but because management now has all the voting shares the company can never be taken over in a hostile transaction. Although any increase in the relative financial rights of the shareholders is no doubt welcome, the voting rights recapitalization in effect gives the public shareholders only about a 5 percent premium for their shares compared to an average of about 50 percent in third-party transactions. Moreover, the offer itself is arguably highly coercive. A shareholder who declines the offer and keeps voting shares will see the financial value of his or her shares diluted by almost half. Clearly, if a shareholder cannot mount an organized campaign to oppose the trade, he or she cannot afford to refuse to take the deal.

One problem with voting rights recapitalizations is that the New York Stock Exchange has traditionally refused to list nonvoting stock for trading. Moreover, several courts have held that takeover defenses that entail violation of stock exchange rules and that cause the company to be delisted constitute irreparable harm to the shareholders and may be enjoined. The credible threat of takeovers being launched against even very large companies, however, led several such companies, among them General Motors, to oppose (and even violate) the rule against listing nonvoting or lesser voting stock. With the extraordinary growth of NASDAQ, it was at least possible that the NYSE might lose many listings because of its rule. The SEC eventually proposed that all stock exchanges be required to adopt a uniform listing standard prohibiting voting rights recapitalizations. The rule was struck down as being beyond the power of the SEC (*Business Roundtable v. SEC*, 905 F.2d 406 (D.C. Cir. 1990)), but the major exchanges with some prodding from the SEC have continued to adhere to it anyway.

§13.16 State Takeover Statutes

States often oppose takeovers of corporations with significant local connections. The first attempts by states to slow down takeover activity led to the enactment by virtually all states of registration requirements for cash tender offers. These registration requirements applied to publicly held corporations with significant local contacts (usually defined in terms of having property with a specified value in the state, having its principal executive offices in the state, being organized under the laws of the state, or having a specified number of shareholders in the state). In *Edgar v. Mite Corporation*, 457 U.S. 624 (1982), the United States Supreme Court effectively invalidated most of these **first-generation state takeover laws** as an unreasonable burden on interstate commerce. Based on this decision, some commentators concluded that the national market for control of publicly held corporations was beyond the scope of state regulation. This, however, did not prove to be the case.

In 1987, the United States Supreme Court upheld the Indiana **control share acquisition statute** (*CTS Corporation v. General Dynamics Corp. of America*, 481 U.S. 69 (1987)). This statute defines a control share acquisition as any acquisition that causes the shareholder to break through the 20 percent, the 33.3 percent, or 50 percent levels of share ownership. A person making an acquisition of control shares of an Indiana corporation does not obtain the right to vote the newly acquired shares unless a majority of disinterested shareholders (excluding both the shares that the acquirer of the control shares owns and the shares that incumbent management owns) vote to grant voting rights to the acquirer. A proposed acquirer may compel a vote by disinterested shareholders on whether voting rights should be granted upon the acquisition if the acquirer agrees to pay for the cost of the shareholders' meeting. The Supreme Court upheld this statute largely under the traditional power of states to regulate internal affairs of domestically created corporations. Following this decision, states rushed to enact similar statutes, amid dire predictions by law and economics scholars that the result would be inefficiency and less competent management.

The precise impact of the Indiana control share acquisition statute and similar statutes is difficult to assess in the abstract. These statutes were clearly enacted with the intention of making takeovers more difficult, but it is not clear that they will have that result. Certainly, the possibility of losing the right to vote newly acquired shares despite a major financial investment may be a serious deterrent to takeover attempts. On the other hand, it may be possible to obtain a vote of the shareholders before the decision to purchase is final. Bidders may prefer to have a vote in advance on their proposed takeover attempt so they can gauge in advance the degree of support they have from the shareholders. It was partly for this reason that Delaware decided to adopt a different type of statute.

Many states have adopted statutes that deter takeovers by regulating the back-end transaction. Many of these statutes are **fair price statutes** that require the price paid to minority shareholders to be not less than the price paid by the interested shareholder. If this price condition is not met, the transaction requires the approval of (1) the board of directors in office before the interested shareholder acquired its shares; (2) a supermajority (e.g., 80 percent) of all voting shares; or (3) a majority of the disinterested shares, that is, those owned by shareholders other than the interested shareholder. These statutes, the terms of which vary from state to state, are generally patterned on the Maryland statute.

A second type of statute prohibits all back-end mergers with an interested shareholder for a specified period of time following the acquisition of shares by the interested shareholder, unless the transaction is approved in one of the ways described in the previous paragraph. Most of these **business combination statutes** are modeled on the New York statute, which prohibits back-end transactions for a period of five years.

Section 203 of The Delaware General Corporation Law, enacted in 1988, is a statute of the New York type. It generally prohibits a wide variety of transactions between the corporation and a shareholder owning more than 15 percent of the corporation's shares within a period of three years after the transaction in which the shareholder acquired the shares. Approval by the board of directors (in office before the acquisition) or by two-thirds of the remaining

shareholders permits a transaction to proceed immediately. The transaction may also proceed immediately if the interested shareholder acquires over 85 percent of the corporation's stock. A similar though much more restrictive Wisconsin statute was upheld in *Amanda Acquisition Corp. v. Universal Foods Corp.*, 877 F.2d 496 (7th Cir.), *cert. denied*, 493 U.S. 955 (1989), and based on that decision, it is generally believed that such statutes are constitutional.

§13.17 State Regulation of Defensive Tactics

An unusual mosaic of state and federal law governs takeovers and defensive tactics. The Williams Act, a federal statute, largely controls the mechanics of tender offers. Attempts by states to interfere are largely foreclosed by the **Mite** decision. Curiously, however, state law largely rules defensive tactics. In this regard, decisions by the Delaware Supreme Court have been particularly influential.

Directors of a target corporation have a potential conflict of interest: On the one hand, their personal positions of profit and honor within a large public entity may evaporate if the bidder is successful. (For this reason, basic decisions as to whether to oppose an offer may be delegated to the directors who are not also officers or employees of the corporation.) The accepted state law principles on defensive tactics are that the adoption of such tactics in the good faith belief that the offer is not in the best interests of the target is a matter of judgment subject to review under the common law "business judgment rule" but that defenses designed to entrench incumbent management are judged by the rigorous fiduciary duties relating to self-dealing. The business judgment rule provides a very lenient standard of review, while the standard of review for self-dealing transactions is considerably more onerous. The line between these two principles is hardly a clear one, because most defensive tactics can be viewed as either legitimate defense or as motivated primarily by a desire on the part of management to stay in power, usually called **management entrenchment**.

The Delaware Supreme Court has held that the decision to impose a poison pill takeover defense in advance of an actual takeover is evaluated under the business judgment rule with the important qualification that the defense must be reasonable in light of the potential threat (*Moran v. Household International, Inc.*, 500 A.2d 1346 (1985)). Thus, offers that involve unfair or coercive partial tender offers may be opposed by virtually any available means (*Unocal Corp. v. Mesa Petroleum Co.*, 493 A.2d 946 (1985)). Although the SEC prohibited the specific tactic used in the *Unocal* case when it adopted its all holders rule, that rule does not affect the scope of the Delaware holding as to permissible defensive tactics against inadequate or coercive offers.

In a third important decision, the Delaware Supreme Court held that quite a different set of principles applies once the board has resolved to sell the company. At that point, the duty of the directors shifts to obtaining the best possible price for the shareholders: The board may not favor one contender for control over another except on the basis of maximizing the price that the target shareholders obtain (*Revlon v. MacAndrews & Forbes Holdings, Inc.*, 506 A.2d 173 (1986)). The Delaware Supreme Court has since reaffirmed that this

principle applies only after the board of directors has decided to sell the company (*Ivanhoe Partners v. Newmont Mining Corp.*, 555 A.2d 1334 (Del. 1987); *Mills Acquisition Co. v. MacMillan, Inc.*, 559 A.2d 1261 (Del. 1989)).

The central issue in determining whether the Revlon rule applies is determining whether the target company is in fact for sale. In *Paramount Communications, Inc. v. Time, Inc.*, 571 A.2d 1140 (Del. 1989), Time and Warner Brothers had agreed to a "strategic combination" of the two companies involving a stock-for-stock merger in which Warner Brothers would be the surviving corporation under the name Time-Warner. Paramount interceded with a hostile tender offer for Time at a substantial premium. Time and Warner then abandoned the merger plan, and Time made a tender offer for Warner and adopted a number of defenses designed to thwart the Paramount bid. Paramount then sued on the theory that the Revlon rule required a fair and open auction for Time. The Delaware Supreme Court disagreed on the grounds that Time had never been for sale and its breakup had never been contemplated. And the various tactics undertaken to preserve the combination of Time and Warner were not enough when viewed in context to trigger a Revlon duty to seek the highest bidder. The case spawned yet another defensive tactic known as the **just say no** defense. Many thought that one way for a target company to avoid an auction under the Revlon rule was simply to deny that the company was for sale and to structure any desired deal as a strategic combination. When that defense was asserted, however, in connection with a proposed combination of Paramount and Viacom in which QVC made an unwelcome competing bid for Paramount, the Delaware Supreme Court noted that in the originally proposed deal, which had been publicly described as a sale, Viacom management would assume complete control over Paramount, and held that the transaction triggered a Revlon duty to maximize the price of the sale thus requiring that QVC be given a fair opportunity to compete for the target Paramount (*Paramount Communications v. QVC Network, Inc.*, 637 A.2d 34 (Del. 1994)). Viacom eventually prevailed. As a result, the focus of Delaware law relating to takeover defenses appears to have shifted to an inquiry into whether the transaction involves a shift of control at the shareholder level.

Although the principles relating to defensive tactics have been largely created under Delaware law, federal courts are often called on to resolve issues relating to defensive tactics in litigation involving federal law issues or diversity of citizenship. Other state courts also have resolved litigation relating to defensive tactics in ways generally consistent with Delaware law. In practice, however, courts have sometimes invalidated takeover defenses on the grounds that they involve entrenchment or they fail to meet the lenient standards of the business judgment rule. For example, the Second Circuit invalidated options on crown jewel assets given to one contender for control when it appeared that the options were granted at a price significantly below the market value of the assets involved (*Hanson Trust PLC v. ML. SCM Acquisition, Inc.*, 781 F.2d 264 (1986)). This decision appears to be based solely on state law. Other decisions involving similar transactions have upheld the tactic. There appears to be no overarching principle in this complex area except evaluation of the motives of the directors and the court's view of the overall fairness of the transaction from the standpoint of target shareholders.

§13.18 Leveraged Buyouts and Going Private

In many takeover battles, one contender is a group of investors that includes incumbent management and that plans, if successful, to continue the enterprise as a privately held, unregistered corporation. These transactions were first described as **going private**, and more recently have come to be known as **leveraged buyouts**. In these deals, a new entity is created in which both individual members of management and outside investors are represented. The new entity obtains unsecured loans required to finance the tender offer. Incumbent management may be required to invest relatively small amounts in the new enterprise but their investments are almost trivial—perhaps a few million dollars in a transaction involving hundreds of millions of dollars. Almost all of the purchase price is borrowed. Once the new entity acquires the publicly held shares and a second step, mop-up merger has been effected, the target corporation is merged with the new entity, which obtains a new loan secured by a lien on the target assets and uses the proceeds to pay off the unsecured loan. The unsecured loan is thus often called **bridge financing** or **mezzanine financing**. The target ends up with the obligation to pay off the loan used to acquire its assets out of its own income or cash flow. These transactions are thus sometimes called **bootstrap acquisitions**. They are also highly leveraged because virtually the entire purchase price is borrowed.

Following a leveraged buyout, the target may sell off portions of its business in order to pay down the new indebtedness. Improvements in earnings and cash flow may arise from savings inherent in not being a reporting corporation (including elimination of various expenses that go with being publicly held), from freedom to focus on longer-term projects, from elimination of potential shareholder suits, and from the discipline of massive debt. The ideal scenario, from the standpoint of management and its partners in the leveraged buyout, is (1) to reduce the burden of the indebtedness created by the buyout by selling off nonessential portions of the target's business; (2) to improve the profitability of the core businesses that remain; and (3) to arrange a new public offering of shares in the restructured target at a significantly higher price than was paid to take the corporation private. In a few instances, this pattern of public to private and then back to public resulted in profits of hundreds of millions of dollars to individuals who originally invested only a small fraction of that amount.

By the mid 1980s, leveraged buyouts (LBOs) had become as common as cash tender offers from third-party bidders. Outside offers from third parties were regularly met with a proposed leveraged buyout in which management participated actively. Issues of fiduciary duty in competitive takeover situations are quite obvious in these situations, where one of the competitors is a management-organized bidder. Needless to say, the board of directors may well be tempted to favor the leveraged buyout offer, thereby increasing both the reality and the appearance of conflict of interest, although the law is quite clear that the board must be neutral and seek only to maximize the price paid to the shareholders.

In determining whether a corporation is a plausible candidate for an LBO, an analysis is typically made of operating cash flow. Indeed, many LBOs involve the taking on of so much debt that the company will show a negative net worth on its balance sheet. In such a case, the deal will depend on obtaining a so-called

solvency letter from an investment bank or accounting firm. If the buyout in fact renders the firm insolvent, payments to the shareholders for their stock may be challenged as fraudulent conveyances or as contrary to corporation law standards governing distributions to shareholders. Indeed, in one failed buyout, it was reported that the shareholders might be required to return the payments they had received more than three years earlier, although as a matter of bankruptcy law such payments have in some cases been held to be exempt settlement payments. That is, some courts have ruled that such payments have the same status as any run-of-the-mill payment for stock as a brokerage firm might credit to an investor who has sold some shares.

§13.19 Where Does All the Money Come From?

One factor that sharply distinguished takeover activity in the 1980s from earlier periods can be stated in one word: cash. Most acquisitions in the 1980s were fueled by the ready availability of cash to enable bidders to buy out target shareholders in transactions that in the aggregate often ran into the billions of dollars. Transactions involving amounts so large as to be almost unimaginable in a private transaction even in the 1970s became routine in the 1980s and 1990s. It is reasonable to ask this question: Where does all the cash come from?

Funds that large corporations raise to finance takeover attempts are easier to explain than those raised by single individuals or small groups with limited personal resources. Many large corporations have accumulated substantial funds from internal operations. The favorable tax rules adopted in the early years of the Reagan administration (rules that were largely repealed by 1986) permitted the growth of internally generated war chests of billions of dollars that were often used to fuel takeover bids. A second important source of internal funds is the sale of unprofitable or nonessential lines of businesses. Over the years, most large corporations acquire a variety of tangential businesses, usually as a byproduct of other transactions. Historically, companies stuck with these small components try to make them profitable rather than disposing of them on the theory that growth in aggregate sales is a mark of successful business operation. In a world of leveraged buyouts, cash flow is paramount. Marginal businesses should be sold, not retained. These transactions may also generate funds available for takeover attempts. A few individuals have also assembled personal fortunes that are sufficient to enable them to launch takeover bids. Many of these fortunes are the product of modest takeovers followed by increasingly large transactions. Some are based on the success of privately owned businesses.

Most of the money used in takeovers in the 1980s was borrowed money, not internally generated money. This was true of most third-party offers as well as virtually all leveraged buyouts. Who is willing to lend this kind of money to finance the apparently risky takeovers? Financing commitments running into billions of dollars may come from a variety of sources. Commercial banks, pension funds, insurance companies, investment bankers, brokerage firms, and the like traditionally have not made speculative loans, but this policy began to change in the 1970s. By the 1980s, these entities often made substantial amounts available to fund takeover attempts in the form of short-term bridge

loans that permitted transactions to proceed with the understanding that longer-term loans—perhaps junk bonds or secured loans in leveraged buyouts—would be obtained to pay off these interim loans. (Some of these sources may also commit large amounts to long-term loans.) A second important source of loan money includes speculators who pool large amounts of funds into trading partnerships in contemplation of engaging in takeover activity. (Perhaps the best known such firm is Kohlberg, Kravis, Roberts (KKR).) This pool of capital has grown steadily as one successful transaction followed another. A third major source of loan funds are foreign lending sources with large dollar accounts arising from the imbalance of foreign trade with the United States. Indeed, foreign corporations have often launched takeover attempts, relying largely on foreign loan sources for their capital.

One brokerage firm (Drexel Burnham Lambert) developed the ability to raise billions of dollars through the placement of less-than-investment-grade debentures—junk bonds, as they are called. This firm developed a large network of financing sources who were willing to advance millions of dollars in funds to finance takeover attempts.

Junk bonds were popular investments because of the high rates of return — perhaps 13 or 14 percent, while investment grade securities had a return of perhaps 9 or 10 percent. The use of junk bonds was severely curtailed by changes to the IRC that limited the amount of interest that could be deducted in connection with acquisition loans. In addition, the Federal Reserve Board (the Fed) ruled that unsecured junk bonds were in effect loans for the purpose of buying stock and thus constituted margin borrowing which by Fed rule is limited to 50 percent of the purchase price of the stock.

The growth of financing sources for takeovers is based in part on the realization that investments in takeover transactions may not be as risky as they first appear. For one thing, financing is based on loan commitments that command substantial commitment fees. If the takeover attempt fails, the potential financier simply pockets the fee and advances no funds. It is thus profitable for the lending sources to make commitments without honoring them. If the proposed takeover is successful, the commitment is called in and funds must be provided, but at that point the assets and cash flow of the target are available to service the loans.

§13.20 Profitable Unsuccessful Takeover Attempts

One paradoxical fact about many takeover attempts in the 1980s is that it was often profitable from the standpoint of a bidder for its takeover bid to fail. Indeed, some of the best-known corporate raiders were widely believed to be more interested in failing than succeeding.

When a target is put into play by a cash tender offer, the probability is high that the target will be taken over by someone. Some bidders may thus make a tender offer with the hope that a bidding contest may develop. If someone else ultimately acquires the target, the unsuccessful bidder simply sells its investment in the target to the successful bidder, usually at a profit. The unsuccessful bidder may also receive additional consideration for discontinuing its offer.

Another possible source of profit from unsuccessful offers involves **green-mail**. After a hostile takeover attempt is launched, negotiations may occur between the bidder and the target. One possible outcome of this negotiation is that the target agrees to buy out the bidder's investment at a profitable price (usually above the now-inflated market price) and the bidder agrees to make no further investments in the target for an extended period. In effect, the target buys peace from the bidder; such payments are usually called greenmail. Greenmail is not illegal, but many observers view it as questionable. Some states have enacted statutes allowing the corporation to recover greenmail payments, and in 1987 Congress imposed a nondeductible excise tax on the receipt of green-mail in an attempt to discourage the practice.

Agreements between a target and a bidder may also take the form of a **standstill agreement** under which the bidder agrees not to increase its holding in the target beyond a specified size for a specified period of time, perhaps 10 years. Some kind of consideration to the bidder typically accompanies a standstill agreement. A standstill agreement often does not prevent the former bidder from profitably selling its shares to another bidder who seeks to obtain control of the target.

§13.21 Are Takeovers Economically or Socially Desirable?

Unlike earlier periods of merger activity where concerns of increased monopoly power were dominant, most economists argued that the 1980s takeover movement was socially desirable and that takeovers should not be prohibited or regulated in any significant way. Indeed, there is an impressive degree of unanimity in the academy that shareholders in the aggregate benefit from takeovers.

Whether the degree of concentration is increased or decreased in specific industries as a result of takeover transactions is difficult to evaluate. In other periods of merger activity, it was generally agreed that economic concentration in many industries was increasing as a result of the transactions taking place. It is not clear that this was true in the 1980s or that it is true today. Indeed, increased monopoly power does not appear to be the goal of most recent takeovers at all. Rather, in the 1980s, the process appears to have been driven by the relationship between the value of the business and the market prices of the securities issued by the corporation. In the 1990s, the urge to merge seems to be generated by strategic considerations such as gaining access to an ensured source of supply, acquiring a new product line, or securing developed expertise in a given area of business in which the bidder is weak.

There are also many deals in which an established company divests itself of a subsidiary or division perhaps because the unit is performing poorly compared with other operations or simply to generate shareholder gains from the spin off of shares in the newly independent company. Another reason for voluntary "deconglomeration" is that a business may fear potential takeover attempts. Potential targets thus attempt to make themselves less attractive targets by voluntarily disposing of nonessential assets that a successful bidder might be expected to sell. In short, just as business combinations have become

consensual, so have bust-up transactions. These transactions clearly reduce the degree of concentration in American industry.

Numerous attempts to explain the takeover phenomenon in economic terms have arisen, but there is no consensus as to a single best explanation for why bidders in hostile takeovers are willing to pay premiums that average 50 percent over market price.

There is one point on which there is broad consensus. If the proper measure of social welfare in corporation law is the maximization of economic returns to shareholders as a group, takeovers improve social welfare. Virtually every empirical study of price movements in connection with takeovers reveals that on the average, shareholders of the target corporation enjoy substantial increases in value. Although shareholders of the bidder usually lose a bit, the gains of the target shareholders significantly exceed any losses suffered by the bidder's shareholders.

The loss suffered by the bidder's shareholders on the average suggests that bidders sometimes pay too much for their targets. This is a phenomenon that is sometimes called the **winner's curse**. This should come as no surprise: If a bidding war arises for a target, the winner will usually be the most optimistic bidder.

The reason why takeovers at substantial premiums over market price arise in the first place is less clear. One plausible explanation is that target corporations are relatively poorly managed, and that the net gain to target shareholders reflects the improvement in target profitability resulting from the change in management. In other words, before the takeover the securities that the target issues are depressed, because of the relatively poor financial outlook of the target. The outlook improves dramatically with the prospect of fresh management, and the price of target shares increases to reflect this improvement in outlook. This theory is strongly endorsed by members of the "Chicago School," an influential group of conservative economists and law professors whose opinions (on takeovers and mergers particularly) today constitute a distinct school of thought. The theory seems both neat and consistent with the efficient capital market hypothesis. The major problem with the theory is that it explains only a relatively small number of takeovers that occurred during the 1980s. Rather, many target corporations appeared to be well-managed companies; indeed, the bidder often announced in advance that it did not plan to make major changes in target management if the takeover was successful.

A somewhat different theory suggests that the ability of bidders to borrow money through junk bonds in order to buy the stock of target shareholders indicates that target companies are overcapitalized with equity. Another suggestion is that shareholders developed a distinct preference for generous dividends, because they were afraid that management would invest available cash in projects with unattractive rates of return. In any event, the substitution of debt for equity, which on balance is what happened in junk bond financed takeovers, has the effect of increasing leverage and forcing the distribution of cash. Although it is not fair to say that under-leveraged companies with excess cash are mismanaged, it is fair to say that investors may have a different opinion as to how such companies should be managed. As for the extra risk of insolvency created by additional junk bond debt, it is not clear that this risk is of serious concern to investors in junk bonds who are receiving stock-like returns. If the company

cannot pay, the junk bond investors will in all likelihood be forced to take stock in a reorganization (which is essentially what their cash bought in the first place). Moreover, in many cases a reorganization may be accomplished privately through a pre-packaged bankruptcy proceeding in which the votes to approve the plan are solicited in advance of filing. Viewed in this way, junk bonds look very much like stock with a promise to pay dividends.

It may be too that investor tastes changed significantly during the 1970s and 1980s. During that period, many investors began to invest in diversified mutual funds and through other institutional vehicles. A diversified investor is more or less indifferent to risk as long as the prospective gain from a transaction is high enough. It matters little that a few companies end up insolvent if other companies make enough more to generate an acceptable net gain. Management, however, tends to view things differently: They have much of their own personal wealth tied up in the company and are naturally reluctant to enter into risky transactions. Thus, the diversification of investors through institutional investing may have created a conflict between investor and management preferences that did not previously exist.

Another possible explanation is that the takeover movement is motivated by empire building on the part of a few entrepreneurs who believe that bigger is better. In the long run, a strategy of growth for growth's sake would seem doomed to fail unless size in some way reflects greater efficiency. Economists argue that an empire building explanation is not consistent with the empirical evidence of real shareholders' gains from the takeover movement.

Another explanation is based on the concept of **synergy**. Two separate businesses may fit together so that the combined value of two together is greater than the sum of the values of the two separately. Although it is possible that synergy may explain a few successful combinations, it does not begin to explain most of the transactions that occurred during the 1980s. Indeed, the argument about synergy was most strongly put forward in the late 1960s and early 1970s during the period when many conglomerates were created; the combination of unrelated business was generally so unsuccessful that much of the takeover activity after that period was prompted by the prospect of gains from buying the combined companies and selling the pieces for amounts in the aggregate that exceeded the value of the whole. Such deals came to be known as bust-up takeovers.

Another possible explanation is that takeovers are caused by failure of the securities markets to reflect accurately the break-up value of targets. This explanation may be inconsistent with the efficient capital market hypothesis, but cannot be dismissed out of hand for that reason. After all, many companies are sold off in pieces for more than they cost to acquire. On the other hand, one would naturally expect the market to ignore break-up value if there were no prospect that break-up would occur.

In addition to the foregoing, some have suggested that takeovers are motivated primarily by tax considerations (particularly the fact that interest on takeover debt may be deductible), peculiarities in financial accounting standards, and the transfer of wealth from other constituencies (such as bondholders) to shareholders.

The most likely explanation of the takeover phenomenon is that several factors are at work and that no single factor explains all transactions.

V

◇

FINANCIAL MARKETS
AND INVESTMENTS

◆ TRADING IN STOCKS AND BONDS

§14.1 Introduction

This chapter describes the public markets for stocks and bonds, beginning with the New York Stock Exchange (NYSE) and other stock exchanges. This is followed by a discussion of the over-the-counter (OTC) market, focusing primarily on the National Association of Securities Dealers Automated Quotation (NASDAQ) system. In recent years, these markets have been supplemented by the development of financial futures and options, primarily through innovative securities introduced by the commodities exchanges. Commodities trading

and futures and these new financial instruments are described briefly in Chapter 16.

The markets discussed in this chapter are **secondary markets** in which persons who already own outstanding shares and wish to sell them deal with persons wanting to buy them. These markets are not the place where a corporation goes to raise new capital through the sale of new securities to the public (although it is common for companies planning a public offering to arrange in advance for listing on an exchange so that trading facilities will be immediately available to investors). Rather, the markets discussed in this chapter provide basic liquidity so that persons who invest in publicly traded securities can be confident that they can dispose of them if and when they wish. (As discussed briefly in Chapter 11, which examines corporate securities, when a corporation issues stock to the public to raise capital, the stock is typically sold directly to investor-customers by an investment bank or brokerage house — or a group or syndicate of such firms — acting as an underwriter.)

§14.2 The Efficient Capital Market Hypothesis

One of the most important insights into how the markets work is the **efficient capital market hypothesis** (**ECMH**), which is sometimes also called simply the **efficient market theory**, and which is also discussed briefly in Chapter 13, which discusses mergers and acquisitions. The implications of this theory are both far-reaching and startling. In brief, the predominant version of the ECMH states that securities prices quickly reflect everything publicly known about individual companies and the economy as a whole. When new information becomes available, the market absorbs and discounts it instantaneously and efficiently. Furthermore, the market accurately assesses the known information and is not misled, for example, by announced changes in accounting principles that affect book earnings but not the real worth of a business. The market's efficiency is explained by the efforts of large numbers of analysts and speculators who follow the market closely and exploit any opportunity to profit from temporary deviations of market prices from the prices that reflect all known information. These temporary deviations provide an incentive for analysts and speculators to continue to search for them, but the deviations are small and their existence is fleeting. In short, the independent efforts of hundreds or thousands of persons to make profits in the market is the driving force toward market efficiency.

There are several different versions of the ECMH. The version described above is called the **semi-strong form** and has the widest degree of acceptance. Under the semi-strong version, market prices do not encapsulate information that is not publicly available (e.g., inside information about the issuer, or the unexpected possibility that a specific takeover offer may be made in the future). The hypothesis therefore does not deny that profits may be made on inside information about the issuer or about planned takeover moves, as long as the information is acted on before it becomes public.

Two other versions of the ECMH are the **weak form** and the **strong form**. The weak form states that past price movements are no indication of future

price movements. Economists largely regard the weak form as proven by statistical analysis. The strong form states that market prices reflect nonpublic information as well as public information. Although few (if any) subscribe to the whole of the strong form, there is evidence, for example, that target company prices tend to rise well before a takeover is announced. To be sure, the increase in price may be due to leaks and illegal insider trading, but that suggests that even nonpublic information is partially reflected in market prices.

The implications of the ECMH in its semi-strong form are startling. First of all, if the theory is correct, one cannot predict the future movement of stock prices based on presently available information; because all current information is already embedded in a security's price, the price will change only because of events or information that cannot now be foreseen. (If the event could be foreseen it would have been already embedded in the current price.) Second, at any instant in time, the next price movement of a stock is as likely to be down as to be up, irrespective of the direction of the previous price movement. Stock prices move randomly, showing no historical pattern. Thus, historical analysis of previous stock price movements (a version of **technical analysis**) is useless for the prediction of future prices. It is true that many persons successfully charge substantial fees for technical analysis, but they are either charlatans or just plain lucky. Third, extensive reading and study of historical information about a company is also a waste of time: That information is already embedded in the price. Fourth, in-and-out trading is a losing strategy, because one cannot beat the market in the long run, and active trading simply runs up brokerage costs. Finally, the goal of many money managers and institutional investors to beat the averages in the long run is impossible: An investor can only do as well as the market as a whole.

There is no doubt that many market professionals do not agree with the ECMH in all of its implications. To be sure, one often hears about mutual fund managers or large investors who have beaten the market 5 or 10 years in a row. Economic theorists tend to reject such anecdotal evidence on the ground that it merely reflects the laws of chance. After all, someone may be able to guess the outcome of 10 coin flips once in a while. There are, however, some anomalies that theory alone cannot explain. For example, the market tends to go up in January. Moreover, initial public offerings tend to increase in price in the aftermarket. Another example was the sharp market break that occurred in October 1987: There appears to have been nothing during the period of that decline that can account for a decline of nearly one-third in the value of many stocks. Nevertheless, the evidence supporting the ECMH at least during periods of normal market activity is great, and it is clear that the theory provides a valuable insight as to how the market operates. The ECMH is accepted as a reasonably accurate description of securities markets by many market professionals and investors. For example, as described in Chapter 15, which discusses mutual funds, many institutional investors now try only to equal the performance of the market, not to beat it.

On the other hand, the theory seems paradoxical. If the market were truly efficient and everyone believed it to be so, then no one would bother to do research and the market would become inefficient. The answer to this **efficiency paradox** is that it is really no paradox at all. At the very least, it makes sense

for investors to do research as a hedge against the possibility that others will stop doing research. Moreover, in the real world investors have no very reliable way of knowing exactly how much time, effort, and money to invest in research. At best, an investor will rely on intuition and hunch in deciding when to stop digging for more information. In other words, investors are likely to compete with each other not only in doing research but in deciding when to stop doing research.

It is also arguable that the ECMH is trivial. After all, the market is the traders who compose it. No officially correct price is ever announced. Thus it is hardly surprising that on the average investors do on the average.

One important point about the ECMH that is not always appreciated is that the studies tending to show the efficiency of the securities markets are largely based on examination of securities that are widely traded on the largest markets, particularly trading in shares of the largest companies registered on the NYSE. Some parts of the OTC market also attract a large amount of interest and probably rival the NYSE markets in efficiency. When one moves into other parts of the NYSE or the over-the-counter market or into local securities traded on regional exchanges, however, there are many fewer analysts following specific stocks, and one would expect the market to be less efficient than it is for the most widely traded stocks. Many publicly held securities may be traded in a **thin market**, with trades occurring infrequently and with only one or two brokers regularly quoting prices.

It is also important to understand that the ECMH does not necessarily apply to investments for purposes of gaining control (or even voice) in a publicly traded company. Tender offers are routinely made for public companies at prices well in excess of the market price of target company shares.

Several theories have been advanced to explain "anomalies" in market pricing. They look to **noise** or **chaos** inherent in active trading markets. In other words, although the interaction of many traders has the effect of ultimately driving market prices to a close to proper level, market prices by their very nature tend to fluctuate as certain theories, opinions, and even fads gain favor among investors. The theory has intuitive appeal given that anecdotal evidence suggests that investors often copy each other's trades. Moreover, it may even be that managers at mutual funds and other large institutional investors are inclined to follow the crowd because it is safer (as a matter of job security) to match the performance of other large traders than it is to strike out on an independent course and possibly underperform compared to other funds. This has led to the proposal of the **arbitrage pricing theory** (**APT**), or the idea that market prices are the result of competition among traders focusing on constantly changing theories of value, and indeed some recent academic work suggests that over the long haul all stocks revert back to a more or less equal rate of return.

In any event, the essential idea behind alternative theories of how the market works is that although a trader may not be able consistently to beat the market, it does not necessarily follow that the market consistently establishes, say, the highest price that a bidder for control would be willing to pay. Indeed, one would not expect the market to do so unless it were reasonable to assume that every company that might be better managed is or will be promptly taken

over. Rather, one might expect that some portion of the current trading price of a company represents its value as a takeover target discounted for the probability that such a bid will occur.

In addition to market anomalies and the takeover phenomenon, there are several large investors, perhaps most notably Warren Buffett, the CEO of Berkshire Hathaway, who have consistently made large gains as a result of large investments in publicly traded companies. In the case of Buffett, such investments have been made for the long term and in some instances have involved Buffett's active participation or at least consultation in the management of the firms in which investments are made. Although such examples are not explainable by a simplistic view of market efficiency, they are consistent with a limited view of what efficiency means, namely, that it is very difficult for passive investors to beat the market through a strategy of active trading.

§14.3 The New York Stock Exchange

The NYSE is a place — a building located at the corner of Wall Street and Broad Street in New York City. All transactions in shares occurring on the NYSE take place (at least formally) in a series of large rooms in this building known collectively as the **floor**. On the floor, there are numerous **posts** at which specific securities are traded and around which members interested in specific stocks congregate.

Only stocks that are listed on the NYSE are traded there. To be listed, a company must meet specific size and share ownership requirements. Among other things, a company must have earnings of at least $2,500,000 for the most recent year, must have an aggregate market value of publicly traded stock of at least $40,000,000, must have at least 1,100,000 publicly held shares, and must ordinarily have at least 2,000 stockholders. In addition, each company must enter into a standard listing agreement with the NYSE that imposes certain obligations on the listing company. Among these obligations is a commitment to make information about developments affecting the company publicly available on a timely basis. Moreover, NYSE **listing standards** require more extensive shareholder voting rights than required by state law. The listing requirements ensure that only the largest and most successful of the publicly held corporations are traded on the NYSE. This is the market for the blue chip stocks that are household names: General Motors, IBM, and so forth. However, among the more than 2,600 companies (and 3,100 stocks) currently listed on the NYSE, there are many that are not widely known.

Only members of the NYSE have the privilege of trading on the floor. Most members are brokerage firms that deal with the general public; transactions are executed on behalf of members of the general public on the floor of the NYSE by representatives of those brokerage firms. Some individuals (called floor traders) also are members of the NYSE and handle trades for other brokers. To be entitled to membership, an individual or firm must buy a seat on the NYSE that entitles the member (or a broker employed by a member firm) to go onto the floor of the NYSE during trading hours and execute transactions. The number of seats is limited, and a limited market of sorts exists for seats. Because

most NYSE members trade on behalf of the public, the value of a seat depends in part on market activity in securities. Since 1990, seats have sold for as much as $1,050,000 and as little as $250,000.

The NYSE retains a hefty share of the volume of stock trading. Its success is based on several factors: (1) it is the most prestigious exchange and many companies desire to be listed there; (2) the NYSE has historically provided a highly successful continuous and orderly market; and (3) the NYSE prohibits members from executing transactions in many listed securities other than on the NYSE floor. Today, the NYSE is a highly computerized operation capable of handling trades of hundreds of millions of shares per day. The following sections describe more fully how this institution operates.

§14.4 A Prototypical NYSE Transaction

Assume that you decide to buy 100 shares of IBM at the currently reported market price of $115 per share. To buy 100 shares of IBM requires $11,500 in cash plus commissions, but you have that amount on deposit with your broker. You therefore call up your broker and instruct him to buy 100 shares of IBM "at the market." This last phrase means that your order will be executed at the market price in effect at the time your order arrives on the trading floor. (You may also give a limit order, that is, an order that will be executed only at a price you specify, if the market reaches that price, as discussed further below.)

An order for 100 shares is known as a **round lot** and is the standard trading unit for shares on the NYSE. One can sell blocks of less than 100 shares; a unit of less than 100 shares is known as an **odd lot** and is handled in a different way than round lots. Market orders for up to 30,000 shares may be handled by computer. In order to describe the mechanics of the NYSE, however, we will assume that your order will be filled in the traditional manner for all trades before 1976 and that continues today for larger orders.

Before the computerization of the NYSE in 1976, your broker would receive your order and telephone it to its New York office (or, if your broker was not a member of the NYSE, to the New York offices of a broker regularly used by your broker to fill orders). The order would then be conveyed by telephone to the NYSE where an employee of your brokerage firm or a floor broker would receive your order. He or she would walk to the post where IBM is traded. At this post is the **specialist** who handles IBM. There are also a number of other brokers surrounding this post who are interested in IBM. Many have orders of their own to fill. Today, the latest price at which IBM traded and the current bid-and-asked prices are on computer screens for all to see. These quotations might be "115 bid 115$\frac{1}{8}$ asked." At this point, one of two things might happen:

1. The broker with your order may signify that he wants to buy 100 IBM at the market. Another broker in the trading crowd at the post may have an order to sell 100 IBM, also at the market. A deal may be struck then and there at a price negotiated on the spot. This price would either be the last price, the bid price, the asked price, or in between, whatever

is agreed on. The identities of the buying and selling brokers and the amount and price of the trade are noted by a floor reporter who sends information electronically about the transaction to the tape, where the transaction will appear in a few seconds, as well as to the involved brokerage firms.

2. The broker with your order may not find another broker with an order to sell that matches your order to buy. At this point, the specialist may step in and complete the transaction, normally at the **asked** (or **offered**) price. (If your order is to sell, it would typically be executed at the **bid** price.) The stock that the specialist supplies may come from either of two sources. The specialist keeps a list of **limit orders** — orders to buy or sell IBM stock at various prices other than the market price at the time the limit order was entered. Your buy order may be used to fill one of the sell orders from this book. Indeed, if your order can be filled from this source, it must be so filled. Alternatively, if the order cannot be filled from this source, the specialist sells the shares needed to complete your order from its own inventory. In other words, public and limit orders have priority over specialist participation. Again, the transaction is noted to a reporter, is confirmed to your brokerage firm, and appears on the tape within seconds of completion.

It is the responsibility of the selling broker to report trades. Thus, trades appearing on the tape are sales and not purchases, although there of course is a purchase for every sale. The significance of sale reporting, however, is that the tape does not reflect the fact that in a sale of, say, 20,000 shares there may have been 5 different purchasers. By the same token, the tape does not reflect the fact that several sales by different sellers may have been to the same purchaser. Such information is very difficult to come by unless one is on the floor, which is one of the reasons that being on the floor is an advantage.

Having completed the purchase, your broker will **clear** the trade that night through a **clearing firm**. That is, the clearing firm will net out purchases and sales for numerous firms. Your broker will usually send you a **confirmation**. The **settlement** actually takes place three days later. At or before that time, you must have sufficient cash or other consideration on deposit with your broker to cover the trade, and your broker must likewise have covered the trade with its clearing firm. As of settlement, you become entitled to the certificate for the shares. You could direct the broker to obtain a certificate for the shares in your name if you plan to hold the shares for a while, or, if you do not give this instruction, the broker simply records on the next statement of your account that you own 100 shares of IBM. You may also arrange to obtain shares registered in your own name but leave them with your broker for safekeeping.

Most investors (about 65 percent) choose to leave their securities on deposit with their broker and registered in their broker's name (sometimes called **street name**) as a matter of convenience, as is discussed more fully in the chapter on securities. This practice is important to the securities industry, because it allows for much more efficient settlement of trades. Indeed, with the volume of trading as high as it now is, it is doubtful that the markets could function if most investors insisted on certificates. Moreover, uncertificated

shares are the primary source of supply for shares that are lent to short sellers. Thus, without the book entry system, it would be much more difficult and expensive to effect a short sale, and the market would be somewhat less efficient. The Uniform Commercial Code makes it clear that if a brokerage house mistakenly (or fraudulently) pledges securities held in its name, for example, in connection with a loan of working capital to the firm, the lender has priority over the true owners of the securities. Although losses from theft or misuse of securities left on deposit with a broker are insured against by the **Securities Investor Protection Corporation** (**SIPC**), a major scandal involving delays or even losses to numerous investors who left securities in street name with brokers could lead many investors to insist on certificated shares in the future and could severely hamper the markets.

Although settlement is three days after the transaction, you are the immediate owner of 100 shares of IBM for most purposes. If you become unhappy with your investment before the three-day period for closing lapsed—even later on the same day—your broker can "close out your position" by entering into a commitment to sell 100 shares of IBM. You would, of course, owe two commissions and if the market declined between the time you purchased and the time you sold, you would lose that amount also.

In the 1960s, the NYSE began the computerization of many aspects of its operations. Indeed, the tremendous growth in trading that has occurred since then would not have been possible otherwise. In 1960, the average daily volume was about 3,000,000 shares; in 1997, it was quite common for 600,000,000 shares to trade in one day, and on October 28, more than 1.2 billion shares were traded.

The NYSE's electronic order delivery system was originally known as the **Designated Order Turnaround** (**DOT**) system, but as a result of upgrading, it is now known officially as **SuperDOT**. It permits member brokers to transmit orders electronically directly to the specialist posts without the intervention of a floor broker. If the order is a market order and is smaller than a designated number of shares of a single stock (currently up to 30,000 shares), the order may be transmitted to the floor electronically. Even larger *limit* orders (of up to 99,999 shares) may also be transmitted to the floor by the SuperDOT system, a feature that is no doubt designed to relieve the specialist of the need to keep track of most such orders.

SuperDOT is not an electronic execution system. Trades do not occur until they are matched with a buyer or seller. Although buy and sell orders both coming in electronically may be matched with each other, that happens in only about 4 percent of trades. It is more typical for a small order arriving by SuperDOT to be taken by a member of the trading crowd or to be batched with other orders as part of a larger trade. Indeed, the specialist may **stop** a market order in order to keep it from being executed if it appears that the electronic order is likely to be filled at a better price because of an imbalance of orders on the floor. (When an order is stopped, the specialist guarantees that the order will not be executed at any worse price than that quoted at the time of the stop.) Thus, quite ironically, one of the advantages of trading on an exchange is that orders may be processed more slowly to give the investor the advantage of **price improvement** or **execution between the quotes**. Studies indicate that investors receive price improvement on the NYSE about 28 percent

of the time, less in very active stocks, but much more in less active stocks. Nevertheless, in 1995, the average SuperDOT market order was executed and reported back to the originating broker in 24 seconds. SuperDOT accounts for 85 percent of all orders and 33 percent of all volume on the NYSE. The prototypical IBM purchase transaction described here would, of course be executed through SuperDOT, and is so small that it would create barely a "blip" in that system.

Finally, SuperDOT has a feature that is primarily used by program traders and arbitrageurs (as described in more detail below). The LIST program allows member firms to use SuperDOT to transmit orders in hundreds of different stocks simultaneously. As discussed below, this allows trading strategies that involve whole portfolios of stock.

Following the October 1987 and October 1989 market crashes, the NYSE, in cooperation with the futures exchanges, instituted a series of so-called **circuit breakers** to be triggered when the stock market rises or falls by 50, 100, 250, and 400 points in the Dow Jones Industrial Average (DJIA) as compared with the previous day's close. The 250- and 400-point circuit breakers were raised to 350 points and 550 points in early 1997 because the DJIA had risen substantially, and the percentages represented by the old numbers had become relatively small. When the circuit breakers were adopted, the DJIA stood at around 2200. Since then the DJIA has traded in the 8,000 range. Thus, at the time the breakers were adopted, a 250-point change represented a 12 percent move in the market, while it is less than a 4 percent move when the market is in the 7000 range. The 50-point and 100-point circuit breakers limit the availability of the DOT system for use in connection with program trading, while the 350-point and 550-point circuit breakers close the market altogether for periods of one and two hours, respectively. (The futures markets discussed below also close more or less simultaneously if one of these is tripped.) The central idea behind the circuit breakers is to limit the influence of program trading in especially volatile markets. The 50-point breaker has been tripped many times, while the 100-point breaker has been tripped a few times. The other breakers were tripped for the first and only time on October 27, 1997.

§14.5 Limit Orders

The above example involved an order to purchase 100 shares of IBM at the market. When placing an order, one may specify the price at which it is to be executed, say a purchase of IBM "at 114 or lower" or a sale of IBM at "116 or higher." These are **limit orders.**

Limit orders are handled quite differently from market orders. Today they are largely entered through the SuperDOT system, but the way they are handled can best be understood by first describing the process in the preelectronic era.

Assume you place a limit order to buy 100 shares of IBM at 114 when the market price is 115½. When the broker arrives at the IBM post with your order, he finds that the market price for IBM is about 1½ points (dollars) above your order price. Obviously no seller is going to sell for 114 under these circumstances. The broker is also not going to wait around at the IBM post for 30

minutes or so to see whether IBM will conveniently drop a point and one-half while he waits. Rather, the broker gives the limit order to the specialist who records it in the limit order book as an offer to buy at 114. (The book formerly was in fact a book, but is now maintained electronically.) If the price of IBM drops to 114, the purchase orders in the limit order book are filled in the order that they were received by the specialist. Because of this priority in execution, it is possible that IBM's price may drop briefly to $114 and yet your order might not be executed if the market then rises.

The limit order book records both offers to buy and to sell at various prices. An investor is normally interested in buying low and selling high. Thus, most limit orders are of the two types described above, that is, "buy at 114 or lower," or "sell at 116 or higher." Not all limit orders are of these types, however. Another type of limit order is a **day order**: for example, "buy at $114 or better but in any event buy at the close of trading at the market." Yet another type of limit order is a **stop order**, which is an order to sell when the price has *declined* to a particular point or to buy when the price has *increased* to a particular point. A stop order to sell may be placed by a person who wants to save a profit or cut a loss by selling when a stock falls in price. Similarly, a person may think that a stock will continue to go up if it breaks through a particular price; hence a stop order to buy may be placed.

Limit orders (other than day orders) are good until cancelled. In other words, they remain on the specialist's book awaiting execution until they are cancelled by the person placing the order. Brokers usually recommend that limit orders that are unlikely to be executed promptly or that have lost their original justification be cancelled.

It is also possible to enter **tick-sensitive orders**. (A **tick** is one unit of movement in price, for most stocks one-sixteenth of a point (**teenies**), although some stocks are quoted in thirty-seconds or even smaller fractions.) Prior to 1996, the standard tick was one-eighth of a point, but the NYSE and other exchanges have decided to move toward decimal quotations and the shift to sixteenths is part of that transition. A **buy-minus** order is an order to buy, but only if the buy can be executed at less than the offer, and a **sell-plus** order is an order to sell, but only if the order can be executed at more than the bid price. In short, tick sensitive orders are orders that may only be executed between the quotes, that is, they are conditioned on the investor getting price improvement.

§14.6 The Role of the Specialist

Specialists have existed on the NYSE throughout most of its history. A **specialist** is charged with the responsibility of maintaining an orderly market for the stocks assigned to them. They are expected to maintain an inventory of assigned stocks and to buy when the market is declining or to sell when the market is rising in order to ensure a **deep and continuous market**. In the absence of specialists, the price of a stock — even a stock as widely traded as IBM — might have erratic fluctuations due to temporary blips in demand or supply arriving at the post. Indeed, there might even be brief periods when there might be only buyers and no sellers, or only sellers and no buyers. In the

absence of a specialist, prices might fluctuate excessively in a manner unrelated to underlying value. Specialists are thus supposed to smooth out artificial fluctuations by trading against the market when necessary to ensure that the market remains orderly. Specialists are not expected to try to prevent market declines (and indeed usually could not do so even if they tried). Their objective is to let the market find its proper level in an orderly way. During the October 1987 crash, some specialists concluded that buying stock was futile and could only bankrupt the specialist without improving the orderly flow of the market. They therefore withdrew from the market for brief periods and requested halts in trading until an acceptable price to reopen trading could be established. A price is acceptable in this context when it clears the market, that is, when it leads to a balance between shares offered for purchase and shares offered for sale at that price without intervention by the specialist.

At first blush, it might seem that specialists are sure to lose money in their trading activities when they trade against the trend. In fact, this is not the case. Although specialists may need to purchase stock for their own account during a price decline, they may ultimately profit if the market recovers and they dispose of that stock at higher price levels. Indeed, studies indicate that market prices tend to be mean-reverting (i.e., prices tend to fall or rise back to some average that is appropriate for the riskiness of the stock in question). (Given that most investors these days are portfolio investors, mean-reversion is hardly surprising.) Thus, over the long haul, the specialist who buys on the way down and sells on the way up should make money. Moreover, most of the time the market is more or less stable (due in part to the activities of specialists) and during such times the specialist functions largely as a market maker buying at the bid and selling at the ask, while brokers in the crowd may trade with each other at or between the specialist's bid and asked quotes.

The second major source of income for specialists is commissions for acting as agent for brokers who place limit orders with them for execution. The specialist earns a commission on the execution of each such order. In January 1996, for example, approximately 63 percent of all executed SuperDOT orders (representing about 75 percent of shares so traded) were limit orders.

The NYSE designates over 50 firms as specialist firms, and about 400 individuals actually perform the functions of specialists on behalf of these firms. There is only one specialist per stock, but with 3,100 listed stocks, specialist firms obviously serve as specialist for many stocks. The largest firm acts as specialist for more than 100 stocks. The individuals who actually perform the specialist functions usually handle four or five stocks each, although an individual specialist may occasionally handle as many as 10 stocks at a time. Specialist firms must meet stringent capital requirements and their performance is closely monitored, particularly during times of market turmoil.

Specialists are **downstairs brokers**, because they deal only with members of the NYSE on the floor but not with members of the general public. The brokerage firms that deal with the public are known as **upstairs brokers**, because some of them have had offices physically located above the trading floor (although most big brokerage houses are no longer housed in the exchange building). Upstairs brokers are often many times larger than the downstairs specialist firms, and the question has arisen whether upstairs firms should be permitted to acquire specialists. The major concern is the fear of leakage of

sensitive market information to the upstairs firm. Several upstairs firms, however, have acquired specialists on regional exchanges and on the New York and American stock exchanges without apparent leakage of information.

Specialists on the NYSE are assigned by the Exchange. In one incident in 1991, an issuer decided to withdraw its listing application when it was assigned a specialist that did not appear on a list of acceptable specialists it had previously submitted to the NYSE. The company continues to trade on the National Market System of NASDAQ. In 1997, the NYSE changed its policies to permit listed companies to have a greater voice in the selection of their specialists.

Many observers question whether it is really necessary to have a specialist who is assigned the exclusive right on the floor to make a market in each NYSE stock. The specialist system is somewhat controversial, because NYSE Rule 390 prohibits members from trading most NYSE-listed stocks for their own account anywhere other than on the NYSE, a practice known as **off-board trading**. (Securities and Exchange Commission (SEC) rules provide that stocks listed after April 26, 1979, are exempt from the rule.) In effect, Rule 390 prohibits NYSE members from competing with specialists by making a market off the Exchange. On the other hand, it can be argued that Rule 390 makes the NYSE more efficient and fair by requiring that all trades cross on the floor, thus ensuring that there is substantial volume and that all investors will have an opportunity to participate in every trade (particularly with block trades discussed below).

Still, few other major stock exchanges use the specialist system. Some (e.g., the Toronto Stock Exchange) have done away with specialists altogether, while others (e.g., the Chicago Stock Exchange) allow for competing specialists. Some exchanges have no market makers of any kind. The International Stock Exchange (formerly the London Stock Exchange), for example, is totally electronic, as is the Cincinnati Stock Exchange. The Tokyo Stock Exchange and the Paris Bourse both have something like a specialist who monitors trading but who cannot trade for his or her own account.

§14.7 Block Trades

A **block trade** is a trade involving a minimum of 10,000 shares. The largest block trade on record involved nearly 49,000,000 shares. Block trades are an increasingly important part of NYSE activity. In 1996, there were over 2.5 million such trades that represented 56 percent of total NYSE trading volume. In 1965, there were only 2,171 such trades, representing about 3 percent of NYSE volume. These startling figures reflect the increasing dominance of **institutional investors** on the NYSE.

Most block trades involve institutional investors such as mutual funds, pension plans, insurance companies, and similar entities, which own about half of the outstanding stock among United States shareholders. As one might expect, institutional investors have a strong incentive to trade among themselves and avoid commissions as well as regulations that may require trades to be split up among many buyers or sellers on an exchange. Thus, most institutional investors use private trading systems when trading among themselves. These private trading systems are discussed more fully below.

Most of the work of putting a block trade together occurs "upstairs," in

the institutional trading departments of the member firms. Some of these departments develop expertise in effecting transactions in stocks of certain types of companies (e.g., utilities or banks). Other departments tend to specialize in stocks of specific companies. Some firms act as **block positioners** and use their own capital to take part (a **stub end**) of a block trade that cannot be entirely placed with institutional investors. Block positioners must register with the NYSE and meet minimum capital requirements.

Salespeople and traders of institutional departments maintain constant communication with many institutional investors. Many maintain direct phone lines to the trading desks of the institutions. When a department receives an order to buy or sell a large block of stock, it contacts institutions to see whether they want to participate on the other side of the trade. An electronic network, **Instinet**, also exists; it connects trading desks of institutional investors that may be used for simultaneous inquiries about possible interest in the block. (Instinet is owned by Reuters, which carefully controls who can trade on the system. Instinet trades are included in the consolidated tape of the NYSE. There are several other electronic trading systems that are described more fully below.) The issuing company itself may be contacted if it has announced a share repurchase program. An inquiry may also be made of the specialist to determine how much of the block might be absorbed by public orders at the contemplated price. Inquiries sometimes generate additional interest on the same side of the transaction as the original block. The managing firm may thus put together an even larger transaction, involving several buyers and sellers on each side of the transaction.

When the transaction is put together "upstairs," it must ordinarily be **crossed** on the NYSE floor. (As discussed above, if a trade that a member firm handles involves a stock listed on or before April 26, 1979, the trade must be made on the NYSE.) Small numbers of shares not otherwise committed may be handled by the specialist or sold to customers of floor brokers present at the post. Crossing the trade on the floor also ensures that public orders for the same stock (held either as limit orders by the specialist or by floor brokers) may participate in the offering if it is favorable for them to do so. If the managing firm is a block positioner, SEC rules allow it to take some or all shares for its own account if the price is at or between the quotes, but the public must be allowed to participate if the block trade is to be executed at a price above the current offer or below the current bid.

§14.8 Regional Exchanges Also Trade in NYSE-Listed Stocks

In addition to the NYSE, there are several **regional stock exchanges**: the Boston Stock Exchange, the Chicago Stock Exchange, the Cincinnati Stock Exchange, the Pacific Stock Exchange, and the Philadelphia Stock Exchange. Regional exchanges may list and freely trade in stocks listed on the Exchange. SEC approval is required for **unlisted trading privileges**, but it is routinely granted. The **Intermarket Trading System** (**the ITS**) is a computer system that provides automated price quotations on these stocks traded in multiple

markets and an automated routing system that sends orders to the market providing the most favorable price. The ITS does not guarantee the best price, however, because trades sent from one market to another are not necessarily treated with the same priority as trades sent directly to that market.

The regional exchanges may also list stocks of companies with a regional following, but there are very few stocks so listed, possibly because listing standards on NASDAQ are so low that most small companies opt for national exposure there. As of October 31, 1996, there were only 12 stocks reported in the *Wall Street Journal* as traded exclusively on a regional exchange.

§14.9 Newspaper Reports of NYSE Trading

The financial pages of a newspaper give considerable information about the trading activity each day on the NYSE, about the trading in specific stocks, and about the specific investment characteristics of each stock traded on the NYSE. This section, based on the *Wall Street Journal* reporting system, describes the information that is available.

Table 14-1 shows the breakdown of trading in NYSE-listed stocks by market, and on a half-hourly basis, for Thursday, October 30, 1997 (a routine but relatively active trading day chosen more or less at random). Over 819,000,000 shares were traded. Trades executed on the regional exchanges are included in the composite figures and are broken down separately. Although the NYSE still accounts for the great bulk of trading, the regional exchanges' share of the market for trades involving less than 3,000 shares has gradually increased to about 65 percent of the trades of that size; of course, when trades of all sizes are concerned, the NYSE still predominates, executing more than 80 percent of trades on most days.

Table 14-1 also shows (in the section titled "Diaries") overall price movements for all stocks traded on October 30, 1997, as well as the previous day and a week earlier. Again, block trades, the last entry, are single trades of 10,000 shares or more; they are indicative of the degree of institutional investor activity.

Table 14-1 also gives information about the most active stocks traded on the NYSE on October 30, 1997, both in terms of total volume and in terms of the largest percentage gainers and losers. Note that there is little overlap between the two lists. This is to be expected, because almost all large percentage gainers or losers are relatively low-priced stocks.

Table 14-2 sets forth trading in some NYSE stocks for October 30, 1997. The symbols and footnotes used in Table 14-2 are explained in Table 14-3, which also gives precise definitions for many of the figures that appear in the report of trading. In Table 14-2, IBM appears near the bottom of the column. The "High–Low–Close–Net Change" data to the far right of the table reflect the latest day's trading. IBM traded at a high of $99\frac{3}{8}$ and a low of $95\frac{9}{16}$; the final trade was at $95\frac{13}{16}$. The "Net Change" figure represents the change between the closing price on the reported day and the closing price on the previous trading day. The net change figure thus is unrelated to the high and low trading prices during the day (**intraday**). The approximate value of IBM traded on this one day was $63904 \times 100 \times$ (say) \$97 or about \$620,000,000.

And that is only a small fraction of all listed stocks; clearly billions of dollars of stocks are traded on the NYSE each day. Whereas the yield for IBM may be calculated from other information shown (by dividing the dividend by the stock price), the **price/earnings (P/E)** ratio cannot be calculated from other information appearing on this page; earnings per share for IBM were reported some time earlier and that number is essential for calculating the P/E ratio. The calculations of yield and P/E ratio are not adjusted daily and are indications of range. Because physical space is at a premium on this page, calculations are not carried out to any degree of precision.

If one looks through the stocks in Table 14-2, one sees that there are companies that show a positive yield but have no P/E ratio. An example is INA Industries. Another company, ICF Kaiser, has a P/E ratio of 27 but no yield. In the case of INA, it appears that although the company had no earnings during the previous year, it pays a dividend of $1.24 per share anyway. In the case of ICF, the reverse is true: The company apparently had earnings during the previous year (of approximately 2/27 or about $.07 per share) but does not pay a dividend.

Finally, brief mention should be made of the preferred stocks that are publicly traded on the NYSE. Many utility companies have outstanding several issues of preferred shares carrying varying rates of dividends. Illinois Power is a good example; it has three different classes of preferred stock that are traded on the NYSE. Presumably these preferreds reflect different financings by Illinois Power at different times. It will be noted that no P/E ratio is set forth for preferreds, because they are limited participation securities with no claim to increased dividends based on increases in earnings. Their value is therefore determined largely by their distribution rights. The yields for these preferreds that a single company issues may vary substantially, depending on their relative priorities and other rights of the specific class, including conversion rights and redemption (call) provisions. The yields on the Illinois Power preferreds vary from 6.2 percent to 9.0 percent.

In general terms, preferred stocks listed on the NYSE are high-grade securities on which continued dividend payments are highly probable. Thus prices and therefore yields are more highly sensitive to interest rates and relative rights than to changes in earnings or prices of common shares.

§14.10 The American Stock Exchange

A second important trading market is the **American Stock Exchange (AMEX)**. The AMEX is considerably smaller than the NYSE. The summaries for its operations on October 30, 1997, are also set forth in Table 14-1. It operates in essentially the same way as the NYSE, but there is no cross-listing of individual stocks between the AMEX and NYSE. Some AMEX stocks are also traded on regional exchanges and price quotations for these stocks are disseminated by ITS. Listing standards for the AMEX are lower than for the NYSE. Thus, most companies listed on the AMEX are smaller than companies on the NYSE. Moreover, most AMEX stocks are lower priced. This is well illustrated by Table 14-4, which reflects trading in stocks on this smaller ex-

Table 14-1

STOCK MARKET DATA BANK 10/30/97

MAJOR INDEXES

†12-MO HIGH	LOW		DAILY HIGH	LOW	CLOSE	NET CHG	% CHG	†12-MO CHG	% CHG	FROM 12/31	% CHG
DOW JONES AVERAGES											
8259.31	6021.93	30 Industrials	7543.01	7381.18	x7381.67	− 125.00	− 1.67	+ 1352.29	+ 22.43	+ 933.40	+ 14.48
3368.33	2133.56	20 Transportation	3143.19	3087.21	3091.65	− 43.54	− 1.39	+ 958.09	+ 44.91	+ 835.98	+ 37.06
247.99	209.47	15 Utilities	243.33	240.73	x241.33	− 1.04	− 0.43	+ 14.60	+ 6.44	+ 8.80	+ 3.78
2620.84	1908.93	65 Composite	2467.79	2424.10	x2424.44	− 34.13	− 1.39	+ 514.75	+ 26.95	+ 398.61	+ 19.68
929.94	664.68	DJ Global-US	875.16	857.63	857.63	− 14.11	− 1.62	+ 192.01	+ 28.85	+ 157.07	+ 22.42
NEW YORK STOCK EXCHANGE											
514.21	373.68	Composite	484.43	475.83	475.83	− 7.10	− 1.47	+ 101.33	+ 27.06	+ 83.53	+ 21.29
643.81	470.85	Industrials	607.11	595.41	595.41	− 7.79	− 1.29	+ 123.30	+ 26.12	+ 101.03	+ 20.44
310.70	247.87	Utilities	295.92	292.10	292.12	− 3.19	− 1.08	+ 40.08	+ 15.90	+ 32.21	+ 12.39
481.05	337.21	Transportation	455.06	448.27	449.71	− 5.03	− 1.11	+ 112.50	+ 33.36	+ 97.41	+ 27.65
493.08	330.70	Finance	463.19	452.47	452.47	− 10.72	− 2.31	+ 120.67	+ 36.37	+ 101.30	+ 28.85
STANDARD & POOR'S INDEXES											
983.12	703.77	500 Index	923.28	903.68	903.68	− 15.48	− 1.68	+ 198.41	+ 28.13	+ 162.94	+ 22.00
1146.82	825.37	Industrials	1076.13	1052.53	1052.53	− 16.15	− 1.51	+ 225.87	+ 27.32	+ 182.56	+ 20.98
211.44	180.93	Utilities	206.52	204.33	204.69	− 1.27	− 0.62	+ 7.14	+ 3.61	+ 5.88	+ 2.96
339.84	242.34	400 MidCap	317.94	313.37	313.47	− 4.47	− 1.41	+ 71.13	+ 29.35	+ 57.89	+ 22.65
192.48	134.54	600 SmallCap	179.79	176.94	177.21	− 2.58	− 1.44	+ 40.29	+ 29.43	+ 31.73	+ 21.81
212.04	151.72	1500 Index	198.91	195.03	195.03	− 3.26	− 1.64	+ 43.02	+ 28.30	+ 35.22	+ 22.04
NASDAQ STOCK MARKET											
1745.85	1201.00	Composite	1602.74	1564.45	1570.41	− 32.34	− 2.02	+ 348.90	+ 28.56	+ 279.38	+ 21.64
1148.21	751.99	Nasdaq 100	1029.76	1000.45	1000.70	− 29.06	− 2.82	+ 248.71	+ 33.07	+ 179.34	+ 21.83
1414.11	971.06	Industrials	1266.61	1244.48	1251.77	− 23.12	− 1.81	+ 175.13	+ 16.27	+ 142.14	+ 12.81
1884.02	1334.04	Insurance	1770.49	1753.76	1765.40	− 8.07	− 0.46	+ 431.36	+ 32.33	+ 299.97	+ 20.47
1977.59	1194.16	Banks	1915.97	1892.79	1910.05	− 17.36	− 0.90	+ 714.56	+ 59.77	+ 636.59	+ 49.99
732.03	475.52	Computer	658.68	640.78	640.78	− 19.24	− 2.92	+ 164.88	+ 34.65	+ 121.99	+ 23.51
312.80	198.06	Telecommunications	295.32	287.32	290.97	− 3.24	− 1.10	+ 82.68	+ 39.69	+ 75.06	+ 34.76
OTHERS											
721.90	541.20	Amex Composite*	676.43	669.49	670.84	− 5.57	− 0.82	+ 109.28	+ 19.46	+ 98.50	+ 17.21
518.94	373.94	Russell 1000	487.71	478.16	478.16	− 8.13	− 1.67	+ 103.78	+ 27.72	+ 84.41	+ 21.44
465.21	335.85	Russell 2000	434.87	427.73	428.66	− 6.21	− 1.43	+ 88.09	+ 25.87	+ 66.05	+ 18.22
551.24	397.80	Russell 3000	517.56	508.08	508.08	− 8.50	− 1.65	+ 109.76	+ 27.56	+ 88.64	+ 21.13
477.08	356.95	Value-Line(geom.)	448.56	442.21	442.28	− 6.28	− 1.40	+ 85.14	+ 23.84	+ 66.96	+ 17.84
9486.69	6841.79	Wilshire 5000	...	...	8763.71	− 137.09	− 1.54	+ 1912.37	+ 27.91	+ 1565.42	+ 21.75

†-Based on comparable trading day in preceding year. *-Replaced previous index eff. 1/02/97.

Table 14-1 (*cont.*)

MOST ACTIVE ISSUES				DIARIES				
NYSE	VOLUME	CLOSE	CHANGE	**NYSE**		THUR	WED	WK AGO
WasteMgt	35,845,900	23 $\frac{1}{4}$	$-$ 5 $\frac{3}{4}$	Issues traded		3,427	3,447	3,418
Compaq	18,674,400	61 $\frac{1}{4}$	$-$ 2 $\frac{3}{16}$	Advances		804	1,991	586
TelcmBrslrs	9,484,500	91	$-$ 13	Declines		2,175	1,088	2,419
EDS Corp	8,434,200	37 $\frac{7}{8}$	$+$ 5 $\frac{1}{4}$	Unchanged		448	368	413
RepInd	7,668,900	31 $\frac{7}{16}$	$-$ 1 $\frac{1}{4}$	New highs		31	49	66
DataGen	7,254,700	19	$-$ 4 $\frac{3}{8}$	New lows		39	21	86
MicronTch	6,517,300	25 $\frac{1}{4}$	$-$ 2	zAdv vol	(000)	127,709	400,075	70,392
IBM	6,390,400	95 $\frac{13}{16}$	$-$ 2 $\frac{7}{16}$	zDecl vol	(000)	556,292	336,002	589,835
Motorola	6,314,600	58 $\frac{3}{16}$	$-$ 3 $\frac{3}{8}$	zTotal vol	(000)	707,817	770,615	669,292
MedPtnr	6,110,900	25 $\frac{3}{4}$	$-$ 1 $\frac{1}{8}$	Closing tick[1]		-218	$+223$	-222
Boeing	6,023,900	47 $\frac{3}{64}$	$-$ $\frac{25}{64}$	Closing Arms[2] (trin)		1.61	1.54	2.03
GenElec	6,010,800	63 $\frac{1}{4}$	$-$ 1 $\frac{5}{8}$	zBlock trades		14,677	15,874	13,950
Sears	5,976,600	41 $\frac{1}{16}$	$-$ $\frac{15}{16}$	**NASDAQ**				
PhilipMor	5,943,100	38 $\frac{7}{8}$	$-$ $\frac{5}{8}$	Issues traded		5,737	5,739	5,729
AT&T	5,546,400	48 $\frac{1}{8}$	$-$ $\frac{1}{4}$	Advances		1,445	2,799	1,008
NASDAQ				Declines		2,929	1,723	3,466
Intel	26,565,800	75 $\frac{3}{4}$	$-$ 4 $\frac{1}{2}$	Unchanged		1,363	1,217	1,255
DellCptr	26,033,800	78	$-$ 5 $\frac{1}{2}$	New highs		42	49	71
PhyCor	22,606,600	24	$-$ 5 $\frac{9}{16}$	New lows		62	31	62
CiscoSys	16,777,600	79 $\frac{15}{16}$	$-$ $\frac{9}{16}$	Adv vol	(000)	154,836	481,026	126,660
AppldMatl	13,236,300	31 $\frac{15}{16}$	$-$ 1 $\frac{11}{16}$	Decl vol	(000)	561,845	375,798	654,694
SunMicrsys	9,931,300	32 $\frac{7}{8}$	$-$ 1 $\frac{1}{2}$	Total vol	(000)	754,106	900,604	818,877
3ComCp	9,522,300	40 $\frac{1}{4}$	$-$ 3	Block trades		11,191	13,089	10,927
Microsoft	9,012,200	128 $\frac{5}{8}$	$-$ 2 $\frac{1}{4}$	**AMEX**				
OracleCp	8,330,500	33 $\frac{3}{4}$	$-$ 1 $\frac{3}{16}$	Issues traded		730	744	765
OxfordHlth	6,903,900	25 $\frac{13}{16}$	$-$ 1 $\frac{3}{8}$	Advances		213	387	144
KLA Tencor	6,644,600	40 $\frac{15}{16}$	$-$ 5 $\frac{5}{16}$	Declines		376	238	466
WorldCom	6,461,500	32 $\frac{15}{16}$	$-$ 1 $\frac{1}{16}$	Unchanged		141	119	155
AscendComm	6,382,300	26 $\frac{3}{8}$	$-$ 2 $\frac{1}{16}$	New highs		14	7	13
AMEX				New lows		7	4	25
SPDR	9,772,900	89 $\frac{15}{16}$	$-$ 2 $\frac{1}{32}$	zAdv vol	(000)	6,661	12,912	4,365
GreyWolf	3,153,800	8	$-$ $\frac{3}{16}$	zDecl vol	(000)	23,618	18,252	24,138
TubosMex	1,666,700	20 $\frac{5}{8}$	$-$ 1 $\frac{9}{16}$	zTotal vol	(000)	31,889	37,659	33,700
ViacomB	1,065,200	29 $\frac{1}{2}$	$-$ $\frac{9}{16}$	Comp vol	(000)	38,327	46,156	44,536
NaborsInd	979,000	42	$+$ $\frac{15}{16}$	zBlock trades		n.a.	742	601

Table 14-1 (*cont.*)

PRICE PERCENTAGE GAINERS ...

NYSE	VOL	CLOSE	CHANGE	% CHG
EDS Corp	8,434,200	$37\,7/8$	$+\ 5\,1/4$	$+$ 16.1
JilinChem	154,900	$15\,1/8$	$+\ 1\,1/2$	$+$ 11.0
GlamisGld	155,600	$5\,1/8$	$+\ 1/2$	$+$ 10.8
AamesFnl	1,343,300	$14\,3/8$	$+\ 1\,1/4$	$+$ 9.5
AmFnl	278,200	$37\,13/16$	$+\ 3\,1/4$	$+$ 9.4
BeijngYan	178,600	$11\,15/16$	$+\ 15/16$	$+$ 8.5
KinrossGld	24,400	$4\,3/8$	$+\ 5/16$	$+$ 7.7
MorganPdts	21,900	$6\,3/16$	$+\ 7/16$	$+$ 7.6
PlacrDome	1,112,200	16	$+\ 1\,1/16$	$+$ 7.1
ScorAdr	4,000	$45\,3/4$	$+\ 3$	$+$ 7.0
GenlSemi	292,200	$11\,1/2$	$+\ 3/4$	$+$ 7.0
ComstkRes	1,206,800	$16\,3/4$	$+\ 1$	$+$ 6.3
BarckGld	2,999,900	$21\,1/8$	$+\ 1\,1/4$	$+$ 6.3
HuanengPwr	215,600	$21\,1/8$	$+\ 1\,1/4$	$+$ 6.3
VarcoInt	429,300	$62\,5/16$	$+\ 3\,5/8$	$+$ 6.2
Homestake	889,000	$12\,3/4$	$+\ 11/16$	$+$ 5.7
TelkomIndo	505,600	$18\,15/16$	$+\ 1$	$+$ 5.6
SignlAprl	15,400	$2\,3/8$	$+\ 1/8$	$+$ 5.6
ChinaTire	64,900	11	$+\ 9/16$	$+$ 5.4
AgnicoEgl	171,800	$7\,3/8$	$+\ 3/8$	$+$ 5.4
NASDAQ NNM				
ACC	3,028,000	$39\,3/8$	$+\ 12\,1/4$	$+$ 45.2
UnionAcptncA	584,600	$6\,1/2$	$+\ 1\,1/4$	$+$ 23.8
Roberds	105,900	4	$+\ 3/4$	$+$ 23.1
NetworkImag.pf	5,100	7	$+\ 1\,1/4$	$+$ 21.7
UnivInt	333,300	$3\,11/16$	$+\ 5/8$	$+$ 20.4
OptionCr	38,600	$4\,5/8$	$+\ 3/4$	$+$ 19.4
LifeBcp	1,425,900	$29\,15/16$	$+\ 4\,9/16$	$+$ 18.0
ArabShld	15,800	$2\,7/8$	$+\ 7/16$	$+$ 17.9
ArtGreetg	76,100	5	$+\ 3/4$	$+$ 17.6
SeeqTch	1,244,800	$3\,7/8$	$+\ 9/16$	$+$ 17.0
Homecorp	36,600	$23\,1/2$	$+\ 3\,1/4$	$+$ 16.0
VividTch	459,900	$12\,3/4$	$+\ 1\,5/8$	$+$ 14.6
EISInt	154,500	8	$+\ 1$	$+$ 14.3
Xetel	115,700	5	$+\ 5/8$	$+$ 14.3
AMEX				
AlldDgtl	35,700	$2\,3/4$	$+\ 11/16$	$+$ 33.3
HrznPharm	63,200	$16\,1/8$	$+\ 2\,1/8$	$+$ 15.2
AmBiltrite	40,100	$25\,3/4$	$+\ 3\,3/8$	$+$ 15.1
SifcoInd	28,700	$21\,1/2$	$+\ 2\,1/4$	$+$ 11.7
HallwdEngyC	6,000	$12\,1/4$	$+\ 1\,1/4$	$+$ 11.4

AND LOSERS

NYSE	VOL	CLOSE	CHANGE	% CHG
WasteMgt	35,845,900	$23\,1/4$	$-\ 5\,3/4$	$-$ 19.8
ChicagoBridge	381,600	$16\,3/4$	$-\ 3\,7/8$	$-$ 18.8
DataGen	7,254,700	19	$-\ 4\,3/8$	$-$ 18.7
WasteMgtInt	363,400	$6\,1/2$	$-\ 1\,3/8$	$-$ 17.5
MedPtnr	6,110,900	$25\,3/4$	$-\ 5\,1/4$	$-$ 16.9
DalTile	218,400	$9\,1/2$	$-\ 1\,3/4$	$-$ 15.6
Calpine	212,800	$16\,1/8$	$-\ 2\,15/16$	$-$ 15.4
Copel	326,500	$12\,1/4$	$-\ 1\,7/8$	$-$ 13.3
TelcmBrslrs	9,484,500	91	$-\ 13$	$-$ 12.5
CocaClFemsa	352,300	42	$-\ 6$	$-$ 12.5
BcoFran	861,900	$24\,1/8$	$-\ 3\,3/16$	$-$ 11.7
NtlMedia	160,300	$5\,1/4$	$-\ 11/16$	$-$ 11.6
Disco	18,000	$36\,1/2$	$-\ 4\,11/16$	$-$ 11.4
BncoRioPltaADS	1,734,300	$10\,3/8$	$-\ 1\,5/16$	$-$ 11.2
GpFnlSerfin	196,600	3	$-\ 3/8$	$-$ 11.1
Spartech	123,800	$15\,7/8$	$-\ 1\,15/16$	$-$ 10.9
PohangIron	623,800	$15\,11/16$	$-\ 1\,7/8$	$-$ 10.7
KoreaElecPwr	747,600	$8\,3/8$	$-\ 1$	$-$ 10.7
Domtar	24,600	$7\,3/8$	$-\ 7/8$	$-$ 10.6
WelptHlth	354,300	$47\,11/16$	$-\ 5\,1/2$	$-$ 10.3
NASDAQ NNM				
Pegasystems	4,012,300	$18\,3/8$	$-\ 9\,3/8$	$-$ 33.8
BancQuadrm	156,400	$3\,3/4$	$-\ 1\,1/4$	$-$ 25.0
7thLevel	1,105,700	$1\,3/4$	$-\ 1/2$	$-$ 22.2
PhysCptr	2,799,400	$5\,1/16$	$-\ 1\,3/8$	$-$ 21.4
APACHEMed	46,000	$2\,3/8$	$-\ 5/8$	$-$ 20.8
Thermatrix	21,400	$2\,3/8$	$-\ 5/8$	$-$ 20.8
FriscoBay	3,000	$2\,3/8$	$-\ 5/8$	$-$ 20.8
PhyCor	22,606,600	24	$-\ 5\,5/8$	$-$ 18.8
MVSIAwt	154,700	3	$-\ 11/16$	$-$ 18.6
JDASftwrGp	1,227,900	$30\,5/16$	$-\ 6\,11/16$	$-$ 18.1
ConcurrentCmpt	1,203,800	$2\,3/4$	$-\ 19/32$	$-$ 17.8
TriTeal	313,000	$3\,1/4$	$-\ 11/16$	$-$ 17.5
BostonChick	5,186,500	$10\,7/16$	$-\ 2\,3/16$	$-$ 17.3
EPMedSys	2,800	$1\,7/8$	$-\ 3/8$	$-$ 16.7
AMEX				
LehmnHldgHKwt98	10,800	3	$-\ 7/16$	$-$ 12.7
USBiosciwt	5,000	$1\,7/8$	$-\ 1/4$	$-$ 11.8
PrimeRes	9,600	$6\,7/8$	$-\ 7/8$	$-$ 11.3
SheffPharm	9,000	$2\,1/16$	$-\ 1/4$	$-$ 10.8
KingPwrGp	11,600	$6\,5/8$	$-\ 3/4$	$-$ 10.2

Table 14-1 (*cont.*)

VOLUME PERCENTAGE LEADERS

NYSE	VOL	%DIF*	CLOSE		CHANGE
CentlLaElec	1,494,600	4334.2	x26 $\frac{1}{16}$	−	$\frac{3}{16}$
CarsnPirSct	1,390,000	3950.8	46 $\frac{1}{8}$	+	1
SpiekerPrpty	3,414,700	2541.6	38 $\frac{5}{8}$	−	$\frac{1}{4}$
IMCO Recyc	575,700	2307.1	18 $\frac{1}{4}$	−	$\frac{9}{16}$
WasteMgt	35,845,900	2009.8	23 $\frac{1}{4}$	−	5 $\frac{3}{4}$
WashPost B	162,700	1791.4	429 $\frac{1}{16}$	−	3 $\frac{11}{16}$
InaCom	2,015,700	1379.0	30	−	2 $\frac{13}{16}$
HnckJ PtPremII	391,200	1358.3	11 $\frac{9}{16}$	.....	
CapMAC	1,027,500	1145.8	30	−	2
LexmarkIntA	3,038,300	1035.4	30 $\frac{1}{2}$	−	2 $\frac{1}{4}$
CadburySch	596,600	946.8	40 $\frac{7}{16}$	−	$\frac{1}{16}$
Proffitts	2,438,200	944.2	27 $\frac{1}{2}$	−	$\frac{5}{8}$
Tokheim	387,600	908.8	16 $\frac{1}{8}$	−	$\frac{1}{4}$
CzchRepblc	228,000	882.5	11 $\frac{1}{2}$	−	$\frac{11}{16}$
RoyalGpTch	670,300	875.4	25 $\frac{1}{2}$	−	$\frac{7}{8}$
DataGen	7,254,700	784.5	19	−	4 $\frac{3}{8}$
MrgnStn 7.82 un	59,600	716.8	25 $\frac{3}{16}$	−	$\frac{1}{8}$
MedPtnr	6,110,900	712.0	25 $\frac{3}{1}$	−	1 $\frac{1}{8}$
ChicagoBridge	381,600	692.9	16 $\frac{3}{4}$	−	3 $\frac{7}{8}$
WheelbrTch	1,064,300	659.4	14 $\frac{3}{16}$	−	1 $\frac{1}{4}$

NASDAQ NNM	VOL	%DIF*	CLOSE		CHANGE
AHL Svcs	861,900	6754.1	17	+	1 $\frac{1}{2}$
Middleby	1,466,200	6252.1	10 $\frac{1}{8}$	−	$\frac{3}{8}$
SuperiorCnsl	1,222,400	4983.0	31	−	1 $\frac{3}{4}$
LifeBcp	1,425,900	2955.9	29 $\frac{15}{16}$	+	4 $\frac{9}{16}$
Pegasystems	4,012,300	2725.8	18 $\frac{3}{8}$	−	9 $\frac{3}{8}$
JustinInd	1,182,100	2162.7	13	−	$\frac{1}{4}$
DMMgt	991,400	2158.4	14 $\frac{1}{4}$	+	$\frac{1}{4}$
PhyCor	22,606,600	2026.6	24	−	·5 $\frac{9}{16}$
HoenigGp	300,800	1628.5	5 $\frac{9}{16}$	+	$\frac{1}{16}$
UnionAcptncA	584,600	1456.3	6 $\frac{1}{2}$	+	1 $\frac{1}{4}$
PhysCptr	2,799,400	1358.8	5 $\frac{1}{16}$	−	1 $\frac{3}{8}$
RamapoFnl	445,400	1354.2	9 $\frac{1}{2}$	+	$\frac{3}{4}$
FstLibFnl	78,300	1225.8	26	+	2 $\frac{1}{4}$
ACC	3,028,000	1216.5	39 $\frac{3}{8}$	+	12 $\frac{1}{4}$
EchoStar	2,114,200	1077.6	18 $\frac{7}{8}$	−	$\frac{5}{8}$
4Health	406,500	1072.3	6 $\frac{1}{4}$	+	$\frac{1}{2}$

AMEX	VOL	%DIF*	CLOSE		CHANGE
GAFnl	85,100	808.6	18 $\frac{7}{8}$	.....	
ThermoVoltek	119,300	779.6	7	+	$\frac{7}{16}$
AckrlyGrp	82,600	645.2	14 $\frac{3}{8}$	+	$\frac{3}{8}$
AmBiltrite	40,100	573.4	25 $\frac{3}{4}$	+	3 $\frac{3}{8}$
Mediq	126,200	556.5	9 $\frac{1}{16}$	+	$\frac{9}{16}$

*Common stocks of $5 a share or more with average volume over 65 trading days of at least 5,000 shares.
a-has traded fewer than 65 days.   b-10,000% or greater

BREAKDOWN OF TRADING IN NYSE STOCKS (9:30 a.m. to 4 p.m. EST)

BY MARKET	Thur	Wed	WK AGO
New York	707,817,320	770,615,420	669,291,930
Chicago	26,931,200	31,781,800	30,613,400
CBOE	21,500	30,900	16,600
Pacific	12,383,700	13,851,500	15,180,400
NASD	50,584,000	61,107,210	56,486,540
Phila	6,774,200	6,937,100	7,400,700
Boston	7,430,600	9,382,200	8,520,500
Cincinnati	7,354,500	8,100,800	9,073,100
Composite	819,296,820	901,806,930	796,583,170

NYSE first crossing 1,228,000 shares, value n.a.)
Second (basket) 3,166,716 shares, value $167,699,824
†The net difference of the number of stocks closing higher than their previous trade from those closing lower; NYSE trading only.
x-Ex-dividend of Travelers Group 15¢ lowered the Industrial average 0.74. Southern Co. 32½¢ lowered the Utility average 0.16. These lowered the Composite average 0.39.
z-NYSE or Amex only.

½-HOURLY	Thur	Wed	WK AGO
9:30-10	81,130,000	102,880,000	81,100,000
10-10:30	88,150,000	92,390,000	73,940,000
10:30-11	66,000,000	71,730,000	59,980,000
11-11:30	51,280,000	60,740,000	53,370,000
11:30-12	51,030,000	55,200,000	39,540,000
12-12:30	47,400,000	54,250,000	32,300,000
12:30-1	37,440,000	39,730,000	35,710,000
1-1:30	33,420,000	34,820,000	44,990,000
1:30-2	33,890,000	55,710,000	44,870,000
2-2:30	43,200,000	44,010,000	35,680,000
2:30-3	43,680,000	39,550,000	47,370,000
3-3:30	57,960,000	49,540,000	54,770,000
3:30-4	73,237,320	70,065,420	65,671,930

Table 14-2

NEW YORK STOCK EXCHANGE

	52 Weeks Hi	52 Weeks Lo	Stock	Sym	Div	Yld %	PE	Vol 100s	Hi	Lo	Close	Net Chg
	25 5/16	17 3/8	Humana	HUM		...	23	2691	21 5/8	20 7/8	20 7/8	– 11/16
	23 15/16	16 5/8	Hunt	HUN	.38	1.8	52	159	22 1/8	21 1/4	21 1/4	– 13/16
	18 1/2	10	Huntco A	HCO	.14	1.0	22	96	14	13 13/16	14	+ 3/16
	9 7/8	3 7/16	HuntgLfSci	HTD		...	7	87	4 1/16	4	4	– 1/16
	1 5/8	9/16	Huntway	HWY		...	14	30	1 7/16	1 7/16	1 7/16	+ 1/16
	7 5/16	7	Hyperion97	HTA	.40	5.6	...	241	7 3/16	7 3/16	7 3/16	...
	7	6 3/8	Hyperion99	HTT	.43	6.4	...	1329	6 7/8	6 3/4	6 3/4	...
	8	7	Hyperion02	HTB	.47	6.0	...	526	7 15/16	7 13/16	7 13/16	– 1/8
	8 7/16	7 1/8	Hyperion2005	HTO	.55	6.8	...	256	8 1/4	8 1/8	8 1/8	– 1/16
	10 1/16	9	HyperionFd	HTR	.75m	8.2	...	540	9 3/16	9 1/8	9 1/8	– 1/16

-I-I-I-

	52 Weeks Hi	52 Weeks Lo	Stock	Sym	Div	Yld %	PE	Vol 100s	Hi	Lo	Close	Net Chg
	27 1/4	22 1/8	IBP Inc	IBP	.10	.4	19	1277	23 3/16	22 7/8	23 1/16	...
	2 7/8	1 3/4	ICF Kaiser	ICF		...	27	305	2 3/16	2	2 1/8	...
	56	18 1/4	ICN Pharm	ICN	.32	.7	20	2511	47 3/4	45 7/8	46 3/4	+ 3/8
	33 3/8	28 1/8	IES Ind	IES	2.10	6.6	14	172	32	31 7/8	32	– 1/8
	25 3/4	23 7/8	IES Util A	IEU	1.97	7.8	...	1	25 5/16	25 5/16	25 5/16	+ 1/16
s	**46 5/8**	**20 5/8**	**IKON**	**IKN**	**.16**	**.6**	**29**	**4321**	**28 13/16**	**26 13/16**	**26 13/16**	**– 1 5/8**
	101 1/2	56 1/4	IKON OfcSol dep pf		5.04	7.3	...	5	70 7/8	69	69	–2
	42 1/2	31 3/8	IMC Global	IGL	.32	.9	17	2635	35	33 15/16	33 15/16	– 15/16
	16 7/8	15 5/6	INA Invest	IIS	1.24	7.4	...	26	16 13/16	16 13/16	16 13/16	+ 1/8
n	53	38 7/8	ING Groep ADR	ING	.49p	...	...	609	41 1/2	40 13/16	41 3/8	– 5/8
n▲	39 3/4	39 3/16	ING Groep wi			...	...	3	40 3/4	40 1/2	40 3/4	+1
	26 1/8	19	INMC MtgHldg	NDE	1.84f	7.7	57	2051	24 1/8	23 3/4	23 15/16	...
	13 5/8	9 1/2	IP Timber	IPT	2.00	18.9	2	773	10 13/16	10 1/2	10 9/16	– 1/4
	13	9 1/2	♣ IRT Prop	IRT	.90	7.4	18	340	12 7/16	11 3/4	12 3/16	– 5/16
n	30	18 1/2	ISPAT Int A	IST		...	...	1321	25	24 5/8	24 3/4	– 1/4
	77 5/8	40 7/8	ITT Corp	ITT		...	21	4469	74	72 3/4	73 3/8	– 9/16
	33 11/16	22 1/8	ITT Ind	IIN	.60	1.9	35	3401	32	31 7/16	31 9/16	– 13/16
	32 13/16	28 1/2	IdahoPwr	IDA	1.86	6.0	14	476	31 5/16	30 3/4	31 3/16	+ 1/8
s	36 11/16	23 1/4	♣ IDEX Cp	IEX	.48	1.4	18	404	35 1/16	33 11/16	33 11/16	– 1
	39	30 1/2	♣ IllCentl	IC	.92	2.6	15	614	36 1/8	35 5/16	35 3/8	– 11/16
	26 5/8	25 3/4	IllPwr MIPS pfA		2.36	9.0	...	70	26 1/8	26 1/8	26 1/8	+ 1/16
	34	27 1/2	IllPwr pfA		2.04	6.2	...	2	32 3/4	32 3/4	32 3/4	– 1 1/4
	25 5/8	24	IllPwr pfT toprs		2.00	8.0	...	46	25 1/8	25 1/16	25 1/16	– 1/16
s	55 5/16	34 3/4	Ill Tool	ITW	.48	1.0	21	3678	49 7/16	48 1/4	48 1/4	– 11/16
	28 5/8	20 1/8	♣ IlNova	ILN	1.24	5.6	10	18734	22 1/4	21 15/16	22 1/8	– 1/8
	33 3/8	21	Imation	IMN		...	32	11548	23	21 3/8	22	+ 5/16
	21	13 5/8	♣ IMCO Recyc	IMR	.20	1.1	19	5757	18 7/16	17 3/4	18 1/4	– 9/16
	7	2 1/4	IMO Ind	IMD		...	dd	4	5 3/8	5 3/8	5 3/8	+ 1/16
s▲	43 1/2	17 1/8	ImperlBcp	IMP	stk	...	27	1649	43 7/8	42 3/4	43 1/2	...
	71 3/8	45	ICI	ICI	2.42e	4.0	20	910	61 3/16	60 13/16	60 13/16	– 1 9/16
	40 5/8	**19 3/4**	**InaCom**	**ICO**		**...**	**14**	**20157**	**32 3/4**	**30**	**30**	**– 2 13/16**
	37 5/8	19 3/4	♣ Inco Ltd	N	.40	2.0	16	4779	20 11/16	20 1/4	20 1/4	– 7/16
	28	14 1/2	♣ IncoLtd VBN	NVB	.32	2.0	...	360	16 3/8	16	16 3/16	– 3/16
	56 1/2	48 3/8	♣ Inco Ltd pfE		2.75	5.6	...	2	49 1/2	49 1/2	49 1/2	...
	9 9/16	8 5/8	IncOpp1999	IOF	.60	6.4	...	721	9 7/16	9 3/8	9 7/16	...
	9 9/16	8 5/8	IncOpp2000	IFT	.63	6.7	...	40	9 1/2	9 7/16	9 7/16	– 1/16
	10 13/16	6 1/2	IndiaFd	IFN	.01e	.1	...	609	8 1/16	7 7/8	7 7/8	– 1/4
	14 1/4	8 5/8	IndiaGrFd	IGF	.08e	.8	...	232	10	9 3/4	9 15/16	– 3/16
	34 1/4	22 5/8	IndiEngy	IEI	1.18f	4.3	15	197	28 3/4	27 9/16	27 5/8	– 1
	26	23 7/8	IndiMich A	IMJ	2.00	8.0	...	19	25 1/4	25 1/16	25 1/16	– 1/8
	12 1/2	5 3/8	♣ IndonesiaFd	IF		...	...	362	6 3/4	6 1/2	6 1/2	– 1/16
	32 1/8	21 1/8	Indosat	IIT	.65e	2.8	...	703	23 3/16	22 13/16	23 3/16	+ 7/16
n	23 1/4	17 3/4	IndlDistrGp	IDG		...	...	185	19 3/8	18 7/8	19	– 5/16
n	20 7/8	14 3/8	IndstriasBach ADS	IBA		...	...	143	17	16 1/2	16 5/8	– 5/8
s	46 1/4	27 1/16	IngersolRand	IR	.60	1.5	16	4178	40 7/8	39 5/8	40 1/4	– 5/8
n	30 1/8	19	IngramMicro A	IM		...	26	3206	29 15/16	28 3/16	28 13/16	– 3/4
	27 1/2	16	♣ InlandStl	IAD	.20	1.0	10	1401	19 3/4	19 7/16	19 1/2	– 1/2
	17 5/8	11 1/4	Innkeepers	KPA	1.04f	6.1	21	1316	17	16 13/16	16 15/16	...
	33 1/8	**13 1/4**	**InptOutpt**	**IO**		**...**	**64**	**2706**	**28 11/16**	**27**	**27 1/16**	**– 1 3/4**
	25 3/4	15 1/4	InsgnaFnl A	IFS		...	77	414	21 11/16	21 3/8	21 11/16	+ 1/16
	9 5/8	7 3/16	InsteelInd	III	.24	3.1	dd	37	7 5/8	7 1/2	7 5/8	– 1/16
	13 3/4	11 7/8	InsrdMuniFd	PIF	.77	5.8	...	317	13 3/8	13 1/4	13 3/8	+ 1/16
	39 1/8	**22**	**IntegHS**	**IHS**	**.02**	**.1**	**17**	**4837**	**33**	**31 3/4**	**31 3/4**	**– 1 3/4**
	6 3/4	3 3/8	Intellicall	ICL		...	dd	24	5 1/4	5 1/8	5 3/16	– 1/16
	13 15/16	11 7/8	♣ IntcapCa	IIC	.75	5.6	...	64	13 1/2	13 3/8	13 7/16	– 1/16
	13 1/16	10 7/8	♣ IntercpCAQty	IQC	.72	5.6	...	47	12 13/16	12 3/4	12 3/4	...
	17	15 1/2	♣ IntcapSec	ICB	1.32	7.9	...	87	16 13/16	16 5/8	16 13/16	+ 1/16
	15 3/16	13 3/8	♣ IntcapInsCA	ICS	.78	5.4	...	10	14 5/16	14 5/16	14 5/16	...
	16 1/2	13 3/4	♣ IntcapMnBd	IMB	.99	6.2	...	74	16 1/16	15 7/8	16	– 1/16
	13 3/4	11 1/2	♣ IntcapInsInco	IIM	.78	5.9	...	136	13 3/16	13 1/8	13 3/16	+ 1/16
	15 3/16	13	♣ IntcapInsMuni	IMS	.81	5.6	...	57	14 3/8	14 3/8	14 3/8	– 1/8
	16 1/4	14 1/2	♣ IntercpMuniTr	IMT	.96	6.3	...	382	15 1/4	15 1/16	15 3/16	– 1/16
	12 11/16	10 7/8	♣ IntercpNYQty	IQN	.69	5.5	...	101	12 5/8	12 9/16	12 5/8	– 1/16
	15 1/2	13 7/8	♣ IntcapQual	IQT	.96a	6.2	...	98	15 7/16	15 3/8	15 3/8	– 1/16
	12 13/16	11	♣ IntercpQty	IQM	.75	6.0	...	112	12 5/8	12 1/2	12 1/2	– 1/16
	15 13/16	14 3/16	♣ IntcapMuni	IQI	.93	6.3	...	435	14 13/16	14 5/8	14 13/16	+ 1/16
s	31 1/8	16 15/16	InterimSvc	IS		...	26	266	27	25 13/16	25 7/8	– 1 1/16
	7 1/2	2 7/8	Intlake	IK		...	2	267	5 3/8	5 1/4	5 3/8	– 1/8
	11 3/16	4 3/8	IntlCeram	ICM		...	...	52	9 7/8	9 3/4	9 7/8	– 1/16
	31 3/8	24 1/2	♣ IntAlum	IAL	1.00	3.4	21	18	29 3/8	29 3/8	29 3/8	– 1/8
s	109 7/16	62 9/16	IBM	IBM	.80	.8	16	63904	99 3/8	95 9/16	95 13/16	– 2 7/16
	27 3/4	26	IBM dep pf		1.88	6.8	...	65	27 3/4	27 143/256	27 5/8	+ 1/16
n	4 1/2	1/16	IntFinBear wt			...	...	379	1/4	3/16	3/16	+ 1/16
	53 7/16	39 7/8	IntFlavor	IFF	1.44	3.0	23	2199	47 15/16	46 5/8	47 9/16	– 3/16
x	26 3/16	15 1/4	IntGameTch	IGT	.12	.5	23	6793	25	23 15/16	24 1/8	– 11/16
	32 7/16	15 1/8	IntMultfood	IMC	.80	2.8	94	289	29 3/16	28 1/4	29 1/16	+ 9/16

	52 Weeks Hi	52 Weeks Lo	Stock	Sym	Div	Yld %	PE	Vol 100s	Hi	Lo	Close	Net Chg
	57 1/8	35 3/4	KnghtRidder	KRI	.80	1.5	13	5750	52 11/16	52	52	– 1 3/16
n	34 3/16	17 1/8	Knoll	KNL		...	...	223	28 3/8	27 3/4	28	– 1/2
	74 3/4	35 5/8	KohlsCp	KSS		...	44	1813	66	63 5/8	65 1/4	+ 11/16
	20 3/8	10 1/8	Kollmrgn	KOL	.08	.5	8	248	17 7/8	17 1/4	17 1/2	– 5/8
	23 3/4	16 1/2	KoorInd	KOR	.44e	2.1	11	1094	21	20 5/8	20 15/16	– 3/16
▼	**22 3/8**	**9 3/16**	**KoreaElecPwr**	**KEP**	**.30e**	**3.6**	**...**	**7476**	**8 7/8**	**8 1/4**	**8 3/8**	**– 1**
▼	7 1/4	3 3/4	KoreaEquity	KEF		...	...	603	3 13/16	3 5/8	3 3/4	– 1/16
▼	**17 7/8**	**8**	**KoreaFd**	**KF**		**...**	**...**	**11997**	**8 1/16**	**7 11/16**	**7 7/8**	**– 3/4**
	9	**4 1/4**	**KoreanInvFd**	**KIF**	**.29e**	**6.3**	**...**	**1633**	**4 11/16**	**4 1/2**	**4 5/8**	**– 3/8**
n	26 1/2	18	KranzRlty pfB		1.22e	4.9	...	3	25	25	25	...
	20 1/8	14 3/4	♣ Kranzco	KRT	1.92	10.0	26	155	19 5/8	19 1/8	19 3/16	– 9/16
s	33 1/4	21 3/16	Kroger	KR		...	20	8821	32 1/8	31 5/16	31 15/16	+ 1/2
	120	65 1/2	Kubota	KUB	.98e	1.3	...	5	75	74 1/4	74 1/4	– 1 1/4
	38 3/8	15 7/8	Kuhlman	KUH	.60	1.7	22	245	35 7/8	34 15/16	34 15/16	– 1 1/16
	171	107	Kyocera	KYO	.98e	.8	...	76	118	116 3/4	118	– 4 1/2

-L-L-L-

	52 Weeks Hi	52 Weeks Lo	Stock	Sym	Div	Yld %	PE	Vol 100s	Hi	Lo	Close	Net Chg
	2 3/4	1	LA Gear	LA		...	dd	419	1 3/16	1 1/8	1 3/16	+ 1/16
	35 5/8	15 3/8	LCI Int	LCI		...	25	7333	25 13/16	24 7/8	24 15/16	– 9/16
	25 7/8	21 1/4	♣ LGE Energy	LGE	1.19f	5.5	17	547	21 13/16	21 5/8	21 11/16	– 1/8
	5 5/8	4 1/4	LLE RoyalTr	LRT	.66e	12.7	...	234	5 3/16	5 1/16	5 3/16	+ 1/16
n	27 1/8	22 3/4	LNR Prop wi			...	...	220	25 1/4	24 1/2	24 3/4	– 3/8
	5 1/4	3 5/8	LSB Ind	LSB	.06	1.3	dd	10	4 1/2	4 1/2	4 1/2	...
	46 7/8	18 5/8	♣ LSI Logic	LSI		...	18	20816	21 15/16	21	21 1/8	– 1
▲	20 5/8	16 1/8	LTC Prop	LTC	1.46	7.1	17	195	20 3/4	20 3/8	20 1/2	– 1/8
n	26 1/2	25	LTC Prop pfA		2.37	9.2	...	184	26	25 7/8	25 7/8	– 1/16
	14 9/16	10	LTV Cp	LTV	.12	1.0	38	1576	12 1/4	11 15/16	12 1/4	+ 1/16
	15/16	3/16	LTV Cp wt			...	...	100	1/4	3/16	3/16	– 1/16
	24 3/8	16	LaQuinta	LQI	.07	.4	17	4617	17 5/8	17	17 3/8	– 7/16
	39	29 1/8	♣ LaZ Boy	LZB	.84	2.3	16	340	37 9/16	37 3/16	37 3/16	– 7/8
	32 1/8	15 1/2	LabChile	LBC	.58e	2.4	...	100	24 1/4	23 3/8	24 1/4	+ 11/16
	4	2 1/4	LabCpAmer	LH		...	...	6404	2 9/16	2 3/8	2 1/2	+ 1/16
n	59 1/4	53 1/2	LabCp pfA		1.18p	...	...	445	55 1/2	54 1/2	55 1/4	+ 1/4
n	60 1/2	55	LabCpAmer pfB		.02p	...	...	1	59 1/2	59 1/2	59 1/2	– 1/2
	11/32	1/32	LabCpAmer wt			...	...	53	1/16	1/16	1/16	...
	26 1/16	20 1/4	LacledeGas	LG	1.30	5.1	18	99	25 1/2	25 3/16	25 1/4	– 5/16
	34 5/16	18 1/2	♣ Lafarge	LAF	.48f	1.6	12	739	30 1/8	29 1/2	29 3/4	– 3/4
	5 15/16	**1 5/8**	**LaidlawEnvr**	**LLE**		**...**	**dd**	**682**	**5 1/16**	**4 13/16**	**4 7/8**	**– 5/16**
n	16 1/2	12 3/4	Laidlaw g	LDW	.05p	...	...	3100	14 3/16	13 15/16	13 15/16	– 3/8
	47 7/8	32 3/8	♣ LakheadPipe	LHP	3.12	7.1	14	566	44 5/16	43 7/8	44 1/16	– 5/16
	8 3/4	6	LamsonSes	LMS		...	36	29	6 9/16	6 9/16	6 9/16	+ 1/16
	32 7/8	21	LandsEnd	LE		...	18	242	31 11/16	31 1/16	31 9/16	+ 3/8
n	37 7/8	27 1/8	LaSallePtnr	LAP		...	...	77	36 11/16	36 7/16	36 11/16	+ 1/16
	36 1/8	24 1/2	LaSalleRe	LSH	2.84	8.5	...	378	34 3/8	33 3/8	33 1/2	– 1 1/8
n	26 7/16	24	LaSalleRe pfA		2.19	8.5	...	101	25 11/16	25 7/16	25 11/16	– 1/16
	14 5/8	9 5/8	LASMO	LSO	.10e	.7	...	123	13 1/2	12 7/8	13 3/8	+ 1/2
	27	25 3/8	LASMO A	LSOA	2.50	9.4	...	30	26 5/8	26 1/2	26 1/2	– 1/8
	16 7/8	12 13/16	LatinAmDllr	LBF	1.50a	10.7	...	391	14 5/8	13 7/8	14 1/16	– 11/16
▼	**19**	**12 7/8**	**♣ LatinAmEqty**	**LAQ**	**.16e**	**1.3**	**...**	**1108**	**13 1/2**	**12 11/16**	**12 3/4**	**– 1 1/8**
	12 1/2	9 3/8	LatAmGrw	LLF	.15e	1.5	...	118	10	9 7/8	9 15/16	– 1/8
	22 1/2	**12 1/4**	**LatinAmDiscv**	**LDF**	**2.00e**	**12.5**	**...**	**1081**	**16 1/4**	**15 5/8**	**15 15/16**	**– 1 1/16**
▼	**21**	**14 1/4**	**♣ LatinAmFd**	**LAM**	**.24e**	**1.7**	**...**	**486**	**14 13/16**	**14**	**14 1/8**	**– 1 7/16**
	14 1/8	10 5/8	LawterInt	LAW	.40	3.6	13	247	11 1/2	11 1/4	11 1/4	– 1/8
	33 11/16	16 3/4	LawyrTitl	LTI	.20	.6	8	106	31 3/8	31	31 3/16	– 1/16
	51 11/16	31 3/4	Lear	LEA		...	17	1018	48 13/16	48 1/8	48 3/8	– 7/16
	22 3/4	5 1/2	LearningCo	TLC		...	dd	8596	19 3/4	18 7/8	19 1/2	– 5/8
s	27 5/8	14 3/8	LeaRonal	LRI	.52	2.0	18	48	25 7/8	25 1/2	25 1/2	– 1/2
	30 1/2	20 3/4	Lee Ent	LEE	.52	2.0	24	199	27 1/2	26 9/16	26 5/8	– 3/4
s	55 1/4	23 7/8	♣ LeggMason	LM	.44	.9	20	1103	49 5/16	47 11/16	49 5/16	+ 3/8
	47 3/4	29 3/8	LeggetPlat	LEG	.56f	1.4	20	541	42 3/8	41 1/8	41 1/8	– 5/8
	1/2	1/8	LehighGp	LEI		...	dd	601	1/4	11/64	1/4	+ 1/64
	56 1/2	24 1/8	LehmnHldg	LEH	.24	.5	11	6029	48 13/16	47 3/8	47 3/8	– 1 3/4
	26 1/16	24 1/2	Lehmn QUICS	LEQ	2.08	8.1	...	214	25 3/4	25 5/8	25 11/16	...
	44 11/16	22	Lennar	LEN	.01e	...	15	1540	40 11/16	39 7/8	40 3/8	– 7/16
n	17 5/8	15	Lennar wi			...	...	106	15 7/8	15 5/8	15 3/4	– 1/4
	36 5/8	23 3/8	LeucdaNat	LUK	.25	.7	28	309	35 1/2	34 3/8	34 3/8	– 1 1/4
s	33 1/8	19	Leviathan un	LEV	1.90f	6.2	25	195	30 1/2	30 1/4	30 7/16	– 3/16
	16 13/16	12 1/8	LexngtnPrpty	LXP	1.16	7.8	19	180	15	14 7/8	14 7/8	– 3/8
	36 5/16	**19 1/8**	**LexmarkInt A**	**LXK**		**...**	**15**	**30383**	**31**	**30**	**30 1/2**	**– 2 1/4**
	39 3/8	23 5/8	♣ Libbey	LBY	.30	.8	16	80	37 7/8	37 11/16	37 13/16	+ 1/8
	4 13/16	3 5/8	LibrteInvst	LBI		...	dd	10	4	4	4	...
	14 3/4	11	♣ LibtyASE	USA	1.30e	10.0	...	1142	13 1/8	12 7/8	13 1/16	– 3/16
	13 7/16	9 1/8	♣ LibtyASG	ASG	1.94e	16.0	...	372	12 1/4	12 1/16	12 1/8	– 1/4
	47 5/16	32 1/4	LibtyCp	LC	.80	1.8	23	303	45 3/16	43 1/4	43 1/2	– 1 11/16
	57 1/4	34 3/4	LibFin	L	.60	1.2	13	174	52 11/16	51 5/16	52 1/8	– 13/16
	27 15/16	21 1/8	LibertyProp	LRY	1.68f	6.1	22	1015	27 3/4	27 1/4	27 11/16	+ 5/16
n	26	24 1/4	LibertyProp pfA		.48p	...	...	61	25	24 7/8	24 7/8	– 1/8
	8 7/16	7 3/4	LibtyTrmTr	LTT	.42	5.1	...	107	8 5/16	8 5/16	8 5/16	...
	56 1/8	33 3/4	♣ LifeReCp	LRE	.52	1.0	16	70	53 7/16	53	53 1/4	– 1/16
s	70 5/16	33 7/8	LillyEli	LLY	.80	1.2	dd	27858	68 15/16	65 1/2	66	– 1 3/4
	24 5/8	16 1/2	LillyInd	LI	.32	1.7	16	149	19	18 7/8	18 15/16	+ 3/16
	25 3/4	16 1/2	Limited Inc	LTD	.48	2.1	15	8988	23 3/8	22 1/4	23 1/4	+ 5/8
	20 1/2	16 3/4	♣ LincNatSec	LNV	.96a	4.8	...	52	19 15/16	19 5/8	19 7/8	+ 1/4
	73 5/8	47	♣ LincNatCp	LNC	1.96	2.9	16	2034	69 3/8	67 7/8	68	– 7/16
	27 5/16	25 1/4	LincNat QUIPS A		2.19	8.3	...	57	26 5/16	26 3/16	26 5/16	+ 1/16
	26 3/4	24 7/8	LincCap TOPrS B		2.09	8.1	...	21	25 7/8	25 11/16	25 7/8	+ 3/16
	14	12 1/4	♣ LincNatInco	LND	1.04m	7.7	...	6	13 9/16	13 7/16	13 9/16	+ 1/16
s	50 1/4	26 21/32	LindsayMfg	LNN	.14	.3	22	40	43 1/8	42 7/8	43	...

Table 14-2 (*cont.*)

COMPOSITE TRANSACTIONS

52 Weeks Hi	52 Weeks Lo	Stock	Sym	Div	Yld %	PE	Vol 100s	Hi	Lo	Close	Net Chg
26 1/4	25 1/16	McDonalds dep pf		1.93	7.6	...	58	25 5/16	25 5/16	25 5/16	...
26 3/8	24 15/16	McDonalds QUIDS	MCZ	2.09	8.3	...	101	25 3/16	25 3/16	25 3/16	...
n 25 7/8	24 1/8	McDonalds sbdb2037	MCJ	1.88	7.4	...	37	25 5/16	25 3/16	25 1/4	- 1/8
n 25 11/16	24 1/4	McDonalds sbdb	MCW	1.88	7.4	...	113	25 5/16	25 3/16	25 1/4	+ 1/16
70 3/16	42 1/2	McGrawH	MHP	1.44	2.2	12	1749	67 1/16	65 7/8	66 7/16	+ 1/16
110 3/8	48 1/2	McKesson	MCK	1.00	1.0	32	1833	105 15/16	103 3/8	105 1/4	- 3/4
27 7/16	18 5/8	McWhorterTch	MWT		...	18	178	26	25 5/8	26	...
75 3/8	49 3/4	Mead	MEA	1.20	1.9	22	2168	63 7/16	62 5/16	62 5/16	- 1 1/4
26 5/8	**15 1/4**	**♣ MdwbrkInsGp**	**MIG**	**.08**	**.3**	**22**	**490**	**23 3/4**	**22 7/8**	**22 7/8**	**- 1 1/4**
21 1/2	12	Medeva	MDV	.38e	2.8	...	142	13 3/4	13 1/4	13 1/2	- 1/8
s 30 1/2	15 1/8	MedAssrnce	MAI		...	16	30	27 7/8	27 1/8	27 7/8	+ 1/2
45 1/16	35 1/8	♣ MeditrPrd	MT	2.89f	6.8	16	1743	43	42 5/16	42 13/16	- 1/8
32	**17 7/8**	**MedPtnr**	**MDM**		**...**	**dd**	**61109**	**28 3/4**	**25 1/2**	**25 3/4**	**- 1 1/8**
n▲ 26 1/16	21 7/16	MedPtnr TAPS	MDX		...	...	10826	26 1/8	24 3/8	24 3/8	- 5/8
s 50 15/16	28 13/16	Medtronic	MDT	.22	.5	37	13559	45 5/8	43 3/16	43 3/8	- 1
50 1/2	32 1/4	♣ MedusaCp	MSA	.60	1.4	12	1997	41 7/8	39 3/4	41 13/16	- 9/16
s 58 3/4	31 3/4	MellonBk	MEL	1.32	2.6	18	12501	52 1/16	50	50 9/16	- 13/16
26 1/2	25 3/16	MellonBk pfK		2.05	8.1	...	10	25 7/16	25 1/4	25 7/16	+ 1/4
35 1/4	19	Memtec	MET	.07e	.2	...	572	31 15/16	31 5/8	31 5/8	- 13/16
9 11/16	8 3/4	MentorIncoFd	MRF	.84	8.9	...	146	9 7/16	9 3/8	9 7/16	...
27 1/2	24 3/4	MEPC QUIPS A		2.28	8.7	...	38	26 3/8	26 5/16	26 5/16	- 3/16
s 53 1/2	32 5/8	MercBcpMO	MTL	1.15	2.4	28	1204	48 15/16	48 1/16	48 3/16	- 1 1/4
69	46 1/8	MercStrs	MST	1.20	2.0	17	589	59 3/4	58 1/2	58 9/16	- 3/8
108 3/16	72 1/4	Merck	MRK	1.80f	2.1	24	36365	90 7/16	87 1/2	87 1/2	- 1 3/16
16	1	MercuryFin	MFN		...	2	4730	1 1/4	1 3/16	1 1/4	- 1/16
s 48 1/8	24 5/16	♣ MercuryGen	MCY	.58	1.4	18	135	42 3/8	41 3/4	41 3/4	- 5/8
s 35	22 1/8	Meredith	MDP	.26	.8	19	2286	34 3/8	32 15/16	34	+ 13/16
5 5/8	3 5/8	MeridnGld	MDG		...	...	408	4 5/16	4	4 1/16	- 1/8
26 3/8	17 1/2	MeridnIndTr	MDN	1.16	5.0	17	42	23 1/4	23	23 1/16	- 1/8
18 1/2	9 7/8	MeridianRes	TMR		...	42	846	13 1/4	12 13/16	13	- 3/8
n 27 5/8	20 7/8	Meritor	MRA		...	...	3085	22 3/16	21 1/8	21 5/8	+ 1/8
s 78 3/16	33 7/8	MerLynch	MER	.80	1.2	14	22533	69	66 1/4	66 1/4	- 2 9/16
24 1/16	16 1/4	MerLySP500 98	MIE		...	...	5	22 3/8	22 3/8	22 3/8	- 1/4
71 7/8	59	MerLySTRYPES99	MLB	4.09	5.9	...	78	70 1/4	69 1/2	69 3/4	- 3/4
n 11 3/16	9 3/8	MerLySP500 MITTS 02	MIM		...	...	600	10 9/16	10 3/8	10 7/16	- 3/16
28 1/16	18 3/4	MerLySTRYPES6	MCO	1.37	5.1	...	50	27	26 1/4	26 3/4	- 1/4
14 7/8	10 1/2	MerLySP500 MITTS	MIX		...	...	27	14 1/16	13 3/4	13 7/8	- 3/16
43	34 7/8	MerLySTRYPES B	IML	2.39	6.5	...	51	37 1/4	36 5/8	36 5/8	- 3/8
31 1/4	28 7/8	MerLyn dep pfA		2.25	7.2	...	141	31 3/16	31 1/8	31 1/8	- 1/8
16 1/8	11	MerLy MITTS	MLC		...	...	69	14 3/4	14 1/2	14 5/8	- 1/8
17 15/16	11 3/4	MerLyEur MITTS	MEE		...	...	124	16 1/4	16 1/8	16 1/8	- 1/8
12 9/16	9 3/4	MerLyTch MITTS	TKM		...	...	103	11 3/8	11	11 1/8	- 1/4
n▼ 10 3/4	8 5/8	MerLynNK MITTS	JEM		...	...	447	8 13/16	8 1/2	8 1/2	- 5/16
n 10	8 1/4	MerLySP MITTSTTS	IEM		...	...	120	8 3/4	8 1/2	8 1/2	- 1/4
n 27	24 3/4	MerLyn TOPrS		2.00	7.7	...	116	25 15/16	25 13/16	25 15/16	+ 1/16
n 26 3/8	24 1/8	MerLynPfCap pf		1.94	7.6	...	289	25 5/8	25 7/16	25 5/8	+ 1/8
23	18 1/4	♣ MerryLdInv	MRY	1.56	7.1	18	337	22 1/8	21 13/16	22	...
28 7/8	24 1/2	♣ MerryLdInv pfC		2.15	8.0	...	11	27	26 1/2	27	+ 1/4
47 3/4	43 1/2	MesaRoyTr	MTR	4.69e	10.1	...	9	46 1/4	45 7/8	46 1/4	+ 1/2
4 7/8	3 9/16	MesabiTr	MSB	.37e	9.9	...	118	3 13/16	3 11/16	3 3/4	- 1/8
26 7/16	24 5/8	MetEdCap pfA		2.25	8.7	...	48	25 13/16	25 11/16	25 13/16	+ 1/8
n 16 1/2	10	Mtls USA	MUI		...	...	373	15 1/16	14 1/2	14 15/16	...
s▼ 10 11/16	7 1/2	Metrogas	MGS	.76r	10.5	...	25	7 1/2	7 1/4	7 1/4	- 1/4
24 7/8	15 1/2	Metromail	ML		...	69	262	20	19 7/8	19 7/8	- 1/8
14 15/16	**9 1/4**	**MexEqIncoFd**	**MXE**	**1.11e**	**9.4**	**...**	**489**	**12 1/4**	**11 9/16**	**11 3/4**	**- 7/8**
23 7/16	13 3/4	MexicoFd	MXF	.40e	2.2	...	4403	18 5/8	17 7/8	18 9/16	- 3/8
60 1/16	**24 7/8**	**MicronTch**	**MU**		**...**	**16**	**65173**	**26 15/16**	**25 1/4**	**25 1/4**	**- 2**
30 1/2	24 5/8	MidAmerApt	MAA	2.14	7.7	28	356	28	27 1/2	27 13/16	- 1/16
27 1/2	24 1/4	MidAmerApt pfA		2.37	8.9	...	5	26 11/16	26 11/16	26 11/16	- 1/16
11	9	♣ MidAmRealty	MDI	.88	8.4	23	36	10 1/2	10 7/16	10 1/2	+ 1/16
17 1/16	9 3/4	MidAtlMed	MME		...	dd	466	14 3/4	14 1/4	14 1/2	- 3/8
14 1/4	9 3/4	♣ MidAtlRltyTr	MRR	.96	7.1	22	141	13 9/16	13 5/16	13 7/16	+ 3/16
65 1/4	44 1/8	MidOcean A	MOC	3.00	4.7	10	280	64 1/4	63	63 3/4	...
18 5/8	14 3/4	MidAmEngy	MEC	1.20	6.8	13	605	17 7/8	17 11/16	17 3/4	- 1/8
n 25 7/8	24	MidAmEngy QUIPS A		2.00	7.9	...	43	25 1/4	25 1/8	25 3/16	- 1/16
26 1/8	24	MidlandBk unA		2.22	8.6	...	36	25 7/8	25 7/8	25 7/8	...
27 15/16	25 7/8	MidlandBk unB		2.56	9.3	...	139	27 11/16	27 9/16	27 9/16	...
26 3/4	24 5/8	MidlandBk unC		2.28	8.6	...	317	26 7/16	26 5/16	26 3/8	...
26 3/4	24 5/8	MidlandBk unD		2.39	9.1	...	671	26 1/2	26 1/4	26 3/8	- 1/16
n 26 13/16	15	MidGames	MWY		...	20	568	21 1/2	21 1/16	21 1/8	- 11/16
s 34 11/16	21 3/4	MdwstExp	MEH		...	14	191	31 3/4	31	31 5/16	- 11/16
x 14 7/8	9 7/8	Mikasa	MKS	.15e	1.1	13	132	14	13 7/8	14	+ 1/4
1 1/8	13/32	MilestnProp	MPI		...	dd	16	11/16	5/8	5/8	- 1/16
1 5/16	7/16	MilestnProp pf		j	...	...	7	1 1/4	1 3/16	1 3/16	- 1/16
24 1/8	16 5/8	Millennium	MCH	.60	2.6	...	1677	23 1/2	23 1/8	23 1/2	...
s 22 7/8	8 3/4	MillerInd	MLR		...	26	2105	10 1/4	9 13/16	10 3/16	+ 3/16
52	33 5/8	Millipore	MIL	.40	1.0	dd	2235	40 5/8	38 1/2	40 7/16	+ 1 7/16
28 7/8	20 1/4	♣ MillsCp	MLS	1.89	7.7	...	867	25 1/8	24 7/16	24 1/2	- 5/16
45 5/8	32 1/8	♣ MinrlTech	MTX	.10	.2	19	500	41	39 1/2	40 11/16	+ 1/2
105 1/2	75 1/4	MinnMngMfg	MMM	2.12	2.3	18	10219	93 5/16	92	92 1/8	- 1 5/16
11 1/16	10 1/4	♣ MinnMuni	MNA	.61a	5.6	...	41	10 15/16	10 15/16	10 15/16	...
36 15/16	27	♣ Minn P&L	MPL	2.04	5.7	15	376	36 1/2	35 15/16	36 1/16	- 1/2
30 3/8	19 7/8	MirageResrt	MIR		...	22	3216	25 1/8	24 1/4	24 3/8	- 5/8
27 5/8	25 11/16	MissnCap MIPS A		2.47	9.3	...	56	26 5/8	26 1/2	26 5/8	+ 1/8
26 1/2	24 3/4	MissnCap MIPS B		2.12	8.1	...	62	26 3/16	26 1/8	26 1/8	+ 1/16
27 1/4	16 3/4	MissChem	GRO	.40	2.2	9	387	18 5/8	17 5/8	18 1/2	...
n 25 1/2	23 5/8	MS PwrCap TOPrS		1.94	7.6	...	15	25 3/8	25 1/4	25 3/8	+ 1/8
29 3/4	18 1/4	♣ MitchlEngy A	MNDA	.48	1.9	cc	47	25 1/8	24 3/4	25 1/16	+ 1/4
22 7/16	18 7/8	NtlPrpnPtnr	NPL	2.10	9.6	...	221	22	21 13/16	21 13/16	- 1/8
n 26 1/8	24 1/4	NtlRural QUICS	NRU	2.00	7.8	...	33	25 3/4	25 9/16	25 9/16	...
n 25 1/4	24 3/4	NtlRural QUICS B	NRV		...	...	161	25 1/8	24 15/16	25 1/8	...
42 7/8	18 1/4	NtlSemi	NSM		...	16	20504	35 5/16	34 3/16	34 1/2	- 1 3/16
52 1/4	33 1/2	NtlSvcInd	NSI	1.20	2.7	19	1835	44 15/16	43 1/2	44	+ 5/16
9 5/8	5 7/16	NtlStand	NSD		...	dd	2	6 1/4	6 1/4	6 1/4	- 1/4
21 1/2	7 1/2	NtlSteel B	NS		...	6	1006	17 3/8	16 3/8	17 1/16	+ 1/4
96 3/8	65 3/8	NtlWstmin	NW	3.66e	4.3	...	151	88 1/4	86	86	- 4 1/16
26 5/8	24 1/8	NtlWstmin pfB		2.19	8.5	...	133	25 5/8	25 3/8	25 5/8	- 1/16
27 3/4	25 1/8	NtlWstmin pfA		2.66	10.0	...	35	26 5/8	26 1/2	26 5/8	+ 1/16
26 3/8	23 3/4	NtlWstmin XA		1.97	7.8	...	209	25 5/16	25 3/16	25 3/16	- 3/16
n 26 1/4	24	NtlWstmin C		2.16	8.4	...	714	25 7/8	25 11/16	25 3/4	- 1/8
10 3/8	8 3/4	NationsBal	NBM	.42	4.3	...	14	9 7/8	9 7/8	9 7/8	...
8 7/8	7 3/4	NationsGov03	NGI	.56	6.6	...	346	8 9/16	8 1/2	8 1/2	...
9 1/8	7 7/8	NationsGov04	NGF	.59	6.9	...	344	8 5/8	8 9/16	8 9/16	...
s 71 11/16	45 7/16	NationsBank	NB	1.52f	2.6	13	18071	60 3/4	58 1/2	58 1/2	- 2 5/8
n 32 15/16	23 3/8	NatwdFnl A	NFS	.12e	.4	...	1280	30 7/8	30 1/8	30 5/8	- 1/8
24 3/4	19 1/2	NatwdHlth	NHP	1.56	7.0	15	694	22 1/4	21 15/16	22 1/4	+ 1/16
s 29 5/16	20	NatuzziInd	NTZ	.15r	.7	...	630	22 5/16	22 1/4	22 5/16	- 1/16
29 1/2	9	Navistar	NAV		...	33	4886	23 3/16	22 1/4	23	- 9/16
61 1/4	55	Navistar pfG		6.00	10.0	...	3	60	59 15/16	60	...
36 1/4	19	NeimanMarc	NMG		...	26	352	33 3/4	32 7/8	32 7/8	- 7/8
x 15 1/4	8 7/8	♣ NelsonThos	TNM	.16	1.4	7	630	11 13/16	11 7/16	11 7/16	- 3/8
22 3/8	11 1/4	♣ NetwkEqpt	NWK		...	14	986	16 3/8	16 1/8	16 3/16	- 5/16
22 9/16	19 3/8	NevPwr	NVP	1.60	7.5	14	313	21 9/16	21 3/16	21 1/4	- 5/16
5 1/2	4 5/8	NewAmFd	HYB	.51	9.8	...	1011	5 1/4	5 1/8	5 3/16	- 1/16
43 3/16	36 3/8	NewCentEngy	NCE	2.32	5.6	34	851	41 9/16	41 1/4	41 1/4	- 1/8
33 13/16	17 5/8	NewEngBusn	NEB	.80	2.7	17	427	30	29 11/16	29 3/4	- 1/4
39 13/16	32 1/2	♣ NewEngElec	NES	2.36	6.2	12	685	38 5/8	38 1/16	38 1/4	- 9/16
31	21 7/8	NewEngInv	NEW	2.12a	7.1	15	92	30 3/8	29 13/16	29 15/16	- 3/16
n 31 11/16	19	NewHolland	NH	.55p	...	...	606	28 1/4	27 7/8	28 1/4	- 1/8
n 25 7/8	24 7/8	NJ EconDev	NJP	1.90	7.5	...	888	25 7/16	25 1/4	25 3/8	...
33 15/16	26 3/4	♣ NewJerRes	NJR	1.60	4.9	15	100	32 13/16	32 5/8	32 13/16	...
25 5/8	21 3/8	♣ NewPlnRlty	NPR	1.46f	6.1	18	604	23 15/16	23 5/8	23 13/16	- 1/8
16 5/8	12 1/4	♣ NewSoAfrFd	NSA	.09e	.7	...	118	12 3/4	12 3/4	12 3/4	...
s 35 1/2	16 3/4	♣ NYBcp	NYB	.60	1.8	16	233	34 5/16	33 1/2	33 3/4	- 11/16
28 5/8	20 3/8	NYSE&G	NGE	1.40	5.3	10	1001	26 11/16	26 1/4	26 9/16	- 1/16
25 3/4	22 1/4	NYSE&G pfE		1.85	7.4	...	2	25	25	25	- 1/4
56 1/4	35 1/8	NYTimes A	NYT	.64	1.2	22	1978	53 13/16	52 1/16	52 3/4	+ 1/8
69 3/8	26 1/2	♣ NewbrNtwk	NN		...	49	10860	51 1/2	49 3/4	50 7/16	- 1 1/16
n 40 3/8	18 3/8	NewcrtCrGp	NCT	.07e	.2	...	409	33 13/16	33 1/8	33 3/8	- 1 1/8
43 13/16	28 1/8	Newell	NWL	.64	1.7	21	4054	38 11/16	36	37 15/16	+ 1 3/8
s 33	16 7/8	♣ NewfieldExpl	NFX		...	23	486	26 5/8	26 1/4	26 1/2	- 3/16
24 7/8	15	NewhallLd	NHL	.40a	1.7	17	52	23 7/16	23 1/4	23 7/16	+ 1/16
51 3/8	34 5/8	NewmtGold	NGC	.48	1.3	44	3994	38 7/16	36 1/2	37 1/2	+ 1
53 1/8	32 7/8	♣ NewmtMin	NEM	.48	1.3	cc	20598	37 1/2	34 15/16	36 1/4	+ 1 1/16
s 42 3/4	16 3/16	NewpkRes	NR		...	47	967	41 5/8	40 1/2	41 5/8	- 9/16
n 26 3/8	13	♣ NewportNews	NNS	.16	.7	24	1000	21 7/8	21 5/16	21 13/16	- 1/16
23	17	NewsCp ADR	NWS	.09e	.5	6	3070	18 3/4	18 5/16	18 5/8	+ 3/16
18 3/4	14	NewsCp ADR pf		.23e	1.3	...	15334	17 5/16	17 1/8	17 5/16	...
25 3/4	24 1/8	Newscorp prA		2.16	8.7	...	197	25	24 7/8	24 15/16	+ 1/16
24	21 1/2	Newscorp prB		1.84e	8.0	...	10	22 7/8	22 13/16	22 7/8	+ 1/16
n 21 1/2	**12 5/8**	**NextLevel**	**NLV**		**...**	**...**	**9265**	**13 5/8**	**12 15/16**	**13**	**- 7/8**
11 1/8	7 7/8	NiaMoPwr	NMK		...	8	1851	9 9/16	9 1/4	9 3/8	- 1/16
53	33	NiaMoPwr pfA		3.40	7.1	...	z170	49	48	48	+ 3/4
53 1/4	35 1/2	NiaMoPwr pfB		3.60	7.1	...	5	51	51	51	- 1/2
58 1/16	38	NiaMoPwr pfC		3.90	7.0	...	1	56 1/8	56	56	- 1/8
73	47 3/4	NiaMoPwr pfE		4.85	7.3	...	z490	66 3/8	66 3/8	66 3/8	- 5/8
98 3/4	76	NiaMoPwr pfI		7.72	8.1	...	z10	95 1/4	95 1/4	95 1/4	...
26 3/4	23	NiaMoPwr pfM		2.38	9.1	...	89	26 1/8	26 1/16	26 1/8	- 1/8
39 9/16	30	NICOR	GAS	1.40	3.7	15	903	38 7/8	37 7/16	37 7/16	- 1 1/8
76 3/8	45	Nike B	NKE	.40	.8	17	13783	48 1/2	46 3/4	47 5/16	- 1/2
52 3/4	31	NineWest	NIN		...	...	1609	34 11/16	34 5/16	34 3/8	- 3/16
38 7/16	13 7/8	99cOnlyStr	NDN		...	33	851	37 7/8	36 1/2	37 7/8	+ 1 1/8
52 1/2	33 3/4	NipponTel	NTT	.21e	.5	...	728	41 1/8	40 3/8	40 3/4	- 1 1/2
25 3/8	23 1/2	Nipsco QDCS A	NIC	1.94	7.8	...	25	24 15/16	24 13/16	24 7/8	...
50	32 1/4	NobleAffil	NBL	.16	.4	23	1213	41 1/2	40 7/16	40 3/4	- 1/4
37 15/16	15 1/2	♣ NoblDrll	NE		...	19	13894	35 7/8	33 1/4	34 3/4	+ 1/2
102 7/16	45 1/8	Nokia		.70e	.8	...	27113	89 1/4	83	84 3/16	- 2 7/16
5 3/8	1 13/16	NordRes	NRD		...	dd	138	2	1 7/8	1 15/16	+ 1/16
s 38 1/8	28 3/16	♣ NorflkSo	NSC	.80	2.5	17	5837	32 9/16	31 1/2	31 9/16	- 3/8
45	39 7/8	NSoRlwy pf		2.60	5.8	...	8	44 3/4	44 1/2	44 3/4	+ 1/4
36 7/16	22	♣ Norrell	NRL	.16	.6	25	842	28 3/4	28	28 3/4	- 1/16
61 1/4	45 5/8	Norsk	NHY	.98e	1.7	...	583	56 1/2	56 1/8	56 1/8	- 1 1/16
27 1/2	14	♣ Nortek	NTK		...	10	261	23 13/16	22 7/8	22 15/16	- 1
60 1/16	**37 1/2**	**NortlInvers**	**NRT**	**4.20e**	**9.1**	**...**	**139**	**49**	**46**	**46 1/4**	**- 3 3/4**
n 29	24 5/8	NrtlInvr ADR	NTL		...	...	14	25 3/4	25	25	- 5/8
35	28	♣ NC Gas	NCG	1.40	4.3	12	20	32 3/4	32 9/16	32 3/4	+ 3/16
17 1/2	12 1/2	NoEuroOil	NET	1.90e	11.0	12	76	17 5/16	17	17 1/4	+ 1/4
s 31 1/2	15 3/8	NorthForkBcp	NFB	.60	2.1	21	1683	29 1/16	28 5/8	29	- 5/8
14 1/4	7 5/8	NE Util	NU		...	dd	2133	11 9/16	11 1/4	11 1/4	- 1/4
35	25 1/2	NorthnBrdr	NBP	2.20	6.7	17	241	32 3/4	32 3/8	32 3/4	- 3/16
52 15/16	44 1/2	♣ NoStPwr	NSP	2.82	5.7	14	1296	50 7/16	49 3/4	49 3/4	- 7/16
56 3/4	48 1/4	♣ NoStPwr pfA		3.60	6.8	...	4	54 3/8	53	53	- 1/2
▲ 65 1/2	59 1/2	NoStPwr pfC		4.10	6.2	...	1	66	66	66	+ 1
113 7/8	57 3/4	NoTelecm	NT	.60	.7	31	7207	90 3/8	87 9/16	87 15/16	- 1 15/16
15/16	5/8	NogateExp g	NGX		...	...	105	3/4	3/4	3/4	- 1/16
127 7/8	71 3/8	♣ NorthrpGrum	NOC	1.60	1.5	23	1765	108 13/16	107 1/16	108 1/8	- 5/16

Table 14-3

EXPLANATORY NOTES

The following explanations apply to New York and American exchange listed issues and the Nasdaq Stock Market. NYSE and Amex prices are composite quotations that include trades on the Chicago, Pacific, Philadelphia, Boston and Cincinnati exchanges and reported by the National Association of Securities Dealers.

Boldfaced quotations highlight those issues whose price changed by 5% or more if their previous closing price was $2 or higher.

Underlined quotations are those stocks with large changes in volume, per exchange, compared with the issue's average trading volume. The calculation includes common stocks of $5 a share or more with an average volume over 65 trading days of at least 5,000 shares. The underlined quotations are for the 40 largest volume percentage leaders on the NYSE and the Nasdaq National Market. It includes the 20 largest volume percentage gainers on the Amex.

The 52-week high and low columns show the highest and lowest price of the issue during the preceding 52 weeks plus the current week, but not the latest trading day. These ranges are adjusted to reflect stock payouts of 1% or more, and cash dividends or other distributions of 10% or more.

Dividend/Distribution rates, unless noted, are annual disbursements based on the last monthly, quarterly, semiannual, or annual declaration. Special or extra dividends or distributions, including return of capital, special situations or payments not designated as regular are identified by footnotes.

Yield is defined as the dividends or other distributions paid by a company on its securities, expressed as a percentage of price.

The P/E ratio is determined by dividing the closing market price by the company's primary per-share earnings for the most recent four quarters. Charges and other adjustments usually are excluded when they qualify as extraordinary items under generally accepted accounting rules.

Sales figures are the unofficial daily total of shares traded, quoted in hundreds (two zeros omitted; f-four zeros omitted.)

Exchange ticker symbols are shown for all New York and American exchange common stocks, and Dow Jones News/Retrieval symbols are listed for Class A and Class B shares listed on both markets. Nasdaq symbols are listed for all Nasdaq NMS issues. A more detailed explanation of Nasdaq ticker symbols appears with the NMS listings.

FOOTNOTES: ▲-New 52-week high. ▼-New 52-week low. a-Extra dividend or extras in addition to the regular dividend. b-Indicates annual rate of the cash dividend and that a stock dividend was paid. c-Liquidating dividend. cc-P/E ratio is 100 or more. dd-Loss in the most recent four quarters. e-Indicates a dividend was declared in the preceding 12 months, but that there isn't a regular dividend rate. Amount shown may have been adjusted to reflect stock split, spinoff or other distribution. ec-Emerging Company Marketplace issue. FD-First day of trading. f-Annual rate, increased on latest declaration. g-Indicates the dividend and earnings are expressed in Canadian money. The stock trades in U.S. dollars. No yield or P/E ratio is shown. gg-Special sales condition; no regular way trading. h-Temporary exemption from Nasdaq requirements. i-Indicates amount declared or paid after a stock dividend or split. j-Indicates dividend was paid this year, and that at the last dividend meeting a dividend was omitted or deferred. k-Indicates dividend declared this year on cumulative issues with dividends in arrears. m-Annual rate, reduced on latest declaration. n-Newly issued in the past 52 weeks. The high-low range begins with the start of trading and doesn't cover the entire period. p-Initial dividend; no yield calculated. pf-Preferred. pp-Holder owes installment(s) of purchase price. pr-Preference. r-Indicates a cash dividend declared in the preceding 12 months, plus a stock dividend. rt-Rights. s-Stock split or stock dividend, or cash or cash equivalent distribution, amounting to 10% or more in the past 52 weeks. The high-low price is adjusted from the old stock. Dividend calculations begin with the date the split was paid or the stock dividend occurred. stk-Paid in stock in the last 12 months. Company doesn't pay cash dividend. un-Units. v-Trading halted on primary market. vi-In bankruptcy or receivership or being reorganized under the Bankruptcy Code, or securities assumed by such companies. wd-When distributed. wi-When issued. wt-Warrants. ww-With warrants. x-Ex-dividend, ex-distribution, ex-rights or without warrants. z-Sales in full, not in 100s.

Table 14-4
American Stock Exchange Composite Transactions

AMERICAN STOCK EXCHANGE

Quotations as of 5 p.m. Eastern Time
Thursday, October 30, 1997

	52 Weeks Hi	Lo	Stock	Sym	Div	Yld %	PE	Vol 100s	Hi	Lo	Close	Net Chg
			-A-B-C-									
	23 3/4	13 5/8	AMC Entn	AEN		...	dd	192	20 1/4	19 5/8	19 7/8	...
	41	26	AMC Entn pf		1.75	5.1	...	51	34 3/8	33 1/2	34 3/8	+ 1/8
n	**6 1/4**	**1 13/16**	♣ **AMTEC**	**ATC**		**...**	**...**	**448**	**1 15/16**	**1 7/8**	**1 7/8**	**- 1/8**
	7 3/8	2 3/4	ARC Int	ATV		...	6	774	5 3/4	5 1/2	5 9/16	- 3/16
n	23 13/16	18 1/4	ARM FnlGp	ARM		...	...	109	21 1/8	20 3/4	21 1/8	+ 1/8
	27	25 1/2	ARM FnlGp pf		2.38	9.0	...	8	26 3/8	26 3/8	26 3/8	- 1/8
	24 3/4	18 5/8	ASR Inv	ASR	2.00	8.8	6	72	23	22 5/16	22 3/4	- 1/8
	10 5/8	8 1/8	♣ AT Plastics g	ATJ	.18	...	...	158	9 3/4	9 1/8	9 3/4	+ 3/16
	24 3/4	13 3/4	Acadiana	ANA	.36	1.6	...	8	22 7/8	22 7/8	22 7/8	+ 1/8
	18 1/2	10	AckrlyGrp	AK	.02	.1	23	826	14 3/8	14	14 3/8	+ 3/8
	19 1/2	8 7/8	♣ AdvMagnet	AVM		...	cc	74	9 3/8	9 1/4	9 5/16	- 3/16
	3 11/16	1 1/8	♣ AdvPhotonix	API		...	dd	62	1 11/16	1 9/16	1 9/16	- 1/8
n	12	10	AegisRlty	AER		...	...	533	11 1/16	10 3/4	10 15/16	+ 1/16
	13 5/8	**2 13/16**	**Aerosonic**	**AIM**		**...**	**27**	**57**	**9 7/8**	**9 1/4**	**9 7/8**	**+ 1/2**
	7 1/2	1 1/4	♣ AirWaterTech	AWT		...	dd	1002	1 9/16	1 3/8	1 3/8	- 1/8
s	10 5/8	5 11/16	Alarmgrd	AGD		...	65	62	8 1/2	8 3/16	8 1/2	+ 3/16
	18 1/4	13	♣ AHaagen	ACH	1.44	8.7	97	199	16 13/16	16 3/8	16 1/2	- 3/16
	3 3/8	**1 1/2**	**AlldDgtl**	**ADK**		**...**	**...**	**357**	**2 7/8**	**2 3/16**	**2 3/4**	**+ 11/16**
	15 7/8	5	AlliedRsrch	ALR		...	7	201	14 1/4	13 7/8	13 15/16	- 3/16
	8 1/4	5 5/8	♣ AllouHlth	ALU		...	11	5	8	8	8	- 1/8
	19 7/8	5 1/2	Alphalnd	AHA		...	dd	655	16	15 1/4	15 1/4	- 9/16
	26 7/8	10 5/8	AltLvgSvc	ALI		...	dd	61	25	24 1/2	24 1/2	- 7/8
n	9	3 5/8	Amerac	AMC		...	...	74	5	4 7/8	5	- 1/8
	14 3/4	10 1/2	AmFPrepFd2	PF	1.33e	9.9	...	1	13 3/8	13 3/8	13 3/8	...
	45	27 1/4	AmBkCT	BKC	1.44	3.2	14	36	44 5/8	44 3/8	44 7/16	- 3/16
▲	**26**	**17 7/8**	**AmBiltrite**	**ABL**	**.40**	**1.6**	**16**	**401**	**26 7/8**	**22 3/8**	**25 3/4**	**+ 3 3/8**
	3 5/8	3 1/16	AmInsMtg	AIA	.28	8.8	11	44	3 1/4	3 3/16	3 3/16	- 1/16
	15 1/4	13 13/16	AmInsMtgII	AII	2.53e	17.9	12	60	14 5/16	14 1/8	14 1/8	- 1/8
	14	10 7/8	AmMtg86	AIJ	4.50e	41.1	9	130	11 1/16	10 15/16	10 15/16	- 1/8
	15 1/8	13 1/8	AmMtg88	AIK	1.08m	8.1	12	17	13 3/8	13 5/16	13 3/8	+ 1/16
	51	33 1/4	AmIsraelPapr	AIP		...	...	8	44 1/4	43 3/4	43 3/4	- 1
	6 1/8	1 5/16	♣ AmPaging	APP		...	dd	107	2 3/8	2 3/16	2 5/16	...
	16 3/4	7 3/4	AmRlestInv	REA	.88f	5.9	12	51	14 7/8	14 5/8	14 7/8	+ 1/8
	6 3/16	2 3/4	AmRestrtPtrs	RMC	.20	5.3	dd	2	3 3/4	3 3/4	3 3/4	- 1/8
	14 7/8	9 1/8	♣ AmSciEngrg	ASE		...	22	42	10 7/8	10 3/4	10 3/4	- 1/4
	2 1/4	5/8	AmShrdHosp	AMS		...	14	314	1 3/4	1 11/16	1 11/16	- 3/16
	22 1/4	5 5/8	AmTchCeram	AMK		...	19	63	17 1/8	16 1/2	16 15/16	- 1/2
	106 1/4	75 3/4	AT&T Fund	ATF	2.80	2.7	...	13	102 1/2	101 1/8	102 1/2	+ 1/8
	6 5/16	4 9/16	♣ AmpalAm A	AISA		...	dd	59	5 3/8	5 1/8	5 1/4	- 1/8
	11 3/8	**2 5/8**	**AmpexCp A**	**AXC**		**...**	**12**	**1213**	**3 7/16**	**3 1/8**	**3 1/4**	**- 1/4**
	16 7/8	11 1/4	Amwest	AMW	.44	3.1	29	3	14 1/4	14 1/4	14 1/4	- 1/16
s	**34 1/4**	**4 15/16**	♣ **AndreaElec**	**AND**		**...**	**43**	**1769**	**21 9/16**	**20 1/4**	**20 5/16**	**- 1 5/16**
	18 1/8	8 5/8	AngelesMtg	ANM	1.20f	7.1	5	8	17 1/8	17	17	...
	4 3/4	1 1/4	AngelesPtMtg	APT		...	dd	367	4 3/4	4 1/8	4 3/16	+ 1/16
	6 3/4	**2 3/8**	**Apogee**	**APG**		**...**	**dd**	**9**	**2 3/8**	**2 3/8**	**2 3/8**	**- 1/8**
n	16 1/4	7 1/4	AppleOrth	AOI		...	...	28	14 1/4	13 7/8	13 7/8	- 3/8
	36 3/4	17 1/4	ArgentBk	AGB	.56	1.6	26	5	34 1/2	34 1/2	34 1/2	...
s	5 7/8	4 1/4	ArizLand	AZL	.25e	4.6	13	11	5 7/16	5 7/16	5 7/16	+ 1/8
	13 1/2	6 1/2	ArmorHldg	ABE		...	...	125	11 7/16	11	11	- 1/2
	3 9/16	1 3/4	♣ ArrhythResrch	HRT		...	14	25	2 1/2	2 7/16	2 7/16	- 1/16
s▲	20 11/16	7 1/8	AssistLivng	ALF		...	cc	1052	20 3/4	19 1/2	19 7/8	- 1/16
	9 1/16	4 1/2	CruiseAm	RVR		...	18	17	8 5/8	8 1/2	8 5/8	- 1/8
n	6 3/16	2 1/4	CrystlIxInt	KRY		...	...	1605	4 5/8	4 3/8	4 113/256	- 1/16
	40	19 3/8	CubicCp	CUB	.38	1.2	23	35	31 1/2	30 5/8	31 3/8	+ 3/8
	12 1/2	8 1/4	CybexIntl	CYB		...	dd	20	11 5/8	11 1/2	11 1/2	- 1/8
	4 1/16	1 3/4	CycommInt	CYI		...	...	1598	2 9/16	2 1/16	2 3/16	+ 1/16
			-D-E-F-									
	15 1/8	9 9/16	DRS Tch	DRS		...	13	94	12 15/16	12 3/8	12 7/8	+ 3/16
	6 3/8	**3 3/4**	**DairyMrtA**	**DMCA**		**...**	**dd**	**50**	**4 5/8**	**4 1/2**	**4 1/2**	**- 3/8**
	6 3/8	3 7/8	DairyMrtB	DMCB		...	dd	2	4 3/4	4 3/4	4 3/4	- 1/8
	2 3/16	3/16	♣ DakotaMin	DKT		...	dd	900	3/8	5/16	3/8	...
	14	4 5/8	DanielsnHldg	DHC		...	dd	12	7 7/8	7 3/4	7 7/8	- 1/8
	35 1/2	20 3/4	♣ DarlingInt	DAR		...	41	20	32 1/2	32	32 1/4	- 1/8
	2 7/16	7/8	Datametrics	DC		...	dd	1214	2 1/16	1 13/16	2	+ 1/8
	12 1/2	7 3/8	DataramCp	DTM		...	8	10	8 3/4	8 5/8	8 3/4	...
	19 3/8	8 3/8	DavCoRestr	DVC		...	33	11	18 15/16	18 13/16	18 15/16	- 1/16
	15 1/2	7 1/2	♣ DaxorCp	DXR	.50p	...	cc	46	11 3/4	11 1/4	11 3/4	+ 1/4
	6 11/16	2 1/4	DaytonMng	DAY		...	...	368	2 11/16	2 9/16	2 5/8	...
s	11	8 1/16	♣ DecoratorInd	DII	.28	2.9	9	1	9 3/4	9 3/4	9 3/4	- 1/8
s	41	20 3/8	DelLabs	DLI	.14	.4	19	7	36 1/4	36	36 1/4	...
	5 1/8	**1 5/8**	**DenAmer**	**DEN**		**...**	**14**	**444**	**3 3/16**	**2 15/16**	**3 1/16**	**+ 3/16**
	49 1/8	27 3/8	♣ DevonEngy	DVN	.20	.5	39	231	44 3/8	43 3/8	43 9/16	- 9/16
	6 3/8	4 1/2	♣ DeWolfe	DWL		...	12	2	5	5	5	- 1/8
	1 1/2	3/8	♣ DgtlComm	DCT		...	dd	109	1/2	7/16	1/2	...
n	11 3/8	4 1/8	♣ DigitalPwr	DPW		...	...	16	8	8	8	...
	16 3/4	5 3/4	♣ Diodes	DIO		...	16	71	13 3/8	13 1/4	13 1/4	- 3/8
n	10 5/8	8 1/2	DiversfCpRes	HIR		...	...	11	8 7/8	8 3/4	8 7/8	- 1/8
	16 15/16	6 1/4	DixonTi	DXT		...	16	51	15 1/8	14 13/16	15	- 3/16
	44 7/8	35	DoleFd ACES	DLA	2.75	6.6	...	32	41 1/2	41	41 3/8	- 1/8
s	**14 3/8**	**10 5/8**	♣ **DrewInd**	**DW**		**...**	**9**	**190**	**11 7/8**	**11 1/8**	**11 1/4**	**- 5/8**
	10 15/16	9 7/16	♣ DreyfMunIn	DMF	.65	6.3	...	153	10 3/8	10 1/4	10 5/16	- 1/16
	10 7/16	8 1/4	♣ DreyfCalMn	DCM	.60	6.0	...	16	10 1/8	10	10	...
	13 3/4	7 1/8	DriverHar	DRH		...	18	2	12 1/8	12 1/8	12 1/8	- 1/4
·	9 5/8	4 5/8	EtzLavud	ETZ		...	...	37	7 7/8	7 5/8	7 5/8	+ 1/8
	8 11/16	**3 7/8**	**EtzLavud A**			**...**	**...**	**20**	**7 1/4**	**7 1/4**	**7 1/4**	**+ 3/8**
	8 7/8	1 3/4	EXX Inc A	EXXA		...	dd	17	4 1/2	4 1/4	4 1/2	...
	8 3/8	1 7/8	EXX Inc B	EXXB		...	...	3	4 1/2	4 1/2	4 1/2	+ 1/8
	12 3/8	5 7/8	♣ EZEM Inc B	EZMB	stk	...	dd	46	6 15/16	6 1/2	6 3/4	+ 1/4
	19 1/2	12 1/4	EasternCo	EML	.52f	3.0	17	14	17 1/2	17 1/4	17 1/2	+ 1/8
	8 3/8	4	EchoBayMn	ECO	.08j	...	dd	6886	4 3/8	4 1/8	4 5/16	+ 3/16
	11 1/8	7 7/16	♣ EcolgyEnvr	EEI	.32	3.0	cc	31	11	10 3/4	10 3/4	- 3/8
n	19 3/8	16 1/8	Edprbrscn A	EBC	.98e	5.8	...	43	17 1/4	17	17	- 5/8
	7 15/16	5 1/16	♣ ElPasoElec	EE		...	9	2162	6 3/16	6 1/16	6 1/8	- 1/8
x	12	9 1/4	♣ ElsworthFd	ECF	1.88e	18.2	...	107	10 7/16	10 1/4	10 5/16	- 1/16
	16 3/4	10 1/4	♣ EmeritusCp	ESC		...	dd	98	15 3/8	15 3/16	15 3/16	- 1/16
	1 7/8	3/8	EmersnRadio	MSN		...	dd	1038	1/2	3/8	7/16	...
	6 13/16	5/8	EmpireCar	EMP		...	dd	32	2 1/8	2 1/16	2 1/8	+ 1/16
	20 1/2	8 1/2	♣ EngyResrch	ERC		...	cc	51	15 7/8	15 1/2	15 5/8	...
	12 1/4	9 7/16	Engex	EGX		...	...	21	9 7/8	9 7/8	9 7/8	- 1/8
	11 3/4	6	EnvrTectncs	ETC		...	82	7	9	9	9	+ 1/8
	5 7/16	1 7/16	Envirotest A	ENR		...	dd	110	5	4 3/4	4 15/16	- 1/16
	21 1/4	12 1/4	EnzoBiochm	ENZ		...	dd	1270	16 3/4	15 13/16	16 1/4	- 1/2
	27 5/16	**15 1/4**	♣ **Equus II**	**EQS**	**.76e**	**3.5**	**...**	**306**	**21 7/8**	**21 1/8**	**21 9/16**	**- 1 5/16**
	10 1/4	1	EssexBcp	ESX		...	dd	225	5 7/8	5 3/16	5 1/2	- 1/16

Table 14-4 (*cont.*)

COMPOSITE TRANSACTIONS

52 Weeks Hi	Lo	Stock	Sym	Div	Yld %	PE	Vol 100s	Hi	Lo	Close	Net Chg
		-J-K-L-									
n 24³⁄₁₆	22¾	JP Mrg COMPS	JPO				4	23⅝	23¾	23⅜	+ ⁷⁄₁₆
4⅞	⅜	JTS Cp	JTS				1136	⅝	⁹⁄₁₆	⅝	
5½	3¹¹⁄₁₆	Jaclyn	JLN			16	2	4⅜	4⅜	4⅜	+ ⅛
3¼	1¹⁵⁄₁₆	JanBellMkt	JBM			18	179	2¹⁵⁄₁₆	2¹¹⁄₁₆	2⅞	+ ⅛
1⅝	½	Jetronic	JET			7	335	1⅜	1¹⁄₁₆	1³⁄₁₆	− ¹⁄₁₆
6¼	3⅛ ♣	Joule	JOL			22	15	5½	5¼	5½	+ ¼
8⅛	3¾ ♣ KBK Cap	KBK			16	5	8⅛	8⅛	8⅛	
6¾	2⅝	KFX Inc	KFX				61	2¹⁵⁄₁₆	2¾	2⅞	− ¹⁄₁₆
23¹⁵⁄₁₆	10¾ ♣ KV Pharm A	KVA			27	137	20⁵⁄₁₆	19⅞	19⅞	− ⅞
23½	10¾ ♣ **KV Pharm B**	**KVB**			28	49	20½	19¾	19¾	− 1¼
n 6⅜	3⅜	KafusEnvr	KS				369	4⅞	4⁹⁄₁₆	4¾	− ¼
34⅝	22⅜	KankakeeBcp	KNK	.48	1.5	15	15	31½	31⅜	31⅜	− ½
s 39	11⁷⁄₁₆	Keanelnc	KEA			49	2083	29¾	28½	29½	− ⁹⁄₁₆
s 14⅜	10⅝	KY FstBcp	KYF	.50	3.6		2	13¾	13¾	13¾	+ ¼
38⅜	10⅛ ♣ KeyEngy	KEG			35	1658	31¾	30⅝	31⅛	− ¾
10⅞	4½ ♣ KillernProp	KPI			6	8	9¹⁄₁₆	9	9	
3¹⁵⁄₁₆	2¹¹⁄₁₆ ♣ **KinarkCp**	**KIN**			19	97	3⁷⁄₁₆	3⅛	3⁷⁄₁₆	+ ³⁄₁₆
n 17	6	KingPwrGp	KPG				116	7½	6	6⅝	− ¾
23⅜	15⅛ ♣ KogerEqty	KE	.60f	2.8	23	59	21½	21¼	21⁵⁄₁₆	− ⁵⁄₁₆
6⅞	4⅛	KrugInt	KRG	stk		10	111	5¾	5⅝	5⅝	− ¼
2¹³⁄₁₆	1⅝ ♣ LXR Biotec	LXR				800	2	1⅞	2	+ ¹⁄₁₆
8¼	3⅞ ♣ LaBarge	LB			11	684	5⅛	4⅞	5	
s 17⅝	9⅝ ♣ LancerCp	LAN			19	251	12⅜	11¾	11⅞	− ⅜
26⁹⁄₁₆	19¼ ♣ Landauer	LDR	1.20	4.7	19	11	25⅜	25¼	25⅜	+ ¹⁄₁₆
5⅜	3³⁄₁₆ ♣ **LaserTch**	**LSR**			29	98	3⅝	3½	3½	− ¼
20⅜	13¼ ♣ LazareKap	LKI			13	102	15⅜	15⅜	15⅜	
14¾	2	**LehmnHldgHK wt98**					108	3¼	2¾	3	− ⁷⁄₁₆
21½	4¼	LehmnHldgSel cwt98					5	16½	16½	16½	− 2½
17½	11 ♣ LilVernon	LVC	.28	1.8	18	102	16⅛	15⅞	16	
4	2⅛ ♣ ecLuxtec	LXU			dd	4	2⅛	2⅛	2⅛	− ⅛
		-M-N-O-									
♥ 4⅞	3	MC Shipping	MCX	.16	5.3	11	107	3	2⅞	3	
12⅛	6	MDC Comm	MDQ				5	6¼	6¼	6¼	− ¼
31	15⅞ ♣ MSB Bcp	MBB	.60	2.2	47	53	28	27¾	27¾	+ ⅛
1⁷⁄₁₆	⅝	MSR Expl	MSR			dd	718	1³⁄₁₆	1¼	1¼	+ ¹⁄₁₆
n 3⅛	1¾	MagicwrksEntn	MJK				21	2⅛	2¼	2¹⁄₁₆	+ ¹⁄₁₆
8⁷⁄₁₆	4	MagHunt	MHR			dd	1305	7¾	6¾	6⅞	
2¹³⁄₁₆	½	MagHunt wt					36	1⁵⁄₁₆	1¼	1⁵⁄₁₆	− ¹⁄₁₆
8	2¹⁵⁄₁₆	MAI Sys	NOW				15	3¾	3¾	3¾	
19½	10¼ ♣ MainePS	MAP	1.00	7.9	dd	10	12¹¹⁄₁₆	12⅝	12⅝	
6	1¹⁵⁄₁₆	MalibuEntn	MBE				47	3⅜	3½	3⅝	− ¹⁄₁₆
n 57¼	45¾	MndCommEx TIMES	TIM				25	50⅞	50½	50⅞	− ⅛
7¾	3¼	MarltonTech	MTY			19	71	6¼	6	6¼	− ³⁄₁₆
n 7¾	4	MarqueeGp	MRT				1059	5¼	4¹⁵⁄₁₆	5¼	
14	12	MA HlthEdu	MHE	.74	5.6		7	13¼	13¼	13¼	− ⅛
5⅜	2½	MatecCp	MXC			dd	3	4⅛	4⅛	4⅛	+ ⅛
19¼	6¾	MaximPharm	MMP				312	14½	13⅝	14½	+ ⅜
9½	1¼	MaximPharm wt					33	6¼	5⅞	6¼	+ ¼
n♥ 2⅛	2¹⁄₁₆	MaxxPete	MMX				70	2	2	2	− ¹⁄₁₆ ·
62⅜	40¾	Maxxam	MXM			11	174	53¹⁄₁₆	52¹¹⁄₁₆	53	− ³⁄₁₆
10¼	7⅜	McRaelnd A	MRIA	.36	3.6	9	25	10	9⅞	10	+ ¼
10¼	7½	McRaelnd B	MRIB			9	3	9¾	9¾	9¾	− ³⁄₁₆
4¾	2½ ♣ MsrmtSpec	MSS			11	120	3⅞	3⅞	3⅞	

52 Weeks Hi	Lo	Stock	Sym	Div	Yld %	PE	Vol 100s	Hi	Lo	Close	Net Chg
6⅛	3¾	RichtonInt	RHT			10	12	6¹⁄₁₆	6	6¹⁄₁₆	− ¹⁄₁₆
12⅞	9⅛	RigelEngy g	RJL				5	10³⁄₁₆	10³⁄₁₆	10³⁄₁₆	− ³⁄₁₆
15½	12⅛ ♣ RivieraHldg	RIV			11	7	14¾	14⅝	14⅝	
n 7⅝	4¾ ♣ **RivieraTool**	**RTC**				179	8	7¼	8	+ ¾
16¾	9	RobtPharm	RPC			dd	432	10⅜	10	10¹⁄₁₆	− ¼
46½	25¾	RogersCp	ROG			20	138	42	41⅛	41½	− ⅞
1¹⁵⁄₁₆	1¼	Rotonics	RMI	.04e	2.7	21	520	1½	1⅜	1½	+ ⅛
4	1⅝ ♣ **RoyalOak**	**RYO**				6241	2⅜	2⅜	2⅜	+ ⅛
n 26¼	24¾	RyceMcrCap pf		.48p			59	25¼ 24¾ 2⁵⁄₁₆		25	− ¼
		-S-T-U-									
▲ 58	39⅝	SJW Cp	SJW	2.28	3.9	12	6	58½	58	58½	+ ½
s 27⅛	9⅝ ♣ **SabaPete**	**SAB**			24	891	11⅛	10⅝	10⅝	− 1¹⁄₁₆
s 25	14⅞ ♣ SagaComm A	SGA			47	3	20¾	20¾	20¾	
13⅛	3½	Salomon DY wt					2	8⅞	8⅞	8⅞	− ⅜
15¾	13⅜	SanDgoGE pfA		1.00	6.6		2	15⅛	15⅛	15⅛	− ¼
14⅜	12½	SanDgoGE pfC		.88	6.1		17	14⅜	14⅜	14⅜	
1¾	¹¹⁄₁₆	SntaFeGamg	SGM			dd	16	¹¹⁄₁₆	¹¹⁄₁₆	¹¹⁄₁₆	
28	14⅛	SantaMonBk	SMO	.48t	1.8	18	76	27¹⁄₂	27¼	27¼	
4	2¹⁄₁₆	ScandnvaCo	SCF				30	3¼	3⅛	3¼	+ ⅛
s 20³⁄₁₆	15½	SchultHome	SHC	.20	1.1	10	31	17¾	17⅝	17⅝	− ⅛
67	41	Scopelnd	SCP	.70a	1.1	4	6	66	66	66	+1
s 13¼	8⅝	ScotlandBcp	SSB	.30a	2.8	18	29	10¾	10⅝	10⅝	− ⅛
n 11⅜	9	Securacom	SFT				158	9¼	9¼	9¼	− ¼
s 13½	9	SelasCp	SLS	.18	1.8	11	68	10⅝	10¹⁄₁₆	10¼	− ⅛
15⅞	6⅞	Selfcare	SLF			dd	128	12⅜	12	12¾	+ ⅝
n 4¼	2⅛	SentryTch	SKV				68	2½	2⅜	2⅜	− ¹⁄₁₆
n 4¼	2¼	SentryTch pfA					9	2⅜	2⅜	2⅜	
9½	3¼ ♣ Servotrnics	SVT			cc	15	8	8	8	
4	2	**SheffPharm**	**SHM**				90	2¼	2¹⁄₁₆	2¹⁄₁₆	− ¼
17⁵⁄₁₆	9⅞	SheltrCmpnt	SST	.06	.4	13	273	17⅛ 16¹⁵⁄₁₆		17⅛	+ ⅛
24	9⅛	**Sifcolnd**	**SIF**	.15e	.7	15	287	21¾	19½	21½	+ 2¼
8⁷⁄₁₆	5⅜	SignalTch	STZ			27	49	5⅞	5⅝	5⅝	
3⅛	½	SilvrdoFod	SLV			dd	306	¹¹⁄₁₆	⅝	¹¹⁄₁₆	
9⅛	5	SkylnChili	SKC	.02p		19	1	6⅜	6⅜	6⅜	
3⅛	1⅞	SloanSupmkt	SLO			4	122	2⅛	2	2⅛	+ ⁷⁄₁₆
10⅞	9⁹⁄₁₆	SmthBrnyInt	SBI	.58	5.6		18	10½	10⁷⁄₁₆	10⁷⁄₁₆	+ ⅛
15	13¾	SmithBarney	SBT	.85	6.0		80	14⅜	14¹⁄₁₆	14¼	− ¼
8½	3¼	SoftnetSys	SOF			46	54	7¹⁵⁄₁₆	7¾	7⅞	+ ⅛
¹⁵⁄₁₆	⁵⁄₁₆	ecSoligenTch	SGT			dd	270	⁹⁄₁₆	½	⁹⁄₁₆	+ ¹⁄₁₆
17³⁄₁₆	14⅛	SoCalEd pfB		1.02	6.0		7	17⅛ 16¹⁵⁄₁₆		17⅛	+ ⅛
18⅜	14¾	SoCalEd pfC		1.06	5.8		4	18⅜	18⅜	18⅜	+ ⅛
19⅛	16	SoCalEd pfE		1.20	7.0		3	17¼	17¼	17¼	+ ¼
24⅝	21⅛	SoCalEd pfG		1.45	5.9		44	24⅝	24¼	24⅝	+ ⅜
26¼	24¾	SoCalEd QUIDS		2.09	8.2		24	25⅜	25⅜	25⅜	− ⅛
20½	12¼	SouthfstBcsh	SZB			dd	5	19½	19¾	19½	+ ¼
19⅞	15⅞	SW GaFnl	SGB	.40	2.1		1	19¼	19¼	19¼	+ ¼
6⅛	1⅞ ♣ SpatialTch	STY			dd	140	1¹⁵⁄₁₆	1⅞	1⅞	− ¹⁄₁₆
2½	1⅛	SpecChem	CHM			dd	20	1¼	1¼	1¼	
⁵⁄₁₆	¹⁄₃₂	SportSupply wt					13	¹⁄₃₂	¹⁄₃₂	¹⁄₃₂	
9½	2½	SportsClub	SCY			99	265	9	8½	8⅞	− ⅜
66¹⁷⁄₃₂ 47⁴¹⁄₆₄		S&P Midcap	MDY	1.52e	2.5		2297	61⁶³⁄₆₄	60½	60½	− 1⁵⁄₆₄
98½ 69¹¹⁄₁₆		SPDR	SPY	1.40e	1.6		97729	92⁹⁄₁₆	89¾	89¹⁵⁄₁₆	− 2⅞
12	8¾	Starett	SHO	.25	2.1	27	69	11¹¹⁄₁₆	11½	11¹¹⁄₁₆	− ¹⁄₁₆
14⅞	9¼	StephanCo	TSC	.08	.6	11	109	13	12⅞	13	+ ³⁄₁₆
3⅜	⁷⁄₁₆	**StevensIntl A**	**SVGA**			dd	216	2⅝	2¼	2⅜	+ ¼

change. Most NYSE stocks sell for more than $20 per share, while most AMEX stocks sell for less than $10 per share. These ranges are maintained over long periods by individual stocks through the device of splitting the stock if it rises in price beyond its traditional trading range.

As corporations grow, it is relatively common for them to be first listed on the AMEX and later, as they continue to grow, to move up to the NYSE. This is a mark of some prestige: One sometimes sees advertisements placed by such companies announcing that in the future their stock will be traded on the more prestigious NYSE. It is more common nowadays, however, for smaller companies to be traded first in the OTC market on the NASDAQ and then to move directly to the NYSE.

The AMEX has been steadily losing business to other markets. In 1985, the AMEX had 4.2 percent of share volume, while the NYSE had 54.7 percent and NASDAQ had 41.1 percent. In 1995, the AMEX share had fallen to 2.6 percent, with the NYSE at 45.1 percent and NASDAQ at 52.3 percent. These numbers are somewhat misleading in that trades on the NYSE and AMEX involve both buyers and sellers in most cases; only about 17 percent of NYSE trades involve a specialist, whereas all NASDAQ trades involve dealers. Nevertheless, it is clear that the AMEX has been losing business. Indeed, NASDAQ has proven to be so attractive that several large companies including Intel and Microsoft have opted to remain there although they easily qualify for listing on the NYSE.

§14.11 The Over-the-Counter Market

The **over-the-counter (OTC) market** is quite unlike the organized exchanges described in the previous sections. There is no single place or location for the over-the-counter market. Rather, it consists of a large number of brokers and dealers who deal with each other by computer or telephone, buying and selling shares for customers or for their own account. A **dealer** is a securities firm that trades for its own account, while a **broker** executes orders for a customer. Large securities firms commonly act both as broker and as dealer in OTC securities, and may act as both a broker and a dealer in the same transaction as long as that fact is disclosed to customers. As a result, the term **broker-dealer** is typically used in statutes and rules dealing with the securities industry. Dealers involved in the OTC market are organized into a semi-public association called the **National Association of Securities Dealers** (**NASD**). By federal law, all broker-dealers must be members of the NASD.

The core of the OTC market is the **market maker**. A market maker is a dealer who stands ready to buy or sell a specific stock at quoted prices; the price at which a market maker is willing to sell (the **asked** or **offered** price) is, of course, somewhat higher than the price at which it is willing to buy (the **bid** price). The difference between the two quotes is called the **spread** and is the source of the market maker's profit. The bigger the spread, the bigger the profit on a purchase and sale. Spreads are directly related to the risk inherent in the quoted stock.

The OTC market was originally completely unregulated and unorganized. Dealers would make a market in specific stocks simply by announcing price

quotations in that stock. The accepted method of communication was through the insertion of representative **bid-and-asked quotations** in a daily publication called the **pink sheets**. A broker with an order to fill would check the pink sheets to see which dealers were making a market and would then telephone one or more of them seeking the best price. For many years, this market functioned quietly, with virtually no information available as to actual prices at which trades occurred or to actual volumes of transactions in specific shares.

Today, most bid-and-asked quotations for OTC stocks appear in the **National Association of Securities Dealers Automated Quotation** (**NASDAQ**) system, a computerized quotation system. However, many quotations for less heavily traded stocks appear on a computerized bulletin board system that the NASD maintains and some that are even less actively traded continue to appear in the pink sheets. Today, pink sheet stocks trade quite infrequently (if at all). Indeed, many are not "publicly traded" in the usual sense. For example, there may be bid prices but no ask prices and vice versa. In any event, a broker with an order to buy or sell an OTC stock finds the best price quotation from a market maker, either from the NASDAQ screen or by using the telephone, and then places the order with the one with the best price. There may be more than one price in the OTC market, because for most stocks there are several market makers. The OTC market thus consists of a web of brokers and dealers dealing with each other by telephone or by computer.

The NASD was originally organized as a **self regulatory organization** (**SRO**) under authority granted in the federal securities laws. Over the years, however, the NASD came to promote NASDAQ as an alternative trading model, and as a result of controversy over trading practices, the regulatory and disciplinary functions of the NASD are formally split into two separate organizations, **NASD Regulation** (**NASDR**) and NASDAQ.

Because the OTC market is a dealer market in which the dealer acts as principal for its own account, dealer compensation was traditionally in the form of **markups** or **markdowns** rather than in the form of **commissions** as charged by brokers. If the dealer is a market maker, it profits on the spread between the bid and ask price, but if the firm that receives an order is not a market maker, the traditional practice was for the firm to contact a market maker, arrange for the purchase or sale of the stock in question, and then resell the stock (in the case of purchase) to the customer at a markup. To be sure, a non–market maker could handle such a trade as a broker, but competitive pressures generally limited the amount of commission that could be charged to about the same as charged by NYSE firms. These days, most OTC trades are brokered and a commission is charged. Indeed, a customer will often be charged a commission even if his or her firm is a market maker in the security.

§14.12 The NASDAQ National Market

As a result of 1975 legislation aimed at deregulating the stock markets, the NASD developed the **NASDAQ National Market** for widely traded securities. The principal market makers for these securities now report actual trades and prices, and the reporting of such transactions is superficially indistinguishable from that of the exchanges. There are over 4,000 stocks in the National Market.

The average National Market stock has 11 market makers, and over 200 heavily traded stocks have 26 or more. To be eligible for listing on the National Market, a company must meet one of two alternative sets of standards. Under the first alternative, the company must have $4,000,000 in tangible assets, income in the most recent year of $400,000, publicly held stock of at least 500,000 shares with a minimum value of $3,000,000, at least 400 shareholders, and 2 market makers. Under the second alternative, a company must have $12,000,000 in assets, 1,000,000 publicly held shares with a value of $15,000,000, an operating history of at least 3 years, at least 400 shareholders, and 2 market makers. The first standard is designed to accommodate start-up companies, whereas the second standard is designed to accommodate established companies without earnings. As one might expect, the standards for continued listing are somewhat relaxed (as they are on the NYSE). To continue to be listed, a company need only have $1,000,000 in tangible assets, 200,000 publicly held shares with a value of at least $1,000,000, and 400 shareholders.

The large national securities firms are major market makers in OTC securities. Some may make markets in more than 1,000 different securities at any one time, ranging from securities traded in the National Market System to securities primarily of regional or local interest. As of the end of 1995, there were 512 active market making firms.

Table 14-1 reflects the October 30, 1997 activity in the NASDAQ National Market, and Table 14-5 shows the price quotations for numerous stocks in that market.

NASDAQ maintains a computerized order system known as the **Small Order Execution System (SOES),** which was developed in response to the 1987 crash when numerous NASDAQ market makers simply refused to accept orders. SOES differs from the NYSE DOT system in that the market maker who receives an SOES order is required to execute the order (up to a quantity of 1,000 shares for most issues). Thus, SOES is a limited automatic execution system. This has led to the emergence of a small number of firms that specialize in taking advantage of discrepancies in pricing among competing market makers, the so-called SOES Bandits. SOES trading accounts for about 7 percent of NASDAQ volume but about 14 percent of trades.

In 1995, the Justice Department began an investigation of NASDAQ to determine whether market makers had colluded to fix prices. The investigation was prompted by an academic study that found "missing eighths" in the quotes of market makers. That is, a statistical survey of quotes determined that market makers appeared to avoid quotes ending in odd eighths (that is, $\frac{1}{8}$, $\frac{3}{8}$, $\frac{5}{8}$, or $\frac{7}{8}$). More precisely, such quotes showed up less often than they should have as a matter of statistical distribution. In addition, the Department of Justice (with the cooperation of some of the same brokerage firms that had come to be known as the SOES Bandits) listened in on trading sessions in which market makers lambasted other market makers for breaking ranks and not maintaining spreads.

One explanation for the "missing eighths" could be an implicit agreement to keep spreads wider than they would otherwise be, thus increasing market maker profit from each trade. On the other hand, it could be that OTC market makers tend to play follow the leader in the same way that commercial banks do in setting the prime rate, and that changes are undertaken very carefully,

Table 14-5

NASDAQ NATIONAL MARKET ISSUES

	52 Weeks Hi	52 Weeks Lo	Stock	Sym	Div	Yld %	PE	Vol 100s	Hi	Lo	Close	Net Chg
	3 3/4	1 1/16	Imunogen	IMGN		...	dd	1071	1 3/8	1 1/4	1 5/16	...
	7 3/4	3 5/8	Imunomed	IMMU		...	dd	1033	4 7/8	4 1/2	4 5/8	− 3/16
	2 3/8	1 1/8	♣ImpactSys	MPAC		...	60	54	1 13/16	1 3/4	1 13/16	− 1/8
	35	12	♣Impath	IMPH		...	49	261	27 3/4	25	27 1/8	+ 1/2
n	19 1/8	16	ImprlCrComrcl	ICMI		...	...	5878	17	16 1/4	16 9/16	− 7/16
	29 1/4	12 3/4	♣**ImperlCred**	ICII		...	18	892	26	24 7/16	24 7/16	− 1 5/16
	7 5/8	1 1/2	ImpGnsng	IGPFF		...	...	90	2 1/4	2 1/8	2 1/8	...
	33 3/4	15 3/4	InFocusSys	INFS		...	19	818	31 3/4	30 1/4	31 3/4	+ 1/4
	2 1/8	7/8	InHomeHlth	IHHI		...	dd	243	1 3/8	1 5/16	1 5/16	...
	10 5/8	6 3/4	InControl	INCL		...	...	132	8 1/8	8	8 1/8	...
	90 1/2	35 1/2	IncytePharm	INCY		...	cc	322	83	77 1/4	82 1/2	+ 1 1/2
	3 15/32	1 5/16	**IndeNet**	INDE		...	dd	3641	2 21/32	2 3/8	2 9/16	+ 1/8
	14	6 3/8	**IndepnHldg**	INHO	.05b	.4	9	30	11 1/2	11	11 1/2	− 1
	17 3/8	8 5/8	IndepndBkMA	INDB	.36f	2.4	17	55	15 3/8	14 7/8	15 1/8	− 1/4
s	33 1/4	18 3/8	♣IndepndBkMI	IBCP	.74b	2.3	18	21	32 1/2	31 1/2	31 1/2	− 1
n	26 1/4	25	IndepCapTr pf	INDBP		...	...	24	26	25 3/4	25 3/4	− 1/4
	44	25 1/2	IndUtd	IUBC	1.04f	2.4	14	2	42 3/4	42 3/4	42 3/4	+ 1/4
	8 3/4	3 1/4	IndigoNV	INDGF		...	...	566	5 7/8	5 5/8	5 3/4	...
	11 7/8	2 5/8	♣Individual	INDV		...	dd	492	5 1/8	4 7/8	4 15/16	+ 1/16
	9 3/4	5 3/8	♣IndivInv	INDI		...	dd	34	7 1/4	7 1/8	7 1/8	...
n	17 7/8	14	IndusInt	IINT		...	...	58	14 1/8	14	14 1/8	+ 1/8
	29 5/8	5 7/8	**IndMatematik**	IMIC		...	...	3355	24 1/2	22 1/4	22 7/8	− 2 1/4
	18 3/8	12	IndBcp	INBI	.56f	3.2	17	32	17 7/8	17 1/4	17 17/32	− 23/32
	16	9 1/4	IndlHldgs	IHII		...	43	361	14 7/8	14 5/16	14 5/16	− 9/16
	9 1/8	2 3/8	IndlHldgs wtB	IHIIZ		...	...	92	8 1/8	7 5/8	8	+ 1/4
n	3 1/2	3/4	IndlHldgs wtC	IHIIL		...	...	10	2 3/4	2 3/4	2 3/4	+ 1/16
	21 3/4	13 1/2	IndlScient	ISCX	.08e	.4	13	12	18 1/2	18 1/2	18 1/2	...
	19 1/2	3 5/8	Infrnce A	INFR		...	dd	540	5 3/4	5 1/2	5 9/16	− 3/16
	24 1/2	9 1/8	♣InfntyFnl	INFN		...	47	275	15 3/4	15 1/4	15 5/8	+ 1/4
	18 5/8	5 1/4	**InfiniumSftwr**	INFM		...	cc	269	16 3/4	15	15	− 1 7/8
	4 7/8	1 5/8	Infonautc A	INFO		...	dd	425	2 11/16	2 1/2	2 5/8	− 1/16
n	16	10 1/4	InfoMgtAssoc	IMAA		...	...	120	13 1/8	12 1/4	12 3/8	− 5/8
sn	37 7/8	7 1/2	**InfoMgtRes**	IMRS	stk	...	68	1435	27 1/4	25	25 7/8	− 1 3/8
	15 3/4	6 1/4	InfoResEngrg	IREG		...	dd	95	10 1/4	9 1/2	9 3/4	− 1/4
	20	11 1/8	♣InfoRes	IRIC	p	...	dd	1884	17 1/8	16 7/8	17 1/16	− 9/16
	12 7/8	5 7/8	InfoStorage	ISDI		...	dd	495	7 3/4	7 1/2	7 3/4	+ 1/4
	27 5/8	5 5/8	**Informix**	IFMXE		...	dd	12303	6 11/16	6	6 1/4	− 1/2
	14 1/2	4 3/8	Infoseek	SEEK		...	dd	4949	10 7/8	9 3/4	10 7/16	− 1/4
	5 3/4	2 27/32	InfuTch	INFU		...	10	10	3	3	3	...
	17 3/8	11 3/4	InglsMkt	IMKTA	.66	5.0	13	554	13 1/2	13 1/8	13 3/16	− 5/16
	37 1/4	13	♣**InhaleThera**	INHL		...	...	3011	31	25	25	− 2 5/8
	7 1/4	2 1/8	**InIndCasino**	INLD		...	7	52	4 5/8	4 1/2	4 5/8	+ 3/8
	4 1/4	1 23/32	**InnerDyne**	IDYN		...	dd	633	3 5/8	3 1/4	3 3/8	− 1/4
	2 1/4	5/8	♣Innodata	INOD	stk	...	dd	8	7/8	7/8	7/8	...
	3 1/4	1 1/2	InnoServ	ISER		...	dd	1	1 13/16	1 13/16	1 13/16	...
n	29 1/2	15 1/4	InnovaCp	INVA		...	...	67	22 1/8	21	21 1/2	− 1/2
	12 5/8	6 3/4	InnovsvDvcs	IDEA		...	dd	36	9 5/16	8 5/8	8 5/8	− 3/8
	9	4	InovativGam	IGCA		...	dd	58	4 3/8	4 1/8	4 5/16	− 1/16
n	17 3/4	15 1/4	InovtvValv	IVTC		...	...	1591	17 1/8	16 1/8	17 1/8	+ 3/8
s	42 7/8	10 5/16	Innovex	INVX	.12	.5	12	4543	26	24 1/2	25 1/2	− 1/2
s	39 3/4	15 1/2	InsightEnt	NSIT		...	35	702	39	37 3/4	38	− 1
	5 3/4	1 5/16	InsigniaSol	INSGY		...	dd	428	2 13/16	2 9/16	2 11/16	+ 1/16
	43	34	Insilco	INSL		...	4	57	36 3/4	35 1/4	36 3/4	+ 1
	6 7/8	3	♣InSiteVisn	INSV		...	...	612	4 1/8	3 5/8	4 1/8	+ 1/16
	3 5/8	2 1/8	InsitufmE	INEI	.06	2.7	5	45	2 7/16	2 1/4	2 1/4	...
	10 3/16	5 3/8	InsitufmTch	INSUA		...	...	125	9 1/2	9	9	− 3/8
n	20 1/2	15 51/64	INSpireInsur	NSPR		...	...	1153	18 5/8	17 1/2	18 3/16	+ 5/16
n	12 1/2	2 1/2	InstrLab	ILABY		...	...	41	2 5/8	2 1/2	2 5/8	...
	14 1/4	6 1/2	**InsAuto**	IAAI		...	42	153	11 1/4	10 7/8	10 7/8	− 5/8
	13 3/4	2 3/4	Integ	NTEG		...	...	574	4 5/8	4 1/2	4 5/8	− 1/8
	6	2 1/2	IntgraLfSci	IART		...	dd	219	4	3 11/16	3 13/16	− 3/16
	2 17/32	1 1/4	IntgrMdAm	INMD		...	dd	166	2 3/16	2 1/16	2 1/8	− 1/16
	44	10 1/4	IntgCircuit	ICST		...	dd	828	32 1/8	30 1/4	31 1/4	− 1
	15 1/2	7 5/8	IntegDvc	IDTI		...	dd	11186	11 3/4	11	11 1/8	− 1/2
	24	11	♣IntegMsr	IMSC		...	19	78	16 1/4	15 3/4	16 1/4	...
n	7 7/8	1 1/2	**IntgtMedRes**	IMRI		...	...	2914	4 5/8	3 9/16	4	− 3/4
	9 7/8	1 1/2	IntgPack	IPAC		...	dd	56	1 7/8	1 3/4	1 3/4	− 1/8
	37 11/16	10 1/8	**IntgProcEqpt**	IPEC		...	dd	4324	23 3/8	21 3/4	21 7/8	− 2
	16 3/8	6 1/2	IntgSilSol	ISSI		...	dd	1425	10	9 1/4	9 3/4	+ 1/8
	17 1/8	7 5/8	♣IntgtSysGp	ISCG		...	31	66	11	10 3/8	11	+ 1/2
	31 1/2	8 1/2	**IntegSys**	INTS		...	cc	4786	18 3/4	17	17	− 2 1/8
	3	1 1/8	Integrity A	ITGR		...	dd	5	1 13/16	1 13/16	1 13/16	+ 5/16
s	102	51 7/8	♣**Intel**	INTC	.12	.2	19	265658	79 31/64	75 5/8	75 3/4	− 4 1/2
s	81 1/2	32 3/8	♣**Intel wt**	INTCW		...	...	25383	58 7/8	55	55 1/8	− 4 7/8
	11 5/8	1 3/8	Intelect	ICOMF		...	71	7875	8 3/4	8	8 1/2	− 5/16
n	10 7/8	2 3/4	InteliData	INTD		...	dd	555	3 7/16	3 1/4	3 5/16	− 1/16
	9 1/8	2 1/4	IntelElec	INEL		...	dd	6057	5 3/16	4 3/4	5	− 3/32
	8 1/2	4	IntlgtMed	IMII		...	dd	394	4 5/8	4 5/8	4 5/8	− 1/8
	25 7/8	8 1/4	**Intelligp**	ITIG		...	58	867	21	19	19	− 2
	26 1/2	12	♣**IntelliQuest**	IQST		...	35	407	17 1/4	15	16 9/32	+ 1 25/32

	52 Weeks Hi	52 Weeks Lo	Stock	Sym	Div	Yld %	PE	Vol 100s	Hi	Lo	Close	Net Chg
	4 3/32	1 5/8	♣**KelleyOG**	KOGC		...	dd	2509	3 9/16	3 5/16	3 5/16	− 3/16
	23 5/8	7 7/8	KelstrmInd	KELL		...	26	3318	21 3/8	20	20 13/16	− 7/16
	38 3/4	23 1/4	♣KellySvc A	KELYA	.88	2.4	18	377	36 1/4	34	36 1/4	+ 3/4
	31 3/8	17 1/4	**KEMET Corp**	KMET		...	16	5233	23 3/8	22	22 1/16	− 1 9/16
n	19	10	KendleInt	KNDL		...	...	1067	15	13 3/8	15	+ 1/2
s	20	7 5/64	KenndyWilsn	KWIC	stk	...	14	2	16 1/4	16 1/4	16 1/4	− 1/2
	18 7/8	9 5/8	KenseyNsh	KNSY		...	dd	948	15 3/8	14 3/8	15	− 1/2
	10 3/8	4 3/8	♣KentekInfo	KNTK	.08	1.0	...	446	8	7 1/2	7 3/4	+ 1/8
	8 1/4	4 1/8	♣**KY ElecStl**	KESI		...	dd	8	7	6 7/8	7	+ 3/8
	16	6 5/8	KeraVision	KERA		...	...	1110	7 1/8	6 5/8	7	− 1/8
n	18 3/4	10 1/8	Kevco	KVCO		...	12	114	14 7/8	14 1/8	14 3/4	+ 5/8
	13 3/4	4 7/8	KewneeSci	KEQU	.16	1.4	12	163	12	11 1/2	11 3/4	+ 1/8
n	10 3/8	7	**KeyFL Bcp**	KEYB		...	...	138	10	9 1/2	9 3/4	+ 3/4
	26 5/8	11 3/4	KeyTch	KTEC		...	26	109	14	13 3/8	13 1/2	− 1/2
	9	4 1/8	KeyTronic	KTCC		...	95	88	4 3/4	4 3/8	4 3/4	...
	22 1/2	12 3/8	KeystnAuto	KEYS		...	30	70	22	21 3/4	21 3/4	− 1/4
	39 5/8	24 1/4	♣KeystnFnl	KSTN	1.04	3.1	20	658	34 7/8	33	34	− 1
	46 7/8	35	KimballInt	KBALB	1.16	2.9	16	106	40 3/4	39 1/2	40 1/8	− 7/8
	19 15/16	11 3/8	KinetCncpt	KNCI	.15	.8	19	99	19	18 3/4	18 15/16	+ 1/16
	8 1/4	4 1/2	**KinardInv**	KINN		...	5	28	6 3/8	5 7/8	6 3/8	+ 1/2
	23 3/4	8	KittyHwk	KTTY		...	24	634	20 1/2	20	20 1/4	+ 1/4
	24 5/8	13 7/8	KlmthFstBcp	KFBI	.32f	1.4	25	260	22 5/8	21 7/8	22 5/8	...
	21 1/8	14 3/4	KnapeVogt	KNAP	.66	3.4	14	5	19 1/2	19 1/2	19 1/2	...
	11	4 1/4	KnckrBockr	KNIC		...	dd	510	7 1/16	6 5/8	6 11/16	− 5/16
	32	18 5/8	KnightTrans	KNGT		...	30	50	28 7/8	28	28 7/8	− 1/2
n	33 3/8	20 3/8	Knightsbrdge	VLCCF	1.26e	4.2	...	712	30 1/8	29 5/8	30	− 3/8
	17 1/4	9 7/8	KoalaCp	KARE		...	18	40	15 1/2	15	15 1/2	...
n	11 3/4	9 3/4	KofaxImage	KOFX		...	...	367	10 1/4	10	10 1/16	− 1/16
n	13 3/4	9 7/8	KollRlEst	KREG		...	...	66	12 1/8	11 5/8	12	...
	36 3/4	15 5/16	♣Komag	KMAG		...	dd	9713	17 9/16	17	17 3/16	− 7/16
	8 13/16	3 3/8	**KooKooRoo**	KKRO		...	dd	2216	4 1/4	3 13/16	3 15/16	− 1/4
	29	7 1/4	♣**Kopin**	KOPN		...	dd	681	21 7/8	20 1/4	20 1/4	− 2 3/8
n	44 7/8	19 1/4	KosPharm	KOSP		...	...	846	37 15/16	36 1/8	36 5/8	− 1 5/8
	15 1/8	5 3/4	KossCp	KOSS		...	13	116	14 1/2	14	14 1/8	+ 1/8
	35 3/4	16 1/4	Kronos	KRON		...	22	292	29 1/2	27	27 7/8	+ 1/8
	58 3/8	12	♣**KulckSoffa**	KLIC		...	53	8347	26 3/4	24	24	− 2 1/8
s	5 1/4	1 161/512	KushnrLck	KLOC		...	cc	611	4 5/8	4 3/8	4 17/32	− 3/32
s	1 1/2	3/8	KushnrLck wtC	KLOCZ		...	...	1	11/16	11/16	11/16	− 1/16

-L-L-L-

	52 Weeks Hi	52 Weeks Lo	Stock	Sym	Div	Yld %	PE	Vol 100s	Hi	Lo	Close	Net Chg
	25 15/16	7 3/8	LCC Int	LCCI		...	dd	127	20 3/4	20	20 3/4	...
	21 3/4	12 1/2	LCS Ind	LCSI	.15	.8	13	136	19 3/4	19	19	− 3/4
n	61 1/2	18 3/4	LHS Gp	LHSG		...	...	167	48	46	46 3/4	− 3/4
	27 3/8	16 27/64	LSB Fnl	LSBI	.34	1.3	15	13	25 5/8	24 1/4	25 5/8	+ 1 3/4
	18 1/8	9 1/2	LSI Ind	LYTS	.25f	1.4	17	1117	17 3/8	17	17 3/8	+ 1/8
	8 7/16	3 15/16	**LTX**	LTXX		...	dd	3122	5 3/4	5 3/16	5 1/4	− 9/16
	57 1/8	30 7/8	LVMH Moet	LVMHY	.50e	1.5	...	175	34 3/4	34	34	− 1/2
	6 5/16	3 1/2	♣LaJollaPhrm	LJPC		...	...	147	5 1/16	5	5 1/16	+ 1/16
	1 1/8	7/16	♣LaJollaPhrm wt	LJPCW		...	...	3	1	1	1	...
	20	14 1/4	♣LabOne	LABS	.72	4.4	38	54	17	16 1/4	16 1/2	+ 1/4
	35 3/8	6 1/2	LaborRdy	LBOR		...	89	3741	34 1/2	30 1/2	33	+ 1 1/4
	6 1/8	2 5/8	LacldStl	LCLD		...	dd	163	5 1/4	5 1/8	5 1/4	...
	17 1/4	10 1/2	LaCrosseFtwr	BOOT	.11f	.7	15	10	14 3/4	14 1/4	14 3/4	...
	19 3/8	11 1/2	LaddFurn	LADF		...	22	21	15 5/8	15 1/8	15 1/8	− 3/8
▼	3	1 1/8	LadyLuck	LUCK		...	dd	1715	1 7/32	1 1/32	1 3/16	− 1/32
n	11 1/2	10	LakeIndCap pf	LKFNP	.10p	...	...	66	10 3/8	10 1/4	10 1/4	− 3/8
n	61 1/4	42	LakeIndFnl	LKFN	.15e	.3	...	46	47	46 3/8	46 7/8	+ 3/8
	9	2 3/4	LakeldInd	LAKE		...	14	96	8	7 1/8	7 3/8	− 3/8
s	26 3/4	11 1/4	LakeviewFnl	LVSB	.13	.5	...	45	25 1/4	24 1/4	24 3/8	...
	67 7/16	23 3/8	**Lam Resrch**	LRCX		...	dd	20222	37 1/2	34 3/4	34 3/4	− 3 1/4
n	23 5/8	15 1/4	LamalieAssoc	LAIX		...	...	123	18 5/8	18	18 5/8	+ 1/8
▲	32 3/4	16	LamarAdvts A	LAMR		...	95	4421	34 1/2	31 1/4	34 1/4	+ 1 1/2
	4 5/8	2 5/16	**LamaurCp**	LMAR		...	dd	291	2 1/2	2 3/8	2 3/8	− 1/8
	54 1/4	36 1/8	LancastrCol	LANC	.76	1.6	16	562	49 5/8	48 5/8	48 5/8	− 1 3/8
	24 11/16	17	♣Lance	LNCE	.96	4.5	22	734	21 5/8	21	21 1/2	+ 1/8
	9 1/8	2 1/4	♣Lancit	LNCT		...	dd	126	3 3/16	2 5/8	3 1/16	− 1/8
	28 1/4	8	LandairSvc	LAND		...	21	127	25	22 5/8	25	+ 1/2
	9 1/2	4	LandecCp	LNDC		...	dd	540	5	4 3/4	4 7/8	...
x	27 5/8	16 1/4	LandmrkBcsh	LARK	.40	1.7	27	8	23 1/4	23 1/4	23 1/4	− 1 3/8
	34 3/8	12 7/8	LandrySeafod	LDRY		...	46	1214	28	26 1/2	27 3/8	− 1/8
	29	21 1/2	♣LandstarSys	LSTR		...	17	484	25 1/2	24 5/8	25	...
	9 1/4	4 1/2	Lanoptics	LNOPF		...	dd	93	4 13/16	4 9/16	4 5/8	...
	10	3 3/8	LanVision	LANV		...	dd	82	6 3/8	6	6	...
n	15 3/8	6	Larscom A	LARS		...	24	913	10 1/2	9 3/4	10 1/16	− 7/16
	14	5 1/2	LarsnDav	LDII		...	dd	608	6 1/4	6	6 1/16	− 3/16
	22 5/8	9 5/8	LaserInd	LASRF		...	16	1530	20 1/8	19	19 3/4	− 5/8
n	9 7/16	5 1/2	LaserPwr	LPWR		...	...	725	8 7/8	8	8 7/8	+ 3/8
	10 1/16	4 15/16	LaserVis	LVCI		...	dd	316	8 1/2	7 7/8	8 1/2	+ 3/8
	6 1/4	1 5/8	**LasrMaster**	LMTS		...	dd	700	3 1/2	2 7/8	3 1/4	+ 1/4
	9 5/8	4 1/8	Laserscope	LSCP		...	22	201	5 7/8	5 3/8	5 5/8	− 1/8

because no one wants to initiate a change that no one else will follow. Indeed, the presence of the SOES Bandits would itself counsel caution in changing quotes. Both the Justice Department and the SEC brought civil actions against NASDAQ and 24 market making firms. The actions were settled, with the defendants agreeing to monitoring of trading practices. Related private actions were also settled with the payment of nearly $1 billion by the offending broker-dealers.

Although the combination of commercial and enforcement activities in one organization was one of the primary criticisms leveled at NASDAQ during these investigations, federal law has long mandated such a structure and that organizations such as the NYSE, the AMEX, and the various regional exchanges all combine such activities under one roof. Indeed, in the commodities markets, the exchanges are responsible for even more of the enforcement activities, including many that are left to the SEC in the securities area. Moreover, and perhaps more important, the combination of commercial and enforcement activities may make more sense than at first appears. The various stock markets compete vigorously with each other, and one of the few ways in which one market can attract more listed companies or more investors is to offer a more trustworthy trading environment. In other words, it is always in the interest of a market to enforce just and equitable principles of trade, and it is unclear that separating traders from enforcement officers is the best way to do that.

§14.13 Other Levels of the OTC Market

There are four levels of the OTC market. The first level is the National Market described above, for which the NASD provides daily information on actual trades and volumes.

The second level is the **NASDAQ SmallCap Market**. There are 1932 issues listed in the SmallCap Market. In order to be listed, a company must have at least $4,000,000 in total assets, $2,000,000 in capital and surplus, a public float of 100,000 shares worth at least $1,000,000, 300 shareholders, and 2 market makers. Published information on these stocks is limited to volume, last trade price, and change in price.

The third level, introduced in 1990, is the NASDAQ Bulletin Board, which provides members with electronic quotations for many stocks previously listed only in the pink sheets. Unlike NASDAQ quotations, Bulletin Board price quotations are not firm.

The fourth and lowest level of the OTC market is the quotations in the daily pink sheets of inactively traded OTC securities as maintained and disseminated by the National Quotation Bureau. This information generally does not appear in financial newspaper reporting. The pink sheets today consist of hundreds of long, skinny pages of bid and asked quotations for inactively traded securities. They may range from insolvent shells to solid, old-line companies that have barely enough outside holdings of shares to justify a listing in the sheets. Better quality companies may be quoted only with a bid notation (possibly the company's own) and no shares offered for sale. Many of the companies listed in the sheets have so few shares publicly held that they are not

registered with the SEC. The pink sheets are published daily, and are the last remnant of the old days of the free-wheeling and unregulated OTC market.

§14.14 The Third Market and the Fourth Market

Despite NYSE Rule 390, a substantial off-board market for NYSE traded stocks has evolved. This market is called the **third market**. (The NASDAQ presumably is the second market.) The third market is in essence an OTC market in NYSE listed stocks. Although NYSE members are prohibited from making a market in NYSE stocks listed on or before April 26, 1979, numerous non-member firms do make markets in such stocks, and NYSE member firms may direct trades to these off-board market makers if they choose to do so. Although third market firms will often guarantee immediate execution at the current bid or offer quoted by the NYSE specialist, they generally do not offer price improvement. (They argue that waiting for price improvement takes time and that prices may change adversely in the meantime, though NYSE specialists often will stop a market order, thus guaranteeing that the investor will get the **national best bid or offer** (**NBBO**) at the time of the stop.) Moreover, many third market firms pay rebates to brokers who send them trades. Such **payment for order flow** is itself controversial, because it suggests that third market firms keep the profits from potential price improvement for themselves and referring brokers. The NYSE has responded to these practices by developing a system that allows investors to designate orders on SuperDOT as NYSE PRIME, that is, that such trades should be executed on the NYSE rather than in the third market. In addition to payment for order flow, several NASDAQ market makers were targeted in investigations by the Justice Department and the SEC in connection with allegations that they maintained wider-than-necessary spreads in OTC stocks as discussed above. Although it is impossible to manipulate spreads in connection with third market trading (where quotes necessarily track those of the NYSE specialist), the scandal gave NASDAQ and the OTC model of trading a black eye and by implication suggests that the specialist system may be more open and honest and better for the investor.

Third market trades in NYSE listed stocks are reported as part of NYSE volume on the **consolidated tape**. The consolidated tape, which was inaugurated on June 16, 1975, as a result of a legislative mandate by Congress, includes all trading in NYSE stocks on the NYSE itself as well as on regional exchanges and in the third market.

There are several **proprietary trading systems** (**PTSs**) used primarily by institutional investors as an alternative to block trading on the NYSE. These systems include Instinet and the **Crossing Network** (also owned by Reuters), **POSIT** (for portfolio system for institutional trading), and the so-called **Arizona Stock Exchange** (**AZX**). These PTSs account for about 1.4 percent of total NYSE volume during regular trading hours. Such private trading among institutions is sometimes called the **fourth market**.

With POSIT, potential buyers and sellers use computers to list their orders. At 11:00 a.m. and 1:30 p.m., the orders, almost all involving 5,000 shares or more, are automatically matched for trades, in most cases at the midpoint between the bid and asked quote at some randomly selected moment. The cost

is about 2 cents per share, half the normal commission paid by institutional investors for trades over the NYSE, and about one-tenth what a small investor is charged for trades on the NYSE.

The growth of private computer-driven electronic trading systems threatens to have major impact on NYSE specialists, other financial middlemen, and a host of lower-level order clerks, traders' assistants, back office recordkeepers, and other employees whose functions may become superfluous. Many floor traders, however, express little fear of these systems, because they regularly get better prices for their customers than electronic systems provide, perhaps in part because trading on the floor allows for a higher level of anonymity for the customer and for the size of the order he or she has placed.

In addition, an increasing amount of trading in NYSE-listed stocks is done in foreign markets. As of late 1993, the NYSE estimated that about 4,500,000 shares per day were traded in London and that 300,000 to 400,000 shares were traded in each of the other major markets (Tokyo, Paris, and Frankfurt). In addition about 3,500,000 shares are traded each day primarily in London as part of portfolio-based ("program") trades (which are discussed in more detail in a later section). These markets, especially the market for portfolio trades, are sometimes called the **fax market**, because many orders are faxed to London for off-exchange execution at the NYSE closing price.

In an effort to recapture some of this business, the NYSE in 1991 instituted two **crossing sessions** after regular trading hours, which allow trades of individual stocks and portfolios of stocks at the closing NYSE price. Crossing Session I, which operates from 4:15 to 5:00 p.m. and handles orders for individual stocks over the SuperDOT system, averaged 247,600 shares per day in 1995, though on one day it accounted for over 14,000,000 shares. Crossing Session II, which operates from 4:00 to 5:15 p.m., handles orders for **baskets** of at least 15 different NYSE stocks valued at a total of $1,000,000 or more (the official definition of a program trade), averaged 1,300,000 shares per day in 1995 and on one day accounted for 27,595,600 shares. It is estimated that Crossing Session II has repatriated over half of the foreign program trading that formerly went to the fax market.

§14.15 Market Indexes

Stock market indexes or averages attempt to measure the general level of stock prices over time. The best known indexes are the Dow Jones Averages, which are actually four different averages: of 30 industrial companies, 20 transportation stocks, 15 utilities, and a composite average of the 65 stocks. The Dow Jones Averages have been calculated since 1896.

The Dow Jones Averages for October 30, 1997, are shown in Table 14-1 as they appear in the *Wall Street Journal*, which is itself published by Dow Jones & Co., Inc. This company also owns the **broad tape**, which is a major news service covering financial, business, and national news, and which is relied on heavily by market professionals during the trading day.

The 65 stocks that make up this average are set forth in Table 14-6, as is the method of calculation of the indexes themselves. In one sense, the **Dow Jones Industrial Average** (**DJIA**) is narrowly based, reflecting the price move-

Table 14-6

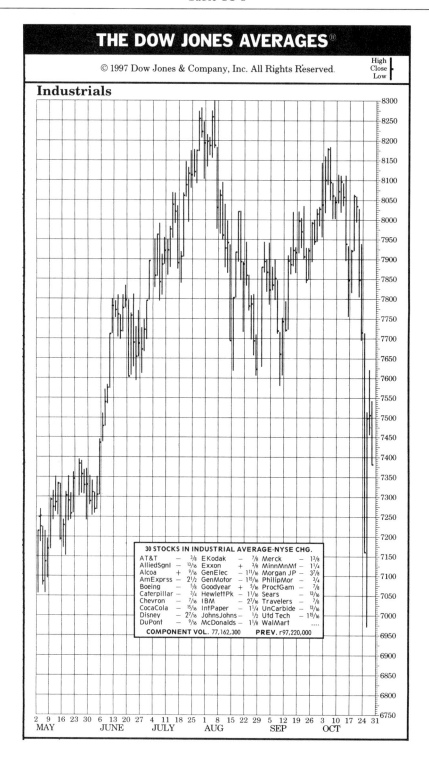

Table 14-6 (*cont.*)

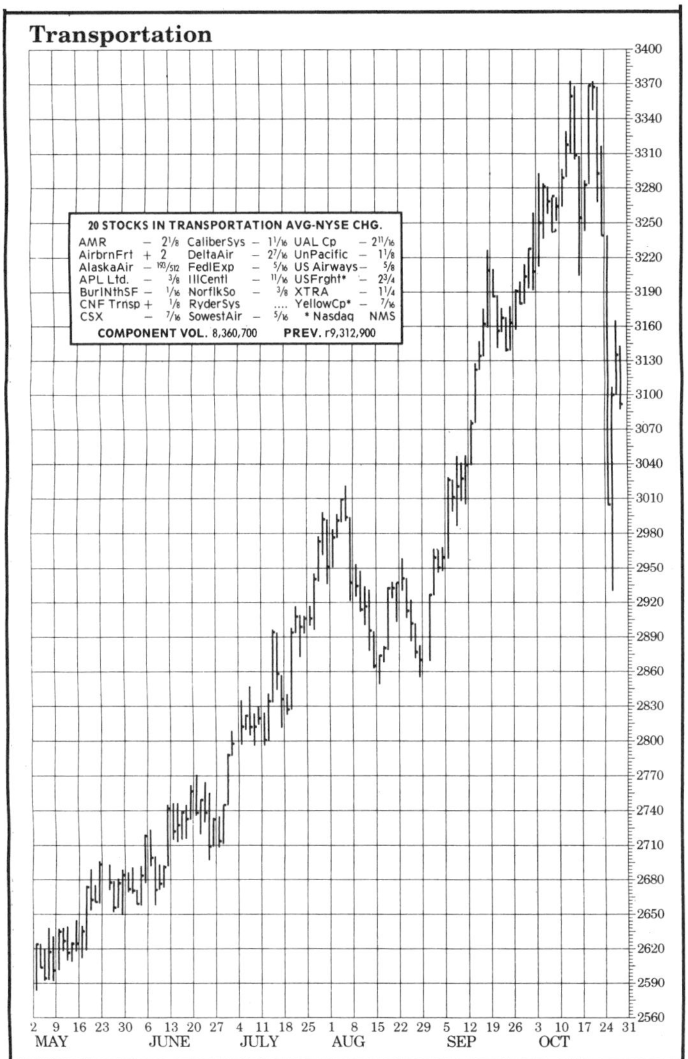
Transportation
20 STOCKS IN TRANSPORTATION AVG-NYSE CHG.
AMR – 2 1/8 CaliberSys – 1 1/16 UAL Cp – 2 11/16
AirbrnFrt + 2 DeltaAir – 2 7/16 UnPacific – 1 1/8
AlaskaAir – 193/512 FedlExp – 5/16 US Airways – 5/8
APL Ltd. – 3/8 IllCentl – 11/16 USFrght* – 2 3/4
BurlNthSF – 1/16 NorflkSo – 3/8 XTRA – 1 1/4
CNF Trnsp + 1/8 RyderSys .... YellowCp* – 7/16
CSX – 7/16 SowestAir – 5/16 * Nasdaq NMS
COMPONENT VOL. 8,360,700 PREV. r9,312,900
3400
3370
3340
3310
3280
3250
3220
3190
3160
3130
3100
3070
3040
3010
2980
2950
2920
2890
2860
2830
2800
2770
2740
2710
2680
2650
2620
2590
2560
2 9 16 23 30 6 13 20 27 4 11 18 25 1 8 15 22 29 5 12 19 26 3 10 17 24 31
MAY JUNE JULY AUG SEP OCT

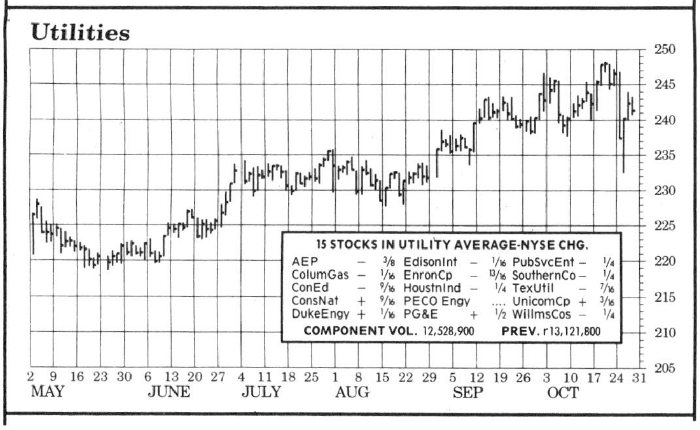
Utilities
15 STOCKS IN UTILITY AVERAGE-NYSE CHG.
AEP – 3/8 EdisonInt – 1/16 PubSvcEnt – 1/4
ColumGas – 1/16 EnronCp – 13/16 SouthernCo – 1/4
ConEd – 9/16 HoustnInd – 1/4 TexUtil – 7/16
ConsNat + 9/16 PECO Engy .... UnicomCp + 3/16
DukeEngy + 1/16 PG&E + 1/2 WillmsCos – 1/4
COMPONENT VOL. 12,528,900 PREV. r13,121,800
250
245
240
235
230
225
220
215
210
205
2 9 16 23 30 6 13 20 27 4 11 18 25 1 8 15 22 29 5 12 19 26 3 10 17 24 31
MAY JUNE JULY AUG SEP OCT

Table 14-6 (*cont.*)

The Dow Jones Averages Hour by Hour

Following are the Dow Jones averages of INDUSTRIAL, TRANSPORTATION and UTILITY stocks with the total sales of each group for the period included in the chart.

DATE	OPEN	10 AM	11 AM	12 NOON	1 PM	2 PM	3 PM	CLOSE	CHG	%	HIGH* (THEORETICAL)	LOW*	HIGHᵘ (ACTUAL)	LOWᵘ
30 INDUSTRIALS: (divisor: 0.25450704)														
Oct 30	7502.15	7435.70	7464.68	7519.68	7493.41	7474.50	7449.70	7381.67	− 125.00	− 1.67	7569.78	7340.42	7543.01	7381.18
Oct 29	7498.56	7510.11	7617.18	7511.33	7549.40	7489.48	7521.40	7506.67	+ 8.35	+ 0.11	7664.08	7409.67	7621.60	7456.08
Oct 28	7160.90	7000.79	7190.86	7274.85	7367.43	7298.91	7428.58	7498.32	+ 337.17	+ 4.71	7553.57	6936.45	7515.02	6971.32
Oct 27	7714.42	7680.78	7608.34	7596.30	7531.72	7387.81	b7361.04	7161.15	− 554.26	− 7.18	7717.37	7150.10	7714.42	7159.92
Oct 24	7849.00	7910.64	7835.49	7726.68	7763.05	7794.23	7770.90	7715.41	− 132.36	− 1.69	7975.47	7645.91	7939.61	7695.51
20 TRANSPORTATION COS.: (divisor: 0.35171330)														
Oct 30	3134.83	3095.74	3116.44	3131.99	3131.81	3119.73	3106.58	3091.65	− 43.54	− 1.39	3158.29	3063.22	3143.19	3087.21
Oct 29	3099.83	3137.14	3161.49	3132.88	3137.50	3115.82	3134.12	3135.19	+ 35.36	+ 1.14	3184.59	3087.39	3165.22	3099.83
Oct 28	3004.93	2933.76	2997.83	3011.86	3069.79	3038.52	3069.26	3099.83	+ 95.25	+ 3.17	3132.70	2913.24	3106.93	2929.94
Oct 27	3239.14	3205.56	3179.61	3157.58	3137.68	3085.83	b3062.86	3004.58	− 234.56	− 7.24	a3228.13	2999.42	3239.50	3004.04
Oct 24	3293.34	3311.29	3292.81	3252.47	3259.58	3266.15	3259.58	3239.14	− 53.49	− 1.62	3324.44	3223.68	3316.80	3238.97
15 UTILITIES: (divisor: 2.2811277)														
Oct 30	242.12	241.55	242.20	242.73	242.92	242.59	242.40	241.33	− 1.04	− 0.43	244.34	239.71	243.33	240.73
Oct 29	240.23	240.26	243.99	242.10	242.56	241.77	243.16	242.37	+ 2.14	+ 0.89	244.94	240.01	244.04	239.99
Oct 28	237.16	232.86	233.05	233.33	236.81	235.82	237.74	240.23	+ 2.79	+ 1.18	241.41	230.92	240.34	232.48
Oct 27	246.42	246.75	245.33	245.36	244.62	241.27	b241.16	237.44	− 9.12	− 3.70	247.63	236.89	246.84	237.41
Oct 24	245.11	245.63	245.79	244.94	245.96	246.45	246.51	246.56	+ 1.48	+ 0.60	247.93	243.74	247.27	244.78
65 STOCKS COMPOSITE AVERAGE: (divisor: 1.4504628)														
Oct 30	2458.07	2435.26	2446.39	2460.64	2456.28	2449.00	2441.68	2424.44	− 34.13	− 1.39	2478.35	2407.77	2467.79	2424.10
Oct 29	2445.17	2456.33	2486.88	2458.40	2466.93	2449.91	2462.15	2458.57	+ 13.40	+ 0.55	2502.22	2426.25	2487.87	2443.14
Oct 28	2358.47	2304.42	2355.11	2373.81	2409.23	2388.81	2421.60	2445.17	+ 86.66	+ 3.67	2464.69	2286.08	2448.57	2300.73
Oct 27	2527.00	2513.47	2491.83	2485.07	2467.10	2423.92	b2413.53	2358.51	− 168.49	− 6.67	a2526.35	2354.46	2527.08	2358.17
Oct 24	2561.08	2577.28	2559.87	2529.97	2539.36	2547.38	2541.60	2527.00	− 33.86	− 1.32	2595.46	2506.61	2582.49	2523.33

**a-Actual high exceeds theoretical due to computational method. b-Value at 2:37 p.m. temp. halt. Mkt. closed at 3:30.

ments of only 30 stocks; it is a **blue chip** average, because the 30 companies are among the largest and most influential in the country. Because of this emphasis on the largest companies, it is not uncommon for the DJIA to move in one direction while the broader-based indexes described in the following section move in the opposite direction.

It is not entirely clear why the DJIA has achieved the prominence that it has. One advantage is its relative antiquity, going back over 100 years. It also has attracted a following because it involves rather dramatic price moves. For example, the DJIA was widely used to describe the collapse of securities prices that occurred in October 1987 following the August 25 high. After a period of increasingly volatile prices, the second week of October 1987 was marked by several trading days of increases in trading volume accompanied by moderate decreases in the DJIA. On Monday, October 19, however, the NYSE suffered its largest one-day loss up to that time as measured by the Dow—508.32 points. It closed on October 19 at 1,738.40, down one-third from its historic high of 2722.42 in August. During the two-week period in October when most of this decline occurred, less than 3 percent of all the outstanding shares registered on the NYSE were traded, but the aggregate loss in value of all NYSE shares was approximately $1 trillion. An even greater point drop occurred on October 27, 1997, when the DJIA fell 554 points, triggering the 350- and 550-point circuit breakers, which resulted in the NYSE closing about a half hour early. Although the drop was a record in terms of points, it was only about 7 percent of the DJIA value of 7715 on the previous day. On the following day, the DJIA

registered its biggest rise in history, climbing 337 points on record volume of more than 1.2 billion shares. Ironically, the circuit breakers had been raised from 250 and 400 points, to 350 and 550 earlier in 1997. Following the events of October 1997, the chairman of the SEC called for further study of whether these triggers were appropriate, suggesting that a percentage test might make more sense given the extraordinary increase in the DJIA since 1987. Although much of the losses suffered during these two episodes reflected only the disappearance of appreciation (so-called paper profits), many traders and investors suffered devastating losses of capital. All losses, whether of paper profits or of capital, are of course felt keenly and have a psychological effect on future economic behavior.

The DJIA can easily be criticized as a market measure. It has traditionally been an average of large industrial companies. As such, it has not always reflected important parts of the market such as growth stocks, has overrepresented the capital goods and energy sectors of the market, and has given too little weight to financial and service companies. The mix of stocks was changed somewhat in 1997, however, in an effort to include more growth stocks, thus increasing the likelihood of increases in the average. Despite its critics, the DJIA remains a venerable and widely watched stock market barometer. Moreover, despite its shortcomings, there is usually very little difference between day-to-day percentage changes in the Dow and changes in the more scientific indexes, thus demonstrating that a little diversification goes a long way.

There are other widely followed indexes besides the DJIA. Table 14-1 sets forth several other indexes as presented by the *Wall Street Journal.* Several of these are broad-based indexes covering hundreds or thousands of stocks. None of them, however, have achieved the wide following of the DJIA. All of them reflected the crashes that occurred in 1987 and 1997, indicating that the decline was marketwide and not limited to the blue chip stocks that compose the DJIA.

The two most widely followed alternative indexes are the **New York Stock Exchange Composite Index (the NYSE Composite)** and the **Standard & Poor's 500 Index (S&P 500)**. These indexes differ conceptually from the DJIA. In the DJIA, a dollar change in the price of a single stock in the average has the same effect as a change of one dollar in the price of any other stock in the average. There is no weighting of the individual stocks by the size of the company or the number of shares outstanding. Both the S&P 500 and NYSE Composite are true indexes in that they measure changes in total market value of the stocks that make up the index, and the index number is the percentage change compared with a base period. The NYSE Composite is indexed to December 31, 1965 (when the base was 50), while the S&P 500 is indexed to the period from 1941 to 1943 (when the base was 10). The NYSE Composite is based on all of the stocks traded on the NYSE; the S&P 500 is based on the 500 largest domestic stocks, which with a few important exceptions are traded on the NYSE.

The **Value Line Composite Index** is based on 1,650 stocks, 300 of which are traded OTC and 100 of which are AMEX stocks. The **Wilshire 5,000** is even broader, covering 5,000 stocks traded on all the principal securities markets. The **Russell 1000, Russell 2000,** and **Russell 3000** are also widely used particularly as a comparison for the performance of various mutual funds.

An important function of these alternative indexes is to serve as the basis for options and futures trading on indexes. This subject is described in the chapter on options and commodities. Trading strategies based on indexes have become so important that the addition of a stock to an index (or its removal) can significantly affect the stock's price. In other words, stock market indexes are not merely statistics. This is not particularly surprising, however, given the importance of diversification in investing. Although it may sound curious, because of diversification, investors (in the aggregate) appear to care much more about how the market as a whole performs than about the prices of individual stocks, which explains why index funds (i.e., funds that try to match the market) have become so popular in recent years.

§14.16 Margin

Buying on **margin** involves borrowing money from your broker to enable you to buy stock or other securities. By obtaining such a loan, an investor may make a larger investment than he or she could have without the loan. Buying on margin creates leverage. Because the loan is secured by a lien on the readily marketable securities purchased, it is a very safe loan from the point of view of the broker and the bank that lends to the broker. (Indeed, the sometimes publicized **broker-loan rate** or **call-money rate**, the rate at which banks lend to brokers with securities as security, tends to be less than the prime rate.)

Margin trading is subject to federal regulation, because it was believed that excessive margin trading before the collapse of the securities markets in 1929 contributed significantly to the magnitude and severity of that collapse. An analysis of the way margin trading may have contributed to the dramatic collapse of securities prices in 1929 is instructive because it both reflects the dangers of leverage and explains how margined securities transactions work.

The late 1920s was a period of unparalleled optimism in the securities markets. Securities prices were going up and seemed to have no way to go but up even further. Many brokers provided purchasers of shares with 90 percent or even higher margin privileges. A person buying 1,000 shares of $10 stock could therefore buy $10,000 worth of stock simply by putting up $1,000 in cash and borrowing $9,000 from the broker. When the price of the stock went from $10 to $12, the investor more than doubled his money: He sold for $12,000 the stock he had purchased for $10,000, returned the $9,000 to the broker and kept $3,000 (minus brokerage commissions and interest) for himself. These transactions occurred time and time again during the 1920s: Buying stock on margin was like finding money. Furthermore, many people pyramided: They would take the potential gain from the run-up in price (without actually selling the stock and liquidating the position) and use that equity to borrow additional margin to buy additional stocks on the 90 percent debt/10 percent equity ratio. To make matters even more dangerous, many persons of very modest means were speculating on margined stocks and pyramiding. This is, of course, classic leverage that is also involved in buying commercial real estate or many businesses. When prices are going up, profits roll in at a fast clip; when prices decline, disaster strikes.

When the first breaks in price occurred in the summer of 1929, many margin purchasers found themselves facing margin calls, that is, requests from the broker to put up more collateral, because the price of the stock had declined and the stock did not fully secure the broker's loan. In the example above, if the price declined to $9 per share, the broker would be seriously at risk: The collateral is worth only $9,000 and declining, while the loan is $9,000 plus accrued interest and increasing steadily (from additional interest charges). Most margin purchasers had no additional capital to deposit with the broker (even if they wished to do so). To cut the potential losses, brokers began selling margined shares to recoup as much as they could. Positive feedback (and panic) resulted, driving down prices even further as more margin calls were triggered, increasing the sharpness of the crash. In the process, many brokerage firms were wiped out along with their customers, because the customers were insolvent and the firms were unable to cover their customer commitments. Brokerage firm failures wiped out the assets of solvent customers, because all accounts were uninsured. Customers became unsecured creditors in the broker's bankruptcy proceeding. The bottom of the market collapse did not occur until 1931 and 1932, when many securities prices had declined by over 70 percent. It was not uncommon for the $10 stock sold in 1929 to be selling for $2 per share or less in 1931.

One lesson learned from the 1929 market debacle was that limits should be placed on the amount of margin customers can borrow on the security of marketable securities of fluctuating value. This regulatory power is vested in the Federal Reserve Board (the Fed). Over the years, the required margin has varied; but the requirement has been stable at 50 percent for over 30 years. This means that today an investor may borrow no more than 50 percent of the purchase price. Lower margin requirements apply to some safer securities such as treasury securities, which require only a 10 percent down payment. Margin requirements are also lower for commodities, although as explained in Chapter 16, margin has a different function in the commodities markets.

If one has $10,000, and wants to buy a $100 stock, one can borrow an additional $10,000 from a broker, and buy 200 shares—$20,000 worth of the stock. From the broker's standpoint, the risk is not very great, because the $10,000 loan is secured by stock worth $20,000. Because the stock is collateral for the loan, the broker will retain possession of the certificate if the stock is certificated or, if not, will simply note in its records that the stock is subject to a security interest. (Needless to say, it is much easier for the investor to borrow against uncertificated stock, which does not need to be delivered to the broker and does not even need to be endorsed by the investor.) Moreover, interest charges on the margin loan create an incentive for investors to close out margined positions if the stock does not move upward promptly.

The effect of 50 percent margin is to double the consequence of each dollar of increase or decline in the stock over what the consequence would have been in an unmargined investment. As was true in 1929, at some point decline may be large enough that the broker will feel compelled to make a margin call. NYSE rules require additional margin when the value of the collateral has declined to the point that the equity in the account is less than 25 percent of the value of the shares. In other words, if one bought 200 shares of a $100 stock on margin

(putting up $10,000 in cash and borrowing the remaining $10,000), a **margin call** would be issued when the stock declined to a value of $13,333 or $66.66 per share. Many brokerage firms, however, make margin calls before this level is reached; several leading brokerage firms require additional margin at 30 or 35 percent rather than at the 25 percent minimum required by the NYSE.

Technically, **initial margin** is the amount that must be put up on the original purchase (50 percent currently), while **maintenance margin** is the point at which a margin call is made to preserve an outstanding position. Both, however, are usually referred to as "margin."

Margin calls are made on the basis of the value of the entire portfolio of securities that the customer maintains with the broker, not on each individual stock. When the value of the portfolio has dropped so that a margin call is necessary, the broker is expected to telephone the customer no later than the next day; depending on the brokerage firm's policies (and the perceived credit-worthiness of the customer), the customer may be allowed a day or two, or as long as a week, to supply the additional capital in the form of either cash or additional marginable securities. If the additional capital is not received, the securities in the account are sold and the proceeds used to repay the outstanding margin loan.

Margin regulations apply to all borrowing to buy securities, including borrowing from banks and other sources — even a friend or family member. When a person borrows money from a bank secured by a lien on shares of stock, for example, he or she must sign a statement that the purpose of the loan itself is not to invest in marketable securities.

Not all stocks may be purchased on margin. The Fed maintains a list of stocks that qualify as security for margin loans. Generally speaking, stocks that trade for less than $5 per share may not be counted toward account equity for margin purposes. And until the late 1960s, OTC stocks could not be bought on margin at all.

Although margin increases risk by enhancing moves both up and down, it can also be used to reduce risk by increasing diversification. That is, an investor with, say, $10,000 to invest could buy 5 round lots of $20 stocks (ignoring commissions) ($20 × 100 shares × 5 stocks = $10,000), but with margin could buy 10 round lots ($20 × 100 shares × 10 stocks = $10,000 cash + $10,000 margin loan). (Although the investor could buy odd lots of many more securities, commission rates on such purchases are significantly higher.) As discussed in more detail in following sections, diversification reduces risk significantly with no sacrifice in return. Thus, margin may make sense for a smallish investor who wishes to manage his or her own account, but who cannot buy enough different stocks to achieve adequate diversification. With thousands of mutual funds available to small investors with as little as $2,500 to invest, diversification is readily available, though in a mutual fund one gives up control over the exact composition of the portfolio.

Aside from allowing the investor to achieve more diversification, margin is a way of increasing leverage at the investor level. Increased leverage should be recognized for what it is: increased risk. The desire to take more risk, however, may be rational: more risk means more return. Thus, an investor who is willing to take more risk than may be available with plain vanilla stocks may leverage a

portfolio with margin. It is now also possible to buy no-load mutual funds on margin. In any event, the decision to invest on margin should be carefully considered. Margin makes sense only if the expected rate of return on the portfolio exceeds the interest rate on the margin loan. Moreover, interest on the margin loan must be paid in cash, while the stocks in the portfolio may only generate paper gains.

It is possible with publicly traded options to achieve much more leverage than with margin. Options are discussed in more detail in Chapter 16.

§14.17 Short Selling

A **short sale** enables an investor to speculate on a price decline to the same extent as the purchase of shares constitutes speculation on a price increase. The idea is simple: A short seller borrows shares from a broker and sells them. When the price declines (if the price declines), the short seller buys shares to replace the shares borrowed and sold. The short seller's profit is the difference between the higher sales price and lower purchase price, less commissions, interest, and any dividends paid on the borrowed stock (all of which are the short seller's obligation). At first blush, it may seem unethical to profit on a decline in prices or to sell something one does not actually own. Yet as long as the person from whom the shares are borrowed consents to the transaction and gets the shares back, no one is hurt. It is no more unethical than borrowing money to finance a profitable business venture. Would anyone suggest that the lender of money should in fairness be entitled to the borrower's profit?

Between 1929 and 1932, many fortunes were made by systematic short selling (or "shorting") of stocks. In these campaigns, known as **bear raids**, traders borrowed shares and sold them, further driving down prices in an already soft market. Profits from successful short sales were used as collateral to short more stock, driving prices down further. This may appear to be predatory behavior. From another perspective, the "shorts" were simply more accurate in predicting the future than were the "longs," who bought shares during this period believing that the worst was over and that prices would be going up. Moreover, it is unclear that short selling in fact permanently drives the price of a stock down. After all, the short seller must eventually buy back the shares, and the price should rise as a result by just as much as the price fell in the first place. Thus, many traders regard open short interest as supportive of the current price of a stock and would be positively inclined to buy stocks that have been sold short to an unusual extent.

The mechanics of short selling require some explanation. First of all, how and from whom does one borrow stock? The answer is that there is a large supply of securities held at brokerage houses that is available for borrowing. These are typically shares held for investors by brokerage firms under the book entry system. If the owner of stock that has been lent decides to sell, the broker must deliver the shares either by getting them back from the short seller, or more commonly by using other shares in the floating supply until the short seller closes out the short position and returns the shares. Large stockholders, including pension funds and mutual funds, also routinely lend shares. The

incentive for lending (aside from fees charged) is that these loans are collateralized with cash from the borrower on which no interest is customarily paid to the stock borrower but on which the lender may earn interest. An institutional investor may lend shares in its portfolio simply to earn interest on the collateral. (A savvy short seller will use securities as collateral, because interest or appreciation may be retained or will negotiate for some interest on a cash deposit. In the commodities markets, traders who borrow physical commodities to cover delivery are said to "rent" the commodity.) There is no downside for the lender, because the short seller — the person borrowing the stock and selling it — is also responsible for any dividends that may be declared on the stock while it is borrowed.

From the standpoint of the short seller, the borrowing of stock is similar to a margin transaction. The borrower must provide collateral equal to 50 percent of the value of the stock being borrowed. Upon receiving the borrowed stock and selling it, the proceeds are retained in the customer's account and cannot be drawn down. No interest is usually paid on the capital in this account, although it may be possible for large short sellers to earn interest by substituting treasury bills or other interest-earning cash equivalents.

If the short seller guesses wrong, and the price of the stock goes up, he or she may face a margin call much as a margin buyer faces a margin call when the stock price goes down. Theoretically, the liability of a short seller is infinite, because there is no maximum limit on the rise of a stock price, while the most a margin buyer can lose is twice the amount of capital invested if the stock drops to zero (assuming a 50 percent margin requirement). These are theoretical maximum losses, however, not realistic ones.

A more serious risk in short selling is that someone buying the same stock will **corner** the market, that is, buy enough of the outstanding stock that it becomes increasingly difficult for short sellers to find shares to buy back to cover their short positions. A corner requires the availability of very large amounts of capital to buy a large proportion of the stock available for public trading, the float, absorbing the short sales made by persons expecting the price to go down further. There have been no attempted corners in recent years in the securities markets, although there have been attempts in the commodities markets. An attempt to corner a stock or a demand for the return of shares at a time when substitute shares are not available (perhaps because they are thinly traded) is sometimes called a **short squeeze** or **squeezing the shorts**.

Financial newspapers publish regular reports of short positions for many widely traded stocks. These reports show uncovered short positions for the week and previous week, thus allowing for easy calculation of changes; they also show the number of days worth of trading volume that would be required to cover outstanding positions, thus giving some indication of how readily available the stock is to cover an open position and how likely it is that a corner will arise. Table 14-7 shows information about short selling as published periodically in the *Wall Street Journal*.

Assuming that uncovered short sales for a given stock have increased in the most recent period, is that a "bullish" or "bearish" sign? (A **bull market** is a rising market, whereas a **bear market** is a falling market.) An increase in uncovered short positions obviously means that many investors thought prices

Table 14-7

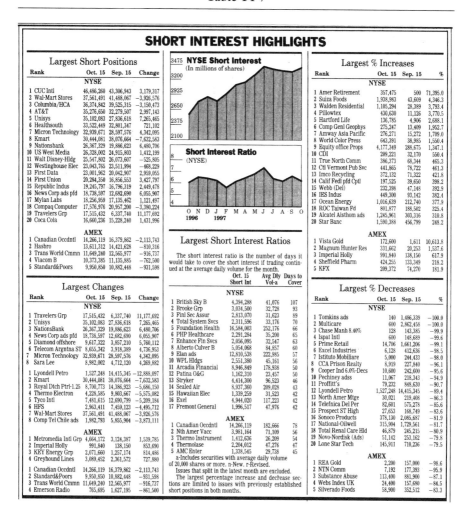

SHORT INTEREST HIGHLIGHTS

Largest Short Positions

Rank		Oct. 15	Sep. 15	Change
	NYSE			
1	CUC Intl	46,486,260	43,306,943	3,179,317
2	Wal-Mart Stores	37,561,491	41,488,067	−3,926,576
3	Columbia/HCA	36,374,842	39,525,315	−3,150,473
4	AT&T	35,276,650	32,279,507	2,997,143
5	Unisys	35,102,083	27,836,618	7,265,465
6	Healthsouth	33,522,449	32,801,347	721,102
7	Micron Technology	32,939,671	28,597,576	4,342,095
8	Kmart	30,444,081	38,076,664	−7,632,583
9	Nationsbank	26,367,329	19,886,623	6,480,706
10	US West Media	26,328,002	24,915,803	1,412,199
11	Walt Disney-Hldg	25,547,802	26,073,607	−525,805
12	Westinghouse Elec	23,043,765	23,511,994	−468,229
13	First Data	23,001,962	20,042,907	2,959,055
14	First Union	20,284,350	16,856,553	3,427,797
15	Republic Indus	19,245,797	16,796,319	2,449,478
16	News Corp ads pfd	18,738,597	12,682,690	6,055,907
17	Mylan Labs	18,256,959	17,135,462	1,121,497
18	Compaq Computer	17,576,976	20,957,200	−3,380,224
19	Travelers Grp	17,515,432	6,337,740	11,177,692
20	Coca Cola	16,660,236	15,228,240	1,431,996
	AMEX			
1	Canadian Occdntl	14,266,119	16,379,862	−2,113,743
2	Hasbro	13,611,312	14,421,628	−810,316
3	Trans World Cmmn	11,649,240	12,565,977	−916,737
4	Viacom B	10,373,385	11,135,885	−762,500
5	Standard&Poors	9,950,850	10,882,448	−931,598

Largest Changes

Rank		Oct. 15	Sep. 15	Change
	NYSE			
1	Travelers Grp	17,515,432	6,337,740	11,177,692
2	Unisys	35,102,083	27,836,618	7,265,465
3	NationsBank	26,367,329	19,886,623	6,480,706
4	News Corp ads pfd	18,738,597	12,682,690	6,055,907
5	Diamond offshore	9,617,322	3,857,210	5,760,112
6	Telecom Argntna ST	8,655,342	3,918,389	4,736,953
7	Micron Technology	32,939,671	28,597,576	4,342,095
8	Sara Lee	8,982,002	4,712,120	4,269,882
1	Lyondell Petro	1,527,248	14,415,345	−12,888,097
2	Kmart	30,444,081	38,076,664	−7,632,583
3	Royal Dtch Ptrl-1.25	8,700,773	14,386,923	−5,686,150
4	Thermo Electron	4,228,585	9,803,667	−5,575,082
5	Tyco Intl	7,481,615	12,690,799	−5,209,184
6	HFS	2,963,411	7,459,123	−4,495,712
7	Wal-Mart Stores	37,561,491	41,488,067	−3,926,576
8	Comp Tel Chile ads	1,982,793	5,855,904	−3,873,111
	AMEX			
1	Metromedia Intl Grp	4,664,172	3,124,387	1,539,785
2	Imperial Holly	991,840	138,150	853,690
3	KEY Energy Grp	2,071,660	1,257,174	814,486
4	Greyhound Lines	3,089,452	2,361,572	727,880
1	Canadian Occdntl	14,266,119	16,379,862	−2,113,743
2	Standard&Poors	9,950,850	10,882,448	−931,598
3	Trans World Cmmn	11,649,240	12,565,977	−916,737
4	Emerson Radio	765,695	1,627,195	−861,500

NYSE Short Interest (In millions of shares)

Short Interest Ratio (NYSE)

O N D J F M A M J J A S O
1996   1997

Largest Short Interest Ratios

The short interest ratio is the number of days it would take to cover the short interest if trading continued at the average daily volume for the month.

		Oct. 15 Short Int	Avg Dly Vol-a	Days to Cover
	NYSE			
1	British Sky B	4,394,288	41,076	107
2	Brooke Grp	3,034,500	32,728	93
3	Finl Sec Assur	2,813,070	31,623	89
4	Total System Svcs	2,311,596	33,176	70
5	Foundation Health	16,584,003	252,176	66
6	PHP Healthcare	2,291,284	35,200	65
7	Enhance Fin Svcs	2,056,095	32,547	63
8	Alberto Culver B	5,054,068	84,857	60
9	Elan ads	12,810,538	222,985	57
10	WPL Hldgs	2,551,380	45,161	56
11	Arcadia Financial	8,946,849	178,938	50
12	Patina O&G	1,162,310	23,457	50
13	Stryker	4,414,300	96,523	46
14	Sealed Air	8,937,360	209,028	43
15	Hawaiian Elec	1,339,259	31,523	42
16	Exel	4,944,020	117,223	42
17	Fremont General	1,996,517	47,976	42
	AMEX			
1	Canadian Occdntl	14,266,119	182,666	78
2	Nth Amer Vacc	3,981,164	71,109	56
3	Thermo Instrument	1,412,636	26,209	54
4	Thermolase	2,204,012	47,276	47
5	AMC Enter	1,338,545	29,738	45

a-Includes securities with average daily volume of 20,000 shares or more. n-New. r-Revised.

Issues that split in the latest month are excluded.

The largest percentage increase and decrease sections are limited to issues with previously established short positions in both months.

Largest % Increases

Rank		Oct. 15	Sep. 15	%
	NYSE			
1	Amer Retirement	357,475	500	71,395.0
2	Suiza Foods	1,938,983	43,609	4,346.3
3	Walden Residential	1,105,294	28,389	3,793.4
4	Pillowtex	430,630	11,126	3,770.5
5	Hartford Life	136,785	4,906	2,688.1
6	Comp Genl Geophys	275,247	13,409	1,952.7
7	Amway Asia Pacific	276,271	15,272	1,709.0
8	World Color Press	643,391	38,985	1,550.4
9	Equity office Props	4,177,349	288,675	1,347.1
10	CDI	209,221	32,170	550.4
11	True North Comm	386,373	68,344	465.3
12	Ctl Vermont Pub Svc	441,865	78,722	461.3
13	Imco Recycling	372,132	71,322	421.8
14	Calif Fedl pfd CptI	197,525	39,650	398.2
15	Webb (Del)	232,398	47,148	392.9
16	IES Indus	449,300	93,142	382.4
17	Ocean Energy	1,016,639	212,740	377.9
18	ROC Taiwan Fd	801,877	188,502	325.4
19	Alcatel Aisthom ads	1,245,961	303,316	310.8
20	Star Banc	1,590,388	456,799	248.2
	AMEX			
1	Vista Gold	172,600	1,611	10,613.8
2	Magnum Hunter Res	331,662	20,253	1,537.6
3	Imperial Holly	991,846	138,150	617.9
4	Sheffield Pharm	424,255	133,349	218.2
5	KFX	209,372	74,270	181.9

Largest % Decreases

Rank		Oct. 15	Sep. 15	%
	NYSE			
1	Tomkins ads	140	1,486,339	−100.0
2	Multicare	600	2,862,458	−100.0
3	Chase Manh 8.40%	128	143,385	−99.9
4	Ispat Intl	600	148,689	−99.6
5	Prime Retail	14,706	1,661,206	−99.1
6	Excel Industries	6,128	412,636	−98.5
7	Istituto Mobiliare	5,000	244,433	−98.0
8	CCA Prison Realty	8,919	227,840	−96.1
9	Cooper Ind 6.0%-Decs	10,600	242,600	−95.6
10	Pechiney adss	11,067	218,343	−94.9
11	Proffitt's	79,232	848,630	−90.7
12	Lyondell Petro	1,527,248	14,415,345	−89.4
13	North Amer Mtge	30,021	219,408	−86.3
14	Telefnica Del Per	82,601	575,278	−85.6
15	Prospect ST High	27,653	168,749	−83.6
16	Sonoco Products	378,130	2,085,687	−81.9
17	National-Oilwell	315,904	1,729,561	−81.7
18	Total Renal Care Hld	46,879	245,215	−80.9
19	Novo-Nordisk (Ads)	51,142	253,162	−79.8
20	Lone Star Tech	145,911	710,236	−79.5
	AMEX			
1	REA Gold	2,200	157,000	−98.6
2	NTN Comm	7,192	177,393	−95.9
3	Substance Abuse	113,400	881,900	−87.1
4	Webs Index UK	24,400	157,680	−84.5
5	Silverado Foods	58,900	352,512	−83.3

Table 14-7 (*cont.*)

	10/15/97	9/15/97	% Chg	Avg Dly Volume
Hong Kong Tele Ads ..	865,731	877,728	−1.4	187,828
Horizon/Cms..........	514,789	269,031	91.3	310,547
Hormel Foods	2,502,695	2,493,039	0.4	76,090
Host Marriott	6,427,007	5,247,871	22.5	1,528,090
Host Marriott Sv	462,716	415,520	11.4	41,042
Household Intl	1,154,948	884,247	30.6	481,014
Houston Industs	4,679,322	6,539,770	−28.4	698,814
Howell Corp	909,001	849,946	6.9	10,328
HSB Group (Hldg)	298,016	423,886	−29.7	34,671
Hudson Foods (A)....	233,389	403,926	−42.2	106,742
Hughes Supply	253,556	125,144	102.6	73,757
Humana Inc............	1,521,885	1,518,385	0.2	557,052
IBP, Inc................	953,809	1,065,213	−10.5	375,633
ICN Pharma Inc.......	4,331,317	4,289,134	1.0	564,438
Idaho Pwr Co	391,112	615,293	−36.4	55,600
IES Industries	449,300	93,142	382.4	61,900
Ikon Off Sol-D/S	129,112	360,600	−64.2	40,528
Ikon Off Solution	4,483,582	4,923,280	−8.9	698,128
Ill Central Corp.......	465,023	257,068	80.9	141,890
Ill Tool Works	4,627,676	4,714,992	−1.9	304,800
Illinova Corp	2,528,999	3,418,238	−26.0	319,357
Imation Corp..........	1,763,399	989,447	78.2	291,623
IMC Global Inc	7,879,963	7,866,022	0.2	341,738
Imco Recycling	372,132	71,322	421.8	27,480
Imper Chem (ads)	1,587,439	2,435,550	−34.8	128,857
Inacom Corp	1,367,746	0	....	42,610
Inco Limited	2,337,170	2,913,282	−19.8	574,585
Industrias Bach	1,126,752	0	....	254,580
ING Groep (Adss) ...	1,355,046	531,945	154.7	78,080
Ingersoll-Rand	2,799,330	2,210,900	26.6	383,052
Ingram Micro	1,149,265	1,155,267	−0.5	78,461
Inland Steel	1,158,930	886,655	30.7	347,252
Inmc Mtge Hldgs......	622,721	515,956	20.7	147,476
Input/Output Inc	1,457,463	2,306,880	−36.8	757,142
Insignia Finl Gr	1,770,639	1,680,200	5.4	93,638
Int Flavors	1,833,184	2,508,971	−26.9	247,500
Integon Corp..........	1,749,225	1,548,538	13.0	48,961
Integrated Hlth	7,973,948	7,923,778	0.6	249,338
Interpublic Gr	5,792,962	6,046,982	−4.2	344,419
Interstate Baker.......	1,494,264	1,096,404	36.3	268,323
Intimate Brands	5,239,801	4,472,763	17.1	207,209
Intl Busin Mach	7,875,722	8,213,231	−4.1	3,704,461
Intl Ceramica-Ads ...	0	161,649	−100.0	7,004
Intl Game Technol	3,493,064	3,525,583	−0.9	740,747
Intl Paper Co..........	6,990,206	7,005,413	−0.2	1,567,819
Intl Rectifier	1,170,077	1,707,257	−31.5	255,166
Iomega Corp	12,109,741	14,218,048	−14.8	2,640,980
Ipalco Enterpr	246,880	543,579	−54.6	71,314
Ispat Intl N.V.	600	148,689	−99.6	221,485
Istituto Mobil	5,000	244,433	−98.0	18,328
Istituto Nazion........	804,991	859,435	−6.3	35,204
ITT Corp..............	864,839	1,038,367	−16.7	1,009,357
ITT Industr (Ind)	653,397	1,012,170	−35.4	234,733
J&L Specialty St......	667,062	696,200	−4.2	52,480
Jefferson-Pilot	1,372,006	854,126	60.6	242,257
JLG Industries	1,846,477	1,723,817	7.1	209,223
John Alden Fin	494,623	512,357	−3.5	173,247
Johnson & Johnson....	7,005,710	7,586,782	−7.7	2,882,361
Johnson Controls	885,097	929,840	−4.8	219,104
Jostens Inc	486,959	341,131	42.7	109,019
JP Foodservice	3,117,091	2,490,956	25.1	88,466
K-III Communcat	453,165	518,599	−12.6	117,052
K2 Inc.	308,600	179,900	71.5	100,361
Kaiser Aluminum	1,020,529	1,315,422	−22.4	356,238
Kansas City Pwr LT ..	620,444	820,878	−24.4	96,485
Kan City SO Ind	s1,534,550	573,097	....	709,900
Kaufman & Broad	805,811	861,265	−6.4	230,128
Kellogg Co.............	7,301,057	7,988,458	−8.6	616,680
Kenneth Cole A	408,255	267,255	52.8	34,223
Kent Electonics.......	652,784	390,099	67.3	159,538
Kerr-McGee Corp	641,101	423,542	51.4	265,652
Keycorp...............	2,600,241	1,891,944	37.4	412,100
Keyspan Ener-Hld	1,100,683	0	....	117,325
Kimberly Clark	5,167,771	4,121,372	25.4	2,088,423
King World Prods	357,659	153,917	132.4	209,804
Kmart Corp	30,444,081	38,076,664	−20.0	2,276,476
Kmart Financ I........	115,619	378,802	−69.5	91,585

were going down; that should be bearish. However, most analysts put an opposite spin on the data. All the uncovered short sales reported for the month have been made and absorbed by the market; they will need to be covered in the future. Thus, an increase in uncovered short sales represents a potential increase in demand, and is a bullish sign.

In some instances, an investor may enter into a short sale by borrowing the stock and selling it although the investor already owns the stock. This is called a **short sale against the box**. (The "box" is a theoretical safe deposit box.) This is primarily a tax maneuver or one designed to hedge against the possibility of a drop in price when for some reason an investor cannot sell his own stock.

Among securities traders, selling shares short while planning to cover in the near future by purchasing shares is as common a market stratagem as purchasing shares while planning to resell them in the near future. Indeed, the terminology of traders suggests equivalence: A trader who owns shares is said to be long, while one who owes shares to the market is said to be short. SEC regulations distinguish between regular security sales from a long position and true short sales in one respect. Aggressive short selling has the capacity to depress a security's price to unrealistically low levels in the short term, particularly in an already declining market. Federal securities law requires that short sales be made only on an **uptick** (i.e., only following a market transaction that was at a higher price than the preceding transaction) or on a **zero uptick** (i.e., only after one or more transactions at a level price if the last previous price movement was an uptick). This provision (dating from the 1930s) is designed to prevent the supposedly depressing effect of sequential short sales.

A similar rule was adopted in 1994 for NASDAQ-listed stocks. This marks a major change in regulatory philosophy from the early 1980s; at that time, there was a movement to repeal the uptick rule in its entirety on the grounds that it restricted the freedom of market forces and was ineffective because the same trading strategy could be achieved by trading in put options (which are discussed in detail in a later chapter).

In 1991, the SEC proposed that short holdings of major investors be disclosed when they exceed 5 percent of the outstanding issue. This proposal, which was not adopted, was in response to an increase in volume of short selling, primarily by securities firms. It has been estimated that some $30 billion in stocks have been sold short, a significant increase from a decade ago. The aggregate of long positions in stocks is approximately $3 trillion. In its proposal to require disclosure of large short positions, the SEC described the following advantages of permitting short selling:

> Short selling provides the market with two important benefits: market liquidity and pricing efficiency. Substantial market liquidity is provided through short selling by market professionals, such as market makers, block positioners, and specialists, who facilitate the operation of the markets by offsetting temporary imbalances in the supply and demand for securities. To the extent that short sales are effected in the market by securities professionals, such short sale activities in effect add to the trading supply of stock available to purchasers and reduce the risk that the price paid by investors is artificially high because of a temporary

contraction of supply. An exchange specialist, for example, is required to maintain price continuity and to minimize the effects of temporary disparities between supply and demand, i.e. to maintain a fair and orderly market. Thus, the specialist may sell short in order to supply stock to satisfy purchase orders. While an over-the-counter ("OTC") market maker is not under the same affirmative obligation to maintain a fair and orderly market, OTC market makers frequently sell short in order to supply stock to fill customers' purchase orders. Similarly, block positioners may provide liquidity in the market through short sales to satisfy large customer purchase orders.

Arbitrageurs contribute to pricing efficiency by utilizing short sales to profit from price disparities between a stock and a derivative security, such as a convertible security or an option on that stock. For example, an arbitrageur may purchase a convertible security and sell the underlying stock short to profit from a current price differential between two economically similar positions. In addition, where an issuer proposes to issue securities (of a class already outstanding) in exchange for the securities of another issuer, pursuant to a merger or exchange offer, arbitrageurs may sell short the security proposed to be issued to hedge their purchases of the security proposed to be acquired.

Short selling also contributes to the pricing efficiency of the equities markets. Efficient markets require that prices fully reflect all buy and sell interest. When a short seller speculates on a downward movement in a security, his transaction is a mirror image of the person who purchases the security based upon speculation that the security's price will rise. Both the purchaser and the short seller hope to profit by buying the security at one price and selling at a higher price—the primary difference being that the sequence of transactions is reversed. Market participants who believe a stock is "overvalued" may engage in short sales in an attempt to profit from the perceived divergence of prices from true economic values. Such short sellers add to stock pricing efficiency because their transactions assure that their perception of future stock price performance (and, inferentially, issuer performance) is reflected in the market price.

Some short selling may be effected for manipulative purposes. (The Commission notes that such manipulative trading practices are prohibited by the general antifraud provisions of the Exchange Act and the rules thereunder.) It appears, however, that historically downward price manipulations have been less frequent than upward manipulations. (Stock market manipulations may involve efforts to achieve an illegal profit by depressing the price of securities through (i) selling activity, including short sales, made for the purpose of inducing the sale of the security by others; or (ii) establishing a short position coupled with publicizing negative, materially misleading statements concerning the issuer.)

§14.18 The Bond Market

Many corporations have outstanding interest-bearing debt that is not due for many years. These publicly held, negotiable securities are technically called **bonds** if the debt is secured or **debentures** if it is unsecured. The term "bond" is typically used, however, to describe both secured and unsecured instruments.

The federal government, state governments, political subdivisions, and governmental agencies such as the Federal National Mortgage Association also issue huge amounts of bonds to finance their activities. The United States Treasury issues notes for maturities of less than 10 years and bonds for longer

maturities. Notes are usually sold by competitive bid at auctions based on yield or interest rate rather than on price. Long-term commercial loans may also be privately negotiated and evidenced by promissory notes rather than negotiable certificates. Most long-term bank loans are of this character. This section, however, deals only with negotiable bonds.

Corporate bonds are issued subject to an **indenture**, which in essence is a loan agreement setting forth the terms of debt securities. Each indenture must comply with strict requirements set forth in the federal securities laws under the jurisdiction of the SEC, and compliance with the indenture is monitored by an **indenture trustee** — usually a bank or trust company — for the benefit of the scattered bondholders.

Before turning to pricing, it is necessary to describe the characteristics of publicly traded debt instruments. Bonds are issued in $1,000 denominations or in multiples of $1,000. Each bond carries with it a right to receive a stated amount of interest every half year (or every full year in some cases). The ratio between this fixed amount and the $1,000 face value is called the **coupon rate**. Historically, bonds were **bearer bonds** (i.e., interest and ultimately principal was payable to whomever possessed the bonds) and the right to receive each semiannual payment was reflected by a coupon attached to the bond; every six months or year the holder would clip off the maturing coupon and submit it for payment. Today, new bonds are issued in **registered** form (i.e., they are **registered bonds**), which means they are issued in the name of a person rather than in bearer form and the interest payments are not represented by negotiable coupons. The issuer simply sends a check to the registered owner periodically for the interest. The Internal Revenue Code (the IRC) now denies an interest deduction to the issuing corporation in connection with bearer bonds, with the result that all bonds are now issued in registered form.

The coupon rate is set when the bond is created and is an integral part of the bond's description. For example, a $1,000 bond that commits the issuer to pay $45 every six months has a coupon rate of 9 percent: $90 per year is 9 percent of the face value of $1,000. This coupon rate is constant for the life of the bond and the bond is usually described as a 9 percent bond.

When bonds are originally issued, the coupon rate is usually fixed at or very close to the then going market interest rate so that the bond initially sells for approximately $1,000. Sales at the **face amount** of the bond are said to be at **par** or at face value. Once the bonds are issued and sold to the public, a market in them develops. As interest rates and risk of nonpayment change, the bonds will fluctuate in price as determined by the market for debt instruments. The market price is unrelated to par or face value. For example, if interest rates are higher than the coupon rate, the bond sells at a discount from par, that is, for less than $1,000. The market price is the price that makes the return that a purchaser of the bond obtains equal the higher market rate of interest. If market interest rates are lower than the coupon rate, the bond sells at a premium, that is, at a price higher than the par value of $1,000.

An illustration may be useful. A small volume of bonds are traded each day on the NYSE and other exchanges. Table 14-8 is an excerpt from the *Wall Street Journal* report of trading for October 30, 1997. The entry "ATT 6s00" means that these are bonds issued by AT&T maturing in the year 2000. The

Table 14-8

NEW YORK EXCHANGE BONDS

Quotations as of 4 p.m. Eastern Time
Thursday, October 30, 1997

Volume $18,787,000

	Domestic Thu.	Domestic Wed.	All Issues Thu.	All Issues Wed.
Issues traded	253	265	261	275
Advances	108	144	109	152
Declines	99	81	106	81
Unchanged	46	40	46	42
New highs	9	9	9	9
New lows	3	1	4	1

SALES SINCE JANUARY 1
(000 omitted)

1997	1996	1995
$18,855,787	$4,715,351	$6,115,682

Dow Jones Bond Averages

–1996– High	–1996– Low	–1997– High	–1997– Low		---1997--- Close	---1997--- Chg.	---1997--- %Yld	--1996-- Close	--1996-- Chg.
106.09	100.99	104.70	101.09	20 Bonds	103.97	– 0.20	7.03	103.16	+ 0.16
102.43	97.46	102.38	97.64	10 Utilities	101.89	+ 0.12	6.99	100.13	+ 0.19
109.94	104.06	107.23	104.54	10 Industrials	106.05	– 0.53	7.06	106.20	+ 0.14

CORPORATION BONDS
Volume, $18,479,000

Bonds	Cur Yld.	Vol.	Close	Net Chg.
ATT 4¾98	4.8	10	99 5/16	+ ⅛
ATT 4⅜99	4.5	26	97⅝	...
ATT 6s00	6.0	235	99¾	– ⅛
ATT 5⅛01	5.3	13	96½	– ¼
ATT 7⅛02	6.9	50	103⅛	– ⅛
ATT 7¾07	7.2	11	107⅞	– ½
ATT 8⅛22	7.8	50	104½	– ¼
ATT 8⅛24	7.8	41	104¼	– 1⅝
ATT 8.35s25	7.7	40	108⅝	– 1⅜
ATT 8⅝31	7.9	130	109	+ 1⅜
Aames 10½02	10.3	85	102	+ 1
AcmeM 12½02	11.6	22	108	– ⅛
AlskAr 6½05	cv	10	149	+ 1
AlskAr 6⅞14	cv	37	106½	– ½
Allwst 7¼14	cv	8	100¼	– ¾
Alza 5s06	cv	40	97½	– 1
AExC 6⅛00	6.1	3	100	+ ¾
Amoco 8⅝16	8.1	20	106⅝	+ 1⅝
Anhr 8⅝16	8.2	10	105	+ ½
AnnTaylr 8¾00	8.8	164	99¾	...
Argosy 12s01	cv	758	87¾	– ½
Argosy 13¼04	13.0	225	102⅛	+ ⅛
AutDt zr12	...	1	63½	– 1½
BkrHgh zr08	...	88	87½	...
BarBks 10⅞03	9.3	5	117½	+ ½
BellPa 7⅛12	7.2	16	99⅛	+ ½
BellPa 7½13	7.4	18	101⅝	– ¼
BellsoT 6½00	6.4	5	101	...
BellsoT 5⅞09	6.1	32	96	+ 1¼
BellsoT 7⅞32	7.5	5	104½	+ ⅝
BellsoT 7½33	7.2	20	103½	+ ⅝
BellsoT 6¾33	7.1	67	95⅛	+ ⅛
BstBuy 8⅝00	8.6	169	100¾	...
BethSt 6⅞99	6.9	2	99½	– ¾
BethSt 8⅜01	8.3	10	101¼	– ¼
BethSt 8.45s05	8.4	59	100½	...
Bevrly 7⅝03	cv	10	101	...
Bevrly 9s06	8.8	10	102½	– 1½
Bluegrn 8¼12	cv	30	94½	+ ½
Bordn 8⅜16	8.1	10	103	+ ¼
BorgWS 9⅛03	9.0	5	102	+ ¼
BoydGm 9¼03	8.9	15	104	– ¾
BrnGp 9½06	9.1	30	104½	+ ½
BwnSh 9¼05	cv	4	102	– 1
CapsCap 6.55s02	cv	50	94	+ ⅞
ChaseM 8s04	7.9	17	101⅞	+ ⅜
ChaseM 7⅞04	7.8	20	101½	– ¼
ChaseM 8s05	7.9	46	101⅜	– ⅛
ChaseM 6¾08	6.8	10	99¼	– ⅞
CPoM 7¼12	7.2	10	101⅛	– ⅞
CPoV 7¼12	7.2	20	100⅝	+ ¼
CPoWas 7¾	7.7	2	100¾	– ¾
ChespkE 9⅛06	8.7	40	104½	+ 1
ChvrnC 9¾17	9.3	132	105	...
ChckFul 7s12	cv	16	102⅛	+ 1⅛
ChryF 13¼99	11.8	19	111⅞	– ¼
ChryF 9½99	9.0	25	106	+ ⅞
Clardge 11¾02f	...	40	96⅝	...
ClrkOil 9½04	9.1	210	104	+ ¼
ClevEl 8¾05	8.6	15	101¾	...
ClevEl 8⅜11	8.1	54	102⅞	+ ⅞
ClevEl 8⅜12	8.2	30	102	...
Coeur 6⅜04	cv	20	88½	+ 1½
CmwE 8s03	7.9	35	101⅝	– ⅜
CmwE 8⅛07J	8.0	10	102	+ ⅞
CompUSA 9½00	9.2	94	103	...
CompMgt 8s03	cv	30	106⅛	+ ⅜
Consec 8⅛03	7.7	45	105½	– 1
CnEn 7½02	7.5	1	100	...
CntlHm 10s06	9.5	15	105	+ ⅞
Convrse 7s04	cv	31	78	– 2
Coty 10¼05	9.8	50	104¾	...
duPnt dc6s01	6.1	65	98⅞	+ ⅛
DukeEn 5⅞01	5.9	10	99⅝	+ ⅞
DukeEn 7s05	7.0	16	100¼	– ⅜
DukeEn 6⅜08	6.5	54	98	+ ⅛
DukeEn 6¾25	7.1	4	94½	+ ½
DukeEn 7s33	7.1	20	98⅛	+ 1
Eckerd 9¼04	8.6	41	107¼	– ⅛
FairCp 12s01	11.8	20	101¾	...
FairCp 13⅛06	12.9	144	101½	+ ⅛
FairCp 13s07	12.5	7	103⅞	+ 1⅞
FedDS 10s01	9.1	5	109⅝	– ⅛
Fldcst 6s12	cv	20	83½	+ 1
FordCr 6⅜08	6.5	103	97⅝	+ ⅞
Ganett 5¼98	5.3	2	99⅝	– ⅜
GEICap 7⅞06	7.2	95	109	– 2⅞
GHost 11½02	11.5	52	99⅝	– ⅛
GHost 8s02	cv	127	84¼	– 1½
GMA 7⅛99	7.1	16	101⅛	+ ⅛
GMA 5.60s99	5.6	40	99⅜	+ ¼
GMA 9⅜00	8.8	1	106⅝	– 1⅜
GMA 7s00	6.9	44	101⅝	+ ½
GMA 5¼01	5.7	5	96⅞	+ ⅝
GMA 7s02	6.9	29	101¼	– ⅝
GMA dc6s11	6.6	15	91¼	+ ¼
GMA zr12	...	2	364½	– ½
GMA zr15	...	20	302⅜	– 3⅛
GenesisH 9¾05	9.3	13	104¾	+ ½
GrandCas 10⅛03	9.5	75	106¼	+ ¾
Hallwd 7s00	7.6	30	92¼	– 1¼
Hallw na13½09B	...	1	99¾	– 3¼
Hlthso 9½01	9.1	11	104¾	...
Hertz 6⅝00	6.6	55	101	+ 1½
Hills 12½03	16.2	80	77	– 1
Hilton 5s06	cv	13	112½	+ 1½
Hollngr 9¼06	9.0	75	103	+ ½
HomeDpt 3¼01	cv	50	125½	– ½
HuntPly 11¾04	10.4	65	113	+ 1
ICN Ph 8½99	cv	1	207	...
ITT Cp 7⅜15	7.6	10	97	...
ITT Cp 7¾25	7.9	170	97⅝	– ¼
IllBel 7⅝06	7.5	7	101	– ¼
IntgHlth 5¾01	cv	1	107¼	– ¾
IBM 6⅜00	6.3	144	100¾	...
IBM 7¼02	7.0	37	104	+ ⅜
IBM 7½13	7.1	20	105⅞	– ⅝
IPap dc5⅛12	6.3	40	81⅝	...
IntShip 9s03	8.8	37	102¾	+ ¾
KaufB 9⅜03	9.2	135	102¼	...
Koppers 8½04	8.1	110	104¾	+ ¼
Leucadia 7¾13	7.5	10	104	+ 2½
LibPrp 8s01	cv	1	132	+ 2
Loews 3⅛07	cv	13	111	– ¼
LglsLt 7.3s99	7.2	25	101¼	+ ⅛
LglsLt 8⅝04	8.4	10	102¼	– ½
LglsLt 8½06	8.4	11	101½	– ¾
LglsLt 8.9s19	8.4	372	105⅝	+ ⅞
LglsLt 9¾21	9.6	46	102	+ ⅛
LglsLt 8.2s23	7.9	160	103⅝	+ ¼
LglsLt 9⅝24	9.4	18	102	...
MacNS 7⅞04	cv	25	100½	...
MarO 7s02	6.9	50	100⅞	– ⅛
Masco 5¼12	cv	8	107	– 1
Mascotch 03	cv	51	87¼	– 2
MerLyStkMk 97	...	25	105⅝	– ⅛
MichB 7¾11	7.7	51	101⅛	– ⅞
MichB 7s12	7.0	6	100¼	+ ¾
MPac 4¼05r	5.0	20	85⅛	– ⅛
Mobil 8⅜01	7.8	40	107⅛	+ ¼
Motrla zr13	...	13	77½	– ½
Nabis 8s00	7.8	10	102¾	– ¼
NatData 5s03	cv	22	99	+ ½
NtEdu 6½11	cv	5	93	– 1
NRut 8½98	8.5	10	100⅜	– ¼
NStl 8⅜06	8.4	23	100	...
Navstr 9s04	8.6	1	104⅜	+ ⅞
NETelTel 6.15s99	6.2	10	99¾	– ¼
NETelTel 6¼03	6.3	15	100	+ ⅛
NETelTel 7⅜07	7.3	18	100¾	...
NJBTl 7¼11	7.2	5	101	+ ¼
NYTel 7¾06	7.6	10	101⅝	...
NYTel 7½09	7.4	15	101⅛	...
NYTel 7s13M	6.9	40	102	– ⅛
NYTel 7⅝23	7.4	15	102⅝	+ ⅛
Noram 6s12	cv	58	89	...
NoPac 3s47r	3.4	15	88	+ 9¼
Novacr 5½2000	cv	16	96	+ ¾
OcciP 10⅛09	8.3	28	122⅛	– 1⅛
OhBIT 7⅞13	7.7	27	102¼	+ ½
OreStl 11s03	10.1	1257	108½	– 1⅝
Oryx 7½14	cv	12	101½	– ½
OwIll 11s03	10.1	10	108½	– ½
PacBell 6¼05	6.3	137	99⅛	+ ⅝
PacBell 6⅞23	7.1	30	96⅞	– ⅛
PacBell 7½33	7.4	64	101¼	...
PacTT 7¼08	7.2	8	101⅛	+ ⅝
ParkElc 5½06	cv	10	95	...
PennTr 9⅝05	15.5	1078	62	– ¼
Pennzl 6½03	3.4	1	194	– 11
Pennzl 4¾03	3.5	2	134	– 2
PhilEl 7⅛23	7.2	10	99	+ 1
PhilEl 7¼24	7.3	80	99	– ½
Primark 8¾00	8.6	137	102	+ ⅛
PSEG 6s00	6.0	33	99½	...
PSEG 6⅞03	6.8	5	100½	+ ⅝
PSvEG 6¾06	6.8	1	100	– 1½
PSEG 7½23	7.5	41	100½	+ ⅛
RJR Nb 8s00	7.9	30	101¾	+ ⅝
RJR Nb 8⅝02	8.2	144	105⅝	– ¼
RJR Nb 7⅝03	7.5	210	101⅛	+ ⅛
RJR Nb 8¾05	8.3	20	105⅛	– ½
RJR Nb 8¾07	8.3	87	106	– ⅛
RJR Nb 9¼13	8.5	25	108¼	– ⅜
RJR Nb 8¾04	8.3	65	105½	+ ½
Rallys 9⅞00	10.1	54	98¼	...
RelGrp 9s00	8.6	93	104¼	+ ¼
Revl 9½99	9.2	218	103⅛	+ ⅛
Rowan 11⅞01	11.4	95	104½	– ⅛
Safwy 9.35s99	9.0	22	104¼	...
Safwy 10s01	9.0	56	111⅛	– ⅛
Safeway 10s02	8.8	84	114	+ 1⅜
Safwy 9.65s04	8.5	23	114	...
Safwy 9⅞07	8.2	10	120	...
Sears 9½99	9.1	8	104½	– ½
Sequa 9⅝99	9.3	20	104	+ 1¼
SvcMer 8⅜01	8.4	10	100	...
SvcMer 9s04	10.7	822	83¾	+ ½
Shoney zr04	...	10	42	+ 2
Showboat 9¼08	9.0	8	103	...
Sizeler 8s03	cv	60	99½	+ ½
SouBell 7⅜10	7.3	13	100⅞	– 1
SouBell 7⅝13	7.5	30	101½	...
SoCG 7½23	7.4	5	101½	+ 1⅞
Southpt 7.1s07	7.3	2	97¼	...
SwBell 6⅝05	6.6	10	101	+ 1⅝
StdCmcl 07	cv	8	91½	+ 1
StdPac 8½07	8.4	10	101	+ ¾
StoneCn 11s99	10.8	140	102⅛	– 1⅜
StoneC 9⅞01	9.7	980	101¾	+ ¼
StoneC 10¾02A	10.6	226	101½	+ ⅜
StoneC 10¾02O	10.1	691	106¾	+ ¼
StoneC 11½04	10.6	77	108	+ 1
SunCo 9⅜16	8.8	4	106⅞	– ¾
TVA 6¼99	6.2	60	100¼	– ⅞
TVA 7.45s01	7.3	5	102⅛	– ¼
TVA 6⅞02	6.8	5	101	...
TVA 6⅞02	6.8	30	101½	+ ⅜
TVA 6⅛03	6.2	51	99⅛	...
TVA 7⅝22	7.4	12	102½	– ⅛
TVA 7¾22	7.5	241	103	...
TVA 8.05s24	7.9	60	102	...
TVA 8⅝29	7.9	370	108⅞	+ ¾
TVA 8¼34	8.1	52	101⅞	– ⅛
TVA 7¼43	7.2	160	101⅛	– ¾
TVA 6⅞43	7.0	95	98	+ 2
TVA 7.85s44	7.4	103	106	+ ⅝

EXPLANATORY NOTES
(For New York and American Bonds)

Yield is Current yield.

cv-Convertible bond. cf-Certificates. cld-Called. dc-Deep discount. ec-European currency units. f-Dealt in flat. il-Italian lire. kd-Danish kroner. m-Matured bonds, negotiability impaired by maturity. na-No accrual. r-Registered. rp-Reduced principal. st, sd-Stamped. t-Floating rate. wd-When distributed. ww-With warrants. x-Ex interest. xw-Without warrants. zr-Zero coupon.

vi-In bankruptcy or receivership or being reorganized under the Bankruptcy Act, or securities assumed by such companies.

Table 14-8 (*cont.*)

Bonds	Cur Yld.	Vol.	Close	Net Chg.
Tenet 8s05	7.8	92	102⅞	– ⅞
Texco 8 1/299J	8.4	10	100¾	+ ¼
TmeWar 7.45s98	7.4	30	100⅛	...
TmeWar 7.95s00	7.8	40	102⅛	– ¾
TmeWar zr13	...	22	48	– ⅛
TollCp 8¾06	8.6	50	101¾	– 1¾
TucEP 7.65s03	7.6	10	100½	...
USX 5¾01	cv	76	97½	+ 1
Viacm 7s03A	7.5	40	93¾	+ ⅝
Viacm 7s03B	7.5	25	93¾	+ ¼
WMX dc2s05	cv	36	82⅞	– 3⅛
Wainoco 12s02	11.4	15	105⅜	+ ⅜
Wainoco 7¾14	cv	18	100	...
Webb 9¾03	9.5	76	102½	+ ¾
Webb 9s06	9.0	61	100¼	– ¼
Webb 9¾08	9.6	884	101¾	– ⅜
Weirton 10⅞99	10.4	30	104½	...
Weirton 10¾05	10.3	8	104¼	– 1⅛
WstbrgC 11s02	10.9	60	100¾	+ ½
WstbrgC 7½04	cv	8	85	– 2
WhlPit 9⅜03	9.2	15	102⅜	– ⅜
WisBl 7¼07	7.2	1	100⅞	+ ⅜
WldColor 9⅛03	8.8	28	104	+ ¼
WldColor 07	cv	63	94	+ ⅞
Wrldcp 7s04	cv	5	65	+ 2
Zenith 6¼11	cv	32	74	– ⅛

FOREIGN BONDS
Volume, $306,000

Inco 7¾16	7.5	131	102¾	– 1¼
TrnMarMx 03	...	16	97½	+ ½
SeaCnt 9½03	9.3	10	102⅝	– ⅜
EmplCA 5s04	...	61	73½	– 3½
Inco cv04	...	6	100½	– 1½
CGDina 8s04	...	25	84	– 2½
TelArg 11⅞04	10.5	5	113¼	– ¾
TrnMarMx 06	...	26	99⅛	– 1⅞

AMEX BONDS

Volume $4,746,000

SALES SINCE JANUARY 1

1997	1996	1995
$321,594,000	$412,263,000	$600,938,000

	Thu.	Wed.	Tue.	Mon.
Issues traded	18	14	25	14
Advances	4	8	9	3
Declines	9	5	13	6
Unchanged	5	1	3	5
New highs	1	0	0	0
New lows	0	0	2	0

Bonds	Cur Yld	Vol	Close	Net Chg.
AdvMd 7¼02	cv	15	93	...
AHaagn 7½01	cv	71	99½	...
AssisLiv cv02	5.5	62	110	+ 2¼
JTS 5¼02	cv	2	37⅝	+ ⅛
MLHK30 99	...	31	101	– 1
SwBell 7¾09	7.6	14	101⅝	...
SwBell 7⅜12	7.4	25	100¼	...
SwBell 7⅝13	7.5	7	101¼	– ⅜
Thrmtrx 3/07	cv	35	100¼	+ ¼
TmeWar zr12	...	5	38	– 1¼
Trump 11¾03f	...	10	97	...
Trump 13⅞05f	...	6	96	+6 15/16
Viacm 9⅛99	9.0	155	101½	– ¼
Viacom 10¼01	9.6	50	107	– ¼
Viacom 8¾01	8.7	90	100⅜	– 1⅜

Bonds	Cur Yld.	Vol.	Close	Net Chg.
Viacom 7¾05	7.9	5	98	– 1
Viacom 8s06	8.1	4143	98⅜	– ½

NASDAQ

Convertible Debentures

Thursday, October 30, 1997

Issue	Vol.	Close	Net Chg.
Agnico 3½04	85	76½	– ¼
Baker 7s02	12	85	– 1
BellSpt 4¼00	45	87⅝	– ⅜
BostChck 4½04	300	73	– 2¼
BostChk zr15	300	21¼	+ ⅛
BostChck 7¾04	2200	83	– 3¾
BoxEngy 8¼02	40	99½	...
CalMicr 5¼03	90	86	– 2
CinFnc 5½02	80	198	+ 3
Convex 6s12	50	97¼	...
DuraPh 3½02	100	113⅝	+ 3⅞
EagleH 6¼01	11	113	– 2
Hechng 5½12	43	39	– 3½
Hexcel 7s11	60	109	– 6
LeasSol 6⅞03	76	92½	+ ¾
MrshSup 7s03	4	107	– ½
OHM 8s06	10	100	+ 3
PhyCor 03	600	93¼	– 8¼
Plat Tech	30	180	...
Synetic 5s07	8	89½	+ 1
SysSftwr 7s02	100	99½	+ ¼
Telxon 7½12	27	106½	+ ½
VLSI 8¼05	25	103½	+ ⅜

coupon rate is 6 percent per year. In other words, the holder of each $1,000 bond receives $60 every year. Trading prices for bonds are quoted without one zero for reasons of space. (The quote may be thought of as a percent of par.) The 6 percent AT&T bond closed at 99¾ or $997.50 for each $1,000 face value bond. How could it be that a bond with a face value of $1,000 and paying $60 annually in interest sells for $997.50? That is the market compensating for the fact that the current market interest rate for a bond with this bond's financial return and risk characteristics is slightly higher than 6 percent.

What is the actual market interest rate for this bond? The column "Cur Yld" (current yield) gives a clue: For the ATT 8⅝31, this column shows an entry of 7.9 percent for the Alabama Power bond. It turns out that the 7.9 percent figure is only an approximation. All interest-bearing bonds have two features. The purchaser who buys the bond is entitled to receive two things: (1) $86.75 every half year from now until the year 2031, and (2) on a specified day in the year 2031, $1,000 in cash. For this combination of two benefits, a purchaser today pays $1,090. The 7.9 percent current yield in the table reflects only the return on $1,090 that the interest payments yield; no account is taken of the fact that in 2031 the holder will also receive $1,000.

The true measure of yield that takes into account both factors is called the **yield to maturity**. The yield to maturity is the interest rate that in a present value calculation would make all the cash payments over the remaining life of a bond—both interest payments and repayment of principal at maturity—equal to the bond's market value.

Calculations of yield to maturity are closely related to present value calculations. The current yield is widely used because (1) it is much easier to calculate than the yield to maturity and (2) when the payment date is far in the future, the difference between the current yield and the yield-to-maturity will rarely be significant. Recall how small the present values of payments due in the distant future are.

The method of calculation of current yield probably explains some apparent anomalies in the table. For example, why does the ATT 6s00 show a current yield of 6.0 percent and price of 99¾ while the ATT 8⅝31 show a current yield of 7.9 percent and a price of 109? Why would the market charge the very same company such different interest rates? The answer is that the 00 bond matures about three years from the date of the quote, while the 31 bond matures in about 34 years. Clearly, the repayment of principal upon maturity is a significant component of value that is ignored by current yield. (Incidentally, the "s" in these designations is simply a place-holder to separate the interest rate from the maturity date. In some older tables, the letter "s" indicated semiannual interest payments.)

Current yield is not shown for convertible bonds that may be exchanged for common stock (or other securities) at a ratio fixed in the bond indenture. Typically, a convertible bond carries a below-market interest rate, because the conversion feature constitutes an added element of return. Thus, it would be misleading to compare the yield, whether current or to maturity, of a convertible bond with that of a nonconvertible bond.

To facilitate price comparisons in active trading in debt securities, traders usually refer to basis points rather than price. A **basis point** is one hundredth of one percent in yield. A price movement of 25 basis points is a change in price equal to a change in the yield to maturity of one quarter of one percent.

When investment grade bonds are bought and sold, it is customary to apportion the interest due as of the date of closing. Bonds that are in default, or are significantly below investment grade, are **dealt in flat**, that is, there is no apportionment of interest and each holder is entitled to any payments received without regard to the period these payments represent.

Most bond trading occurs over-the-counter rather than on the NYSE. The NYSE has a "nine bond rule" that provides that transactions involving more than nine bonds may be executed off the NYSE floor. Thus, the published quotations in Table 14-8 do not reflect the prices at which the vast majority of bond trades actually occurred: Indeed most publicly traded bonds are not even listed on the NYSE, but rather are traded through dealers in an OTC market.

Investments in corporate bonds by individual investors may appear attractive because of their relatively high interest rate and relatively low risk of default. There are, however, potential pitfalls for individual investors. There may be little liquidity where the number of bonds being purchased is small; over-the-counter traders may not be interested in purchasing bonds in units of less than $100,000 of face value (which is considered a round lot for corporate bonds) except at a discount. This risk can usually be avoided by investing in a bond fund. An investment in a bond fund, however, is not precisely equivalent to an investment in a bond, because a bond fund has no maturity date. This difference can be significant as a matter of tax treatment, because the repayment of bond principal

at maturity is tax-free, whereas cashing out a bond fund may not be if there is a gain.

§14.19 Junk Bonds

Junk bonds are bonds that are below investment grade as determined by one or more investment rating services. They have been widely used in recent years to raise very large amounts of capital—billions of dollars in many cases—for takeover bids by outsiders. In these situations, the cash flow that the corporation being acquired generates is usually the source of funds to service the debt represented by the junk bonds. The risk of default is significantly higher with junk bonds than with investment grade securities, ranging from a low of about 0.6 percent in 1994 to a high of 10.3 percent in 1991 after the secondary market for junk bonds collapsed. Nevertheless, junk bonds pay a higher rate of return than investment grade bonds with lower risk on the average than common stocks. Thus, as long as one invests in a diversified portfolio (as one always should), junk bonds may be an appropriate investment even for conservative investors. Indeed, there are many investment funds that specialize in junk bonds, thus allowing even the small investor access to this market.

§14.20 Zero Coupon Bonds

The bonds issued by Motorola shown in Table 14-8 ("Motrla") are examples of **zero coupon bonds**. These are bonds that are issued at deep discounts from par value and do not pay interest. A "zero" issued by Motorola and due in 2013 can be purchased for $775 for a $1,000 bond. The difference represents interest that is in effect paid in a lump sum in 2013 when the bond matures. Because zeros by definition do not pay current interest, there is no current yield.

An individual buying a zero must include in his or her tax return each year the amount of imputed interest payable on the investment although it is not received until maturity. As a result, zeros are attractive investments only for tax-exempt entities, particularly Keogh plans and individual retirement accounts (IRAs) owned by individuals.

Brokerage firms invented zeros by stripping interest-bearing coupons from long-term government bonds and selling the stripped bond and the interest coupons separately. Such securities are known by colorful feline acronyms: certificates of accrual on treasury securities are known as **CATS**, while treasury investment growth receipts are known as **TIGRs**. In response, the United States Treasury decided to issue its own zeros — Separate Trading of Registered Interest and Principal of Securities, or **STRIPS**. Zeros based on government securities are attractive, because there is virtually no risk of nonpayment at maturity. The same cannot be said for corporate zeros, such as those issued by Allied Chemical Corporation.

Zeros that are publicly traded fluctuate in price in response to changes in interest rates and are very volatile. For example, a 20-year bond selling at par might be stripped of its coupons and be sold at $146 per $1,000 bond to yield

9.55 percent to maturity. If the price of the unstripped bond rises from $1,000 to $1,010, the price of the stripped zero would rise about $28, or a price increase of nearly 20 percent over the original $146 price.

Deep discount bonds are similar to zeros except that they pay current interest rates well below effective market interest rates. The discount may arise either because the bond was issued with a coupon rate below the market rate (in which case the discount is called original issue discount and carries the adverse tax consequences described above) or because the market rate for a bond of comparable risk has risen since the bond was issued (in which case the discount is called market discount and income tax is payable only when the difference is received). When a bond trades at a discount because the default risk has increased since issuance, the bond is sometimes called a **fallen angel**.

§14.21 Short-Term Debt

Some short-term debt obligations do not involve a separate payment of interest by the borrower. Rather, the borrower simply agrees to pay a specific amount—say, $10,000 in 30 days—and then sells this obligation at whatever price it can get at an auction or by a negotiated sale. A person may buy such an obligation for, say $9,930. The $70 difference in price is the interest. The effective interest rate for the 30-day period is a little less than 8 percent per year. That interest is computed by comparing the amount invested ($9,930) and the interest earned ($70). Rather confusingly, interest rates on transactions of this type are often quoted as the percentage the discount bears to the face amount—$70 as a fraction of $10,000 rather than as a fraction of $9,930. The difference is usually not great, but the latter quotation slightly understates the true rate of interest on the investment. Quoted interest rates on short-term discounted debt are usually annualized for convenience of making comparisons. This effective annual interest rate is sometimes called the **coupon-equivalent yield**, the **bond-equivalent yield**, or the **investment yield**. The calculation normally reported (that compares the interest received to the face amount of the bill) is usually called the **discount rate**.

The United States government is a major issuer of debt instruments at a discount. The United States Treasury issues discount instruments—known as **Treasury bills** (also called **T-bills** or simply bills)—with maturities as short as three months. Large volumes of discounted bills due in six months or one year are also sold each month. The minimum purchase is $10,000 of face value and a round lot is $5,000,000 of face value. These instruments are viewed as entirely riskless and the price is established solely on the basis of market interest rates in the economy. The higher the interest rates, the greater the discount and, hence, the lower the price a $10,000 bill would command.

Secondary markets in discounted securities are made by securities dealers in all maturities of Treasury issues so that holders may sell securities before they mature. This secondary market also enables persons to make investments in these short-term interests at times when the Treasury is not making a direct offering in the primary market. New issues may be purchased directly from the United States Treasury without payment of any commissions or fees through

the Treasury Direct program. The price and yields are established by auctions that the government conducts on a regular basis. Information about this program may be obtained from the nearest Federal Reserve Bank or directly from the Treasury's Bureau of the Public Debt.

Short-term discounted instruments are also sold by state and local governments, corporations, and other entities. Corporate short term debt is often called **commercial paper**.

§14.22 Municipal Bonds

Bonds issued by states, municipalities, and state-created taxing authorities are called municipal bonds. They are attractive investments primarily because interest on them is exempt from federal income taxation. Because of this tax-exempt feature, municipals carry significantly lower interest rates than taxable bonds of the same risk.

Some municipals that a specific state issues may also be exempt from state income taxes as well as from municipal income taxes. These bonds are sometimes referred to as **double tax exempt** or **triple tax exempt** bonds. Such bonds should normally be purchased only by persons who can take full advantage of the multiple tax exemptions.

In the Tax Reform Act of 1986, Congress restricted the purposes for which municipal bonds that are entitled to federal tax exemption may be used. Because the tax exemption is an important part of the value of municipals, it is important to obtain reliable advice as to the tax status of specific municipals before any investment is made.

Tax-exempt municipal bonds are predominantly investments for the affluent taxpayer in high tax brackets. As with corporate bonds, the small investor should normally invest in municipals through a mutual fund. Many such funds are structured to offer double and triple tax exempt status to investors in particular states.

§14.23 Risk in Fixed-Income Investments

There are four basic types of risks with fixed-income investments:

1. *Interest rate risk*. If interest rates rise, the value of bonds and fixed-income investments go down. The worst thing to do is to buy long-term fixed-income investments at the low point in the interest rate cycle. One minimizes interest rate risk by purchasing short term and avoiding long term securities. For example, a bond with a 7 percent coupon purchased at par ($1,000) will decline by the following amounts with a one percent rise in interest rates:

> A 3-year bond will decline to $973.80
> A 5-year bond will decline to $959.40
> A 7-year bond will decline to $947.20
> A 10-year bond will decline to $932
> A 30-year bond will decline to $886.90

In general, yields and interest rates are higher for bonds with longer maturities. For example, in November 1996, 30-year Treasury bonds yielded 6.65 percent, whereas a bond maturing in November 1997 yielded 5.52 percent. But the longer a bond's maturity, the greater its price volatility.

A stripped treasury—a treasury bond that has been converted into a zero coupon bond by selling off the stream of interest payments is sold at a substantial discount to reflect the yield. The yield to maturity of a regular treasury — a treasury bond that still carries the right to interest payments — is calculated on the assumption that future interest payments are invested at a constant rate. Of course, future interest rates are not stable. Variations in the differences between the yields to maturity of zero treasuries and regular treasuries may therefore reflect a market estimate of the future trends in interest rates. If it is believed that rates are likely to go down, the yield to maturity of the zero should be slightly above the yield to maturity of the interest-bearing treasury, and vice versa, if it is expected that interest rates are likely to rise.

In the early 1990s, there was a spectacular decline in the interest rates paid on all kinds of interest-bearing deposits, **certificates of deposit (CDs)**, and fixed-income investments. In the late 1980s, six-month CDs might have paid interest at the rate of 7 percent or even more in some instances; by 1991, rates had declined to 5 percent, and a year later had declined to between 2 and 3 percent. These very low rates made fixed-income investments unattractive and made equity investments more attractive. Billions of dollars of maturing CDs were not renewed, with money often placed temporarily in interest-bearing demand deposits and then moved to alternative uninsured investments—stocks, bonds, mutual funds, and annuities—that offer a higher yield. This trend out of CDs became so strong that many banks set up in-house brokerage services in an effort to capture the funds represented by maturing CDs. Although these brokerage firms may be closely affiliated with specific banks, the investments that they offer are traditional mutual funds and the like, which are both uninsured and more risky than the CDs in which the funds were previously invested.

2. *Credit risk.* There is a danger that companies issuing fixed income securities will default and be unable to pay off the securities when they mature. There may also be a credit risk in high-rate municipal bonds. Credit risk does not necessarily involve actual default. Any change in the economic terms of a debt security that increases the risk of default causes a decline in the security's market price. This, too, is credit risk.

A good example involved a proposal by Marriott Corporation in 1992 to divide into two different corporations: Marriott International, Inc. which would manage Marriott's vast hotel chain, and Host Marriott Corporation, which would own Marriott real esate. Most of the Marriott long-term debt would be assumed by Host Marriott Corporation, while Marriott International, Inc., would receive a significant fraction of Marriott's current cash flow, but would assume virtually none of Marriott's outstanding long-term debt. On the day of the announcement, Marriott's 10 percent bonds maturing in 2012, which Marriott had sold to investors just six months earlier, declined in price from 110 to 80, a loss of $300 for each bond with a face amount of $1,000. Standard & Poor's Corporation announced that it would lower the credit rating of the

Marriott bonds if the division occurred. Even though this transaction was not prohibited by any covenant in the bond indentures, the uproar and litigation that followed this proposal were so substantial that Marriott found it necessary to make significant changes in the proposed corporate split. Litigation was based on the argument that Marriott withheld relevant information when the bonds had been sold six months earlier. The indenture trustee for one bond issue resigned; Merrill Lynch withdrew as an adviser to Marriott, apparently because of concern that in the future, institutional investors would not purchase debt securities underwritten by Merrill Lynch if Merrill Lynch was associated with the Marriott plan. Even though Marriott's plan did not succeed as first formulated, it reveals the limited value of standard covenants designed to protect bondholders against credit risk. It also reveals, however, that bondholders are not without some political pressure of their own.

Credit risk also exists in the case of debt securities that foreign governments issue (e.g., Russian bonds issued before 1917) or by state or municipal governments. Although defaults on government obligations are relatively rare, the risk nevertheless exists.

Credit risk is usually measured through one or more rating companies that estimate the risk involved in investing in specific debt instruments and then "rate" the investment, using a code consisting of alphabetical (or alphabetical and numerical) ratings. The two principal rating systems and their codes for fixed-income investments are set forth in the following table:

	Moody's	S&P
Highest quality	Aaa	AAA
High grade	Aa	AA
Upper medium grade	A	A
Medium grade	Baa	BBB
Speculative	Ba	BB
Uncertain position	B	B
Poor	Caa	CCC
Speculative to a high degree	Ca	CC
Extremely poor prospects	C	C
In default	—	D

Moody's applies numerical modifiers — 1, 2, and 3 — in the generic classifications Aa through B; 1 indicates that the security ranks at the higher end of the rating category, while 3 indicates that the issue ranks at the lower end. Standard and Poor's uses a plus (+) or minus (−) for ratings of AA through CCC to provide further gradations of quality within a specific grade. High-quality bonds are generally rated AAA through AA in Standard and Poor's, while medium quality bonds are ranked as A through BBB. Junk or high-yield bonds are assigned ratings of BB through C, if they are rated at all.

3. *Prepayment risk.* The issuer may refinance high interest rate obligations for the same reason that a homeowner decides to refinance a mortgage. Hence, a security that does not have a significant credit risk but is paying attractive rates should be examined closely to make sure that the obliger cannot call or prepay the obligation.

The most common mistake unsophisticated bond buyers make is to buy a

bond on the basis of yield but without regard to callability. In times of low interest rates (e.g., the early 1990s), the most reliable and conservative indication of value is **yield to call**, that is, the yield until the time before maturity that the bonds may be redeemed (if any), because high coupon bonds will almost certainly be called as soon as legally possible. For example, in 1991, the prepayment rates on mortgage-backed securities issued by the Federal National Mortgage Association jumped to 17.36 percent from 7.67 percent in 1990. The yields of these funds, which in earlier years were well over 12 percent, thus declined as high rate mortgages were refinanced and replaced by lower rate mortgages.

The general rule of thumb is that if an older bond has a coupon rate 1.5 percent above a new bond, the odds are strong that the old bond will be called in a transaction financed by the issue of new bonds. The United States Treasury stopped issuing callable bonds in 1985. Municipal bonds typically have an optional call beginning 10 years after the issue date. They may also contain an extraordinary call provision if they were issued to finance a project such as housing, which may be paid off early. Municipals often pay $1,020 for each $1,000 of face value when called, except that extraordinary calls pay at par. Corporate bonds are usually callable.

4. *Currency risk.* Investors who consider high returns available from investments in foreign countries should take into account the possibility that foreign currencies might be devalued, with the consequence that a portion of the investment may be lost. Mexico treasury bills may yield 15 percent, for example, but if the peso is devalued, as it has been in the past, there will be an automatic reduction in the value of the principal of the investment that may well eclipse any gain from the high yield. That is currency risk.

CHAPTER 15

INVESTMENT STRATEGIES FOR THE SMALL INVESTOR

§15.1 Introduction

This chapter focuses on investing. Investing must be distinguished from trading. To be sure, there are many traders who make a living (or try to) from buying and selling — but not holding — securities and other financial instruments. Moreover, trading is important to investors, because investors must use the trading markets to build a portfolio of investments and to adjust that portfolio from time to time as new money is invested, or as investments are cashed out, or simply to keep the portfolio in balance as some investments rise and others fall in value. Thus, an investor will care very much about getting the best price on any individual trade. But an investor cares mostly about longer-term risk and return.

This chapter first addresses the general topics of diversification and risk. It

then describes a variety of investment companies and other investment vehicles that offer investors a prepackaged diversified portfolio of investments at various levels of risk. These include closed-end funds, open-end funds (known as mutual funds), unit investment trusts, real estate investment trusts, and hedge funds. The chapter then discusses various short-term funds and nonequity investments, including money market funds. Next, the chapter addresses a variety of issues that arise when one chooses to manage one's own investments rather than investing through professionally managed funds, including when one should consider such a strategy, dealings with brokerage houses, and the use of investment advisers. Finally, the chapter considers some of the special issues that arise for individuals who have received stock options as part of their compensation.

§15.2 Risk and Diversification

There are many different investment strategies for the small investor. It is assumed in this discussion that the typical small investor is relatively **risk averse**. That is, the investor is not willing to take large risks simply because the expected return is higher than with less risky investments. In most of the strategies described below, the investor's goal is to obtain a better return, either in the form of income or capital appreciation, than can be obtained from a riskless or virtually riskless investment. Obviously, one needs first to establish investment objectives and then make investments that are consistent with those objectives. Plausible investment goals include:

1. *Preservation of assets.* When safety is the most important concern, one may simply invest the entire amount in money market accounts, insured bank money market accounts or certificates of deposit, and short-term United States Treasury securities. The specific selection may depend on relative yields and the likelihood that the investor may require access to funds in the near future.

2. *Income.* When the primary goal is to earn investment income at minimal risk to principal, one might choose mutual funds concentrating in longer-term government securities, municipal bonds, quality corporate bonds, and high-income stocks such as utilities and blue chips (both domestic and foreign). One might also consider investing a portion of the principal in limited partnership interests investing in positive cash-flow-producing types of real estate investments.

3. *Growth.* When a person is willing to take a greater risk of loss of assets in exchange for the possibility of greater growth of principal assets, one might choose mutual funds that emphasize capital appreciation (although the performance of many of these funds historically has been disappointing) or direct investments in common stocks and real estate investments.

4. *Aggressive growth.* When a person is willing to assume a high risk of asset depreciation in exchange for higher growth or speculative increase in asset value, one might choose developmental projects such as real estate, investing either through stock or by direct purchases. One might also invest in stocks that are rumored to be candidates for takeover bids.

In general terms, the greater the risk of an investment, the higher its return

must be. In investing, there is no such thing as a free lunch. Markets generally price investments efficiently; an investment that has a significantly higher yield than another must, somewhere, carry with it some additional element of risk. This is neatly illustrated by Table 15-1, which graphs the relationship between risk and return for the most common classes of investments.

Once an investor has determined the level of risk he or she desires, it is important to invest in a diversified portfolio of investments at that level of risk. That does not necessarily mean, however, that one must construct a portfolio of only investments that individually carry the desired risk and return combination. For example, if one puts half of one's portfolio in stocks (with a historical return of about 10 percent over the long haul) and half in government securities (with a historical return of zero percent after inflation), the blended return on the entire portfolio can be expected to be about 5 percent after inflation. Thus, while the investor has reduced the risk of the portfolio, it has been at the sacrifice of return. An investor who invests in an all-stock portfolio takes on more risk, but it is the level of risk that must be assumed to achieve (say) a 10 percent return.

Diversification largely eliminates the risk of massive losses because a single investment performs poorly, but it does not provide protection against a market-wide decline in values. With a diversified portfolio of as few as 20 stocks, an investor can enjoy the same rate of return as with an investment in a single stock while avoiding as much as 90 percent of the risk that goes with an investment

Table 15-1

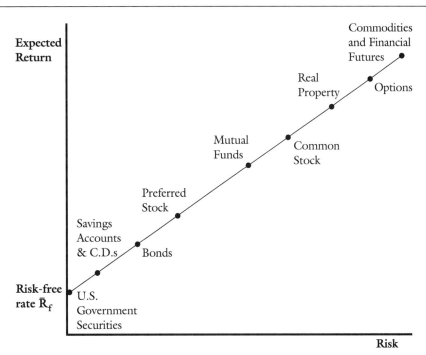

in a single stock portfolio. No investor should take more risk than necessary for a given level of return. Thus, it makes no sense for an investor to put all of his or her eggs in one basket. (Indeed the law of trusts has long recognized that a trustee who fails to diversify may be held liable to the trust.)

Although such exotic-sounding ideas as the efficient capital market hypothesis (ECMH) and modern portfolio theory may seem to be more of academic interest than of practical value, they actually have profound implications even for the small investor. Simply stated, the ECMH holds that it is impossible to beat the market consistently on the basis of publicly available information. The evidence supporting this proposition is overwhelming, although the theory does have its limitations as discussed more fully in the chapters on mergers and acquisitions and trading in stocks and bonds. It is important to understand that the ECMH does not mean that one cannot make money investing in stocks or other securities. Rather, it means that one can only expect to make a market rate of return.

Although an investor can reduce risk significantly by choosing 10 or 20 stocks or other securities even at random, there has emerged a large body of learning, known as **modern portfolio theory** (**MPT**), about how diversification works and how portfolios should be structured for maximum risk-reduction effect. MPT implies that an investor can eliminate company-specific risk. In other words, a well-diversified investor takes only the risk that the market as a whole will rise or fall. One important insight that comes from MPT is that because it is possible to eliminate company-specific risk, securities are priced in the market as if such risk were not present. In other words, the market pays no additional return to investors who bet heavily on individual companies, that is, investors who engage in stock-picking strategies. This is not to say that one cannot win big with such a strategy. Rather, it is only to say that unless one has reliable inside information, the odds are longer than the prize is worth.

Taken together, these theories suggest that it makes no sense for the small investor (or perhaps even the large investor) to try to predict the performance of individual companies or even the market as a whole. All that an investor should do is choose the level of risk or return desired and invest in a well-diversified portfolio of instruments bearing that risk. (One need only focus on one or the other measure, because the ECMH implies that instruments of comparable risk will be priced to yield comparable returns.) In other words, these theories taken together strongly suggest that an investor should buy and hold.

Risk is a slippery concept. The critical reader will have noticed that the idea that stocks return 10 percent over the long haul seems inconsistent with the idea that they are riskier. The answer to this seeming paradox is that risk is a time-sensitive concept. Even a diversified portfolio may have considerable risk over a period of 1 or 2 years, but much less risk over a period of 20 years. If the market on the average is focusing on (say) a 5-year risk horizon, an investor who is willing to hold for a longer period assumes less risk, although that does not necessarily guarantee the historical rate of return.

Diversification has sometimes also been applied at the company level as a matter of business strategy. Some businesspeople figure that if it makes sense for an investor to diversify, then it also makes sense for a company to do the

same thing in order to smooth out its earnings. That is not necessarily so. Investors can easily assemble a portfolio of companies making various products and thus hold precisely the constellation of businesses that they desire to hold. Similar acquisitions and divestitures are very expensive at the company level. Moreover, they result in a company that offers prepackaged diversification that may appeal only to limited numbers of investors. (It is like a package in a supermarket containing a banana and an apple; a few may be interested in buying both, but many will prefer other combinations.) Finally, diversification may ultimately distract management from its task of doing the best possible job managing the company's operations. It stands to reason that a CEO faced with running two or more unrelated operations will have less time to focus on each. All this is not to say that there is no such thing as synergy in business. Rather, it is only to say that synergy and diversification are two different things. Similar arguments can be made about many firm-level strategies involving the purchase and sale of derivative instruments. They may be designed to hedge against risks that diversified investors have already hedged against. Thus, reducing risk at the firm level may lead to a drop in a stock's market price rather than an increase.

A small investor may not be able to diversify effectively by purchasing small amounts of different publicly traded securities that different companies issue. The trading units for round lots may be too large for effective investment of small amounts of funds. And extra commissions charged on odd lot transactions make that alternative unattractive. In some cases, a small investor may be able to construct a sufficiently large portfolio by buying on margin, as explained in Chapter 14, the chapter that discusses trading in stocks and bonds. There is, however, a very easy way to achieve diversification with an investment of as little as $1,000 in some cases by investing in one or more investment companies or mutual funds. The following sections describe a number of such investments available to small investors.

§15.3 Investment Companies

An **investment company** is a corporation or other entity that invests in securities of other corporations. An investment company therefore has at any given time a portfolio of securities and usually some cash or cash-equivalent assets awaiting investment. Investment companies are themselves entities that issue shares. (Many investment companies are organized as Massachusetts business trusts or as Maryland corporations.) Investors may purchase these shares and thereby obtain instant diversification, because the shares that an investment company issues in effect constitute investment in the portfolio owned by the investment company. Because the value of the investment company's portfolio is known, it is also relatively easy to determine the net asset value of each share of the investment company's stock. One simply values all the holdings in the investment company's portfolio and divides by the number of outstanding shares. A mutual fund is one type of investment company, but there are many others.

Not all companies that invest in securities are investment companies. If a company invests exclusively in controlling interests in several operating companies and itself has no other business, it is called a holding company. A company

that has business operations and also invests free cash in securities is not an investment company either, as long as its earnings are primarily attributable to its business orperations and not its investments. If an investment company is closely held by a few shareholders, it may be deemed to be a **personal holding company** for tax purposes. The investment companies described in the balance of this chapter are primarily publicly held companies. Publicly held investment companies are subject to a substantial degree of regulation by the Securities and Exchange Commission (the SEC) under the Investment Company Act of 1940. Some investment companies limit themselves to fewer than 100 investors or to only investors with a net worth of more than $3,000,000 in order to be exempt from SEC regulation. Such funds are called **hedge funds** and are discussed briefly below.

The investment goals of a publicly held investment company—the objective of its portfolio activities — are publicly stated. They may be to maximize long-term capital appreciation, to maximize current income, to invest in a diversified portfolio of public utility stocks, to invest in long-term investment grade bonds, or some combination of these. Investment companies generally do not seek controlling positions; most are diversified investors that limit their investments in portfolio companies to a small fraction (usually less than 5 percent) of the voting shares of each portfolio company.

Investment companies earn profits from two principal sources: trading profits from buying and selling portfolio securities and dividends or interest from investments. Investment companies that distribute substantially all of their earnings each year to shareholders are not themselves subject to tax. Rather, they are conduits whose income (e.g., capital gain, tax-exempt municipal bond interest) is passed through to the shareholders. Thus, an investor who seeks only tax-exempt municipal bond income may invest in an investment company that invests only in such bonds, and the dividends that the shareholder receives are exempt from income tax to the extent they represent interest on tax-exempt municipal bonds. Management fees are subtracted from income prior to their distribution to shareholders and are not separately itemized in the distribution process.

An investment company itself has shareholders. It must hold shareholders' meetings, elect directors and officers, and so forth. Most investment companies contract with a brokerage firm or investment banker to obtain investment advice for a fee: The brokerage firm or investment banker may also handle share transfer and other related costs of the investment company operation. Of course, fees are also charged for these services.

Publicly held investment companies are broken down into two broad categories discussed in the following sections: closed-end companies and open-end companies. Open-end companies are usually called mutual funds.

§15.4 Closed-End Investment Companies

Closed-end companies are the oldest type of investment companies. Their unique characteristic is that they have outstanding a fixed number of their own

shares that are traded either on a securities exchange or over the counter. Closed-end funds lost their popularity as a result of the collapse of securities prices in the 1930s, but in the last few years a number of new closed-end funds have been created. Many of these new closed-end funds concentrate in foreign securities of specific countries. Closed-end companies are also known as publicly traded funds, because their shares are listed on securities exchanges or traded in the over-the-counter (OTC) market like any other securities.

An investor who decides to invest in a closed-end fund simply places an order with a broker to purchase the desired number of shares in the market in which the shares of the closed-end company are traded. A shareholder who decides to liquidate his or her interest in the closed-end company places an order to sell the shares in the appropriate market. In either event, investing in a closed-end fund or disposing of such an investment involves merely the payment of standard brokerage fees for executing the transactions. Table 15-2 taken from the *Wall Street Journal* shows prices for numerous closed-end funds.

The market price for shares issued by closed-end investment companies fluctuates according to market conditions, and may be either higher or lower than the net asset value of the shares. Shares of a closed-end fund are said to trade at a discount if the market price for its shares is less than the net asset value per share. Closed-end fund shares are said to trade at a premium if the market price of the fund shares is higher than the net asset value.

The attractiveness of many closed-end funds is that they sometimes trade at deep discounts from net asset value. If the discount narrows, an investor may have a substantial paper profit that is not based on a change in the net asset value of the fund shares. On the other hand, many closed-end companies trade at discounts over long periods, and a seemingly advantageous investment may turn out disadvantageous if the discount remains stable or increases.

Illustrative of the trading markets for closed-end funds are the tactics that professional traders typically follow. Basically, they "play" the discount, buying when the discounts widen and selling or short-selling when the discounts narrow or when prices creep up so that the shares are trading at a premium over net asset value. One experienced trader suggests the following trading strategy: One should buy when (1) the discount is 75 percent greater than the average discount over the previous six months and (2) the discount exceeds 3 percent for a balanced fund, 5 percent for a junk bond fund, and 10 percent for a country fund.

Several new closed-end funds have been launched in recent years. Experience demonstrates that it rarely pays to subscribe to a brand new issue of a closed-end fund at net asset value. After a period of price stabilization at or above the issue price (during which the issue is marketed), the fund shares are permitted to seek their own level in the market, which usually is significantly less than net asset value. Investors that originally subscribed suffer the loss caused by the market's discounting of the shares. On the other hand, a number of new country-oriented or region-oriented closed-end funds consistently traded at significant premiums over net asset value.

Table 15-2
Mutual Fund Quotations

CLOSED-END FUNDS

Friday, October 31, 1997

Closed-end funds sell a limited number of shares and invest the proceeds in securities. Unlike open-end funds, closed-ends generally do not buy their shares back from investors who wish to cash in their holdings. Instead, fund shares trade on a stock exchange. The following list, provided by Lipper Analytical Services, shows the ticker symbol and exchange where each fund trades (A: American; C: Chicago; N: NYSE; O: Nasdaq; T: Toronto; z: does not trade on an exchange). The data also include the fund's most recent net asset value, its closing share price on the day NAV was calculated, and the percentage difference between the market price and the NAV (often called the premium or discount). For equity funds, the final column provides 52-week returns based on market prices plus dividends. For bond funds, the final column shows the past 12 months' income distributions as a percentage of the current market price. Footnotes appear after a fund's name. a: the NAV and market price are ex dividend. b: the NAV is fully diluted. c: NAV, market price and premium or discount are as of Thursday's close. d: NAV, market price and premium or discount are as of Wednesday's close. e: NAV assumes rights offering is fully subscribed. v: NAV is converted at the commercial Rand rate. w: Convertible Note-NAV (not market) conversion value. y: NAV and market price are in Canadian dollars. All other footnotes refer to unusual circumstances; explanations for those that appear can be found at the bottom of this list. N/A signifies that the information is not available or not applicable.

Fund Name (Symbol)	Stock Exch	NAV	Market Price	Prem /Disc	52 week Market Return
General Equity Funds					
Adams Express (ADX)	♣N	28.63	23¹³/₁₆	− 16.8	26.7
Alliance All-Mkt (AMO)	N	31.24	30¹/₁₆	− 3.8	68.1
Avalon Capital (MIST)	O	13.74	13	− 5.4	18.2
Baker Fentress (BKF)	♣N	24.05	20¹/₁₆	− 16.6	21.5
Bergstrom Cap (BEM)	A	156.35	139	− 11.1	26.0
Blue Chip Value (BLU)	♣N	10.08	10⁹/₁₆	+ 4.8	33.9
Central Secs (CET)	A	29.96	31⁵/₈	+ 5.6	33.8
Corp Renaissance (CREN)-c	O	7.33	4⁷/₈	− 33.5	−38.1
Engex (EGX)	A	13.65	10¹/₈	− 25.8	−9.0
Equus II (EQS)	♣A	31.39	22⁷/₁₆	− 28.5	48.0
Gabelli Equity (GAB)	N	11.28	10⁹/₁₆	− 6.4	25.0
General American (GAM)	♣N	30.76	26¹/₂	− 13.8	27.4
Librty AllStr Eq (USA)	♣N	13.51	13	− 3.8	29.7
Librty AllStr Gr (ASG)	♣N	12.79	12³/₁₆	− 4.7	46.7
MFS Special Val (MFV)	N	15.03	19	+ 26.4	19.6
Morgan FunShares (MFUN)-c	O	11.86	10³/₄	− 9.4	26.5
Morgan Gr Sm Cap (MGC)	♣N	14.03	13	− 7.3	39.7
NAIC Growth (GRF)-c	C	10.63	16⁷/₁₆	+ 54.6	69.9
Royce Value (RVT)	♣N	17.71	15¹/₂	− 12.5	37.2
Royce,5.75 '04Cv-w	N	136.86	116³/₁	− 15.0	21.8
Salomon SBF (SBF)	N	20.05	18¹/₄	− 9.0	28.7
Source Capital (SOR)	N	51.46	48¹/₁₆	− 6.5	30.9
Tri-Continental (TY)	♣N	33.93	27³/₄	− 18.2	24.1
Zweig (ZF)	♣N	12.09	12¹/₄	+ 1.3	22.3
Specialized Equity Funds					
C&S Realty (RIF)	♣A	11.97	12¹/₈	+ 1.3	22.5
C&S Total Rtn (RFI)	♣N	18.70	17¹³/₁₆	− 4.7	23.4
Centrl Fd Canada (CEF)-ac	♣A	4.07	3⁷/₈	− 4.8	−16.0
Delaware Gr Div (DDF)	N	17.73	17³/₄	+ 0.1	15.8
Delaware Grp GI (DGF)	N	16.96	17¹⁵/₁₆	+ 5.8	20.5
Duff&Ph Util Inc (DNP)-a	N	8.92	9¹²/₁₆	+ 10.0	24.4
Emer Mkts Infra (EMG)	♣N	N/A	11³/₄	N/A	11.4
Emer Mkts Tel (ETF)	♣N	N/A	15¹⁵/₁₆	N/A	6.9
First Financial (FF)	N	20.72	22¹/₁₆	+ 6.5	68.1
Gabelli GI Media (GGT)	N	9.98	8¹/₈	− 18.6	25.9
H&Q Health Inv (HQH)	♣N	21.62	17¹/₈	− 20.8	20.9
H&Q Life Sci Inv (HQL)	♣N	17.65	14⁵/₁₆	− 18.9	11.0
INVESCO GI Hlth (GHS)	♣N	21.37	17⁵/₁₆	− 19.0	29.1
J'Han Bank (BTO)	♣N	N/A	42⁹/₁₆	N/A	57.8
J'Han Pat Globl (PGD)	♣N	N/A	12⁹/₁₆	N/A	8.9
J'Han Pat Sel (DIV)	♣N	N/A	15¹/₈	N/A	11.9
Nations Bal Tgt (NBM)	N	11.42	9¹⁵/₁₆	− 13.0	21.3
Petroleum & Res (PEO)	♣N	44.11	40¹/₄	− 8.8	24.3
Royce Micro-Cap (OTCM)	♣O	11.93	10⁷/₈	− 8.8	44.8
SthEastrn Thrift (STBF)	♣O	N/A	23³/₄	N/A	69.7
Thermo Opprtunty (TMF)	A	12.26	10³/₄	− 12.3	−24.8

Fund Name (Symbol)	Stock Exch	NAV	Market Price	Prem /Disc	52 week Market Return
Clemente Global (CLM)-c	N	11.82	9³/₁₆	− 22.3	21.1
Czech Republic (CRF)	N	15.33	12	− 21.7	−5.7
Dessauer Glbl Eq (DGE)	N	11.34	11³/₈	+ 0.3	N/A
Economic Inv Tr (EVT)-cy	T	158.61	106¹/₂	− 32.9	43.9
Emer Mkts Grow (N/A)	z	59.83	N/A	N/A	N/A
Emerging Mexico (MEF)-c	N	11.86	9	− 24.1	34.8
Europe (EF)	♣N	20.72	16¹/₂	− 20.4	11.5
European Warrant (EWF)-c	N	N/A	16⁷/₈	N/A	65.9
F&C Middle East (EME)-c	N	21.33	17¹/₂	− 18.0	41.4
Fidelity Em Asia (FAE)	♣N	11.59	9³/₄	− 15.9	−26.7
Fidelty Ad Korea (FAK)	♣N	4.84	4¹³/₁₆	− 0.6	−52.8
First Australia (IAF)	A	9.35	7⁷/₁₆	− 20.5	−15.8
First Israel (ISL)	♣N	N/A	13	N/A	23.8
First Philippine (FPF)	N	8.18	8⁷/₁₆	+ 3.1	−36.4
France Growth (FRF)	N	13.86	11¹/₁₆	− 20.2	17.3
GT Glbl Estn Eur (GTF)	N	18.62	16³/₈	− 12.1	31.5
Germany Fund (GER)	♣N	17.47	14⁵/₁₆	− 18.1	24.2
Germany, Emer (FRG)	♣N	12.65	10⁵/₈	− 16.0	37.4
Germany, New (GF)	♣N	18.73	14¹⁵/₁₆	− 20.2	22.4
Global Small Cap (GSG)	A	16.79	12⁷/₈	− 23.3	17.1
Growth Fd Spain (GSP)	♣N	17.99	15¹/₂	− 13.8	36.1
Herzfeld Caribb (CUBA)	♣O	6.52	5⁷/₁₆	− 16.6	13.2
India Fund (IFN)	N	9.29	8¹/₄	− 11.2	20.2
India Growth (IGF)-dp	N	11.75	10¹/₈	− 13.8	−10.3
Indonesia (IF)-o	♣N	N/A	7³/₈	N/A	−16.9
Irish Inv (IRL)	N	19.98	15³/₄	− 21.2	17.7
Italy (ITA)	N	12.30	9¹/₂	− 22.8	18.1
Jakarta Growth (JGF)	N	4.74	5⁵/₈	+ 18.7	−29.0
Japan Equity (JEQ)-c	♣N	6.99	7³/₈	+ 5.5	−22.6
Japan OTC Equity (JOF)	N	5.41	5⁷/₁₆	+ 0.5	−27.0
Jardine Fl China (JFC)	♣N	N/A	10⁵/₁₆	N/A	N/A
Jardine Fl India (JFI)-c	♣N	9.10	7¹³/₁₆	− 14.1	11.6
Korea (KF)	N	8.16	8³/₁₆	+ 0.3	−49.4
Korea Equity (KEF)	N	3.55	3¹¹/₁₆	+ 3.9	−47.3
Korean Inv (KIF)	N	4.55	4⁷/₁₆	− 2.5	−45.4
Latin Amer Disc (LDF)	N	17.66	16¹/₄	− 8.0	40.4
Latin Amer Eq (LAQ)	N	13¹¹/₁₆	N/A	0.7
Latin Amer Growth (LLF)	N	12.62	10	− 20.8	4.1
Latin Amer Inv (LAM)	♣N	N/A	15¹/₈	N/A	−3.2
Malaysia (MF)	N	6.74	8⁹/₁₆	+ 27.0	−37.6
Mexico (MXF)-c	N	N/A	18⁹/₁₆	N/A	34.3
Mexico Eqty&Inc (MXE)-c	N	15.01	11³/₄	− 21.7	35.4
Morgan St Africa (AFF)	N	19.66	15¹/₄	− 22.4	28.9
Morgan St Asia (APF)	N	10.00	8¹/₁₆	− 19.4	−19.8
Morgan St Em (MSF)	N	16.31	13⁷/₁₆	− 17.6	−1.8
Morgan St India (IIF)	N	10.37	9³/₈	− 9.6	4.2
Morgan St Russia (RNE)	N	31.38	27¹¹/₁₆	− 11.8	55.3
New South Africa (NSA)	♣N	16.44	13	− 20.9	0.7
Pakistan Inv (PKF)	N	6.28	5³/₁₆	− 17.4	1.2
Portugal (PGF)	♣N	N/A	16⁷/₈	N/A	31.7
ROC Taiwan (ROC)-c	N	10.81	8³/₈	− 23.1	−13.7
Royce Global Trust (FUND)-c	♣O	6.71	5¹¹/₁₆	− 15.2	30.0
Schroder Asian (SHF)-c	N	9.19	8¹/₄	− 10.9	−31.8
Scud Spain & Por (IBF)	N	16.04	13³/₈	− 16.6	49.5
Scudder New Asia (SAF)	N	12.62	10¹/₂	− 16.8	−15.3
Scudder New Eur (NEF)	N	19.95	15¹/₂	− 22.3	13.2
Singapore (SGF)-d	♣N	7.88	8¹¹/₁₆	+ 10.2	−25.2
Southern Africa (SOA)	N	19.79	15⁷/₈	− 19.8	11.0
Spain (SNF)	N	17.14	14¹/₈	− 17.6	46.5
Swiss Helvetia (SWZ)	♣N	31.17	23⁷/₈	− 23.4	18.9
TCW/DW Emer Mkts (EMO)	N	13.58	12⁷/₁₆	− 8.4	20.0
Taiwan (TWN)-c	N	23.44	17¹¹/₁₆	− 24.5	−17.2
Taiwan Equity (TYW)-c	♣N	12.17	9¹⁵/₁₆	− 18.3	0.6
Templeton China (TCH)-c	N	10.97	9⁵/₈	− 12.3	−17.3
Templeton Dragon (TDF)	N	N/A	12¹¹/₁₆	N/A	−5.0
Templeton Em App (TEA)-c	N	14.32	13¹/₁₆	− 8.8	14.0
Templeton Em Mkt (EMF)	N	N/A	19⁷/₁₆	N/A	10.0
Templeton Russia (TRF)-c	N	37.92	39⁹/₁₆	+ 4.3	95.1
Templeton Vietnm (TVF)	N	N/A	9³/₄	N/A	−14.3
Thai (TTF)	N	5.56	10	+ 79.9	−45.5
Thai Capital (TC)	♣N	3.88	6¹/₈	+ 57.9	−49.0
Third Canadian (THD)-cy	T	21.76	18³/₄	− 13.8	21.7
Turkish Inv (TKF)	N	8.76	7³/₈	− 13.0	41.9
United Corps Ltd (UNC)-acy	T	71.87	49	− 31.8	36.6
United Kingdom (UKM)	♣N	16.43	13¹/₈	− 20.1	13.2

Table 15-2 (*cont.*)

Fund Name (Symbol)	Stock Exch	NAV	Market Price	Prem /Disc	12 Mo Yield 9/30/97
Colonial Intmdt (CIF)-a	♣N	7.28	7⁹/₁₆	+ 3.9	8.3
Corp Hi Yld (COY)	♣N	14.02	14⁵/₁₆	+ 2.1	9.9
Corp Hi Yld II (KYT)	N	N/A	13³/₈	N/A	9.5
Debt Strategies Fund (DBS)	N	10.04	10³/₁₆	+ 1.5	N/A
Franklin Univ (FT)-c	N	10.27	9⁷/₁₆	− 8.1	8.8
High Inc Adv (YLD)	♣N	N/A	6⁵/₁₆	N/A	9.9
High Inc Adv II (YLT)	♣N	N/A	6¹/₂	N/A	10.9
High Inc Adv III (YLH)	♣N	N/A	7¹/₂	N/A	9.7
High Inc Opp (HIO)	♣N	12.31	12¹/₁₆	− 2.0	9.3
High Yld Income (HYI)	N	7.57	7³/₄	+ 2.4	9.6
High Yld Plus (HYP)-a	N	8.83	9¹/₄	+ 4.8	9.1
Kemper High Inc (KHI)	N	9.45	10¹/₈	+ 7.1	8.9
Managed High Inc (MHY)	♣N	11.82	11³/₄	− 0.6	9.3
Managed High Yld (PHT)	N	14.22	13¹⁵/₁₆	− 2.0	9.0
Morgan St Hi Yld (MSY)-a	N	15.56	15¹/₁₆	− 3.2	8.8
New Amer Hi Inc (HYB)	N	N/A	5¹/₄	N/A	8.5
Prospect St High (PHY)	♣N	3.97	4¹/₈	+ 3.9	10.0
Putnam Mgd HiYld (PTM)	N	14.70	15³/₁₆	+ 3.3	8.8
Salomon HIF (HIF)	N	15.05	16³/₄	+ 11.3	9.0
Senior Hi Inc (ARK)	N	9.29	9³/₄	+ 5.0	9.2
USF&G Pacholder (PHF)-c	♣A	17.70	17⁷/₁₆	− 1.5	9.7
VKAC Hi Inc (VIT)	N	6.42	7⁷/₁₆	+ 15.8	9.4
VKAC Hi Inc II (VLT)	N	8.38	9¹⁵/₁₆	+ 18.6	9.7
Zenix Income (ZIF)	N	6.94	8¹/₈	+ 17.1	9.0
Other Domestic Taxable Bond Funds					
ACM Mgd $ (ADF)	N	14.36	13¹/₂	− 6.0	9.8
ACM Mgd Income (AMF)	N	9.52	10¹/₁₆	+ 5.7	8.9
Alliance Wld $ (AWG)	♣N	16.00	15⁷/₈	− 0.8	8.1
Alliance Wld $ 2 (AWF)	N	13.68	13¹/₈	− 4.1	13.1
Allmerica Secs (ALM)	N	11.79	10⁹/₁₆	− 10.4	8.1
BEA Income (FBF)	♣N	8.40	8¹/₂	+ 1.2	8.9
BEA Strategic Gl (FBI)	♣N	10.67	10	− 6.3	8.7
CNA Income (CNN)-c	N	10.81	11³/₄	+ 8.7	8.2
Colonial Intrmkt (CMK)	♣N	11.46	10³/₄	− 6.2	9.1
Duff&Ph Util Cor (DUC)	N	14.42	13¹³/₁₆	− 4.2	8.5
Franklin Mul-Inc (FMI)-a	N	11.22	9⁹/₁₆	− 14.8	8.0
Franklin Pr Mat (FPT)-ac	N	10.13	9¹/₁₆	− 10.5	6.7
Highlander Inc (HLA)-c	♣A	14.69	13¹/₈	− 10.7	8.6
J Han Income (JHS)	♣N	16.62	15³/₄	− 5.2	7.7
J Han Investors (JHI)	♣N	21.79	20⁷/₈	− 4.2	7.6
Kemper Multi Mkt (KMM)	♣N	10.80	10⁵/₁₆	− 4.5	8.7
Kemper Strat Inc (KST)	♣N	14.90	20¹/₁₆	+ 34.6	9.0
Lincoln Income (LND)-c	N	13.96	13⁹/₁₆	− 2.8	8.1
MFS Charter (MCR)	N	10.64	9³/₄	− 8.4	8.3
MFS Intmdt (MIN)	N	7.76	7	− 9.8	8.3
MFS Multimkt (MMT)	N	7.79	7¹/₈	− 8.5	8.7
MassMutual Corp (MCI)	N	N/A	43⁹/₁₆	N/A	4.7
MassMutual Part (MPV)	N	N/A	11¹/₈	N/A	5.5
Op Fd Multi-Sec (OMS)	N	N/A	10¹/₈	N/A	8.7
Putnam Mas Inc (PMT)	N	9.26	8¹/₂	− 8.2	8.3
Putnam Mas Int (PIM)	N	8.69	8	− 7.9	8.1
Putnam Prem Inc (PPT)	N	8.84	8¹/₂	− 3.8	8.1
USLife Income (UIF)	N	10.65	9¹/₂	− 10.8	8.3
VKAC Inc Tr (ACD)	N	8.09	7¹¹/₁₆	− 5.0	8.6
Zweig Total Rtn (ZTR)	♣N	8.52	9⁵/₁₆	+ 9.3	7.5
World Income Funds					
Americas Inc Tr (XUS)-c	♣N	8.97	8³/₁₆	− 8.7	7.6
BlckRk North Am (BNA)-c	N	12.48	10⁵/₈	− 14.9	7.9
Bull&Bear Global Inc (BBZ)	♣A	7.91	8⁵/₁₆	+ 5.1	8.3
Dreyfus Str Govt (DSI)	♣N	N/A	9¹/₄	N/A	8.9
Emer Mkts Float (EFL)	N	15.58	15³/₈	− 1.3	10.3
Emer Mkts Inc (EMD)	N	19.16	16¹⁵/₁₆	− 11.6	12.9
Emer Mkts Inc II (EDF)	N	15.65	14¹⁵/₁₆	− 4.6	10.1
First Aust Prime (FAX)-a	A	8.85	8¹/₈	− 8.2	10.1
First Commonwlth (FCO)-a	N	13.94	12⁷/₁₆	− 10.8	8.0
Global Hi Inc $ (GHI)	N	15.16	12³/₄	− 15.9	10.0
Global Partners (GDF)	N	15.15	13¹¹/₁₆	− 9.7	10.4
Kleinwort Aust (KBA)-a	♣N	9.51	8⁵/₁₆	− 12.6	9.4
Lat Am $ Income (LBF)	N	13.15	14¹/₄	+ 8.4	10.5
Morg St Em Debt (MSD)	N	14.12	13¹/₂	− 4.4	9.3
Morgan St Glbl (MGB)	N	15.26	14¹/₄	− 6.6	9.1
Op World Bond (OWB)	N	8.28	8¹/₁₆	− 2.6	8.3
Salomon SBG (SBG)	N	10.31	9⁵/₁₆	− 9.7	9.4

Fund Name (Symbol)	Stock Exch	NAV	Market Price	Prem /Disc	12 Mo Yield 9/30/97
Salomon SBW (SBW)	N	15.66	13¹³/₁₆	− 11.8	10.8
Scudder Wrld Inc (SWI)	N	13.38	13¹³/₁₆	+ 3.2	9.6
Strategic Gl Inc (SGL)	N	14.05	11¹¹/₁₆	− 16.8	9.6
Templeton Em Inc (TEI)	N	N/A	11¹¹/₁₆	N/A	10.6
Templtn Gl Govt (TGG)	N	N/A	7¹/₂	N/A	7.0
Templtn Glbl Inc (GIM)	N	N/A	7¹/₂	N/A	8.0
Worldwide $Vest (WDV)	♣N	15.40	12¹³/₁₆	− 16.8	9.4
National Muni Bond Funds					
ACM Muni Secs (AMU)	N	13.46	14¹/₈	+ 4.9	6.4
Amer Muni Income (XAA)-c	♣N	14.56	12¹⁵/₁₆	− 11.1	5.8
Amer Muni Tm II (BXT)-d	N	11.65	10¹⁵/₁₆	− 6.1	5.7
Amer Muni Tm III (CXT)-c	♣N	11.36	10¹³/₁₆	− 4.8	5.3
Amer Muni Tm Tr (AXT)-c	N	11.59	11¹/₁₆	− 4.6	5.9
Apex Muni (APX)	N	10.56	10⁷/₁₆	− 4.7	6.5
BlckRk Ins 2008 (BRM)	N	16.55	15⁵/₁₆	− 8.2	5.2
BlckRk Ins Muni (BMT)	N	11.10	10⁵/₈	− 4.3	5.9
BlckRk Inv Q Mun (BKN)	N	15.32	13³/₄	− 12.7	5.9
BlckRk Muni Tgt (BMN)	N	11.14	10⁵/₈	− 4.6	5.9
Bull&Bear Muni Inc (BBM)	♣A	16.70	14¹/₁₆	− 15.8	5.1
Colonial Hi Inc (CXE)-a	♣N	8.45	8³/₈	− 0.9	6.6
Colonial Inv Gr (CXH)	♣N	11.17	10⁹/₁₆	− 5.4	6.1
Colonial Mu Inc (CMU)-a	♣N	7.41	7⁵/₈	+ 2.9	6.7
Dreyfus Income (DMF)	♣A	N/A	N/A	N/A	6.3
Dreyfus St Munis (LEO)	N	N/A	10¹¹/₁₆	N/A	6.4
Dreyfus Str Muni (DSM)	♣N	N/A	10²/₁₆	N/A	6.4
Duff&Ph Util TF (DTF)	N	16.29	16	− 1.8	6.0
Greenwich St Mun (GSI)	N	11.91	11¹/₄	− 5.5	6.4
Ins Muni Income (PIF)	N	15.11	13⁵/₁₆	− 11.9	5.8
InterCap Ins Bd (IMB)	♣N	15.53	16	+ 3.0	6.0
InterCap Ins Muni (IIM)	N	14.69	13¹/₄	− 9.8	5.9
InterCap Ins Sec (IMS)	♣N	15.54	14³/₈	− 7.5	5.6
InterCap Ins Tr (IMT)	N	15.96	15¹/₄	− 4.4	6.5
InterCap Q Inc (IQI)	♣N	15.91	14⁷/₈	− 6.5	6.6
InterCap Q Inv (IQT)	N	15.50	15⁵/₁₆	− 1.2	6.3
InterCap Q Sec (IQM)	N	14.31	12¹/₂	− 12.6	5.8
Inv Grd Muni Inc (PPM)	N	16.79	15	− 10.7	6.0
Kemper Muni Inc (KTF)	N	12.32	13⁹/₁₆	+ 10.1	6.4
Kemper Strat Mun (KSM)	N	12.30	12⁷/₈	+ 4.7	6.3
MFS Muni Inco (MFM)	N	8.51	9¹/₁₆	+ 6.5	7.1
Managed Munis (MMU)	♣N	12.41	11⁹/₁₆	− 6.8	6.2
Managed Munis 2 (MTU)	N	12.33	11⁷/₁₆	− 7.2	6.2
Merrill Hi Inc (N/A)	-z	11.52	N/A	N/A	N/A
Merrill Mun Str (N/A)	z	10.87	N/A	N/A	N/A
Muni Partners (MNP)	N	14.58	13	− 10.8	6.1
Muni Partners II (MPT)	N	14.10	12⁵/₈	− 10.5	5.9
Muni Prem Inc (PIA)	♣N	10.32	9³/₄	− 5.5	6.2
MuniAssets (MUA)	N	14.61	13⁷/₁₆	− 8.0	6.3
MuniEnhanced (MEN)	N	12.13	11⁷/₁₆	− 5.7	6.2
MuniHoldings (MHD)	N	15.82	15⁵/₁₆	− 3.2	N/A
MuniInsured (MIF)	A	10.06	8⁷/₈	− 11.8	5.7
MuniVest (MVF)	A	9.96	9¹¹/₁₆	− 2.7	6.3
MuniYield (MYD)	♣N	16.09	15⁷/₈	− 1.3	6.3
MuniYield Ins (MYI)	N	15.84	14¹³/₁₆	− 6.5	6.2
MuniYield Qual (MQY)	N	15.17	14⁷/₁₆	− 4.8	6.2
MuniYld Qual II (MQT)	N	15.46	14³/₈	− 7.0	6.3
Municipal Adv (MAF)	N	14.64	13³/₁₆	− 9.9	6.0
Municipal High (MHF)	♣N	9.76	9⁷/₈	+ 1.2	6.3
Municipal Inc (TFA)	♣N	10.08	9¹/₈	− 10.1	6.3
Municipal Inc II (TFB)	♣N	10.30	9¹/₄	− 10.2	6.1
Municipal IncIII (TFC)	N	9.94	9³/₁₆	− 7.6	6.2
Municipal Op (OIA)	♣N	8.63	8³/₄	+ 1.4	6.8
Municipal Op II (OIB)	♣N	8.95	8¹/₂	− 5.0	7.0
Municipal Op III (OIC)	N	9.95	9⁵/₈	− 3.3	7.4
Munivest II (MVT)	N	14.59	13⁷/₈	− 4.9	6.3
Nuveen Ins Opp (NIO)	♣N	15.78	15¹³/₁₆	+ 0.2	6.2
Nuveen Ins Pr 2 (NPX)	♣N	13.60	12⁷/₁₆	− 8.5	5.8
Nuveen Ins Qual (NQI)	♣N	15.68	15¹¹/₁₆	0.0	6.2
Nuveen Inv Qual (NQM)	♣N	15.77	15⁹/₁₆	− 1.3	6.5
Nuveen Muni Adv (NMA)	♣N	15.68	15¹⁵/₁₆	+ 1.6	6.4
Nuveen Muni Inc (NMI)	N	12.02	12⁹/₁₆	+ 4.5	6.1
Nuveen Muni Mkt (NMO)	♣N	15.85	16¹/₈	+ 1.7	6.4
Nuveen Muni Val (NUV)	♣N	10.29	9⁵/₈	− 6.5	6.0
Nuveen Perf Plus (NPP)	♣N	15.22	14¹⁵/₁₆	− 1.9	6.7

§15.5 Open-End Investment Companies (Mutual Funds)

An **open-end investment company** is unlike a closed-end fund in two respects: First, an open-end company does not have a fixed number of shares outstanding. Rather, an open-end company stands ready at any time to issue new shares to persons desiring to invest in the fund. New shares are sold at **net asset value** (**NAV**), although in some cases a sales charge or **load** must also be paid at purchase. Second, an open-end company stands ready to redeem shares at net asset value at any time for investors who wish to liquidate their positions, although some funds charge an exit fee, the amount of which may depend on how long the fund shares have been held. Such companies are open-ended because they have no fixed number of shares although some funds do close themselves to further purchases by new investors when they become unwieldly to manage or when the managers perceive a lack of investment opportunities to which new cash may be devoted. Open-end funds are usually called **mutual funds**.

Open-end funds are not publicly traded on exchanges. Rather, a person who wishes to invest in a mutual fund deals directly with the fund itself and receives newly issued shares. When a person decides to liquidate his or her interest in such a fund, the investor again contacts the mutual fund and arranges to have his or her shares redeemed. Mutual funds are sold directly by the fund or through brokers who receive part of any sales load that is charged.

The obvious advantage of an open-end fund is that because the fund itself agrees to redeem shares at net asset value, there can be no discount. When closed-end funds trade at significant discounts, enterprising speculators have sometimes purchased large amounts of the shares on the open market and then successfully forced the closed-end fund to amend its articles of incorporation to become an "open-end" fund (thereby automatically eliminating the discount from net asset value).

Table 15-3 is an excerpt from the *Wall Street Journal* showing quotations for many mutual funds. In this table, "NAV" stands for net asset value per share; because there is no market trading in open-end fund shares, there are no share price quotations as is the case with closed-end funds. "Net Chg" shows the change in net asset value from the previous day. The heading "Inv Obj" refers to the investment objectives of the fund; a key to investment objective abbreviations appears in Table 15-4. The heading "YTD % Ret" shows the year-to-date return as a percent of current NAV including both increases in NAV and distributions (which may be either in the form of dividends or capital gains). The next four columns show percent returns for the indicated periods of four weeks, one year, three years, and five years, all calculated in the same fashion as the year-to-date return. In each case, these figures assume reinvestment of any distributions. The letters appearing adjacent to the return figures are in essence grades comparing the performance of the fund over the indicated period with other funds of the same objective. An A indicates a fund in the top one-fifth, while an E indicates a fund in the bottom one-fifth. The column headed "Max Init Chrg" shows the sales load for the fund, as explained below. The column headed "Exp Ratio" (expense ratio) shows the percentage of the fund value that is paid for management fees and promotional expenses on an annual basis. This

number includes only asset-based charges; it does not include direct expenses such as brokerage commissions. Some mutual fund charts also show a **turnover ratio** for the portfolio, that is, the number of times per year that the entire portfolio is bought or sold. This number is quite useful to investors in determining how actively the fund is managed and to what extent the managers attempt to pick stocks or follow a buy and hold strategy.

Until relatively recently, the fees that mutual funds charged were strictly regulated by the SEC. There were two types of funds: **load funds** and **no-load funds**. A load is an additional charge imposed on an investor when he or she invests in the fund; it is sometimes called a **front-end load**, because it is usually imposed on the purchase of the mutual fund shares. Historically, the load was about 8 percent above the net asset value for small investments, and decreased gradually for larger investments. Load funds can be easily identified from Table 15-3 as the ones showing a number other than zero for maximum initial charge. Load funds are heavily advertised and recommended by brokers who receive a commission from the load. For example, the AAL Mutual family of funds in Table 15-3 are all load funds. An investment in one of these funds would need to increase in value by at least 4 percent plus annual expenses shown in the last column before an investor could break even.

No-load funds are funds that offer to sell shares at net asset value. They are sold without extensive advertising and usually without the intervention of a broker, so that the investor has to locate the desired investment on his or her own and contact the manager of the no-load fund directly. Many investment advisers recommend that investors invest in no-load funds suitable for their investment needs in order to avoid paying the sales load. However, the actual investment performance of the two types of funds does not unambiguously indicate that this strategy leads to a higher net return.

In recent years, the SEC has relaxed the rules relating to sales charges, and many mutual funds have switched to more complex pricing structures. Many funds have reduced their front-end loads but have imposed a **back-end redemption charge** or **exit fee** on redemptions occurring within a specified period after the investment is made. In addition, SEC Rule 12b-1 allows mutual funds to deduct certain marketing and distribution costs directly from assets; in effect this imposes the costs of distribution (**12b-1 fees**) on existing fund holders rather than on new investors. Funds adopting this practice in Table 15-3 are marked with a "p." With a variety of costs being imposed, some in a hidden manner without complete disclosure, the comparison of costs between alternative mutual fund investments has become treacherous, and the formerly sharp line between load and no-load funds has become blurred to some extent.

Table 15-3 shows that mutual fund managers create "families" of mutual funds, each with their own investment objective. The goal is to provide a fund that meets the investment objectives of numerous diverse groups of investors with different short-term and long-term goals. Most fund families permit free transfer of investments from one fund in the family to another fund in the same family without service charge. In this way, the manager hopes to retain control over investment funds even when the goal of the investor changes because of changes in individual circumstances.

Table 15-3

LIPPER INDEXES

Thursday, October 30, 1997

EQUITY INDEXES	PRELIM. CLOSE	PERCENTAGE CHG. SINCE PREV.	WK AGO	DEC. 31
Capital Appreciation	1816.75	− 1.45	− 4.91	+ 16.71
Growth Fund	5952.23	− 1.54	− 4.74	+ 21.66
Small Cap Fund	627.15	− 1.47	− 5.29	+ 14.79
Growth & Income	5726.22	− 1.43	− 4.43	+ 20.40
Equity Income Fd	3056.19	− 1.19	− 3.80	+ 19.66
Science and Tech Fd	519.66	− 2.87	− 8.57	+ 11.89
International Fund	602.16	− 1.90	− 4.52	+ 6.55
Gold Fund	99.57	+ 0.74	− 13.85	− 31.49
Balanced Fund	3536.68	− 0.80	− 2.72	+ 15.41
Emerging Markets	85.10	− 3.58	− 13.10	− 7.92
'BOND INDEXES				
Corp A-Rated Debt	735.99	+ 0.28	+ 0.65	+ 7.84
US Government	278.01	+ 0.30	+ 0.87	+ 7.32
GNMA	301.91	+ 0.15	+ 0.47	+ 7.63
High Current Yield	749.42	− 0.22	− 1.32	+ 10.82
Intmdt Inv Grade	202.28	+ 0.23	+ 0.55	+ 7.22
Short Inv Grade	185.99	+ 0.07	+ 0.22	+ 5.34
General Municipal	529.31	+ 0.16	+ 0.71	+ 6.73
High Yield Municipal	257.20	+ 0.14	+ 0.61	+ 7.23
Short Municipal	114.38	+ 0.01	+ 0.15	+ 3.61
Global Income	199.08	+ 0.09	− 0.05	+ 3.11
International Income	126.57	+ 0.32	+ 1.41	+ 2.28

'Indexes are based on the largest funds within the same investment objective and do not include multiple share classes of similar funds. The Yardsticks table, appearing with Friday's listings, includes all funds with the same objective.

Source: Lipper Analytical Services, Inc. The Lipper Funds Inc. are not affiliated with Lipper Analytical Services.

NAV	Net Chg	Fund Name	Inv Obj	YTD %ret	4Wk %ret	Total Return 1Yr	3Yr-R	5Yr-R	Max Init Chrg	Exp Ratio
		AAL Mutual A:								
9.99	+0.03	Bond p	IB	+7.6	+0.8	+8.5 C	+8.5 D	+6.0 E	4.00	0.98
24.89	−0.37	CGrowth p	GR	+22.3	−4.2	+30.9 B	+24.4 B	+15.9 D	4.00	1.06
10.37	−0.01	HiYBdA	HC	NS	−0.3	NS ..	NS ..	NS ..	4.00	NA
11.39	−0.08	Intl p	IL	+3.9	−6.3	+7.1 C	NS ..	NS ..	4.00	2.10
15.85	−0.27	MidCap p	MC	+16.7	−6.4	+22.5 C	+22.4 B	NS ..	4.00	1.35
11.46	+0.02	MuniBd p	GM	+7.3	+0.2	+9.2 A	+10.0 A	+7.5 B	4.00	0.89
13.32	−0.22	SmCap p	SC	+18.9	−5.3	+27.5 C	NS ..	NS ..	4.00	2.06
12.28	−0.08	EqInc p	UT	+9.8	−4.0	+15.6 D	+12.8 E	NS ..	4.00	1.15
		AAL Mutual B:								
24.76	−0.38	CGrowth p	GR	NS	−4.3	NS ..	NS ..	NS ..	0.00	NA
11.31	−0.08	Intl p	IL	NS	−6.3	NS ..	NS ..	NS ..	0.00	NA
15.76	−0.26	MidCap	MC	NS	−6.5	NS ..	NS ..	NS ..	0.00	NA
13.24	−0.21	SmCap p	SC	NS	−5.4	NS ..	NS ..	NS ..	0.00	NA
		AARP Invst:								
20.95	−0.16	BalS&B	BL	+17.4	−3.0	+22.5 A	+18.0 B	NS ..	0.00	0.88
15.24	+0.02	BdInc	AB	NS	+0.3	NS ..	NS ..	NS ..	0.00	NA
54.40	−0.93	CaGr	GR	+29.3	−6.9	+37.3 A	+25.0 B	+18.0 C	0.00	0.90
16.92	−0.15	DivGr	GI	NS	−3.5	NS ..	NS ..	NS ..	0.00	NA
15.84	−0.04	DivInc	MP	NS	−1.3	NS ..	NS ..	NS ..	0.00	NA
15.21	+0.02	GiniM	MG	+6.7	+0.7	+7.7 C	+8.1 D	+5.8 C	0.00	0.64
17.95	−0.24	GlblGr	GL	+10.1	−7.9	+15.2 C	NS ..	NS ..	0.00	1.75
55.72	−0.85	GthInc	GI	+24.8	−5.4	+33.0 A	+24.6 C	+20.2 A	0.00	0.69
16.26	+0.03	HQ Bd	AB	+6.8	+0.8	+7.6 E	+9.1 E	+6.8 E	0.00	0.91
16.41	−0.27	IntlSkt	IL	NS	−5.9	NS ..	NS ..	NS ..	0.00	NA
19.41	−0.18	SmCoStk	SC	NS	−4.0	NS ..	NS ..	NS ..	0.00	NA
18.39	+0.03	TxFBd	NM	+6.5	+0.1	+8.2 B	+9.0 C	+7.2 C	0.00	0.66
17.17	−0.30	USStkI	GI	NS	−5.8	NS ..	NS ..	NS ..	0.00	NA
		AHA Funds:								
15.59	−0.17	Balan	BL	+18.2	−3.3	+24.6 A	+20.7 A	+15.2 A	0.00	0.23
21.76	−0.36	DivrEq	GR	+25.4	−5.6	+32.7 A	+27.2 A	+20.1 B	0.00	0.17
10.03	+0.02	Full	AB	+8.0	+0.9	+9.1 C	+9.7 D	+7.5 C	0.00	0.21
10.22	+0.01	Lim	SB	+5.4	+0.5	+6.4 C	+7.0 C	+5.5 C	0.00	0.12
		AIM Funds A:								
49.33	−0.93	Agrsv p	SC	+15.1	−7.7	+16.9 D	+23.5 B	+27.6 A	5.50	1.11
26.10	−0.22	Bal p	BL	+21.5	−2.9	+26.3 A	+23.9 A	+18.3 A	4.75	1.15
30.61	−0.51	BlChp p	GI	+23.8	−5.9	+29.2 C	+25.9 B	+17.8 C	5.50	1.26
14.41	−0.18	CapDev p	SC	+24.1	−5.1	+30.6 B	NS ..	NS ..	5.50	NA
13.26	−0.22	Chart p	GI	+20.9	−6.5	+28.1 C	+23.5 C	+16.5 D	5.50	1.12
28.77	−0.61	Const p	MC	+13.9	−8.6	+18.3 D	+20.2 C	+19.1 B	5.50	1.14
17.06	−0.43	GlAgGr	GL	+4.2	−10.9	+8.7 E	+19.0 A	NS ..	4.75	1.83
16.47	−0.40	GlGr p	GL	+10.1	−9.0	+16.3 B	NA ..	NS ..	4.75	1.93
10.93	...	GlInc p	WB	+6.5	+0.2	+9.1 A	+11.8 B	NS ..	4.75	1.25
17.68	−0.15	GlUtil p	UT	+13.1	−4.4	+20.1 A	+17.3 A	+11.1 C	5.50	1.17
17.45	−0.31	Grth p	GR	+18.1	−7.4	+23.1 D	+21.8 D	+14.2 E	5.50	1.18
10.14	−0.03	HYld p	HC	+10.5	−0.4	+14.9 B	+13.9 B	+12.3 B	4.75	0.97
8.53	...	Inco p	GT	+9.5	+0.1	+13.3 A	+13.4 A	+9.7 B	4.75	0.98
9.43	+0.03	IntGov p	IG	+7.6	+0.9	+8.3 B	+8.5 B	+5.9 C	4.75	1.08
16.51	−0.42	IntlEq p	IL	+4.1	−9.7	+10.5 B	+10.8 A	+15.5 A	5.50	1.58
10.08	+0.01	LimM p	SG	+5.1	+0.6	+5.9 D	+6.3 D	+5.0 D	1.00	0.54
8.28	+0.01	Muni p	GM	+5.6	+0.4	+6.9 E	+7.6 E	+6.7 D	4.75	0.80
14.98	−0.23	Sumit	GR	+23.3	−6.7	+28.4 C	+24.4 B	+17.6 C	8.50	0.70
11.01	+0.01	TeCt p	SS	+5.5	+0.3	+6.8 E	+7.3 E	+6.6 D	4.75	0.72
10.97	+0.01	TFInt	IM	+5.6	+0.2	+6.7 C	+6.6 E	+5.8 D	1.00	0.56
35.07	−0.77	Valu p	GR	+20.3	−5.7	+26.5 C	+21.9 D	+19.8 B	5.50	1.11
22.42	−0.36	Weing p	GR	+21.1	−6.8	+26.3 D	+22.6 C	+15.2 D	5.50	1.12
		AIM Funds B:								
26.05	−0.22	Bal t	BL	+20.7	−2.9	+25.2 A	+23.0 A	NS ..	0.00	1.97
30.41	−0.51	BlChp t	GI	+23.0	−5.9	+28.3 C	NS ..	NS ..	0.00	NA
14.30	−0.18	CapDev t	SC	NA	NA	NA ..	NA ..	NA ..	0.00	NA
13.22	−0.21	Chart t	GI	+20.1	−6.5	+27.1 D	NS ..	NS ..	0.00	1.94
16.78	−0.42	GlAgGr t	GL	+3.7	−10.9	+8.1 E	NA ..	NS ..	0.00	2.37
16.21	−0.40	GlGr t	GL	+9.6	−9.0	+15.7 C	NA ..	NS ..	0.00	2.48
10.92	...	GlInc t	WB	+6.0	+0.1	+8.5 B	+11.2 B	NS ..	0.00	1.75
17.66	−0.15	GlUtil t	UT	+12.4	−4.5	+19.2 B	+16.4 B	NS ..	0.00	1.96
16.79	−0.30	Grth t	GR	+17.2	−7.4	+22.1 E	+20.8 D	NS ..	0.00	2.03
10.14	−0.02	HYld t	HC	+9.9	−0.5	+14.1 C	+13.0 C	NS ..	0.00	1.68
8.51	...	Inco t	GT	+8.6	+0.1	+12.4 A	NA ..	NS ..	0.00	1.80
9.43	+0.02	IntGov t	IG	+6.8	+0.9	+7.5 C	NA ..	NS ..	0.00	1.84
16.14	−0.41	IntlEq t	IL	+3.5	−9.8	+9.6 C	NA ..	NS ..	0.00	2.35
8.29	+0.01	Muni t	GM	+5.0	+0.3	+6.0 E	NA ..	NS ..	0.00	1.61
34.56	−0.76	Valu t	GR	+19.5	−5.8	+25.5 D	+20.9 D	NS ..	0.00	1.94
22.05	−0.36	Weing t	GR	+20.3	−6.8	+25.3 D	NS ..	NS ..	0.00	1.95
		AIM Funds C:								
77.01	−0.56	AdvFlex t	MP	+17.1	−4.0	+22.0 A	+18.6 B	+14.2 B	0.00	2.26
49.67	+0.14	AdvInc t	AB	+6.3	+0.8	+7.0 E	+8.6 E	+6.1 E	0.00	1.51
56.92	−0.66	AdvIntV t	IL	+6.5	−9.8	+15.9 A	NS ..	NS ..	0.00	2.50
96.76	−1.41	AdvLgCp t	GI	+20.8	−5.8	+26.7 D	+21.8 D	+16.8 D	0.00	2.26
58.90	−0.50	AdvMulF t	MP	+14.0	−5.3	+22.5 A	+17.5 B	NS ..	0.00	2.45
63.98	−0.26	AdvRlEst t	SE	+14.7	−4.4	NA ..	NS ..	NS ..	0.00	2.40
20.42	−0.47	PrGrthB t	GR	+25.5	−8.8	+38.6 A	+28.6 A	+20.0 B	0.00	2.32
26.87	−0.05	QusarB t	SC	+19.5	−4.3	+24.0 D	NA ..	+22.0 B	0.00	2.62
13.48	−0.06	ReEInvB t	SE	+16.3	−4.6	+37.4 B	NS ..	NS ..	0.00	NA
7.60	...	ST MIb t	WB	+3.5	−0.4	+5.7 B	+3.5 E	+3.3 E	0.00	2.00
16.20	−0.15	StrBalB t	BL	+9.5	−2.8	+12.9 E	+12.3 E	+9.5 E	0.00	2.10
51.96	−1.32	TechB t	TK	+8.4	−13.4	+17.1 D	NA ..	NS ..	0.00	2.44
12.46	−0.32	WldPrivB t	IL	+12.3	−9.6	+19.9 A	+9.6 B	NS ..	0.00	2.83
		Alliance Cap C:								
14.17	−0.07	CpBdC t	AB	+8.1	−3.8	+10.9 A	+12.9 A	NS ...	0.00	1.90
9.10	−0.29	GlbDIGvC p	WB	−2.6	−17.6	+3.4 D	NA ..	NS ..	0.00	2.35
7.56	+0.02	GovtC t	LG	+6.2	+0.9	+6.9 E	+7.1 E	NS ..	0.00	1.71
3.41	−0.04	GrInc t	GI	+20.1	−6.6	+30.7 B	NA ..	NS ..	0.00	1.76
35.99	−0.63	GwthC t	GR	+19.9	−4.8	+29.0 C	+22.5 C	NS ..	0.00	2.00
12.46	−0.11	InBldC t	SE	+14.0	−4.0	+18.6 E	+15.8 E	+10.7 E	0.00	2.93
10.49	+0.01	InsMuC t	NM	+6.8	+0.3	+8.4 B	+10.8 A	NS ..	0.00	1.72
16.29	−0.41	IntlC t	IL	+0.2	−9.3	+3.3 E	+3.5 D	NS ..	0.00	2.53
9.44	+0.01	LtdMtGC t	IG	+5.2	+0.7	+5.8 E	+4.7 E	NS ..	0.00	2.92
8.62	...	MrtgC t	MG	+6.4	+0.5	+7.3 D	+8.2 D	NS ..	0.00	2.38
11.04	+0.01	MuCA C t	SS	+7.7	+0.4	+9.5 A	+10.7 A	NS ..	0.00	1.47
10.18	+0.01	MuFLC t	SS	+7.7	+0.6	+9.3 A	+11.4 A	NS ..	0.00	1.43
10.18	+0.01	MuNJC t	SS	+7.3	+0.3	+8.7 A	+10.2 A	NS ..	0.00	1.52
10.10	+0.01	MuNYC t	SS	+8.2	+0.4	+10.0 A	+10.5 A	NS ..	0.00	1.34
10.19	+0.01	MuOHC t	SS	+8.5	+0.4	+10.4 A	+10.6 A	NS ..	0.00	1.45
10.93	+0.01	NtlMuC t	GM	+7.4	+0.4	+9.3 A	+10.6 A	NS ..	0.00	1.39
7.80	−0.07	NAGvC t	WB	+8.1	−6.3	+14.1 A	+10.5 B	NS ..	0.00	3.04
20.45	−0.47	PrGrthC t	GR	+25.5	−8.8	+38.7 A	NA ..	NS ..	0.00	2.32
26.88	−0.05	QuasarC t	SC	+19.5	−4.4	+24.0 D	NA ..	NS ..	0.00	2.61
13.48	−0.06	ReEInvC t	SE	+16.3	−4.6	NA ..	NS ..	NS ..	0.00	NA
51.95	−1.32	TechC t	TK	+8.4	−13.4	+17.1 D	NA ..	NS ..	0.00	2.44
17.07	−0.14	**AmanaIncome**	EI	+15.6	−5.8	+19.3 E	+16.8 E	+12.6 E	0.00	1.44
26.32	−0.12	**AmUtlFd**	UT	+8.0	−2.6	+12.5 E	+14.1 D	+8.9 E	0.00	1.27
		Amer AAdvant Funds:								
16.11	−0.13	BalInst	BL	+15.2	−2.8	+19.9 C	+18.4 B	+14.8 A	0.00	0.62
21.47	−0.33	GrIncInst	GI	+20.0	−5.5	+27.6 C	+23.6 C	+19.0 B	0.00	0.62
17.06	−0.11	IntlInst	IL	+11.1	−5.9	+18.9 A	+15.0 A	+18.2 A	0.00	0.85
10.16	+0.03	BdInst	IB	NA	NA	NA ..	NA ..	NA ..	0.00	NA
9.63	+0.01	LtdTrInst	SB	+5.3	+0.3	+6.3 C	+6.5 D	+5.5 C	0.00	0.60
15.96	−0.12	BalPlan	BL	+14.8	−2.9	NA ..	NA ..	NS ..	0.00	0.97
21.22	−0.32	GrInPlan	GI	+19.7	−5.5	NA ..	NA ..	NS ..	0.00	0.94
		Amer Century:								
19.39	−0.19	Balanced	BL	+14.0	−3.1	+15.9 E	+15.3 E	+11.5 E	0.00	0.99
19.88	−0.40	EqGro	GR	+25.8	−6.4	+35.0 A	+28.3 A	+20.6 A	0.00	0.63
7.41	−0.07	EqInc	EI	+20.3	−4.9	+28.9 A	NA ..	NS ..	0.00	1.00
7.97	+0.21	GlGold	AU	−29.2	−16.8	−31.6 C	−11.8 C	+1.5 D	0.00	0.62
24.72	−0.46	IncGro	GI	+24.3	−6.4	+32.3 A	+27.4 A	+20.0 A	0.00	0.62
12.82	−0.09	NatRes	NR	+8.8	−6.6	+11.8 C	NA ..	NS ..	0.00	0.76
15.80	−0.09	Real	SE	+18.5	−5.7	+39.8 A	NS ..	NS ..	0.00	1.00
6.13	−0.09	StrAgg	GI	+12.5	−5.5	+15.2 E	NS ..	NS ..	0.00	1.20
5.48	−0.03	StrConv	MP	+10.1	−2.1	+12.3 E	NS ..	NS ..	0.00	1.01
5.88	−0.06	StrMod	BL	+11.7	−3.8	+14.7 E	NS ..	NS ..	0.00	1.10
12.81	−0.12	Util	UT	+14.6	−3.1	+20.5 A	+16.6 B	NS ..	0.00	0.71
7.79	−0.12	Value	GI	+19.7	−6.8	+28.9 C	+25.0 B	NS ..	0.00	1.00
		Amer Century Benham:								
10.62	...	AZIntMu	IM	+4.9	0.0	+6.3 D	NA ..	NS ..	0.00	0.66
9.73	+0.04	Bond	AB	+7.8	+0.7	+8.7 C	+10.1 C	+7.1 D	0.00	0.79
9.79	+0.02	CaHYMu	SS	+8.2	+0.4	+10.2 A	+10.3 A	+8.5 A	0.00	0.51
10.49	+0.02	CaInsTF	NM	+6.9	+0.3	+8.7 A	+10.0 A	+7.9 A	0.00	0.49
11.33	+0.01	CaIntTF	IM	+5.6	0.0	+7.0 B	+7.6 B	+6.4 B	0.00	0.48
11.62	+0.03	CaLgTF	SS	+7.3	+0.3	+9.3 A	+10.0 A	+8.1 A	0.00	0.48
10.33	...	CaLtdTF	SM	+4.3	+0.1	+5.3 B	+5.4 C	+4.7 C	0.00	0.49
11.32	+0.06	IntlBnd	WB	−4.0	+2.6	−2.6 E	+7.6 C	+7.1 C	0.00	0.83
10.59	+0.01	FlIntMu	IM	+6.4	+0.2	NA ..	NA ..	NS ..	0.00	0.65
10.67	+0.01	GNMA	MG	+7.5	+0.7	+8.9 A	+9.7 A	+7.0 A	0.00	0.55
10.46	+0.01	Int TF	IM	+5.6	+0.3	+7.1 B	+7.2 D	+6.1 C	0.00	0.60
10.07	+0.02	IntTrBd	IB	+7.2	+0.5	+8.1 C	+8.5 D	NS ..	0.00	0.74
10.51	+0.02	ITreas	IG	+6.9	+1.0	+7.6 C	+8.1 C	+6.1 C	0.00	0.51
10.75	+0.02	Lg TF	GM	+7.1	+0.5	+8.9 B	+9.5 B	+7.4 B	0.00	0.59
10.11	...	Ltd TF	SM	+4.5	+0.3	+5.3 B	+5.1 D	NS ..	0.00	0.38
10.34	+0.06	LTreas	LG	+11.3	+1.8	+12.5 A	+13.1 A	+9.4 A	0.00	0.60
10.19	+0.02	PrmBnd	AB	+7.5	+0.8	NA ..	+10.1 C	NS ..	0.00	0.45
9.49	+0.01	SGov	SG	+5.1	+0.5	+5.8 D	+6.5 D	+4.7 E	0.00	0.70
9.80	...	STreas	SG	+5.1	+0.5	+5.9 D	+6.3 D	+5.0 D	0.00	0.61
86.97	+0.18	Tg2000	LG	+6.0	+0.8	+6.8 E	+9.4 B	+7.5 B	0.00	0.53
66.09	+0.33	Tg2005	LG	+9.5	+1.5	+10.6 A	+13.8 A	+10.6 A	0.00	0.58
50.93	+0.45	Tg2010	LG	+12.7	+2.1	+14.5 A	+17.5 A	+12.8 A	0.00	0.68
40.29	+0.43	Tg2015	LG	+16.4	+3.3	+19.0 A	+21.1 A	+15.2 A	0.00	0.65
28.77	+0.31	Tg2020	LG	+19.7	+3.1	+22.4 A	+23.9 A	+17.0 A	0.00	0.61
23.78	+0.33	Tg2025	LG	+21.1	+4.1	+23.5 A	NS ..	NS ..	0.00	0.67
		Amer Century 20th:								
25.11	−0.56	Gift	SC	+3.0	−10.9	+2.4 E	+13.5 E	+22.0 B	0.00	0.98
27.40	−0.59	Grwth	GR	+25.2	−7.4	+27.3 C	+18.5 E	+13.1 E	0.00	1.00
14.73	−0.22	Heritage	GR	+22.0	−7.4	+29.1 C	+19.8 D	+16.9 C	0.00	0.99
8.70	−0.18	IntDisc	IL	+18.2	−8.3	+24.2 A	+17.0 A	NS ..	0.00	1.88
9.16	−0.21	Intl Gr	IL	+15.1	−8.3	+21.5 A	+11.5 A	+15.1 A	0.00	1.65
5.27	−0.13	New Opp	CP	+3.5	−10.5	NS ..	NS ..	NS ..	0.00	NA
47.60	−0.73	Select	GI	+23.5	−5.6	+27.4 C	+20.2 E	+14.5 E	0.00	1.00
32.94	−0.91	Ultra	GR	+17.3	−8.8	+19.5 E	+21.7 D	+19.7 B	0.00	1.00
14.31	−0.30	Vista	MC	−1.4	−10.6	+0.8 E	+15.4 E	+13.3 E	0.00	0.99
		Amer Express IDS A:								
10.02	−0.17	BluCpA	GI	+18.9	−6.5	+23.9 E	+24.5 C	+18.5 B	5.00	0.89
5.29	...	BondA	AB	+8.6	+0.2	+10.3 B	+11.8 A	+9.5 A	5.00	0.84
5.32	+0.01	CalA	SS	+6.2	+0.4	+7.8 D	+8.4 D	+6.8 D	5.00	0.80
10.16	−0.04	DEIA	EI	+16.5	−2.6	+22.6 E	+18.3 E	+16.9 C	5.00	0.93
13.57	−0.21	DiscvA	MC	+20.9	−7.4	+27.7 B	+20.4 C	+14.8 D	5.00	1.00
5.23	−0.22	EmgMkA	EM	+2.2	−17.1	NS ..	NS ..	NS ..	5.00	NA
15.13	−0.20	EqSelA	GI	+21.2	−5.8	+27.2 C	+22.7 D	+16.7 D	5.00	0.87
13.27	−0.11	EqValA	GI	+19.3	−3.9	+26.8 D	NS ..	NS ..	5.00	0.89
4.59	−0.02	ExtlA	HC	+12.4	−0.1	+15.0 B	+15.3 A	+12.4 A	5.00	0.94
5.05	+0.01	FdlnA	SG	+6.6	+0.6	+7.6 A	+8.3 A	+6.3 A	5.00	0.91
5.29	−0.06	GlBal	GL	+7.8	−4.4	NS ..	NS ..	NS ..	5.00	NA
6.25	−0.01	GlBdA	WB	+2.6	−0.5	+4.7 C	+9.2 C	+8.0 B	5.00	1.20
6.82	−0.16	GloGrA	GL	+1.8	−8.6	+5.0 E	+4.0 E	+10.3 E	5.00	1.37
32.19	−0.63	GwthA	GR	+19.0	−9.2	+24.8 D	+26.5 A	+20.5 A	5.00	1.04
4.64	+0.01	HiYdA	HM	+7.3	+0.6	+8.8 D	+9.2 C	+6.9 D	5.00	0.70
5.58	+0.01	InsrA	NM	+5.6	+0.4	+7.1 E	+8.6 D	+6.9 D	5.00	0.75
10.46	−0.26	IntlA	IL	+0.3	−10.3	+4.3 D	+4.6 D	+10.2 D	5.00	1.31
5.50	...	MassA	SS	+6.2	+0.3	+7.8 D	+8.6 C	+7.0 C	5.00	0.86
12.11	−0.18	MgdAllA	MP	+10.0	−5.3	+14.6 D	+11.8 E	+11.3 D	5.00	0.80
5.52	+0.01	MichA	SS	+5.6	+0.4	+7.3 E	+8.5 D	+7.0 C	5.00	0.82
5.37	...	MinnA	SS	+6.4	+0.4	+7.9 D	+8.6 C	+6.9 D	5.00	0.80
15.06	−0.06	MutlA	BL	+15.0	−2.4	+20.2 C	+17.1 C	+13.5 C	5.00	0.87
5.26	+0.01	NYA	SS	+6.8	+0.3	+8.5 B	+7.9 E	+6.4 E	5.00	0.82
24.31	−0.36	NwDA	GR	+17.4	−5.4	+21.7 E	+24.1 C	+18.7 B	5.00	0.94
5.46	+0.01	OhioA	SS	+5.9	+0.5	+7.5 D	+8.3 D	+6.7 D	5.00	0.85
8.02	−0.01	PreMtA	AU	−36.7	−14.3	−39.5 D	0.0 A	+10.6 A	5.00	1.50
9.84	−0.09	ProgA	CP	+20.1	−3.8	+28.5 B	+20.4 C	+16.1 D	5.00	1.04
6.36	−0.13	RschOpA	GR	+17.3	−6.7	+21.3 E	NS ..	NS ..	5.00	NA
9.26	+0.01	SelectA	AB	+7.2	+0.3	+8.4 D	+10.5 B	+8.2 B	5.00	0.89

Table 15-3 (*cont.*)

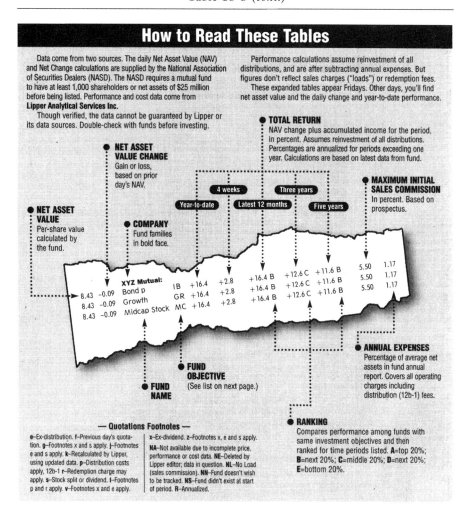

How to Read These Tables

Data come from two sources. The daily Net Asset Value (NAV) and Net Change calculations are supplied by the National Association of Securities Dealers (NASD). The NASD requires a mutual fund to have at least 1,000 shareholders or net assets of $25 million before being listed. Performance and cost data come from **Lipper Analytical Services Inc.**

Though verified, the data cannot be guaranteed by Lipper or its data sources. Double-check with funds before investing.

Performance calculations assume reinvestment of all distributions, and are after subtracting annual expenses. But figures don't reflect sales charges ("loads") or redemption fees.

These expanded tables appear Fridays. Other days, you'll find net asset value and the daily change and year-to-date performance.

● **NET ASSET VALUE CHANGE**
Gain or loss, based on prior day's NAV.

● **TOTAL RETURN**
NAV change plus accumulated income for the period, in percent. Assumes reinvestment of all distributions. Percentages are annualized for periods exceeding one year. Calculations are based on latest data from fund.

● **MAXIMUM INITIAL SALES COMMISSION**
In percent. Based on prospectus.

● **NET ASSET VALUE**
Per-share value calculated by the fund.

● **COMPANY**
Fund families in bold face.

4 weeks

Three years

Year-to-date

Latest 12 months

Five years

XYZ Mutual:

8.43	-0.09	Bond p	IB	+16.4	+2.8	+16.4 B	+12.6 C	+11.6 B	5.50	1.17
8.43	-0.09	Growth	GR	+16.4	+2.8	+16.4 B	+12.6 C	+11.6 B	5.50	1.17
8.43	-0.09	Midcap Stock	MC	+16.4	+2.8	+16.4 B	+12.6 C	+11.6 B	5.50	1.17

● **ANNUAL EXPENSES**
Percentage of average net assets in fund annual report. Covers all operating charges including distribution (12b-1) fees.

● **FUND OBJECTIVE**
(See list on next page.)

● **FUND NAME**

● **RANKING**
Compares performance among funds with same investment objectives and then ranked for time periods listed. **A**=top 20%; **B**=next 20%; **C**=middle 20%; **D**=next 20%; **E**=bottom 20%.

— Quotations Footnotes —

e–Ex-distribution. **f**–Previous day's quotation. **g**–Footnotes x and s apply. **j**–Footnotes e and s apply. **k**–Recalculated by Lipper, using updated data. **p**–Distribution costs apply, 12b-1 **r**–Redemption charge may apply. **s**–Stock split or dividend. **t**–Footnotes p and r apply. **v**–Footnotes x and e apply.

x–Ex-dividend. **z**–Footnotes x, e and s apply. **NA**–Not available due to incomplete price, performance or cost data. **NE**–Deleted by Lipper editor; data in question. **NL**–No Load (sales commission). **NN**–Fund doesn't wish to be tracked. **NS**–Fund didn't exist at start of period. **R**–Annualized.

Table 15-4

MUTUAL FUND OBJECTIVES

Categories compiled by The Wall Street Journal, based on classifications by Lipper Analytical Services Inc.

STOCK FUNDS

Capital Appreciation (CP): Seeks rapid capital growth, often through high portfolio
turnover.
Growth (GR): Invests in companies expecting higher than average revenue and earnings
growth.
Growth & Income (GI): Pursues both price and dividend growth. Category includes S&P
500 Index funds.
Equity Income (EI): Tends to favor stock with the highest dividends.
Small Cap (SC): Stocks of lesser-known, small companies.
MidCap (MC): Shares of middle-sized companies.
Sector (SE): Environmental; Financial Services; Real Estate; Specialty & Miscellaneous.
Global Stock (GL): Includes small cap global. Can invest in U.S.
International Stock (IL) (non-U.S.): Canadian; International; International Small Cap.
European Region (EU): European markets or operations concentrated in Europe.
Latin America (LT): Markets or operations concentrated in Latin America.
Pacific Region (PR): Japanese; Pacific Ex-Japan; Pacific Region; China Region.
Emerging Markets (EM): Emerging market equity securities (based on economic
measures such as a country's GNP per capita).
Science & Technology (TK): Science, technology and telecommunications stocks.
Health & Biotechnology (HB): Health care, medicine and biotechnology.
Natural Resources (NR): Natural resources stocks.
Gold (AU): Gold mines, gold-oriented mining finance houses, gold coins or bullion.
Utility (UT): Utility stocks.

TAXABLE BOND FUNDS

Short-Term (SB): Ultrashort obligation and short, short-intermediate investment grade
corporate debt.
Short-Term U.S. (SG): Short-term U.S. Treasury; Short, short-intermediate U.S. gov-
ernment funds.
Intermediate (IB): Investment grade corporate debt of up to 10-year maturity.
Intermediate U.S. (IG): U.S. Treasury and government agency debt.
Long-Term (AB): Corporate A-rated; Corporate BBB-rated.
Long-Term U.S. (LG): U.S. Treasury; U.S. government; zero coupon.
General U.S. Taxable (GT): Can invest in different types of bonds.
High Yield Taxable (HC): High yield high-risk bonds.
Mortgage (MG): Ginnie Mae and general mortgage; Adjustable-Rate Mortgage.
World (WB): Short world multi-market; short world single-market; global income;
international income; Emerging-Markets debt.

MUNICIPAL BOND FUNDS

Short-Term Muni (SM): Short, short-intermediate municipal debt; Short-intermediate
term California; Single states short-intermediate municipal debt.
Intermediate Muni (IM): Intermediate-term municipal debt including single-state funds.
General Muni (GM): A variety of municipal debt.
Single-State Municipal (SS): Funds that invest in debt of individual states.
High Yield Municipal (HM): High yield low credit quality.
Insured (NM): California insured, New York insured, Florida insured, all other insured.

STOCK & BOND FUNDS

Balanced (BL): A balanced portfolio of both stocks and bonds with the primary objective
of conserving principal.
Stock/Bond Blend (MP): Multi-purpose funds such as balanced target; convertible;
flexible income; flexible portfolio; global flexible and income funds that invest in both
stocks and bonds.

Most mutual funds are actively managed. That means the fund manager shifts investments aggressively in order to maximize the return to investors. The usual yardstick for performance is whether the fund exceeds the market performance of one of the broad market averages, usually the Standard & Poor's 500 stock index. The efficient capital market hypothesis suggests that fund managers cannot hope to beat the market averages consistently, and indeed most mutual funds have not been able to consistently exceed these market averages. One study in the late 1970s showed, for example, that 90 percent of the managed funds fared worse than the Standard & Poor 500 index over a 10-year period.

In recent years, there has been a strong trend toward **index funds** that are not actively managed but hold a portfolio that is structured so that it closely mimics the mix of stocks in one or more broad market indexes. An index fund may also be more attractive to sophisticated investors, because it involves significantly less trading than a managed fund, and brokerage commissions, investment advice, and other costs are significantly reduced. The tremendous growth in mutual funds in recent years is in part the result of the increased use of index funds by pension plans and other institutional investors who are seeking only a market level return on their investments.

§15.6 Unit Investment Trusts

A **unit investment trust** is usually a vehicle for fixed income investments, particularly municipal bonds, though some unit investment trusts may hold mortgage-backed securities and corporate bonds. A unit investment trust has a fixed portfolio of securities, all with the same or similar maturities. They are "unmanaged" in the sense that they invest in a portfolio of securities and hold them until they mature or are called for redemption. Unit investment trusts have fixed life spans that vary from 1 to 30 years. When the unit investment trust receives payments of principal or interest, the amounts are paid to the investors and not reinvested. Unit investment trusts are created by a sponsor, which is usually a brokerage firm. Units are sold publicly and the sponsor usually maintains a secondary market so that investors may liquidate their investment before maturity.

Unit investment trust units are sold on a dollar price basis that includes a sales charge of 3 to 5 percent. The longer an investor holds the trust units, the lower the impact of the sales charge on the yield. Many unit trusts invest in diversified portfolios, while others concentrate on single-state issues that offer income that is double or triple tax-exempt for residents of those states. (**Double tax exempts** are issues exempt from federal and state income taxes; **triple tax exempts** are issues exempt from federal, state, and city income taxes.) Single-state issues may lack the protection that wider diversification provides. Some unit investment trusts may contain bonds that are less than investment grade or are in default so that, as with all investments, some preliminary investigation is desirable. Many single-state issues, for example, may contain hospital bonds that are vulnerable to default.

Unit investment trusts are attractive investments for small investors, be-

cause they permit the investment of modest amounts in a diversified or predictable portfolio. Because bonds held by unit investment trusts may be callable, advertised high yields are not guaranteed. It is likely that older high-yielding securities will in fact be called before they mature, thereby reducing the yield available on the balance of the investment.

Because unit investment trusts are unmanaged (i.e., because there is no trust-level trading), they have very low expenses. The median management fee for a conventional no-load fund is about 1.2 percent, whereas the median fee for a unit investment trust is about 0.2 percent.

Although these trusts typically impose sales charges and have limited life, in many cases investors who hold their units until maturity may roll them over into a new unit investment trust for a reduced fee.

§15.7 Real Estate Investment Trusts

A **real estate investment trust** (**REIT**) is not strictly an investment company, but is similar in some respects. REITs invest in real estate rather than in securities. They compete directly with investment companies for the small investor's dollars, because they provide a fair amount of instant diversification in relatively conservative real estate investments and a return that is typically competitive with or exceeds mutual fund returns. A number of REITs are publicly held; about 85 of them are publicly traded on securities exchanges. As a result, interests in REITs are easy to buy and easy to sell, and they provide the benefits of owning real estate without management responsibilities.

REITs have had a checkered career. In the 1970s and 1980s, they were sometimes formed to serve as tax shelters or to develop and construct commercial real estate ventures, ventures that usually failed. The form that is popular in the 1990s is called an equity REIT and is a conservative manager of completed and operating income-producing properties. Such a REIT may own 15 or 30 properties in a number of different communities. Although the managers take a cut of the income, the yield on well-managed REITs is between 5 and 10 percent per year, an attractive return given the yields generally available on other conservative investments in the 1990s. If a REIT distributes substantially all its income to its investors, it is treated as a conduit in exactly the same way as investment companies are.

Care must be taken in the selection of a REIT, because some REITs are saddled with problem properties carried over from the real estate booms and busts. Others have invested heavily in office buildings, which are a drag on the market in many communities.

§15.8 Hedge Funds

A **hedge fund** is in essence a private investment company. The typical hedge fund is a limited partnership with no more than 99 investors or with only investors with a net worth of $3,000,000 or more. Under federal law (the Investment Company Act of 1940), a fund with more than 100 investors must register and comply with an array of regulations unless the investors are qualified

high net worth individuals or institutions. Thus hedge funds are often limited to 99 investors (and presumably one general partner) precisely to avoid such regulation.

The name "hedge fund" comes from the hedging strategies pursued by the early funds. The original hedge fund, set up in the 1940s, invested half in long positions and half in short positions in an effort to minimize risk. In the 1980s, hedge funds were used more as a way of gaining leverage, that is, as a way of using borrowed funds to augment the investment pool. Both practices are severely restricted for (public) registered funds. Federal law prohibits a registered fund from effecting short sales (with unimportant exceptions). Federal law also specifies that a registered company may have no more than a 1/2 debt/equity ratio (or 1/1 preferred/common ratio in the case of a closed-end company). In many types of transactions, it is possible (though not necessarily wise) to gain leverage of 10/1 or even 100/1. One of the concerns about the proliferation of hedge funds is that through leveraging they are able to control a large percentage of the trading in important markets.

Although hedge funds are largely exempt from SEC regulation, they do in many cases fall within the jurisdiction of the Commodities Futures Trading Act (CFTC), because their investments in commodities (such as stock index futures) qualify them as commodities pools. The CFTC has, however, routinely granted exemptions from its rules for hedge funds.

Hedge funds typically require a large investment ($500,000 or more) from each investor and offer limited withdrawal privileges. The managers of the fund usually take a large percentage of gains (often as much 20 percent) as their compensation. Managers often receive no compensation unless there are gains, and in many cases carryover losses must be made up before any compensation may be paid (the "high water mark" rule). Most hedge funds seem to be quite conservatively managed (as one might expect of a fund with very wealthy clients) and seem on the average to beat the broader market by a few percentage points. Because hedge funds are unregulated, those who run them are beyond the SEC's supervisory jurisdiction.

§15.9 Mutual Funds and Risk

Mutual funds provide instant diversification for the small investor at relatively nominal cost. The major problems with the small investor's use of this investment vehicle are, first, the difficulty of ascertaining the actual cost of alternative mutual fund investments, and second, the bewildering variety of different families of funds, and the equally bewildering variety of funds with varying investment objectives within each family.

Although one of the primary reasons for investing in a mutual fund is diversification, some recently introduced funds have announced a strategy of minimal diversification. These funds invest in 35 to 50 stocks, rather than the typical 200 to 500, on the theory that fund managers can more easily follow the stocks in the portfolio and structure the portfolio better in terms of overall risk. These funds may also have more of an impact on company-level decision-making, including that associated with takeovers.

Risk is arguably the most important factor for an investor to consider when

choosing an investment, but it can be very difficult to determine the risk level of a specific mutual fund. To be sure, most funds are sufficiently diversified so that there is little risk from individual stocks in the fund. Nonetheless, every fund carries some level of market risk. If it is mostly invested in well-established companies, fund values will tend to move by the same or even lesser percentages than broad-based market indexes. If the fund is invested in smaller and younger growth companies, the value of a share in the fund will likely exhibit wider swings than the market as a whole. An investor has little to go on other than the fund name and avowed strategy (both of which tend to be unreliable) together with the raw listing of stocks in the portfolio.

Attempts to quantify mutual fund risk have been controversial, with much disagreement about what to quantify. There are various kinds of risk, including interest rate risk, default risk, currency risk, and volatility. A particular fund may be low risk by one measure but high risk by another.

A domestic stock fund may have considerable volatility. But then the question arises how to measure volatility risk. One possibility is standard deviation, a statistical measure that blends the probability of price swings with their size to give a single figure (usually stated in percentage form) that is roughly equal to the limit in price changes (or any other changes for that matter) that will be experienced two-thirds of the time. In other words, standard deviation provides a measure of what might be called normal price swings.

Another possible measure of a fund's risk is its **beta coefficient**. The beta coefficient is a measure of the tendency of the fund (or even an individual security) to move with changes in some benchmark index. Thus, a fund with a beta of 1.0 moves by the same percentage as the market, whether up or down. A fund with a beta of 2.0 moves twice as much, and a fund with a beta of 0.5 moves half as much. For example, if the S&P 500 is up by 2 percent on a given day, a fund with a beta of 2.0 should be up by 4 percent, while a fund with a beta of 0.5 should be up by 1 percent. The same relationship should hold on the downside.

With both standard deviation and beta, the big question is: Over what period of time (in the past) does one look to see how the fund has performed? Proposals have focused on one year and five years, while one of the major mutual fund rating agencies prefers to use three years. The period of time chosen may lead to very different answers, which is why fund managers tend to use several different time periods when they themselves attempt to assess risk. Of course, there is no reason all three could not be disclosed to investors. But it is unclear how an investor should interpret information that a fund has a beta of 2.0 over the last five years but only 1.0 over the last year. Such information could indicate either that the fund has become more conservative or that the fund contains a few stocks that during the past year moved against the market by enough to throw the percentages off.

One proposed way to deal with the problem of changing fund risk is to require that mutual fund prospectuses be filed monthly. Presumably, the idea behind monthly filing is that risk measurement would be based on the portfolio as it stands at the date of filing. That is, a mutual fund would be required to calculate what its performance would have been over past periods if it had held the stocks in its latest portfolio. The problem with this disclosure, however, is

that a fund that (for example) seeks to buy distressed stocks that have fallen dramatically in price (perhaps on the theory that they are now undervalued) may appear to be very risky, even though the drop in price occurred before the fund's acquisition. On the other hand, if the acquired stocks fell in price at a time when the rest of the market was rising, inclusion of such stocks as part of the fund's constructive portfolio could make the fund appear to be quite conservative. Of course, the various possible combinations of these effects could lead to any result in between as well.

One major mutual fund rating agency, Morningstar, uses six different factors to assess fund risk: stock concentration, sector concentration, standard deviation, beta, p/e ratio, and highest monthly loss. Even these are no guarantee that all forms of risk will be evident even to the professional manager. For example, one manager confided to the press that he had been overconcentrated in stocks of companies with large amounts of debt and that as a result the fund had performed poorly when investors began to shun such companies. Lipper Analytic Services, Inc. has developed a classification of mutual funds that has been adopted by the *Wall Street Journal* in reporting mutual fund results. This classification is set forth in Table 15-4.

With mutual funds, one cannot always trust the label. Popular words — "growth," "value," "aggressive growth," and "balanced" — do not have clear content and portfolios described by any of these terms may include a variety of different securities with widely varying risk and yield characteristics. "Growth" typically refers to the shares whose earnings are expected to grow faster than average over time, while "value" refers to shares that are attractively priced on the basis of traditional value measures such as dividend yield, price-earnings (P/E) ratios, or price-to-book values. However, many "growth" funds have extensive holdings of income-producing stock, while "value" funds may have shares that are very "pricey" based on traditional measures. A person who desires a "low risk" investment may inadvertently end up with a fund that has a much higher degree of risk than expected. One "balanced" fund, for example, has an average P/E ratio as high as 33 and a price-to-book ratio of 11 to 1. These are astronomical numbers when compared with the S&P 500 with a P/E ratio of 19 and a price-to-book ratio of 3.8 to 1. A "balanced" fund, one might assume, would be relatively similar to the S&P index.

Although there is no express legal requirement that a mutual fund be accurately named, a mutual fund must state its avowed investment policy in its articles of incorporation. Statements of purpose can be quite general and can leave a lot of wiggle room. Thus, one worry about mutual fund investing is whether one can count on a fund pursuing the strategies that are implicit in its name or that are stated (or suggested) in sales literature. On the other hand, it is entirely possible that a fund manager may in good faith change his or her mind and may even conclude that the announced strategy is diametrically opposed to prudence at some point. A too-tightly worded statement of purpose may in such a case prevent the manager from serving investors well. In an effort to deal with some of these concerns, eight large mutual fund managers, acting through the Investment Company Institute (ICI), the industry's trade association, have developed a two-page fund profile to be distributed in tandem with the fund prospectus.

§15.10 Mutual Fund Investment Strategies

Practically speaking, it makes little sense for a small investor to worry much about past fund performance. Theory suggests that picking a fund based on past performance is rather like trying to predict the next flip of a coin on the basis of past flips. Several long-term studies of mutual fund performance have shown that funds do not beat the market any more often or consistently than one would expect as a matter of statistical chance. This is not, however, an especially surprising finding. The "market" is, after all, nothing more than the traders who compose it. Thus, the idea that on the average one will do about the average is to be expected. The efficient market theory, therefore, does not imply that no single fund will ever beat the market several years in a row. Rather, it simply means that the number of funds that do so will be about what one would expect at random. Incidentally, this may be one reason why many fund managers set up several funds with different focuses. The more funds one has under management, the better the chances that one or more of the funds will significantly outperform the market and can be used to promote sales in future years.

If the investor ignores performance, however, what should the investor worry about? The answer is that when choosing a mutual fund, the single most important consideration, after deciding what level of risk one wants, are fees and expenses. Such information is readily available in the financial press and through discount brokerage houses.

As discussed above, there are essentially four types of fees that a mutual fund may charge: a sales load, an exit fee, a management fee, and a 12b-1 fee. The first two are direct charges to investors, while the latter two are charges borne by the fund. In addition, the fund pays brokerage commissions and similar fees entailed by individual trades. Some indication of the extent of these expenses can be found in the fund's turnover ratio. Most funds turn over their portfolios about once a year, but some funds turn over two or more times in a year, while others fall far short of once a year. Other things being equal, a fund with low turnover is likely to perform better than one with high turnover (at least if one believes in the efficient market theory).

The use of exit fees, in particular, has been the subject of numerous investor complaints. Exit fees raise the cost of transfer of funds from one mutual fund family to another or from one brokerage firm to another; the complaint has generally been that brokers do not disclose the existence of exit fees when persuading the investor to make the initial investment.

A number of former no-load funds now levy exit fees, marketing fees, distribution fees, and low loads of perhaps 3 percent. Nevertheless, many true no-load mutual funds still exist. Exit fees should be distinguished from sales loads. In many cases (perhaps most), exit fees are payable only if the investor redeems within a relatively short period of time. Thus, the fee may work to the advantage of other investors by discouraging redemptions and allowing the fund manager to invest more available funds in longer-term investments and to keep less in cash. Moreover, in some cases exit fees are added to the fund and not paid to the manager or broker (as sales loads are). For the investor who is prepared to hold a fund investment for the long haul, exit fees may actually increase return.

Mutual funds increasingly offer investors a choice as to how fees are to be paid: either a traditional front-end load or an exit fee coupled with a 12b-1 fee drawn from annual earnings. This choice may seem baffling to an investor, because a rational solution depends on unknowable future events: How long will the investor wish to stay in the investment?

For example, Alliance Capital Management's Multi-Market Trust offers Class A shares with a 3 percent upfront load plus a three-tenths of one percent 12b-1 fee, or Class B shares with no upfront load, but a 1 percent 12b-1 fee plus a declining exit fee that begins at 3 percent. In the long run, these should come out to about the same thing, but there may be significant difference on various short-run options. The following table, based on a $10,000 investment in a basic value fund assuming a 10 percent return by the fund and the payment of various sales charges, shows that the difference in fees is time sensitive:

Value of Shares if Redeemed at Year-End

Year	Class A (6.5% front end load)	Class B (1% 12b-1 fee plus 4% declining exit fee)
1	$10,285	$10,459
2	11,314	11,514
3	12,445	12,674
4	13,689	13,949
5	15,058	15,351
6	16,364	16,725
7	18,221	18,222
8	20,043	19,853

In this example, the hefty upfront charge applied to Class A shares means that the Class B shares are $610 ahead of the Class A after one year; however, the exit fee cuts this advantage of the Class B if they are liquidated after one year. This advantage of the Class B nevertheless continues for seven years; after that time the continuing 12b-1 charges pushes the Class B share permanently below the Class A shares.

As a rule of thumb, if a fund has a front-end load of 4.5 percent or less, it is usually cheaper to pay the load than a one percent 12b-1 fee. For investors that may cash out early, it is usually cheaper to pay the 12b-1 charge than a 5 percent or more front-end load, unless there is a heavy exit fee in addition to the 12b-1 charge. When rule 12b-1 was originally approved, the assumption of the SEC was that these charges would permit more selling effort, more growth in the size of funds, and a concomitant reduction in fees. Everything has happened as expected, except the reduction in fees.

Similar considerations of fees and expenses should be paramount in choosing a variable annuity. (As discussed in the earlier chapter on annuities and retirement plans, annuities are a close substitute for mutual funds.) Variable annuity operating expenses tend to be somewhat higher than expense ratios for mutual funds, but this difference results at least partly from the fact that a variable annuity also carries a death benefit. Moreover, a variable annuity grows

tax free, while gains on a mutual fund may be reduced by taxes, although usually only to the extent of distributions. Sales and redemption charges in the insurance industry also tend to be higher than sales loads and exit fees in the mutual fund industry. Moreover, comparative information is very difficult to come by for insurance companies, in part because they are regulated state by state, but the *Wall Street Journal* runs a weekly listing of prices, returns, and operating expenses for most major variable annuities.

In addition to fees and expenses, however, another very important factor in choosing an insurance company is the adequacy of its capitalization. Until recently, this information was not assembled in any standardized fashion, but a uniform formula for calculating the risk-based capital ratio has now been promulgated by the National Association of Insurance Commissioners for use in determining when state regulators should step in to "rehabilitate" an ailing company. Ironically, insurers have generally been forbidden from disclosing this information themselves, because state regulators have been concerned that it will be used to persuade consumers that insurers are somehow safer bets than they really are. The information is available, however, through private advisory services and some public rating firms.

Because of the way they are organized, investment companies (mutual funds, including both open-end and closed-end funds) do not carry with them the risk of undercapitalization that goes with insurance companies. A mutual fund holds its investments in trust for the investor-shareowners, and there is no commingling of investments for other purposes (e.g., underwriting the insurance component of a whole life policy). Moreover, an open-end mutual fund is required to pay out the net asset value of a share (less any redemption fee) on demand determined at the end of the business day. On the other hand, this potential for cash outflow on demand may lead an open-end mutual fund to keep more of its funds in cash. Closed-end funds that may only be liquidated by selling the shares to other investors (in a secondary market such as the New York Stock Exchange (NYSE)) need not worry about cash-outs, but such funds usually trade at less than their net asset value.

Because many mutual funds are sold through brokers, some of the same conflict of interest problems arise as in connection with other investments. Specifically, brokers may be tempted to recommend that investors buy the funds that carry the highest commissions or that they sell one mutual fund and buy another in order to generate additional commissions. The practice of churning mutual funds to generate commissions is sometimes referred to as twisting, and because of the high sales loads that some funds carry, it can be even more of a drain on return than conventional churning of individual stocks. As a general rule, much less trading can be justified in connection with a mutual fund or other less risky investments precisely because they are less risky and therefore tend to change in price less than individual stocks. On the other hand, when an investor decides to switch from, say, a growth strategy to an income strategy, perhaps because the investor's circumstances have changed or even simply because the investor has had a change of heart, then switching mutual funds may make sense.

The decision to invest as an individual or through a mutual fund appears to be significantly related to the generation in which one grew up. Babyboomers

seem to prefer investing through funds, whereas their parents appear to prefer individual investing. And it is unclear what "Generation X" will turn out to prefer. There are many potential reasons for the different generational preferences, but it would seem that if the trends hold true over the next few years, more and more investment dollars will flow into funds and out of individually managed accounts.

Individual investors often diversify among different classes or categories of investments in order to achieve a blended risk and return combination and to minimize the effects of a decline in value of any one category of investment. A plausible balanced portfolio for an investor with capital in the range of $100,000 might include 25 percent in riskless insured investments, 25 percent in long-term bonds or mutual funds specializing in longer-term bonds, 40 percent in conservative stocks with some growth potential, and 10 percent in individual growth stock or strongly growth-oriented mutual funds. These percentages may change significantly, of course, with specific investment goals and with changes in economic conditions. A relatively young investor, for example, may have a larger percentage of his or her portfolio in growth stocks and a smaller percentage in the lower-yielding category of long-term bonds or bond funds.

Finally, it is unclear that it makes much sense to diversify among mutual funds. To the extent that the investor mixes mutual funds of differing objectives (i.e., with differing risks), all that one is doing is creating some sort of blended return for a unique level of risk. It is unlikely that any small investor is able to fine-tune risk at this level on any rational basis. To the extent that the investor mixes mutual funds with similar investment objectives in hopes of gaining more diversification, it is doubtful that diversification makes much difference beyond 200 to 300 different stocks. Moreover, because so many funds are indexed to the market (either fully or largely), it is unclear whether one does in fact gain any additional diversification. In many cases, the different funds will have invested in the very same underlying stocks and other instruments so that the net result of diversifying among such funds will simply be the multiplication of record-keeping headaches for the investor. On the other hand, if the strategy is to construct a customized portfolio using so-called **sector funds**, that is, to invest industry by industry or country by country rather than company by company, then purchasing several mutual funds may make sense. Moreover, to the extent the investor can costlessly move among mutual funds with differing investment strategies, it is possible to play one's hunches about market movements without penalty unless, of course, one guesses wrong. But if for one reason or another one wants or needs to invest in managed funds, it may make sense to diversify among funds in order to reduce the risk that one fund manager may pursue a particularly disastrous strategy or may indeed diverge from the fund's announced strategy.

§15.11 Money Market Funds

One type of mutual fund that has become extremely popular is the virtual equivalent of an uninsured savings account: the **money market fund**. The development of this type of mutual fund is a good illustration of the problems

of government regulation when faced with free market forces. For many years the United States government regulated the maximum interest rates that commercial banks and savings and loan associations could pay on savings accounts. The maximum rate was $5\frac{1}{2}$ percent. This created no real problem until the early 1980s, when competitive interest rates rose to 12 percent, or even higher in some areas. At first, regulated banks and savings and loan associations were overjoyed, as they paid $5\frac{1}{2}$ percent interest on deposits which they could lend out at rates as high as 15 or 16 percent. That joy proved to be very short-lived, however, as mutual fund managers, investment banks, and brokerage firms devised a new type of mutual fund that promised market rates of interest for depositors in a virtually risk-free investment. All at once, the regulated banks and savings and loan associations were faced with a severe liquidity crisis as millions of savers withdrew funds from regulated savings accounts in order to invest them in these new accounts. The federal government quickly realized that if these long-standing financial institutions were to survive at all, they would have to be permitted to compete effectively with the new-fangled money market funds for savings. Thus, the development of the money market fund was the cause for deregulation of bank interest rates in the early 1980s. The competitive bank and savings and loan programs that were developed in response to the money market fund are described in the following section.

A money market fund is a mutual fund that invests only in short-term, virtually riskless investments. These funds bear names such as "cash management accounts" or "liquid assets funds." Most money market funds are very large, with hundreds of millions or billions of dollars of assets. They invest in such items as negotiable bank certificates of deposit issued by large commercial banks, bankers' acceptances, commercial paper, short-term time deposits with foreign banks, and U.S. treasury notes and bills. Investments are usually in units of at least $10,000,000, and often in amounts of $100,000,000 or more. Because all of these investments have very short maturities, measured in days rather than months or years, the risk of default or collapse is very low. Money market funds may also have specialized portfolios to a limited extent. Some funds invest solely in short-term tax-exempt municipal anticipation notes or similar securities in order to provide a tax-exempt yield on a pure money market fund investment. Of course, the yield on tax-exempt funds is significantly lower than the yield on taxable money market funds.

One unique aspect of money market funds is that the trading unit is one dollar and earnings are reflected not by increases in the value of the trading unit but by adding more trading units to the account. The result is that an investor who holds, for example, 3,456 shares of a money market fund thinks in terms of having a deposit of $3,456. Additional trading units are added to the fund in proportion to its size in one dollar units. Depositors are permitted to write checks on the account without limitation, although small checks under $100 are usually prohibited. Whenever a check is presented, the required number of trading units are redeemed into dollars. The whole arrangement is indeed very close to a bank account. Although money market funds are not insured against loss by the United States government, investment advisers generally view these investments as cash equivalents, given the gilt-edged nature of the investments that form the portfolios of these funds and the short maturity periods.

Nevertheless, in 1990, a major publicly held company, Integrated Resources, defaulted on its commercial paper, leaving two money market funds facing potential losses that could have reduced the net asset value of a share below one dollar. In both cases, the parent companies immediately rushed in to make up the losses, leaving the money market funds' record of never having lost money intact. The immediate consequence was that money markets upgraded the quality of the commercial paper in their portfolios. The secondary consequence was that issuers of commercial paper with lower credit ratings found it increasingly difficult to raise working capital by issuing commercial paper. Several other money market funds also would have "broken the buck" (often because of investments in derivatives), but these funds have also been propped up by their sponsors with infusions of cash. One small money market fund that broke the buck went out of business in 1994, paying investors a little over $0.90 per share. (The fund dealt exclusively with a partnership of banks that in fact owned the fund.)

Government-only funds invest exclusively in securities issued by the United States government and its agencies. An extremely risk-averse investor might consider shifting cash to one of these funds because the risk of default is virtually eliminated.

The significance of breaking the buck lies in the fact that most investors treat such funds as equivalent to a checking or savings account. Thus, in addition to SEC requirements that money market funds invest only in top-quality securities with low volatility and that they maintain an average maturity of 90 days or less, the requirement that share values be maintained at one dollar dictates that the relative value of the fund must be stated in terms of yield, which effectively prohibits the fund from declining in value below one dollar per share. Otherwise the yield would be negative and a depositor would be entitled to something less than the amount of the deposit upon withdrawal.

§15.12 Insured Money Market Accounts and Certificates of Deposit

Interest-bearing deposits in commercial banks and savings and loans institutions are virtually riskless investments to the extent they are insured by the Federal Deposit Insurance Corporation (FDIC). The maximum deposit currently covered is $100,000. Banks and thrifts now offer a variety of different accounts; the two most widely used are a traditional passbook account that pays perhaps 4 percent per year and requires no minimum balance, and an account with a minimum balance (often $2,000) that pays floating interest rates that generally depend on market interest rates. The latter type of account may be called a **money market account**, a **money market checking account**, or a variety of other names that emphasize that it provides a floating interest rate based on market rates; it is the traditional banking institutions' response to the money market fund described in the previous section. Usually a depositor is entitled to write a limited number of checks on the account without penalty or service charge. Some institutions may also provide free transferability from a

money market account to a checking account at the same institution, or vice versa. Some accounts provide an automatic periodic transfer of excess funds in a checking account to a money market account. This is called a **sweep**. Traditional checking accounts are non-interest-bearing and excess funds should not be deposited in them.

Banks and savings institutions also offer competitive interest rates on **certificates of deposit** (**CDs**) that pay somewhat higher interest rates than on passbook or money market accounts. CDs are usually issued in round-number denominations, say, $1,000, $5,000, $10,000, and larger amounts. Interest rates on larger-denomination CDs may be somewhat higher than on smaller denominations. A CD differs from a traditional interest-bearing savings account in that the investor agrees to leave the specified amount with the bank for a specified period (e.g., one month, six months, a year, or longer). Withdrawals before the expiration of the period are usually permitted subject to a forfeiture of a substantial portion of the interest otherwise earned on the CD.

When investing sums in excess of $100,000, the federally insured bank account or CD does not provide protection against a partial loss in the event of bank failure. Although bank failures may seem to be a remote possibility, when dealing with large sums of money even remote risks should be avoided. If the amount involved is not too large, complete protection can be obtained by making separate $100,000 deposits in different insured institutions or in accounts under different names in a single institution.

When the amount is so large that it is unwieldy to break it into $100,000 units, there are alternative investments that are either riskless or carry such slight risk of default that they are viewed as riskless. These investments include Treasury bills or notes and high-quality **commercial paper**. Commercial paper is unsecured debt maturing on a specific day in the future no more than nine months from the date of issue. Commercial paper that large finance companies or major industrial corporations issue is also generally viewed as a risk-free short-term investment. The yield is somewhat higher than for Treasury bills, which are entirely risk-free.

A similar investment is a **bankers' acceptance** — a short-term interest-bearing note whose payment has been guaranteed by a major commercial bank. Acceptances arise out of commercial transactions, usually large international sales transactions. Payment may also be guaranteed by the parties to the underlying transaction and possibly by a lien on the goods themselves. Like high-quality commercial paper, bankers' acceptances are generally viewed as risk-free; the yield is also somewhat higher than for Treasury bills.

A person investing very large sums of money on a short-term basis (over $100,000) may consider a **repurchase agreement** (**repo**). A repo is a loan structured as a sale; a bank "sells" an investor riskless securities — usually Treasury instruments — while simultaneously agreeing to buy them back at a later date for a higher price. The difference in price represents interest to the investor. Repos may be overnight transactions or may continue for as long as a year.

Repos are widely used to avoid the risk of bank failure on investments in excess of $100,000. The theory is that if the bank fails while a repo is open, the customer simply keeps the securities sold to it. In this kind of transaction, it is therefore important that the securities involved be in some way set aside

for the investor, usually through a third-party escrow account. The investor should also get a list of the securities sold, including certificate numbers. Otherwise, a bankruptcy trustee or receiver may later argue that the transaction was really an unsecured loan. Repos generally earn somewhat more than banks pay on insured CDs for the same period.

A **reverse repo** is a repo from the standpoint of the dealer who is seeking to borrow securities in order to sell them. A dealer wishes to sell securities it borrows when it anticipates a price decline so that it can replace the securities at a lower price. In other words, it wishes to engage in a short sale of the securities that are the subject of the transaction.

During periods of low interest rates, the returns available on bank CDs may fall to unusually low levels because of the relative lack of competition for such funds. Most savers who invest in CDs do not tend to move quickly from bank to bank or to other investments, and banks may have much less need for CD funds during low-interest periods. Thus banks may cut the rates they offer for these funds more than the amount rates are falling in the broader market.

At the very least, one should check the rates being offered at several banks before **rolling over** a CD (i.e., before redepositing the principal in a new CD upon maturity of the old CD). Many financial publications publish the highest rates being offered around the country, so one is not limited to local banks. In addition, many securities firms sell **brokered CDs**. That is, the securities firm negotiates with a bank to offer an attractive interest rate in exchange for the securities firm's finding depositors. The securities firm in effect sells participations in these CDs that often pay higher returns than those available to individuals at a bank. Although many brokered CDs are insured by the FDIC, some investments in brokered CDs may be part of a larger CD that may be partially uninsured because of limitations on the amount of insurance per depositor.

An investor who wishes to consider alternatives to CDs might investigate short-term bond funds, tax-exempt funds, conservative stock funds, and money market funds. Although these investments are not guaranteed, they carry very low levels of risk because of the quality of the issuers and because of diversification. Generally speaking, bigger funds are better than smaller funds in that a smaller fund may suffer a rash of withdrawals that requires the fund to dispose of its better-quality securities.

When investing in a bond fund it is important to check the fund's **duration**. Duration is a measure of the average length of time over which the bonds in the fund will mature. The longer a fund's average duration, the more sensitive the fund is to interest rate changes. As with a single bond, a short time to maturity means that the prospect of principal repayment looms relatively large in valuing the bond. That is not to say that the fund will distribute the proceeds; rather, it will typically reinvest them in more bonds. The point is that the longer the period until maturity, the more important the present value of the periodic payments becomes. Thus as interest rates in the economy rise, as they are bound to do eventually if they have fallen to especially low levels, the value of a longer-term fund will fall more quickly than the value of a similar but shorter-term fund. Such a fund is therefore riskier than a fund with a shorter duration.

Another source of higher returns in periods of low interest rates (and

indeed in all periods) is lending to family members who otherwise would borrow funds from a bank or other commercial source. Investing, after all, is often really nothing more than lending sums of money to banks or other firms in need of it. If a family member has a genuine need and is responsible, why not cut out the middle person? The lender may be able to get a higher rate than a bank would pay on a deposit, and the borrower may be able to get a lower rate than a bank would charge for interest. This same idea leads many small business owners to lend some portion of their investment to their businesses (though in the context of business, there may be additional tax considerations depending on the legal form of business). The idea of intrafamily lending and borrowing as a substitute for investing assumes that family members will charge and pay interest at or near market rates. It is not uncommon to feel that charging interest is for the commercial world and not something that family members should insist on or expect. But clearly, if an intrafamily loan is prompted by a family member's need for an investment opportunity (and incidentally benefits the borrowing family member), such feelings are irrational and quite destructive of the opportunity. It is probably better, if such feelings cannot be overcome, to stick to commercial sources.

An intrafamily loan may also take the form of a home equity loan, thus allowing the borrower to deduct interest payments for tax purposes (which may mean that the lender can obtain a somewhat higher rate of return). Presumably, an intrafamily home equity loan may be set up even if a commercial home equity loan is already outstanding. The only limitation is that the total amount outstanding may not exceed the purchase price of the house plus improvements. Of course, such a loan would need to be junior to any existing loan. That is, such a loan would need to be secured by a third mortgage if there is a first mortgage and another home equity loan outstanding.

When making an intrafamily loan, it is important to follow the formalities, particularly for tax purposes, However, following formalities is also important because in the event of the borrower's bankruptcy, it is much more likely that the loan will be respected as a bona fide claim and not merely an effort to divert assets. Moreover, the parties are more likely to respect the relationship if it is formalized. In the case of a home equity loan, it is important to check the terms of the senior mortgages to be sure that additional borrowing is allowed. If it is not, such a loan may constitute an event of default and trigger a demand for payment on the first mortgage.

§15.13 Individual Investing

Despite the wide variety of investment services and products available to small investors, many continue to manage their own portfolios. Indeed, statistics seem to indicate that roughly half of all securities are held and traded by individual investors. Although the purchase of mutual fund shares is generally sound advice for the small investor desiring a diversified portfolio, the question thus arises: How large of a nest egg should an investor have in order to build a diversified portfolio on one's own? The answer is $25,000 or $30,000, which should be invested in a judicious selection of stocks. Above all, the temptation

to engage in trading to "fine tune" the portfolio must be sternly resisted. When selecting investments, each stock should be unrelated to the maximum extent possible both in terms of line of business and cyclical factors. By the purchase of shares in the $15 to $25 range, a portfolio with reasonable diversification may be created with minimum transaction costs.

Is this worth the effort, given the easy availability of mutual funds? Probably not, if one is to include the value of the investor's time; however, if one expects his or her portfolio to become larger through the infusion of fresh funds from time to time, it may be sensible to start a small diversified portfolio at an early stage. There are a number of other reasons why managing one's own portfolio, with or without the help of an investment adviser, may make sense. For one thing, an individual investor may be able to take on more risk (through margin borrowing or otherwise) than can be had through a mutual fund, although it is possible to buy mutual funds on margin through some brokerage houses. Moreover, and probably more important, the investor can often achieve a much higher level of tax deferral simply by buying and holding growth stocks, although such a strategy also increases risk. Taxes may also be minimized by careful timing of sales of gainers and losers, so that during any given tax year, capital gains roughly equal capital losses. Presumably, mutual funds also seek to balance gains and losses to minimize taxes for their investors, though it is obviously impossible for a fund to adjust for other aspects of an individual's tax situation.

Other advantages of individual investing include control over investment strategy and the ability to invest based on one's own views or insights into particular segments of the market. By managing one's own account, the expenses that go with investing in mutual funds can be avoided. Aside from sales and redemption charges, which may be avoided by investing in no-load funds, all funds are charged a management fee by their adviser, and many funds pay a so-called 12b-1 fee for promotional services. Moreover, like other investors, funds also pay commissions when they trade. Although individual investors generally pay commissions that are higher than those paid by institutional investors such as mutual funds, it is always possible to minimize commissions by using a discount broker. Moreover, funds sometimes pay higher commissions than necessary in exchange for so-called soft-dollar services such as customized investment advice that is sometimes of dubious value. (Indeed some such services are conveniently offered to fund managers at attractive resort locations or on a cruise.)

Perhaps more important than commission rates is the frequency of trading (or **turnover**). An informal review of no-load growth funds suggests that a turnover rate between 100 and 200 percent is quite normal. Moreover, many fund managers engage in **window dressing** or selling off stocks that have performed poorly just before the end of a reporting period in order to avoid the need to show such stocks in the portfolio as reported to shareholders. In other words, some funds may choose to sell at a low price just to avoid controversy.

The individual investor may also enjoy increased flexibility in trading. Large funds necessarily hold large blocks of shares in individual companies and thus often cannot trade quickly, because the market reacts to big trades. (One expert has suggested that mutual funds vastly understate trading costs, because calcu-

lations routinely ignore the price effect of trading. For example, in one reported case, speculators sold short stocks held by a large mutual fund that had announced that it was almost fully invested, because it was thus thought likely to liquidate some of its holdings.)

A related worry about mutual funds is that they may be overdiversified. A little diversification goes a long way. Studies indicate that 20 different stocks are enough to eliminate virtually all company-specific risk as long as the stocks are spread among industries. It stands to reason that a fund that is invested in 500 different stocks cannot follow all of these stocks as closely as a fund that holds only 50 stocks. Although financial theory suggests that it may make sense to simply buy and hold the market, the success of that theory depends on a significant number of investors continuing to do market research.

Funds that grow too large may be forced to buy ever riskier securities at the fringes in order to maintain portfolio balance without allowing positions to grow too large in any one security (which might necessitate more active management than is consistent with the fund's style). If a fund were to experience significant withdrawals, however, the fund might well choose to sell the most liquid (and presumably safest) securities first (on the theory that such sales will entail the smallest losses), even though the effect on remaining investors is to increase the risk in the fund. These tactics led to the closing of one money market fund, but there is no reason that a similar dynamic could not befall a stock fund.

Finally, advocates argue that if diversification makes sense, more diversification makes more sense, and one should diversify globally and over a wide variety of investment types. Recent studies, however, raise questions about the wisdom of global diversification, at least in down markets, because foreign markets tend to follow U.S. markets when prices are down. As for diversifying among more widely differing investments, such a strategy does not allow for fine-tuning risk. If everybody invested in a portfolio of everything, everyone would enjoy the same return. But clearly some investors are willing to take more risk for more return. In short, the logic of diversification can be taken too far, and there must be some point at which further diversification makes no sense.

Although the advantages of individual investing may seem quite marginal, on balance it appears that an investor who holds a diversified portfolio and refrains from trading except when absolutely necessary (to balance the portfolio or to gain tax advantages) may do better over the very long haul than the typical mutual fund investor.

Many brokers and financial planners advise investing a specific amount at regular intervals, say, $100 every pay period, an investment plan that is called **dollar cost averaging**. This plan may protect the investor from the danger of investing large amounts at a market peak, and presumably from failing to invest at a market trough. Dollar cost averaging will result each month in the investor buying more shares when prices are low and fewer shares when prices are high.

Although regular investing may be a good way to discipline oneself to save more, the advantages of dollar cost averaging are more psychological than real. Indeed, a recent long-term study concluded that an investor would do better 64.5 percent of the time by putting all available funds into the market at once rather than spreading the investments out over time. Thus, if one finds that for

one reason or another it is necessary to invest a large sum of money all at once, the study suggests that it is better to put it all into the market of one's choice. Incidentally, if one desires to invest in the stock or bond market but wants to take one's time deciding precisely how, it is always possible to buy stock index or bond futures to lock in current market levels.

Individual investing is a broad concept and a wide variety of arrangements may be made with brokers regarding how one's account is handled. Moreover, there are many different kinds of brokerage houses, ranging from the full-service firm to the no-frills discounter. A full-service brokerage house offers research and investment advice, whereas the no-frills discounter does not. A full-service house may also offer other benefits. For example, if the firm has an investment banking department that underwrites offerings, an investor who has an account at that firm may be offered shares in such offerings, whereas investors at other firms may only be able to buy in the secondary market at higher prices.

When opening an account, NASD rules require a brokerage house to obtain certain information from the investor that is designed to help determine the customer's sophistication, investment goals, and capacity to bear risk. With respect to risk, the broker will want to know (quite legitimately) about income, net worth, dependents, and other personal factors. Similar information may be required if the customer chooses to trade in different securities (such as options) or if the customer wishes to open a margin account.

Most full-service brokerage houses offer both **discretionary accounts** and **nondiscretionary accounts**. A discretionary account allows the broker to order trades without consulting with the investor. Discretionary accounts are increasingly rare and probably quite unwise in a world in which independent investment advisers may readily be retained. Retaining an investment adviser (who typically charges a percentage fee based on the size of the account being handled) will often more than pay for itself in saved commissions and fees at the brokerage level. Moreover, an investment adviser and a broker will tend to monitor each other's recommendations and may thus avoid the excesses that might tempt one of them acting alone (e.g., overtrading an account or investing in high-commission, high-risk securities). It is a good idea when opening an account to read and retain a copy of all such forms executed in connection with the account. Not only do the forms explain the customer's rights and obligations in great detail, they also establish a record of the customer's investment goals that may be crucial if any dispute later arises about the broker's handling of the account.

§15.14 Commission Rates, Best Execution, and Churning

The hazards of individual investing should not be underestimated. Individual investors pay much higher commission rates than mutual funds do, and commissions often are not clearly stated on monthly statements or confirmation slips. A large institutional investor may pay as little as one cent a share, whereas an individual investor making a $10,000 trade may pay as little as $40 at a discount broker or as much as $200 at a full-service broker. In all fairness,

however, the trade at the discount broker may not be at the best possible price, so the overall difference in price may be less dramatic than it appears.

With respect to OTC stocks, many brokers charge a commission even for stocks in which they make a market. In addition, when individual investors purchase or sell OTC stocks and bonds, they often pay the ask price when they buy and receive the bid price when they sell, while institutional investors can usually negotiate a price between the quotes. In other words, individual investors do not get **best execution**.

The same is increasingly true of NYSE stocks. Stocks listed on or after April 19, 1979, may be traded away from the exchange, a practice called **off-board trading**. This trading has led to the development of competing market makers who actively seek "order flow" and sometimes pay a small finder's fee to referring brokers for orders sent to them rather than to the exchange floor. The practice is known as **payment for order flow**. As with ordinary OTC orders, these orders are executed at (rather than between) the quotes (which is why market makers are willing to pay for referrals). In early 1995, the SEC reacted to payment for order flow by adopting a rule requiring disclosure in investor trade confirmations of the aggregate referral fees that the broker receives but not requiring any statement of the fee that the specific trade generates.

Although quotes are readily available for stocks (so that one can at least know what the spread is), it can be difficult to find out what the spread is for a bond. Most bonds are bought and sold in-house by brokerage firms. Moreover, trading in bonds tends to be more one-sided. Investors usually buy and hold bonds, and thus brokerage houses tend to sell many more bonds than they buy.

The SEC has taken steps to encourage exchange trading of bonds, but it is unclear whether a significant exchange-based market will develop. Brokers often tout bonds they are offering as being commission free, but clearly they have no reason to sell products that do not make them money somehow. Thus, it is virtually never the case that one could immediately sell a bond back to the broker for the full price paid. The difference may be thought of as either spread or commission, but as far as the investor is concerned it is the same thing—a transaction cost.

In the end, inferior execution may not be that big a problem for most individual investors. A one-eighth point difference on a $20 stock is less than 0.7 percent, which, given average gains for stocks over the long haul, will be recouped in less than a month. Nevertheless, the difference is just another way that trading costs mount up for the individual investor.

One of the most common problems experienced by individual investors is excessive trading or **churning**, which is a problem because most brokers are compensated solely by commission. Although most brokerage houses pay their salespeople a modest salary for a year or so during training or when starting out, most houses pay no base salary at all thereafter. Thus, a broker makes money only if his or her customers trade. To be sure, it is always up to the customer in the end whether to trade (except in the rather unusual case of a discretionary account), but investors have a way of placing trust in their brokers and many tend to follow their broker's advice quite blindly (in some cases seemingly ignoring the commissions that are subtracted from their accounts).

Many brokerage houses have responded to the danger of churning by their brokers by offering so-called wrap accounts to customers who engage in active trading. With a wrap account, an active trader may pay a fixed fee periodically in lieu of commissions on individual trades.

§15.15 Investment Advice

In addition to churning, another danger of individual investing is the difficulty of obtaining reliable advice about possible investments. Many investors who choose to maintain their own portfolio do so because they think a good broker will occasionally have access to nonpublic information, or at the very least will learn of material information before the market price reflects the news. Trading on inside information is clearly illegal if disclosure of the information constitutes a breach of fiduciary duty. Although an investor who merely gains the benefit of inside information without reason to know that advice is based on it probably will not be held liable, the risk to the broker and the brokerage house is considerable. One should therefore be skeptical about any hint that information is ahead of the market and should always ask oneself why such information would be offered. Often, the answer will be that the broker is simply trying to generate a trade and a commission.

As a practical matter, there is virtually no way for a small investor to be ahead of the market with respect to new information. Companies routinely discuss developments by conference call with brokers and analysts. The result is that the market almost always adjusts to information before it can filter down to the investor on the street. Even if the information is relatively fresh, it is unlikely that one can act fast enough if the broker is required to consult with the investor. Indeed, it is even unlikely that a broker who is authorized to act alone can act with enough speed to capture much of a benefit. In any event, the hazards of letting the broker act alone probably outweigh the occasional benefit.

Whatever the value of potential access to better information, there are numerous forces at work that may compromise the quality of information that is available to individual investors. As a matter of law, brokers are limited to making recommendations only for investments for which they have a **reasonable basis**. In practice, the reasonable basis requirement means that a given brokerage firm will be limited in the stocks that its brokers may recommend by the list of stocks for which the house has a current research report. And because of the potential for liability to investors, most brokerage firms are quite vigilant in enforcing such limitations. This does not mean, of course, that an investor cannot buy or sell a stock that the brokerage firm does not follow. It only means that the investment advice that one may expect to obtain at any one firm is limited to the securities that the firm follows.

Brokerage firms may be more inclined to recommend stocks in which they make a market or for which they are serving as an underwriter or in which they have a substantial inventory. Another factor to consider in evaluating advice is that analysts often own the stocks they tout. Thus, they have some incentive to see that others buy the same stock. On the other hand, it may be a good sign

that an analyst has enough confidence in his or her own advice to follow it. Although brokers are prohibited from **front-running**, that is, trading ahead of a customer order that is expected to affect the market, it is not now illegal to buy ahead of one's own recommendation, though short-term trading by investment advisers without disclosure of the practice to clients has been held to be a violation of federal securities law.

Finally, it is important to understand the point of view of the analyst. Some analysts focus on underlying value (**fundamentals**), while others focus on market forces (**technical factors**). In one incident reported in the *Wall Street Journal*, analysts at a single firm using different methods simultaneously recommended buying and selling the same stock.

§15.16 The Suitability Rule

In addition to the requirement that the broker have a reasonable basis for recommending a security, stock exchange and NASD rules require a broker to recommend only investments that are suitable for an investor's personal circumstances and investment goals. What is suitable for an investor depends both on the amount of risk that an investor can afford to take as well as the amount of risk that the investor wants to take. Violations of the **suitability rule** are clearly grounds for discipline of the broker. Many arbitration panels have found violations of the rule to justify compensation to aggrieved investors. And at least one state court has found a violation of the suitability rule (together with state law fiduciary duty) in a broker's failure to ensure that a customer account was sufficiently diversified.

Despite the suitability rule, brokers may tend to recommend securities that for one reason or another are unsuitable for the investor. Riskier securities generally carry higher commissions, markups, spreads, and discounts, which means that both the broker and the house make greater profits from selling riskier rather than safer investments. There have been numerous examples of brokers overselling in-house products.

§15.17 Investing in Initial Public Offerings

Evidence indicates that on the average, **initial public offerings** (**IPOs**) of stock outperform the market on a risk-adjusted basis. In other words, an investment in an IPO is more likely to show a profit than other stock investments of comparable risk. In many cases, the increase in price of such offerings is dramatic. For example, in late 1993, shares of Boston Chicken more than doubled in value on the day they were issued. Thus, it is not surprising that investors are anxious to purchase such shares and, accordingly, are miffed when they cannot get in on such deals.

There are complex forces at work in the IPO market that cause it to behave as it does and that carry significant risks for investors. One of the reasons that IPOs tend to be underpriced is that the investment bankers who **underwrite** (distribute) such offerings have a keen interest in seeing the stock sold quickly

(seeing the stock "go out the window" in the argot of Wall Street). In most cases, underwriters purchase the offered stock from the issuer and resell it, a practice that is known as a **firm commitment** underwriting. Thus, the underwriter must ordinarily keep what is not sold. Initial prices therefore tend to be set on the low side. Moreover, in a **fixed-price offering**, which is the more or less standard practice in part because of the structure of securities law, the price must be set so as to satisfy the most reluctant investor. It is also important that a public offering indeed be public, that is, widely distributed. Otherwise, it is open to charges of fraud. Perhaps more important, if the price of the stock goes down in the aftermarket, investors are more likely to sue (and win) under the more or less strict liability provisions of the Securities Act of 1933. Finally, for a variety of reasons, the owners and managers of the company going public are likely to prefer that the price of the stock increase after the offering, though it may well mean that they receive less for the stock that is sold in the first place, a cost about which surprisingly few issuers complain.

As one might expect, investment banks are under intense pressure to allocate IPO bargains to their best customers. Thus, one reason that many investors cannot get in on such deals (aside from the fact that there is never enough to go around) is that investment banks quite naturally allocate what they have to those customers with whom they have long and loyal relationships or to influential political or other persons whose favor the underwriter seeks. Indeed, it is these relationships that enable the investment banks to assure issuers that they will be able to market their stock. On the other hand, to continue to participate in attractive IPOs, loyal customers may sometimes be called on to invest in stocks that they might otherwise be reluctant to purchase. Moreover, investment banks, consistent with their issuer clients, have an interest in not seeing the price of newly issued stock fall in the aftermarket.

Investment bankers are anxious to assure themselves that the customers to whom they sell IPO shares will not immediately resell the shares for a quick profit. This practice is known as **flipping**, which tends to cause the price to fall and leads to all the same worries as would selling the stock for too high a price in the first place. Aside from potential liability under the federal securities laws, an investment bank might suffer damage to its reputation for purposes of attracting future clients. Thus, investment bankers want to be assured that investors will keep the stock they buy for a decent interval. Indeed, one of the complaints that is sometimes heard from those who are "lucky" enough to be allocated shares in an IPO is that they are sometimes subtly coerced into keeping the shares longer than they might like.

§15.18 Penny Stocks

Generally speaking, a **penny stock** is a low-priced high-risk stock that is sold through brokerage houses specializing in such issues. The rule of thumb is that a penny stock is a stock that sells for less than five dollars per share. But the difficulty in defining a penny stock is apparent from SEC rules, which define penny stock by means of nine categories of what they are not.

The problem with penny stocks has tended to be not so much with the

stocks themselves as with the firms through which they are sold. Thus, SEC rules relating to penny stocks are directed to brokerage houses. The rules require special disclosures by the brokerage house to their customers in connection with the risk, firmness of price quotations, and compensation. The rules also require special disclosures to investors in periodic account statements and preservation of information with regard to the firm's sales staff. The rules also provide for certain exemptions for firms whose business is not primarily in connection with penny stocks and for certain limited offerings.

The SEC has adopted special rules to deal with **blank check offerings** of penny stocks. A blank check offering is an offering to raise funds for purposes to be determined. Under SEC rules, funds raised from a blank check offering must be placed in escrow until the offering is completed and until business assets accounting for at least 80 percent of the funds have been acquired. The definition of penny stock includes blank check offerings at any price (not only those at less than $5).

Broker-dealers who sell penny stocks have been known by a variety of names, including **boiler room** and **bucket shop**, and they have usually relied on **cold calling**, that is, calling potential customers with whom the firm has no prior relationship in an effort to sell the stock of the day. These firms may engage in high pressure sales tactics designed to sell a particular stock rather than conducting genuine research. Individual employees of boiler rooms often move from firm to firm as one operation is shut down and another opens up, or the firms themselves disband after a stock has been sold and then re-form under a new name to sell a new stock.

§15.19 Mistakes That Unsophisticated Investors Make

Persons making their initial forays into the world of investing should be aware of the most common mistakes that unsophisticated investors make (as seen through the eyes of a sophisticated professional):

1. *Investing in last year's hot stock or mutual fund.* In other words, one should beware of purchasing yesterday's favorite just before the trend changes; one should invest on the basis of estimates of the future, not what was trendy in the past.

2. *Taking profits too quickly.* Timing, of course, is everything in speculation, but a common error is to become nervous that a paper profit will disappear overnight and to take the profit prematurely.

3. *Failing to cut losses.* What someone paid for a stock is irrelevant. The question is whether the person would buy the stock today. If the answer is no, sell it. A common misconception is to hold a losing investment waiting for it to go back up "so I can come out even."

4. *Assembling a stock portfolio without an investment objective.* One has to establish an investment objective and then monitor and update the portfolio with this objective in mind.

5. *Buying too many mutual funds.* Mutual funds provide instant diversification within a specific investment objective. But the purchase of, say, three different growth funds, three growth-and-income funds, four bond funds, and

three international funds is consistent only with the objective of indexing to the economy generally.

6. *Buying a one-product stock after insufficient research.* If the product turns out not to be a commercial success, the entire investment is likely to be lost.

7. *Believing one can time the market.* The long-term trend of the market has been basically upward; moving totally out of the market and then coming back in is less likely to be successful than staying in for the long haul. Cost averaging by making purchases at regular intervals is likely to be more successful than trying to time the market.

8. *Excessively relying on recommendations of brokerage firms.* Brokerage firms make four or five "buy" recommendations for every "sell" recommendation. Most "sell" recommendations are made only after the stock has declined significantly in price — and when it is too late. Yet, selling is an essential aspect of portfolio management. Brokerage firms are reluctant to make "sell" recommendations in part because of concern about relationships with the issuer, including participating in subsequent financings and having a reliable source of information, and in part because most investors are purchase-oriented rather than sale-oriented, with the result that "sell" recommendations do not generate as much business as "buy" recommendations.

CHAPTER 16

OPTIONS, COMMODITIES, FUTURES, AND OTHER ESOTERICA

§16.1 Introduction

This chapter describes a variety of investment vehicles, including options, futures, and options on futures. Many of these vehicles are extremely high-risk investments: They are attractive from a speculative standpoint primarily because they combine relatively small initial investments with a substantial potential for gain or loss. As such they are suitable investments only for the sophisticated. These investment devices may also be used, however, to "hedge" established positions, that is, to protect existing investments from changes in value. In this context, they are conservative rather than speculative in character.

The instruments that this chapter discusses are called derivatives, because their value may be based on, or derived from, price movements in individual stocks or on changes in stock indexes that reflect a portfolio of publicly traded stocks. Elaborate computer-based trading strategies were developed during the 1980s to take advantage of these instruments by trading them in tandem with the underlying securities. These strategies link the markets for derivatives with the traditional markets for securities and have increased the volume of trading in traditional markets. Indeed, many observers believed that these strategies were contributing forces to the October 1987 market crash, although others have argued that market linkage in fact makes all markets more stable.

Some of the investments vehicles that this chapter describes are of com-

paratively recent origin. Others, such as trading in commodities futures, have existed for more than a century.

This chapter deals only with standard options and futures that are traded on established markets. This is the tip of an iceberg. A vast, and largely unregulated, over-the-counter market for custom-made derivatives also exists. Some of these are so complicated that the risks involved may not be well understood even by the persons who create them.

§16.2 Standardized Securities Options: Puts and Calls

The easiest way to describe how standardized securities options work is to use a real-life example. Table 16-1 is the portion of the listed options quotations page of the *Wall Street Journal* that shows trading in options for IBM for October 30, 1997.

There are two types of publicly traded options: (1) **call options** are options to purchase IBM stock at a fixed price for a limited period, and (2) **put options** are options to sell IBM stock at a fixed price for a limited period. The left-hand column of Table 16-1 simply names the stock in question (IBM) and the closing price for that stock on the New York Stock Exchange (NYSE) ($95^{13}/_{16}$) for reference purposes. The second column, "Strike," is the price at which a specific option in question is exercisable, sometimes called the **exercise price**. The **strike price** is fixed when the option is created and remains unchanged during the life of the option. IBM options shown expire at the close of trading on the third Friday of the months of November, December, January, and April.

The columns under "Call–Last" and "Put–Last" are closing market prices for IBM options at the listed strike prices expiring in the month in question. Thus, for IBM there are options potentially being traded at 11 different strike prices at 5-dollar intervals between 70 and 120, expiring at as many as 3 different times. Thus, there are 33 different potential call options on IBM stock. Similarly, there are 33 different potential put options, or a total of 66 different options on IBM in all (although neither put nor call options are traded at all the possible variations). In short, information about a large number of different options is crammed into a small amount of space in Table 16-1.

Puts and calls are traded in blocks of options on 100 shares. The option unit on 100 shares is called a **contract**. The price quotations in Table 16-1, however, are on a per share rather than a per contract basis, although the volume is the number of contracts traded.

On October 30, 1997, the price of the IBM November 110 call option was 1/2 or $0.50 per share. The price of a contract for this option was therefore $50. Obviously, a purchase of several hundred contracts would be feasible for even a person with modest means.

A person who purchased an IBM November 110 call contract would have acquired, at a cost of $50 (plus commissions), the right to purchase 100 shares of IBM at $110 per share at any time until expiration on Friday, November 21, 1997 (the third Friday of the month).

Let us assume for the moment that the speculator has reason to believe that there will be a substantial run-up in IBM in the next week. Indeed, she

Table 16-1

LISTED OPTIONS QUOTATIONS

Thursday, October 30, 1997

Composite volume and close for actively traded equity and LEAPS, or long-term options, with results for the corresponding put or call contract. Volume figures are unofficial. Open interest is total outstanding for all exchanges and reflects previous trading day. Close when possible is shown for the underlying stock on primary market. **CB**-Chicago Board Options Exchange. **AM**-American Stock Exchange. **PB**-Philadelphia Stock Exchange. **PC**-Pacific Stock Exchange. **NY**-New York Stock Exchange. **XC**-Composite. **p**-Put.

MOST ACTIVE CONTRACTS

Option/Strike			Vol	Exch	Last	Net Chg	a-Close	Open Int
M C I	Nov	37 1/2	14,361	CB	1/2	– 1/16	35 9/16	69,874
M C I	Nov	35	12,455	CB	1 1/2	– 1/4	35 9/16	54,528
M C I	Nov	35	p 11,082	CB	7/8	– 1/16	35 9/16	12,453
G M	Dec	50	7,802	CB	16	– 4 5/8	66 1/8	8,221
Intel	Nov	85	6,785	AM	1 1/4	– 5/8	75 3/4	29,825
Compaq	Nov	65	p 5,944	PC	6 3/4	+ 2 3/8	61 1/2	10,231
TelBrasl	Dec	125	5,265	XC	4	– 2 1/4	94 3/16	791
DellCptr	Nov	85	5,194	PB	4	– 2	78	4,054
Intel	Dec	70	p 4,859	AM	2 3/4	+ 1 3/8	75 3/4	1,333
DellCptr	Nov	80	p 4,832	PB	7 1/8	+ 2 3/8	78	5,885
Compaq	Nov	65	4,765	PC	3	– 5/8	61 1/2	8,642
Amoco	Jan 99	75	4,590	CB	20 7/8	+ 4 1/8	91	261
Intel	Nov	80	p 4,477	AM	6 3/8	+ 3	75 3/4	20,468
I B M	Nov	90	p 4,368	XC	2 1/8	+ 13/16	95 13/16	13,432
Cisco	Nov	80	4,319	XC	3 3/4	– 1/4	79 15/16	7,988
I B M	Nov	95	p 4,304	XC	3 7/8	+ 1 3/16	95 13/16	10,941
TelBrasl	Nov	120	4,212	XC	2 7/8	– 1 5/8	94 3/16	3,305
Amoco	Nov	75	4,205	CB	17 1/8	– 1 5/8	91	4,444
Intel	Nov	80	4,162	AM	2 1/2	– 1 1/2	75 3/4	12,067
I B M	Nov	100	4,126	XC	2 5/16	– 13/16	95 13/16	13,159

Option/Strike			Vol	Exch	Last	Net Chg	a-Close	Open Int
Compaq	Nov	75	3,758	PC	5/8	– 3/16	61 1/2	26,411
Intel	Nov	90	3,743	AM	5/8	– 1/8	75 3/4	31,251
A M D	Nov	25	p 3,666	PC	4 1/4	+ 2 1/8	22 3/16	3,384
WDigit	Nov	30	3,599	AM	2	– 3/4	29 7/16	657
G T E	Dec	42 1/2	3,520	AM	1 15/16	– 3/16	42 1/8	10,100
AplMat	Nov	35	3,506	PC	1 9/16	– 13/16	31 15/16	8,052
Intel	Nov	75	p 3,480	AM	3 1/2	+ 1 7/8	75 3/4	8,286
BostChkn	Nov	15	p 3,470	XC	4 3/4	+ 1 1/4	10 7/16	8,773
Pfizer	Nov	75	3,356	AM	1 1/2	+ 3/16	71 3/4	4,019
Oracle	Nov	35	p 3,251	CB	2 1/4	+ 3/4	33 3/4	3,902
ConAgr	Dec	25	3,170	AM	7	+ 2 3/4	31 1/2	5,005
ConAgr	Jun	25	3,170	AM	7 7/8	...	31 1/2	...
G M	Mar	50	3,161	CB	16 3/8	– 1 3/8	66 1/8	205
WDigit	Nov	30	p 3,146	AM	2 9/16	+ 5/16	29 7/16	878
DellCptr	Nov	80	3,076	PB	6	– 3	78	2,633
TchDta	Dec	45	3,059	PC	1 7/8	– 1 1/8	42	3,032
DellCptr	Nov	90	3,052	PB	2 7/8	– 1 1/4	78	7,267
Compaq	Nov	70	p 3,047	PC	10 1/2	+ 2	61 1/2	17,425
Chiron	Jan	20	3,040	XC	1 7/16	– 3/16	19 1/16	6,872
Intel	Nov	85	p 2,984	AM	10	+ 3 1/2	75 3/4	18,161

wsj.com Complete equity option listings and data are available in The Wall Street Journal Interactive Edition at **http://wsj.com** on the Internet's World Wide Web.

Option/Strike		Exp.	–Call– Vol.	–Call– Last	–Put– Vol.	–Put– Last
ACC Cp	30	Dec	222	9	...	...
39 3/8	35	Nov	491	5 5/8	43	1 3/4
39 3/8	35	Dec	312	7 1/4	...	...
39 3/8	40	Dec	367	3 3/8	50	3 7/8
ASM Litho	65	Apr	...	...	220	12 1/4
AT&T	45	Nov	1660	3 5/8	234	13/16
48 3/16	50	Nov	755	15/16	28	2 1/4
48 3/16	50	Dec	1774	2	34	2 7/8
Aames	12 1/2	Dec	403	2 7/8	20	15/16
14 3/8	15	Dec	347	1 1/2	81	1 3/4
Abbt L	65	Nov	368	9/16	20	5
AccuStff	25	Dec	750	3 3/4	...	...
AdvFibCm	30	Nov	30	2 9/16	263	2 1/8
A M D	25	Nov	1714	1	3666	4 1/4
Advnta	30	Nov	45	2 1/16	650	1
AdvanB	30	Nov	385	1 1/8	...	...
Agourn	45	Nov	257	3	13	2 7/8
Airtch	30	Apr	550	10	...	...
Altera	45	Nov	2315	1 3/8	2065	5 1/8
AmerOn	70	Nov	40	9	393	2 1/16
75 5/8	70	Jan	424	12 1/4	166	4 3/4
75 5/8	75	Nov	375	5 3/8	575	3 7/8
75 5/8	80	Nov	228	2 3/4	70	6 3/4
75 5/8	85	Nov	302	1 9/16	160	9 7/8
75 5/8	90	Nov	664	11/16	...	...
75 5/8	95	Nov	430	3/8	10	18 1/2
AmExpr	80	Dec	662	3 1/2	90	4 1/2
Amrtch	65	Jan	...	...	255	3 1/2
Amgen	45	Dec	8	4 1/8	215	1 5/16
47 7/16	50	Nov	257	11/16	1	3 1/2
Amoco	75	Nov	4205	17 1/8	...	...
Analog	30	Nov	200	1 1/2	155	1 3/8
AppleC	17 1/2	Nov	537	7/8	100	1 7/16
16 1/2	20	Nov	217	1/4	146	3 3/8
16 1/2	35	Jan	740	1/16	...	...
Aplbee	25	Feb	464	1	...	...

Option/Strike		Exp.	–Call– Vol.	–Call– Last	–Put– Vol.	–Put– Last
75 3/4	80	Jan	849	5	257	8 1/8
75 3/4	85	Nov	6785	1 1/4	2984	10
75 3/4	85	Dec	2395	2 1/4	109	10 1/8
75 3/4	85	Jan	1164	3 1/2	531	11 3/4
75 3/4	85	Apr	503	6	94	12 1/4
75 3/4	90	Nov	3743	5/8	212	14 3/8
75 3/4	90	Dec	446	1 3/8	37	14
75 3/4	90	Jan	737	2 1/4	127	15 3/8
75 3/4	90	Apr	435	4 5/8	16	15
75 3/4	95	Nov	1114	1/4	140	17 5/8
75 3/4	95	Dec	418	11/16	3	17
75 3/4	95	Jan	441	1 5/8	...	...
75 3/4	100	Dec	212	3/8	...	...
75 3/4	100	Jan	422	1 1/16	68	22
75 3/4	100	Apr	217	2 5/8	10	21 3/4
75 3/4	102 1/2	Jan	250	3/4	10	24 5/8
75 3/4	110	Jan	42	9/16	250	31 3/8
I B M	70	Jan	79	26 7/8	278	5/8
95 13/16	75	Jan	33	25 1/8	682	1
95 13/16	80	Nov	...	...	616	11/16
95 13/16	80	Dec	2	18	220	1
95 13/16	85	Nov	21	12 1/4	925	1 1/8
95 13/16	85	Dec	...	...	200	1 13/16
95 13/16	85	Jan	...	...	454	2 1/4
95 13/16	90	Nov	1891	8	4368	2 1/8
95 13/16	90	Dec	25	10 5/8	398	3 1/8
95 13/16	90	Jan	168	10	244	3 7/8
95 13/16	95	Nov	808	4 1/2	4304	3 7/8
95 13/16	95	Dec	434	6 3/8	194	5 1/8
95 13/16	95	Jan	159	7 3/4	553	5 3/8
95 13/16	100	Nov	4126	2 5/16	2354	6 1/2
95 13/16	100	Dec	758	4 1/8	71	7 3/8
95 13/16	100	Jan	765	5 1/8	69	8 1/8
95 13/16	105	Nov	2308	1 1/8	181	10 1/2
95 13/16	105	Dec	736	2 1/2	12	9
95 13/16	105	Jan	536	3 1/2	70	10
95 13/16	110	Nov	770	1/2	713	14 5/8
95 13/16	110	Jan	636	2 1/4	40	14 1/2
95 13/16	115	Jan	363	1 5/8	...	...
95 13/16	120	Jan	251	7/8	...	...

fully expects that the price of IBM will rise 50 points in the next two weeks—from $95^{13}/_{16}$ to $145^{13}/_{16}$. This may sound unlikely, and indeed it is, but it is not impossible. Such increases in price commonly occur in takeover-candidate stocks in very short periods of time.

Assume also that our speculator has only about $10,000 to invest. If she were to buy IBM common stock, she can afford to purchase only 100 shares at $95.81. If she can arrange a margin purchase, she can buy an extra 100 shares. If the price of IBM in fact rises to $145^{13}/_{16}$, our speculator will have made $5,000 less commissions on a straight purchase; if she makes a margin purchase, she will make about $10,000 less commissions and interest. These are certainly tidy profits for a two-week investment.

But consider what happens if the speculator takes $10,000 and buys IBM November 110 call options: She can buy 220 contracts and thereby obtain the right to buy 20,000 shares. Now, when the price goes up 50 points, our speculator is able to exercise the call option and buy 20,000 shares at 110 per share and immediately sell them for $145^{13}/_{16}$. The net profit after deducting the $10,000 cost of the options is more than $700,000.

One can obviously get rich quickly on call options if one can correctly predict when a big run-up in price will occur. Indeed, those who made fantastic profits on inside information about takeovers often used call options to maximize their gains. It should be added that the SEC views such trading as being illegal, and violators are subject to civil and criminal penalties.

It is not necessary for the speculator to exercise the options to purchase the shares and then immediately resell; the options themselves can be sold. Thus, the profit can be realized by the speculator whether or not she has the capital to exercise the options. Indeed, one would expect the IBM November 110 calls to be trading at about $36 per share ($3,600 per contract) in the example given because the expiration date is very close. If the option had longer to run, the price would be even higher, because there is a chance that IBM stock will rise even higher before expiration. When the price of the underlying stock is greater than the strike price of a call option, the option is said to be **in the money**.

There is no danger that the option writer will renege; his or her performance is guaranteed by both the exchange on which the option is traded and the broker who arranged for the option to be written. Nor is there much danger that an investor will allow a valuable option to go unexercised before it expires; brokerage firms regularly sweep option customers accounts and sell all options that are in the money shortly before expiration.

There must be a downside to get-rich-quick trading in options. Indeed there is. What happens if the speculator is wrong and the price of IBM remains stable? If the speculator bought the stock itself, she is about even: IBM has remained stable in price and the investment can be recovered (less commissions) simply by selling the stock. Even if the speculator had bought an extra 100 shares on margin, she still would lose only a little interest in addition to commissions. But if the speculator had bought call options, they would have expired on November 21, and she would have lost the entire investment.

The IBM call option used in the last example is an **out of the money** option, because IBM would need to rise more than $14^{3}/_{16}$ points in price before

the option has any value. The November 90 IBM option, on the other hand, is in the money, because the stock is selling at $95^{13}/_{16}$ and the option has an intrinsic value of $5^{13}/_{16}$. This option sold for 8 on October 30: The difference between $5^{13}/_{16}$ and 8 represents a **premium** for the possibility that IBM may increase in price before the option expires. The difference is sometimes called the **time value** of the option to distinguish it from the option's **intrinsic value**.

The person who commits to sell IBM shares at the option of the purchaser is called the **writer** of the option. When a person writes an option and sells it, the writer receives the sales price of the option: The writer of the IBM calls described above pockets the $10,000 sales price for the options (less a brokerage commission). If the option expires valueless, the writer keeps the $10,000, thereby improving the yield on his or her portfolio. If IBM unexpectedly moves up in price and the option is exercised, the writer will of course be required to sell the shares at 110 (the strike price). The writer still has a profit, but all profits above the strike price inure to the purchaser of the call option. Writing call options at above-market strike prices is generally profitable in stable or declining markets, because few or none of them will be exercised. If the market rises, the writer receives the strike price and the option purchaser receives the entire value of the stock above the strike price.

Some investors write call options without actually owning the shares. This is called going naked or writing **naked options**, and is considerably more risky than writing covered options — options for which the writer already owns the shares. Writing a naked call option on IBM common stock is analogous, in terms of risk, to a short sale of IBM stock. If the price moves up, both the short seller and the writer of the uncovered call are required to buy IBM stock to close out the transaction. Because the broker selling the uncovered call option is responsible for delivery of the shares if the call is exercised, it is essential that the writer of an uncovered call post margin and that that margin be increased if the price of the underlying IBM stock rises during the life of the option.

Call options may also be used to speculate on a variety of potential takeover candidates by persons with limited financial resources. A person having identified, say, 10 companies that are likely takeover candidates may purchase call options on all 10 stocks at a cost considerably less than directly investing in the stocks themselves. If one or two of the 10 actually become takeover candidates, the gain on these calls may well exceed the cost of all of the call options. Of course, if none of the 10 actually become takeover candidates during the period of the options, the speculator may easily lose his or her entire investment.

Probably the most common strategy among options traders is to buy near-to-the-money options to speculate on smaller moves in the price of a stock. Although it is almost inconceivable that IBM would rise from $95.81 to $145.81 per share, it would not be at all unusual for it to rise by $5 even on a single day. If a trader were to buy a $95 call and sell it after the stock had risen to $100, the trader could make a $5 per share profit (ignoring commissions) on this one-day investment. Assuming that the option does not expire at least for a few more days, the price of the option is likely to rise by just about the same amount as the price of the stock on any given day. Of course, it may also fall. Indeed, the trader who buys a $95 call option can even make a profit

if the stock only moves up to $96 or $97 (again ignoring commissions), because the option itself may be sold for the premium, which declines marginally each day until expiration, other things equal.

Call options may be purchased in order to hedge short sale positions. It will be recalled that a short seller borrows shares and sells them, hoping prices will decline so that he or she can replace the borrowed shares at a lower price. A short seller gets squeezed when prices move up rather than down; if the short seller is concerned about this prospect he or she can reduce or eliminate the risk by buying a call option on the same stock. If the price goes up, the loss on the short sale position will be offset by the gain on the call. Whether this is desirable depends on how expensive the call is, because that is the "premium" for this type of insurance.

A put option enables the purchaser of the put to profit on market declines. A put is the mirror image of a call option. The writer of a put option commits to buy the stock at the strike price for the specified period at the option of the buyer of the option. In a call, the writer commits to sell and the buyer of the call has the option whether to buy. In a put, the writer commits to buy and the buyer of the put has the option whether to sell.

For example, from Table 16-1 it will be seen that the IBM January 85 put option sold at $2\frac{1}{4}$. If a person bought this put, and the price of IBM declined to 70, the holder of the put would show a profit equal to the difference between 85 and 70, minus the cost of the put option. In the vernacular, the holder of the put could "buy IBM at 70 and put it to the writer at 85." That is why it is called a put.

Table 16-1 shows the inverse relationship between puts and calls. When a call is in the money and has intrinsic value, the corresponding put must, by definition, be out of the money, and vice versa.

Because the writer of a put option only commits to purchase a stock at a specified price, there is no precisely analogous concept to writing naked call options on the put side. The writing of puts, however, can create devastating losses if there is a sudden strong downward movement in the stock's price. The risk involved in writing put options is not apparent in a generally rising market. Such a market existed from early 1982 through August 1987. Many brokers recommended to relatively unsophisticated clients during this period that the clients write put options to increase the investment yield of their portfolios. It seemed to be a relatively safe way of increasing investment return. In the abrupt market decline that occurred in October 1987, many of these investors' savings were wiped out as brokerage firms liquidated their accounts in order to meet obligations under put contracts, and some investors ended up owing their brokerage firms substantial amounts as well. The writing of put options in excess of available at-risk capital is sometimes referred to as writing naked put options as an analogy to the risk involved in writing naked call options in a rising market.

The writer of a put option can limit future losses by buying an offsetting put option or by writing a call option. In a period of sharp market decline such as occurred in October 1987, the prices of puts advanced so rapidly (and the process of communicating securities orders was often so constricted) that these strategies were, as a practical matter, unavailable to at-risk put writers.

Puts may be purchased to shield portfolio positions from price declines;

for example, a person with 100 shares of IBM who fears a short-term decline in the stock but who does not want to sell the shares, may purchase a put option for 100 shares. If the price does decline, the loss of value in the underlying stock will be offset to some extent by the rise in value of the put, although the precise amount of protection depends on the terms of the particular put purchased.

In 1990, the **Chicago Board Options Exchange (CBOE)** began trading in long-term put-and-call options, called **long-term equity anticipation securities (LEAPS)**. These options have expiration periods of as long as two years. The strike price for LEAPS is usually set quite far away from the stock's current price—for example, when a stock is trading at 50, LEAPS calls may be quoted at 60 and puts at 40. A one-year call option on a $95 blue chip stock with a strike price of $105 might be around $600. In order for the investor to break even, the stock would need to reach $111 by expiration, a 17 percent rise in price, although the value of the option itself might increase if the stock were to rise significantly in price soon after the purchase of the option. In any event, with LEAPs, the trade-off is that larger price swings are necessary rather than the quicker ones needed to make a profit with conventional short-term options.

In general, the purchaser of a put or call option risks only the money he or she has invested in the option. If the price moves in the wrong direction, the holder of the option simply allows the option to expire unexercised. The writer of an option, on the other hand, is much more at the mercy of market forces.

The following chart may be useful in assessing the relationship between investment strategies and standardized securities options:

To profit on expected fluctuations in securities prices, if the price is going up, an investor should:

1. Buy the stock
2. Buy the stock on margin
3. Buy calls
4. Write puts

If the price is going down, an investor should:

1. Sell the stock
2. Sell the stock short
3. Write calls
4. Buy puts

One can speculate simultaneously on upward and downward movements by the purchase of options (a strategy known as a straddle). One may buy, for example, a November 100 IBM put for 6½ and a November 110 call for $0.50. The straddle thus costs 7 per share plus commissions. One makes money on this straddle if the price of IBM drops below 100 or rises above 110. One loses only if IBM steadily trades in the range between 100 and 110 for the balance of the option period.

A **synthetic position** is a combination of options that roughly equals ownership of the underlying security. A speculator in a potential takeover stock, for example, may buy a call with a strike price near the current market price of the stock while simultaneously selling or writing a put option at the same price. This combination, which approximates ownership of the security itself, is usually considerably less expensive to create (even if the margin requirement for writing the put is taken into account) than purchasing the stock directly or on margin.

Another options strategy is a **covered strangle** or **covered write**: selling both a call option and put option on a stock the speculator already owns. On a $60 stock, the speculator might write a call option at $65 and a put option at $55. Because the stock is already owned, it serves as collateral for writing the put option. In effect, the speculator pockets two premiums at the risk of being compelled to sell her stock when the price approaches $65 or add to her holding if the price declines toward $55. In a broad sense, a covered strangle is the converse of going naked. An **uncovered strangle** is the sale of both a call option and a put option when the speculator does not already own the stock. Some investors may be concerned that an uncovered strangle does not provide protection against substantial losses if the stock were to explode or collapse in price. Such an investor may obtain considerable protection by adding "wings," purchasing out of the money puts and calls to cap the maximum exposure in either direction.

Another interesting strategy minimizes the cost of a planned investment of, say, 200 shares of a stock currently selling at $37 per share. The strategy consists of the purchase of 100 shares, while at the same time selling a long-term call at 45 and a long-term put at 25. There are three possible outcomes: If the stock remains between 45 and 25, the investor keeps the stock and the purchase price is reduced by the two premiums on the options. If the price goes above 45, the stock will be called away but the investor has realized a gain of $20 per share on 100 shares, plus the two premiums. If the price declines to 25, the investor will be compelled to buy another 100 shares, but the price of these shares is $25 minus the two premiums, and the average price of the 200 shares is below the $37 per share that the investor would have paid if he or she had bought the 200 shares as originally planned. Of course, if the stock does not thereafter go above $25, the original plan to buy 200 shares at $37 per share was a terrible idea anyway.

A **married put** permits a speculator to engage in a bear raid similar to that made famous in the 1930s. A married put involves the simultaneous purchase of the underlying shares and of deep-in-the-money puts. For example, a speculator might purchase 100,000 shares of a $75 stock and 1,000 put contracts (puts on 100,000 shares) at 90. The cost of this put might be $13.50 per share. The speculator then sells the 100,000 shares gradually, in a manner designed to create apprehension from other shareholders and encourage them to sell. Because no short sale is involved, the sales may occur sequentially without regard to the uptick rule that applies to short sales. The expectation is that the profits on the puts will exceed the loss incurred from selling the shares at gradually declining prices. Some brokerage firms decline to trade in married puts, and the strategy described above seems to be manipulative and in probable violation of the federal securities law.

Why does an options market exist if the efficient market theory is so well accepted? When considered as stand-alone investments, options are far riskier than stocks because they last for only a short period, because they depend for their value solely on increases or decreases in market price, and because one loses the entire premium paid if the option expires worthless. To be sure, buying call options is an inexpensive way to buy stock, in the sense that one need only pay a few dollars or even cents per share to buy a chance at market gains in excess of the exercise price. But this is in fact a very expensive way to invest when one considers the fact that if the stock does not increase to the exercise price, the option expires worthless and the premium is lost. If one buys the stock and it fails to increase in price or increase in price as much as expected, one still has the stock and will have lost nothing other than the interest that may have been earned on the money in the meantime. Studies of option trading continue to indicate that option buyers—both put and call buyers—lose money in more than 60 percent of all transactions. A speculator in options thus faces long odds in an efficient market.

A plausible answer to the question of why an options market exists is that options are ideal for hedging rather than direct investment. Of course, the fact that options may make sense for one purpose does not mean they cannot be used (or misused) for another purpose. A conservative investor may use options as a way of insuring against the possibility that a particular stock or a portfolio of stocks will rise or fall in price. In addition, an investor who wants to increase the return from a portfolio may sell (write) options allowing others to buy or sell. By doing so, the investor receives the premium from the buyer of the option and agrees to buy or sell the stock in question if the optionholder exercises. In sense, the writer of the option is betting against price movements in the stock and getting paid to do so by those who are worried about price movements, a tactic that is perfectly consistent with the efficient market theory. Speculators (as opposed to hedgers) may also participate in the market, and although it may be very risky from their point of view, hedgers welcome their participation, because the more trading there is in options, the cheaper it is to use them to hedge.

§16.3 Options on Indexes, Foreign Currencies, and Interest Rates

Options trading can be extended to any product that fluctuates in price. Rather than writing an option on a single stock, one can write an option on a portfolio of stocks, that is, on a stock index. One can write an option on foreign currencies (whose values fluctuate with respect to U.S. dollars and with respect to each other). One can write options on Treasury notes or Treasury bonds (whose values fluctuate in response to interest rate changes, because they are viewed as riskless investments). Indeed, options are traded on all of these. Table 16-2 is a partial listing of trading in these nonstock options as reported by the *Wall Street Journal*. The only real difference in operation between traditional securities options described in the previous section and these nonstock options

Table 16-2

CBOE INTEREST OPTIONS

Thursday, October 30, 1997

OPTIONS ON SHORT-TERM INTEREST RATES (IRX)

Strike	Calls-Last			Puts-Last		
Price	Nov	Dec	Jan	Nov	Dec	Jan
50	....	....	....	....	7/8	....

Total call volume 0   Total call open int. 41
Total put volume 100   Total put open int. 374
IRX levels: High 50.30; Low 49.40; Close 50.20, −0.30

30 YEAR TREASURY YIELD OPTION (TYX)

Strike	Calls-Last			Puts-Last		
Price	Nov	Dec	Jan	Nov	Dec	Jan
60	2⅛	2 13/16	....	9/16	1⅛	....
62½	....	1⅜	1 13/16	....	2⅛	....
65	....	11/16	....	....	....	....
67½	....	....	....	....	5⅞	....

Total call volume 213   Total call open int. 3,158
Total put volume 222   Total put open int. 1,585
TYX levels: High 61.87; Low 61.35; Close 61.64, −0.57

Thursday, October 30, 1997

EXCHANGE RATES

The New York foreign exchange selling rates below apply to trading among banks in amounts of $1 million and more, as quoted at 4 p.m. Eastern time by Dow Jones and other sources. Retail transactions provide fewer units of foreign currency per dollar.

Country	U.S. $ equiv.		Currency per U.S. $	
	Thu	Wed	Thu	Wed
Argentina (Peso)	1.0014	1.0014	.9986	.9986
Australia (Dollar)	.7008	.6989	1.4269	1.4308
Austria (Schilling)	.08237	.08173	12.140	12.236
Bahrain (Dinar)	2.6738	2.6525	.3740	.3770
Belgium (Franc)	.02815	.02799	35.528	35.725
Brazil (Real)	.9042	.9062	1.1060	1.1035
Britain (Pound)	1.6705	1.6720	.5986	.5981
1-month forward	1.6683	1.6698	.5994	.5989
3-months forward ...	1.6640	1.6657	.6010	.6004
6-months forward ...	1.6576	1.6591	.6033	.6027
Canada (Dollar)	.7095	.7133	1.4095	1.4019
1-month forward ...	.7105	.7144	1.4075	1.3998
3-months forward ...	.7127	.7166	1.4032	1.3954
6-months forward ...	.7154	.7195	1.3978	1.3899
Chile (Peso)	.002378	.002409	420.50	415.05
China (Renminbi)	.1203	.1203	8.3136	8.3132
Colombia (Peso)	.0007753	.0007753	1289.82	1289.84
Czech. Rep. (Koruna) .				
Commercial rate	.03041	.03035	32.888	32.949
Denmark (Krone)	.1528	.1518	6.5465	6.5895
Ecuador (Sucre)				
Floating rate	.0002378	.0002378	4205.00	4205.00
Finland (Markka)	.1926	.1925	5.1917	5.1952
France (Franc)	.1736	.1727	5.7595	5.7900
1-month forward	.1739	.1730	5.7494	5.7804
3-months forward ...	.1746	.1736	5.7290	5.7595
6-months forward ...	.1753	.1744	5.7030	5.7334
Germany (Mark)	.5824	.5782	1.7170	1.7295
1-month forward ...	.5834	.5792	1.7140	1.7265
3-months forward ...	.5854	.5812	1.7081	1.7206
6-months forward ...	.5881	.5839	1.7004	1.7127
Greece (Drachma)	.003694	.003666	270.74	272.76
Hong Kong (Dollar)	.1295	.1294	7.7210	7.7295
Hungary (Forint)	.005135	.005118	194.73	195.38
India (Rupee)	.02754	.02753	36.305	36.325
Indonesia (Rupiah)	.0002747	.0002759	3640.00	3625.00
Ireland (Punt)	1.4997	1.4963	.6668	.6683
Israel (Shekel)	.2821	.2831	3.5445	3.5325
Italy (Lira)	.0005928	.0005896	1687.00	1696.00
Japan (Yen)	.008328	.008284	120.08	120.72
1-month forward	.008364	.008319	119.57	120.21
3-months forward ...	.008440	.008396	118.48	119.11
6-months forward ...	.008552	.008507	116.94	117.55
Jordan (Dinar)	1.4094	1.4094	.7095	.7095

Table 16-2 (*cont.*)

CURRENCY TRADING

Country	U.S. $ equiv. Thu	U.S. $ equiv. Wed	Currency per U.S. $ Thu	Currency per U.S. $ Wed
Kuwait (Dinar)	3.3047	3.3003	.3026	.3030
Lebanon (Pound)	.0006532	.0006531	1531.00	1531.25
Malaysia (Ringgit)	.2904	.2920	3.4435	3.4250
Malta (Lira)	2.5740	2.5543	.3885	.3915
Mexico (Peso)	....	....	....	....
Floating rate	.1200	.1212	8.3300	8.2500
Netherland (Guilder) ..	.5165	.5126	1.9360	1.9510
New Zealand (Dollar) .	.6234	.6222	1.6041	1.6072
Norway (Krone)	.1427	.1417	7.0058	7.0573
Pakistan (Rupee)	.02296	.02296	43.560	43.560
Peru (new Sol)	.3736	.3729	2.6766	2.6815
Philippines (Peso)	.02874	.02817	34.800	35.500
Poland (Zloty)	.2903	.2878	3.4445	3.4750
Portugal (Escudo)	.005708	.005675	175.20	176.20
Russia (Ruble) (a)	.0001699	.0001699	5887.00	5885.00
Saudi Arabia (Riyal) ..	.2665	.2666	3.7520	3.7515
Singapore (Dollar)	.6329	.6337	1.5800	1.5780
Slovak Rep. (Koruna) .	.03003	.02998	33.297	33.357
South Africa (Rand) ...	.2066	.2080	4.8410	4.8080
South Korea (Won)	.001036	.001010	964.95	990.25
Spain (Peseta)	.006895	.006844	145.04	146.11
Sweden (Krona)	.1331	.1331	7.5142	7.5117
Switzerland (Franc) ...	.7157	.7102	1.3973	1.4080

Country	U.S. $ equiv. Thu	U.S. $ equiv. Wed	Currency per U.S. $ Thu	Currency per U.S. $ Wed
1-month forward ...	.7180	.7124	1.3927	1.4038
3-months forward ...	.7226	.7171	1.3839	1.3945
6-months forward ...	.7291	.7235	1.3715	1.3822
Taiwan (Dollar)	.03232	.03243	30.944	30.835
Thailand (Baht)	.02513	.02548	39.800	39.250
Turkey (Lira)	.00000553	.00000549	180675.00	182190.00
United Arab (Dirham)	.2723	.2723	3.6725	3.6725
Uruguay (New Peso) ..	....	....	....	....
Financial	.1018	.1018	9.8250	9.8250
Venezuela (Bolivar) ...	.002007	.002002	498.33	499.50
SDR	1.3838	1.3784	.7226	.7255
ECU	1.1465	1.1383	....	....

Special Drawing Rights (SDR) are based on exchange rates for the U.S., German, British, French , and Japanese currencies. Source: International Monetary Fund.

European Currency Unit (ECU) is based on a basket of community currencies.

a-fixing, Moscow Interbank Currency Exchange.

The Wall Street Journal daily foreign exchange data for 1996 and 1997 may be purchased through the Readers' Reference Service (413) 592-3600.

OPTIONS
PHILADELPHIA EXCHANGE

	Calls Vol.	Calls Last	Puts Vol.	Puts Last
ADllr				70.41
50,000 Australian Dollar EOM-European.				
70 Nov	...	...	100	0.90
ADollr				70.41
50,000 Australian Dollars-European				
72½ Oct	...	...	100	2.40
SFranc				71.42
62,500 Swiss Franc EOM-European style.				
69½ Oct	20	1.98	...	...
69½ Nov	20	2.35	...	...
62,500 Swiss Francs-European style.				
71 Oct	...	...	200	0.28
72 Oct	...	...	250	0.88
Australian Dollar				70.41
50,000 Australian Dollars-cents per unit.				
72 Nov	...	...	20	2.03
British Pound				166.75
31,250 Brit. Pound EOM-European				
165 Oct	20	1.94	...	...
166 Nov	20	2.30	...	...
31,250 Brit. Pounds-European Style.				
164 Nov	...	...	10	0.47
31,250 Brit. Pounds-cents per unit.				
160 Nov	100	6.60	...	...
161 Dec	...	...	10	0.69
162 Dec	100	5.12	...	...
164 Dec	...	...	100	1.26
166 Nov	...	...	10	1.15
168 Nov	32	0.87	...	...
Canadian Dollar				71.02
50,000 Canadian Dollars-cents per unit.				
71 Nov	200	0.35	200	0.30
71½ Dec	10	0.31	...	...
72 Dec	40	0.22	...	...
73 Dec	31	0.05	...	...
73 Mar	15	0.32	...	...
French Franc				173.48
250,000 French Francs-European Style				
17 Nov	...	...	30	0.60
17¼ Nov	20	2.14	...	...

	Calls Vol.	Calls Last	Puts Vol.	Puts Last
GMark-JYen				69.93
62,500 German Mark-Japanese Yen cross.				
69 Nov	6	1.18	...	...
German Mark				58.12
62,500 German Mark EOM-European style.				
58 Nov	...	...	25	0.81
62,500 German Marks EOM-European style.				
57½ Oct	25	0.74	...	...
57½ Nov	25	1.20	50	0.58
58½ Oct	10	0.23	...	...
62,500 German Marks EOM-cents per unit.				
56 Oct	75	2.30	...	...
56½ Oct	75	1.82	...	...
57 Oct	200	1.30	...	...
62,500 German Marks-European Style.				
58½ Nov	16	0.48	...	...
58½ Dec	200	0.94	...	...
59 Mar	640	1.36	...	...
59½ Dec	400	0.52	...	...
60 Dec	10	0.35	...	...
60 Mar	640	1.00	...	...
62,500 German Marks-cents per unit.				
55 Mar	...	...	15	0.46
56 Nov	12	2.17	50	0.12
56 Dec	4	2.40	5	0.25
56½ Nov	12	1.76	65	0.17
57 Nov	200	1.21	...	...
57 Mar	56	2.54	51	0.90
57½ Nov	340	1.17	...	...
58 Dec	380	1.06	...	...
60 Dec	5	0.49	...	...
60 Mar	400	0.90	...	...
61 Dec	4	0.27	...	...
Japanese Yen				83.11
6,250,000 J.Yen EOM 100ths of a cent per unit.				
83½ Oct	275	0.26	...	...
6,250,000 J.Yen EOM 100ths of a cent per unit.				
84 Oct	200	0.10	...	...

	Calls Vol.	Calls Last	Puts Vol.	Puts Last
6,250,000 J.Yen-100ths of a cent per unit.				
81½ Nov	...	...	4	0.34
82 Dec	...	...	4	0.82
82 Mar	...	...	7	1.46
87 Dec	8	0.44	...	...
6,250,000 J.Yen-EuropeanStyle.				
90 Nov	...	...	15	6.20
Swiss Franc				71.42
62,500 Swiss Francs-European Style.				
65 Nov	19	6.89	...	...
66 Dec	4	6.08	165	0.10
66½ Nov	10	5.23	...	...
67 Nov	25	4.77	...	...
68 Nov	...	...	12	0.07
68 Dec	14	4.00	4	0.30
68 Mar	...	...	10	0.65
68½ Nov	40	3.06	...	...
69 Nov	12	2.80	30	0.20
69 Dec	...	...	4	0.41
70 Nov	32	1.83	78	0.40
70 Dec	14	2.12	20	0.78
70 Mar	...	...	15	1.10
71 Nov	98	1.10	...	...
71 Dec	...	...	10	0.93
71½ Nov	8	0.90	...	...
72 Nov	...	...	90	1.30
72 Dec	...	...	29	1.35
72 Mar	...	...	15	1.93
73 Dec	10	0.79	5	1.85
74 Dec	...	...	12	2.66
76 Mar	...	...	4	4.35
62,500 Swiss Francs-cents per unit.				
69 Dec	...	...	160	0.41
69 Mar	...	...	34	0.96
70 Dec	...	...	14	0.88
70 Mar	...	...	26	1.30
70½ Dec	...	...	45	0.83
71 Dec	...	...	50	0.96
71 Mar	...	...	25	1.73
76 Dec	25	0.30	...	...
Call Vol 5,963		**Open Int** ... 94,552		
Put Vol 1,856		**Open Int** ... 100,922		

is that one cannot usually receive or deliver the underlying securities or commodities when the option is exercised; one simply settles up in cash.

Options on stock indexes were introduced in the 1980s and quickly became extremely popular. (Trading in stock indexes themselves is discussed below in connection with commodities and futures.) Table 16-3 shows options traded on the CBOE. The original S&P 500 option was an **American option** contract with a life of approximately eight months, exercisable any time during the life of the option. In 1988, it was changed to a **European option**—it may be exercised only on the expiration date of the option. The advantage of the European option is that institutional investors writing options as part of hedging transactions are assured that the option remains in existence until its expiration date and cannot be "called away" before that time.

The American Stock Exchange (AMEX) and the CBOE conduct trading in long-term stock index options. These options have lives as long as three years, as compared with the maximum of nine months for most index option contracts. In addition, the face amounts of the longer index options are much smaller: The AMEX's LT20 is one-twentieth of the major market index, while the CBOE's OEX LEAPS represent one-tenth of the value of the S&P 100 index and its SPX LEAPS one-tenth of the value of the S&P 500 index. These options are designed to permit hedging of smaller portfolios.

The possibility of using puts and calls on individual stocks to hedge against price movements has previously been noted. Is there any social benefit to the trading of index options described in this section? Or are they pure gambling on random movements in abstract numbers? These questions have evoked some controversy. Basically, options package the risk components of investments in units that can be traded separately from the underlying units. Index options permit investors with large and diversified portfolios to hedge against broad price movements. Thus, for persons who invest in diversified portfolios, index options are arguably more important for hedging purposes than are options on individual stocks, although index options may seem like naked gambling on statistics.

§16.4 Commodities Markets

Commodities trading, primarily based in Chicago, and to a lesser extent in New York, has existed for more than a century. In recent years, these markets have been broadened to include trading in a variety of financial products. This section deals with traditional commodities trading; the following section briefly discusses financial products.

The traditional commodities market consists of two separate markets. The market for commodities available today—commodities located in warehouses or storage silos—is the **cash market** or **spot market**. Table 16-4 shows cash market prices for October 30, 1997. This market is used by suppliers, producers, and users of the various commodities that are traded. Most of the trading and speculative interest in commodities is not in the cash market, however, but in the futures market.

Table 16-5 shows the quotations for the futures markets for several agricultural commodities. Unlike the spot market, the **futures market** reflects

Table 16-3

INDEX OPTIONS TRADING

Thursday, October 30, 1997

Volume, last, net change and open interest for all contracts. Volume figures are unofficial. Open interest reflects previous trading day. p–Put c–Call

CHICAGO

Strike	Vol.	Last	Net Chg.	Open Int.
CB MEXICO INDEX(MEX)				
Dec 90p	10	2⁷/₁₆	+ ⁷/₈	10
Nov 100p	101	4¹/₂	+ 2³/₁₆	50
Dec 100p	3	6¹/₂	+ 3³/₈	161
Nov 105p	7	7	+ 4³/₄	...
Dec 105p	100	8¹/₂	+ 4⁵/₈	162
Nov 110c	200	5¹/₄	− 3⁷/₈	12
Nov 110p	300	6¹/₂	+ 3	150
Dec 110p	19	8¹/₂	+ 2³/₈	40
Mar 110c	2	11⁷/₈	+ 1³/₈	10
Nov 115c	13	3¹/₂	− 4¹/₈	...
Nov 115p	5	8¹/₄	+ 3¹/₄	31
Nov 120c	20	2¹/₈	+ ¹/₁₆	20
Nov 125c	10	1³/₁₆	− ¹/₂	47
Mar 125p	1	20³/₈	+12	30
Mar 150p	4	43¹/₄	+23⁷/₈	10
Call Vol.	245	Open Int.		2,646
Put Vol.	550	Open Int.		1,122
CB TECHNOLOGY(TXX)				
Nov 220p	2	5⁷/₈		...
Nov 230p	4	11³/₈	+ 5¹/₂	2
Dec 240c	10	8³/₄	− 1³/₄	...
Dec 260c	10	2³/₈	− ⁷/₈	...
Call Vol.	20	Open Int.		1,737
Put Vol.	6	Open Int.		146
DJ INDUS AVG(DJX)				
Nov 64c	50	11¹/₂	+ ¹/₄	50
Nov 64p	1,156	¹¹/₁₆	+ ³/₈	73
Dec 64p	5	1¹/₁₆	+ ³/₈	3,445
Nov 66p	59	¹³/₁₆	+ ³/₈	501
Dec 66p	700	1¹/₈	+	...
Nov 68p	40	1	+ ³/₈	490
Mar 68c	100	9¹/₂	+	...
Mar 68p	20	2⁷/₁₆	+ ⁷/₁₆	4
Nov 70c	196	4⁵/₈	− 1¹/₈	192
Nov 70p	1,052	1⁵/₈	+ ¹/₂	2,256
Dec 70p	44	1¹⁵/₁₆	+ ³/₈	1,769
Nov 72c	75	3⁷/₈	− ³/₈	739
Nov 72p	473	2	+ ⁵/₈	4,607
Dec 72c	50	5¹/₈	− ¹/₂	1,932
Dec 72p	5,680	2⁵/₈	+ ¹¹/₁₆	2,280
Mar 72c	25	7¹/₈	− ¹/₄	872
Mar 72p	24	3³/₄	+ ³/₄	269
Jun 72p	3	4¹/₄	− ³/₄	52
Nov 73c	103	3	− ³/₄	626
Nov 73p	361	2¹/₈	+ ¹/₂	2,044
Dec 73c	32	4¹/₂	+ ¹/₈	389
Dec 73p	98	3	+ 1¹¹/₁₆	694
Nov 74c	248	2⁵/₁₆	− ⁷/₁₆	832
Nov 74p	1,801	2¹¹/₁₆	+ 1³/₁₆	2,499
Dec 74c	899	3¹/₂	− ¹/₄	1,810
Dec 74p	878	3³/₈	+ 1	2,364
Mar 74c	29	6	− ¹/₈	118
Mar 74p	15	4³/₈	+ ⁵/₈	71
Nov 75c	858	1¹¹/₁₆	− ⁵/₈	1,840
Nov 75p	2,739	3	+ ¹³/₁₆	7,758
Dec 75c	1,134	2⁷/₈	− ¹/₄	1,977
Dec 75p	1,517	4	+ 1	2,875
Nov 76c	1,420	1³/₈	− ⁵/₁₆	1,684
Nov 76p	1,265	3⁵/₈	+ 1¹/₈	2,458
Dec 76c	19	2¹³/₁₆	+ ¹/₁₆	1,925
Dec 76p	56	4³/₈	+ 1	2,206
Mar 76c	11	4⁷/₈	+	258
Mar 76p	79	5	+ ³/₈	84
Nov 77c	164	15/₁₆	− ³/₈	950
Nov 77p	188	4¹/₄	+ 1	2,914
Dec 77c	9	2¹/₄	− 3⁵/₁₆	772
Dec 77p	21	4³/₈	+ ⁵/₈	441
Nov 78c	177	³/₄	−	3,231
Nov 78p	309	4¹/₂	+ 1	2,465
Dec 78c	12	1⁵/₈	+ ¹/₄	5,992
Dec 78p	116	5³/₈	+ 1	861
Mar 78p	1	6	+ 1	559
Nov 79c	692	¹/₂	+	3,153
Nov 79p	24	6¹/₄	+ 2	1,981
Dec 79c	53	1¹/₄	− ¹/₈	1,588
Nov 80c	118	⁵/₁₆	− ¹/₁₆	19,816
Nov 80p	274	6³/₈	+ 1	10,321
Dec 80c	34	1¹/₈	− ³/₈	6,720
Dec 80p	66	7	+ 1¹/₈	6,592
Mar 80c	1,068	2¹³/₁₆	+	6,713
Mar 80p	575	7¹/₄	+ ¹/₄	10,003
Jun 80p	5	8¹/₄	+ 4	4,010
Nov 81c	50	¹/₄	−	5,063
Nov 81p	43	7¹/₂	+ 2¹/₈	3,939
Nov 82c	626	³/₁₆	−	14,854
Nov 82p	5	7¹/₂	+ ³/₄	4,216
Dec 82c	24	⁹/₁₆	+	23,905
Dec 82p	10	8¹/₄	+ 1¹/₈	16,005
Mar 82c	2,451	2¹/₈	− ¹/₁₆	21,372
Dec 83p	10	8¹/₂	+ ¹/₂	50
Dec 84c	528	³/₈	+ ¹/₈	772
Call Vol.	11,465	Open Int.		164,749
Put Vol.	20,411	Open Int.		123,671

RANGES FOR UNDERLYING INDEXES

Thursday, October 30, 1997

	High	Low	Close	Net Chg.	From Dec. 31	% Chg.
DJ Indus (DJX)	75.43	73.81	73.82	− 1.25	+ 9.34	+ 14.5
DJ Trans (DTX)	314.32	308.72	309.17	− 4.35	+ 83.60	+ 37.1
DJ Util (DUX)	243.33	240.73	241.33	− 1.04	+ 8.80	+ 3.8
S&P 100 (OEX)	883.82	862.81	862.81	−16.64	+142.83	+ 19.8
S&P 500 -A.M.(SPX)	923.28	903.68	903.68	−15.48	+162.94	+ 22.0
CB-Tech (TXX)	232.96	224.32	224.38	− 8.58	+ 24.50	+ 12.3
CB-Mexico (MEX)	111.97	105.57	106.05	− 5.92	+ 24.09	+ 29.4
CB-Lps Mex (VEX)	11.20	10.56	10.61	− 0.59	+ 2.41	+ 29.4
MS Multintl (NFT)	504.38	490.94	490.94	− 8.79	+ 92.49	+ 23.2
GSTI Comp (GTC)	149.10	144.76	144.81	− 4.25	+ 28.36	+ 24.4
Nasdaq 100 (NDX)	1029.76	1000.70	1000.70	−29.06	+179.34	+ 21.8
NYSE (NYA)	484.43	475.83	475.83	− 7.10	+ 83.53	+ 21.3
Russell 2000 (RUT)	434.87	427.73	428.66	− 6.21	+ 66.05	+ 18.2
Lps S&P 100 (OEX)	88.38	86.28	86.28	− 1.66	+ 14.28	+ 19.8
Lps S&P 500 (SPX)	92.33	90.37	90.37	− 1.55	+ 16.30	+ 22.0
S&P Midcap (MID)	317.94	313.39	313.47	− 4.47	+ 57.89	+ 22.7
Major Mkt (XMI)	779.39	763.23	763.23	−12.77	+ 95.44	+ 14.3
Leaps MMkt (XLT)	77.94	76.32	76.32	− 1.28	+ 9.54	+ 14.3
Hong Kong (HKO)	....	....	207.78	− 8.36	− 65.47	− 24.0
Leaps HK (HKL)	....	....	20.78	− 0.83	− 6.54	− 23.9
IW Internet (IIX)	269.48	261.35	262.72	− 6.72	+ 18.64	+ 7.6
AM-Mexico (MXY)	122.90	115.08	115.74	− 7.16	+ 26.02	+ 29.0
Institut'l -A.M.(XII)	1002.10	977.12	977.12	−17.04	+184.44	+ 23.3
Japan (JPN)	....	....	168.29	− 4.81	− 28.80	− 14.6
MS Cyclical (CYC)	489.12	480.54	480.54	− 8.58	+ 91.98	+ 23.7
MS Consumr (CMR)	404.66	395.01	396.35	− 3.82	+ 60.40	+ 18.0
MS Hi Tech (MSH)	460.82	444.64	444.66	−15.48	+ 61.62	+ 16.1
Pharma (DRG)	496.58	481.15	484.24	− 3.06	+124.78	+ 34.7
Biotech (BTK)	170.52	165.04	166.42	− 4.10	+ 22.12	+ 15.3
Comp Tech (XCI)	460.64	444.68	444.91	−15.73	+104.99	+ 30.9
Gold/Silver (XAU)	90.83	87.17	90.46	+ 4.15	− 26.29	− 22.5
OTC (XOC)	743.21	724.31	724.33	−19.08	+141.46	+ 24.3
Utility (UTY)	267.95	264.53	266.06	− 1.19	+ 9.50	+ 3.7
Value Line (VLE)	855.86	844.37	844.37	−11.49	+161.75	+ 23.7
Bank (BKX)	710.37	693.15	693.15	−22.75	+155.47	+ 28.9
Semicond (SOX)	312.26	292.62	292.62	−19.64	+ 52.32	+ 21.8
Top 100 (TPX)	861.96	841.03	841.04	−14.95	+161.96	+ 23.9
Oil Service (OSX)	132.78	126.17	130.12	+ 1.34	+ 58.17	+ 80.9
PSE Tech (PSE)	302.26	294.67	294.79	− 8.98	+ 52.60	+ 21.7

Strike	Vol.	Last	Net Chg.	Open Int.
DJ TRANP AVG(DTX)				
Nov 305p	10	5¹/₄	+ 1³/₄	500
Mar 305p	50	12⁷/₈	+ 9⁵/₈	200
Nov 310p	10	6⁵/₈	+ 1³/₄	44
Nov 315p	1	9¹/₂	+ 1¹/₂	44
Mar 325p	50	19³/₄	+ 5¹/₄	1
Call Vol.	0	Open Int.		1,319
Put Vol.	121	Open Int.		1,032
MS MULTINATIONAL(NFT)				
Dec 490p	36	19¹/₄	+ 4¹/₂	100
Dec 500p	44	23	− 6¹/₄	46
Dec 505c	1	22	+	...
Dec 515p	2	25	+ 5⁵/₈	2
Dec 520c	29	12	− 14⁵/₈	100
Call Vol.	30	Open Int.		2,441
Put Vol.	82	Open Int.		1,905
NASDAQ-100(NDX)				
Dec 760p	18	5¹/₈	+ 3⁵/₈	249
Dec 790p	5	5³/₈	+ 1³/₄	244
Dec 800p	5	6³/₈	− 1¹/₂	213
Dec 870p	2	12¹/₂	+ 2	36
Dec 900p	47	9	+	37
Dec 900p	2	18¹/₂	+11	42
Dec 910p	11	6¹/₄	+	1
Dec 910c	4	16³/₈	+ 3⁷/₈	10
Dec 920c	191	13¹/₂	+ 7¹/₂	11
Dec 920c	75	12⁷/₁₆	− 9¹/₇₈	75
Dec 930p	73	15¹/₂	+	641
Dec 930p	900	24	+ 11⁷/₈	1,205
Jan 930p	900	33¹/₄	+	200
Nov 940p	22	17	+ 8	12
Dec 940p	4	24	− 2⁵/₈	76
Nov 950p	47	15¹/₄	+ 6¹/₈	83
Nov 960p	1	19	+ 11³/₄	35
Nov 970p	3	18⁷/₈	+ 7⁷/₈	27
Nov 980p	81	27¹/₂	+ 14¹/₄	90

Strike	Vol.	Last	Net Chg.	Open Int.
Nov 990c	15	37¹/₂	− 16¹/₂	80
Nov 990p	60	34	+ 18	255
Dec 990p	105	38⁵/₈	+ 7¹/₄	1,837
Jan 990p	2	42³/₈	+	...
Nov 1010c	185	29¹/₂	− 25⁷/₈	624
Nov 1010p	72	38	+ 14³/₈	843
Dec 1010p	2	46³/₈	+ 11³/₄	750
Jan 1010p	5	45	+	...
Nov 1020c	1,544	31	− 18	39
Nov 1020p	1,123	42	+ 17¹/₈	847
Dec 1020c	10	50	+ 17¹/₂	2
Dec 1020p	3	52	+ 24	234
Nov 1030p	9	42	+ 12	749
Dec 1030p	13	60	+ 18¹/₈	71
Nov 1040c	22	17¹/₂	− 15¹/₂	479
Nov 1040p	6	51¹/₂	+ 17¹/₂	296
Dec 1040c	20	42	− 87³/₄	4
Dec 1040p	20	54	+ 14¹/₂	330
Nov 1050c	46	23	− ¹/₈	2,111
Nov 1050p	29	61³/₈	+ 25⁵/₈	152
Dec 1050c	4	32¹/₂	− 6¹/₂	44
Dec 1050p	4	62⁵/₈	+ 22⁵/₈	551
Nov 1060c	181	59³/₈	+ 25⁵/₈	253
Dec 1060c	2	33⁵/₈	− 1³/₈	311
Nov 1070c	54	13	+	373
Nov 1080c	6	8¹/₂	− 4³/₄	261
Dec 1080p	20	82³/₄	+ 29	852
Nov 1090c	22	6³/₄	− 4	548
Dec 1090c	5	18¹/₂	− 5³/₄	60
Nov 1100c	124	4	− 3¹/₄	1,684
Nov 1100p	36	102	+ 27	552
Dec 1100c	101	17¹/₂	− 2¹/₄	119
Nov 1110c	212	3¹/₄	− 3	1,246
Nov 1120c	113	2⁷/₈	− 1¹/₂	773
Dec 1150c	5	2¹/₂	+ 1³/₁₆	969
Dec 1150c	9	5³/₄	− 5³/₈	132

Strike		Vol.	Last	Net Chg.	Open Int.
Nov	1160 c	2	2 3/16	+ 3/16	269
Nov	1170 c	15	3/4	− 1/4	628
Dec	1200 c	650	3	+ 3/8	804
Dec	1240 c	8	1 1/4	− 13/16	85
Call Vol.		**3,261**	**Open Int.**		**19,608**
Put Vol.		**4,109**	**Open Int.**		**29,566**
		RUSSELL 2000(RUT)			
Dec	375 p	10	4 1/8	...	209
Nov	400 c	250	29 1/2	− 6 1/4	708
Dec	400 p	9	7 5/8	+ 2 1/8	627
Nov	405 p	20	3 7/8	− 3/8	260
Nov	410 p	263	6 3/8	+ 2 1/2	1,354
Dec	410 c	10	31 7/8	+ 7 1/2	209
Dec	410 p	25	10 3/8	+ 4 1/8	785
Nov	415 c	2	19	+ 1 1/4	300
Nov	420 p	1,240	7 3/4	− 3 1/2	110
Dec	420 c	3	23 1/4	...	1,165
Jan	420 p	4	15 5/8	+ 12 1/4	10
Nov	425 c	4	12 1/2	− 3 1/2	824
Nov	425 p	1	7	+ 1	378
Dec	425 p	166	14	+ 1 3/4	302
Jan	425 c	1	25	+ 6	1
Nov	430 c	5	12 3/4	− 5/8	24
Nov	430 p	6	10 3/4	+ 3	911
Dec	430 c	255	17	− 3/4	255
Dec	430 p	250	15	+ 1 3/4	472
Nov	435 c	33	7 3/4	− 1 1/4	251
Dec	435 c	10	13	− 2	189
Dec	435 p	57	16 5/8	+ 2 1/8	41
Nov	440 c	12	5 3/4	− 3/4	370
Nov	440 p	1,001	14	+ 3 1/8	1,154
Dec	440 c	4	10 1/4	− 4 3/4	900
Dec	440 p	20	19 3/4	− 3 1/2	1,515
Nov	445 c	5	4	− 3/4	57
Nov	450 c	20	2 3/8	− 5/8	1,033
Nov	450 p	1	21 1/4	+ 5 5/8	450
Dec	450 c	18	8 1/8	− 3/8	1,044
Dec	450 p	41	26 3/8	+ 7 7/8	567
Jan	450 c	5	9 5/8	− 2 1/8	26
Nov	455 c	20	2 1/8	+ 5/16	246
Dec	455 c	23	5 1/8	+ 1 3/4	503
Nov	470 c	4	1/2	− 1/2	601
Nov	475 c	2	1/2	− 9/16	172
Call Vol.		**686**	**Open Int.**		**20,996**
Put Vol.		**3,114**	**Open Int.**		**23,440**
		S & P 100 INDEX(OEX)			
Nov	760 p	7,107	9 1/2	+ 4	11,221
Dec	760 p	699	16 1/2	+ 7	1,510
Jan	760 p	23	15 1/4	+ 4 1/2	68
Nov	780 c	2	106 7/8	...	10
Nov	780 p	1,735	11 1/2	+ 4	2,574
Dec	780 p	12	16	+ 4 1/2	518
Nov	800 c	31	88 1/4	− 4 3/4	115
Nov	800 p	8,199	14 1/2	+ 5 3/4	19,015
Dec	800 c	1	90	− 15 1/2	78
Dec	800 p	351	21	+ 7	3,142
Jan	800 p	33	27	+ 12 1/8	19
Nov	810 p	2,251	15 1/2	+ 5 1/2	5,557
Dec	810 p	34	23	+ 6 3/4	1,713
Nov	820 c	45	73	− 2	558
Nov	820 p	5,139	18	+ 7 1/4	8,246
Dec	820 p	97	24 3/4	+ 7 1/2	1,577
Jan	820 p	313	26 1/4	+ 5 1/4	1,179
Feb	820 p	1	31 1/4	+ 3 1/2	130
Nov	830 c	111	62	− 3	753
Nov	830 p	1,693	19 3/4	+ 7 1/2	7,001
Dec	830 c	10	77	− 3 1/8	44
Dec	830 p	88	28	+ 8 1/2	1,004
Nov	840 c	527	50 3/4	− 2 1/4	1,385
Nov	840 p	2,975	22 7/8	+ 9 5/8	7,186
Dec	840 p	340	29 1/4	+ 7 1/4	2,295
Feb	840 c	110	74	− 7 1/2	1,263
Feb	840 p	8	34	+ 7	178
Nov	850 c	313	37	− 10 3/8	2,191
Nov	850 p	4,030	26	+ 10 1/2	11,305
Dec	850 p	101	33 1/2	+ 8 1/8	2,801
Jan	850 p	11	33 5/8	+ 6 5/8	180
Feb	850 p	2	40 1/2	+ 8 1/2	199
Nov	860 c	2,136	29 1/2	− 9 1/4	2,836
Nov	860 p	4,144	30	+ 11 1/2	7,644
Dec	860 c	7	53	+ 7/8	406
Dec	860 p	74	35 3/8	+ 7 5/8	979
Jan	860 p	5	36	+ 9 5/8	369
Feb	860 p	2	43 1/2	+ 6	190
Nov	865 c	270	29	− 9 1/2	386
Nov	865 p	1,364	29 1/2	+ 10	2,471
Nov	870 c	2,125	25	− 7	1,959
Nov	870 p	2,648	34 1/8	+ 12 1/8	7,767
Dec	870 c	16	41	− 11	1,040
Dec	870 p	202	44	+ 13	1,430
Jan	870 c	2	47	− 3	233
Jan	870 p	30	44	+ 7 1/4	472
Nov	875 c	961	23	− 5	1,049
Nov	875 p	1,511	37	+ 14	4,617
Nov	880 c	2,025	18	− 7	3,348
Nov	880 p	2,740	38 5/8	+ 13 1/2	8,823
Dec	880 c	134	35 7/8	− 3/8	902
Dec	880 p	263	44 1/2	+ 10 3/4	2,854
Jan	880 c	68	45	− 2	256
Jan	880 p	50	43	+ 2 5/8	1,147
Nov	885 c	597	19	− 3	1,714
Nov	885 p	1,039	42 5/8	+ 15 1/8	2,753
Nov	890 c	1,319	14	− 6	4,138
Nov	890 p	672	44	+ 14	6,531
Dec	890 c	218	30	− 1 3/8	417

Strike		Vol.	Last	Net Chg.	Open Int.
Dec	930 c	790	13 1/4	− 2 3/4	1,801
Dec	930 p	12	74	+ 11 7/8	2,302
Jan	930 c	3	23 3/4	+ 2	249
Jan	930 p	7	85	+ 21	971
Nov	935 c	772	2 5/8	− 1 1/4	4,531
Nov	935 p	25	75 1/4	+ 19 3/4	667
Nov	940 c	3,234	2 1/8	− 7/8	8,627
Nov	940 p	74	73 7/8	+ 9 7/8	1,384
Dec	940 c	75	9 7/8	− 1 5/8	3,237
Jan	940 c	400	19 1/4	− 1 1/8	1,719
Feb	940 c	8	29 1/8	− 1 7/8	279
Nov	945 c	917	1 5/8	− 5/8	3,117
Nov	950 c	1,203	1 1/4	− 1/2	10,947
Nov	950 p	31	73 7/8	+ 7/8	239
Dec	950 c	1,210	8 7/8	− 3/4	593
Jan	950 c	12	17	+ 1/2	1,220
Feb	950 p	10	103	+ 6	5
Nov	955 c	143	1	− 1/2	4,670
Nov	955 p	1	78	− 4 1/4	4
Nov	960 c	3,291	13/16	− 5/16	8,364
Dec	960 c	7	5 1/2	− 1/2	3,073
Jan	960 c	2	13 1/8	+ 1 1/8	660
Feb	960 c	1	20 1/4	+ 3 3/4	210
Nov	970 c	674	9/16	− 1/8	7,506
Dec	970 c	88	4 1/2	− 1	918
Nov	980 c	707	7/16	− 1/16	9,558
Dec	980 c	36	4 1/8	− 1/4	1,332
Jan	980 c	53	8 1/4	− 5/8	1,861
Nov	990 c	634	1/4	− 1/8	8,734
Dec	990 c	97	2 1/4	− 3/8	1,195
Jan	990 c	34	6	− 1 1/2	385
Nov	1010 c	222	1/8	...	4,084
Dec	1010 c	35	1 7/16	− 1/16	1,772
Nov	1020 c	100	1/16	...	3,752
Nov	1030 c	76	1/16	− 1/16	2,261
Dec	1030 c	50	1/2	− 1/4	215
Call Vol.		**45,586**	**Open Int.**		**200,773**
Put Vol.		**53,048**	**Open Int.**		**192,048**
		S & P 500 INDEX-AM(SPX)			
Dec	500 p	74	1	+ 7/16	12,359
Dec	525 p	95	3/4	− 1/8	6,271
Dec	550 p	1,360	1 1/8	+ 1/4	11,848
Dec	575 p	83	1 1/2	+ 1/2	4,710
Dec	600 p	856	2	+ 3/4	19,390
Dec	625 p	510	2 1/2	+ 1/2	9,010
Dec	650 p	75	3	+ 5/8	9,564
Dec	675 p	622	5	+ 2 3/4	18,188
Nov	700 p	1,495	3	+ 1 1/2	6,967
Dec	700 c	4	207	− 17	1,567
Dec	700 p	4,748	6	+ 1 3/4	24,481
Dec	720 p	4	5 3/4	+ 1	8,186
Dec	725 p	45	6	+ 1 1/2	15,189
Dec	730 p	13	6 5/8	+ 1 5/8	2,407
Dec	740 p	41	10	+ 4 1/2	4,438
Nov	750 p	870	6 1/4	+ 3	6,290
Dec	750 p	2,172	8	+ 4	23,867
Dec	755 p	15	8 1/2	+ 4 7/8	163
Dec	760 p	94	9	+ 1 1/4	2,700
Dec	765 p	50	10 3/8	− 14 5/8	363
Dec	770 p	23	9 1/2	+ 1 1/2	5,401
Dec	775 p	14	11	+ 2 7/8	9,780
Dec	780 p	9,516	11	+ 3	4,118
Dec	795 p	243	11 1/2	+ 2 1/4	2,025
Nov	800 c	7	120	− 8 1/2	261
Nov	800 p	8,961	9	+ 3 1/4	6,347
Dec	800 p	9,714	15	+ 5	27,544
Nov	810 p	218	9 1/2	+ 3 1/4	3,976
Jan	810 c	3	117 1/8	...	3
Jan	810 p	10	16	+ 3	206
Nov	820 p	836	12 1/2	+ 6 1/2	7,425
Dec	820 c	5	118	+ 1	32
Dec	820 p	5,917	16	+ 3	4,370
Dec	825 p	113	18	+ 7	15,632
Nov	830 p	705	11	+ 3	9,706
Dec	830 p	4	14	+ 5 3/4	4,656
Jan	830 p	5	20	...	300
Nov	840 p	731	14 1/2	+ 6 1/2	7,260
Dec	840 p	291	18	+ 2	8,147
Nov	850 c	253	68	− 11	739
Nov	850 p	14,632	15	+ 4 1/2	19,004
Dec	850 p	2,434	22	+ 5 1/2	43,352
Jan	850 p	2	22 3/8	+ 4 3/8	1,243
Dec	855 p	5	20	+ 7	1,923
Nov	860 c	30	60	− 12	257
Nov	860 p	1,699	18	+ 7 1/2	4,562
Dec	860 p	1,209	25	+ 7	9,988
Jan	860 p	155	26	+ 7	520
Dec	865 c	2	67	− 10 1/8	5
Dec	865 p	2,536	21 1/2	+ 3 1/2	5,034
Nov	870 p	951	19	+ 7	9,457
Dec	870 p	602	29 1/4	+ 9 1/4	4,717
Jan	870 c	3	78	+ 10	6
Jan	870 p	3	30	+ 11 1/2	4
Dec	875 c	12	72	+ 4	8,118
Dec	875 p	10,274	30	+ 11	14,268
Nov	880 p	1,943	21	+ 6 1/8	13,266
Dec	880 p	119	25 1/2	+ 4 1/4	4,560
Nov	890 c	227	40	− 5	1,040
Nov	890 p	4,553	21	+ 5	9,205
Dec	890 p	313	30	+ 4	11,858
Jan	890 c	1	60	− 7	163
Jan	890 p	4	37	+ 9	159
Nov	900 c	3,001	29	− 9	13,401
Nov	900 p	3,950	27	+ 8 3/8	24,849
Dec	900 c	70	51	+ 1	27.780

Table 16-4

CASH PRICES

Thursday, October 30, 1997
(Closing Market Quotations)

GRAINS AND FEEDS

	Thur	Wed	Year Ago
Barley, top-quality Mpls., bu	uz	z	z
Bran, wheat middlings, KC ton	u80-83	80-83	93.00
Corn, No. 2 yel. Cent. Ill. bu	bpu2.68½	2.69	2.58½
Corn Gluten Feed, Midwest, ton	60-78	60-78	93.00
Cottonseed Meal, Clksdle, Miss. ton	175.00	180.00	180.00
Hominy Feed, Cent. Ill. ton	80.00	81.00	81.00
Meat-Bonemeal, 50% pro. Ill. ton	250.00	250.00	265.00
Oats, No. 2 milling, Mpls., bu	uz	z	z
Sorghum, (Milo) No. 2 Gulf cwt	u500-14	502-17	4.81
Soybean Meal, Cent. Ill., rail, ton 44%	u211-22	211½-22½	229.50
Soybean Meal, Cent. Ill., rail, ton 48%	u226-34	226½-34½	237.50
Soybeans, No. 1 yel Cent.-Ill. bu	bpu6.76½	6.79½	6.61
Wheat, Spring 14%-pro Mpls. bu	u4.35	4.37¼	4.43¼
Wheat, No. 2 sft red, St.Lou. bu	bpu3.59	3.57½	3.52
Wheat, hard KC, bu	3.80¾	3.80½	4.64
Wheat, No. 1 sft wht, del Port Ore	u3.97	3.96	3.93

FOODS

Beef, Carcass, Equiv.Index Value, choice 1-3,550-700lbs.	u102.14	101.00	106.69
Beef, Carcass, Equiv.Index Value, select 1-3,550-700lbs.	u92.30	90.96	95.21
Broilers, Dressed "A" lb.	ux.5090	.5130	.5970
Broilers, 12-Cty Comp Wtd Av	u.5568	.5568	.6208
Butter, AA, Chgo., lb.	u1.95	1.95	1.25
Cocoa, Ivory Coast, $metric ton	1,779	1,796	1,565
Coffee, Brazilian, NY lb.	n1.52	1.55	1.26
Coffee, Colombian, NY lb.	n1.62	1.65	1.33
Eggs, Lge white, Chgo doz.	u.73-78	.71-76	.80½
Flour, hard winter KC cwt	10.25	10.20	11.15
Hams, 17-20 lbs, Mid-US lb fob	ua.7	.72	z
Hogs, Iowa-S.Minn. avg. cwt	u45.75	44.75	52.75
Hogs, Omaha avg cwt	u45.00	45.50	54.00
Pork Bellies, 12-14 lbs Mid-US lb	u.64	.63-64	.59¼
Pork Loins, 14-18 lbs. Mid-US lb	u92-98	92-100	1.04
Steers, Tex.-Okla. ch avg cwt	uz	70.00	71.00
Steers, Feeder, Okl Cty, av cwt	u83.88	83.88	63.88
Sugar, cane, raw, world, lb. fob	13.24	13.14	11.15

FATS AND OILS

Coconut Oil, crd, N. Orleans lb.	xxn.29¼	.29½	.40
Corn Oil, crd wet/dry mill, Chgo.	u.25½-26	.25½-26	.22¼
Grease, choice white, Chgo lb.	b.21	.21	.16¾
Lard, Chgo lb.	.24	.24	.21
Palm Oil, ref. bl. deod. N.Orl. lb.	n.27¼	.27¼	.27
Soybean Oil, crd, Central Ill. lb.	u2443-503	2478-538	.21⅜
Tallow, bleachable, Chgo lb.	.26	.25	.17½
Tallow, edible, Chgo lb.	.26	.26	.21¼

FIBERS AND TEXTILES

Burlap, 10 oz 40-in NY yd	n.3000	.3000	.3400
Cotton 1 1/16 str lw-md Mphs lb	.6955	.6918	.6980
Wool, 64s, Staple, Terr. del. lb.	u2.60	2.60	1.90

METALS

Aluminum ingot lb. del. Midwest	p.75¾-6¾	.75¾-6¾	.65½

	Thur	Wed	Year Ago
Copper			
high gr lb., Cmx sp price	.91	.91	.93
Copper Scrap, No 2 wire NY lb	h.74	.74	.76
Lead, lb.	p.46013	.46111	.49140
Mercury 76 lb. flask NY	q180-95	180-95	260.00
Steel Scrap 1 hvy mlt Chgo ton	139-40	139-40	126.50
Tin composite lb.	q3.6866	3.6989	3.9928
Zinc Special High grade lb	q.61000	.61000	.51500

MISCELLANEOUS

Rubber, smoked sheets, NY lb.	n.50½	.50½	.66½
Hides, hvy native steers lb., fob	u86-90	84-90	96.25

PRECIOUS METALS

Gold, troy oz			
Engelhard indust bullion	317.94	314.68	380.80
Engelhard fabric prods	333.84	330.41	399.84
Handy & Harman base price	316.75	313.50	379.50
Handy & Harman fabric price	332.59	329.18	398.48
London fixing AM 314.00 PM	316.75	313.50	379.50
Krugerrand, whol	a318.50	315.50	378.50
Maple Leaf, troy oz.	a327.50	324.50	391.00
American Eagle, troy oz.	a327.50	324.50	391.00
Platinum, (Free Mkt.)	406.00	407.00	381.00
Platinum, indust (Engelhard)	408.00	406.00	381.00
Platinum, fabric prd (Engelhard)	508.00	506.00	481.00
Palladium, indust (Engelhard)	213.00	221.00	119.00
Palladium, fabrc prd (Englhard)	228.00	236.00	134.00
Silver, troy ounce			
Engelhard indust bullion	4.825	4.765	4.830
Engelhard fabric prods	5.308	5.242	5.313
Handy & Harman base price	4.805	4.750	4.820
Handy & Harman fabric price	5.286	5.225	5.302
London Fixing (in pounds)			
Spot (U.S. equiv.$4.8060)	2.8820	2.8755	2.9610
3 months	2.9135	2.9050	3.0030
6 months	2.9445	2.9365	3.0445
1 year	3.0120	3.0000	3.1355
Coins, whol $1,000 face val	a3,496	3,453	3,386

a-Asked. b-Bid. bp-Country elevator bids to producers. c-Corrected. h-Reuters. n-Nominal. na-Not available. p-Producer price via Platt's Metals Week. q-Platt's Metals Week. r-Rail bids. u-U.S. Dept. of Agriculture. x-Less than truckloads. z-Not quoted. xx-f.o.b. tankcars.

trading in standard units for delivery at specific times in the future. The futures market for corn is a good example. Table 16-5 reflects trading in 5,000 bushel units of corn for future delivery in December 1997, March, May, July, September, and December of 1998. On October 30, 1997, one could buy or sell corn in 5,000-bushel units for future delivery in December 1997 for $2.7975 per bushel or corn for delivery in December 1998 for $2.9025 per bushel. These transactions must be in the standard 5,000-bushel units. Assume that you decide to purchase 5,000 bushels of corn for December 1998 delivery. As a result of this transaction you have made a commitment to buy 5,000 bushels of corn next December; if the purchase were actually carried out, the transaction would involve $14,512.50 ($2.9025 × 5,000). On the other hand, it is essential to realize that you have not actually bought any corn in the physical sense: You have simply committed yourself to buy corn next December at $2.9025 per bushel.

Both the Chicago Board of Trade (where your purchase was executed) and the **futures commission merchant** (**FCM**) (the equivalent of a broker) that placed your order are responsible for the performance of your obligation to buy the corn. (Commodities futures may also be traded through larger brokerage firms that typically have FCM units or relationships with FCMs who handle their orders.) Therefore, when you "buy the future," that is, when you enter into the contract to buy 5,000 bushels of corn next December, you must post some money to ensure that you will carry out your commitment. When you buy the future, you will be required to put up perhaps 10 percent of the total purchase price of $14,512.50, or $1,451.25 in cash. This up-front payment is called margin, but it differs in a fundamental way from a margin purchase of stock. In a purchase of stock on margin, the broker is lending the investor funds to purchase shares, and the margin required is a down payment on the purchase price. In a margin transaction for stock, interest is charged on the unpaid balance. In the case of margin in a commodities future transaction, no credit is extended to buy anything; the margin in this context is somewhat analogous to a performance bond. Further, no interest is charged on a commodities future transaction, because no funds have been advanced by the broker.

The futures market does not differentiate between buyers and sellers with respect to margin: If you believe that corn prices are going down, you can sell the future, that is, enter into a contract to sell 5,000 bushels of corn in December. The terms would be precisely the same as if you had purchased corn: You would need to post about $1,451.25 margin.

A speculator who expects the price of a commodity to go up buys a futures contract for that commodity; a person who expects the price to go down sells a futures contract. One can buy or sell commodities for future delivery in the futures market, speculating on the prices of commodities for years without ever acquiring, owning, or selling the commodities themselves. A speculator in corn, for example, never needs to own a single grain of real corn despite a lifetime of trading in corn futures.

Virtually none of the delivery obligations that futures contracts create actually leads to delivery of the commodity. To see how this works, let us follow through on the preceding hypotheticals to show a speculation in corn futures. Let us assume first that you buy a corn futures contract for $2.9025 per bushel.

Over the summer, there is a drought, the potential corn harvest declines, and the price of corn increases. By November 1998, the price of December 1998 corn has risen to $3.15 per bushel. Clearly, you have made a profit, but how do you realize upon it? In the world of commodities futures, you do not "assign" or "turn in" or "sell" your contract to buy. Nor do you await delivery and then sell the corn itself on the spot market. Rather, you simply enter into another futures contract to sell December corn at $3.15 per bushel. When this transaction is executed, you have netted out or closed out your position. Because you now have commitments both to buy and to sell the standard trading unit of December 1998 corn, you do not owe the market any corn and the market does not owe you any corn. At that point, your account with your broker reflects only the purchase of December corn for $14,512.50 and the sale of December corn for $15,750 ($3.15 × 5,000) for a profit of $1,257.50. You are neither long nor short in corn. Your cash account with the broker, available for future commodities speculation now contains $2,688.75, the profit on the transaction in December corn plus the $1,451.25 cash originally put up as the performance bond.

This process of netting out works equally well if you originally sold a corn future. You simply buy a corn future with the same maturity, and your position is netted out. This process is so well established that it is reflected in the commission structure for commodities futures: Only a single commission is charged for the dual step of buying a future and then closing it out. Thus, if a position has not been closed out and the date of delivery is drawing near, one avoids the nuisance of accepting or tendering delivery by entering into an offsetting contract. This is not to say that deliveries under futures contracts never occur. If a user of corn, a producer of corn oil, say, decides it needs the corn in December, it simply does not net out its position; then delivery of 5,000 bushels of real corn is required under the standardized futures contract. A speculator who fails to net out similarly would need to make or accept delivery. This transaction, however, would be in the form of a warehouse receipt: A speculator who is long in corn runs no risk of awakening one morning to see a truck pulling up with 5,000 bushels of corn to be dumped in his or her front yard.

For every futures transaction, there must be both a buyer and a seller. (The same is true with options.) The process, however, is as totally anonymous as on a securities exchange: The buyer has no idea of the identity of the seller and vice versa. Indeed, because the exchange guarantees each trade, it in effect becomes the buyer for each seller and the seller for each buyer, once the transaction has been verified. There is also no limit on the number of futures contracts that can be written. Theoretically, there may be more open contracts to deliver grain in the future than all the grain that actually exists in the world. Usually, however, the numbers are more modest. Table 16-5 provides information as to the number of open futures contracts on October 30, 1997, that is, the number of pairs of buy and sell commitments. As the table shows, there were 24,896 December 1998 contracts, and a total of 407,039 contracts for all expiration dates, 542 more than the day before, indicating that many contracts had been closed out by offsetting purchases or sales.

Futures trading may lead to huge speculative gains or losses on rather small

Table 16-5

FUTURES PRICES

Thursday, October 30, 1997

Open Interest Reflects Previous Trading Day.

GRAINS AND OILSEEDS

CORN (CBT) 5,000 bu.; cents per bu.

	Open	High	Low	Settle	Change	Lifetime High	Lifetime Low	Open Interest
Dec	280½	280¾	275½	279¾	− 1½	310	227½	200,086
Mr98	290¾	290¾	285	289	− 2	305	236	105,646
May	296¾	296¾	290½	294¾	− 2¼	310	241¾	30,751
July	300½	300½	295	299	− 1¾	315½	245	40,602
Sept	288½	290	288	290	− 1	301	244	3,624
Dec	287½	290½	285	290¼	+ ½	299½	247	24,896

Est vol 70,000; vol Wed 65,599; open int 407,039, +542.

OATS (CBT) 5,000 bu.; cents per bu.

	Open	High	Low	Settle	Change	Lifetime High	Lifetime Low	Open Interest
Dec	162	162	156½	156¾	− 4¾	183	143	6,964
Mr98	170	170	165¼	165¾	− 4¾	180	148¼	4,198
May	172½	172¾	169	169	− 5½	182½	151	858

Est vol 1,500; vol Wed 801; open int 12,497, +542.

SOYBEANS (CBT) 5,000 bu.; cents per bu.

	Open	High	Low	Settle	Change	Lifetime High	Lifetime Low	Open Interest
Nov	689	689	680	685	− 4	750	577	36,318
Ja98	695	695	687	692½	− 3½	752	583	64,083
Mar	703	703	694½	699½	− 4	749	593	23,106
May	704	706	700½	705	− 4¾	745	601	17,122
July	715	715	706	711½	− 5	751	611½	14,208
Nov	682	686	679½	683	− 3½	717	597	6,646

Est vol 60,000; vol Wed 67,931; open int 162,011, +3,846.

SOYBEAN MEAL (CBT) 100 tons; $ per ton.

	Open	High	Low	Settle	Change	Lifetime High	Lifetime Low	Open Interest
Dec	222.00	222.50	219.50	222.20	− .40	239.50	186.00	39,358
Ja98	219.00	219.20	216.80	218.90	− 1.00	237.50	185.50	22,100
Mar	215.10	216.00	213.70	214.70	− 1.80	234.00	184.50	19,997
May	215.10	215.30	213.00	214.00	− 1.70	231.00	185.50	17,452
July	215.50	216.50	214.60	215.70	− 1.60	231.50	188.50	11,488
Aug	216.00	217.00	215.60	216.10	− 1.50	231.50	189.00	2,690

Est vol 15,000; vol Wed 16,947; open int 118,272, +297.

SOYBEAN OIL (CBT) 60,000 lbs.; cents per lb.

	Open	High	Low	Settle	Change	Lifetime High	Lifetime Low	Open Interest
Dec	25.30	25.35	25.00	25.03	− .35	27.50	21.72	54,072
Ja98	25.30	25.38	25.18	25.24	− .31	27.45	21.98	26,171
Mar	25.45	25.55	25.38	25.45	− .26	27.50	22.20	14,073
May	25.50	25.60	25.40	25.50	− .23	27.55	22.35	9,152
July	25.60	25.60	25.45	25.50	− .28	27.40	22.40	8,797

Est vol 14,000; vol Wed 15,916; open int 114,388, +775.

WHEAT (CBT) 5,000 bu.; cents per bu.

	Open	High	Low	Settle	Change	Lifetime High	Lifetime Low	Open Interest
Dec	358	361½	355	359¾	+ 1	473½	334¾	53,886
Mr98	372	375½	369½	374¼	+ 1	470	343¾	26,402
May	379	385	377	381¾	+ 1½	439½	345½	6,077
July	380½	385	379¾	384¼	+ 1½	425	333	14,372
Dec	395½	399	394½	397	+ 1	417	368	2,949

Est vol 15,000; vol Wed 10,445; open int 103,854, −104.

WHEAT (KC) 5,000 bu., cents per bu.

	Open	High	Low	Settle	Change	Lifetime High	Lifetime Low	Open Interest
Dec	366	372	365	370¼	+ ¼	498	340	27,343
Mr98	379	384½	378¾	383¼	+ ¼	491	350	15,657
May	386½	390½	385½	390	+ 1½	450	350	4,795

Est vol 5,330; vol Wed 5,512; open int 54,854, −752.

WHEAT (MPLS) 5,000 bu.; cents per bu.

	Open	High	Low	Settle	Change	Lifetime High	Lifetime Low	Open Interest
Dec	390	392	387½	390	− 2¼	479	349	13,572
Mr98	399	401	397	400	− 1	469	361	7,096
May	401	406	401	404	+ ½	440	363	1,510

Est vol 3,804; vol Wed 2,236; open int 23,286, +80.

CANOLA (WPG) 20 metric tons; Can. $ per ton

	Open	High	Low	Settle	Change	Lifetime High	Lifetime Low	Open Interest
Nov	380.00	381.70	378.80	379.00	− 3.40	410.00	332.20	8,412
Ja98	386.60	387.70	384.30	384.40	− 4.40	395.00	337.00	22,879
Mar	391.30	391.50	387.60	387.80	− 4.90	398.20	339.00	3,858
May	395.10	396.00	392.50	392.50	− 4.10	400.50	341.00	842
July		....	....	393.20	− 3.80	402.50	366.00	343

Est vol 6,100; vol Wd 6,091; open int 36,363, −672.

WHEAT (WPG) 20 metric tons; Can. $ per ton

	Open	High	Low	Settle	Change	Lifetime High	Lifetime Low	Open Interest
Dec	172.50	173.40	172.50	173.40	+ .10	183.30	147.80	3,242
Mr98	175.50	176.00	175.00	176.00	....	183.80	150.00	3,389
May	177.00	178.40	177.00	178.40	+ .10	184.40	152.50	1,591
July	178.00	179.40	178.00	179.00	− .50	184.50	170.30	1,997

Est vol 734; vol Wd 1,046; open int 10,239, +99.

BARLEY-WESTERN (WPG) 20 metric tons; Can. $ per ton

	Open	High	Low	Settle	Change	Lifetime High	Lifetime Low	Open Interest
Dec	151.30	152.50	151.20	152.20	− .50	158.70	123.50	5,956
Mr98	154.30	155.50	154.10	155.20	− .40	161.00	126.30	5,598
May	155.80	156.60	155.80	156.60	− .40	162.00	128.70	1,868
July	157.50	157.80	157.30	157.80	− .50	158.40	145.00	166

Est vol 1,100; vol Wd 1,506; open int 13,691, +1,026.

LIVESTOCK AND MEAT

CATTLE-FEEDER (CME) 50,000 lbs.; cents per lb.

	Open	High	Low	Settle	Change	Lifetime High	Lifetime Low	Open Interest
Oct	76.70	76.90	76.70	76.80	− .07	83.15	66.10	1,486
Nov	77.00	77.72	76.95	77.67	+ .65	84.30	68.35	6,090
Ja98	77.35	78.25	77.35	78.20	+ .85	84.95	76.25	5,527
Mar	77.35	78.15	77.32	78.10	+ .67	84.50	76.00	2,689
Apr	77.65	78.45	77.65	78.37	+ .72	84.45	77.60	1,000
May	78.60	79.25	78.60	79.05	+ .55	84.40	78.40	725
Aug	80.40	81.00	80.35	81.00	+ .40	83.25	80.20	266

Est vol 3,386; vol Wd 3,183; open int 17,810, +243.

CATTLE-LIVE (CME) 40,000 lbs.; cents per lb.

	Open	High	Low	Settle	Change	Lifetime High	Lifetime Low	Open Interest
Dec	66.85	67.25	66.47	67.22	+ .47	73.02	65.25	39,414
Fb98	68.07	68.40	67.75	68.35	+ .40	73.92	67.15	24,214
Apr	71.55	72.07	71.52	72.02	+ .50	75.55	71.00	14,367
June	69.22	69.70	69.15	69.67	+ .42	72.37	68.50	10,861
Aug	69.30	69.65	69.30	69.55	+ .20	72.15	68.60	3,571
Oct	71.55	72.00	71.55	71.92	+ .37	74.05	71.42	1,164

Est vol 11,530; vol Wd 20,158; open int 93,592, +2,610.

HOGS-LEAN (CME) 40,000 lbs.; cents per lb.

	Open	High	Low	Settle	Change	Lifetime High	Lifetime Low	Open Interest
Dec	62.00	62.85	61.80	62.82	+ 1.17	73.90	60.02	19,309
Fb98	61.90	62.77	61.75	62.72	+ 1.07	71.90	60.52	9.858
Apr	59.05	59.70	58.95	59.67	+ .90	68.15	57.00	4,024
June	66.25	66.95	66.15	66.92	+ .95	73.70	62.10	2,334
July	65.15	65.60	64.90	65.50	+ .75	71.75	63.40	911
Aug	63.70	64.50	63.70	64.50	+ .80	69.85	62.17	228
Oct	59.45	59.70	59.45	59.62	+ .17	64.90	58.00	338

Est vol 5,567; vol Wd 4,670; open int 37,072, −258.

PORK BELLIES (CME) 40,000 lbs.; cents per lb.

	Open	High	Low	Settle	Change	Lifetime High	Lifetime Low	Open Interest
Feb	64.50	66.00	63.90	65.82	+ 1.47	81.02	58.55	6,024
Mar	64.50	65.70	63.80	65.55	+ 1.47	79.40	58.80	958
May	64.50	65.90	64.00	65.20	+ 1.05	79.00	60.40	282
July	64.92	66.55	64.50	66.47	+ .77	79.00	61.10	146

Est vol 2,655; vol Wd 2,247; open int 7,442, −60.

FOOD AND FIBER

COCOA (CSCE)-10 metric tons; $ per ton.

	Open	High	Low	Settle	Change	Lifetime High	Lifetime Low	Open Interest
Dec	1,603	1,615	1,580	1,587	− 16	1,777	1,342	33,117
Mr98	1,643	1,648	1,618	1,625	− 14	1,803	1,373	29,043
May	1,663	1,668	1,642	1,646	− 14	1,817	1,399	13,587
July	1,682	1,685	1,662	1,665	− 14	1,835	1,485	3,947
Sept	1,703	1,703	1,703	1,685	− 14	1,836	1,456	4,806
Dec	1,702	1,702	1,702	1,703	− 14	1,863	1,510	8,878
Mr99	1,718	1,718	1,718	1,723	− 14	1,901	1,634	8,129
May	1,735	1,738	1,735	1,738	− 14	1,911	1,688	2,193
July	1,755	1,759	1,755	1,759	− 8	1,759	1,705	551
Sept	1,773	1,778	1,773	1,778	− 4	1,778	1,773	363

Est vol 8,911; vol Wd 7,770; open int 104,614, −66.

COFFEE (CSCE)-37,500 lbs.; cents per lb.

	Open	High	Low	Settle	Change	Lifetime High	Lifetime Low	Open Interest
Dec	149.25	151.00	148.00	148.15	− 2.45	226.00	97.00	11,194
Mr98	138.75	141.00	138.50	138.75	− 1.75	203.00	96.25	8,301
May	135.50	137.00	135.50	135.50	− 1.00	195.00	101.00	2,790
July	132.75	134.00	132.75	132.75	− .25	191.00	120.00	1,916
Sept	129.50	130.75	129.50	129.75	+ .25	186.00	122.50	920
Dec	127.00	127.50	127.00	126.75	+ .10	150.25	124.75	640

Est vol 5,059; vol Wd 6,319; open int 25,771, −119.

SUGAR-WORLD (CSCE)-112,000 lbs.; cents per lb.

	Open	High	Low	Settle	Change	Lifetime High	Lifetime Low	Open Interest
Mar	12.06	12.30	12.03	12.30	+ .30	12.19	10.13	94,054
May	12.00	12.19	11.96	12.18	+ .23	12.12	10.20	27,740
July	11.84	12.00	11.83	11.98	+ .16	11.98	10.30	19,199
Oct	11.74	11.90	11.74	11.90	+ .19	11.97	10.45	21,198
Mr99	11.58	11.70	11.58	11.70	+ .12	11.87	10.41	5,720
May	11.53	11.53	11.53	11.65	+ .12	11.68	10.75	563
July		....	....	11.62	+ .11	11.68	11.41	348

Est vol 55,788; vol Wd 44,309; open int 168,822, +8,172.

SUGAR-DOMESTIC (CSCE)-112,000 lbs.; cents per lb.

	Open	High	Low	Settle	Change	Lifetime High	Lifetime Low	Open Interest
Jan	22.15	22.17	22.05	22.05	− .10	22.53	22.02	3,554
Mar	22.20	22.20	22.15	22.15	− .05	22.51	22.05	3,164
May	22.40	22.40	22.35	22.35	− .06	22.56	22.15	2,589
July	22.60	22.60	22.59	22.59	− .02	22.67	22.36	3,099
Sept	22.59	22.59	22.59	22.59	− .06	22.68	22.35	2,090
Nov		....	....	22.33	− .12	22.51	22.00	670
Ja99		....	....	22.30	− .08	22.44	22.24	195

Est vol 227; vol Wd 1,479; open int 15,396, +108.

COTTON (CTN)-50,000 lbs.; cents per lb.

	Open	High	Low	Settle	Change	Lifetime High	Lifetime Low	Open Interest
Dec	71.85	72.44	71.75	72.05	+ .37	80.10	70.80	47,313
Mr98	73.25	73.80	73.10	73.40	+ .31	81.00	72.36	17,615
May	74.10	74.40	74.05	74.15	+ .25	81.00	73.20	9,876
July	74.70	75.15	74.70	74.78	+ .18	79.25	73.85	9,802
Oct	75.55	75.55	75.55	75.60	+ .20	78.00	74.40	870
Dec	75.50	75.80	75.50	75.79	+ .22	76.60	73.30	10,295
Mr99		....	....	76.68	+ .18	77.25	74.75	269

Est vol 14,000; vol Wd 7,384; open int 96,078, +181.

Table 16-5 (*cont.*)

	Open	High	Low	Settle	Change	Lifetime High	Lifetime Low	Open Interest
Apr	2.300	2.350	2.285	2.335	+ .005	2.460	1.825	9,628
May	2.210	2.255	2.200	2.240	....	2.350	1.830	8,093
June	2.210	2.235	2.190	2.220	....	2.330	1.745	7,836
July	2.210	2.240	2.195	2.220	....	2.325	1.852	8,082
Aug	2.210	2.235	2.200	2.225	....	2.325	1.845	7,489
Sept	2.210	2.235	2.210	2.230	....	2.320	1.850	5,495
Oct	2.240	2.265	2.225	2.265	+ .005	2.350	1.840	4,780
Nov	2.390	2.410	2.355	2.405	+ .007	2.480	1.915	3,034
Dec	2.540	2.550	2.530	2.554	+ .009	2.615	1.950	6,493
Ja99	....	....	....	2.575	+ .009	2.634	2.085	5,605
Feb	2.450	2.460	2.450	2.468	+ .009	2.540	2.025	3,500
Mar	....	....	....	2.339	+ .008	2.420	1.945	2,813
Apr	....	....	....	2.225	+ .007	2.300	1.910	1,496
May	....	....	....	2.185	+ .006	2.270	1.960	2,297
June	....	....	....	2.180	+ .001	2.300	1.860	2,457
July	....	....	....	2.180	+ .001	2.276	1.960	1,911
Aug	....	....	....	2.180	....	2.240	1.975	2,044
Sept	....	....	....	2.191	....	2.257	1.970	2,085
Oct	....	....	....	2.213	....	2.265	2.042	1,763
Nov	....	....	....	2.326	....	2.388	2.140	1,040
Dec	....	....	....	2.460	....	2.521	2.213	3,788
Ja00	....	....	....	2.500	....	2.531	2.295	3,333
Mar	....	....	....	2.300	....	2.315	2.119	751

Est vol 56,138; vol Wed 121,603; open int 237,527, −15,401.

BRENT CRUDE (IPE) 1,000 net bbls.; $ per bbl.

	Open	High	Low	Settle	Change	Lifetime High	Lifetime Low	Open Interest
Dec	19.85	20.23	19.78	20.10	+ .46	21.62	18.10	64,302
Ja98	19.93	20.21	19.84	20.13	+ .42	21.42	18.18	47,715
Feb	19.85	20.10	19.78	20.04	+ .38	21.20	18.18	18,147
Mar	19.77	19.95	19.66	19.90	+ .36	20.95	18.24	6,886
Apr	19.59	19.70	19.59	19.77	+ .35	20.62	18.24	5,471
May	19.43	19.47	19.43	19.64	+ .34	20.42	18.33	5,152
June	19.30	19.40	19.30	19.51	+ .23	20.00	18.10	9,072
July	19.31	19.42	19.22	19.42	+ .24	19.80	18.32	2,739
Aug	19.13	19.33	19.13	19.34	+ .23	19.80	18.58	2,564
Sept		....	....	19.27	+ .23	19.36	18.36	2,158
Oct		....	....	19.21	+ .24	19.34	19.00	1,244
Nov		....	....	19.16	+ .26	19.15	18.85	410

Est vol 44,276; vol Wd 47,340; open int 165,860, +1,393.

GAS OIL (IPE) 100 metric tons; $ per ton

	Open	High	Low	Settle	Change	Lifetime High	Lifetime Low	Open Interest
Nov	180.00	181.50	179.75	181.00	+ 2.50	192.50	165.00	27,511
Dec	181.00	182.25	180.75	182.00	+ 2.25	194.00	160.50	21,941
Ja98	182.50	183.00	182.00	183.00	+ 2.00	195.00	168.00	14,252
Feb	182.50	182.50	181.50	182.50	+ 1.50	194.50	169.00	8,592
Mar	180.25	180.25	179.25	180.25	+ 1.25	191.00	168.00	5,945
Apr	176.75	176.75	176.75	177.75	+ 1.50	185.25	166.25	3,392
May	175.25	175.25	174.75	175.50	+ 1.50	183.75	16500	1,632
June	174.50	175.00	174.00	174.75	+ 1.50	183.25	163.50	7,142
July		....	....	175.50	+ 1.50	183.00	163.75	1,575
Aug		....	....	176.50	+ 1.50	182.00	169.00	1,819
Sept		....	....	177.75	+ 1.25	184.00	170.00	368
Oct		....	....	179.25	+ 1.25	179.75	178.00	701
Dec		....	....	180.00	+ 1.25	186.00	173.00	3,949

Est vol 14,861; vol Wd 19,453; open int 98,869, +4,77.

INTEREST RATE

TREASURY BONDS (CBT)-$100,000; pts. 32nds of 100%

	Open	High	Low	Settle	Change	Lifetime High	Lifetime Low	Open Interest
Dec	117-21	118-19	117-21	118-05	+ 19	119-02	100-08	617,654
Mr98	118-02	118-07	117-17	117-28	+ 19	118-24	104-21	73,570
June	....	....	....	117-16	+ 19	118-02	104-03	11,715
Sept	....	....	....	117-06	+ 20	116-18	103-22	2,029
Dec	....	....	....	116-29	+ 21	117-01	103-13	4,704

Est vol 695,000; vol Wed 656,513; open int 708,738, +987.
Note: Tues.Vol. should have been 1,062,845

TREASURY BONDS (MCE)-$50,000; pts. 32nds of 100%

	Open	High	Low	Settle	Change	Lifetime High	Lifetime Low	Open Interest
Dec	118-08	118-17	117-27	118-12	+ 21	118-27	105-20	18,522

Est vol 6,945; vol Wed 12,441; open int 18,549, −411.

TREASURY NOTES (CBT)-$100,000; pts. 32nds of 100%

	Open	High	Low	Settle	Change	Lifetime High	Lifetime Low	Open Interest
Dec	111-13	111-30	111-13	111-22	+ 13	112-12	104-10	373,009
Mr98	111-06	111-19	111-06	111-13	+ 13	111-30	105-24	25,491
June	....	....	....	111-09	+ 13	110-29	106-26	102

Est vol 170,007; vol Wed 153,156; open int 398,602, −342.

5 YR TREAS NOTES (CBT)-$100,000; pts. 32nds of 100%

	Open	High	Low	Settle	Change	Lifetime High	Lifetime Low	Open Interest
Dec	108-06	08-185	108-06	08-115	+ 8.0	109-06	04-005	232,765
Mr98	108-10	08-145	08-045	08-095	+ 8.5	108-27	106-07	5,443

Est vol 87,304; vol Wed 92,633; open int 238,208, +5,796.

2 YR TREAS NOTES (CBT)-$200,000, pts. 32nds of 100%

	Open	High	Low	Settle	Change	Lifetime High	Lifetime Low	Open Interest
Dec	03-287	04-017	103-28	103-30	+ 3.0	104-09	02-265	37,516

Est vol 4,200; vol Wed 3,315; open int 37,546, +327.

30-DAY FEDERAL FUNDS (CBT)-$5 million; pts. of 100%

	Open	High	Low	Settle	Change	Lifetime High	Lifetime Low	Open Interest
Oct	94.505	94.505	94.500	94.500	....	94.510	93.900	5,624
Nov	94.47	94.47	94.46	94.47	+ .01	94.48	93.88	8,659
Dec	94.45	94.46	94.43	94.45	+ .02	94.48	93.78	5,185
Ja98	94.44	94.45	94.43	94.44	+ .02	94.47	93.97	2,603
Feb	94.46	94.46	94.44	94.45	+ .03	94.48	93.84	2,180
Mar	94.42	94.43	94.41	94.41	+ .03	95.30	94.13	313
May	94.39	94.40	94.37	94.38	+ .03	94.43	94.15	229

Est vol 4,444; vol Wed 3,224; open int 24,837, −85.

MUNI BOND INDEX (CBT)-$1,000; times Bond Buyer MBI

	Open	High	Low	Settle	Change	Lifetime High	Lifetime Low	Open Interest
Dec	121-26	122-05	121-13	121-23	+ 12	122-19	109-22	21,105
Mr98	120-27	120-28	120-10	120-17	+ 10	121-08	116-29	245

Est vol 2,500; vol Wed 4,668; open int 21,350, +520.
The index: Close 121-25; Yield 5.58.

TREASURY BILLS (CME)-$1 mil.; pts. of 100%

	Open	High	Low	Settle	Chg	Discount Settle	Discount Chg	Open Interest
Dec	95.13	95.18	95.10	95.11	+ .03	4.89	− .03	5,436
Mr98	95.28	95.28	95.19	95.22	+ .02	4.79	− .02	4,568
June	95.26	95.26	95.16	95.16	+ .03	4.84	− .03	481

Est vol 918; vol Wed 2,375; open int 10,507, +823.

LIBOR-1 MO. (CME)-$3,000,000; points of 100%

	Open	High	Low	Settle	Chg	Discount Settle	Discount Chg	Open Interest
Nov	94.38	94.40	94.36	94.37	+ .01	5.63	− .01	36,485
Dec	94.26	94.26	94.20	94.23	+ .02	5.77	− .02	14,983
Ja98	94.36	94.38	94.34	94.36	+ .03	5.64	− .03	4,393
Feb	94.34	94.35	94.34	94.33	+ .03	5.67	− .03	1,313
Mar	....	....	....	94.32	+ .04	5.68	− .04	691
Apr	....	....	....	94.30	+ .03	5.70	− .03	186
May	....	....	....	94.27	+ .04	5.74	− .04	150
June	....	....	....	94.26	+ .04	5.74	− .04	300

5 YR. FRENCH GOVT. BONDS (MATIF)
FFr 500,000; 100ths of 100%

	Open	High	Low	Settle	Change	Lifetime High	Lifetime Low	Open Interest
Dec	97.38	97.48	97.25	97.34	+ .35	97.48	97.25	54,445
Mr98	....	....	....	97.09	+ .35	....	....	605

Est vol 35,908; vol Wd na; open int 55,050, +2,919.

10 YR. FRENCH GOVT. BONDS (MATIF)
FFr 500,000; 100ths of 100%

	Open	High	Low	Settle	Change	Lifetime High	Lifetime Low	Open Interest
Dec	98.90	99.12	98.82	98.98	+ .42	100.58	96.84	112,629
Mr98	98.40	98.48	98.38	98.44	+ .42	99.80	97.46	8,760

Est vol 140,790; vol Wd 132,909; open int 121,389, −1,682.

PIBOR-3 MONTH (MATIF) FF5,000,000

	Open	High	Low	Settle	Change	Lifetime High	Lifetime Low	Open Interest
Dec	96.27	96.28	96.24	96.26	+ .04	96.76	93.16	44,026
Mr98	95.98	96.02	95.96	96.00	+ .06	96.66	93.79	51,365
June	95.74	95.77	95.72	95.75	+ .07	96.48	93.39	33,150
Sept	95.55	95.59	95.54	95.56	+ .06	96.33	92.90	18,394
Dec	95.41	95.44	95.39	95.42	+ .07	96.13	93.77	24,755
Mr99	95.26	95.29	95.24	95.27	+ .07	95.93	93.52	46,234
June	95.10	95.15	95.08	95.13	+ .09	95.73	93.37	12,958
Sept	94.96	95.00	94.94	94.97	+ .07	95.56	94.23	8,781
Dec	94.79	94.82	94.79	94.83	+ .09	95.37	94.45	7,524
Mr00	94.68	94.68	94.68	94.71	+ .09	95.21	94.43	6,466
June	....	....	....	94.63	+ .09	95.04	94.36	2,580
Sept	....	....	....	94.52	+ .09	94.70	94.28	436

Est vol 61,713; vol Wd 69,796; open int 256,669, +2,627.

3 YR. COMMONWEALTH T-BONDS (SFE)-A$100,000

	Open	High	Low	Settle	Change	Lifetime High	Lifetime Low	Open Interest
Dec	94.74	94.79	94.70	94.77	+ .07	94.88	94.00	410,042
Mr98	....	....	....	94.70	+ .07	94.35	94.35	456

Est vol 31,186; vol Wd 39,411; open int 410,498, −17,564.

EUROYEN (SIMEX)-Yen 100,000,000 pts. of 100%

	Open	High	Low	Settle	Change	Lifetime High	Lifetime Low	Open Interest
Dec	99.48	99.49	99.48	99.49	+ .15	99.49	94.78	130,722
Mr98	99.46	99.49	99.46	99.49	+ .30	99.49	95.65	123,409
June	99.41	99.45	99.41	99.45	+ .40	99.45	95.60	94,415
Sept	99.34	99.39	99.34	99.39	+ .50	99.39	95.50	74,627
Dec	99.24	99.28	99.24	99.28	+ .50	99.28	96.37	65,415
Mr99	99.10	99.14	99.10	99.14	+ .50	99.14	96.24	38,343
June	98.95	98.99	98.95	98.99	+ .50	98.99	96.65	20,747
Sept	98.81	98.83	98.81	98.83	+ .50	98.83	96.99	8,381
Dec	....	....	....	98.68	+ .50	98.66	97.23	3,627
Mr00	....	....	....	98.53	+ .50	98.47	97.10	1,905
June	....	....	....	98.38	+ .50	98.36	97.39	1,143
Sept	....	....	....	98.25	+ .50	98.18	97.94	567

Est vol 24,977; vol Wd 19,333; open int 563,301, +372.

BOBL-MED.TERM BOND (DTB)-DM 250,000; DM per $

	Open	High	Low	Settle	Change	Lifetime High	Lifetime Low	Open Interest
Dec	103.65	103.89	103.58	103.73	+ .20	104.89	102.42	412,419
Mr98	102.94	103.12	102.94	103.02	+ .27	103.53	101.77	27,732

Est vol 208,195; vol Wd 168,121; open int 440,151, +34,318.

CURRENCY

JAPAN YEN (CME)-12.5 million yen; $ per yen (.00)

	Open	High	Low	Settle	Change	Lifetime High	Lifetime Low	Open Interest
Dec	.8333	.8396	.8328	.8360	+ .0032	.9320	.8135	102,896
Mr98	.8500	.8501	.8460	.8471	+ .0032	.9375	.8269	1,033
June	....	....	....	.8584	+ .0032	.9090	.8510	230

Est vol 16,076; vol Wd 26,903; open int 104,160, −1,491.

DEUTSCHEMARK (CME)-125,000 marks; $ per mark

	Open	High	Low	Settle	Change	Lifetime High	Lifetime Low	Open Interest
Dec	.5800	.5859	.5787	.5827	+ .0029	.6610	.5343	62,885
Mr98	.5880	.5885	.5827	.5854	+ .0030	.6160	.5383	2,685
June	.5880	.5880	.5870	.5879	+ .0030	.5995	.5490	2,655
Sept	....	....	....	.5901	+ .0030	.5875	.5687	113

Est vol 30,914; vol Wd 29,604; open int 68,314, −927.

CANADIAN DOLLAR (CME)-100,000 dlrs.; $ per Can $

	Open	High	Low	Settle	Change	Lifetime High	Lifetime Low	Open Interest
Dec	.7150	.7152	.7101	.7116	− .0037	.7685	.7075	67,996
Mr98	.7153	.7176	.7132	.7148	− .0038	.7670	.7108	3,308
June	.7190	.7190	.7160	.7172	− .0038	.7470	.7138	628
Sept	....	....	....	.7192	− .0038	.7463	.7155	326

Est vol 10,058; vol Wd 10,153; open int 72,351, −592.

BRITISH POUND (CME)-62,500 pds.; $ per pound

	Open	High	Low	Settle	Change	Lifetime High	Lifetime Low	Open Interest
Dec	1.6680	1.6728	1.6588	1.6640	− .0038	1.6970	1.5630	49,415
Mr98	1.6580	1.6620	1.6540	1.6480	− .0038	1.6840	1.5680	355

Est vol 6,279; vol Wd 10,150; open int 49,841, −2,173.

SWISS FRANC (CME)-125,000 francs; $ per franc

	Open	High	Low	Settle	Change	Lifetime High	Lifetime Low	Open Interest
Dec	.7129	.7215	.7115	.7176	+ .0055	.7740	.6602	47,382
Mr98	.7253	.7282	.7202	.7241	+ .0055	.7450	.6754	2,431
June	....	....	....	.7305	+ .0055	.7135	.6750	264
Sept	....	....	....	.7366	+ .0055	.7310	.6965	116

Est vol 20,228; vol Wd 26,811; open int 50,193, +780.

AUSTRALIAN DOLLAR (CME)-100,000 dlrs.; $ per A.$

	Open	High	Low	Settle	Change	Lifetime High	Lifetime Low	Open Interest
Dec	.6981	.7064	.6962	.7035	+ .0032	.7860	.6825	20,393

Est vol 471; vol Wd 1,416; open int 20,444, −844.

MEXICAN PESO (CME)-500,000 new Mex. peso, $ per MP

	Open	High	Low	Settle	Change	Lifetime High	Lifetime Low	Open Interest
Dec	.11700	.11790	.11010	.11578	− 00155	.12720	.09850	24,084
Mr98	.11100	.11300	.10750	.11060	− 00180	.12340	.0970	12,545
June	.10500	.10800	.10440	.10550	− 00280	.11985	.09200	1,758
Sept	.09900	.10500	.09900	.10300	− 00160	.11680	.08000	2,923
Dec	.09900	.09900	.09900	.09990	− 00120	.11440	.08000	776

Est vol 8,338; vol Wd 12,593; open int 43,086, +368.

INDEX

DJ INDUSTRIAL AVERAGE (CBOT) $10 times average

	Open	High	Low	Settle	Chg	High	Low	Open Interest
Dec	7380.0	7575.0	7350.0	7365.0	− 187.0	8252.0	6870.0	7,266
Mr98	7450.0	7630.0	7438.0	7438.0	− 191.0	8335.0	6970.0	962
June	7530.0	7710.0	7517.0	7517.0	− 195.0	8320.0	7070.0	76
Sept	7610.0	7800.0	7599.0	7599.0	− 199.0	8410.0	7150.0	43

Est vol 10,500; vol Wd 17,471; open int 8,347, +616.
The index: High 7543.01; Low 7381.18; Close 7381.67 −125.00

S&P 500 INDEX (CME) $500 times index

	Open	High	Low	Settle	Chg	High	Low	Open Interest
Dec	923.50	928.50	902.00	903.10	− 21.15	992.25	753.00	196,602
Mr98	916.00	939.00	912.00	912.35	− 21.55	100260	854.40	6,387
June	930.00	948.00	922.00	922.20	− 21.80	101200	864.25	1,581
Sept		....	....	931.35	− 22.65	102295	884.00	251
Dec		....	....	941.75	− 22.50	103625	895.00	266
June		....	....	964.50	− 22.50	106115	959.35	98

Est vol 93,284; vol Wd 100,635; open int 205,210, −688.
Indx prelim High 923.28; Low 903.68; Close 903.68 −15.48

MINI S&P 500 (CME) $50 times index

	Open	High	Low	Settle	Chg	High	Low	Open Interest
Dec	924.50	928.50	902.00	903.00	− 21.25	992.25	844.00	15,354

Est vol 14,020; vol Wd 16,646; open int 15,545, +578.

investments. In the above example, there was a return of $1,237.50 on a $1,451.25 investment in one year: That is a return of over 85 percent. Of course, the buyer assumed a considerable risk. If the price of corn had declined, the loss could easily have exceeded the initial investment. If the price of December corn had declined to $2.50, for example, the buyer would have incurred a loss of $2,012.50. If it had dropped to $2.30, the loss would have been $3,012.50. Before losses of these magnitudes would occur, however, the FCM would make sure that the buyer had sufficient assets to cover the loss—either free capital or freshly posted additional margin made after a margin call—or the broker would close out the transaction on its own.

Speculation is possible in commodities futures, because (1) commodities often exhibit substantial price movements, and (2) a purchaser's or seller's net gain or loss on a futures transaction is measured by the price movement of a large amount of the commodity, but the actual capital invested is usually about 10 percent of the total value of the commodity. Again, it is a species of leverage, although in this case there is no actual use of borrowed capital.

Margin calls are common in the commodities futures business, because only a small deposit is required to carry a substantial position. In the foregoing example, a $1,451.25 deposit enables one to speculate on price movements on 5,000 bushels of corn worth 10 times the amount of the deposit. In this market, each person's account is **marked to market** on a daily basis. Marked to market simply means that the margin position of the account is recalculated each day. The price used is the price set forth in the "Settle" column of Table 16-5. If the price moves in a favorable direction, the account, when marked to market, will show a surplus over the minimum needed to carry the position: That surplus may be withdrawn or used to buy additional futures contracts. In other words, one can "pyramid" a successful futures speculation very easily. If the price moves in an unfavorable direction, the margin in the account is marked down.

Trading in commodities futures is quite unlike trading on the NYSE and other securities exchanges. The Chicago Board of Trade is a place where traders come to trade, in many cases solely for their own account.

Trading for each commodity takes place in a separate pit, with traders arranged within the pit according to the month of the contract they are trading. Trading is by **open outcry** and hand signals, with purchasers and sellers of the futures often trading on small price movements. You may have seen photographs of this hectic process—traders screaming and shouting in the pits. Repeated outcries of price are necessary, because prices remain valid only during the outcry. Because of price volatility and the small margins required to acquire futures positions, this trading is hectic and fortunes may be made or wiped out in very short periods of time. Traders (unlike speculators) do not ordinarily carry a net long or short position past the end of a trading session. In the jargon of the market, a trader rarely "goes to bed" with a position. Although proprietary trading is the rule on the commodities exchanges, it is illegal on the securities exchanges to hold a seat for purposes of trading primarily for your own account.

There are no specialists or market makers on the commodities exchanges, nor are there firm bid and ask quotations. Perhaps because of these differences, the commodities exchanges limit the maximum price movements that can occur

in a single day in most contracts. Trading is suspended when the maximum change in a single day occurs. Prior to 1989, such limits were unknown in the securities markets, but so-called circuit breakers were instituted by the NYSE in response to the crashes of 1987 and 1989. Indeed, these circuit breakers, which are coordinated with trading in stock index futures on the commodities exchanges, were instituted largely because of the fear that trading in stock index futures tended to cause the stock market to move in tandem.

Commodities futures are widely used by producers and users of commodities to **hedge** against future price changes. A farmer growing corn, for example, may know that his corn will be harvested and ready to market in July 1998. The futures price for July corn is $2.90. If that price is acceptable to the farmer for his crop, he can lock it in by purchasing July corn futures in the approximate amount of his expected harvest. He may even be required to do so by his bank if he has borrowed to finance the crop. If the price of corn declines, the farmer will sell his corn at a loss but recoup that loss on the profit on the futures contract. (It is almost always impractical, because of transportation costs to deliver the corn to the purchaser of the contract.) If the price goes up, the farmer has a loss on the futures contract, but is able to sell his harvested corn above $2.90. Because the farmer does not know in advance what the size of his harvest will be, it is not possible to set up a perfect hedge, and banks do not usually require a complete hedge. Moreover, the hedge may be imperfect if the variety or quality of the corn that the farmer grows differs from the type of corn that is specified in the standard contract or if the price available to the farmer at his delivery location differs from that quoted at the standard delivery location (which for grains is usually Toledo, Ohio). Farmers may also get a better break if they buy crop insurance and hedge only a portion of the crop with futures.

A manufacturer that uses corn in its manufacturing process may similarly ensure itself of reliable raw material prices for an extended period in the future by buying futures contracts. Farmers or users of commodities may also hedge by buying or selling commodities "for forward delivery" at fixed prices without using the standardized futures market. But trading in standardized futures contracts, unlike trading in securities, is restricted by law to trading on a registered commodities exchange. In other words, there can be no legal third market in futures. Because hedgers own the commodity in which they are trading, they are not required to post as much margin as are speculators; generally the required deposit is about half that required from speculators.

Futures trading resembles option trading, but there are important differences. An option does not commit the purchaser of the option to do anything; if the price moves in the wrong direction, the purchaser of the option simply lets it expire. A futures contract, on the other hand, commits the purchaser and seller to close out the position: If the price moves in the wrong direction, the purchaser or seller of the futures contract must take a loss that grows steadily as the price moves further in the wrong direction.

The margin required in a futures transaction is also superficially analogous to the purchase price of an option. Again, however, there is a difference. The price paid for an option is the cost of the right to enter into a transaction: The premium becomes the property of the writer of the option. The margin required

in a futures contract is a guarantee of performance and remains the property of the person entering into the contract.

In a futures contract, both sides of every contract are subject to the risk of market forces. Moreover, commodities futures trading is "stacked" against the small outside speculator. About 90 percent of all individual commodity speculators lose money; the average lifetime of an individual futures account is less than a year. There are numerous trading systems or strategies that are commercially available for a fee, but the results of these systems or strategies are indifferent, despite advertising claims to the contrary. An article in the *Wall Street Journal* describes the situation faced by the small investor in this market: "In the best of times, an individual futures-market speculator, like a casino gambler, has a less than even chance of making money in the futures markets. The odds always favor the house, or the markets." Also, other participants in this market are sophisticated, powerful, and have superior access to information in the market. Huge grain-trading companies or banks actively participate in this market; they have nearly instant access to market-moving information, and their multi-million-dollar trades may themselves dramatically effect future prices in seconds, usually when it is advantageous to them. Further, professional futures-pit speculators are present on the trading floor and may make split-second trading decisions based on price changes before an individual speculator has time to pick up the phone and call a broker. Individual speculators must pay commissions on their transactions, while other participants in the market do not. Futures contracts expire every few months, and positions are bought and sold, often on a daily basis. Commissions are charged on each purchase and sale. Thus, it is not unusual for an individual's futures account to be eaten up by commissions in less than a year. The *Journal* article quotes an administrative law judge for the Commodity Futures Trading Commission as stating "You've got to be out of your gourd to trade futures."

§16.5 Financial Futures and Options to Buy Futures

Today, most of the action in the futures business is in financial and index futures. Standardized contracts to buy or sell foreign currencies at stated times in the future—British pounds in 25,000 pound units, Canadian dollars in $100,000 units, Japanese yen in 12,500,000 yen units—are actively traded. Interest rate futures in Treasury bonds, and 5-year Treasury notes are traded in $100,000 units; Treasury bills are traded in $1,000,000 units. All of these financial futures can be bought or sold for approximately 10 percent down as a way of hedging against or speculating on interest rates or foreign exchange rates.

From a dollar standpoint, the most active trading is in stock index futures and government securities futures. Table 16-5 reflects trading in these contracts. A major difference between traditional commodities futures and these financial futures is that they settle in cash for the difference between the contract price and the price at expiration.

Because futures carry with them the risk of loss from adverse price movements in excess of the amount initially invested, a logical development is the

496

creation of put and call options on futures. Table 16-6 is an example of price quotations for options on futures contracts.

§16.6 Arbitrage and Program Trading

The development of index options and index futures opens up a variety of computerized trading strategies. **Arbitrage** is the process of taking advantage of small price differences in equivalent securities. Such differences may arise from different maturity dates on equivalent securities, trading in different geographical markets, or trading in securities with different forms but equivalent or interrelated values. Index options, index futures, and the underlying securities that compose the indexes all trade simultaneously in different markets. It would be impossible for an individual to determine whether the prices of the 500 stocks that make up the S&P 500 stock index are above or below what they should be given the price in the futures market for the index. Computers, however, allow for arbitrage transactions across markets of this type. Computerized trading programs may involve the simultaneous purchase of several hundred securities (in round lots via SuperDOT) that mimic the S&P 500 index with the simultaneous sales of S&P 500 index futures. This kind of trading is known as **program trading**. Because there are many arbitrageurs involved in program trading, and because many programs may dictate the simultaneous purchase or sale of large amounts of stock on the NYSE, program trading may have been a factor in the October 1987 market crash. On the other hand, it has also been argued that program trading has the effect of linking the stock and futures markets, causing gaps in prices between the two to narrow, making both markets more efficient, and ultimately reducing volatility in both. Thus, although there was heavy program trading during the 1997 crash, there was little worry afterwards that it had somehow caused or worsened the fall in prices.

In essence, program trading involves buying stocks or futures, according to which is cheaper at the moment, and selling the other which is selling at a relatively high price. If futures are relatively cheap, one buys futures and sells stocks. The profit in the transaction is thus locked in because the trader can use the proceeds of the stock sale to close out the cheaper futures contracts, keeping the difference. Prior to 1987, most such trades were "unwound" only when the futures expired, causing huge increases in volume on so-called triple-witching days when many futures, options, and futures options expired simultaneously. These problems were addressed by changing the expiration of futures and other derivative instruments to the opening of trading on the expiration day rather than the closing, thus allowing the prices of stocks a full trading day to adjust to the massive volume. Moreover, it seems quite likely that specialists on the floor of the NYSE (and market makers in the over-the-counter (OTC) market to the extent that certain index stocks are traded there) quickly came to understand the dynamics of program trading and adjusted to it. Indeed, to the extent that program trading increases volume on the NYSE and in other stock markets, specialists and market makers benefit. Finally, traders also discovered that program trading itself tended to cause the gap to close between the prices of futures and the prices of stocks, so that the trade could be unwound shortly after it was made by simply entering into the opposite transaction.

Table 16-6

FUTURES OPTIONS PRICES

Thursday, October 30, 1997

AGRICULTURAL

CORN (CBT)
5,000 bu.; cents per bu.

Strike Price	Calls-Settle Dec	Mar	May	Puts-Settle Dec	Mar	May
260	20⅞	32⅝	39½	1⅛	3¾	5
270	12⅝	25½	32¾	2⅞	7	8
280	6⅜	19½	26⅞	6⅞	10¾	12
290	3⅛	15	21⅝	13⅜	16	16½
300	1⅝	11¼	17½	21¾	22¼	22¼
310	1	8½	14½	31	29¼	....

Est vol 25,000 Wd 13,473 calls 12,338 puts
Op int Wed 245,868 calls 225,611 puts

SOYBEANS (CBT)
5,000 bu.; cents per bu.

Strike Price	Calls-Settle Jan	Mar	May	Puts-Settle Jan	Mar	May
625	69¾	79½	86½	2⅝	5½	8
650	48	59	67	5¾	10	13½
675	30⅜	42	51¼	13	18	21½
700	17¼	29¼	38½	24¾	29	34
725	9½	20½	29	41¾	45⅛	48
750	5⅛	13½	21	62¼	63½	65

Est vol 13,000 Wd 4,273 calls 3,275 puts
Op int Wed 75,074 calls 74,741 puts

SOYBEAN MEAL (CBT)
100 tons; $ per ton

Strike Price	Calls-Settle Dec	Jan	Mar	Puts-Settle Dec	Jan	Mar
200	22.50	20.00	17.50	.50	1.25	3.00
210	13.15	11.15	10.50	1.15	2.60	6.00
220	5.00	5.50	6.50	3.00	6.75	11.15
230	1.50	2.50	4.00	9.40	13.75	19.15
240	.40	1.00	2.50	18.40	22.25	27.50
250	.30	.60	1.50	....	....	....

Est vol 2,750 Wd 2,027 calls 924 puts
Op int Wed 27,495 calls 32,218 puts

SOYBEAN OIL (CBT)
60,000 lbs.; cents per lb.

Strike Price	Calls-Settle Dec	Jan	Mar	Puts-Settle Dec	Jan	Mar
2400	1.130	1.450	1.850	.090	.230	.400
2450	.750	1.070	1.530	.200	.350	.590
2500	.450	.800	1.250	.400	.560	.800
2550	.230	.560	1.030	.710	.820	1.100
2600	.140	.380	.840	1.090	1.150	....
2650	.080	.270	.700	1.550	1.530	....

Est vol 1,033 Wd 1,206 calls 801 puts
Op int Wed 31,988 calls 32,090 puts

WHEAT (CBT)
5,000 bu.; cents per bu.

Strike Price	Calls-Settle Dec	Mar	May	Puts-Settle Dec	Mar	May
340	21	39¼	48¾	1	5½	....
350	12¾	32¼	42	3	8¼	10¾
360	6½	26	35¼	7	12	14¼
370	3½	20½	30	13½	16½	18½
380	1½	16	25	21¾	21½	23¼
390	¾	12½	20¾	31	28	....

Est vol 4,800 Wd 2,102 calls 1,601 puts
Op int Wed 65,443 calls 45,859 puts

COTTON (CTN)
50,000 lbs.; cents per lb.

Strike Price	Calls-Settle Dec	Mar	May	Puts-Settle Dec	Mar	May
70	2.15	4.09	....	.10	.75	1.00
71	1.32	3.39	....	.27	.99	1.28
72	.60	2.77	....	.65	1.40	1.63
73	.32	2.23	3.15	1.27	1.83	2.04
74	.14	1.76	2.65	2.09	2.35	2.50
75	.08	1.36	2.20	3.03	2.93	3.03

Est vol 3,000 Wd 1,080 calls 548 puts
Op int Wed 54,997 calls 43,276 puts

ORANGE JUICE (CTN)
15,000 lbs.; cents per lb.

Strike Price	Calls-Settle Dec	Jan	Feb	Puts-Settle Dec	Jan	Feb
60	....	12.45	....	....	.50	....
65	....	8.35	....	....	1.40	....
70	....	5.55	....	....	3.50	....
75	....	3.45	7.60	....	6.20	....
80	....	2.25	....	....	9.90	....
85	....	1.45	....	....	14.10	....

Est vol 1,500 Wd 1,093 calls 397 puts
Op int Wed 46,270 calls 11,955 puts

37,500 lbs.; cents per lb.

Strike Price	Calls-Settle Dec	Jan	Mar	Puts-Settle Dec	Jan	Mar
140	8.70	5.20	8.70	.55	6.45	9.95
145	4.95	3.40	6.90	1.80	9.65	13.15
150	2.51	2.20	5.60	4.00	13.45	16.85
155	1.20	1.50	4.50	8.05	17.75	20.75
160	.40	1.00	3.70	12.25	22.25	24.95
165	.20	.70	3.00	17.05	26.95	29.25

Est vol 3,135 Wd 1,069 calls 1,271 puts
Op int Wed 31,541 calls 28,145 puts

SUGAR-WORLD (CSCE)
112,000 lbs.; cents per lb.

Strike Price	Calls-Settle Dec	Jan	Mar	Puts-Settle Dec	Jan	Mar
1150	.81	.83	.94	.01	.03	.14
1200	.35	.44	.62	.05	.14	.32
1250	.09	.18	.39	.29	.38	.59
1300	.02	.07	.23	.72	.77	.93
1350	.01	.03	.14	1.21	1.23	1.34
1400	.01	.01	.10	1.71	1.71	1.80

Est vol 19,704 Wd 7,043 calls 2,261 puts
Op int Wed 111,780 calls 68,497 puts

COCOA (CSCE)
10 metric tons; $ per ton

Strike Price	Calls-Settle Dec	Jan	Mar	Puts-Settle Dec	Jan	Mar
1500	89	132	156	2	7	31
1550	46	92	123	9	17	48
1600	16	63	89	29	38	70
1650	7	40	68	70	65	93
1700	4	24	52	117	99	127
1750	1	15	38	164	140	163

Est vol 1,963 Wd 1,551 calls 459 puts
Op int Wed 40,394 calls 21,321 puts

Strike Price	Calls-Settle Nov	Dec	Jan	Puts-Settle Nov	Dec	Jan
175	6.55	9.75	12.45	.55	2.75	4.45
180	3.00	6.70	9.55	2.00	4.70	6.55
185	1.10	4.30	7.30	5.10	7.30	9.30
190	.40	2.65	5.50	9.40	10.65	12.50
195	.10	1.85	4.10	14.10	14.85	16.10

Est vol 220 Wd 0 calls 0 puts
Op int Wed 6,505 calls 4,090 puts

LIVESTOCK

CATTLE-FEEDER (CME)
50,000 lbs.; cents per lb.

Strike Price	Calls-Settle Oct	Nov	Jan	Puts-Settle Oct	Nov	Jan
75	....	....	....	0.00	....	....
76	0.80	2.00	3.22	0.00	0.32	1.05
77	0.00	....	....	0.20	....	....
78	0.00	0.75	2.00	1.20	1.07	1.80
79	0.00	....	....	2.20	....	....
80	0.00	0.12	1.00	3.20	2.45	2.77

Est vol 578 Wd 126 calls 343 puts
Op int Wed 4,481 calls 11,448 puts

CATTLE-LIVE (CME)
40,000 lbs.; cents per lb.

Strike Price	Calls-Settle Nov	Dec	Feb	Puts-Settle Nov	Dec	Feb
65	....	2.60	....	....	0.40	0.70
66	....	1.85	....	....	0.62	0.95
67	0.70	1.22	....	....	1.00	1.30
68	0.30	0.75	2.10	1.07	1.52	1.75
69	0.12	0.45	1.57	....	2.22	2.22
70	....	0.25	1.20	....	3.00	2.82

Est vol 2,319 Wd 911 calls 1,246 puts
Op int Wed 20,237 calls 24,664 puts

HOGS-LEAN (CME)
40,000 lbs.; cents per lb.

Strike Price	Calls-Settle Dec	Feb	Apr	Puts-Settle Dec	Feb	Apr
61	2.57	3.30	....	0.77	1.60	....
62	1.90	2.72	1.60	1.07	2.00	3.87
63	1.37	2.25	....	1.55	2.52	....
64	0.97	1.82	1.05	2.15	3.07	5.27
65	0.67	1.45	....	2.82	....	....
66	0.40	1.10	0.67	3.55	4.32	6.87

Est vol 300 Wd 221 calls 86 puts
Op int Wed 5,836 calls 6,548 puts

METALS

COPPER (CMX)
25,000 lbs.; cents per lb.

Strike Price	Calls-Settle Nov	Dec	Jan	Puts-Settle Nov	Dec	Jan
86	5.85	6.95	7.80	.90	1.85	2.60
88	4.35	5.70	6.60	1.40	2.55	3.35
90	3.05	4.55	5.50	2.10	3.40	4.25
92	2.00	3.60	4.55	3.05	4.45	5.25
94	1.30	2.80	3.75	4.35	5.60	6.40
96	.80	2.15	3.05	5.85	6.95	7.70

Est vol 650 Wd 266 calls 104 puts
Op int Wed 9,064 calls 3,075 puts

GOLD (CMX)
100 troy ounces; $ per troy ounce

Strike Price	Calls-Settle Dec	Jan	Feb	Puts-Settle Dec	Jan	Feb
305	13.80	16.80	18.00	1.60	2.80	3.70
310	9.60	12.50	13.20	2.40	3.80	4.50
315	6.10	9.70	10.20	3.90	6.00	6.50
320	4.00	6.90	7.70	6.80	8.20	9.00
325	2.60	4.90	6.00	10.40	11.20	12.20
330	1.30	3.20	4.20	14.10	14.60	15.50

Est vol 25,000 Wd 16,680 calls 7,152 puts
Op int Wed 344,155 calls 124,733 puts

SILVER (CMX)
5,000 troy ounces; cts per troy ounce

Strike Price	Calls-Settle Dec	Jan	Mar	Puts-Settle Dec	Jan	Mar
425	62.0	67.1	68.5	.2	1.0	3.1
450	38.5	44.4	48.8	1.0	3.0	7.6
475	17.0	26.0	32.7	5.5	9.0	16.2
500	6.3	13.5	22.0	19.5	21.3	29.8
525	2.3	7.6	14.7	40.2	40.1	47.0
550	1.3	4.4	10.0	64.2	61.4	66.7

Est vol 2,400 Wd 3,303 calls 1,605 puts
Op int Wed 73,023 calls 32,063 puts

INTEREST RATE

T-BONDS (CBT)
$100,000; points and 64ths of 100%

Strike Price	Calls-Settle Dec	Mar	Jun	Puts-Settle Dec	Mar	Jun
116	2-30	3-40	4-08	0-20	1-51	2-42
117	1-48	....	....	0-38	....	....
118	1-11	2-36	3-07	1-01	2-44	....
119	0-46	....	....	1-36	....	....
120	0-27	1-46	2-19	2-17	3-52	....
121	0-15	....	....	....	....	....

Est. vol. 160,000;
Wd vol. 100,879 calls; 72,528 puts
Op. int. Wed 530,967 calls; 450,603 puts

T-NOTES (CBT)
$100,000; points and 64ths of 100%

Strike Price	Calls-Settle Dec	Mar	Jun	Puts-Settle Dec	Mar	Jun
109	2-47	3-02	3-24	0-03	0-41	....
110	1-53	2-22	2-46	0-09	0-61	....
111	1-04	1-49	2-12	0-24	1-23	....
112	0-33	1-19	....	0-53	1-57	....
113	0-15	0-60	....	1-34	....	....
114	0-06	0-41	....	2-25	....	....

Est vol 25,000 Wd 21,047 calls 15,939 puts
Op int Wed 209,046 calls 226,771 puts

5 YR TREAS NOTES (CBT)
$100,000; points and 64ths of 100%

10700	1-27	1-52	....	0-05	0-35	....
10750	1-00	1-32	....	0-09	0-45	....
10800	0-41	1-13	....	0-19	0-58	....
10850	0-26	0-60	....	0-34	....	....
10900	0-14	0-48	....	0-54	....	....
10950	0-06	0-37	....	....	....	....

Est vol 10,000 Wd 4,335 calls 5,742 puts
Op int Wed 56,122 calls 55,069 puts

Strike Price	Calls-Settle Dec	Jan	Feb	Puts-Settle Dec	Jan	Feb
121	0-12	0-30	0-46	2-40	2-46	2-62
122	0-07	0-18	0-31	3-35	3-34	3-47

Vol Th 11,491 calls 100 puts
Op int Wed 56,789 calls 26,965 puts

GERMAN GOVT BOND (LIFFE)
$250,000 marks; pts. of 100%

Strike Price	Calls-Settle Dec	Jan	Feb	Puts-Settle Dec	Jan	Feb
10150	1.28	1.02	1.23	0.20	0.67	0.88
10200	0.91	0.75	0.96	0.33	0.90	1.11
10250	0.60	0.53	0.73	0.52	1.18	1.38
10300	0.37	0.36	0.55	0.79	1.51	1.70
10350	0.21	0.23	0.40	1.13	1.88	2.05
10400	0.11	0.14	0.28	1.53	2.29	2.43

Vol Th 41,754 calls 29,338 puts
Op int Wed 223,357 calls 270,026 puts

CURRENCY

JAPANESE YEN (CME)
12,500,000 yen; cents per 100 yen

Strike Price	Calls-Settle Nov	Dec	Jan	Puts-Settle Nov	Dec	Jan
8250	1.36	1.96	....	0.26	0.87	....
8300	1.01	1.66	....	0.41	1.06	1.13
8350	0.72	1.39	2.51	0.62	1.29	1.31
8400	0.50	1.16	....	0.90	1.56	1.51
8450	0.35	0.96	1.95	1.25	1.85	1.74
8500	0.25	0.79	1.72	1.65	2.18	....

Est vol 6,714 Wd 4,237 calls 2,043 puts
Op int Wed 62,908 calls 55,014 puts

DEUTSCHEMARK (CME)
125,000 marks; cents per mark

5750	0.97	1.32	1.77	0.20	0.55	0.74
5800	0.62	1.02	....	0.35	0.75	0.91
5850	0.40	0.78	....	0.63	1.01	....
5900	0.23	0.58	0.97	0.96	1.31	1.42
5950	0.12	0.43	....	....	....	....
6000	0.07	0.33	0.62	....	2.05	....

Est vol 4,126 Wd 3,239 calls 3,572 puts
Op int Wed 39,721 calls 53,953 puts

CANADIAN DOLLAR (CME)
100,000 Can.$, cents per Can.$

Strike Price	Calls-Settle Nov	Dec	Jan	Puts-Settle Nov	Dec	Jan
7000	1.18	....	....	....	0.11	0.13
7050	....	....	....	....	0.20	....
7100	0.32	0.54	....	0.16	0.38	....
7150	....	0.31	....	0.45	0.65	....
7200	0.05	0.18	....	0.89	1.02	....
7250	0.02	0.11	....	1.36	1.44	....

Est vol 1,506 Wd 1,307 calls 617 puts
Op int wed 15,930 calls 7,884 puts

BRITISH POUND (CME)
62,500 pounds; cents per pound

16400	2.74	3.62	3.96	0.34	1.22	....
16500	1.98	2.96	3.42	0.58	1.56	....
16600	1.34	2.38	2.94	0.94	1.98	....
16700	0.86	1.90	2.50	1.46	2.50	....
16800	0.52	1.48	2.14	....	3.08	....
16900	....	1.16	1.80	....	....	....

Est vol 1,519 Wd 1,077 calls 887 puts
Op int Wed 26,950 calls 25,922 puts

SWISS FRANC (CME)
125,000 francs; cents per franc

Strike Price	Calls-Settle Nov	Dec	Jan	Puts-Settle Nov	Dec	Jan
7100	1.13	1.64	....	0.37	0.88	....
7150	0.82	1.36	....	0.56	1.10	....
7200	0.57	1.11	1.83	0.81	1.35	....
7250	0.40	0.90	....	....	....	....
7300	0.28	0.73	....	1.52	1.96	....
7350	0.19	....	....	....	....	....

Est vol 1,909 Wd 1,608 calls 1,913 puts
Op int Wed 20,683 calls 16,137 puts

BRAZILIAN REAL (CME)
100,000 Braz. reais; $ per reais

Strike Price	Calls-Settle Nov	Dec	Jan	Puts-Settle Nov	Dec	Jan
895	....	....	....	....	....	....
900	....	....	....	0.02	....	....

Est vol 0 Wd 0 calls 0 puts
Op int Wed 0 calls 31,081 puts

MEXICAN PESO (CME)
500,000 new Mex. pesos; $ per MP

1150	3.50	4.45	....	....	3.70	....
1162	....	....	....	....	4.10	....
1175	....	3.15	....	....	4.90	....
1188	....	2.55	....	....	....	....
1201	....	1.95	....	....	6.17	....

Est vol 939 Wd 2,738 calls 852 puts
Op int Wed 18,991 calls 16,734 puts

INDEX

DJ INDUSTRIAL AVG (CBOT)
$100 times premium

Strike Price	Calls-Settle Nov	Dec	Jan	Puts-Settle Nov	Dec	Jan
72	35.50	43.50	....	19.50	28.50	31.75
73	....	37.00	....	22.40	32.00	35.50
74	23.00	31.50	....	26.25	36.00	....
75	17.50	26.50	....	30.75	41.00	43.50
76	13.00	21.00	....	36.25	46.50	....
77	9.50	18.00	....	43.00	51.50	....

Est vol 1,700 Wd 1,764 calls 5,348 puts
Op int Wed 29,027 calls 20,167 puts

S&P 500 STOCK INDEX (CME)
$500 times premium

895	34.30	45.65	....	26.25	37.60	....
900	31.10	42.60	....	28.00	39.50	....
905	28.00	39.50	....	29.90	41.40	....
910	25.10	36.55	....	31.95	43.40	43.50
915	22.35	33.75	....	34.20	45.55	....
920	19.75	31.05	....	36.60	47.80	48.00

Est vol 12,811 Wd 6,468 calls 25,207 puts
Op int Wed 59,186 calls 128,341 puts

§16.7 Hedging and Portfolio Insurance

A second major source of index futures trading prior to the October 1987 collapse in securities prices was a variety of strategies known as **portfolio insurance**. It is widely believed that these strategies also contributed to the October 1987 market break and were largely unsuccessful in preventing substantial losses.

An institutional investor that holds a portfolio of securities similar to that reflected in the S&P 500 index may hedge that position by selling S&P 500 index futures in much the same way that a farmer with a long position in the form of a crop in the ground can hedge against a price decline. Portfolio insurance (sometimes called **dynamic hedging**) does not strive to produce a riskless portfolio. Rather, it attempts to offset the potential decline while not eliminating the possibility of gain (as a true hedge does) in the case of a market rise. This is accomplished by buying or selling with the movement of the market: selling index futures when prices are declining and buying futures when prices are rising. During the October 1987 market collapse, these strategies became impossible to execute, because they dictated sales of index futures in volumes that the market was unable or unwilling to absorb. When the market began to decline, portfolio insurance programs caused massive sell orders to be sent to the futures exchanges. The price of stock index futures thus began to decline, and because each sale of a stock index future represented a large sale of stock, the price of futures moved downward much more rapidly than the prices of the individual stocks in the index. When the gap between futures prices and the prices of the underlying stocks became sufficiently large, program trades (designed to lock in profits by simultaneously buying futures and selling stocks) were triggered, causing the price of stocks to fall further, and causing the entire process to repeat itself. These problems have been largely alleviated by the imposition of coordinated trading halts on the stock and futures exchanges, and, perhaps more important, by traders' having learned the limitations of such strategies and the markets themselves.

§16.8 Other Trading Strategies Involving Options or Futures

The creation of a variety of derivative securities has dramatically changed the securities markets for large investors. It is usually much cheaper in terms of commissions and other expenses to effect major changes in a large portfolio by transactions in the futures market or options market than by the sale and purchase of many different securities. For example, a debt portfolio can be converted rapidly to equity by simultaneously selling bond futures and buying stock index futures. Of course, commission costs will be incurred if the underlying debt portfolio is ultimately liquidated and the equity investment substituted. However, these transactions may be delayed indefinitely through the use of index futures.

Tactical Asset Allocation (**TAA**) is the name sometimes given to an

investment strategy for large institutional investors that concentrates on classes of investments (e.g., equities, debt securities, and money market funds or cash equivalents) rather than on specific securities. These programs are computer-driven and rely on the purchase and sale of financial futures rather than on transactions in the underlying securities themselves.

The continued improvement in computer technology has led to increasingly sophisticated arbitrage trading strategies. The people who develop quantitative—mathematically based—investment strategies are often called **quants** or **rocket scientists**.

§16.9 Swaps and Derivatives

A **swap** is a transaction in which two parties enter into an agreement providing for the exchange of defined streams of payments over a specified period of time. Typically, a fixed stream is swapped for a stream that varies with interest rate fluctuations, or vice versa. Through careful specification of payment streams, a customer of a bank may hedge against unprotected interest rate or currency exchange rate fluctuations and also arbitrage differences in world capital markets to obtain higher yields or lower borrowing costs.

The swap of a floating rate obligation for a fixed-rate obligation, or vice versa, permits companies to hedge against risks caused by fluctuations in interest rates. For example, Kohlberg Kravis Roberts (KKR), a takeover firm, issued large amounts of floating rate debt in connection with its acquisition of RJR Nabisco even though the cash flow from which these obligations were to be repaid was not interest rate sensitive. KKR hedged its variable rate obligations created in the RJR Nabisco acquisition by an interest rate cap. KKR paid a fee to a bank in return for the bank's agreement that if interest rates exceeded a certain level, the bank would pay the excess interest to KKR. The bank in turn took the fee it received from KKR and invested it in futures that increased in value with interest rate increases, thereby hedging its payment obligation to KKR. The global market for derivative securities—swaps, options, futures, and custom-made financial interests—has revolutionized how corporate and financial institutions handle risk.

Banks typically act in the capacity of principal in these transactions, though they promptly trade out their positions with other customers so as to minimize their exposure to fluctuations of interest or currency rates. In large transactions of this type, there is always some risk that one party may default; large and financially secure banks are necessary parties to these transactions, because they guarantee the parties against default by another party.

It is difficult for bank examiners and others even to gauge the risk that derivative contracts carry, because these transactions often do not fit the traditional definitions of assets and liabilities. Because the risk in these transactions is potentially great, the suggestion has been made that banks should be required to conduct these activities through an affiliate that is not insured by the Federal Deposit Insurance Corporation.

The concern about derivative securities and the risk inherent in them is in part generational. Banking officials who compose the senior management of

most institutions generally are not familiar with the computer-driven markets for derivative securities and do not trust them; younger officials are more confident that serious problems will not arise. Only time will tell who is correct.

Although most swaps are arranged one-on-one in the vast OTC market for derivatives, the Chicago Board of Trade began trading futures swap contracts in June 1991. These contracts are for three-year and five-year interest rate swaps and are designed to permit hedging of long-term positions. In shorter-term swaps, a participant usually can hedge an exposed position through interest rate or Eurodollar futures.

Derivative instruments have been around for a long time in the form of options and futures contracts. The real change is that such instruments are increasingly traded privately and outside the confines of established exchanges. Until 1992, federal law prohibited the trading of futures contracts other than on a registered futures exchange. However, it has never been entirely clear just what a future is. A contract to sell wheat at a date in the future for a price set now or by reference to some benchmark price in the future is not necessarily a futures contract, though it may become one by virtue of being traded or tradeable. The current derivatives market was in effect created when bigger players found it desirable to arrange their own off-exchange or OTC trades and argued that the resulting instruments were not "futures contracts."

The reasons for avoiding exchange transactions are numerous and varied. Often, there is no exchange-traded contract that precisely matches the risks that one or the other of the parties wants to hedge. Further, there are practical limits on the variety of futures contracts that may be traded (particularly the need to have a ready pool of speculators to help provide liquidity), and many exchange-traded instruments are simply close substitutes for the commodity that a hedger really wants to hedge. (For example, a lemon grower might hedge some of his or her risk by buying or selling futures in frozen concentrated orange juice.)

No doubt cost is another reason for avoiding an exchange. As on any exchange, one must deal through a member broker, who charges a commission. Moreover, when one trades on an exchange, one must comply with exchange rules, such as those requiring margin, the good faith deposit that all traders must put down and maintain in order to keep a position open. This is not to say that the futures exchanges tend to over-regulate trading. Margin deposits make a good deal of sense in that they provide security that a trade will be honored. And the futures exchanges have no interest in dampening trading more than necessary. On the other hand, a billion-dollar corporation may see the need to make a margin deposit as almost gratuitous in that it knows (or should know) it will always be good for any loss that might be incurred. In short, with OTC derivatives, there may be no margin requirement at all though participants in this market expend considerable time and money checking the credit of those with whom they trade and generally will not trade if there is any risk of a possible default. Nevertheless, OTC trading may carry higher levels of risk, particularly if a trader has entered into trades with a variety of partners or if the trader has failed to "get it right" in constructing an elaborate hedge.

Finally, the futures exchanges may be opposed to OTC derivatives transactions for competitive (or anticompetitive) reasons: The more business that is siphoned off by those who arrange their own trades elsewhere, the less business

there will be on the exchanges. In all fairness, there may be a legitimate worry here. As bigger trades are accomplished away from the exchange, the market on the exchange becomes thinner and trading becomes riskier for those who trade on the exchanges, and smaller players may be left with a less-efficient market in which to hedge their smaller risks. In the end, however, most OTC trades are so specialized that they probably could not be accomplished very easily if at all by using the standardized contract traded on the exchanges. Ever since the advent of exchange-traded stock options (in 1973) and stock index futures (in 1982), the SEC and the CFTC have been more or less in competition over which agency will have control over new instruments that have some of the characteristics of both securities and futures. This struggle has been complicated by the fact that the Commodities Futures Trading Commission (CFTC) has exclusive jurisdiction over futures, while the SEC has only jurisdiction over exchanges. In any event, the Futures Trading Practices Act of 1992 gives the CFTC the authority to exempt certain OTC transactions in futures, and the CFTC has adopted rules for exempting swaps and hybrids from CFTC regulation. Generally speaking, the swap rules focus on the status of the parties to the transaction, whether the transaction is part of a class of fungible or standardized transactions, and whether the transaction is entered into on a multilateral transaction facility. The hybrid rules also focus on the status of the parties to the transaction and on whether the noncommodity portion of the transaction predominates over the commodity portion (as well as requiring immediate settlement of the trade).

It is important to understand that the word "derivative" is used to refer to a wide variety of complex securities, some of which do not quite fit some of the simpler definitions of the word. Although it is usually said that a derivative is a security the price or return of which is derived from the price or return of one or more other securities, the word is often also used to describe securities that are created by breaking up other securities into smaller pieces. Thus, while virtually all commentators would agree that publicly traded stock index futures are derivatives (although they are among the least worrisome ones), many commentators would also classify a collateralized mortgage obligation (CMO) that pays a return based on the timely interest payments on a pool of residential mortgages as a derivative. In one sense, the latter security is not a derivative, because it makes no reference to any other security for purposes of determining the return to be paid. But in another sense, such a security is a derivative, because the return is based on the contractual obligation of the creator of the CMO to calculate current interest payments and pass them on to the holders of securities tied to that slice of the returns. By this definition, of course, even such familiar securities as Treasury strips would be seen as derivatives.

As a result of numerous recent scandals, the risks of derivatives are often overestimated and mischaracterized. It has been estimated that there is as much as $25 trillion in derivative instruments outstanding globally. This figure, assuming it is accurate, is the nominal (or notional) amount of derivatives. That is, it is the face amount on which the gain or loss from the derivative instrument will be calculated. For example, in the case of an exchange-traded stock index future on the S&P 500, the nominal amount is $500 times the value of the index. If the index stands at 800, then the nominal value of a contract is

$400,000. Although it is theoretically possible that such an amount could be lost by the purchaser, such a result would only come to pass if all of the underlying stocks fell to zero. Although in some sense there is $400,000 at risk, there is virtually no chance that such an amount could be lost. Focusing on the nominal amount of derivatives outstanding is rather like estimating the size of the life insurance market by adding up the face amount of all the policies outstanding. One must keep in mind that a $100,000 policy may only involve the outlay of $300 per year by the insured.

Moreover, there is a tendency to think that derivatives losses somehow simply happen. In fact, derivatives are a zero sum game. For every loser there is a winner, though the losers make the headlines and the winners often prefer to remain in the shadows. To be sure, derivatives dealers make money by selling derivatives. That is, they do not sell such securities at cost. As with any other product, derivatives are sold at a markup (or markdown as the case may be). Thus, someone who buys a derivative instrument is getting something worth less than the purchase price. The real question is how much less? But whatever the markup, that amount is indeed gone forever as far as the buyer is concerned (short of litigation alleging some sort of fraud in the original purchase).

The growing number of scandals relating to derivatives has resulted from many different problems. The collapse of the Barings Bank involved stock index futures, which are actively traded on public futures exchanges and thus are subject to few doubts as to pricing. Ironically, some reports indicate that the Barings collapse may have been caused by slavish adherence to a market model at a time when the markets were not behaving as the model said they would. Under any other circumstances, such discipline might be seen as quite conservative. Ironically, disciplined buying and selling of stock index futures according to market models is precisely the mechanism by which portfolio insurance was supposed to have worked prior to the 1987 crash. Some have suggested that portfolio insurance made the crash worse. Coincidentally, it was reported in 1994 that a second generation of portfolio insurance, sometimes called delta hedging, has come into wide use among traders. (The "delta" refers to the slope of the line defined by the premium and the duration of an option.) It is unclear whether the demise of Barings was an isolated event or was related to strategies that may actually be quite common.

The problems at Gibson Greetings and Proctor & Gamble, both involving derivatives sold by Bankers Trust, appear to have arisen as a result of misrepresentations about risk and price and do not involve questions of the propriety of such instruments for such buyers. Indeed, it has been reported that some companies have been hurt by their reluctance to become involved in the derivatives market. For example, Merck, which sells half of its products overseas, is said to have lost as much as $900,000,000 per year in revenues in the mid-1980s as a result of failing to hedge against currency risks.

Perhaps the most serious derivatives-induced problem is that of Orange County, which declared bankruptcy as a result of losses primarily in CMOs. Other local government entities (including several school boards) and small colleges have also suffered serious losses from investments in similar derivatives. Most of these cases appear to have been the result of overzealous sales efforts on the part of brokers who apparently do not understand derivative instruments

but are nonetheless paid high commissions to sell them. These incidents have prompted calls for more vigorous enforcement of suitability requirements in connection with institutional investors (particularly governments). Until now, the suitability rule was generally thought to protect only individual investors, although the various versions of the rule as adopted by the National Association of Securities Dealers (NASD) and the exchanges do not so limit the scope of the rule. It also seems likely that derivatives losses will lead to legal restrictions on the kinds of investments that various government entities may make. Such rules may have negative consequences, because local governments and similar agencies often face risks that may be able to be hedged against by the use of derivatives.

The Orange County bankruptcy may have much broader implications for municipal finance than simply tighter regulation of investment practices. It appears that the affluent county's strategy has been to attempt to avoid obligations rather than to raise taxes and pay up as has been the invariable practice in the past by other troubled municipalities. At the very least, such hardball tactics can be expected to raise interest rates that must be paid by other state and local governments, and may cause Congress to consider whether continuing tax exemption for these entities makes sense. Finally, it appears that the credit rating agencies maintained Orange County's top rating even though it was known that the county had undertaken risky investment strategies. This revelation may in itself have the effect of raising interest rates on state and local government obligations and prompting more scrutiny by rating agencies of investment strategies in the future.

Derivatives dealers have taken significant steps toward self-regulation in an effort to avoid government regulation. In 1994, major dealers agreed to a Wholesale Transactions Code of Conduct sponsored by New York Federal Reserve Bank. In 1995, six major derivatives firms and the SEC and CFTC entered into a more elaborate agreement touching on four areas: internal monitoring, enhanced reporting, capital adequacy, and informing customers. Under the agreement, dealers report their portfolio structure, their 20 largest positions by trading partner, and their internal estimates of risk. This information will not, however, be available to the public. Because capital adequacy is directly related to risk, one crucial issue in regulating derivatives is the system or model used to measure risk. But because risk measurement is the primary focus of competition among derivatives dealers, it was agreed that firms may use their own proprietary systems as long as they meet certain minimum requirements and the results are verifiable by an outside auditor.

The need for regulation aside, accounting for derivatives is another complicated issue. In the case of exchange-traded derivatives, there is little doubt as to what they are worth on any given day. But OTC derivatives are another matter. In October 1994, the Financial Accounting Standards Board (FASB) adopted a new rule (Statement of Financial Accounting Standard (SFAS) No. 117) requiring disclosure of derivatives holdings, how they are accounted for on the balance sheet, gains or losses therefrom, and the purpose for which they are held (i.e., hedging or speculation). With respect to derivatives held for speculation, the new rule requires that the value of derivatives be disclosed as well. Although there is no requirement that the method of valuation be dis-

closed, the rule encourages risk disclosure that would allow users of financial statements to compare derivatives exposure firm to firm. The FASB rule is part of an increasing trend toward requiring current value accounting rather than historical cost accounting, at least in those areas where fluctuations in market prices are critical.

In the end, it should be remembered that most derivatives trading is undertaken for hedging purposes and thus is risk-reducing rather than risk-enhancing. But no hedge is perfect. For example, there is no futures market for lemons, but frozen concentrated orange juice is a close substitute. Still, even the best-intentioned hedge may sometimes backfire for reasons that are difficult to appreciate in advance. Moreover, it can be very difficult for an outsider to determine whether an elaborate position is in fact a hedge or a highly risky speculation. Ultimately, it is impossible to ensure that derivatives will not be used for speculation, and indeed, speculators serve the quite legitimate function of assuming risk for hedgers (presumably at a price). Thus, it is far from clear that one would want to ban speculation in derivatives.

VI

THE PRACTICE OF CORPORATE LAW

CHAPTER 17

◆ THE PRACTICE OF LAW AS A BUSINESS

§17.1 Introduction

Many of this book's readers are law students who plan to make their living and their careers in the practice of law after they graduate and pass the bar examination. However, many of these students do not have a clear understanding of the economics of the practice of law. They may have the clear idea that a lawyer tries cases, gives advice, or becomes a criminal lawyer or a prosecutor. They also know about broad areas of practice (e.g., personal injury (PI), workers' compensation (workers' comp), family law, business law, general practice, commercial litigation, white collar crime, and so forth). But many students have little idea about how the practice of law translates into dollars that may be used to support a family and pay off large education loans.

Many newly minted lawyers plan to seek employment with one of the large, commercial law firms found in large cities. This chapter is primarily devoted to a discussion of the economics of practice by these law firms in the 1990s. These firms do commercial and transactional work and litigation with respect to business and securities transactions; they may have lawyers who do estate planning and trusts, but they do not typically do criminal defense work or

personal injury work from the plaintiff side. This chapter also briefly discusses job alternatives to large law firm practice.

§17.2 An Introduction to the Economics of Legal Practice

The economics of large law firm practice have changed dramatically in the last couple of decades. The number of lawyers in large law firms has increased much more rapidly than the amount of legal business available to them. The last comment deserves some elaboration.

It is undoubtedly true today, as it has been in the past, that many individuals and small businesses in American society have need of legal services for commercial matters but are not receiving them. However, unless a client has the financial ability and willingness to pay for legal services (or has the type of case that is itself likely to generate a substantial recovery), sophisticated legal services are not likely to be available as an economic matter. The simple fact is that law firm services today are expensive: A relatively inexperienced associate's time may be charged at $100 per hour, and the services of an experienced senior partner in a major big city firm may routinely be charged at three or four times that rate (or even more in some cases). Unfortunately, many civil disputes involve relatively small amounts and cannot justify expensive legal services. There are a few government-financed legal services that may handle small commercial claims, and some lawyers may be willing to assist pro bono in small commercial disputes, but this is not very common today and does not begin to fill the need.

Because the supply of legal services has increased while the realistic demand has not, many law firms find themselves in increasingly competitive circumstances. They must scramble and discount if they wish to keep desirable clients and attract new ones. Previously, commercial enterprises usually paid legal fees that were billed without serious question; these enterprises themselves now face serious competition, and they realize that they must control costs to remain competitive. As a result, legal fees have come under the microscope of cost-cutting or cost-saving. Alternative billing techniques that depart from the simple hourly rate are very common, and law firms offer them both to existing clients and important new ones. In an earlier era, businesses usually relied primarily or exclusively on a single firm for legal services; today, large businesses divide their legal work among several different large firms, increasing the sense of competition among the chosen firms and enabling the business to shop specific cases or problems to obtain the best price. As a result, the practice of law has become much more of a business and less of a profession than it was a couple of generations ago. In a word, it is much more cut-throat out there than it used to be.

At one time, many lawyers prided themselves that they practiced law in the grand manner, to benefit mankind and not with an eye on their personal pocketbooks. Although most of these statements probably should be taken with a grain of salt, no matter what period is involved, it clearly seems to be true that lawyers were more willing two decades ago to take cases without the hope or expectation of a substantial fee than they are today. This is largely a product

of the changing economics—the increased commercialization—of the business of the practice of law.

§17.3 Job Opportunities for the Recent Graduate

Let us assume that you have graduated from law school and have successfully passed the bar. Where do you look for a job in the legal profession? Most graduates will look for jobs with large big city firms—the principal topic of this chapter. There are other alternatives, of course. Some may seek employment with a government agency or with a solo practitioner or a small firm with a handful of lawyers. These opportunities are so diverse and individualistic as to defy systematic analysis. Some may decide to seek employment in a small town; typically, small town firms are quite small, and practice may be both intellectually satisfying and financially remunerative. A few may hang out their shingle and seek to find legal work as a solo practitioner. Finally, some may decide to take employment with a governmental agency.

Once, freshly minted lawyers could usually find employment in the offices of in-house legal counsel in large commercial enterprises; however, as discussed below, inside legal counsel jobs today are highly sought after, quite competitive, and rarely offered to lawyers just starting out. There is no shortage of experienced lawyers interested in these jobs — jobs that may provide a considerable degree of job security and possible rapid advancement.

If a new lawyer cannot find a job and is unwilling to take a chance on solo practice, there are less-prestigious law-related jobs available today — most notably, temporary or **contract lawyers**. If this is unattractive, the new lawyer probably will be forced to find a job that is not directly related to his or her legal training.

§17.4 The Traditional Law Firm

In describing law practice in large law firms today, it is useful to begin with a description of the traditional firm of the 1950s and 1960s and then describe the tumultuous changes in the practice of law that have occurred since then. The competitiveness of large firm practice is a relatively recent phenomenon.

Two generations ago, the traditional law firm was a general partnership in which all partners shared the benefits and burdens of the law practice. Under well-established partnership principles, each partner was personally liable for all obligations of the partnership, including malpractice claims arising from actions of associates or other partners, and claims based on partnership contracts. However, malpractice was not a major concern; lawyers were rarely sued for malpractice, and many firms did not even bother to carry malpractice insurance, which was then incredibly inexpensive in contrast to present premiums.

By modern standards, traditional law firms of the 1950s and 1960s were small. A large firm might have 30 or so partners and 10 or 15 associates; a medium-size firm was one with perhaps 12 or 15 partners and associates combined. Firms usually had only a single office (although some firms had small

branch offices in other cities, particularly if a major client had offices in that city). All the partners in a firm knew each other personally and typically prided themselves on acting civilly and with respect toward each other. The firm structure was usually informal; many firms did not have written partnership agreements, and in effect decisions were made through a committee, by a trusted senior partner, or by some form of consensus of all the partners. When partnership decisions needed to be made, it was easy to fit all the firm's partners around a single table. When the decision involved who should be promoted from associate to partner, all the existing partners would have had at least some contact with and personal knowledge about each candidate.

Law firms during this period were entirely male. There were very few female law school graduates to begin with, but as a matter of policy, most firms simply declined to interview or hire female lawyers. These firms believed that their clients would refuse to accept a female lawyer in a professional relationship. Justice Sandra Day O'Connor of the United States Supreme Court has graphically described that the only jobs she was offered after graduating from law school in the early 1950s were secretarial ones.

There was great stability in firm membership. There was relatively little lateral movement by lawyers from one firm to another, and a person elected to be a partner in an established partnership reasonably expected to spend his entire productive career with that firm. As long as the partner remained productive, he could expect to receive a fair share of the partnership income; if his billings temporarily declined (e.g., because of ill health), the firm might carry him until he recovered.

In these traditional firms of the 1950s and 1960s, there was a fair amount of specialization among lawyers. The country lawyer or lawyer in general practice who did not hesitate to represent clients no matter what area of law was involved had largely disappeared from major law firms by World War II. Although most lawyers had areas of specialization, it was not uncommon for an individual lawyer to feel comfortable representing clients with problems in several quite different legal areas (e.g., taxation, antitrust, and securities law). As the legal system was becoming more complex during this period, however, lawyers generally found it increasingly difficult to retain proficiency in several different areas, and therefore there was a tendency to narrow areas of practice and increase the degree of specialization.

Firms generally had established relationships with specific clients that were treasured and cultivated. These relationships were often of long standing and based on a firm lawyer also serving as the general counsel of the business. When a single business relied on more than one firm, each firm's areas of responsibility were generally clear-cut and there was little or no competition among the firms. These relationships were usually based on a handshake or on oral understandings.

The firm typically did not commit in advance to a price for its services on specific matters; a new client might be advised of each lawyer's normal billing rate, but the amount of time to be spent was not normally estimated or established in advance. The amount actually billed after the work was completed was decided by the firm and the lawyer with responsibility for the matter. The bill typically stated that it was for services rendered without any itemization of

costs, charges, or identification of who actually performed the work. The size of the bill might be based on the amount of time spent, but more subjective factors were also common: the lawyer's assessment of the result achieved, the complexity of the matter, and what fee the matter will bear. Of course, billing disputes occurred from time to time, but they were not common. When they did occur, disputes were usually negotiated out as both firm and client recognized the importance of the continuing relationship. Lawyers were encouraged to keep time records, but sometimes these important records were skeletal or fragmentary, and some lawyers prided themselves on never keeping time records and billing on the basis of what they believed their services were worth.

Traditional law firms did not have formal retirement policies for aging lawyers. A partner might continue to practice until his seventies, or even longer, although as age limited his skills, other partners might suggest that he should retire or accept **of counsel** status, which was a gentle way of being told he no longer was carrying his share of the firm. Upon retirement, the senior lawyer usually became of counsel and the firm might maintain an office for his use and provide him with secretarial assistance. A lawyer who was of counsel might come in to the office one or two days a week to pick up his mail, and usually maintained some contact with the remaining partners. Firms generally did not have retirement plans that provided direct financial benefits for the aging lawyer; rather, each lawyer was expected to make whatever financial provision he desired for his retirement during his productive years with the firm. Because partners were viewed as self-employed, they also were not eligible for social security benefits.

This picture of the traditional law firm remained reasonably accurate throughout the 1970s, although the trend toward specialization continued and many law firms grew steadily during this period, reaching a size much larger than had been previously known. The development of the megafirm with hundreds of lawyers, however, can be traced to events that became dominant in the 1970s and 1980s.

§17.5 Training of Associates

In the 1950s and 1960s, as now, a newly minted member of the bar that was invited to join a law firm began as an employee of the firm and not as a partner—he was an **associate**. This status involved both an apprenticeship and a probationary period. The associate learned how to practice law by watching and assisting the experienced partners; at the same time, the partners evaluated the ability of associates in terms of whether they should be made a partner (i.e., whether the associate should ultimately be admitted to the firm as a partner to share the risks and benefits of that firm's practice).

The training process usually involved extensive mentoring. At first, a partner or senior associate very closely supervised the work of the associate, who gradually would be given more discretion and authority. One important aspect of this process was exposing the associate to real life situations. A litigation associate would accompany the experienced partner to depositions and the courtroom. He would assist the litigation partner in interviewing witnesses and

preparing the case for trial, but primarily he was there to learn. He later would be permitted to handle simple depositions and routine litigation matters on his own. A transactional associate would be exposed to complex transactions by working with the partner on real transactions, although the partner himself was fully capable of handling the task on his own. In this way, the associate would learn how to register a securities offering for an initial public offering (IPO) or prepare a complex contract for the purchase or sale of a business that would protect the client's needs and goals. Although it was not always obvious to the client, an important aspect of this process of training young lawyers was that the client paid for a major part of the training of the young associate, because the ultimate fee included the services of both the supervising lawyer and the associate.

Many firms had formal **rotation** programs for new associates to acquaint them with the areas of firm practice. An associate might thereafter have a voice in which department or area of practice he wished to specialize in.

A new lawyer typically could expect to remain an associate for 6 to 10 years, depending on the tradition in the specific law firm. If he seemed clearly unqualified to become a partner, he might be terminated in the first year or so of his employment with the firm; otherwise, he was virtually assured of employment until the partnership decision was made. Toward the end of this period, the associate's duties were similar to those of a partner: He was expected to handle most matters on his own and begin to develop his own client base. He might serve as a mentor for new associates.

By today's standards, associates did not have to work very hard. An associate might bill 1,600 hours during a year; that figure reflects, of course, that associates did not bill for every hour they were working in the firm. Today, many firms expect an associate to bill in the neighborhood of 2,000 hours per year.

If the associate passed this probationary period, he became a partner with the expectation of remaining with the firm until he retired. If the associate was found wanting, he would politely but firmly be told that there was no future for him at the firm, and that he should look elsewhere for employment. It was not uncommon for an associate who was passed over for a partnership to have spent nearly a decade with the firm. He was a skilled and trained lawyer. The firm might help to place such an associate with a client's legal office or with a smaller or lesser firm, or simply cast the associate loose to find a new job on his own. In the traditional firm, it was up-or-out with a vengeance; if one did not make partner, one was gone. There was no middle ground for the young lawyer.

§17.6 The Transition to Today

Today, large law firms are in many ways a quite different business form from the law firms of the 1950s and 1960s described in the previous sections. Firms today are much larger than firms a generation ago, and the relationships among partners are much more impersonal and profit-oriented than before. The relationship between associates and their firms has also changed; it is much more complex and variegated than in the traditional firm with its strict up-or-out policy. Specialization has also increased dramatically and firms are departmen-

talized; formal rotation programs for associates disappeared long ago, and, if an associate wishes exposure to different areas of practice today, he or she may have to arrange to move physically from one department to another within the firm itself.

Perhaps the most important single difference between the 1950s and 1960s and today is that the control over the pricing of legal services today has largely shifted from being under the virtually complete control of the firm to being largely dominated, reviewed, and controlled by large and sophisticated clients. Clients shop among law firms for the best and cheapest legal services, and firms compete directly and vigorously for legal business. This spirit of competition directly affects the personal relationships within law firms; the feelings of permanence and lifetime commitment on the part of partners has been replaced by an emphasis on production and **rain-making** (i.e., bringing in client business).

These dramatic changes in law firms and the roles of lawyers did not occur overnight. However, with the benefit of hindsight, it is clear that the changes did occur very rapidly and unexpectedly. They can be traced largely to developments that occurred during the 10- to 15-year period between the mid 1970s and the late 1980s. The 1990s has been a period of continued experimentation by law firms as they attempt to adjust to new and quite different economic conditions. The pattern during this critical period was boom and bust similar in form to what has periodically occurred in the real estate and securities markets. The boom began in the 1970s when the demand for legal services began to increase dramatically. Firms responded (not unnaturally) by both raising their fees and growing in size by hiring additional associates and attracting laterals. Competition for high quality associates became particularly intense, and salaries increased to previously unheard-of levels — virtually doubling to as much as $85,000 per year in the largest firms — in a few years as firms competed to attract the strongest and best graduates.

Firms discovered that it was very profitable to grow by increasing the number of associates. The demand for legal services was growing rapidly, and firms discovered that the costs of new associates could be multiplied and passed on to clients without objection. Many firms adopted the practice of billing time for associates at three times their salary and fringe benefits — one-third for the associate, one-third for administrative costs, and one-third to be divided as additional profits among the partners. Under this regime, the ratio of associates to partners increased rapidly, from 1:1 in the traditional firm of the 1960s to 3:1 or 4:1, or even higher in some instances. Growth in the number of associates simply meant greater profits for the firm and its partners. Firms thus had every incentive to grow rapidly by increasing the number of associates relative to the number of partners, a process known as leveraging.

As word spread about the salaries new lawyers were commanding, the law schools began to receive a flood of additional applications for admission. At about the same time, jobs were tightening in many traditional academic areas and many young persons with master's or doctor's degrees decided to change their career goal and go to law school. Law schools responded to the increased attractiveness of a legal education by increasing standards for admission and the number of students admitted to law school. Tuition increased and several new law schools were opened during this period. The number of law school gradu-

ates began to rise, but jobs were plentiful and the cycle of growth continued. During this period, the government developed guaranteed student loan programs that permitted many law students to finance virtually their entire legal education through loans on which principal payments began only after graduation. The booming market for young lawyers alleviated any concern about repayment of these loans and many law students took advantage of these generous programs.

The late 1980s were the salad days for law firms, for partners, for associates, and for law schools. Legal services were a major growth industry. Firms expanded, and reexpanded; salaries and benefits for associates continued to rise; associates were hired with a view toward future growth as much as present needs. Firms created expensive summer internship programs for law students completing their first and second years of law school to encourage them to join the firm upon graduation. Firms that were growing rapidly committed themselves to additional expensive office space to ensure space for future expansion. Indeed, the growth of legal services was a contributing factor to the boom in new office space during the 1980s in many cities; law firms were viewed as desirable tenants and their commitments to rent space helped the financing of many speculative new buildings.

In the early 1990s, this balloon was punctured by a recession that occurred quite unexpectedly. The demand for legal services abruptly and unexpectedly failed to continue to grow; law firms found themselves overstocked with lawyers and expensive office space that they could not use. Some of the more overextended firms laid off new associates, an action that was unheard of previously. Some firms paid new hires a bonus not to come as an associate or as a summer intern. The period of expansion of the job market for law students had ended. Almost immediately, the tightening of the market for legal services had consequences for law school graduates and students. Although new jobs did not dry up completely, they did become more difficult to find and more competitive; education loans suddenly became potentially burdensome; and many individuals reconsidered the decision to apply to law school.

Virtually overnight, the market for legal services changed from a seller's market to a buyer's market. That situation has continued to prevail throughout the 1990s, leading to serious implications for both young lawyers and legal education generally.

§17.7 Growth of In-House Legal Services

Before describing the changes in law firms resulting from the tightening of the market for legal services at the end of the 1980s, it is useful to sketch the changes in relationship between large law firms and their corporate clients that shaped the unexpected change in supply and demand for legal services. This involves the relationship between inside or house counsel (attorneys employed by the corporation) and outside law firms. The changes described in this section occurred roughly contemporaneously with the changes in the practice of law described in the previous sections and had significant impact on the speed with which the change occurred.

As the modern corporation developed, it became clear that it had need for

continuing legal advice and legal representation. Traditionally, this was provided by a law firm. As late as the 1950s and 1960s, it was common for a large corporation to have historical connections with a specific law firm that did (or oversaw) virtually all the corporation's significant legal activities. All of the important legal work of the corporation was in fact handled by or under the direction of the favored law firm or a favored specific partner in the firm. These relationships continued over long periods; often, one or more partners of the law firm were also members of the board of directors of the corporation and, if the corporation employed a lawyer as general counsel, that person was often a partner in the law firm or had prior association with the firm. Sometimes the firm maintained office space within the corporate offices, or vice versa. These arrangements have not entirely disappeared; they are sometimes found today in smaller businesses, and occasionally in larger ones as well.

By the 1950s, most large corporations had created not only the office of **general counsel** or **chief legal officer** (**CLO**)—who was a full-time employee of the corporation—but also skeletal legal staffs to assist the general counsel. However, these staffs were almost always small and handled only the most routine legal matters. For example, they might be involved in the preparation of minutes of meetings of the board of directors, the preparation of simple patent applications and routine contracts, the closing of real estate transactions, and the searching of titles of potential oil and gas leases. More substantial legal matters were always handled by outside lawyers.

In this setting, the outside law firm handled virtually all of the interesting, challenging, and significant legal work (and a great deal of the routine work as well). That firm also was regularly involved in selecting specialized or local counsel, when that was felt to be necessary, and overseeing the performance of these attorneys. The internal legal staff had virtually no challenging work and became the backwater of the legal profession. This view of the position of the inside legal staff was certainly shared by the partners and associates of the dominant law firm. The law firm might successfully place associates who did not make partner on the client's inside legal staff in order to cement the continuing relationship and at the same time provide a suitable spot for the junior attorney where he or she could do little harm. Even with the upgrading of the internal legal staffs (described below) that has occurred in recent years, a tinge of this old attitude may continue to exist in some lawyers today, but to the extent it still exists, that attitude is quite mistaken.

The systematic upgrading of internal legal staffs in terms of quality, size, and prestige was largely fueled by the same economic considerations that affected law firms. During the 1960s and 1970s, large corporations faced an explosion of regulatory activity and products liability litigation. During this period, the corporate general counsel and the favored law firm were not only forced to become familiar with new regulatory requirements but also increasingly to practice preventive rather than reactive law. The lawyers found themselves increasingly involved in the establishment and monitoring of legal compliance systems or participating in corporate planning discussions about future economic activities so that legal problems could be anticipated and prepared for. Initially, virtually none of this important work could be trusted to the inside legal staffs as they were then constituted.

As the quantity of legal work increased with the burst of regulatory and

litigation activity in the 1970s and 1980s, the bills for legal services that law firms submitted to corporations grew dramatically, contributing to the rapid expansion of law firms described earlier. However, during the same period, many corporations found that there was an urgent need to control costs: They were facing increased domestic and foreign competition as well as problems caused by rapid technological change and government regulation. Control over costs through improved efficiency, downsizing, and outsourcing seemed essential if the corporation was to survive and thrive. Cost-conscious corporate executives quickly realized that legal costs were getting out of hand, and the most obvious way to reduce these costs was to improve the capability of the inside legal staff to handle more matters and to monitor the work of expensive outside lawyers.

Upgrading the capability of inside legal staff is not very different from upgrading the capability of an independent law firm. Imaginative general counsel must be hired to increase the legal staff in size and improve its quality, salaries must be improved, and systematic attempts must be made to attract more competent lawyers, train them in much the way associates in law firms are trained, and give them more challenging work. As legal costs continued to rise, more and more corporations adopted this approach.

Many outside law firms initially welcomed the trend toward the upgrading of internal legal staffs, because at the time legal business was booming and the improved internal staff freed the firm's partners, associates, and paralegals from many routine matters. However, the development of substantial in-house legal staffs quickly strained traditional relationships with outside law firms and compelled the forging of new cooperative techniques between the inside and outside attorneys. Inside counsel was not only doing work that previously had been done profitably by associates at the law firm, but also were taking over work that previously justified the investment of significant time by individual partners.

To consider the most extreme scenario, picture a senior partner of a law firm in the 1960s with a historic relationship with a corporation that had only a tiny internal legal department. That partner was in a most enviable position: He presumably had the complete confidence of the management and the individual members of the board of directors. For many years, the firm had handled virtually all the corporation's legal work, although much of the work had been routine and in fact delegated to senior associates. Now, new inside general counsel are appointed specifically to reduce overall legal costs by moving work to an increasingly sophisticated internal law department and by moving isolated pieces of work to other less-costly law firms. Assume that one major source of legal work involves the regular and routine acquisitions of smaller firms by the corporation in order to obtain desired locations or desired products or inventory. Such an acquisition program is traditionally a major source of remunerative and recurring legal business for law firms. The first step by the new general counsel is the assignment of a newly hired inside lawyer to assist the outside firm in one or more acquisitions. After a few transactions, the outside firm is told that the inside lawyer is now in overall charge of the acquisition program and will report directly to the general counsel and indirectly to the corporate officer charged with overall responsibility for acquisitions; the law firm is promised that it will be consulted if any unusual problems arise, but they usually do not. Gradually, inside counsel entirely take over more and more

acquisitions work so that eventually most deals are handled entirely without the assistance of outside counsel and the amount of work performed by the firm and the senior partner for the client noticeably declines.

If one puts oneself in the position of the senior partner of the outside firm in this scenario, it is easy to see why there might be some bitterness and friction. The outside firm has in effect trained the inside lawyer to take over a portion of the firm's business. When this pattern recurs in other areas of specialized work, such as managing litigation, tax, and securities regulation, relationships often became increasingly strained. Perhaps the senior partner or the firm with historic connections with the client tried to return to the good old days by getting the general counsel fired or at least having his or her responsibilities cut back. Generally, such efforts did not succeed, because the inside general counsel had effectively reduced the cost of legal services without any noticeable diminution in quality. Indeed, efforts to undermine the position of the general counsel often made matters worse, because the basis for the unhappiness of the senior partner and the outside firm would be fully understood by top management, which could not be expected to be sympathetic.

Once the historic ties between law firm and client were broken and the independence of inside counsel firmly established, it was common for the corporation, through its general counsel, gradually to place legal work with other firms in an effort to obtain the best legal services at the best price. As a result, the historic ties declined further.

Today, most large corporations routinely place outside legal work with several different law firms. Many corporations, of course, still have close historical connections with specific law firms that provide a substantial amount of continuing legal work for the corporation, with legal fees running into the hundreds of thousands or millions of dollars per year. It is clear, however, that this pattern is not what it was 25 years ago. Inside staff has responsibility for many substantive matters, often including the handling of litigation, that only a few years ago would routinely be delegated to outside counsel. If legal fees have increased, it is because the corporation's need for legal services of the type now provided by outside counsel has increased.

As inside counsel become increasingly involved in placing legal work with competing law firms, they necessarily become directly involved in fee arrangements. The traditional method of billing is based on hourly rates for the lawyers involved. Inside counsel view straight hourly billings with skepticism, because it encourages over-staffing of a job and padding of bills. When such billing is followed, inside counsel may seek to limit the number of lawyers assigned to the work, establish a maximum number of hours that the client will be billed — (so-called **capped billing**), or insist that only certain specific lawyers be assigned the work. These controls quickly spelled an end to the once-common practice of assigning inexperienced lawyers to a project as part of their learning experience. The cost of training new lawyers no longer could be transferred to clients.

As inside counsel have developed alternative sources for legal services, creating competition among law firms, a variety of novel billing techniques have developed that permit direct comparisons of fee proposals by different firms: **fixed fees**, **capped fees**, **volume discount arrangements** (particularly for re-

curring litigation issues), **incentive billing** (with fees for successful outcomes higher than for less successful ones), **value billing**, **task billing**, **partial contingency fees**, **blended rates**, and so forth.

The development of sophisticated inside counsel has not only reduced the available work for law firms, but also increased the competition among law firms as inside counsel have attempted to obtain needed expert outside legal services at the best price.

§17.8 A Snapshot of the Large Law Firm

At this point it is useful to describe a typical large, big city law firm today and contrast it with the traditional firm existing a generation or so ago.

1. *Size.* Perhaps the most visible difference between the modern law firm and the older firm is that large law firms today are behemoths — hundreds of lawyers scattered in offices around the world. A mid-size firm today is one with 60 to 100 lawyers. The very largest firms are full-service firms that can provide legal services for a client in many legal areas and in many different countries, from employment law to complex litigation, from estate planning to structuring complex corporate transactions, as well as the legal, economic, and social implications of doing business in Mexico under the North American Free Trade Agreement (NAFTA) or opening a new plant in Mongolia or Russia. This increase in size and diversity is largely a result of the need to provide services for large publicly held businesses over a wide range — to ensure that a large volume of regular legal business will continue to come the firm's way. Mid-size firms, in contrast, tend to be **boutiques**, specializing in litigation or in one or more areas of law.

2. *Relations among partners.* One consequence of size is that the close personal relationships among partners that generally existed in traditional firms have largely disappeared. Large firms today tend to be impersonal. It is not uncommon for many partners in a large firm to know neither the names nor the faces of many of their co-partners. Firm retreats in which all partners spend a few days with each other may be necessary simply to introduce partners to each other! The size and impersonality of very large firms has changed the motivations of both partners and associates. A sense of loyalty to the firm has diminished; money is the important thing. If a firm falters, why take a chance that things will get better? Leave, if you can.

3. *Departmentalization and specialization.* Law practice in a large firm is a series of specialized practices. A firm may provide full-service coverage for its clients, but it is impossible for a single lawyer to remain current on developments in many legal areas today. Large firms are divided into groups or sections based on areas of specialized practice. One group of lawyers may form the intellectual property group, another will specialize in transactional work, or commercial litigation, estates and trusts, environmental law, and so forth. Lawyers in one specialized area may have little contact or interchange with lawyers in other areas. Although a partner working in the intellectual property section, for example, may not know the partners working in the litigation section, he or she will know and work closely with the other lawyers in the intellectual property

section. Friendships and loyalty exist at the department level even if they do not exist across the firm. When a new associate is hired by a firm, he or she is usually assigned to a section, and thus is involved in a specialty from the outset. Many firms, however, permit new associates to transfer from one specialty area to another within limits in order to find a slot for the associate in which he or she is happiest.

4. *Increased mobility of individual partners.* It is unusual today for a lawyer to spend a lifetime in a single firm. Partners come and go. Many lawyers today have been partners in two or three different firms, and expect that they will move again. Successful partners may feel little compulsion to remain with a firm when faced with an attractive offer from a competing firm if many of his co-partners are not known to him. Less-successful partners may find they are no longer wanted; they may be requested to leave the firm and find some other connection. Success today tends to be measured by developing clients who are personally loyal to the partner and who may be expected to go with him or her if the partner decides to seek greener pastures. What counts today are mobile or **portable** billings.

Partners may decide to leave a firm for a variety of reasons. They may become dissatisfied with their present firm for some reason and cast about openly for another connection. For example, they may feel that their personal compensation does not adequately reward the amount of business they bring in. Or, there may be real or imagined personal slights. Dissatisfaction may also be more general. They may find the institutional and centralized structure of the firm too confining. Or, they may simply feel restless and that it is time to move to a new environment.

Today, lawyers who are rainmakers or those who have developed a valuable specialization often receive unsolicited proposals to change firms. A successful partner may be approached by a **head hunter** who proposes that greener pastures may be found in a competing firm. Such a proposal is itself flattering, and it is not surprising that in an era of great mobility that a successful lawyer might seriously consider a lateral move even if he is not particularly unhappy.

It is also not uncommon for a whole section of partners and associates practicing in a specialized area such as white collar crime or intellectual property to move in a single group to a different firm. It is as although a whole minifirm decided to move to greener pastures. When the rainmakers in the section decide to go, the partners and associates that largely service the clients may decide to go also. A firm that loses one or more sections or groups of partners may find itself critically wounded by the defections and unable to continue as a separate viable entity as other partners and sections also decide to bail out.

5. *The desire to enter a small firm practice.* Partners in a large firm may find themselves increasingly constrained by the economics and politics of large firm practice. This disaffection may lead an entire section or group to split off to form a small, specialized firm on its own. Sometimes one or two mobile partners may themselves decide to form a new firm and hire junior lawyers from outside. The attractiveness of a smaller firm is that the senior partners will be in control of their own destinies. They will be both manager and rainmaker. They may feel that their operating costs will be lower in a small firm, and therefore they

will be able to capture more of the revenue their services and contacts provide. These spin-off firms may continue to have good relations with the parent firm and cooperate on specific matters.

6. *Formal partnership agreements.* Another consequence of firm growth is that almost all large firms today have carefully drafted partnership agreements. The default provisions of state partnership statutes are designed basically for the informal two-person or three-person business; they are simply not adequate to resolve many practical problems that arise in large law firms with hundreds of partners. There must be clear rules about mandatory retirement policies and what happens upon the death of a partner. There must be express authority to expel a nonperforming partner, a management structure that is binding upon all partners, and so forth. With hundreds of partners, the firm simply cannot rely on the good faith and good sense of individual partners to work out problems as they arise. It is interesting that although a large firm may have partners that specialize in partnership law, including drafting of partnership agreements for large firms, the firm will usually retain another law firm to prepare its partnership agreement. This avoids possible later legal attacks on the terms of the partnership agreement, avoids the appearance of conflict of interest, and ensures that provisions have been objectively developed.

7. *Centralization of management.* Management of a large firm is tradition-ally centralized in a management committee or in a single managing partner, or very commonly in both. The general partners as a group typically have minor roles to play in large law firm management; they may be entitled to vote on major questions (such as the selection of members of the **management com-mittee** and the **managing partner** or whether a specific partner should be expelled). When the partners do have the power to vote on an issue, votes are usually weighted by sizes of partnership interest, although some partnership agreements provide for counting votes on a per capita basis. Decisions may be based on a majority vote or, depending on the issue involved, on the affirmative vote of some higher percentage. Management participation rights of general partners in a law firm are thus similar to rights of limited partners in a limited partnership or shareholders in a corporation. Day-to-day management of the firm is usually vested in the managing partner (sometimes the title is chairman or executive director or a similar title). Typically, the managing partner has grown up in the law firm, has been imbued with knowledge of the firm's culture and manner of operation, and is respected by the leading partners. The man-aging partner is also usually a senior partner in the firm, although some man-aging partners are relatively young; the confidence of partners generally is more important than the age of the managing partner. A few firms have experimented with nonlawyer managers who have formal management training and experi-ence, but these experiments have not been very successful.

The managing partner must ensure the smooth internal working of the firm. He or she has the responsibility of running a business that involves hundreds of lawyers and a support staff that may number in the thousands. The managing partner must ensure that the secretarial and support staff, office space, computer equipment, and the like, are adequate for the size of the operation. He or she must ensure that the firm's cash flow is adequate and that lines of credit are available to carry the firm over rough spots, that billings are made

promptly and systematically, that conflicts of interest are avoided, that confidentiality rules are understood and followed, internal personnel clashes are resolved, fees negotiated with major clients and fee disputes resolved; and so forth. The managing partner may be involved in a variety of personnel problems, discussions with underperforming or unhappy partners, the promotion of associates, and so forth. The managing partner is also the official spokesperson for the firm, and normally will be extensively involved in contacts with potential clients and negotiations with possible lateral hires. The managing partner is usually assisted by a management committee that is both a group of senior advisers and a monitor of the performance of the managing partner. The management committee usually consists of partners from various offices and various sections or departments of the firm selected by a vote of the partners. In addition to firm-wide managing partners and management committees, firms may designate office managers for each office that the firm maintains. These may be known as branch managing partners, but their duties are not firm-wide but relate to local staff management, billing supervision, partner and personnel counseling within that office, and so forth.

The position of managing partner is a high visibility and prestigious position in most firms. It was particularly attractive and glamorous during the salad days of firm growth in the 1980s. The job has become much less attractive, however, as managing partners have had to face unpleasant problems of downsizing, negotiation with powerful clients who feel that they should have a major voice in the setting of fees, and dealing with rainmakers who have little inherent loyalty to the firm. It is also a time-consuming job and some highly successful partners have been reluctant to assume these responsibilities for fear that their personal practices will suffer as they devote substantially all their time to internal management matters. For this reason, some firms prefer to select as managing partners lawyers who are close to retirement and who do not expect to return full-time to practice when their managerial stint is completed.

8. *Slicing up the pie.* The large law firm is, of course, a business. To be successful, it must keep its lawyers who perform the essential services happy. Perhaps no topic is more sensitive, more controversial, and the subject of greater talk and speculation within law firms than the compensation of individual partners. The method of determining each partner's slice of the pie varies widely from firm to firm. At one extreme is the you-eat-what-you-kill approach, tying compensation closely to total billings by individual partners. At the other extreme is the lock-step in which all partners with the same seniority receive the same size slice without regard to their productivity. Yet another alternative is a straight percentage method: A partner with a 1.775 percent interest in the partnership receives 1.775 percent of the net profits. These are extremes; much more common are arrangements that provide a standard draw plus a year-end distribution that is based on some weighting of the two basic variables: rainmaking and billings.

Firms may also take a variety of subjective factors into account in the compensation decision. These factors include overall service or benefit to the firm, future potential, protection of morale of other partners, and client satisfaction (i.e., providing the greatest benefit to clients at reasonable prices, thereby improving the long-term relationship with the client). Once a firm moves away

from the mechanical calculation of compensation, a critical issue becomes who makes the decisions. Most firms have created a **compensation committee** whose members may not be eligible for discretionary bonuses. The managing partner and management committee may perform this function in some firms. If a compensation committee is used, it is essential that that committee work closely with the managing partner and the management committee, because if there is any difference in policies followed by the management committee and the compensation committee, the individual partners will almost certainly follow the money rather than follow the managers.

A partner who brings an important client to a firm may legitimately expect a reward for doing so This reward would be over and above the services he or she performs for that client during the year. This **finding bonus** may continue for several years. However, if other lawyers primarily provide services to the client and the client remains with the firm, the continuation of the override would become increasingly questionable, because it is likely that the lawyers actually performing the work would explain why the client has remained with the firm.

9. *The expulsion of partners.* At one time, the ultimate goal of every associate was making partner. Acceptance into the partnership was a virtual lifetime guarantee of security of employment and income. No longer. Partners who are marginal producers are quickly pruned. Law firm agreements typically provide for expulsion of partners by a decision of the management committee and a vote of partners. Firms do not hesitate to exercise this power when a partner is perceived as resting on his or her oars, just not fitting in, or having made a mistake that has cost the firm an important client. This point was vividly made to one of the authors when a junior partner in a major Chicago firm complained that the only lawyers in his firm that had any job security were associates in their third, fourth, and fifth years (before the partnership decision was made). Although this junior partner was primarily responsible for the preparation of witnesses in massive products liability litigation, he felt he had little job security as a partner.

10. *Mandatory retirement.* Law firms have also needed to address the problem of retirement of aging partners. Many firms have a mandatory retirement age, often preceded by a period of reduced activity during which the partner is expected to gradually reduce his or her practice and transfer continuing clients to younger members of the firm. The critical age may be set at 60 or even younger. Firms also have formal retirement plans, typically of the defined contribution variety. At an earlier time, some firms experimented with unfunded plans, but these plans effectively imposed the obligation to fund senior partners retirement on younger partners who were at the height of their earning power. Many of these younger partners decided to migrate to other firms to avoid the reduction of their compensation necessitated by the unfunded retirement plan.

11. *The changing roles of associates.* The chaotic developments of the late 1980s and early 1990s have also changed law firm practices with respect to associates. During the salad days of the 1980s, law firms tried to maintain an associate/partner ratio of 3 or 4 to 1; some firms had even higher leverage. As the availability of routine legal work declined and clients began to closely monitor law firm billing, firms found that it was not practicable to continue this

kind of leverage. Firms reduced the ratio to 1 to 1 or even lower, and some firms completely withdrew from the associate market, planning to grow through **lateral** hires rather than through associates. This conscious decision to reduce the ratio of associates to partners resulted in significantly fewer jobs being available to law school graduates during the transition years of the early 1990s.

From the standpoint of training and promotion of associates, the most important change has been the decline in mentoring by partners and senior associates at the expense of clients because of the tightening of cost controls. The mentoring that now occurs is basically at the cost of the firm itself, and the investment that firms have in individual associates has therefore increased significantly. As discussed below, firms have found that the old up-or-out rules of the past are no longer in the best interests of the firm and a variety of retention policies have been developed for valuable associates who will not become partners.

Another major factor that has influenced law firm policies with respect to associates is the increase in the number of female law school graduates, from practically zero in the 1950s and 1960s to nearly 50 percent in most law schools today. Firms have found it necessary to develop maternity and child-raising policies to permit the retention of female associates who are juggling child-raising and a legal career. Even so, the attrition of female associates in most law firms is much higher than for their male counterparts, and there are many fewer senior partners who are female than one would expect simply from the number of female associates hired.

Some firms in large cities have experimented with joint training of young associates, particularly in litigation and transactional skills. Today, the tab for this training is largely borne by the firm itself, not by its clients. Today, young associates from participating firms may learn these skills through intensive several-day seminars conducted by leading trial lawyers from these firms. The seminar may involve role-playing, mock depositions or cross examinations, and work on actual transactions. Whether this cooperative effort will succeed, given the competitiveness among firms, remains to be seen.

Because the costs of associate training falls largely on law firms, the probationary period for associates has typically been shortened to four or five years. However, many firms have moved to a three-step rather than two-step progression to full partnership; in addition, firms have created permanent nonpartner positions so that their investment in associates who fail to make partner is not totally lost. These developments are described immediately below.

12. *Income and equity partners.* Clients not unnaturally prefer to have partners rather than associates handle their legal matters. Of course, the shortening of the probationary period for associates inevitably means that younger lawyers are designated as partners and thus able to deal directly and more effectively with clients. At the same time, their compensation may continue to be largely based on salary and annual bonus, because their production and experience does not justify their sharing in firm income to the same extent as more experienced partners.

In an effort to accommodate these conflicting goals, many firms have created a two-tier partnership status: **Equity partners** are the senior partners who own the firm and share predominantly in its success or failure, while

income partners are the younger lawyers who do not share in the business risk of the law firm and who receive a salary plus a year-end bonus in much the same way senior associates previously did. Income partners have some of the benefits of partnership: They may attend firm meetings, serve on most firm committees, and are given information about the firm's economic picture. However, they do not share in losses or in profits (except to the extent of a bonus) and may not serve on the significant firm committees that deal with management and compensation. Customarily, an income partner is ultimately promoted to equity partner, but some income partners may remain in that status throughout their legal careers.

Firms that have elected to practice as professional corporations or limited liability companies may create a similar two-tier system, with shareholders and senior shareholders. One LLC firm describes persons who are basically income partners as **participating associates**, a neutral phrase that may be used without regard to the legal form used by the law firm. Some firms have not created two-tier partnership track, but reach the same result internally.

13. *Permanent associates.* In addition to the creation of the intermediate status of income partner, firms increasingly have abandoned the up-or-out rule for associates, and have tried to recoup their investment in training costs by retaining associates indefinitely. If an associate has shown ability in one or more specialties, but is not viewed as potentially of partner caliber, particularly in terms of rainmaking, he or she may be offered a permanent position in the firm on a salaried basis. The title of these lawyers may be **senior attorney** or **senior counsel**, although some may be called simply **staff attorney** and others may be given the more prestigious title of **of counsel**. These positions may be either part time or full time. Female attorneys with extensive child-care obligations may elect this status with the expectation that they may later be moved into a partnership position when their family responsibilities make full-time work feasible.

§17.9 The Concern About Unlimited Liability

As indicated earlier, in the traditional law firm of the 1950s and 1960s, the unlimited liability that is the essence of the partnership relation was not a matter of serious concern. In the large law firm, however, this is no longer true, and many firms have adopted alternative legal forms in an effort to provide partners with a shield against personal liability. These shields protect the personal assets of the individual partner but not the value of his or her interest in the partnership. There is no way to provide protection for assets owned by innocent partners that the firm actually holds.

The concern about potential personal liability arises from several different sources. The most important is concern about malpractice. American society has become increasing litigious over the last few decades, and the possibility that a firm will be sued for malpractice has increased correspondingly. Indeed, there are firms in many cities that specialize in plaintiffs malpractice litigation against lawyers. Insurance against malpractice claims is generally viewed as essential for large law firms. But that insurance is extremely expensive and does

not give complete peace of mind, because it is always possible that someone will screw up on a really massive matter and the claim may exceed the policy limits. These concerns are not theoretical: At least two large law firms settled malpractice claims in connection with the savings and loan litigation for amounts in excess of their malpractice coverage. Because malpractice insurance is so expensive, some lawyers and law firms have consciously decided not to purchase such insurance on the theory that without insurance they are less likely to be made the target of a malpractice claim.

In the large firm, malpractice insurance is necessary, because no partner can have personal confidence in every one of his or her 100 or so co-partners. Hence, there is a risk that partners will be held personally liable for actions of persons they may not even know. Unlimited liability in the partnership form is also of concern because of contract liabilities. Many law firms have signed expensive leases or committed themselves to guarantee the compensation of lateral partners. Some of these commitments were made during the salad days of the late 1980s and are now burdensome to the firms involved. Further, even with respect to conservative contract liabilities, there is always a risk that even a large and successful firm that has been in existence for decades may collapse with the loss of rainmakers, followed by other partners bailing out, leaving all the partners facing substantial contract liabilities.

The first device that gave limited liability to some lawyers arose in the 1960s when most states enacted **professional corporation (P.C.)** or **professional association (P.A.)** statutes that permitted certain service professionals, including lawyers, to incorporate their practices. The motivating force behind these statutes, however, was not the desire to obtain limited liability but rather a tax-motivated goal of obtaining tax deductions for corporate-type retirement plans for individual partners. In many states today, these statutes also provide limited liability for partners as an incidental consequence of incorporation. The tax advantages of incorporating a professional practice have long ago disappeared, but professional corporations continue to exist because of the benefit of limited liability.

In the 1990s, a new business form, the **limited liability company (LLC)** was authorized by statute in every state. The LLC combines desirable partnership-type income taxation with limited liability for all members. In many (but by no means all) states, lawyers may practice as LLCs. Among the states that do not permit lawyers to practice as LLCs are California, Oregon, Rhode Island, and Delaware.

Yet a third device that permits law firm partners to limit their personal liability is the **limited liability partnership (LLP)**, which was first developed in Texas but has been adopted by most states. The LLP statute as originally enacted in Texas provides for an election by partnerships that shield innocent partners from malpractice liabilities. That was shortly followed by the broadening of this shield in Minnesota and New York to provide partners a shield against both tort and contract liabilities. These broad shield LLP statutes proved to be extremely popular, and in 1996, amendments to the Revised Uniform Partnership Act were proposed recognizing the broad shield type of LLP statute.

Thus, three types of business forms for lawyers now exist that may give them protection against unlimited personal liability. This protection is generally

limited to partners who are not themselves involved in malpractice. However, the practice of law in some states is directly regulated by the state Supreme Court and a few state courts have concluded that it is unethical for lawyers to practice law in any form of limited liability entity. In these states, there is apparently no way for lawyers to protect themselves from unlimited liability.

Sophisticated clients and law firm creditors are well aware of this movement toward limited liability for individual lawyers in law firms. The issue of limited liability may become an element of bargaining with respect to fees. It is not uncommon for fee arrangements or contractual documents such as leases to contain specific provisions requiring all or some partners to personally guarantee the performance of the contract despite the use of a limited liability entity by the firm. Similarly, there may be provisions in a contract with a law firm that is a general partnership dealing with release of potential personal liability of innocent members of the firm. The client may negotiate for a reduction in fees in exchange for contractual releases of innocent partners from personal liability.

Leases of office space for large firms have been a continuing problem in the limited liability area. In the 1980s, as the law business boomed, law firms were viewed as very desirable tenants and many firms persuaded landlords to accept nonrecourse leases. With the change in market conditions at the end of the 1980s, the attitude of landlords has changed. Law firms are perceived as being difficult and sometimes unreliable tenants, and landlords may insist that at least some of the senior partners personally guarantee the performance of the lease if a firm is conducting its business in the form of an LLC or a broad shield LLP. This personal guarantee may cover all obligations of the firm under the lease or be limited to the value of the tenant concession package, which consist of benefits that the landlord provides to encourage the firm to move to the new location: free rent, tenant improvement allowances, allowances to satisfy outstanding rental obligations to other landlords, and other cash allowances to tenants. In the case of a large law firm requiring, say, 100,000 square feet of office space, this tenant concession package may easily involve millions of dollars of benefits, so that personal guarantees are not entered into lightly.

§17.10 Alternatives to Law Firm Employment

The decline in law firm hiring at the end of the 1980s came as a shock to many law students who had chosen a legal career based on stories of high salaries and numerous job opportunities. The shock was particularly severe for students who had borrowed funds for their legal education and faced the prospect of repaying the loans without any guarantee that they would have a high paying job. Of course, legal jobs did not dry up totally. Honor graduates from the more prestigious law schools continued to find jobs without difficulty, but students in the bottom half of their graduating classes, particularly in less prestigious schools, faced disaster.

What should a new lawyer do if he or she fails to locate a job at a large law firm despite a major and continuing effort extending over several months? Of course, one could give up the idea of practicing law and go into business management, open one's own business, or go back to school to study something

else. These are not necessarily bad ideas, because many persons in positions of responsibility in government and business have law degrees although they may never have practiced. What is of interest here, however, is avenues by which a person can practice law although no large firm was willing to offer him or her a job. As noted above, one may well find employment in a smaller firm in either a large city or a small community. In addition, there are two avenues by which one can obtain practical experience that might open up job opportunities as lawyers in the future: solo practice and working as a temporary or contract lawyer.

§17.11 Solo Practice

A lawyer who has passed the bar may always hang out his or her **shingle** and begin the practice of law without any prior experience (except possibly working at a law firm for a summer while in law school). This is undoubtedly doing it the hard way in today's specialized environment, although at one time it was an accepted method of starting a practice, particularly in smaller communities.

As a general proposition today, young lawyers should spend some time in an apprenticeship under the oversight of a more experienced lawyer before striking out on their own. Legal apprenticeship of this type is a good idea, because law schools generally do not try to teach law students the mundane and nitty-gritty details of practicing law and representing clients. A recent law school graduate may not know where the courthouse is, to use a common expression. The so-called McCrate Report, prepared by the American Bar Association, has recommended that law schools provide more detailed and practical training, but that is not very likely to occur in the foreseeable future.

In considering solo practice, young lawyers must realize that they will starve if they do not have clients. Some cities have programs that permit lawyers to sign up to represent indigent criminal defendants for a modest fee; however, that is bare subsistence, at best. One must get paying clients to survive. Unfortunately, one is not likely to get many clients simply by opening an office and waiting for walk-in clients. One typically has to "network" to get paying clients who largely select lawyers based on recommendations from other people, or on the basis of family, personal or neighborhood ties. It is possible to survive as a solo practitioner with little or no experience, but it is very difficult.

§17.12 Contract Lawyers

The development of contract lawyering appears to be a recent phenomenon. The idea is basically simple. A placement agency offers to supply qualified lawyers to law firms or solo practitioners for a fee. The lawyers are employed by the placement agency, which is responsible for taxes, withholding, and other employment-related matters. The success of this new business obviously depends on there being a supply of unemployed qualified lawyers and a need by law firms for temporary assistance. These conditions exist as this is written.

Many lawyers who fail to find employment with a firm, and who do not wish to test the rigors of solo practice, have found that serving as a contract lawyer provides a bridge into more traditional law practice. **Contract lawyers** are often referred to as **temporaries** (or **temps**).

From the standpoint of successful solo practitioners and small law firms, temps are attractive because they permit temporary or seasonal needs for lawyer services to be met without making permanent hires. Firms faced with additional work that may be temporary today are well aware of the over-staffing problems that occurred at the end of the 1980s. A typical situation is a firm with a major case that hires temps to perform more or less routine legal services in connection with the case while permitting its partners and associates to handle higher paying work. A decision to hire temps may also be prompted by on-staff illness, maternity leaves, special projects, or seasonal increases in workload, as in tax firms during March and April. Solo practitioners with a litigation practice may use temps exclusively to assist them, overseeing their work but paying the placement agency a relatively small amount for the services being provided.

A temp may end up working for several months under the supervision of an experienced lawyer on a specific case. A temp who performs well in these situations may be offered a permanent job at a later time. Even where no permanent offer is forthcoming, the temp has gained valuable experience as well as entries on one's resume and possible letters of recommendation. The attractiveness of becoming a temp does not lie in the salary, which usually is on an hourly basis and may not significantly exceed the salary of paralegals. However, some income is always better than no income, and the experience of being a temp may well lead to a job in the future, either directly or through recommendations.

The use of temporary lawyers may create ethical and legal issues both for the contract lawyer and for the employing firm. If a temp works under the direction of a lawyer or law firm for an extended period, whether the temp has in fact become an employee for tax and unemployment compensation purposes may become an issue. Ethical issues may also arise, but the practice of using temporary lawyers is so new that the full ramifications have not been explored. Obviously a temp who has worked on one side of a case should not accept temporary employment with the other side to work on the same case. But all sort of ethical issues short of this extreme situation can readily be envisioned.

◆ MASTER WORD LIST